AF270262

REVELATION

WISDOM COMMENTARY

Volume 58

Revelation

Lynn R. Huber
with Gail R. O'Day

Amy-Jill Levine
Volume Editor

Barbara E. Reid, OP
General Editor

A Michael Glazier Book

LITURGICAL PRESS

Collegeville, Minnesota

www.litpress.org

1　　2　　3　　4　　5　　6　　7　　8　　9

Library of Congress Cataloging-in-Publication Data

Names: Huber, Lynn R., author. | O'Day, Gail R., author. | Levine, Amy-Jill, 1956– editor. | Reid, Barbara E., editor.

Title: Revelation / Lynn R. Huber with Gail R. O'Day ; Amy-Jill Levine, volume editor, Barbara E. Reid, OP, general editor.

Description: Collegeville, Minnesota : Liturgical Press, [2023] | Series: Wisdom commentary ; volume 58 | "A Michael Glazier Book." | Includes bibliographical references and index. | Summary: "This commentary on Revelation provides a feminist interpretation of Scripture in serious, scholarly engagement with the whole text, not only those texts that explicitly mention women. It addresses not only issues of gender but also those of power, authority, ethnicity, racism, and classism"— Provided by publisher.

Identifiers: LCCN 2023007039 (print) | LCCN 2023007040 (ebook) | ISBN 9780814682098 (hardcover) | ISBN 9780814682340 (epub) | ISBN 9780814682340 (pdf) | ISBN 9780814669761 (pdf)

Subjects: LCSH: Bible. Revelation—Commentaries.

Classification: LCC BS2825.53 .H84 2023 (print) | LCC BS2825.53 (ebook) | DDC 228/.07—dc23/eng/20230701

LC record available at https://lccn.loc.gov/2023007039

LC ebook record available at https://lccn.loc.gov/2023007040

"Revelation demands an exegetical practice that enables
the interpreter to be drawn more and more deeply
into the text, its view of God, and a world
shaped by the awesome mystery of God."

—Gail R. O'Day, "Teaching and Preaching the Book of Revelation"
Word & World 25, no. 3 (2005): 252

*In memory of Gail R. O'Day, who taught me to be drawn
more deeply into the text without getting lost.*

Contents

Acknowledgments

This project has taken a long time. The most obvious reason for this is the death of my mentor, friend, and co-author Gail R. O'Day. We were excited about working on this project together and started it together, but almost all the commentary was written, sadly, after she was gone. Given her role in the beginning of this project, as I wrote I routinely thought, "What Would Gail Do?" and I looked to her work for inspiration.[1] At the same time, I know parts of the final product would make Gail shake her head and roll her eyes, although she would be proud of the book overall. All mistakes and ill-advised decisions are my own, of course.

Foremost among the people to be acknowledged for supporting this project is Tom Frank, Gail's friend, spouse, and co-adventurer. With a shared love of art and nature and a shared sense of humor, their life together was full of beauty and laughter. The glimpses I saw of Tom's tenderness toward Gail as she battled cancer were inspiring. I am thankful to have my own co-adventurer and loving spouse, Mel Ah Mu. Mel has been a constant source of support for me, helping me weather various difficulties that coincided with this journey. Mel keeps me grounded and encourages me to be more than someone who writes about Revelation. She helps me see things in new ways, and I am so grateful that she is willing to share with me her knowledge, perspective, and love.

---

1. Gail R. O'Day, "Revelation," in *Theological Bible Commentary*, ed. Gail R. O'Day and David L. Petersen (Louisville: Westminster John Knox, 2009), 471–79, and "Teaching and Preaching the Book of Revelation," *WW* 25 (2005): 246–54.

So many people have had a positive impact on this project. I am grateful for every one of them, although I am sure I will forget someone in listing names. I am thankful for the work and patience of those who contributed pieces to this commentary or who agreed to let me include excerpts from their work, including Elizabeth O'Donnell Gandolfo, Rhiannon Graybill, Jacqueline M. Hidalgo, Barbara Rossing, Shanell T. Smith, Hanna Stenström, Eric A. Thomas, and the late Lynne St. Clair Darden. Dr. Darden passed away before this project was even near completion. I hope she realized how thankful I was for her contribution. Editors Barbara Reid and Amy-Jill Levine were unbelievably understanding as this project stretched out longer than expected. As the volume editor, Amy-Jill offered many insights that were key to my thinking and made this book better in the end. Erin Palmer, a former student and now friend, was an immensely helpful reader, editor, and sounding board. She read chapters and offered solid guidance. I am very appreciative of all her time, effort, and insight. Other former and current students who worked with me while I wrote this commentary and who have listened to ideas or read sections of this work include Hannah Allen, Virginia Beall, Zachary Gianelle, Candace Hall, Olivia Lancashire, Shelby Lewis, Phoebe Mock, Molly Morrison, Rachel Mullenix, Jasper Serenity Myers, Victoria Oakley, Adam Plant, Filippos Rempoutzakos, and Alex Villegas. I often wrote with them, and other students, in mind. Hopefully, they see how some of their questions and interests shaped this work.

I have a great community of friends and colleagues who have offered time and support. Kent Brintnall and Rhiannon Graybill have been endlessly supportive and patient. They offered constructive criticism and helped me refine some of my key ideas. In addition, as I was tying up loose ends, they offered some quick feedback. Good friends Evan Gatti, Amy Johnson, and Kirstin Ringelberg cheered me on as I finished this project while balancing teaching, administrative work, and pandemic realities. Others who have shared time, thoughts, encouragement, or inspiration include Jennifer Bird, Greg Carey, Libby Conyer, Melissa Harl Sellew, Juan Hernández Jr., Jacqueline M. Hidalgo, Susan Hylen, Steve Friesen, Ingrid Esther Lilly, Joseph Marchal, Shelly Matthews, Robert Royalty, Jean-Pierre Ruiz, Shepherd Tsosie, Eric A. Thomas, Ekaputra Tupamahu, and Robyn Whitaker. I have an incredible network of people I know through social media, especially Facebook and Twitter. There have been times when people on those platforms have prompted me to read something new or think about a topic from a new perspective. This virtual community has been invaluable, and I am thankful for the scholarly generosity I have experienced there. Again, any shortcomings or missteps in the following pages are entirely my own.

I am also grateful for the support of Elon colleagues (present and past) who helped make this project possible, including Amy Allocco, Steve Bednar, Michael Carignan, Geoffrey Claussen, Barbara Gaither, Baris Kesgin, Ariela Marcus-Sells, Andrew Monteith, Tom Mould, Brian Pennington, Sumeyye Pakdil, Rebecca Todd Peters, Jeffrey Pugh, L. D. Russell, Maureen Vandermaas-Peeler, Pamela Winfield, Tammy Womack, and Annetta Womble. The librarians at Elon, including Joan Ruelle, Patrick Rudd, and Lynn Melchor, are amazingly resourceful, and this project would not have come to fruition without them. In addition, the various forms of material support I received from Elon were invaluable. Thank you to President Connie Book, Associate Provost Tim Peeples, Associate Provost Paul Miller, Dean of the College of Arts and Sciences Gabie Smith, former Provosts Steven House and Aswani Volety, and former Associate Provost Brooke Barnett.

Finally, thank you to whoever picks up this commentary and journeys through the text with it. I hope you find something in these pages that sheds new light on Revelation or that encourages you to look at the text in a new or different way. More important, even though John warns about adding or subtracting to this book (Rev 22:18-19), please feel free to read Revelation through the lenses of your own experience, critical mind, and commitment to equity and justice.

Lynn R. Huber
June 1, 2022

Images and Image Permissions

Figure 1: Myrtice West, *Thou Art Worthy, O Lord, to Receive Glory and Honor and Power*, oil on cloth, 47x35, United States, c. 1980. Photo courtesy of Rollin Riggs. Used with permission from Rollin Riggs.

Figure 2: Sebasteion Relief of Claudius and Britannia, Aphrodisias, Turkey, first century CE. Photo: G. Petruccioli. Used with permission from New York University Excavations at Aphrodisias.

Figure 3: The Woman Clothed in the Sun and the Male Child, *Bamberg Apocalypse*, Reichnau, ca. 1010. Staatsbibliothek Bamberg, Msc.Bibl.140,

v26. Photo: Gerald Raab. Available under the Creative Common License CC-BY-SA 4.0.

Figure 4: Silver Denarius of Domitian depicting Domitia (obverse) and son (reverse), Rome, 82–83 CE. American Numismatics Society 1975.226.78. https://numismatics.org/collection/1975.226.78. Photo: American Numismatic Society, New York. Used with permission from the American Numismatic Society.

Figure 5: Beatus of Liébana, "The Great Prostitute," *Commentary on the Apocalypse*, Spain, ca. 945. The Morgan Library & Museum. MS M.644, fol. 194v. Purchased by J.P. Morgan (1867–1943) in 1919. Photo: The Morgan Library & Museum, New York. Used with permission from the Morgan Library & Museum.

Figure 6: Gertrude Morgan, *Rev. 19 Chap.*, crayon and pencil on paper, United States, ca. 1960. Collections of the Louisiana State Museum, 1981.106.009. Photo: Louisiana State Museum, New Orleans, LA. Used with permission from the Collections of the Louisiana State Museum.

Text Permissions

" 'Alas'—Not 'Woe' for the Earth," from *The Rapture Exposed* by Barbara R. Rossing, copyright © 2004, 2005, is reprinted by permission of Basic Books, an imprint of Hachette Book Group, Inc.

The excerpt from *The Woman Babylon and the Marks of Empire* by Shanell T. Smith and published in 2014 by Fortress is considered fair use.

Abbreviations

Ancient Sources

1 Melanc.	Dio Chrysostom, *Melancomas I (Or. 29)*
1 Tars.	Dio Chrysostom, *First Tarsic Discourse (Or. 33)*
Ab urbe cond.	Livy, *Ab Urbe Condita (Roman History)*
Ann.	Tacitus, *Annals*
Ant.	Josephus, *Jewish Antiquities*
Ant. Rom.	Dionysius of Halicarnassus, *Roman Antiquities*
Ap. Met.	Apuleius, *Metamorphoses (The Golden Ass)*
Apoc. Pet.	Apocalypse of Peter
Aug.	Suetonius, *The Deified Augustus*
Cal.	Suetonius, *Caligula*
CIL	*Corpus Inscriptionum Latinarum*
Civ.	Augustine, *City of God*
Con. prae.	Plutarch, *Coniugalia praecepta (Advice to a Bride and Groom)*
De Myst.	Iamblichus, *De Mysteriis*
Dial.	Justin, *Dialogue with Trypho*
Dom.	Suetonius, *Domitian*
Edict.	Justinian, *Edicta*
Ep.	Pliny the Younger, *Epistles*
Ep.	Seneca, *Moral Epistles*
Epigr.	Martial, *Epigrams*
Expositio	Joachim of Fiore, *Expositio in Apocalypsim*
Fist.	Hippocrates, *Fistulas*

Flacc.	Philo, *Against Flaccus*
Geog.	Strabo, *Geography*
Gyn.	Soranus, *Gynecology*
Haer.	Irenaeus, *Against Heresies*
Heracl.	Euripides, *Children of Hercules*
Hist. Rom.	Dio Cassius, *Roman History*
Herm. *Sim.*	Shepherd of Hermas, *Similitude*
Hist.	*Herodotus, Histories*
Hist. eccl.	Eusebius, *Ecclesiastical History*
Is. Os.	Plutarch, *Isis and Osiris*
Jov.	Jerome, *Adversus Jovinianum libri II*
Jul.	Suetonius, *The Deified Julius*
J.W.	Josephus, *The Jewish War*
Leg.	Cicero, *De legibus (On the Laws)*
Leg.	Plato, *Leges (Laws)*
Ling.	*Varro, De Lingua Latina (On the Latin Language)*
Lives	Diogenes Laertius, *Lives of the Eminent Philosophers*
Mor.	Plutarch, *Moralia*
Mul.	Hippocrates, *De morbis mulierum (Female Diseases)*
Nat.	Pliny the Elder, *Natural History*
Or. Graec.	Tatian, *Oratio ad Graecos (Pro Hellēnas)*
Ov. Met.	Ovid, *Metamorphoses*
Parad.	Cicero, *Stoic Paradoxes*
Praescr.	Tertullian, *Prescription against Heretics*
Rep.	Plato, *Republic*
Res gest. divi Aug.	*Res Gestae Divi Augusti (The Deeds of the Divine Augustus)*
Rhet. Her.	*Rhetorica ad Herennium*
Sat.	Horace, *Satires*
Sat.	Juvenal, *Satires*
SEG	Supplementum Epigraphicum Graecum
Spec. Laws	Philo, *On the Special Laws*
Spect.	Tertullian, *The Shows*
Virg.	Tertullian, *The Veiling of Virgins*

Modern Sources

AJA	*American Journal of Archaeology*
AYB	Anchor Yale Bible
BCE	Before the Common Era
BCT	*Bible and Critical Theory*
Bib	*Biblica*
BibInt	*Biblical Interpretation*
BibInt	Biblical Interpretation Series
BICS	*Bulletin of the Institute of Classical Studies*
BNTC	Black's New Testament Commentary
BR	*Biblical Research*
BSNA	Biblical Scholarship in North America
CBQ	*Catholic Biblical Quarterly*
CE	Common Era
CH	*Church History*
CRR	*Critical Research on Religion*
CurBR	*Currents in Biblical Research*
CW	*Classical World*
ExpTim	*Expository Times*
FCNTECW	Feminist Companion to the New Testament and Early Christian Writings
FCB	Feminist Companion to the Bible
GBS	Guides to Biblical Scholarship
GR	*Greece and Rome*
Hebr. Stud.	*Hebrew Studies*
HTR	*Harvard Theological Review*
IFT	Introductions in Feminist Theology
Int	*Interpretation*
JBL	*Journal of Biblical Literature*
JFSR	*Journal of Feminist Studies in Religion*
JHS	*Journal of the History of Sexuality*
JAOS	*Journal of the American Oriental Society*
JR	*Journal of Religion*

JRS	*Journal of Roman Studies*
JSJ	*Journal for the Study of Judaism in the Persian, Hellenistic, and Roman Period*
JSNT	*Journal for the Study of the New Testament*
JSOTSup	Journal for the Study of the Old Testament Supplement series
JSQ	*Jewish Studies Quarterly*
KJV	King James Version
LNTS	Library of New Testament Studies
NCBC	New Cambridge Bible Commentary
Neot	*Neotestamentica*
NovT	*Novum Testamentum*
NTS	*New Testament Studies*
OBT	Overtures to Biblical Theology
PL	Patrologia Latina
PRSt	*Perspectives in Religious Studies*
RRelRes	*Review of Religious Research*
SBL	Society of Biblical Literature
SemeiaSt	SemeiaStudies
SLA	*Studies in Late Antiquity*
ST	*Studia Theologica*
SymS	Symposium Series
TAPA	*Transactions of the American Philological Association*
USQR	*Union Seminary Quarterly Review*
WBC	Word Biblical Commentary
WCS	Wisdom Commentary Series
WUNT	Wissenschaftliche Untersuchungen zum Neuen Testament
WW	*Word and World*
YCS	Yale Classical Studies

Contributors

Lynne St. Clair Darden (d. 2017) was assistant professor of New Testament at Interdenominational Theological Seminary in Atlanta, Georgia. She authored *Scripturalizing Revelation: An African American Postcolonial Reading of Empire*, SemeiaSt 80 (SBL Press, 2015) and numerous articles and book chapters on womanist and postcolonial biblical interpretation.

Elizabeth O'Donnell Gandolfo is the Earley Associate Professor of Catholic and Latin American Studies at Wake Forest University School of Divinity in Winston-Salem, North Carolina. She is the author of *The Power and Vulnerability of Love: A Theological Anthropology* (Fortress, 2015), co-author with Laurel Marshall Potter of *Re-Membering the Reign of God: The Decolonial Witness of El Salvador's Church of the Poor* (Lexington Books, 2022), and co-editor of *Parenting as Spiritual Practice and Source for Theology: Mothering Matters* (Cham, Switzerland: Springer International, 2017).

Rhiannon Graybill is associate professor of religious studies and the W. J. Millard Professor of Religion at Rhodes College in Memphis, Tennessee. She is a scholar of the Hebrew Bible and author of *Are We Not Men? Unstable Masculinity in the Hebrew Prophets* (Oxford, 2016) and *Texts after Terror: Rape, Sexual Violence, and the Hebrew Bible* (Oxford, 2021) and co-editor of multiple volumes related to biblical studies, gender, and sexuality.

Jacqueline M. Hidalgo is professor of Latina/o/x studies and religion and the director of Oakley Center for Humanities & Social Sciences at Williams College in Willamstown, Massachusetts. She is the author of *Latina/o/x Studies and Biblical Studies* in Brill Research Perspectives in

Biblical Interpretation 3.4 (2020) as well as *Revelation in Aztlán: Scriptures, Utopias, and the Chicano Movement* (Palgrave Macmillan, 2016). With Efrain Agosto she co-edited a volume on *Latinxs, the Bible, and Migration* (Palgrave Macmillan, 2018), and she has written widely on the Bible and scriptures more broadly in Latina/o/x communities.

Barbara R. Rossing is professor of New Testament at the Lutheran School of Theology at Chicago. Her publications include *The Rapture Exposed: The Message of Hope in the Book of Revelation* (Basic Books, 2004); *The Choice Between Two Cities: Whore, Bride and Empire in the Apocalypse* (Trinity Press International, 1999); two volumes of the New Proclamation commentary (Fortress, 2000 and 2004); a nine-session Bible study, *Journeys through Revelation: Apocalyptic Hope for Today* (Presbyterian Women, 2010); and multiple articles and book chapters on Revelation and ecology.

Shanell T. Smith is the author of *The Woman Babylon and the Marks of Empire* (Fortress, 2014) and *Touched: For Survivors of Sexual Assault Like Me Who Have Been Hurt by Church Folk and for Those Who Will Care* (Fortress, 2020). A doctoral expert and institutional consultant, Smith is the founder of Shanell T. Smith Consulting, LLC. Smith offers private and group coaching programs to help doctoral students, irrespective of discipline, successfully navigate through the various stages of their program with clarity, strategic direction, and in the healthiest way possible.

Hanna Stenström is docent and associate professor in biblical studies at University College Stockholm. She is the author of multiple articles and book chapters on feminist interpretation of the Bible in both English and Swedish. In addition, Stenström works as part of the editorial staff of the Swedish Church Magazine and in the Swedish Women's Ecumenical Council's magazine ELSA. She is a co-author of Tala Väl (Speak Well), a preaching blog on the Bible aimed at helping preachers in the Church of Sweden to avoid repeating anti-Jewish stereotypes and supersessionist theology.

Eric A. Thomas is a graduate of Drew University where he completed the PhD in New Testament with concentrations in Africana and Women and Gender Studies. He has authored several essays on Revelation, the Gospel of Mark, and queer Africana biblical interpretation. Thomas serves on the Society of Biblical Literature's Committee for LGBTIQ+ Scholars and Scholarship and is an activist and pastor at Siloam Presbyterian Church in Brooklyn, New York.

Foreword

"Come Eat of My Bread . . . and Walk in the Ways of Wisdom"

Elisabeth Schüssler Fiorenza

Harvard University Divinity School

Jewish feminist writer Asphodel Long has likened the Bible to a magnificent garden of brilliant plants, some flowering, some fruiting, some in seed, some in bud, shaded by trees of age old, luxurious growth. Yet in the very soil which gives it life the poison has been inserted. . . . This poison is that of misogyny, the hatred of women, half the human race.[1]

To see Scripture as such a beautiful garden containing poisonous ivy requires that one identify and name this poison and place on all biblical texts the label "Caution! Could be dangerous to your health and survival!" As critical feminist interpretation for well-being this Wisdom Commentary seeks to elaborate the beauty and fecundity of this

---

1. Asphodel Long, *In a Chariot Drawn by Lions: The Search for the Female in the Deity* (London: Women's Press, 1992), 195.

Scripture-garden and at the same time points to the harm it can do when one submits to its world of vision. Thus, feminist biblical interpretation engages two seemingly contradictory insights: The Bible is written in kyriocentric (i.e., lord/master/father/husband-elite male) language, originated in the patri-kyriarchal cultures of antiquity, and has functioned to inculcate misogynist mind-sets and oppressive values. At the same time it also asserts that the Bible as Sacred Scripture has functioned to inspire and authorize wo/men[2] in our struggles against dehumanizing oppression. The hermeneutical lens of wisdom/Wisdom empowers the commentary writers to do so.

In biblical as well as in contemporary religious discourse the word *wisdom* has a double meaning: It can either refer to the quality of life and of people and/or it can refer to a figuration of the Divine. Wisdom in both senses of the word is not a prerogative of the biblical traditions but is found in the imagination and writings of all known religions. Wisdom is transcultural, international, and interreligious. Wisdom is practical knowledge gained through experience and daily living as well as through the study of creation and human nature. Both word meanings, that of capability (wisdom) and that of female personification (Wisdom), are crucial for this Wisdom Commentary series that seeks to enable biblical readers to become critical subjects of interpretation.

Wisdom is a state of the human mind and spirit characterized by deep understanding and profound insight. It is elaborated as a quality possessed by the sages but also treasured as folk wisdom and wit. Wisdom is the power of discernment, deeper understanding, and creativity; it is the ability to move and to dance, to make the connections, to savor life, and to learn from experience. Wisdom is intelligence shaped by experience and sharpened by critical analysis. It is the ability to make sound choices and incisive decisions. Its root meaning comes to the fore in its Latin form *sapientia*, which is derived from the verb *sapere*, to taste and to savor something. Hence, this series of commentaries invites readers to taste, to evaluate, and to imagine. In the figure of *Chokhmah-Sophia-Sapientia-Wisdom*, ancient Jewish Scriptures seek to hold together belief in the "one" G*d[3] of Israel with both masculine and feminine language and metaphors of the Divine.

---

2. I use wo/man, s/he, fe/male and not the grammatical standard "man" as inclusive terms and make this visible by adding /.

3. I use the * asterisk in order to alert readers to a problem to explore and think about.

In distinction to traditional Scripture reading, which is often individualistic and privatized, the practice and space of Wisdom commentary is public. Wisdom's spiraling presence (*Shekhinah*) is global, embracing all creation. Her voice is a public, radical democratic voice rather than a "feminine," privatized one. To become one of Her justice-seeking friends, one needs to imagine the work of this feminist commentary series as the spiraling circle dance of wisdom/Wisdom,[4] as a Spirit/spiritual intellectual movement in the open space of wisdom/Wisdom who calls readers to critically analyze, debate, and reimagine biblical texts and their commentaries as wisdom/Wisdom texts inspired by visions of justice and well-being for everyone and everything. Wisdom-Sophia-imagination engenders a different understanding of Jesus and the movement around him. It understands him as the child and prophet of Divine Wisdom and as Wisdom herself instead of imagining him as ruling King and Lord who has only subalterns but not friends. To approach the N*T[5] and the whole Bible as Wisdom's invitation of cosmic dimensions means to acknowledge its multivalence and its openness to change. As bread—not stone.

In short, this commentary series is inspired by the feminist vision of the open cosmic house of Divine Wisdom-Sophia as it is found in biblical Wisdom literatures, which include the N*T:

> Wisdom has built Her house
> She has set up Her seven pillars . . .
> She has mixed Her wine,
> She also has set Her table.
> She has sent out Her wo/men ministers
> to call from the highest places in the town . . .
> "Come eat of my bread
> and drink of the wine I have mixed.
> Leave immaturity, and live,
> And walk in the way of Wisdom." (Prov 9:1-3, 5-6)

---

4. I have elaborated such a Wisdom dance in terms of biblical hermeneutics in my book *Wisdom Ways: Introducing Feminist Biblical Interpretation* (Maryknoll, NY: Orbis Books, 2001). Its seven steps are a hermeneutics of experience, of domination, of suspicion, of evaluation, of remembering or historical reconstruction, of imagination, and of transformation. However, such Wisdom strategies of meaning making are not restricted to the Bible. Rather, I have used them in workshops in Brazil and Ecuador to explore the workings of power, Condomblé, Christology, imagining a the*logical wo/men's center, or engaging the national icon of Mary.

5. See the discussion about nomenclature of the two testaments in the introduction, pages xxix–xl.

Editor's Introduction to Wisdom Commentary

"She Is a Breath of the Power of God" (Wis 7:25)

Barbara E. Reid, OP

General Editor

Wisdom Commentary is the first series to offer detailed feminist interpretation of every book of the Bible. The fruit of collaborative work by an ecumenical and interreligious team of scholars, the volumes provide serious, scholarly engagement with the whole biblical text, not only those texts that explicitly mention women. The series is intended for clergy, teachers, ministers, and all serious students of the Bible. Designed to be both accessible and informed by the various approaches of biblical scholarship, it pays particular attention to the world in front of the text, that is, how the text is heard and appropriated. At the same time, this series aims to be faithful to the ancient text and its earliest audiences; thus the volumes also explicate the worlds behind the text and within it. While issues of gender are primary in this project, the volumes also address the intersecting issues of power, authority, ethnicity, race, class, and religious belief and practice. The fifty-eight volumes include the books regarded as canonical by Jews (i.e., the Tanakh); Protestants (the "Hebrew Bible" and the New Testament); and Roman Catholic, Anglican, and Eastern

Orthodox Communions (i.e., Tobit, Judith, 1 and 2 Maccabees, Wisdom of Solomon, Sirach/Ecclesiasticus, Baruch, including the Letter of Jeremiah, the additions to Esther, and Susanna and Bel and the Dragon in Daniel).

A Symphony of Diverse Voices

Included in the Wisdom Commentary series are voices from scholars of many different religious traditions, of diverse ages, differing sexual identities, and varying cultural, racial, ethnic, and social contexts. Some have been pioneers in feminist biblical interpretation; others are newer contributors from a younger generation. A further distinctive feature of this series is that each volume incorporates voices other than that of the lead author(s). These voices appear alongside the commentary of the lead author(s), in the grayscale inserts. At times, a contributor may offer an alternative interpretation or a critique of the position taken by the lead author(s). At other times, they may offer a complementary interpretation from a different cultural context or subject position. Occasionally, portions of previously published material bring in other views. The diverse voices are not intended to be contestants in a debate or a cacophony of discordant notes. The multiple voices reflect that there is no single definitive feminist interpretation of a text. In addition, they show the importance of subject position in the process of interpretation. In this regard, the Wisdom Commentary series takes inspiration from the Talmud and from *The Torah: A Women's Commentary* (ed. Tamara Cohn Eskenazi and Andrea L. Weiss; New York: URJ Press and Women of Reform Judaism, The Federation of Temple Sisterhoods, 2008), in which many voices, even conflicting ones, are included and not harmonized.

Contributors include biblical scholars, theologians, and readers of Scripture from outside the scholarly and religious guilds. At times, their comments pertain to a particular text. In some instances they address a theme or topic that arises from the text.

Another feature that highlights the collaborative nature of feminist biblical interpretation is that a number of the volumes have two lead authors who have worked in tandem from the inception of the project and whose voices interweave throughout the commentary.

Woman Wisdom

The title, Wisdom Commentary, reflects both the importance to feminists of the figure of Woman Wisdom in the Scriptures and the distinct wisdom that feminist women and men bring to the interpretive process. In the Scriptures, Woman Wisdom appears as "a breath of the power of God, and a pure emanation of the glory of the Almighty" (Wis 7:25), who was present and active in fashioning all that exists (Prov 8:22-31; Wis 8:6). She is a spirit who pervades and penetrates all things (Wis 7:22-23), and she provides guidance and nourishment at her all-inclusive table (Prov 9:1-5). In both postexilic biblical and nonbiblical Jewish sources, Woman Wisdom is often equated with Torah, e.g., Sirach 24:23-34; Baruch 3:9–4:4; 38:2; 46:4-5; 2 Baruch 48:33, 36; 4 Ezra 5:9-10; 13:55; 14:40; 1 Enoch 42.

The New Testament frequently portrays Jesus as Wisdom incarnate. He invites his followers, "take my yoke upon you and learn from me" (Matt 11:29), just as Ben Sira advises, "put your neck under her [Wisdom's] yoke and let your souls receive instruction" (Sir 51:26). Just as Wisdom experiences rejection (Prov 1:23-25; Sir 15:7-8; Wis 10:3; Bar 3:12), so too does Jesus (Mark 8:31; John 1:10-11). Only some accept his invitation to his all-inclusive banquet (Matt 22:1-14; Luke 14:15-24; compare Prov 1:20-21; 9:3-5). Yet, "wisdom is vindicated by her deeds" (Matt 11:19, speaking of Jesus and John the Baptist; in the Lukan parallel at 7:35 they are called "wisdom's children"). There are numerous parallels between what is said of Wisdom and of the *Logos* in the Prologue of the Fourth Gospel (John 1:1-18). These are only a few of many examples. This female embodiment of divine presence and power is an apt image to guide the work of this series.

Feminism

There are many different understandings of the term "feminism." The various meanings, aims, and methods have developed exponentially in recent decades. Feminism is a perspective and a movement that springs from a recognition of inequities toward women, and it advocates for changes in whatever structures prevent full flourishing of human beings and all creation. Three waves of feminism in the United States are commonly recognized. The first, arising in the mid-nineteenth century and lasting into the early twentieth, was sparked by women's efforts to be involved in the public sphere and to win the right to vote. In the 1960s and 1970s, the second wave focused on civil rights and equality for women. With the third wave, from the 1980s forward, came global feminism and the emphasis on the contextual nature of interpretation. Now a fourth wave is emerging, with a stronger emphasis on the intersectionality of women's concerns with those of other marginalized groups and the increased use of the internet as a platform for discussion and activism.[1] As feminism has matured, it has recognized that inequities based on gender are interwoven with power imbalances based on race, class, ethnicity, religion, sexual identity, physical ability, and a host of other social markers.

Feminist Women and Men

Men as well as nonbinary people who choose to identify with and partner with feminist women in the work of deconstructing systems of domination and building structures of equality are rightly regarded as feminists. Some men readily identify with experiences of women who are discriminated against on the basis of sex/gender, having themselves had comparable experiences; others who may not have faced direct discrimination or stereotyping recognize that inequity and problematic characterization still occur, and they seek correction. This series is pleased to include feminist men and nonbinary persons both as lead authors and as contributing voices.

Feminist Biblical Interpretation

Women interpreting the Bible from the lenses of their own experience is nothing new. Throughout the ages women have recounted the biblical stories, teaching them to their children and others, all the while interpreting them afresh for their time and circumstances.[2] Following is a very brief sketch of select foremothers who laid the groundwork for contemporary feminist biblical interpretation.

One of the earliest known Christian women who challenged patriarchal interpretations of Scripture was a consecrated virgin named Helie, who lived in the second century CE. When she refused to marry, her

---

1. See Martha Rampton, "Four Waves of Feminism" (October 25, 2015), at https:// www.pacificu.edu/magazine/four-waves-feminism; and Ealasaid Munro, "Feminism: A Fourth Wave?," *Political Insight* (September 2013), https://journals.sagepub .com/doi/pdf/10.1111/2041-9066.12021.

2. For fuller treatments of this history, see chap. 7, "One Thousand Years of Feminist Bible Criticism," in Gerda Lerner, *Creation of Feminist Consciousness: From the Middle Ages to Eighteen-Seventy* (New York: Oxford University Press, 1993), 138–66; Susanne Scholz, "From the 'Woman's Bible' to the 'Women's Bible,' The History of Feminist Approaches to the Hebrew Bible," in *Introducing the Women's Hebrew Bible*, IFT 13 (New York: T&T Clark, 2007), 12–32; Marion Ann Taylor and Agnes Choi, eds., *Handbook of Women Biblical Interpreters: A Historical and Biographical Guide* (Grand Rapids: Baker Academic, 2012).

parents brought her before a judge, who quoted to her Paul's admonition, "It is better to marry than to be aflame with passion" (1 Cor 7:9). In response, Helie first acknowledges that this is what Scripture says, but then she retorts, "but not for everyone, that is, not for holy virgins."[3] She is one of the first to question the notion that a text has one meaning that is applicable in all situations.

A Jewish woman who also lived in the second century CE, Beruriah, is said to have had "profound knowledge of biblical exegesis and outstanding intelligence."[4] One story preserved in the Talmud (b. Ber. 10a) tells of how she challenged her husband, Rabbi Meir, when he prayed for the destruction of a sinner. Proffering an alternate interpretation, she argued that Psalm 104:35 advocated praying for the destruction of sin, not the sinner.

In medieval times the first written commentaries on Scripture from a critical feminist point of view emerge. While others may have been produced and passed on orally, they are for the most part lost to us now. Among the earliest preserved feminist writings are those of Hildegard of Bingen (1098–1179), German writer, mystic, and abbess of a Benedictine monastery. She reinterpreted the Genesis narratives in a way that presented women and men as complementary and interdependent. She frequently wrote about the Divine as feminine.[5] Along with other women mystics of the time, such as Julian of Norwich (1342–ca. 1416), she spoke authoritatively from her personal experiences of God's revelation in prayer.

In this era, women were also among the scribes who copied biblical manuscripts. Notable among them is Paula Dei Mansi of Verona, from a distinguished family of Jewish scribes. In 1288, she translated from Hebrew into Italian a collection of Bible commentaries written by her father and added her own explanations.[6]

Another pioneer, Christine de Pizan (1365–ca. 1430), was a French court writer and prolific poet. She used allegory and common sense

---

3. Madrid, Escorial MS, a II 9, f. 90 v., as cited in Lerner, *Feminist Consciousness*, 140.

4. See Judith R. Baskin, "Women and Post-Biblical Commentary," in *The Torah: A Women's Commentary*, ed. Tamara Cohn Eskenazi and Andrea L. Weiss (New York: URJ Press and Women of Reform Judaism, The Federation of Temple Sisterhoods, 2008), xlix–lv, at lii.

5. Hildegard of Bingen, *De Operatione Dei*, 1.4.100; PL 197:885bc, as cited in Lerner, *Feminist Consciousness*, 142–43. See also Barbara Newman, *Sister of Wisdom: St. Hildegard's Theology of the Feminine* (Berkeley: University of California Press, 1987).

6. Emily Taitz, Sondra Henry, and Cheryl Tallan, *The JPS Guide to Jewish Women 600 B.C.E.–1900 C.E.* (Philadelphia: JPS, 2003), 110–11.

to subvert misogynist readings of Scripture and celebrated the accomplishments of female biblical figures to argue for women's active roles in building society.[7]

By the seventeenth century, there were women who asserted that the biblical text needs to be understood and interpreted in its historical context. For example, Rachel Speght (1597–ca. 1630), a Calvinist English poet, elaborates on the historical situation in first-century Corinth that prompted Paul to say, "It is well for a man not to touch a woman" (1 Cor 7:1). Her aim was to show that the biblical texts should not be applied in a literal fashion to all times and circumstances. Similarly, Margaret Fell (1614–1702), one of the founders of the Religious Society of Friends (Quakers) in Britain, addressed the Pauline prohibitions against women speaking in church by insisting that they do not have universal validity. Rather, they need to be understood in their historical context, as addressed to a local church in particular time-bound circumstances.[8]

Along with analyzing the historical context of the biblical writings, women in the eighteenth and nineteenth centuries began to attend to misogynistic interpretations based on faulty translations. One of the first to do so was British feminist Mary Astell (1666–1731).[9] In the United States, the Grimké sisters, Sarah (1792–1873) and Angelina (1805–1879), Quaker women from a slaveholding family in South Carolina, learned biblical Greek and Hebrew so that they could interpret the Bible for themselves. They were prompted to do so after men sought to silence them from speaking out against slavery and for women's rights by claiming that the Bible (e.g., 1 Cor 14:34) prevented women from speaking in public.[10] Another prominent abolitionist, Isabella Baumfree, was a former slave who adopted the name Sojourner Truth (ca. 1797–1883); she quoted the Bible liberally in her speeches[11] and in so doing challenged cultural assumptions and biblical interpretations that undergird gender inequities.

---

7. See further Taylor and Choi, *Handbook of Women Biblical Interpreters*, 127–32.

8. Her major work, *Women's Speaking Justified, Proved and Allowed by the Scriptures*, published in London in 1667, gave a systematic feminist reading of all biblical texts pertaining to women.

9. Mary Astell, *Some Reflections upon Marriage* (New York: Source Book Press, 1970, reprint of the 1730 edition; earliest edition of this work is 1700), 103–4.

10. See further Sarah Grimké, *Letters on the Equality of the Sexes and the Condition of Woman* (Boston: Isaac Knapp, 1838).

11. See, for example, her most famous speech, "Ain't I a Woman?," delivered in 1851 at the Ohio Women's Rights Convention in Akron; Modern History Sourcebook, https://sourcebooks.fordham.edu/mod/sojtruth-woman.asp.

Another monumental work that emerged in nineteenth-century England was that of Jewish theologian Grace Aguilar (1816–1847), *The Women of Israel*,[12] published in 1845. Aguilar's approach was to make connections between the biblical women and contemporary Jewish women's concerns. She aimed to counter the widespread antisemitic notion that women were degraded in Jewish law and that only in Christianity were women's dignity and value upheld. Her intent was to help Jewish women find strength and encouragement by seeing the evidence of God's compassionate love in the history of every woman in the Bible. While not a full commentary on the Bible, Aguilar's work stands out for its comprehensive treatment of every female biblical character, including even the most obscure references.[13]

The first person to produce a full-blown feminist commentary on the Bible was Elizabeth Cady Stanton (1815–1902). A leading proponent in the United States for women's right to vote, she found that whenever women tried to make inroads into politics, education, or the work world, the Bible was quoted against them. Along with a team of like-minded women, she produced her own commentary on every text of the Bible that concerned women. Her pioneering two-volume project, *The Woman's Bible*, published in 1895 and 1898, urges women to recognize that texts that degrade women come from the men who wrote the texts, not from God, and to use their common sense to rethink what has been presented to them as sacred.[14]

Nearly a century later, *The Women's Bible Commentary*, edited by Carol A. Newsom and Sharon H. Ringe (Louisville: Westminster John Knox, 1992), appeared. This one-volume commentary features North American feminist scholarship on each book of the Protestant canon. Like Cady Stanton's commentary, it does not contain comments on every section of the biblical text but only on those passages deemed relevant to women. It was revised and expanded in 1998 to include the Apocrypha/Deuterocanonical books, and the contributors to this new volume reflect the global face of contemporary feminist scholarship. The revisions made in the third edition, which appeared in 2012, represent the profound

---

12. The full title is *The Women of Israel or Characters and Sketches from the Holy Scriptures and Jewish History: Illustrative of the Past History, Present Duties, and Future Destiny of the Hebrew Females, as Based on the Word of God.*

13. See further Eskenazi and Weiss, *The Torah: A Women's Commentary*, xxxviii; Taylor and Choi, *Handbook of Women Biblical Interpreters*, 31–37.

14. While Cady Stanton's work was groundbreaking in its feminist approach, it nonetheless reflected racist and antisemitic attitudes she and the like-minded white Christian women who worked with her held.

advances in feminist biblical scholarship and include newer voices (with Jacqueline E. Lapsley as an additional editor). In both the second and third editions, *The* has been dropped from the title.

Also appearing at the centennial of Cady Stanton's *The Woman's Bible* were two volumes edited by Elisabeth Schüssler Fiorenza with the assistance of Shelly Matthews. The first, *Searching the Scriptures: A Feminist Introduction* (New York: Crossroad, 1993), charts a comprehensive approach to feminist interpretation from ecumenical, interreligious, and multicultural perspectives. The second volume, published in 1994, provides critical feminist commentary on each book of the New Testament as well as on three books of Jewish Pseudepigrapha and eleven other early Christian writings.

In Europe, similar endeavors have been undertaken, such as the one-volume *Kompendium Feministische Bibelauslegung*, edited by Luise Schottroff and Marie-Theres Wacker (Gütersloh: Gütersloher Verlagshaus, 2007), featuring German feminist biblical interpretation of each book of the Bible, along with Deuterocanonical apocryphal books, and several extrabiblical writings. This work, now in its third edition, was translated into English.[15] A multivolume project, The Bible and Women: An Encyclopaedia of Exegesis and Cultural History, edited by Mary Ann Beavis, Irmtraud Fischer, Mercedes Navarro Puerto, and Adriana Valerio, is currently in production. This project presents a history of the reception of the Bible as embedded in Western cultural history and focuses particularly on gender-relevant biblical themes, biblical female characters, and women recipients of the Bible. The volumes are published in English, Spanish, Italian, and German.[16]

---

15. *Feminist Biblical Interpretation: A Compendium of Critical Commentary on the Books of the Bible and Related Literature*, trans. Lisa E. Dahill, Everett R. Kalin, Nancy Lukens, Linda M. Maloney, Barbara Rumscheidt, Martin Rumscheidt, and Tina Steiner (Grand Rapids: Eerdmans, 2012). Another notable collection is the three volumes edited by Susanne Scholz, *Feminist Interpretation of the Hebrew Bible in Retrospect*, Recent Research in Biblical Studies 7, 8, 9 (Sheffield: Sheffield Phoenix, 2013, 2014, 2016).

16. The first volume, on the Torah, appeared in Spanish in 2009, in German and Italian in 2010, and in English in 2011 (Atlanta: SBL). The other available volumes are as follows: *Feminist Biblical Studies in the Twentieth Century*, ed. Elisabeth Schüssler Fiorenza (2014); *The Writings and Later Wisdom Books*, ed. Christl M. Maier and Nuria Calduch-Benages (2014); *Gospels: Narrative and History*, ed. Mercedes Navarro Puerto and Marinella Perroni; Amy-Jill Levine, English ed. (2015); *The High Middle Ages*, ed. Kari Elisabeth Børresen and Adriana Valerio (2015); *Early Jewish Writings*, ed. Eileen Schuller and Marie-Theres Wacker (2017); *Faith and Feminism in Nineteenth-Century Religious Communities*, ed. Michaela Sohn-Kronthaler and Ruth Albrecht (2019); *The Early Middle Ages*, ed. Franca Ela Consolino and Judith Herrin (2020); *Prophecy and Gender in the Hebrew Bible*, ed. L. Juliana Claassens and Irmtraud Fischer (2021); and

Another groundbreaking work is the collection The Feminist Companion to the Bible Series, edited by Athalya Brenner (Sheffield: Sheffield Academic, 1993–2015), which comprises twenty volumes of commentaries on the Old Testament. The parallel series, Feminist Companion to the New Testament and Early Christian Writings, edited by Amy-Jill Levine with Marianne Blickenstaff and Maria Mayo Robbins (Sheffield: Sheffield Academic, 2001–2010), contains thirteen volumes. These two series are not full commentaries on the biblical books but comprise collected essays on discrete biblical texts.

Works by individual feminist biblical scholars in all parts of the world abound, and they are now too numerous to list in this introduction. Feminist biblical interpretation has reached a level of maturity that now makes possible a commentary series on every book of the Bible. In recent decades, women have had greater access to formal theological education, have been able to learn critical analytical tools, have put their own interpretations into writing, and have developed new methods of biblical interpretation. Until recent decades the work of feminist biblical interpreters was largely unknown, both to other women and to their brothers in the synagogue, church, and academy. Feminists now have taken their place in the professional world of biblical scholars, where they build on the work of their foremothers and connect with one another across the globe in ways not previously possible. In a few short decades, feminist biblical criticism has become an integral part of the academy.

Methodologies

Feminist biblical scholars use a variety of methods and often employ a number of them together.[17] In the Wisdom Commentary series, the authors will explain their understanding of feminism and the feminist reading strategies used in their commentary. Each volume treats the biblical text in blocks of material, not an analysis verse by verse. The entire text is considered, not only those passages that feature female characters or that speak specifically about women. When women are not apparent in the narrative, feminist lenses are used to analyze the dynamics in the text between male characters, the models of power, binary ways of thinking,

---

Rabbinic Literature, ed. Tal Ilan, Lorena Miralles-Maciá, and Ronit Nikolsky (2022). For further information, see https://www.bibleandwomen.org.

17. See the seventeen essays in Caroline Vander Stichele and Todd Penner, eds., *Her Master's Tools? Feminist and Postcolonial Engagements of Historical-Critical Discourse* (Atlanta: SBL, 2005), which show the complementarity of various approaches.

and the dynamics of imperialism. Attention is given to how the whole text functions and how it was and is heard, both in its original context and today. Issues of particular concern to women—e.g., poverty, food, health, the environment, water—come to the fore.

One of the approaches used by early feminists and still popular today is to lift up the overlooked and forgotten stories of women in the Bible. Studies of women in each of the Testaments have been done, and there are also studies on women in particular biblical books.[18] Feminists recognize that the examples of biblical characters can be both empowering and problematic. The point of the feminist enterprise is not to serve as an apologetic for women; it is rather, in part, to recover women's history and literary roles in all their complexity and to learn from that recovery.

Retrieving the submerged history of biblical women is a crucial step for constructing the story of the past so as to lead to liberative possibilities for the present and future. There are, however, some pitfalls to this approach. Sometimes depictions of biblical women have been naïve and romantic. Some commentators exalt the virtues of both biblical and contemporary women and paint women as superior to men. Such reverse discrimination inhibits movement toward equality for all. In addition, some feminists challenge the idea that one can "pluck positive images out of an admittedly androcentric text, separating literary characterizations from the androcentric interests they were created to serve."[19] Still other feminists find these images to have enormous value.

One other danger with seeking the submerged history of women is the tendency for Christian feminists to paint Jesus and even Paul as liberators of women in a way that demonizes Judaism.[20] Wisdom Commentary

---

18. See, e.g., Alice Bach, ed., *Women in the Hebrew Bible: A Reader* (New York: Routledge, 1999); Tikva Frymer-Kensky, *Reading the Women of the Bible* (New York: Schocken Books, 2002); Carol Meyers, Toni Craven, and Ross S. Kraemer, eds., *Women in Scripture* (Grand Rapids: Eerdmans, 2001); Irene Nowell, *Women in the Old Testament* (Collegeville, MN: Liturgical Press, 1997); Katharine Doob Sakenfeld, *Just Wives? Stories of Power and Survival in the Old Testament and Today* (Louisville: Westminster John Knox, 2003); Mary Ann Getty-Sullivan, *Women in the New Testament* (Collegeville, MN: Liturgical Press, 2001); Bonnie Thurston, *Women in the New Testament: Questions and Commentary*, Companions to the New Testament (New York: Crossroad, 1998).

19. J. Cheryl Exum, "Second Thoughts about Secondary Characters: Women in Exodus 1.8–2.10," in *A Feminist Companion to Exodus to Deuteronomy*, FCB 6, ed. Athalya Brenner (Sheffield: Sheffield Academic, 1994), 75–97, at 76.

20. See Judith Plaskow, "Anti-Judaism in Feminist Christian Interpretation," in *Searching the Scriptures: A Feminist Introduction*, vol. 1, ed. Elisabeth Schüssler Fiorenza with Shelly Matthews (New York: Crossroad, 1993), 117–29; Amy-Jill Levine, "The

aims to enhance understanding of Jesus as well as Paul as Jews of their day and to forge solidarity among Jewish and Christian feminists.

Feminist scholars who use historical-critical methods analyze the world behind the text; they seek to understand the historical context from which the text emerged and the circumstances of the communities to whom it was addressed. In bringing feminist lenses to this approach, the aim is not to impose modern expectations on ancient cultures but to unmask the ways that ideologically problematic mind-sets that produced the ancient texts are still promulgated through the text. Feminist biblical scholars aim not only to deconstruct but also to reclaim and reconstruct biblical history as women's history, in which women were central and active agents in creating religious heritage.[21] A further step is to construct meaning for contemporary women and men in a liberative movement toward transformation of social, political, economic, and religious structures.[22] In recent years, some feminists have embraced new historicism, which accents the creative role of the interpreter in any construction of history and exposes the power struggles to which the text witnesses.[23]

Literary critics analyze the world of the text: its form, language patterns, and rhetorical function.[24] They do not attempt to separate layers

---

New Testament and Anti-Judaism," in *The Misunderstood Jew: The Church and the Scandal of the Jewish Jesus* (San Francisco: HarperSanFrancisco, 2006), 87–117.

21. See, for example, Phyllis A. Bird, *Missing Persons and Mistaken Identities: Women and Gender in Ancient Israel* (Minneapolis: Fortress, 1997); Elisabeth Schüssler Fiorenza, *In Memory of Her: A Feminist Theological Reconstruction of Christian Origins* (New York: Crossroad, 1994); Ross Shepard Kraemer and Mary Rose D'Angelo, eds., *Women and Christian Origins* (New York: Oxford University Press, 1999).

22. See, e.g., Sandra M. Schneiders, *The Revelatory Text: Interpreting the New Testament as Sacred Scripture*, rev. ed. (Collegeville, MN: Liturgical Press, 1999), whose aim is to engage in biblical interpretation not only for intellectual enlightenment but, even more important, for personal and communal transformation. Elisabeth Schüssler Fiorenza (*Wisdom Ways: Introducing Feminist Biblical Interpretation* [Maryknoll, NY: Orbis Books, 2001]) envisions the work of feminist biblical interpretation as a dance of Wisdom that consists of seven steps that interweave in spiral movements toward liberation, the final one being transformative action for change.

23. See Gina Hens-Piazza, *The New Historicism*, GBS, Old Testament Series (Minneapolis: Fortress, 2002).

24. Phyllis Trible was among the first to employ this method with texts from Genesis and Ruth in her groundbreaking book *God and the Rhetoric of Sexuality*, OBT (Philadelphia: Fortress, 1978). Another pioneer in feminist literary criticism is Mieke Bal (*Lethal Love: Feminist Literary Readings of Biblical Love Stories* [Bloomington: Indiana University Press, 1987]). For surveys of recent developments in literary methods, see Terry Eagleton,

of tradition and redaction but focus on the text holistically, as it is in its present form. They examine how meaning is created in the interaction between the text and its reader in multiple contexts. Within the arena of literary approaches are reader-oriented approaches, narrative, rhetorical, structuralist, post-structuralist, deconstructive, ideological, autobiographical, and performance criticism.[25] Narrative critics study the interrelation among author, text, and audience through investigation of settings, both spatial and temporal; characters; plot; and narrative techniques (e.g., irony, parody, intertextual allusions). Reader-response critics attend to the impact that the text has on the reader or hearer. They recognize that when a text is detrimental toward women there is the choice either to affirm the text or to read against the grain toward a liberative end. Rhetorical criticism analyzes the style of argumentation and attends to how the author is attempting to shape the thinking or actions of the hearer. Structuralist critics analyze the complex patterns of binary oppositions in the text to derive its meaning.[26] Post-structuralist approaches challenge the notion that there are fixed meanings to any biblical text or that there is one universal truth. They engage in close readings of the text and often engage in intertextual analysis.[27] Within this approach is deconstructionist criticism, which views the text as a site of conflict, with competing narratives. The interpreter aims to expose the fault lines and overturn and reconfigure binaries by elevating the underling of a pair and foregrounding it.[28] Feminists also use other post-modern approaches, such as ideological and autobiographical criticism.

Literary Theory: An Introduction, 3rd ed. (Minneapolis: University of Minnesota Press, 2008); Janice Capel Anderson and Stephen D. Moore, eds., *Mark and Method: New Approaches in Biblical Studies*, 2nd ed. (Minneapolis: Fortress, 2008); Michal Beth Dinkler, *Literary Theory and the New Testament*, AYBRL (New Haven: Yale University Press, 2019).

25. See, e.g., J. Cheryl Exum and David J. A. Clines, eds., *The New Literary Criticism and the Hebrew Bible* (Valley Forge, PA: Trinity Press International, 1993); Edgar V. McKnight and Elizabeth Struthers Malbon, eds., *The New Literary Criticism and the New Testament* (Valley Forge, PA: Trinity Press International, 1994).

26. See, e.g., David Jobling, *The Sense of Biblical Narrative: Three Structural Analyses in the Old Testament*, JSOTSup 7 (Sheffield: University of Sheffield Press, 1978).

27. See, e.g., Stephen D. Moore, *Poststructuralism and the New Testament: Derrida and Foucault at the Foot of the Cross* (Minneapolis: Fortress, 1994); *The Bible in Theory: Critical and Postcritical Essays* (Atlanta: SBL, 2010); Yvonne Sherwood, *A Biblical Text and Its Afterlives: The Survival of Jonah in Western Culture* (Cambridge: Cambridge University Press, 2000).

28. David Penchansky, "Deconstruction," in *The Oxford Encyclopedia of Biblical Interpretation*, ed. Steven McKenzie (New York: Oxford University Press, 2013), 196–205. See, for example, Danna Nolan Fewell and David M. Gunn, *Gender, Power, and Promise:*

The former analyzes the system of ideas that underlies the power and values concealed in the text as well as that of the interpreter.[29] The latter involves deliberate self-disclosure while reading the text as a critical exegete.[30] Performance criticism attends to how the text was passed on orally, usually in communal settings, and to the verbal and nonverbal interactions between the performer and the audience.[31]

From the beginning, feminists have understood that interpreting the Bible is an act of power. In recent decades, feminist biblical scholars have developed hermeneutical theories of the ethics and politics of biblical interpretation to challenge the claims to value neutrality of most academic biblical scholarship. Feminist biblical scholars have also turned their attention to how some biblical writings were shaped by the power of empire and how this still shapes readers' self-understandings today. They have developed hermeneutical approaches that reveal, critique, and evaluate the interactions depicted in the text against the context of empire, and they consider implications for contemporary contexts.[32] Feminists also analyze the dynamics of colonization and the mentalities of colonized peoples in the exercise of biblical interpretation. As Kwok Pui-lan explains, "A postcolonial feminist interpretation of the Bible needs to investigate the deployment of gender in the narration of identity, the negotiation of power differentials between the colonizers and the colonized, and the reinforcement of patriarchal control over spheres

---

The Subject of the Bible's First Story (Nashville: Abingdon, 1993); David Rutledge, *Reading Marginally: Feminism, Deconstruction and the Bible*, BibInt 21 (Leiden: Brill, 1996).

29. See David Jobling and Tina Pippin, eds., *Semeia 59: Ideological Criticism of Biblical Texts* (Atlanta: Scholars Press, 1992); Terry Eagleton, *Ideology: An Introduction* (London: Verso, 2007).

30. See, e.g., Ingrid Rosa Kitzberger, ed., *Autobiographical Biblical Criticism: Between Text and Self* (Leiden: Deo, 2002); P. J. W. Schutte, "When *They*, *We*, and the *Passive* Become *I*—Introducing Autobiographical Biblical Criticism," *HTS Teologiese Studies / Theological Studies* 61 (2005): 401–16.

31. See, e.g., Holly E. Hearon and Philip Ruge-Jones, eds., *The Bible in Ancient and Modern Media: Story and Performance* (Eugene, OR: Cascade, 2009).

32. E.g., Gale Yee, ed., *Judges and Method: New Approaches in Biblical Studies* (Minneapolis: Fortress, 1995); Warren Carter, "Matthaean Christology in Roman Imperial Key: Matthew 1.1," in *The Gospel of Matthew in Its Roman Imperial Context*, ed. John Riches and David C. Sim (London: T&T Clark, 2005); Warren Carter, *The Roman Empire and the New Testament: An Essential Guide* (Nashville: Abingdon, 2006); Elisabeth Schüssler Fiorenza, *The Power of the Word: Scripture and the Rhetoric of Empire* (Minneapolis: Fortress, 2007); Judith E. McKinlay, *Reframing Her: Biblical Women in Postcolonial Focus* (Sheffield: Sheffield Phoenix, 2004).

where these elites could exercise control."[33] Methods and models from sociology and cultural anthropology are used by feminists to investigate women's everyday lives, their experiences of marriage, childrearing, labor, money, illness, etc.[34]

As feminists have examined the construction of gender from varying cultural perspectives, they have become ever more cognizant that the way gender roles are defined within differing cultures varies radically. As Mary Ann Tolbert observes, "Attempts to isolate some universal role that cross-culturally defines 'woman' have run into contradictory evidence at every turn."[35] Some women have coined new terms to highlight the particularities of their socio-cultural context. Many African American feminists, for example, call themselves *womanists* to draw attention to the double oppression of racism and sexism they experience.[36] Similarly, many US Hispanic feminists speak of themselves as *mujeristas* (*mujer* is Spanish for "woman").[37] Others prefer to be called "Latina feminists."[38] As a gender-neutral or nonbinary alternative, many today use Latinx or Latine. *Mujeristas*, Latina and Latine feminists emphasize that the context

33. Kwok Pui-lan, *Postcolonial Imagination and Feminist Theology* (Louisville: Westminster John Knox, 2005), 9. See also Musa W. Dube, ed., *Postcolonial Feminist Interpretation of the Bible* (St. Louis: Chalice, 2000); Christl M. Maier and Carolyn J. Sharp, *Prophecy and Power: Jeremiah in Feminist and Postcolonial Perspective* (London: Bloomsbury, 2013); L. Juliana Claassens and Carolyn J. Sharp, eds., *Feminist Frameworks and the Bible: Power, Ambiguity, and Intersectionality*, LHBOTS 630 (London: Bloomsbury T&T Clark, 2017).

34. See, for example, Carol Meyers, *Rediscovering Eve: Ancient Israelite Women in Context* (New York: Oxford University Press, 2013); Luise Schottroff, *Lydia's Impatient Sisters: A Feminist Social History of Early Christianity*, trans. Barbara and Martin Rumscheidt (Louisville: Westminster John Knox, 1995); Susan Niditch, *"My Brother Esau Is a Hairy Man": Hair and Identity in Ancient Israel* (Oxford: Oxford University Press, 2008).

35. Mary Ann Tolbert, "Social, Sociological, and Anthropological Methods," in *Searching the Scriptures*, 1:255–71, at 265.

36. Alice Walker coined the term (*In Search of Our Mothers' Gardens: Womanist Prose* [New York: Harcourt Brace Jovanovich, 1967, 1983]). See also Katie G. Cannon, "The Emergence of Black Feminist Consciousness," in *Feminist Interpretation of the Bible*, ed. Letty M. Russell (Philadelphia: Westminster, 1985), 30–40; Renita J. Weems, *Just a Sister Away: A Womanist Vision of Women's Relationships in the Bible* (San Diego: Lura Media, 1988); Nyasha Junior, *An Introduction to Womanist Biblical Interpretation* (Louisville: Westminster John Knox, 2015).

37. Ada María Isasi-Díaz (*Mujerista Theology: A Theology for the Twenty-First Century* [Maryknoll, NY: Orbis Books, 1996]) is credited with coining the term.

38. E.g., María Pilar Aquino, Daisy L. Machado, and Jeanette Rodríguez, eds., *A Reader in Latina Feminist Theology* (Austin: University of Texas Press, 2002).

for their theologizing is *mestizaje* and *mulatez* (racial and cultural mixture), done *en conjunto* (in community), with *lo cotidiano* (everyday lived experience) of Latina women as starting points for theological reflection and the encounter with the divine. Intercultural analysis has become an indispensable tool for working toward justice for women at the global level.[39]

Some feminists are among those who have developed interpretations from the perspectives of lesbian, gay, bisexual, transgender, queer and/or questioning, intersex, asexual, and other ways people choose to identify (LGBTQIA+). These approaches focus on issues of sexual identity and use various reading strategies. Some point out the ways in which categories that emerged in recent centuries are applied anachronistically to biblical texts to make modern-day judgments. Others show how the Bible is silent on contemporary issues about sexual identity. Still others examine same-sex relationships in the Bible by figures such as Ruth and Naomi or David and Jonathan. In recent years, queer theory has emerged; it emphasizes the blurriness of boundaries not just of sexual identity but also of gender roles. Queer critics often focus on texts in which figures transgress what is traditionally considered proper gender behavior.[40]

Feminists have also been engaged in studying the reception history of the text[41] and have engaged in studies in the emerging fields of disability theory and of children in the Bible.

39. See, e.g., María Pilar Aquino and María José Rosado-Nunes, eds., *Feminist Intercultural Theology: Latina Explorations for a Just World*, Studies in Latino/a Catholicism (Maryknoll, NY: Orbis Books, 2007). See also Michelle A. Gonzalez, "Latina Feminist Theology: Past, Present, and Future," *JFSR* 25 (2009): 150–55. See also Elisabeth Schüssler Fiorenza, ed., *Feminist Biblical Studies in the Twentieth Century: Scholarship and Movement*, The Bible and Women 9.1 (Atlanta: SBL Press, 2014), who charts feminist studies around the globe as well as emerging feminist methodologies.

40. See, e.g., Bernadette J. Brooten, *Love Between Women: Early Christian Responses to Female Homoeroticism* (Chicago: University of Chicago Press, 1996); Mary Rose D'Angelo, "Women Partners in the New Testament," *JFSR* 6 (1990): 65–86; Deirdre J. Good, "Reading Strategies for Biblical Passages on Same-Sex Relations," *Theology and Sexuality* 7 (1997): 70–82; Deryn Guest, *When Deborah Met Jael: Lesbian Biblical Hermeneutics* (London: SCM, 2005); Teresa J. Hornsby and Ken Stone, eds., *Bible Trouble: Queer Reading at the Boundaries of Biblical Scholarship* (Atlanta: SBL, 2011); Joseph A. Marchal, "Queer Studies and Critical Masculinity Studies in Feminist Biblical Studies," in *Feminist Biblical Studies in the Twentieth Century*, ed. Schüssler Fiorenza, 261–80.

41. See Sharon H. Ringe, "When Women Interpret the Bible," in *Women's Bible Commentary*, ed. Carol A. Newsom, Sharon H. Ringe, and Jacqueline E. Lapsley, 3rd ed. (Louisville: Westminster John Knox, 2012), 5; Taylor and Choi, *Handbook of Women Biblical*

Feminists also recognize that the struggle for women's equality and dignity is intimately connected with the struggle for respect for Earth and for the whole of the cosmos. Ecofeminists interpret Scripture in ways that highlight the link between human domination of nature and male subjugation of women. They show how anthropocentric ways of interpreting the Bible have overlooked or dismissed Earth and Earth community. They invite readers to identify not only with human characters in the biblical narrative but also with other Earth creatures and domains of nature, especially those that are the object of injustice. Some use creative imagination to retrieve the interests of Earth implicit in the narrative and enable Earth to speak.[42]

Biblical Authority

By the late nineteenth century, some feminists, such as Elizabeth Cady Stanton, began to question openly whether the Bible could continue to be regarded as authoritative for women. They viewed the Bible itself as the source of women's oppression, and some rejected its sacred origin and saving claims. Some decided that the Bible and the religious traditions that enshrine it are too thoroughly saturated with androcentrism and patriarchy to be redeemable.[43]

In the Wisdom Commentary series, questions such as these may be raised, but the aim of this series is not to lead readers to reject the authority of the biblical text. Rather, the aim is to promote better understanding of the contexts from which the text arose and of the rhetorical effects it has on people in contemporary contexts. Such understanding can lead to a deepening of faith, with the Bible serving as an aid to bring flourishing of life.

Language for God

Because of the ways in which the term "God" has been used to symbolize the divine in predominantly male, patriarchal, and monarchical modes, feminists have designed new ways of speaking of the divine. Some have

---

Interpreters; Yvonne Sherwood, "Introduction," in *The Bible and Feminism: Remapping the Field*, ed. Yvonne Sherwood with Anna Fisk (New York: Oxford University Press, 2017).

42. E.g., Norman C. Habel and Peter Trudinger, *Exploring Ecological Hermeneutics*, SymS 46 (Atlanta: SBL, 2008); Mary Judith Ress, *Ecofeminism in Latin America*, Women from the Margins (Maryknoll, NY: Orbis Books, 2006).

43. E.g., Mary Daly, *Beyond God the Father: A Philosophy of Women's Liberation* (Boston: Beacon, 1985).

called attention to the inadequacy of the term *God* by trying to visually destabilize our ways of thinking and speaking of the divine. Rosemary Radford Ruether proposed *God/ess*, as an unpronounceable term pointing to the unnameable understanding of the divine that transcends patriarchal limitations.[44] Some have followed traditional Jewish practice, writing *G-d*. Elisabeth Schüssler Fiorenza has adopted *G*d*.[45] Others draw on the biblical tradition to mine female and non-gender-specific metaphors and symbols.[46] In Wisdom Commentary, there is not one standard way of expressing the divine; each author will use her or his preferred ways. The one exception is that when the tetragrammaton, YHWH, the name revealed to Moses in Exodus 3:14, is used, it will be without vowels, respecting the Jewish custom of avoiding pronouncing the divine name out of reverence.

Nomenclature for the Two Testaments

In recent decades, some biblical scholars have begun to call the two Testaments of the Bible by names other than the traditional nomenclature: Old and New Testament. Some regard "Old" as derogatory, implying that it is no longer relevant or that it has been superseded. Consequently, terms like Hebrew Bible, First Testament, and Jewish Scriptures and, correspondingly, Christian Scriptures or Second Testament have come into use. There are a number of difficulties with these designations. The term "Hebrew Bible" does not take into account that parts of the Old Testament are written not in Hebrew but in Aramaic.[47] Moreover, for Roman Catholics and Eastern Orthodox believers, the Old Testament includes books written in Greek—the Deuterocanonical books, considered Apocrypha by Protestants.[48] The term "Jewish Scriptures" is inadequate because these

44. Rosemary Radford Ruether, *Sexism and God-Talk: Toward a Feminist Theology* (Boston: Beacon, 1993).

45. Elisabeth Schüssler Fiorenza, *Jesus: Miriam's Child, Sophia's Prophet; Critical Issues in Feminist Christology* (New York: Continuum, 1994), 191n3.

46. E.g., Sallie McFague, *Models of God: Theology for an Ecological, Nuclear Age* (Philadelphia: Fortress, 1987); Catherine Mowry LaCugna, *God for Us: The Trinity and Christian Life* (San Francisco: HarperCollins, 1991); Elizabeth A. Johnson, *She Who Is: The Mystery of God in Feminist Theological Discourse* (New York: Crossroad, 1992). See further Elizabeth A. Johnson, "God," in *Dictionary of Feminist Theologies*, ed. Letty M. Russell and J. Shannon Clarkson (Louisville: Westminster John Knox, 1996), 128–30.

47. Gen 31:47; Jer 10:11; Ezra 4:7–6:18; 7:12-26; Dan 2:4–7:28.

48. Representing the *via media* between Catholic and reformed, Anglicans generally consider the Apocrypha to be profitable, if not canonical, and utilize select Wisdom texts liturgically.

books are also sacred to Christians. Conversely, "Christian Scriptures" is not an accurate designation for the New Testament, since the Old Testament is also part of the Christian Scriptures. Using "First and Second Testament" also has difficulties, in that it can imply a hierarchy and a value judgment.[49] Jews generally use the term Tanakh, an acronym for Torah (Pentateuch), Nevi'im (Prophets), and Ketuvim (Writings).

In Wisdom Commentary, if authors choose to use a designation other than Tanakh, Old Testament, and New Testament, they will explain how they mean the term.

Translation

Modern feminist scholars recognize the complexities connected with biblical translation, as they have delved into questions about philosophy of language, how meanings are produced, and how they are culturally situated. Today it is evident that simply translating into gender-neutral formulations cannot address all the challenges presented by androcentric texts. Efforts at feminist translation must also deal with issues around authority and canonicity.[50]

Because of these complexities, the editors of the Wisdom Commentary series have chosen to use an existing translation, the New Revised Standard Version (NRSV),[51] which is provided for easy reference at the top of each page of commentary. The NRSV was produced by a team of ecumenical and interreligious scholars, is a fairly literal translation, and uses inclusive language for human beings. Brief discussions about problematic translations appear in the inserts labeled "Translation Matters." When more detailed discussions are available, these will be indicated in footnotes. In the commentary, wherever Hebrew or Greek words are used, English translation is provided. In cases where a wordplay is involved, transliteration is provided to enable understanding.

49. See Levine, *The Misunderstood Jew*, 193–99.

50. Elizabeth Castelli, "*Les Belles Infidèles*/Fidelity or Feminism? The Meanings of Feminist Biblical Translation," in *Searching the Scriptures*, 1:189–204, here 190.

51. The volumes of Wisdom Commentary produced through 2023 use the edition of NRSV published in 1989; subsequent volumes use the updated edition, NRSVue, released in 2021.

Art and Poetry

Artistic expression in poetry, music, sculpture, painting, and various other modes is very important to feminist interpretation. Where possible, art and poetry are included in the print volumes of the series. In a number of instances, these are original works created for this project. Regrettably, copyright and production costs prohibit the inclusion of color photographs and other artistic work.

Glossary

Because there are a number of excellent readily available resources that provide definitions and concise explanations of terms used in feminist theological and biblical studies, this series will not include a glossary. We refer you to works such as *Dictionary of Feminist Theologies*, edited by Letty M. Russell and J. Shannon Clarkson, and volume 1 of *Searching the Scriptures*, edited by Elisabeth Schüssler Fiorenza with the assistance of Shelly Matthews. Individual authors in the Wisdom Commentary series will define the way they are using terms that may be unfamiliar.

A Concluding Word

In just a few short decades, feminist biblical studies has grown exponentially, both in the methods that have been developed and in the number of scholars who have embraced it. We realize that this series is limited and will soon need to be revised and updated. It is our hope that Wisdom Commentary, by making the best of current feminist biblical scholarship available in an accessible format to ministers, preachers, rabbis, teachers, scholars, and students, will aid all readers in their advancement toward God's vision of dignity, equality, and justice for all.

Acknowledgments

There are a great many people who have made this series possible: first, Peter Dwyer, retired director of Liturgical Press, and Hans Christoffersen, editorial director of Liturgical Press, who have believed in this project and have shepherded it since it was conceived in 2008. I am grateful to Therese L. Ratliff, the Press's director and CEO, who is now championing this project.

Editorial consultants Athalya Brenner-Idan and Elisabeth Schüssler Fiorenza have not only been an inspiration with their pioneering work but have encouraged us all along the way with their personal involvement. Volume editors Mary Ann Beavis, Carol J. Dempsey, Amy-Jill Levine, Linda M. Maloney, Song-Mi Suzie Park, Ahida Pilarski, Sarah Tanzer, and Lauress Wilkins Lawrence have lent their extraordinary wisdom to the shaping of the series, have used their extensive networks of relationships to secure authors and contributors, and have worked tirelessly to guide their work to completion. Others who have contributed greatly to the shaping of the project are Linda M. Day, Gina Hens-Piazza, Mignon Jacobs, Seung Ai Yang, and Barbara E. Bowe of blessed memory (d. 2010). Editorial and research assistant Susan M. Hickman provided invaluable support with administrative details and arrangements at the outset of the project. I am grateful to Brian Eisenschenk and Christine Henderson who assisted Susan Hickman with the Wiki. I am especially thankful to Lauren L. Murphy and Justin Howell for their work in copyediting; and to the staff at Liturgical Press, especially Colleen Stiller, retired production manager; Angie Steffens, production manager; Elizabeth Elin, production coordinator; Stephanie Lancour, production editor; Julie Surma, desktop publisher; and Tara Durheim, marketing director.

Prologue

Reading Revelation, with its cascade of images and zigzagging course, reminds us (Gail and Lynn) of following alongside or paddling down a river. While we have a general sense of where we are headed, twists surprise us. There is a sense of anticipation as we move along with the book's narrative; parts of the river are unexpectedly calm, and others threaten navigators with rushing currents. As feminist commentators, we see ourselves as our readers' guides. On the one hand, we want to equip our readers for the things we expect they will encounter as they move through the text and share insights—both our own and those learned from others—about its history, environment, and significance.

On the other hand, we want to balance this preparation with an openness to discovery, even when discovery might lead to difficult places. We want to encourage our fellow travelers to experience fully the sights, sounds, smells, and even tastes of what they encounter on the journey as we provide a framework for understanding these experiences. We hope our readers discover Revelation along with us, recognizing that no two journeys are exactly alike because of the different expectations we carry with us as we head downstream.

Commentaries on Revelation often begin by noting how, despite being called a "revelation," the text obscures more than it may reveal. This irony points to the fact that Revelation resists giving simple answers. Consequently, over time readers have found in its pages a variety of meanings, many that even contradict one another. The admission that this book is obscure or mysterious potentially sets up commentators as adepts who magically unveil the book's meaning for readers. We want to avoid putting ourselves in that role, although we acknowledge we have spent considerable time and effort studying Revelation and its contexts. We want to share what we know so that readers can navigate Revelation with confidence, but we also want our readers to be able to find new meaning within the book's pages. While we serve as guides through this text, we hope readers develop their own sense of Revelation's currents as well.

In addition to this spirit of discovery, we bring feminist commitments and interpretive practices with us as we head along this river. First and foremost, we understand our journey as part of our work "to end sexist oppression."[1] As bell hooks explains, this work includes a "commitment to reorganizing society so that the self-development of people can take precedence over imperialism, economic expansion, and material desires."[2] It requires acknowledging that sexist oppression is intertwined with other oppressions, including racism, classism, heterosexism, ableism, ageism, religious bias, and other social sins that keep people from living life abundantly. To dismantle one form of oppression, we must work to dismantle all. Interpreting Revelation is not the only way we participate in the project of dismantling oppressions, but in our roles as biblical scholars and educators we seek to help our readers and students look for ways Revelation and its interpretations participate in and challenge the exploitation and marginalization of humans, especially women, girls, and individuals across the LGBTQIA+ continuum.[3] To this end, and because we recognize that texts, like rivers, are shaped by a landscape mostly hidden from sight, we employ a "hermeneutic of suspicion" as we approach Revelation.[4] Things below the text's surface, such as first-century assumptions about gender and class, contribute to systems of oppression, so we must be cautious when it comes to reading the text, especially when the surface appears calm. We need to look carefully for rocks and shoals, the ways of thinking and parts of the narrative that

---

1. bell hooks, *Feminist Theory: From Margin to Center*, 2nd ed. (London: Pluto Press, 2000), 26.

2. hooks, *Feminist Theory*, 26.

3. "LGBTQIA+" refers to the range of sexual and gender identities that exist outside of heterosexuality, including lesbian, gay, bisexual, trans, intersex, asexual, and queer identities, and binary understandings of sex, such as trans identity. The plus sign notes that "LGBTQIA" is only a partial list of non-straight identities.

4. Elisabeth Schüssler Fiorenza, *Bread Not Stone: The Challenge of Feminist Biblical Interpretation*, 2nd ed. (Boston: Beacon Press, 1995), 15–16.

have contributed to the domination and suppression of others and the degradation of our world.

At the same time, we try to resist oversuspicious readings that assume Revelation holds only oppressive possibilities and that we must passively accept where the streams of interpretation take us or jump off the boat.[5] While we want to understand and appreciate what John, the author and narrator of Revelation, is doing and how he does it, we refuse to unthinkingly adopt his vision as the only way of imagining Revelation's meaning. As Jacqueline M. Hidalgo observes, Revelation might best be understood as *a* revelation of Jesus Christ rather than *the* revelation of Jesus Christ.[6]

In our interpretation, we strive to embrace a type of reading that Mitzi J. Smith describes as "talking-back" or "sassing" the text: "We need to celebrate sass and talk-back in women of color as well as in White women as a legitimate form of agency and method of truth telling rather than punishing women for speaking truth boldly in the face of corrupt, biased, life-threatening and denying authority."[7] Smith identifies the Syrophoenician woman who "talks back" to Jesus (see Mark 7:24-30) and Sandra Bland, the Black woman who repeatedly asked a police officer why he was arresting her after he stopped her car for a burned-out taillight in 2015, as interpretive role models. To these models, we add the model of Jesus himself as depicted in John's Gospel, since he spoke boldly (παρρησίᾳ) to those who challenged him *and* those he counted as friends (John 7:26, KJV).[8]

Building on Smith's suggestion that sass or talking-back is a viable interpretive technique, we recommend "reading" the text. "Reading" is a queer way of challenging voices of authority and cultural assumptions about appropriateness. Reading something or someone involves calling out hypocrisy with humor and wit. Revelation is a text that many take *very seriously*. Revelation itself, however, uses humor, irony, and parody to contextualize and disarm the powerful (see sidebar on "Phallic Humor

---

5. Rhiannon Graybill, *Texts after Terror: Rape, Sexual Violence, and the Hebrew Bible* (New York: Oxford University Press, 2021), 22–23.

6. Jacqueline M. Hidalgo, *Revelation in Aztlán: Scriptures, Utopias, and the Chicano Movement* (New York: Palgrave Macmillan, 2016), 234.

7. Mitzi J. Smith, *Womanist Sass and Talk Back: Social (In)Justice, Intersectionality, and Biblical Interpretation* (Eugene, OR: Cascade Books, 2018), 44.

8. Gail R. O'Day, "Jesus as Friend in the Gospel of John," *Int* 58 (2004): 144–57.

in the Roman World").[9] Similarly, Adele Reinhartz, in her 2020 presidential address to the Society of Biblical Literature, recommended a "hermeneutics of chutzpah," a willingness to embrace agency as biblical interpreters to question and speak our minds to the text and its interpreters.[10] Sass, humor, and chutzpah are necessary tools for feminist scholars of all sorts, especially those who study Revelation!

Finally, our experience of Revelation is shaped by when, where, how, and why we navigate it. As the ancient philosopher Heraclitus famously proclaimed, "It is impossible to step twice in the same river" (as quoted by Plutarch, *The E at Delphi* 392). The experience of interpreting Revelation is not the same today as it was one year ago, let alone two thousand years ago. Our current reasons for embarking on this journey may differ from our past motivations for engaging the text. Our readings change as we return to the text time and again after conversing with another person or experiencing another life event. The realities around us impact how we read the book's currents and whether we approach it eagerly or with trepidation. We understand that our readers similarly come to the text with varying levels of experience, ranging from little to no knowledge of what lies ahead to a very keen awareness of the book and its impact. No matter how you come to this book, we hope that your experience of Revelation yields new discoveries.

Navigating Revelation with Others

Feminist criticism begins with the recognition that the historical and social contexts of the interpreter shape their interpretations. Our context allows us to see some aspects of a text while hiding or obscuring others. Engaging the interpretations of those with perspectives or vantage points different from our own necessarily offers us new insights into the text, even when reading a text with which we are very familiar. Because of this, the Wisdom Commentary series features "contributing voices" from interpreters who offer their perspectives on parts of the text as

9. Sarah Emanuel, *Humor, Resistance, and Jewish Cultural Persistence in the Book of Revelation: Roasting Rome* (Cambridge: Cambridge University Press, 2020). For the use of humor as a queer and feminist interpretive strategy, see Reta Ugena Whitlock, "Introduction: Loving, Telling, and Reconstructing the South," in *Queer South Rising: Voices of a Contested Place*, ed. Reta Ugena Whitlock (Charlotte, NC: Information Age, 2013), xxxi.

10. Adele Reinhartz, "The Hermeneutics of Chutzpah: A Disquisition on the Value/s of 'Critical Investigation of the Bible,'" *JBL* 140 (2021): 13–14.

a way of augmenting the readings provided by the primary authors. The scholars who offer perspectives here are colleagues we respect and whose work we recommend. In addition, throughout this book, we intentionally note and draw on other excellent scholars, including those whose names might not appear regularly in nonfeminist commentaries. Amid the multiple perspectives we engage, we privilege the voices of women, feminists, scholars of color, and scholars who identify as part of the LGBTQIA+ community. By privileging these voices, we hope to embody the claim made by feminist philosopher Sara Ahmed that "citation is feminist memory."[11] The footnotes and bibliography feature those who have helped us better understand Revelation from a feminist perspective and as a text both implicated in systems of oppression and potentially helpful in dismantling those same systems. There are some instances when we cite interpretations with which we disagree, and we occasionally cite some sources that perpetuate oppressive interpretations as a way of providing specific examples. The context of the citation should signal this disagreement.

Women have long negotiated Revelation's twists and turns, even though many of the most cited works on this book are by men. Women's interpretations are as varied as the places and times from which they approach the narrative, and not all women readers of Revelation bring feminist interpretive goals to the text. Two of the earliest known female interpreters, Priscilla and Maximilla, were second-century prophets living in Asia Minor; they experienced visions, advocated celibacy, and announced the descent of the heavenly Jerusalem, as described in Revelation's closing chapters, was imminent. Their Revelation-infused teachings, which Christian tradition condemned (e.g., Eusebius, *Hist. eccl.* 5.14), shaped the lives of followers even as late as the eighth century.[12] Like Priscilla and Maximilla, Hildegard of Bingen, a twelfth-century abbess, author, healer, and artist, experienced prophetic visions replete with imagery drawn from Revelation. Hildegard opens *Scivias*, a lengthy account of her visions, with a description of how, at age forty-three, she experienced a command to "say and write what you see and hear," much like John's testimony in Revelation (1:11, 19).[13] The list of other

11. Sara Ahmed, *Living a Feminist Life* (Durham, NC: Duke University Press, 2017), 15.

12. Christine Trevett, *Montanism: Gender, Authority and the New Prophecy* (Cambridge: Cambridge University Press, 2002).

13. Hildegard, *Scivias*, trans. Columba Hart and Jane Bishop, The Classics of Western Spirituality (New York: Paulist Press, 1990), Declaration.

visionary and prophetic women inspired by Revelation include women from throughout history: Hadewijch of Brabant, a medieval Flemish poet and lay nun (or Beguine); Rebecca Cox Jackson, a visionary associated with the Shakers who led a multiracial religious community along with her female partner; Sister Gertrude Morgan, a street preacher and visual artist who lived and worked in New Orleans; and Myrtice West, a self-taught artist from Alabama who painted vivid scenes from Revelation under divine direction.[14] Other women whose interpretations of Revelation are extant include the seventeenth-century English author and prophet Anna Trapnel and the nineteenth-century poet Christina Rossetti.[15] We can imagine that these women represent just a portion of the female-identified interpreters who have engaged Revelation's text and imagery across the centuries, as the interpretive insights of many women have been lost to history.

In the introduction to *A Feminist Companion to the Apocalypse of John*, Amy-Jill Levine notes how, early in her career, she observed that women biblical scholars, including Elisabeth Schüssler Fiorenza, Adela Yarbro Collins, and Josephine Massyngbaerde Ford, "clustered around the book of Revelation."[16] While these interpreters engaged a variety of questions related to the book, including its authorship and function, subsequent feminist work on Revelation focuses heavily on John's use of gendered imagery, especially depictions of Jezebel and Babylon, who is represented as a woman and sex-worker. Much of this work explores whether Revelation, with its negative portrayals of women, holds the possibility of "good news" for women. As Hanna Stenström asks, does the book of Revelation provide women, specifically feminists, a usable vision of the future?[17] Even though feminist scholars differ in their answer to this ques-

---

14. Lynn R. Huber, *Thinking and Seeing with Women in Revelation*, LNTS 475 (London: Bloomsbury, 2013); Rebecca Jackson, *Gifts of Power: The Writings of Rebecca Jackson, Black Visionary, Shaker Eldress*, ed. Jean McMahon Humez (Amherst: University of Massachusetts Press, 1987).

15. Judith L. Kovacs and Christopher Rowland, *Revelation: The Apocalypse of Jesus Christ* (Malden, MA: Blackwell, 2004), 62.

16. Amy-Jill Levine, "Introduction," in *A Feminist Companion to the Apocalypse of John*, ed. Amy-Jill Levine with Maria Mayo Robbins, FCNTECW 13 (London: T&T Clark, 2009), 1. For a more recent introduction to feminist interpretation of Revelation, see Susan E. Hylen, "Feminist Interpretation of Revelation," in *The Oxford Handbook of the Book of Revelation*, ed. Craig R. Koester (New York: Oxford University Press, 2020), 461–82.

17. Hanna Stenström, "Feminists in Search for a Usable Future: Feminist Reception of the Book of Revelation," in *The Way the World Ends? The Apocalypse of John in*

tion, today, there are still many female-identified scholars of Revelation specifically and apocalyptic literature more generally. The relatively large number of women working on Revelation calls into question published articles and essays on the book that fail to include any women authors.[18]

In *Revelation: Vision of a Just World*, published in 1991, Elisabeth Schüssler Fiorenza provides the first feminist commentary on the entire book of Revelation. In this deceptively slim volume, Schüssler Fiorenza outlines how Revelation offers both a visionary critique of the socio-economic and political oppression experienced by the text's first audiences and a theological vision of hope and justice that is meaningful to Christians across centuries. While the text is replete with violent images, Schüssler Fiorenza argues that these are a "fitting" response to the political situation in which John and his audiences lived.[19] Without understanding this interpretive context, readers of Revelation risk misinterpreting the book's symbolic language and mistakenly applying Revelation literally in contexts where Christians exercise power and privilege. For example, Schüssler Fiorenza explains that Revelation's gendered images—the depictions of the Woman Clothed in the Sun, Babylon, and the New Jerusalem as the Bride of Christ—must be understood as part of Revelation's overarching rhetorical aims, which are part of John's vision of justice and not John's perspectives on women; rather, they are the seer's appropriation of prophetic traditions in which images of women symbolize cities and political institutions.[20]

Tina Pippin's approach to Revelation is often put in contrast to Schüssler Fiorenza's work. In her 1992 monograph *Death and Desire: The Rhetoric of Gender in the Apocalypse of John*, however, Pippin does not challenge the claim made by Schüssler Fiorenza and others that Revelation's original audiences lived under duress during Roman imperial rule.

Culture and Ideology, ed. William John Lyons and Jorunn Økland (Sheffield: Sheffield Phoenix, 2009), 240–66.

18. I would name all the women I know working on Revelation but would inevitably leave someone out. Suffice to say that four out of the last five chairs or co-chairs of the "John's Apocalypse and Cultural Contexts, Ancient and Modern" section of the Society of Biblical Literature have been women, including Leslie Baynes, Michelle Fletcher, Olivia Stewart Lester, and me.

19. Elisabeth Schüssler Fiorenza, *Revelation: Vision of a Just World* (Minneapolis: Fortress, 1991).

20. See also Elisabeth Schüssler Fiorenza, *The Book of Revelation: Justice and Judgment* (Minneapolis: Fortress, 1998), 205–36.

Instead, she challenges the assumption that the original historical setting is the best or the only context for understanding John's vision. Rather, Pippin recommends that feminist interpreters attend to the ways this biblical book continues to inform the lives of women, including women condemned as "whorish" for failing to meet the standard of purity presented in Revelation's vision of the Woman Clothed in the Sun (Rev 12) or compared to Jezebel, the teacher mentioned in Revelation 2, for "threatening" male leaders through their very existence. She approaches Revelation as a participatory reader, following the text's many "mood swings" and entering the narrative to see, hear, touch, and taste along with John.[21] As a result, her reading of the text foregrounds how women readers experience Revelation within a world that has been shaped by its rhetoric and imagery, including the labeling of women comfortable with their sexuality as "Jezebel."[22]

At the same time, Pippin addresses how John manipulates readers' desire to encourage them, presumably male and heterosexual, to choose fidelity to the Lamb in anticipation of becoming part of a future utopia. Using stereotypical images of women, John shifts loyalty away from the dominating imperial power, represented in the guise of the woman Babylon, by revealing her to be a "bitch-witch."[23] This takes a gruesome turn when John encourages his hearers to revel in the brutal destruction of Babylon, envisioned as a woman, at the hands of "kings of the earth" who strip her naked and burn her flesh. Moreover, the utopic vision of Revelation culminates in a city built upon women's passivity that is devoid of women, as it is populated by male virgins who follow the Lamb.[24] Given these scenes, even though Revelation includes a condemnation of imperial political powers, Pippin concludes that Revelation is not a liberatory vision for women. Revelation's message simply cannot be divorced from its use of gendered imagery.

The writings of Schüssler Fiorenza and Pippin shape much of the feminist conversation about Revelation that follows in their wake. Typically, their views are depicted as diverging streams, a move that Shanell T.

---

21. Tina Pippin, *Death and Desire: The Rhetoric of Gender in the Apocalypse of John* (Louisville: Westminster John Knox, 1992), 15–16.

22. Tina Pippin, *Apocalyptic Bodies: The Biblical End of the World in Text and Image* (London: Routledge, 1999), 32.

23. Pippin, *Death and Desire*, 61.

24. Pippin, *Death and Desire*, 73.

Smith describes as the "Great Whore Debate."[25] Smith notes that feminist scholars often stake their claims regarding Revelation's relevance to women on whether they read the image of Babylon primarily as an image of a city (Schüssler Fiorenza) or a woman (Pippin). As Smith also observes, however, both views emerge from a common source: the recognition that Revelation's imagery impacts the lives of real people, especially women. Both Pippin and Schüssler Fiorenza, like the feminist readers who interact with their works, have a commitment to the "so what" of the text, to the reason readers, especially those who identify as and with women, should care about the words and images found in Revelation's pages. This commitment includes the recognition that, as part of the Christian canon, John's narrative functions as an authoritative text for many individuals and communities, including those with very different goals. As such, it has been used to challenge repressive regimes, such as those in Apartheid South Africa, and to defend the exclusion of some, such as gay men and lesbians, from Christian communities.[26] Like Smith, Schüssler Fiorenza, and Pippin, we take seriously that interpretations of Revelation can impact the lives and communities of its readers.

While Schüssler Fiorenza's work on Revelation has become foundational in the field of Revelation studies in general, many feminist scholars follow Pippin's lead by focusing on John's use of gendered imagery, specifically the images of women. The complexity of these images has yielded a rich interpretive tradition. Feminist scholars have examined the similarities between Revelation's imagery and Roman depictions of sex-workers and brides,[27] John's dependency on ancient goddess traditions,[28] and his appropriation of prophetic depictions of

25. Shanell T. Smith, *The Woman Babylon and the Marks of Empire: Reading Revelation with a Postcolonial Womanist Hermeneutics of Ambiveilence* (Minneapolis: Augsburg Fortress, 2014), 74.

26. For the former, see Allan Aubrey Boesak, *Comfort and Protest* (Philadelphia: Westminster John Knox, 1987). For the latter, see Kevin DeYoung, *What Does the Bible Really Teach about Homosexuality?* (Wheaton, IL: Crossway, 2015), 13–14.

27. E.g., Jennifer A. Glancy and Stephen D. Moore, "How Typical a Roman Prostitute Is Revelation's 'Great Whore'?," *JBL* 130 (2011): 551–69; Lynn R. Huber, "Gazing at the Whore: Reading Revelation Queerly," in *Bible Trouble: Queer Reading at the Boundaries of Biblical Scholarship*, ed. Teresa J. Hornsby and Ken Stone (Atlanta: SBL, 2011), 301–20; Lynn R. Huber, *Like a Bride Adorned: Reading Metaphor in John's Apocalypse* (New York: T&T Clark, 2007).

28. E.g., Mary Ann Beavis, "Jezebel Speaks: Naming the Goddesses in the Book of Revelation," *Feminist Companion to Apocalypse of John*, ed. Levine with Robbins,

cities as women (e.g., Ezek 16 and 23; Isa 47).[29] Other feminist scholars have addressed the linguistic implications of John's gendered language and how John's depiction of women parallels the creation of monsters in literature and film.[30] Additionally, feminist interpreters have turned their attention to how Revelation's "women" influence later texts and traditions, including how modern sex-workers and medieval visionaries read Revelation's gendered images.[31]

Conversations about gender and Revelation include attention to the ways the text constructs masculinity, those characteristics that are culturally associated with manhood and being an ideal man. Stephen D. Moore has highlighted, for example, the text's hypermasculinized depictions of God and Christ, including a vision of the Son of Humanity in Revelation 1 that Moore compares to a steroid-taking bodybuilder. Moore even broaches the issue of whether John's fascination with domination and submission might reflect a personal crisis of masculinity.[32] Christopher Frilingos similarly explores the complex masculinity of the slaughtered Lamb, Revelation's primary metaphor for Christ. Lauded as a messianic Lion, a figure of masculine strength, the Lamb simultaneously appears feminized as an object on display for the eyes of others.[33] We will argue that the Lamb, therefore, appears as a nonbinary figure who cannot be reduced to either a male or female identity.

131–46; Adela Yarbro Collins, "Feminine Symbolism in the Book of Revelation," *BibInt* 1 (1993): 20–33.

29. E.g., Caroline Vander Stichele, "Re-Membering the Whore: The Fate of Babylon According to Revelation 17.16," in *Feminist Companion to Apocalypse of John*, ed. Levine with Robbins, 106–20.

30. Jorunn Økland, "Why Can't the Heavenly Miss Jerusalem Just Shut Up?," in *Feminist Companion to Apocalypse of John*, ed. Levine with Robbins, 88–105, and Michelle Fletcher, "Flesh for Franken-Whore: Reading Babylon's Body in Revelation 17," in *The Body in Biblical, Christian and Jewish Texts*, ed. Joan E. Taylor (London: Bloomsbury, 2014), 144–64.

31. E.g., Pippin, *Apocalyptic Bodies*; Avaren Ipsen, *Sex Working and the Bible* (London: Routledge, 2014); Huber, *Thinking and Seeing with Women in Revelation*.

32. Stephen D. Moore, "The Beatific Vision as a Posing Exhibition: Revelation's Hypermasculine Deity," *JSNT* 60 (1995): 27–55; Stephen D. Moore, *God's Beauty Parlor: And Other Queer Spaces in and around the Bible* (Stanford: Stanford University Press, 2001).

33. Christopher A. Frilingos, "Sexing the Lamb," in *New Testament Masculinities*, ed. Stephen D. Moore and Janice Capel Anderson (Atlanta: SBL, 2003), 297–317; Lynn R. Huber, "Sexually Explicit? Re-Reading Revelation's 144,000 Virgins as a Response to Roman Discourses," *Journal of Men, Masculinities and Spirituality* 2 (2008): 3–28.

As we will see, especially in our discussion of chapters 2–3, Revelation assumes male-identified audience members by using imagery, such as the victor language associated with athletics, that evokes ancient conversations about what it meant to be a "good man." Given this assumption, an understanding of ancient masculinity impacts how Revelation might have been heard in its original context. To some, attention to how texts construct masculine identities initially seems contrary to a feminist project, since male figures in the text have already received plenty of attention. Attending to the ways an author uses cultural notions of masculinity to persuade hearers is, however, an important part of challenging sexist, transphobic, and homophobic interpretations. Feminist interpretation must engage gender broadly and resist focusing only on women and female imagery.

While the perspectives of White feminists such as Schüssler Fiorenza and Pippin have played an important role in the history of feminist interpretation of Revelation, womanist, Latinx, Asian, Jewish, postcolonial, and queer scholars expand and complicate the conversation about Revelation's liberatory potential, or lack thereof. These interpreters examine how race, class, ethnicity, and sexuality intersect with gender in Revelation and how readers' intersectional identities shape conversations with the text. Postcolonial feminist scholars observe, for example, how Revelation's gendered imagery both replicates and perpetuates imperial and colonial ways of thinking and acting. These imperial and colonial "discourses," ways of communicating, present women's bodies, figurative and literal, as something to be conquered and controlled. Jean K. Kim, for example, reads Revelation's sex-worker imagery in relation to the sex industry that traditionally surrounds US military bases. Kim explores how depictions of cities and nations as women, such as the depiction of Rome as a female sex-worker, are interwoven with the treatment of colonized women in similarly negative terms by both colonizing and native men.[34] Also engaging in a feminist postcolonial critique and focusing on the text as a whole, theologian Catherine Keller describes how Revelation's apocalyptic script, the rhetorical patterns and images it employs, fuels the impulse toward colonization, including the one that set Columbus on his journey and led others to follow in his wake to what would be called

---

34. Jean K. Kim, " 'Uncovering Her Wickedness': An Inter(Con)Textual Reading of Revelation 17 from a Postcolonial Feminist Perspective," *JSNT* 73 (1999): 61–81.

the Americas.[35] Pushing the conversation even further is Jacqueline M. Hidalgo, who examines how Chicanx communities of the 1960s and 1970s thought with and revisioned the images of New Jerusalem in Revelation as a way of claiming their ancestral and future homeland, Aztlán, which overlaps with the southwestern United States.[36] At the same time, these liberatory visions can replicate the sexism of Revelation, which uses feminine imagery to envision utopia.[37] Hidalgo recognizes an ambivalence in how Revelation is deployed in and in response to colonial contexts.

The ambivalence inherent in interpretations of Revelation, which simultaneously offer hope of liberation and the continued oppression of some, is highlighted in the work of womanist interpreter Shanell T. Smith. In *The Woman Babylon and the Marks of Empire* (2014) Smith describes how Revelation, specifically the image of Babylon, is a place of tension for African American women readers, since it describes an experience of being both victim of and participant in empire.[38] Echoing the work of W. E. B. Du Bois,[39] who describes a veil through which Black folks see the White world for what it is, Smith describes her position in relation to Revelation as "ambi*veil*ence."[40] This neologism draws together the postcolonial idea of ambivalence, that colonized people both adopt and resist the ways of their colonizers, and the image of the veil, which plays an important role in Revelation as an "unveiling." Through this term, Smith captures how her encounter with Revelation reveals her own double-consciousness as both colonized and colonizer, oppressed and oppressor, just as Babylon can be understood as occupying these dual identities. While some people might choose to hold Revelation at arm's length, relegating the book's meaning entirely to its original historical context or focusing only on the book's more palatable imagery,[41] Smith allows that the text might serve as a reflective, albeit cloudy, mirror.

35. Catherine Keller, *Apocalypse Now and Then: A Feminist Guide to the End of the World* (Boston: Beacon Press, 1996). See also Catherine Keller, "The Breast, the Apocalypse, and the Colonial Journey," *JFSR* 10 (1994): 53–72.

36. Hidalgo, *Revelation in Aztlán*, 16–18.

37. Hidalgo, *Revelation in Aztlán*, 194.

38. Smith, *Woman Babylon*, 4.

39. Hidalgo, *Revelation in Aztlán*, 16–18.

40. Smith, *Woman Babylon*, 11.

41. The lectionary, for example, includes only Revelation's scenes of heavenly worship. See Gail R. O'Day, "Teaching and Preaching the Book of Revelation," *WW* 25 (2005): 248.

The idea that Revelation serves as a cloudy mirror appears in the work of another womanist scholar, Clarice J. Martin. Using the metaphor of the mirror, Martin examines how Revelation's imagery of enslavement, specifically the reference to "human souls" on the list of Babylon's cargo (18:13), reflects enslaved Africans' experience of being kidnapped and shipped to the Americas as chattel. At the same time, the connection to enslavement in the Americas helps readers see and understand Revelation in its first-century setting.[42] Despite the temporal distance between Revelation and the modern world, there are points of resonance that can be heard especially by interpreters who have experienced injustice and oppression, and their knowledge makes clear how Revelation demands resistance.[43]

The feminist and womanist observation that Revelation makes a claim on readers underscores for us the responsibility that comes with writing a commentary. Our words have the potential to impact how other readers engage the text. We can potentially perpetuate the text's problematic elements, and we can help our readers see opportunities to find justice in the text, even though we want to resist the impulse to "rescue" Revelation by explaining away or mitigating the book's sharp edges. Mostly, we want to encounter and engage what the book potentially reveals about God's work in the world, even if our experiences of God and the world do not align completely with this vision. Since our perspectives and assumptions about Revelation's meaning come into play when we interpret the text, we want to take a moment to articulate our contexts and histories with Revelation.

Exploring Revelation Together

We began envisioning this work in 2013, sketching together a few of the main ideas about Revelation we wanted to convey. Among these ideas is the irony that Revelation's persuasive power comes from the way John invites readers into his all-encompassing vision, a task facilitated by his use of metaphor and imagistic language. This invitation means John cannot control what readers do with his revelation, which has led to a rich interpretative tradition. We talked together about how we saw

---

42. Clarice J. Martin, "Polishing the Unclouded Mirror: A Womanist Reading of *Revelation 18:13*," in *From Every People and Nation: The Book of Revelation in Intercultural Perspective*, ed. David Rhoads (Minneapolis: Fortress, 2005), 82–109.

43. Martin, "Polishing the Unclouded Mirror," 105.

our role as authors. Gail specifically liked the imagery of author as guide and of text as river. We wanted to introduce readers both to John's world and to how some interpreters, especially women, have negotiated their way through the book. In addition, we set out to find a balance between offering strong readings of the text and allowing our readers to make up their own minds about Revelation's meaning. Shortly after outlining these ideas, however, Gail began to experience symptoms related to an aggressive form of brain cancer and spent the subsequent years fighting the inevitable. She died in September 2018, when we had only begun to envision the work ahead of us. Even though I have written most of the volume, readers will occasionally see me slip into the language of "we" and "us," since she was the person who made this commentary possible as my teacher, mentor, and friend. I hope it conveys some of her sense of the importance and meaning of Revelation.

Lynn R. Huber: Raised in an evangelical Christian context, I was introduced to Revelation very early. I was taught to be always ready for Jesus's return, that he would come "like a thief in the night" (1 Thess 5:2; cf. Rev 16:15), and I spent most nights in bed cataloguing potential sins so that I could repent and be saved. The year before starting Northwest Nazarene College (now University) in Nampa, Idaho, I was part of a children's ministry team in my evangelical church's regional conference. Some of my team members encouraged me to read Edgar C. Whisenant's *88 Reasons Why the Rapture Is in 1988*, a popular booklet circulating among evangelicals that argued the rapture would occur in September 1988.[44] I was suspicious but concerned. The timing seemed unfortunate since Jesus's return coincided with my first week of college. I was frightened about the possibility of being away from family for the "big day," sad that I would miss out on a college experience, and equally concerned I would be left behind. I was relieved when the appointed week came and went. Eventually, it was my church's teachings about women and my coming out as queer, not apocalyptic disappointment, that prompted me to explore other ways of being a faithful Christian. Given this, it wasn't until I began PhD coursework in New Testament at Emory University that I had reason to return to the book of Revelation, since my mentor and eventual co-author, Gail R. O'Day insisted I take her seminar on the

---

44. Edgar C. Whisenant, *88 Reasons Why the Rapture Is in 1988* (Nashville: World Bible Society, 1988).

book. Under her guidance, I came to appreciate Revelation in a different way. Having experienced the power of Revelation's imaginary landscape firsthand, I was intrigued by the text's use of metaphor and imagery to shape how its audiences should think and act. Since then, much of my scholarly work has focused on Revelation's gendered metaphors, including the ways interpreters recycle them. In addition to this focus, I am interested in exploring how readers on the LGBTQIA+ spectrum experience and engage the text and in using the insights of queer theory, a critical and activist perspective, to engage the text.

Gail R. O'Day: Unlike Lynn's experiences, my family and church did not include faith fearmongering to promote "good" behavior and hence ensure salvation. Revelation was first and foremost a captivating book that I really enjoyed studying in divinity school and doctoral work, a literary, theological, and historical fascinator with deep ties to life in the Roman Empire. I wrote some of my favorite graduate course papers on Revelation. There are pluses and minuses to this history with Revelation. The pluses are that I engage John's imagery without a history of it as a fire-and-brimstone threat to overcome—the book's language dazzles me, and I try to follow where it leads. This personal history guided the way I shaped my doctoral seminars on Revelation. The minuses are that it takes a great act of imagination on my part to enter a social world in which Revelation has been used to instill fear. Here my students have helped me. When I teach Revelation to MDiv students, for their first assignment I ask them to write their "Revelation story"—their history with this biblical book—and their reasons for taking the course. Their stories have unveiled aspects of Revelation that would not otherwise be visible to me. One student related how, as an adolescent, he fell under the influence of the Left Behind series of books with its interpretation of Revelation: if he came home from school and his mother was not in the house, he immediately panicked that she had been taken in the "rapture" and he was now all alone. It is with students like this in mind, along with their faith communities, that I approach Revelation's text.

As the idea of the guide and our use of river imagery suggest, both of us enjoy the outdoors. Gail hiked all forty-eight of New Hampshire's 4,000-foot (about 1.22 kilometer) peaks, and I have enjoyed birdwatching and hiking since college. We both love dogs, and we are both feminists, even though we represent different generations of feminist thought. Studying Revelation, a text that seemingly describes the abuse of the natural world and that some describe as misogynistic, might seem like an odd choice for us; however, we both come to the text with an interest in exploring unfamiliar landscapes, from the ancient worlds of Revelation's author and audience to the otherworldly places of the text, including the heavenly throne room and even the opening to the abyss. Likewise, we share an interest in how authors and artists use imagery, metaphor, and indirect language, such as irony and double entendre, to reveal and persuade. Finally, both of us have a passion for art and poetry and are interested in the ways Revelation and creativity coalesce.

As Christian interpreters, we believe that Revelation mediates the human experience of the uncontainable and unknowable mystery of God.[45] The text may offer readers the opportunity to encounter the divine as well as revealing how Christians before us encountered the divine. This theological claim does not exclude the need to understand the ways the river is shaped by its banks, the tides of the ocean that feed back into it, and the human-made works that impact it. In other words, while we acknowledge Revelation as a sacred text, we emphasize the importance of attending to how it draws on, replicates, and challenges the historical and cultural norms and ideas around it.

Gail was an ordained minister in the United Church of Christ and worked for over thirty-five years teaching in seminary settings. She understood her role as teacher of Bible and preaching to be one of preparing religious leaders to create the revelatory encounter that occurs within the writings of the New Testament. As an expert on the Gospel of John, Gail emphasized how that Gospel provided opportunities for those reading or hearing the text to experience and respond to the revelation of Christ, just as characters in the narrative, such as the Samaritan woman, experienced and responded to the Word. For Gail, there was a revelatory power in texts like John and Revelation that she wanted to maintain as she communicated what these ancient writings meant. In this way, her approach to biblical interpretation was characterized by a commitment to the belief, to quote a slogan of the UCC, that "God is still speaking."

I am, likewise, a member of the United Church of Christ, even though I was raised in evangelical churches and worked with a Nazarene ministry for a semester in college and a church during seminary. I appreciate the power of the Christian tradition, including its symbols and narratives, and I enjoy teaching about the New Testament, especially Revelation, in

---

45. O'Day, "Teaching and Preaching Revelation," 248.

Christian congregational settings. In addition, I see myself as accountable to other LGBTQIA+ Christians, especially those who were raised in nonaffirming churches. These are "my people." I take pride in the fact that I have been able to mentor feminist and queer students called to various forms of ministry.

Trigger Warnings and an Invitation

Some of my students have said, sometimes jokingly and other times not, that Revelation should come with a trigger warning. I understand this concern. As a book that describes violence, including sexual violence and the violence that comes with war, and as a book that uses derogatory language for women and has been used to ostracize Jewish communities, Revelation risks reminding people of real hurt they have experienced in the past or that they are currently experiencing. As a book that uses the metaphor of enslavement to describe faithfulness, Revelation potentially diminishes the horror of being enslaved and occludes slavery's persistence into the modern world. As a book that has been used by some people to condemn others on account of their identity or actions, Revelation potentially makes readers recall their own experiences of being condemned. And as a text that describes environmental destruction and disasters, Revelation can evoke people's real anxieties about the current state of the natural world. A trigger warning could help forestall some of these negative experiences. Trigger warnings can, however, close conversation and predetermine how someone engages the material that prompts such a warning. That, arguably, defeats the purpose of writing a commentary on Revelation. Instead of shutting down conversation, even about texts that some might characterize as difficult or oppressive, the hope with this book is to start and nurture conversation.

Specifically discussing how feminist scholars approach biblical stories of rape and sexual violence, in *Texts after Terror* Rhiannon Graybill highlights the range of complicated feelings these texts can arouse in a reader, describing them as "fuzzy, messy, and icky." She uses this language precisely because it is nontechnical and a little ambiguous, alluding to a variety of negative feelings or affects, including shame, fear, dread, and even confusion.[46] Even though we understand that some people

---

46. Graybill, *Texts after Terror*, 9–10. See also Rhiannon Graybill, "Fuzzy, Messy, Icky: The Edges of Consent in Hebrew Bible Rape Narratives and Rape Culture," *BCT* 15 (2019): https://www.bibleandcriticaltheory.com/issues/vol-15-no-2-2019-bible

want to avoid these types of negative feelings, we know that for others it remains important to be able to hear and react to Revelation, even if it evokes hard-to-pinpoint feelings. In fact, we believe there is productive possibility in encountering Revelation in an environment, such as through the pages of a feminist commentary or in a classroom or Bible study, where there is space to have these experiences and to respond in ways that align with our feminist commitment that the work of dismantling oppression is God's work. With this in mind, we (I am taking the liberty of speaking for Gail) invite you to join this journey through John's vision of "the things that must happen soon."

Lynn R. Huber and Gail R. O'Day

-and-critical-theory/fuzzy-messy-icky-the-edges-of-consent-in-hebrew-bible-rape
-narratives-and-rape-culture/.

Authors' Introduction

Getting Our Bearings: Putting Revelation in Context

Like both humans and rivers, texts have histories that involve innumerable intersecting events and encounters. While we cannot trace all the influences within a book as rich and detailed as Revelation, knowledge of some of its history, context, and rhetorical features helps make sense of what we encounter in the act of reading. In the following pages, we explore some of the "who, where, when, to whom, why, and how" of Revelation, highlighting facets relevant to the directions we take on our journey through this book. This introduction is not an exhaustive look at the world of John's audiences; instead, it is dipping our paddle into the stream to get a feel for what's ahead.

Who?

Revelation's author identifies himself as "John" (1:1, 9) and plays an active role in narrating the text, reporting what he sees and hears, and participating as a character in the action (e.g., 1:17; 7:14; 11:1). John even recounts his visceral responses to what he sees and describes. He weeps (5:4) and experiences amazement (17:6). The book is like a script for a dramatic monologue with the author as both narrator and character in events that unfold around him. Given this first-person perspective,

Revelation's audiences experience everything through John's eyes and hear everything in his voice.

John's narrative presence gives the reader or hearer of Revelation a sense of really knowing the Seer, one way people describe John; however, John reveals little about his identity. What biblical scholars claim about John draws on hints gleaned from the text. For instance, we refer to John using masculine pronouns, since he describes himself as a brother (ἀδελφός) to his audience members (1:9). Scholars also look for clues about John's identity in the accounts of early Christian commentators, such as Irenaeus and Eusebius. Writing in the second through fourth centuries CE, these authors were trying to establish the church's authority in a shifting historical and political context. Consequently, we must weigh these authors' claims with our understanding of their rhetorical concerns and the historical context.

John informs his hearers that he is writing from Patmos (1:9), an island in the Mediterranean off the coast of Asia Minor (modern Turkey), but other than that, we know little about where John is from or his background. Justin (who died around 165 CE) and Irenaeus (who died around 200 CE) assume the Seer is John, the disciple of Jesus (Justin, *Dial.* 81.4; Irenaeus, *Haer.* 3.11.1; 3.16.5, 8; 5.30.3).[1] Eusebius, writing in the late third and early fourth centuries CE, associates this John, both disciple and author of Gospel and Apocalypse, with Ephesus (*Hist. eccl.* 2.22.5). Despite these early accounts, the connection between these two Johns is unclear. Revelation's author provides his name, but the author of the Gospel never claims the name "John" and circumspectly identifies himself as the "beloved disciple" (John 21:20). While John's unique place in Jesus's inner circle of disciples makes this connection with "the beloved" a possibility, there are other candidates for this "pet name," including Lazarus, Mary Magdalene, and even Thomas. In other words, no one is entirely sure whether the author of the so-called "Gospel of John" was actually John, which is why some modern scholars use "Fourth Gospel" to describe the book. Even more unclear is whether the author of the Fourth Gospel also penned Revelation. Even though Eusebius eventually agrees that John the disciple authored the Gospel, Revelation, and the Johannine epistles, he notes that some early interpreters had doubts. The differences in writing style, Revelation's prose being much less

---

1. Craig R. Koester, *Revelation: A New Translation with Introduction and Commentary,* AYB 38A (New Haven: Yale University Press, 2014), 66.

sophisticated than the Gospel, raised such serious questions for some that they rejected it (Eusebius, *Hist. eccl.* 7.25.9-14). Moreover, as even Eusebius admits, there were multiple people named John in Asia Minor during the first century, including a certain John who was an elder in the Christian community at Ephesus (3.39.4-6). Ultimately, we are left asking, "Will the real John of Revelation please stand up?"

Even though evidence for the same John penning both the Gospel and Revelation remains murky and most modern scholars reject the possibility, there are provocative thematic connections between the two books. One of the most obvious is the depiction of Christ as a lamb. In the Gospel, John the Baptizer announces to his disciples as Jesus walks by, "Here is the Lamb [ἀμνός] of God who takes away the sin of the world" (John 1:29; cf. John 1:36). The significance of this imagery culminates in Jesus's crucifixion on the Day of Preparation, when lambs for the Passover meal were sacrificed in the temple (John 19:31).[2] The image of Christ as lamb plays a central role in Revelation, although this text uses another term, ἀρνίον, to describe the Lamb who will share God's throne (5:6). Both texts also describe Christ as the Word of God (John 1:14; Rev 19:13) and envision such a close relationship between God and Christ that the boundary between the two sometimes blurs (e.g., John 8:58; 14:10-11; 18:5-6; Rev 5:6; 7:17). Reading these texts together, therefore, can yield some interesting insights.

The question of any biblical text's authorship raises the issue of what one gains by associating a particular book with a particular author. Does attributing Revelation to Jesus's disciple grant it more authority or make it more significant? Does the idea that both books come from one hand illuminate their facets? Looking at medieval traditions that assumed Jesus's disciple wrote both the Gospel and Revelation sheds light on how these connections can prompt a reader to think about the texts in interesting ways. According to one medieval tradition, the wedding at Cana that inaugurates Jesus's mission in the Gospel is John's own wedding (John 2:1-11). John leaves his bride at the altar, however, and follows Jesus, remaining faithfully celibate for the entirety of his life.[3] This devotion, poignantly represented as John reclining by Jesus at the table (John 13:23-25), leads to John being blessed with the vision that begets Revelation, an idea expressed in this late medieval song: "Saint John,

2. Gail R. O'Day and Susan Hylen, *John* (Louisville: Westminster John Knox, 2006), 183.

3. Jeffrey F. Hamburger, *St. John the Divine: The Deified Evangelist in Medieval Art and Theology* (Berkeley: University of California Press, 2002), 160.

who was a noble martyr, / on Christ's lap asleep lay he, / so saw the
privacy of heaven, / he is called to the banquet."[4] Revelation emerges
from the loving relationship between John, the beloved disciple and
Gospel writer, and Jesus.

Just as questions continue to swirl around John's identity, John's place
of origin remains shrouded in mystery. Presuming that he was a disciple
of Jesus, some scholars suggest John came to Asia Minor from Judea. In
her popular book *Revelations*, Elaine Pagels describes John fleeing after
the war against Rome left the country "ravaged."[5] This aligns with the
picture painted by early Christian authors who thought the Seer and the
Gospel writer were one and the same and potentially accounts for the
war imagery that pervades the book. There is, however, no unequivocal
evidence for this. Revelation's language even fails to offer clues. John
writes in *koine* or "common" Greek, which tells us little since this was
the *lingua franca* of the ancient Mediterranean. It remains possible that
John's first language was Aramaic; however, that too fails to narrow
things down much since Aramaic was associated with a variety of locations, including Judea, Syria, Asia Minor, and other parts of the Levant.

In addition to a seemingly encyclopedic knowledge of Jewish Scripture, which he draws on throughout his narrative, John shows some
familiarity with the Hebrew language. John, for instance, transliterates
both the Hebrew name "Megiddo" (מגידו), an ancient town referenced
in Scripture (e.g., Josh 12:21), and the Hebrew term for "mountain" (הר)
into the Greek, combining the terms into the single place name "Armageddon" (Ἀρμαγεδών) (16:16). Still, how much more Hebrew John
knew remains unclear and does little to pinpoint his hometown or even
country. Although these things point to the likelihood of the Seer being
Jewish, we simply do not know if he was from Judea or one of the many
other Jewish communities spread throughout the Mediterranean world.

Where?

Scholars may not know where John originally comes from, but he
claims to be writing from an island off the coast of Asia called Patmos

---

4. Richard K. Emmerson, "Introduction: The Apocalypse in Medieval Culture,"
in *The Apocalypse in the Middle Ages*, ed. Richard K. Emmerson and Bernard McGinn
(Ithaca: Cornell University Press, 1992), 329n16.

5. Elaine Pagels, *Revelations: Visions, Prophecy, and Politics in the Book of Revelation*
(New York: Penguin, 2012), 7.

(1:9). While some have assumed that Patmos was a penal colony,[6] it was an inhabited island that had all the features found in cities on the mainland, including a gymnasium. The island was also home to a temple of Artemis.[7] Whether it was or was not used as a place to banish political prisoners is simply uncertain. John's time on Patmos may have been a form of exile, although it is unclear whether this was forced or self-imposed. It is even possible that he went to the island to teach and preach since he claims to be on the island "because of the word of God and the testimony of Jesus" (Rev 1:9).[8]

While John wrote from a small island that was somewhat removed from the activity of the mainland (it was about a day of travel by sea from Ephesus),[9] the people he addressed were ancient urbanites living in some of the wealthiest and politically influential cities of Asia Minor—Ephesus, Smyrna, Pergamum, Thyatira, Sardis, Philadelphia, and Laodicea (1:4, 11). Both Ephesus and Smyrna were vital port cities, and Ephesus carried the distinction of being the capital of the province of Asia at the time Revelation was written. The city also bore the title "first and greatest metropolis of Asia," an epithet it wholeheartedly embraced. Ephesus and Smyrna were prosperous and culturally rich, which prompted Pliny the Elder to describe them as the luminaries of Asia (*Nat.* 5.120). Pergamum likewise possessed historical significance as the seat of the kingdom of Pergamum. The king of Pergamum, Attalus III, bequeathed his kingdom to the Republic of Rome in 133 BCE (Strabo, *Geogr.* 13.4.2) and so paved the way for Asia to come under Roman authority. The other cities named by John similarly played their respective roles in maintaining the network of Roman power within Asia Minor. They were communication and transportation hubs as well as important commercial centers. Each of these cities produced goods for local sale and for export to Rome and other Roman provinces. Goods such as those listed among Babylon's cargo in Revelation 18:11-13, like marble, linen, purple, and olive oil, were all produced in the province and sold across

6. E.g., Ben Witherington III, *Revelation*, NCBC (Cambridge: Cambridge University Press, 2003), 9.

7. Ian Boxall, *Patmos in the Reception History of the Apocalypse* (Oxford: Oxford University Press, 2013), 232–34.

8. Boxall, *Patmos in the Reception History*, 33.

9. Walter Scheidel and Elijah Meeks, "ORBIS: The Stanford Geospatial Network Model of the Roman World," https://orbis.stanford.edu/#working.

the Mediterranean.[10] Thus, when we think about Revelation's earliest audiences, we should think about people living in cities with complex social, political, and economic networks.

When?

At first glance, the date for Revelation seems easy to determine since one of the earliest authors to discuss the book, Irenaeus, associates it with the end of Emperor Domitian's reign (*Haer.* 5.30.3).[11] This suggests Revelation comes from the early to mid-90s since Domitian reigned from 81 to 96 CE. Many contemporary scholars agree with this, noting Domitian's supposed appetite for being called "lord and god" (Suetonius, *Dom.* 13.2), an attitude that Revelation clearly criticizes.[12] The imperial hubris that John characterizes in terms of blasphemy and misguided worship (13:5-8) could easily be associated with other Roman emperors and, for that matter, any number of political figures across history. Thus, while Revelation can make sense when read in relation to Domitian's reign, it is wise to be cautious about tying the text too close to this period and Domitian's activities.

In fact, there are a few major events from the second half of the first century CE that could have inspired John's visionary account of the conflict between God's people and earthly political powers. Some scholars link the book to the reign of Nero (54–68 CE), another supposed megalomaniacal emperor. According to the Roman historian Tacitus, writing in the second century, Nero punished Jesus followers for a fire that burned Rome, subsequently crucifying the supposed arsonists and setting their crosses afire (*Ann.* 15.44).[13] A textual reference to a political figure who survives a "mortal wound" (13:12), which should lead to death, is often presumed to be a reference to Nero's suicide and a tradition that he would somehow return to rule over Rome. More recently, scholars have argued for the possibility that Revelation's date should be linked to the Jewish war with Rome (66–73 CE), which led to the destruction of

10. Barbara Levick, "The Roman Economy: Trade in Asia Minor and the Niche Market," *GR* 51 (2004): 182.

11. Steven J. Friesen, *Imperial Cults and the Apocalypse of John: Reading Revelation in the Ruins* (Oxford: Oxford University Press, 2001), 140–43.

12. David A. deSilva, *Seeing Things John's Way: The Rhetoric of the Book of Revelation* (Louisville: Westminster John Knox, 2009), 52.

13. Other accounts of this fire do not include references to Nero's persecution of Christians (Suetonius, *Nero* 38; Dio Cassius, *Hist. Rom.* 62.16-18).

the temple in 70 CE.[14] John's description of "the nations," i.e., gentiles, trampling over the "holy city" (11:2) suggests some connection between Revelation and this period of upheaval.

The connection drawn between Revelation and the reigns of Nero and Domitian responds to John's explicit criticisms of Roman imperial claims of power and influence as well as the apparent eagerness with which the cities and people of Asia Minor accepted these claims. Stephen D. Moore characterizes Asia Minor's relationship to the Roman Empire as "hegemonic," which he defines as a kind of "consent to domination."[15] Asia Minor had a long tradition of ascribing divinity to royalty,[16] which continued when its cities came under Roman control. Thus, when Octavian, more commonly known by the title Augustus, became Roman emperor in 27 BCE, a few cities, including Pergamum and Ephesus, sought the privilege of erecting temples in honor of him and Rome, personified as the goddess Roma (Dio Cassius, *Hist. Rom.* 51.20.6-9). The ritual practices associated with these temples, such as sacrifices, hymns, and processions, which modern scholars refer to as "imperial cults," were an important part of civic identity in Asia Minor. The cities' most influential citizens, including women, were granted roles and titles, such as priest and high priestess, as a reward for their support of the empire.[17] Even though the imperial cults limited priesthood to wealthy upper-class citizens, the cults were visible to everyone in big and small ways.

The imperial cults and the widespread promotion of imperial claims in Asia Minor are arguably some of the most important things going on at the time of Revelation; however, as Steven J. Friesen demonstrates, this

14. For a thorough discussion of dating Revelation, including a compelling argument for dating the book to the Jewish War, see John W. Marshall, *Parables of War: Reading John's Jewish Apocalypse* (Waterloo, ON: Wilfrid Laurier University Press, 2001), 88–97.

15. Stephen D. Moore, "Mimicry and Monstrosity," in *Untold Tales from the Book of Revelation: Sex and Gender, Empire and Ecology,* ed. Stephen D. Moore (Atlanta: SBL, 2014), 17.

16. S. R. F. Price, *Rituals and Power: The Roman Imperial Cult in Asia Minor* (Cambridge: Cambridge University Press, 1984), 31.

17. For a discussion of women's participation in the cults, see Steven J. Friesen, "High Priestesses of Asia and Emancipatory Interpretation," in *Walk in the Ways of Wisdom: Essays in Honor of Elisabeth Schüssler Fiorenza,* ed. Shelly Matthews, Cynthia Briggs Kittredge, and Melanie Johnson-Debaufre (Harrisburg, PA: Trinity Press International, 2003), 136–50.

kind of adulation was characteristic of much of the first century CE.[18] Therefore, even though pinpointing a relatively exact date for Revelation is tempting, given the magnitude of all of these events and the variety of critiques leveraged in the text, it is reasonable to assume that multiple things unfolding within the second half of the first century motivated John's visionary account.

To Whom?

John provides a little more information about his audiences than he does about himself. Or, at least, the text offers its view of who the intended audiences might be by addressing "the seven churches [ἐκκλησίαις] that are in Asia" (1:4). (See "Translation Matters: ἐκκλησία.") These assemblies share with John a commitment to following Jesus, who they believe "loves us and freed us from our sins" (1:5). We avoid calling members of these communities "Christians," as you may have noticed, since in the late first century that designation was employed primarily by those outside of the Jesus movement (Acts 11:26; 26:28; 1 Pet 4:16). Likewise, Revelation never uses the term. As feminists, we try to respect individuals' and communities' privilege in naming themselves since naming is an exercise of power. Further, the modern idea of being "Christian" carries associations that have accrued over the past two thousand years and do not apply to the assemblies addressed by John. Among these is the assumption that Christianity is a tradition distinct from Judaism. Even though it is impossible to fully distance ourselves from modern conceptions of Christianity, we try to use language that is more general and that aligns with how John characterizes those he addresses, such as "the faithful."[19] By being intentional in this way, we hope to be mindful of the temporal distances between ourselves and those first hearers of Revelation.

Even though the cities of Revelation include the most prominent urban centers of Asia Minor, not everyone living within the assemblies was of equal economic class and social status. We know that some Jesus followers living in Asia Minor were wealthy and of high status. The Acts of the Apostles mentions one of these individuals, a businesswoman named Lydia from Thyatira, who is described as a "dealer in purple

18. Friesen, *Imperial Cults*, 147–50.

19. For a discussion of how John refers to audience members, see Peter S. Perry, "The People of God in the Book of Revelation," in *The Oxford Handbook of the Book of Revelation*, ed. Craig R. Koester (New York: Oxford University Press, 2020), 325–40.

cloth" (16:14). Purple cloth was a costly good, and Lydia might have been a wealthy woman since only those with political power were allowed to wear the color.[20] Acts also mentions that members of Lydia's "household," a reference that likely included enslaved people as well as biological dependents, were baptized as Jesus followers along with her (Acts 16:15). Behind this brief description of new converts from Asia Minor is a range of social and class statuses, revealing just a bit of the potential diversity in the assemblies located in these cities. Thus, as we consider how Revelation may have been heard by its earliest audiences, we should envision it being heard by people from all walks of life with different and sometimes competing concerns and hopes.

Gender, Sex, and Marital Status

Highlighting the categories of gender and sex is a hallmark of feminist interpretation, which aims to understand and consequently diminish sexism and gender oppression. Feminists emphasize the saturation of gender within culture, pointing out how gender shapes everything from family relations to political structures and impacts people at all levels of society, from elites to those who are enslaved and/or impoverished. Gender is culturally constructed, which means that communities determine and police what constitutes the "right" ways to enact gendered identities, which are often linked to the way an individual's body is interpreted by others.[21] This means that assumptions about gender as well as expectations about sex are shaped by time and place. So let's turn to a brief introduction to gender in the first century.

20. Kelly Olson, *Dress and the Roman Woman: Self-Presentation and Society* (London: Routledge, 2008), 6.

There is a debate among scholars about Lydia's social status. Some, e.g., Shelly Matthews, *First Converts: Rich Pagan Women and the Rhetoric of Mission in Early Judaism and Christianity, Contraversions: Jews and Other Differences* (Stanford: Stanford University Press, 2001), 85–89, argue that she was well off, one of many rich women patrons featured in Luke's two volumes (e.g., Luke 8:3; Acts 12:12; 17:4, 12). Others, such as Luise Schottroff, "Lydia: A New Quality of Power," in *Let the Oppressed Go Free: Feminist Perspectives on the New Testament*, trans. Annemarie S. Kidder (Louisville: Westminster John Knox, 1993), 131–37, see her as a poor woman who produced luxury goods for others.

21. These are ideas associated with the work of Judith Butler. See, for example, *Undoing Gender* (New York: Routledge, 2004).

The ancient view of gender can be envisioned as a kind of sliding scale with one end higher than the other.[22] For Romans, "men" (*vir* in Latin) were at the top of the scale and everyone else, whom we might describe as "non-men," fell farther down the scale.[23] Gender was not "fixed"; individuals could theoretically move up and down the scale. Presumed biological sex and certain nonbiological factors, however, like social status and class, made it impossible for some non-men to move into the category of men.

In addition to having unambiguous male sex characteristics, being a man required meeting several social conditions, such as being adult, free, and having citizenship. Citizenship as part of gender identity might seem unusual to modern readers, but it conferred the political power and legal rights an individual required to be a man, such as the right to own property and marry. Citizenship in the Roman world was complex, and someone could be both a Roman citizen and a citizen of their home city, just as Paul the apostle claimed citizenship of both Rome and the city Tarsus in Cilicia (Acts 16:37-38; 21:29; 22:25-28).[24] Despite this, even multiple citizenships were not sufficient for being a man; an individual's actions and affectations, including speaking voice and bodily comportment, contributed to whether he was considered a man since these were believed to signal one's virtue. For instance, a low speaking voice was considered more manly than a higher voice, supposedly revealing a speaker's courage and sexual self-control.[25] Gender, in other words, was a *slippery* scale, and individuals could easily lose hold of manhood and move into the category of non-men based on their actions and how those were perceived by others. Thus, in Revelation 2–3, John encourages audience members that he sees as being wishy-washy or weak to embrace masculine virtues, such as endurance (see pp. 37–39).

Roman gender was, in many ways, constructed in relation to others. While the ability to control one's appetites was important to being a man

22. For a discussion of the ancient gender scale focused especially on those who defy gender categories, see Joseph A. Marchal, *Appalling Bodies: Queer Figures before and after Paul's Letters* (New York: Oxford University Press, 2019), 37–45.

23. Craig A. Williams, *Roman Homosexuality* (New York: Oxford University Press, 1999), 163.

24. Andreea Ştefan, "The Case of Multiple Citizenship Holders in the Graeco-Roman East," in *Citizens in the Graeco-Roman World*, ed. Lucia Cecchet and Anna Busetto, Mnemosyne Supplements, History and Archaeology of Classical Antiquity 407 (Leiden: Brill, 2017), 110–31.

25. These ideas are found through Maud W. Gleason, *Making Men: Sophists and Self-Presentation in Ancient Rome* (Princeton: Princeton University Press, 1995), 83.

(i.e., ideal men were not supposed to drink or eat to excess), the ability to control and dominate others, materially, physically, and even sexually, was key. Men were expected to dominate women and other non-men, including non-Romans, the enslaved, and those whose affections placed them in the non-men category. As Joseph A. Marchal explains, "This model appears almost as a zero-sum system of power," with those at the top exercising power over all the "lesser embodied entities" below them.[26] Further, since the system of control was not solely based on sex and gender, Elisabeth Schüssler Fiorenza famously described the system as a "kyriarchy," which builds on the Greek word for "lord" or "master" (κύριος, *kyrios*). In contrast to the more common term "patriarchy," kyriarchy includes the domination of enslavers over the enslaved, the wealthy over the poor, the ruler over the ruled as well as the husband over the wife, father over mother and children, etc.[27]

Even though ancient gender was not based entirely on anatomy, ancient medical experts theorized that the typical female body determined the characteristics of femininity. In contrast to men, women, along with other non-men, were assumed to be passive, soft, and receptive. Women were supposedly colder and, consequently, less active than men, and their uteruses were envisioned as "inside out" penises, designed to be penetrated and impregnated (Galen, *On the Usefulness of the Parts of the Body* 14.6-7). A woman's biology meant that she, according to ancient logic, was less powerful than a man and unable to control herself or her desires. Being a woman generally meant needing oversight by a man, whether one's father, brother, husband, or another male guardian. The inability of women or girls to control themselves sexually provided justification for girls being betrothed and married as young as twelve, even though male partners were usually twenty or older.[28] This social convention was backed by ancient science. The physician Soranus, for one, recommended that the onset of menstruation was time for a girl to no longer be kept a virgin (i.e., it was time for her to marry) since she might act on desires that would lead to pregnancy (*Gyn.* 1.8.33).

26. Marchal, *Appalling Bodies*, 38. See also Jonathan Walters, "Invading the Roman Body: Manliness and Impenetrability in Roman Thought," in *Roman Sexualities*, ed. Judith P. Hallett and Marilyn B. Skinner (Princeton: Princeton University Press, 1997), 29–43.

27. Elisabeth Schüssler Fiorenza, *Empowering Memory and Movement: Thinking and Working across Borders* (Minneapolis: Augsburg Fortress, 2014), 108.

28. Judith Evans Grubbs, *Women and the Law in the Roman Empire: A Sourcebook on Marriage, Divorce and Widowhood* (London: Routledge, 2002), 88.

Even with such a clear hierarchy, gender in the ancient world was not set in stone. Men could easily act in ways that caused others to see them as "non-men," which was described negatively as being "soft," "effeminate," or "womanish." Paul even includes gender nonconforming males, "womanish men" (μαλακοί), in a list of the types of people who will not inherit the kingdom of God (1 Cor 6:9-10), a text now described as an anti-LGBTQIA+ "clobber text."[29] "Not men" could move up the scale if their social status changed or if they embraced masculine virtues. Some Romans understood this movement as having a bodily effect.[30] Seneca the Younger, for example, cited a physician who attributed increasing numbers of women with gout and baldness to their adopting the habits of men (*Ep.* 95.20-22). A non-man who moved too far up the gender scale entered a kind of danger zone in which they were considered deviant or even monstrous.[31] Suffice to say, the social stigma caused by moving too far up or even down the scale was a tool for keeping those at the top in power.

In modern contexts, sexuality is often thought of as an identity that an individual inhabits or embraces related to their gender and the gender of their sexual partners. Sexual identity, many assume, remains relatively stable, even though it may take time for an individual to "figure out" their sexual identity or to "come out," given societal privileging of heterosexuality. These assumptions are not particularly helpful for understanding ancient sex or familial configurations since sex in the ancient world was understood more in terms of acceptable power relations than sexual identity.[32] Sex was imagined as always needing to include (at least) two partners of unequal status with the more powerful person, usually a man, playing the active and penetrative role, while the individual with a lower social status, the non-man, supposedly remained passive and receptive. As long as he was on top, figuratively and literally, a man could have sex with a sex-worker or his enslaved person without stigma. If, however, a man was known to let others penetrate

29. The NRSV translation of 1 Cor 6:9 is somewhat puzzling, rendering μαλακοί as "male prostitutes." For a discussion of this verse, see Marchal, *Appalling Bodies*, 168.

30. Diana M. Swancutt, "*Still* before Sexuality: 'Greek' Androgyny, the Roman Imperial Politics of Masculinity and the Roman Invention of the *Tribas*," in *Mapping Gender in Ancient Religious Discourses*, ed. Todd Penner and Caroline Vander Stichele, BibInt 84 (Boston: Brill, 2007), 11–61; Bernadette J. Brooten, *Love Between Women: Early Christian Responses to Female Homoeroticism* (Chicago: University of Chicago Press, 1996), 45.

31. Swancutt, "*Still* before Sexuality," 20.

32. Deborah Kamen and Sarah Levin-Richardson, "Lusty Ladies in the Roman Imaginary," in *Ancient Sex*, ed. Ruby Blondell and Kirk Ormand (Columbus: Ohio State University Press, 2015), 231–52.

him, if he was a "bottom" in popular terms, his status as a man was at risk. Likewise, a woman who acted dominant in sex or desired other women was considered sexually deviant and even monstrous. Some men described these women, called *tribades*, as having penises with which they penetrated others (e.g., Martial, *Epigr.* 1.90).[33] As is often the case, the dominant view of socially acceptable sex was only part of the story, and it is possible to catch a glimpse of those people who lived outside the norms through the inscriptions scratched on walls and in the lines of love spells written on papyrus.[34]

As we will see when we turn to Revelation's text, even though John works within this ancient understanding of gender, his vision often pushes at and plays with traditional gender expectations. Divine figures in Revelation, for example, will defy gender norms (e.g., the One Like a Son of Humanity, the Lamb), and John will call audience members to embrace a complicated gender identity as male virgins who become the Lamb's Bride.

Ancient ideas about sex were shaped by the assumption that elites would marry and have children. Marriage legislation initiated under Emperor Augustus, which continued to be relevant throughout the first century, required marriage for male citizens between the ages of twenty-five and sixty and female citizens between twenty and fifty.[35] Even though Roman marriage law applied to citizens, the expectation that one would partner and procreate meant there were also marriage relationships apart from citizenship, *de facto* marriages consisting of cohabitation apart from legal marriage.[36] Likewise, those in Jewish communities often married under the auspices of local Jewish leaders.[37] As Revelation's final vision of the faithful is one of a wedding (19:6-8; 21:1-10), the expectations around marriage and family certainly play a role in John's message.

Despite the importance of marriage in Revelation's context, the marriage bed was not the only option for men wanting sex. There were strict penalties for women who committed adultery, such as exile or confiscation of property, and men that had sex with women that effectively "belonged" to other citizen men (e.g., husbands, fathers of unmarried

---

33. Swancutt, "*Still* before Sexuality," 38.

34. Brooten, *Love Between Women*, 77–96.

35. Evans Grubbs, *Women and Law in Roman Empire*, 84.

36. Beryl Rawson, "Roman Concubinage and Other de Facto Marriages," *TAPA* 104 (1974): 279–305.

37. Michael L. Satlow, *Jewish Marriage in Antiquity* (Princeton: Princeton University Press, 2001), 68–90.

girls). Despite this, men were free to have sex with sex-workers and the enslaved in their households, a practice we would define as rape. While a man's status could be put in jeopardy if he were perceived as being unable to control his sexual urges, ancient graffiti in brothels, taverns, and baths points to the flourishing of sex-work in the ancient world.[38]

Even though we privilege the category of gender, reading Revelation only for gender is insufficient since that approach fails to recognize that women, even ancient women, exercise varying levels of power based on class, status, ethnic origin, etc. Given the real likelihood of demographic diversity in the communities addressed in Revelation, we find the idea of "intersectionality" helpful for imagining the individuals within these groups. As Kimberlé Crenshaw explains, "intersectional" is not an identity but a way of understanding "the multiple grounds of identity when considering how the social world is constructed."[39] In any social context, including the communities of Jesus followers in ancient Asia Minor, individuals inhabit multiple identities based on their ethnicity, class, gender, religious identity, sexuality, education level, etc. Because each person has multiple identities, their levels of power and privilege shift as they engage with others. For example, while ancient women were generally subordinate to men, an ancient woman who was free could exercise authority over anyone who was enslaved, male or female. This woman may experience disadvantages based on gender, but her class provides her with certain advantages. Similarly, while an adult male Roman citizen may generally be at the top of the social hierarchy in ancient Asia Minor, his power and status may be threatened by joining the Jesus movement, a religious community that eschewed participating in socially significant organizations and activities, such as the imperial cults. As we read Revelation together, remembering that the original hearers were negotiating complex identities and shifting power hierarchies can help us understand the potential impact of the narrative's demands on the lives of these first hearers.

Class and Status

The pictures of urban communities of Jesus followers painted by Paul and other New Testament authors offer a glimpse of what life may have

38. Sarah Levin-Richardson, *The Brothel of Pompeii: Sex, Class, and Gender at the Margins of Roman Society* (Cambridge: Cambridge University Press, 2019).

39. Kimberlé Crenshaw, "Mapping the Margins: Intersectionality, Identity Politics, and Violence against Women of Color," *Stanford Law Review* 43 (1991): 1245.

looked like for those in Revelation's earliest audiences. These portrayals suggest that urban assemblies included people from a range of classes, statuses, and backgrounds. Households in these communities would have included people considered elite and those who were enslaved or formerly enslaved, as we see in 1 Corinthians 1:11 when Paul mentions Chloe and those in her household, a likely allusion to those she has enslaved or freed persons for whom she is now patron.[40] Names of the elite stand out in the New Testament writings (Onesimus in the letter to Philemon being an exception), but most people in the empire lived at or near subsistence level. They had "the resources needed to produce enough calories in food to maintain the human body," but little else.[41] In this vein, Paul notes that some within the early communities of the faithful were unable to afford to eat when there was a shared meal (1 Cor 11:21). Those in the upper economic echelons, who comprised around 3 percent of the population, and those who had moderate surplus income (around 7 percent of the total population), such as merchants, traders, artisans, and some veterans, also participated in these assemblies. Since much of our information about the ancient world comes from those in the top 3 percent, we will need to make a special effort to listen to the voices of the silent majority. Since John says little about poverty but spends considerable time decrying the wealth of Rome (chap.18), uncritical reading of Revelation might lead to the conclusion that all those living in the Roman Empire enjoyed the "dainties and . . . splendor" John associates with Rome (18:14). That would be an incorrect impression.

The "greatness" of the Roman world depended on the labor of countless enslaved peoples. Romans were not the first, nor the last, people to enslave people; however, as Walter Scheidel argues, "To a much greater extent than other slave-rich systems, the Roman elite relied on their own military forces to procure a captive labour force."[42] Rome and the empire's inhabitants required enslaved labor to produce the raw materials for the infrastructure and massive building projects that characterized the time period, but enslaved people also held jobs as educators, cooks,

40. Jennifer A. Glancy, *Slavery in Early Christianity* (Oxford: Oxford University Press, 2002), 49.

41. Steven J. Friesen, "Poverty in Pauline Studies: Beyond the So-Called New Consensus," *JSNT* 26 (2004): 343.

42. Walter Scheidel, "The Roman Slave Supply," in *The Cambridge World History of Slavery*, vol. 1: *The Ancient Mediterranean World*, ed. Keith Bradley and Paul Cartledge (Cambridge: Cambridge University Press, 2011), 297. For the difference between ancient Greek and Roman enslavement, see Orlando Patterson, *Slavery and Social Death* (Cambridge, MA: Harvard University Press, 1982), 30.

scribes, and the like. Given the prevalence of enslavement in the first-century Mediterranean, Revelation's audiences undoubtedly included enslaved and formerly enslaved, those sometimes described as "freed," as well as enslavers. Estimates of the enslaved population in the Roman provinces, such as the province of Asia, range from 10 to 20 percent of the population, although enslaving people was generally limited to the upper classes.[43] Being enslaved or free was one of Rome's most important social distinctions, trumping ethnic, religious, or familial identities. For instance, Jews enslaved by Romans at the time of the first revolt against Rome (66–70 CE) would have been stripped of their Jewish identity by their enslavers.[44] Socially, the enslaved person was forced to become whomever or whatever the enslaver needed or wanted, even if they attempted to hold on to their cultural and religious traditions. We therefore use the language of "enslaved people" and "enslavement" to underscore how this status was not, for the most part, a choice but typically was imposed on one person by another or on one group by another.[45] The "slave" identity is important for understanding Revelation since John draws on the imagery of enslavement to depict those who are faithful to God and the Lamb, something we address later in our journey (e.g., 7:3).

Manumission (being released from slavery or buying oneself out of enslavement) was possible, even though freed individuals were still beholden to the households of their enslavers, who were considered their patrons. Signaling this connection, freed people generally kept the name of their former enslaver and may have continued to work for them.[46] In theory, this relationship facilitated the incorporation of the formerly enslaved into free society.[47] In practice, however, things were much more complicated. Looking at the funerary inscriptions commemorating the formerly enslaved, classicist Rose MacLean observes that while they assimilated to and embraced the values and lifestyle of the enslaving class, they did so by transforming the expectations that had been placed upon them, such as being industrious and obedient, into virtues worthy of

---

43. Scheidel, "Roman Slave Supply," 291–92.

44. Catherine Hezser, *Jewish Slavery in Antiquity* (Oxford: Oxford University Press, 2006), 28.

45. Katherine A. Shaner, *Enslaved Leadership in Early Christianity* (New York: Oxford University Press, 2018), 123n4.

46. Hezser, *Jewish Slavery in Antiquity*, 47.

47. Rose MacLean, *Freed Slaves and Roman Imperial Culture: Social Integration and the Transformation of Values* (Cambridge: Cambridge University Press, 2018), 3.

remembering.[48] Manumission did not erase the memory of enslavement, and full assimilation was difficult, if not impossible. Even though John does not specifically acknowledge the presence of freed people or the currently enslaved among his audience members, his use of enslavement imagery to characterize faithfulness raises the question of how those who had experienced enslavement and gained freedom or who only knew enslavement would respond to the idealization of the practice.

Ethnicity and Religious Identity

Although Revelation concludes the Christian canon, it was written during the Jewish "prehistory" of Christianity.[49] This was a time before Christianity could be conceived of as something distinct from Jewish tradition, when following Jesus was part of some people's experience of Judaism. Although it is likely that some members of the assemblies receiving Revelation were not Jewish, the book should be understood as part of first-century Mediterranean Judaism in all its diversity.

Ancient Jewish diversity becomes especially evident when looking at how Jewish groups related to the dominant cultures around them. For instance, although describing a situation in Judea, the book of 1 Maccabees reveals Jewish ambivalence toward practices associated with the gymnasium, which was a hallmark of Greek culture and especially popular in Asia Minor (see the discussion related to Rev 2–3). Because the gymnasium required young men to exercise together in the nude, some saw membership as contrary to being a faithful Jew; others, however, disguised evidence of circumcision to participate in the activities held within this important cultural space (1 Macc 1:11-15). In other words, Jews living within the ancient Mediterranean did not agree on every aspect of their shared identity and forged a variety of ways of being Jewish in a predominantly non-Jewish world. Revelation should be understood as John's attempt at convincing his audiences to align being faithful to the God of Israel, his Messiah, and the social and political realities unfolding in the first century.

Some of the Jewish communities of Asia Minor stretched back to the third century BCE (Josephus, *Ant.* 12.147-53) and were understood as an important part of the city's culture. Members of these communities would have spoken *koine* Greek, and there is evidence of Jews holding

---

48. MacLean, *Freed Slaves and Roman Imperial Culture*, 171.
49. Marshall, *Parables of War*, 174.

important civic roles in some of the province's cities.[50] Despite this, the Jews of ancient Asia Minor were still set apart in many ways.[51] Practices such as not working on the sabbath and meeting in their own communities for worship marked the Jews of Asia Minor as other or different. This sense of otherness was augmented by the fact that many Jews associated themselves to their ancestral land by sending a yearly payment or tax to the temple in Jerusalem and sometimes going on pilgrimage in conjunction with delivering this tax.[52] The Jewish connection to the temple plays a role in Revelation, when John is prompted to measure this space (11:1-2), even though Revelation was likely written after its destruction in 70 CE. These ways of connecting at least symbolically to Judea possibly contributed to a sense among their neighbors that Jews were "foreign," an idea reinforced, ironically, by Roman decrees reminding others of the right of Jews to maintain the traditional practices that set them apart.[53]

Because of their "otherness," the Jews of ancient Asia Minor, like others throughout the empire, were subject at times to derision. In her book on humor in Revelation, Sarah Emanuel describes how Roman authors mocked Jews and Jewish cultural practices, including jokes about Jewish circumcision and abstinence from eating pork.[54] The satirist and poet Horace, for instance, simply referred to "circumcised Jews" as a way of highlighting their supposed strangeness (e.g., *Sat.* 1.9.69).[55] Emanuel argues that these subtle forms of dehumanization, when coupled with the violence and destruction of the Roman war in Judea, contributed to a kind of communal trauma among ancient Jews that colors much of the book of Revelation.

At the same time, some non-Jews, including groups described as "God-fearers" or "God-worshipers," opted to join their Jewish neighbors worshiping the God of Israel. These gentiles participated in Jewish religious practices such as observing the sabbath and venerating the Jewish God (Acts 10:11, 13:16) and even contributed to Jewish organizations. One inscription from Asia Minor, although later than the book of Revelation, lists God-fearers among those who donated money to what may have

50. Paul Trebilco, *Jewish Communities in Asia Minor* (Cambridge: Cambridge University Press, 1991), 173–74.

51. Erich S. Gruen, *Diaspora: Jews amidst Greeks and Romans* (Cambridge, MA: Harvard University Press, 2002), 243–44.

52. Gruen, *Diaspora*, 100.

53. Trebilco, *Jewish Communities in Asia Minor*, 8–9.

54. Sarah Emanuel, *Humor, Resistance, and Jewish Cultural Persistence in the Book of Revelation: Roasting Rome* (Cambridge: Cambridge University Press, 2020), 68.

55. Gruen, *Diaspora*, 51.

been an ancient equivalent to a soup kitchen, and another commemorates a donation made by a Roman woman to decorate a Jewish community building, perhaps a synagogue.[56] Some in Revelation's audiences were likely God-fearers or gentiles who involved themselves in their local Jewish communities, since the Jesus movement had already spread to gentiles in the early 40s CE.[57] Still, although Revelation's audiences likely included Jews and gentiles, John envisions them through the lenses of Jewish tradition (e.g., 1:6; 7:4-8).

Living within the cities of Asia Minor would mean familiarity with a variety of religious traditions, including the worship of gods within the Greek and Roman pantheon (these deities sometimes overlapped) and from other parts of the Mediterranean world. The title *In the Land of a Thousand Gods*, a book by ancient historian Christian Marek, offers an apt description of the region's religious landscape.[58] Local cults included deities such as Cybele, an ancient mother goddess also known as Magna Mater, whose power made her popular in Rome (e.g., Ovid, *Fasti* 4.305-44). There was Artemis of Ephesus, whose appearance includes a massive collar made of bulbous appendages that look like breasts (without nipples) but also suggest bulls' testicles or eggs.[59] Whatever these ornaments were, they signaled the goddess's connection to fertility and abundance. Her main shrine in Ephesus was one of the seven wonders of the ancient world, and it served as a sanctuary for fugitives. Modern goddess worshipers continue to visit the site of the temple, where a single pillar stands, to honor Artemis.[60] Other practices popular in Asia Minor included the worship of Isis and Serapis and Dionysus.[61] Domestic religious rituals in which family spirits and household deities, along

56. Dietrich-Alex Koch, "The God-Fearers between Facts and Fiction: Two Theosebeis-Inscriptions from Aphrodisias and Their Bearing for the New Testament," *ST* 60 (2006): 62–90.

57. Paul, who addressed gentile communities in his letters, is our evidence for this. His earliest extant letter is First Thessalonians, which addressed a gentile community living in Macedonia (modern Greece) and which is often dated to the early 40s.

58. Christian Marek, *In the Land of a Thousand Gods: A History of Asia Minor in the Ancient World*, trans. Steven Rendall (Princeton: Princeton University Press, 2016).

59. Michael Immendörfer, *Ephesians and Artemis: The Cult of the Great Goddess of Ephesus as the Epistle's Context*, WUNT 2.436 (Tübingen: Mohr Siebeck, 2017), 148–50.

60. Kathryn Rountree, "Goddess Pilgrims as Tourists: Inscribing the Body through Sacred Travel," *Sociology of Religion* 63 (2002): 475–96.

61. Beate Dignas, *Economy of the Sacred in Hellenistic and Roman Asia Minor* (Oxford: Oxford University Press, 2002), 111.

with worship of Hecate at crossroads, existed together with all manner of deities and religious practices, local and imported. People in John's audiences would be familiar with these traditions which would continue to shape their worldviews.

As we navigate the text of Revelation, we will see and discuss more about the world in which John's audiences lived and worshiped. Even though there are times when we might imagine that Revelation's audience members look familiar, we always want to remember that the ancient context is not our own. Historical context provides the backdrop both for understanding what John has to say about God, Christ, and faithfulness, and for illuminating his assumptions about power and gender. Hearing this text and God's word in it requires us to understand and account for the very different world we inhabit.

Why?

The simple answer to the question of why John wrote Revelation is that "One Like a Son of Humanity" told him to write (1:19). When a vision of the risen Christ, complete with eyes like flames of fire, tells you to write, it is probably a wise idea to heed that command! Despite this easy answer, when modern scholars ask about an ancient author's reason for writing they are interested in the rhetorical purposes of the text. That is, we are interested in knowing the event or issue, or set of events and issues, that prompts an author to engage in constructing this specific communicative exchange. As I often ask my students, why would any author expend the time and effort required to write a book?

A common answer to the question of John's rhetorical purpose is that Revelation responds to the Roman persecution of Jesus followers. This was an early explanation for the book's genesis (e.g., Eusebius, *Hist. eccl.* 4.26.9; Irenaeus, *Haer.* 5.30.3) and is an idea that has grown in popularity over the past two centuries. A variety of media perpetuate the idea, including the long-popular *Foxe's Book of Martyrs*, first published in 1563, and movies like *Quo Vadis* (1951), which depicts an early Christianity under siege from Roman imperial powers. The connections drawn between Revelation and both Nero and Domitian's reigns are related to this perspective, since ancient biographers depicted both emperors as wantonly cruel and eager to eradicate those who refused their demands for veneration (e.g., Tacitus, *Ann.* 15.44; Suetonius, *Dom.* 10-11). Moreover, John's references to the faithful being beheaded and to the saints' blood easily lend themselves to this kind of explanation (e.g., 6:9-11; 17:6; 20:4).

Despite the popularity of this "persecution explanation," modern Revelation scholars offer a more complicated answer to the question of John's motivation. This more nuanced response stems from two important recognitions: (1) that ancient portraits of Nero and Domitian as bloodthirsty villains[62] were penned by biographers seeking to bolster the popularity of subsequent rulers and cannot be taken at face value;[63] and (2) that the Roman Empire's persecution of Christians really began after Revelation was on the scene. The most important piece of evidence for this second recognition is a set of letters from 112 CE between Pliny, a governor of the province of Bithynia within the region of Asia Minor, and Emperor Trajan. This correspondence makes clear that at the time there was no official policy outlining how Roman officials should deal with the Christians and that Roman officials were not being encouraged to seek out Jesus followers for persecution. The idea that at the end of the first century Roman soldiers were sweeping the empire for Christians to torture and kill is simply not true. Still, the correspondence between Pliny and Trajan does reveal that Roman officials (or at least Pliny) held Christians in low esteem, as inflexible and obstinate, and that some who refused to renounce their faith had been executed (Pliny, *Ep.* 10). Despite this, it was not until the reign of Decius (ca. 250 CE) and then Diocletian (ca. 303 CE) that there would be an empire-wide effort to suppress Christianity.[64]

Even though the empire-sponsored persecution of Christians was yet to come, John's reason for writing Revelation may still stem from incidents of violence and his sense that persecution loomed on the horizon. John references the death of a Jesus follower named Antipas (2:14) who quite possibly met a fate like the one Pliny described. John also describes those faithful to God who have been "slaughtered" and anticipates that their number will grow (6:9-11). It is possible that some in John's audiences feared for their livelihoods and lives. Some may even have tried to curry favor with those in power by demonstrating their loyalty, even believing it to be God's will that they honor the emperor (1 Pet 2:17).

---

62. The biographer Suetonius even depicts the emperor Domitian sitting in seclusion stabbing flies with a sharp stylus (*Dom.* 3.1).

63. Leonard L. Thompson, *The Book of Revelation: Apocalypse and Empire* (New York: Oxford University Press, 1990).

64. For a discussion of early Christian persecution, see Candida Moss, *The Myth of Persecution: How Early Christians Invented a Story of Martyrdom* (New York: HarperOne, 2013).

They might have seen this as a strategy for avoiding violence or persecution. It is also possible that John wrote to warn his hearers of coming conflict, trying to shake them out of a perceived complacence about the events unfolding around them. Whatever the exact purpose may be and whether it was justified or not, Revelation exudes a real sense of life-or-death crisis.

Furthermore, those in Revelation's audiences may have experienced threats closer to home from neighbors. Refusing to honor civic gods, including honoring imperial family members, implied that Jesus followers were willing to risk the well-being of their communities by drawing the ire of these gods. They were perceived as superstitious and atheist.[65] In some cases, their presence in a city was seen as a threat to those whose lives depended on the "sacred economy." Acts 19, for instance, depicts Paul's companions in Ephesus being "dragged" before city officials by silver workers who made statues of the goddess Artemis and who feared preaching about the Christ would be detrimental to their livelihoods. The town clerk stops the silver workers by insisting that the men "are neither temple robbers nor blasphemers of our goddess" (Acts 19:37-38). Although violence is avoided, the story reveals how conflict between Jesus followers and local communities could lead to violence and death. It is also simultaneously possible that some communities tolerated and even accepted Jesus followers, especially if they were part of local synagogues. Still, John works to convince his audiences that the conflicts some Jesus followers may be experiencing could lead to more deadly situations.

How?

One of the notable things about Revelation's narrative is John's almost excessive reuse of Scripture. The book bursts at the seams with images, allusions, and phrases drawn from the texts of the Hebrew Bible.[66] John

65. Pablo Richard, "Reading the *Apocalypse*: Resistance, Hope, and Liberation in Central America," in *From Every People and Nation: The Book of Revelation in Intercultural Perspective*, ed. David Rhoads (Minneapolis: Fortress, 2005), 150.

66. Scholars often use the language of "Hebrew Bible" to describe the Scriptures used by John, which would eventually become part of the Jewish and Christian bibles. It is important to realize, however, that when John was writing there was not a fixed canon; i.e., there wasn't a "Bible" or single collection of authoritative texts that could have been bound into a book. Additionally, not all the books that eventually become a part of the Scriptures that Christians call the "Old Testament" were written in Hebrew. Still, for simplicity's sake, we will often use "Hebrew Bible" to describe

does this without clearly quoting past texts and he fails to cite any of his sources! Michelle Fletcher argues, however, that John is not using past texts like pieces of evidence in a term paper; rather, John creates Revelation as a pastiche, a work of art that imitates past styles and combines past voices into a new, creative piece. This type of engagement makes the new seem familiar and effectively communicates multiple layers of meaning.[67] As we engage the text, we highlight some of the possible allusions, although sometimes we are only able to scratch the surface.

As we suggested at the outset, Revelation's narrative flows like a meandering river, making countless twists and turns as it progresses. In fact, the word "meander" comes from the name of the Meander River in Turkey, not too far from ancient Laodicea (Strabo, *Geogr.* 12.8.15). Since most of us modern readers have the privilege of a written text, we tend to approach Revelation from "above." We can easily see the book's structure because the written text serves as a kind of map and because we have a sense of where the narrative is leading. The winding narrative of Revelation was, however, meant to be heard and experienced as it unfolds. John writes, "Blessed is the one who reads aloud the words of the prophecy, and blessed are those who hear and who keep what is written in it" (1:3). Hearing the narrative, the audience moves forward chronologically, only to be prompted to glance back at past images and events and thus effectively linking the past, present, and future. For example, many of the items promised to "those who conquer" in the messages to the seven communities in chapters 2–3 appear in the new Jerusalem in chapters 21–22, which prompts auditors to think back to the attitudes cultivated in those earlier episodes. By the time we reach chapter 22, all the images and ideas that were introduced at the outset appear again, like items carried by our river's current. Despite wanting to experience Revelation as it progresses, having a general sense of its course allows us to approach the text analytically. The view from above helps us see how the book tries to persuade its hearers.

Revelation opens with John experiencing a vision that includes the Son of Humanity dictating to him seven messages to communities in Asia Minor (chaps. 2–3). Immediately after the messages end, John is taken up

---

the Scriptures on which John draws. For a helpful discussion of the problems with language such as "Hebrew Bible," see "Nomenclature for the Two Testaments" in the introduction to this commentary series by Barbara E. Reid (pp. xxxix–xl).

67. Michelle Fletcher, *Reading Revelation as Pastiche: Imitating the Past* (London: Bloomsbury, 2017), 1–4.

into heaven (4:1), and Revelation's structure and focus shift: the limited perspective John had on Patmos is enlarged by the changed location. From this heavenly perch, John's focus oscillates between worship in heaven, primarily in the throne room, and events that happen on, near, or in relation to the earth.

The narrative includes enumerated events that function somewhat like navigational buoys. These include four series of seven: seven messages, seven seals, seven trumpets, and seven plagues. John explicitly counts the seals, trumpets, and plagues, and each series brings an increasing amount of destruction. Although these markers imply order and progression, they are not always reliable. At times, we encounter unexpected features before reaching the buoy. In the cases of the seven seals and trumpets, for example, interludes or extended visions occur between the sixth and seventh events. Sometimes no marker appears where we expect it. John mentions "three woes" in Revelation 8:13: "Then I looked, and I heard an eagle crying with a loud voice as it flew in midheaven, 'Woe, woe, woe to the inhabitants of the earth, at the blasts of the other trumpets that the three angels are about to blow!'" John subsequently identifies the first (9:12) and the second woe and warns of the third (11:14), but the third never appears. Revelation's explicit numbering can give a *false* sense of order; its markers are misleading.

Revelation's nonlinear structure hints at a queer sense of time, promising to resist the standard ordering of events in linear and predictable fashion. Historically, lesbian, gay, bisexual, and other individuals who find themselves outside of "straight" have been forced to organize their life trajectories in ways that challenge the script for when life events are "supposed" to happen, a script that author Elizabeth Freeman terms "chrononormativity." This way of organizing life is designed by a dominant culture to maximize human productivity, according to Freeman.[68] This script dictates when a person should partner and start a family and is a script that queer-identified individuals, including cisgender women who resist cultural expectations to marry and have babies, are forced to resist. Even once gay couples have the legal right to marry, many still challenge chrononormativity and embrace alternate ways of doing life, such as postponing marriage until after having a career, having children before being partnered, embracing serial monogamy. Those who adopt

---

68. Elizabeth Freeman, *Time Binds: Queer Temporalities, Queer Histories* (Durham, NC: Duke University Press, 2010), 3.

this perspective typically regard it not just as a personal decision; rather, the refusal of chononormativity is politically powerful, signaling a refusal to simply be a productive pawn controlled by the dominant culture. Similarly, Revelation's nonlinear patterns coincide with its resistance to Roman perspectives on history and time.

In addition to having an unwieldly narrative structure, Revelation's language sets it apart from other New Testament writings. One reason early interpreters questioned whether Revelation was written by the author of the Fourth Gospel was its writing style, which is markedly different from the more elegant Gospel (Eusebius, *Hist. eccl.* 7.25.22-27). John's language includes obvious grammatical errors and awkward turns of phrase. Andrew of Caesarea, writing in the early seventh century, admitted that Revelation did not always "measure up . . . to the rules,"[69] an understatement (*Commentary on the Apocalypse* 24.72). While John may have been a native Aramaic or Hebrew speaker, his less-than-ideal Greek could be intentional and political. *Koine*, the type of Greek John employed, could serve as a tool of domination. Used by the armies of Alexander the Great in the fourth century BCE to unite the Mediterranean world under his rule, *koine* remained the common language in the Eastern Mediterranean as Rome's power began to spread. Perhaps John's unusual use of *koine* signals his resistance to the dominant culture and those who use the language to regulate and dominate those living in Asia Minor.[70] Still, it is possible that Revelation's grammatical problems and awkward phrasing simply reflect John's unfamiliarity with Greek.

This commentary follows the language of the NRSV translation of Revelation, even though there are places we disagree with or want to nuance that translation. We explain these points of difference in sections throughout the commentary labeled as "Translation Matters." Many of these differences are in places where there is an important point to be made for readers committed to feminist interpretation and the process of uncovering how the text has been used to mask or perpetuate oppression, whether based on gender, sexuality, or class.

Since John claims to describe things he sees from above, the perspective of heaven, a place not accessible to the average human and a place beyond our linguistic competence, he necessarily uses simile and metaphor. John uses the word ὡς, meaning "like" or "as," over seventy

---

69. Thank you to Juan Hernández Jr. for drawing my attention to this.
70. Allen Dwight Callahan, "The Language of Apocalypse," *HTR* 88 (1995): 453–70.

times and ὅμοιος, "like" or "similar to," at least twenty times.[71] For example, a voice John hears coming out of heaven sounds *like* a trumpet (1:10), and the moon becomes *like* blood (6:12). In addition, Revelation employs layers of metaphorical imagery throughout. John constructs his vision by describing things with images of things they are not, drawing on characteristics from both the source image and the thing being described, the target. At the beginning of Revelation 13, for example, a Beast emerges from the sea and John describes its horns, bear-like feet, and a lion's mouth. John is not writing a field manual for identifying unusual animals. Rather, John blends this Beast imagery with characteristics of a political or kingly figure, such as crown imagery, to make claims about political figures. Even though John does not explicitly state, "Politicians are beasts," the imagery encourages audiences to recognize, to see, the connections. Such conceptual metaphors or blends are powerful because they activate the audience members' imaginations and encourage them to envision things the way the author chooses.

Metaphors also invite an audience into the process of interpretation, such that metaphors can easily be taken in a direction the author never intended. For example, Revelation's depiction of the "marriage of the Lamb" (19:7), which suggests an equation between the concept "marriage" and that of a relationship between God and God's followers, led some medieval readers to imagine the sexual consummation of the marriage, depicting an erotic kind of union between God and the soul, an aspect of the concept "marriage" untapped by John.[72] In light of the pliability of Revelation's metaphorical language, readers necessarily make interpretive choices.

By equating two different things, metaphors include elements of both "is" and "is not." Life *is* a path, but it is also *not* really a path. Given this ambivalence, at times it might be necessary to resist some of the equations made by Revelation's metaphors, especially if they force us to envision things in ways that are sexist, racist, ableist, etc. Ironically, by using metaphor to shape how his audiences think about things, effectively affirming the equation of unlike things, John simultaneously invites those listening to resist these equations. By saying, for example,

71. Literary theorists often discuss the difference between simile and metaphor. For our purposes, however, we approach them as related ways of communicating previously held conceptual metaphors.

72. Lynn R. Huber, *Thinking and Seeing with Women in Revelation*, LNTS 475 (London: Bloomsbury, 2013), 115–26.

"Rome is a sex-worker," John is trying to encourage us to think about Rome in a very specific way, but because he is using a metaphor, equating a city with a type of woman, the reader can just as easily say, "No, John, Rome is not *really* a sex-worker." These decisions, as we will see, have ethical implications.[73]

Revelation in the Canon

Even though its position at the end of the collected texts of Christian Scripture suggests its importance as a kind of "final word" on the Bible, Revelation's status within this collection has not always been certain. Church historian Eusebius references a document in which Clement I (d. 99 CE) writes that early Christians were divided in their opinions about whether Revelation was Scripture (*Hist. eccl.* 3.24.18) as well as noting Dionysius of Alexandria's (d. 265 CE) discussion of those who call Revelation fraudulent because it seems more obscuring than revealing (5.25.1). Dionysius also mentions that Revelation may not actually be by John; rather, it could have been penned by a certain Cerinthus, who taught that the coming kingdom of Christ would be an earthly reign, replete with feasting, drinking, and even sexual passion (5.25.2-3). Even though these are not firsthand accounts, they indicate the contested nature of Revelation as Scripture and even some uncertainty about the character of the person behind the book. Confirming these reports are canon lists outlining books that Christians should understand as authoritative. Revelation is noticeably absent from a list generated by the Synod of Laodicea, which gathered in this city during the second half of the fourth century.[74] Syrian Christians, moreover, have generally eschewed Revelation, and it only became part of the Peshitta, the primary Syriac version of the New Testament, in 1905.

At various times throughout history, other authoritative voices within Christian tradition have called into question Revelation's relevance. Martin Luther, in the preface to Revelation for his 1522 translation of the New Testament, expressed what a lot of people have wanted to say about the book but were afraid to put in print: "They are supposed to

---

73. Susan E. Hylen, "Metaphor Matters: Violence and Ethics in Revelation," *CBQ* 73 (2011): 777–96.

74. Edmon L. Gallagher and John D. Meade, *The Biblical Canon Lists from Early Christianity: Texts and Analysis* (Oxford: Oxford University Press, 2017), 127–30.

be blessed who keep what is written in this book [Rev 1:3]; and yet no one knows what that is, to say nothing of keeping it."[75]

Despite Luther suggesting that there were "many far better books available for us to keep,"[76] Revelation remains in the canon. That fact, however, does not necessarily mean it plays an equal role in every Christian tradition or in every church. Revelation's inclusion in the Revised Common Lectionary, used by many mainline Christian churches, is limited to Revelation's introductory matter (1:4-8), images of worship in the throne room (5:11-14), the image of the innumerable crowd before the throne (7:9-17), and visions of the heavenly Jerusalem (2:1-6, 10; 22:1-5, 12-14, 16-17, 20-21).[77] Churches that follow the lectionary might hear only a relatively small portion of the text within the context of worship. Even some Christians who follow the lectionary might, however, find Revelation's text a powerful prophetic tool for understanding the world and the role of the Christian within it. The authors of *Unveiling Empire: Reading Revelation Then and Now*, Catholic scholars writing out of their commitment to social justice, note that they "*care* about the meaning of Revelation" as individuals "trying in our own ways from different outposts of empire to live lives faithful to the Crucified and Risen One."[78] In other Christian traditions, Revelation might be engaged more frequently but in a more personal way. In a publication from the Church of Jesus Christ of Latter-Day Saints, for instance, the author notes Revelation's ability to help believers see the full scope of divine and earthly history; however, he explains that knowing every detail behind the book's imagery is "not paramount in our study of the scriptures."[79] In contrast, for some evangelical Christian churches—namely, those that believe the end times are nearing and that Revelation provides a description of these times—attention to the details of Revelation *is* paramount and much time is spent trying to discern the book's meaning. Simply put, the canonicity of Revelation means different things for different readers.

75. Martin Luther, "Preface to the Revelation of St. John (I)," in *Luther's Works: Word and Sacrament I*, vol. 35, ed. E. Theodore Bachmann (Philadelphia: Fortress, 1960), 398–99.

76. Luther "Preface," 399.

77. *Revised Common Lectionary Daily Readings: Proposed by the Consultation on Common Texts* (Minneapolis: Augsburg Fortress, 2005).

78. Wes Howard-Brook and Anthony Gwyther, *Unveiling Empire: Reading Revelation Then and Now* (Maryknoll, NY: Orbis Books, 1999), xix.

79. David A. Edwards, "Joseph Smith and the Book of Revelation," *Ensign* (December 2015): 65.

Canonicity is a feminist issue since it concerns who has the authority to speak. Compiling a canon is an attempt at consolidating power by limiting the variety of voices invited into the conversation. As Elisabeth Schüssler Fiorenza observes, early Christian efforts at canonization were part of an imperial attempt at legitimating Christianity, and church leaders involved in this process intentionally excluded women's voices.[80] Even though Luther probably might not agree, some of the "far better books" that could have been canonized instead of Revelation were likely penned by women. As we navigate through Revelation in this commentary, we think it is important to remember that not all early Christians eagerly endorsed this book. While some found it a powerful expression of their understanding of God and the Lamb, others were not impressed. Remembering these differing perspectives can help us shift our perspective as we engage the text. Instead of thinking that we must agree with every bit of Revelation without question, we are invited to have multiple perspectives on the text and to consider carefully what is at stake in accepting John's worldview and his theological and christological claims.

80. Elisabeth Schüssler Fiorenza, "New Testament Canon Formation and the Marginalization of Wo/Men," in *Gospels: Narrative and History*, ed. Mercedes Navarro Puerto, Marinella Perroni; ed. Amy-Jill Levine, English ed., The Bible and Women: An Encyclopaedia of Exegesis and Cultural History (Atlanta: SBL Press, 2015), 19.

Revelation 1

Introducing the Apocalypse

Revelation opens with a series of introductions. John introduces audience members to Revelation as a visionary account or an "apocalypse" communicated by God, and John introduces himself as the seer and narrator of this vision. He introduces those hearing his visionary account to figures they will encounter in the heavenly throne room and offers an initial vision of the risen Christ, a figure central to this text. John even begins to introduce hearers to images of their future selves. Through these multiple introductions, John establishes his *ethos*, trustworthiness in ancient rhetoric, as the one who communicates this vision and the authority of his vision.[1] In this opening chapter, modern readers also make acquaintance with John's first audiences, the communities to whom he addresses this apocalyptic letter, and get an initial glimpse into how John understands his relationship to these communities.

These introductions prepare Revelation's audiences, ancient and modern, for the journey that unfolds as they experience the narrative. From the beginning, John invites his audiences to see and hear his report, and eventually, John will prompt those encountering the text to taste, smell, and even feel along with him. This appeal to the senses creates a reading experience distinct among the New Testament writings; reading

---

1. Greg Carey, *Elusive Apocalypse: Reading Authority in the Revelation to John* (Macon, GA: Mercer University Press, 1999), 93–133.

Revelation is an immersive experience. In the summer of 2000, I experienced this aspect of Revelation while visiting an art museum in Passau, Germany, that hosted a multimedia exhibit titled *Apokalypse zwischen Himmel und Hölle*, or *Apocalypse between Heaven and Hell*.[2] The museum invited visitors to watch a video that combined medieval apocalyptic images, mostly taken from artwork and manuscripts from the surrounding area, with a soundtrack of readings from Revelation punctuated by booming thunder and dramatic music. Visitors saw, heard, and felt the apocalypse in a way that I think John would have appreciated. The experience helped me understand how Revelation asks audiences to come to the narrative open to experiencing its message bodily, through all the senses. This feature is, arguably, one way Revelation aligns with feminist commitments and practices, which embrace a holistic view of human experience that includes material, spiritual, and intellectual ways of knowing. In fact, throughout this narrative journey, John emphasizes how theological commitments make bodily claims. Hearing the text with one's ears is not sufficient; John will demand his audiences see his vision and live accordingly.

Lifting the Veil on the Apocalypse (1:1-11)

The very first word of this book is ἀποκάλυψις, or "apocalypse" in English. Sometimes it is used as a title for the book—*Apocalypse of John*. Many translations of Revelation begin with the word "the," even though ancient Greek versions lack the definite article. However, the book should begin with "a" instead of "the," preserving the original Greek and acknowledging that this book offers one of several "revelations" of Jesus Christ.[3]

Even though widespread use of "apocalypse" suggests cataclysmic events and the end of the world, the ancient Greek word is more similar in meaning to ἀνακάλυψις or "anacalypsis," which describes the moment in an ancient Greek wedding when the groom lifted the veil that covered the bride's head and face.[4] The similarity between these terms anticipates

---

2. Herbert W. Wurster and Richard Loibl, *Apokalypse: Zwischen Himmel Und Hölle* (Regensburg: Friedrich Pustet, 2000), 28–30.

3. See also Jacqueline M. Hidalgo, *Revelation in Aztlán: Scriptures, Utopias, and the Chicano Movement* (New York: Palgrave Macmillan, 2016), 234.

4. Karen K. Hersch, *The Roman Wedding: Ritual and Meaning in Antiquity* (Cambridge: Cambridge University Press, 2010), 100; John Howard Oakley and Rebecca

^{1:1}The revelation of Jesus Christ, which God gave him to show his servants what must soon take place; he made it known by sending his angel to his servant John, ²who testified to the word of God and to the testimony of Jesus Christ, even to all that he saw.

³Blessed is the one who reads aloud the words of the prophecy, and blessed are those who hear and who keep what is written in it; for the time is near.

⁴John to the seven churches that are in Asia:

Grace to you and peace from him who is and who was and who is to come, and from the seven spirits who are before his throne, ⁵and from Jesus Christ, the faithful witness, the firstborn of the dead, and the ruler of the kings of the earth.

To him who loves us and freed us from our sins by his blood, ⁶and made

---

a bridal unveiling in Revelation's final chapters. There, audience members will witness the appearance of a bride who marries the Lamb, one of the ways John depicts Christ (21:1-2, 9-10). More important, they will learn that this bride is a metaphor for the community of those faithful to God and Christ, effectively whom John calls them to become. Talk about audience participation! Moreover, just as an ancient bride saw her new husband when her veil was lifted, Revelation's Bride learns more about the identity of her partner, the Lamb, as the veil over "her" eyes is lifted throughout the narrative. Of course, this idea of bridal unveiling is different from many modern weddings, where the future partners may have taken months and years to get to know one another or have even lived together. Clearly, we come to Revelation with different expectations and experiences from John.

Building on the visual connotation of "apocalypse," the Greek text of the first three verses of Revelation emphasizes showing and seeing. God gives Jesus this revelation or apocalypse to *show* those who are faithful to God, described as his "slaves" (See "Translation Matters: δοῦλος"), what must soon take place. Likewise, the Greek word behind "made it known," σημαίνω, invokes the idea of communicating through signs or signals. We might imagine this as a reference to the divine using a kind of sign language to communicate with John.

H. Sinos, *The Wedding in Ancient Athens* (Madison: University of Wisconsin Press, 1993), 30. See also Brian K. Blount, *Revelation: A Commentary* (Louisville: Westminster John Knox, 2009), 27–28, who associates this idea with the undressing of a bride on her wedding night and the stripping of Jesus at the crucifixion.

us to be a kingdom, priests serving his God and Father, to him be glory and dominion forever and ever. Amen.

⁷Look! He is coming with the clouds;
every eye will see him,
even those who pierced him;
and on his account all the tribes
of the earth will wail.
So it is to be. Amen.

⁸"I am the Alpha and the Omega," says the Lord God, who is and who was and who is to come, the Almighty.

⁹I, John, your brother who share with you in Jesus the persecution and the kingdom and the patient endurance, was on the island called Patmos because of the word of God and the testimony of Jesus. ¹⁰I was in the spirit on the Lord's day, and I heard behind me a loud voice like a trumpet ¹¹saying, "Write in a book what you see and send it to the seven churches, to Ephesus, to Smyrna, to Pergamum, to Thyatira, to Sardis, to Philadelphia, and to Laodicea."

Visual language is not the only type of communication noted here, as God conveys this unveiling to John so that he can testify to or about all the things he saw (v. 2), eventually making the visual revelation something spoken *and* heard (v. 3). A blessing pronounced on the one who reads Revelation aloud and those who hear it highlights the importance of the testimony. This multi-modal delivery offers a glimpse into the world of Revelation's audiences in which there would have been widely varying levels of literacy.[5] By hearing the text read aloud in a communal setting, Revelation's audiences envision along with John in their mind's eye, seeing what he sees and describes.[6] The oral and aural aspects of the text contribute to its persuasive power, as they allow those listening to envision the things John sees. By presenting a particular vision of how things are *and* will be, a vision different from the world that the audience inhabits, the text exercises control and sets rules.

The opening verses of Revelation describe the book's chain of transmission or witness.[7] This can be understood as a conventional way of highlighting the authority of an ancient sacred text. Just as, according to

5. Pieter J. J. Botha, *Orality and Literacy in Early Christianity* (Eugene, OR: Wipf and Stock, 2012), 43–48.

6. Robyn J. Whitaker, *Ekphrasis, Vision, and Persuasion in the Book of Revelation*, WUNT 2.410 (Tübingen: Mohr Siebeck, 2015), 7–9.

7. Blount, *Revelation*, 27.

tradition, God reveals the Torah to Moses who passes it down to others,[8] this book originates with God and is shared by a chain of messengers, including Jesus Christ, an angel, and then John himself. For some interpreters, John's claim that Revelation comes from God means that this book holds more authority than other New Testament books and provides a lens through which other books should be read. The medieval abbot and apocalyptic writer Joachim of Fiore, for example, described Revelation as the key to all things past and present (Joachim, *Expositio* f. 3r).[9] Similarly, many modern conservative Christian readers see Revelation as the culmination of Christian Scripture, offering God's key to the present and impending future.[10] This kind of privileging of Revelation discounts John's use of earlier scriptural traditions, which he weaves throughout the narrative. Rather than reading John's acknowledgment of God's role in Revelation as a way the author asserts the importance of his text, the chain of transmission can be understood as John decentering his authority.[11] This is something that John will do again later in the narrative, when he depicts his role in transmitting this vision as one of reception and passivity, a kind of queer prophetic digression (Rev 10; see pp. 135–44).

The reference to "Jesus Christ" in Revelation's chain of witnesses reflects the book's focus on Jesus's significance as one who is God's Messiah. John shows little or no interest in the activities associated with Jesus in gospel traditions, such as healing, exorcism, and teaching. Instead, John refers to "his Christ" (τοῦ χριστοῦ αὐτοῦ), which the NRSV translates into English as "his Messiah," to characterize Jesus as the one through whom God is visible and works (11:15; 12:10), a role like the one inhabited by Jesus in John's Gospel (e.g., John 14:9). The English terms "Christ" and "Messiah" are interchangeable to some extent since the Greek term translates the Hebrew word for "Messiah," a term used to describe someone whom God anoints. Elsewhere in Revelation, "Christ" functions like a name for Jesus, who has been resurrected and now resides with God in heaven (e.g., 1:5; 20:4).

---

8. Michael D. Swartz, "Chains of Tradition from *Avot* to the *'Avodah Piyutim*," in *Jews, Christians, and the Roman Empire: The Poetics of Power in Late Antiquity*, ed. Natalie B. Dohrmann and Annette Yoshiko Reed (Philadelphia: University of Pennsylvania Press, 2013), 189.

9. Lynn R. Huber, *Like a Bride Adorned: Reading Metaphor in John's Apocalypse* (New York: T&T Clark, 2007), 9–10.

10. E.g., Tim LaHaye, *Revelation Unveiled* (Grand Rapids: Zondervan, 2010), 10–11.

11. Craig R. Koester, *Revelation: A New Translation with Introduction and Commentary*, AYB 38A (New Haven: Yale University Press, 2014), 224.

Christ's importance in Revelation is, ironically, communicated through the ambiguity of a simple English preposition, "of," that does not even appear as a specific word in the Greek phrase Ἀποκάλυψις Ἰησοῦ Χριστοῦ. Since the declension of an ancient Greek noun indicates its grammatical function in a sentence, the Greek phrase translated here as "a revelation of Jesus Christ" does not include a word equivalent to "of." "Of" is implied in the grammatical form, genitive case, of the proper noun Jesus Christ. This form suggests that Jesus is *both* a link in the chain of transmission (the apocalypse is his) *and* part of what is revealed within its narrative (it is a revelation of him). This dual understanding of Jesus as revealer and revealed is exemplified in chapters 2–3, where the Son of Humanity, one of Revelation's depictions of Christ, delivers messages to the seven communities and describes himself (in the third person) in the messages. The idea that Christ is both revealer and revealed continues in the next verse, which states that John "testified to the word of God and the testimony of Jesus Christ" (v. 2).

Throughout Revelation, "the testimony of Jesus" is something the faithful are called to "hold" or "keep" (1:9; 12:7; 19:10; 20:4). This testimony is not a collection of Jesus's teachings or sermons, like those found in the Gospels of Matthew, Mark, and Luke. Instead, Jesus's testimony refers, first, to his death and resurrection. Throughout the book, John pairs the language of testimony or witness with references to violence and death (see "Translation Matters: μάρτυς"). I say more about this term in reference to 1:5, where Jesus is described as "the faithful witness, the firstborn of the dead." Second, the idea of Jesus's testimony recalls his revelation in the Gospel of John. In the opening verses of the Fourth Gospel, Jesus famously appears as God's Word (λόγος, 1:1-18). As the Word of God in the flesh, Jesus makes God known through his words, actions, attitudes, death, and then resurrection. Characters in John's Gospel are confronted by this revelatory "Word" when they encounter Jesus and respond with either belief or unbelief.[12] In a somewhat similar way, "Jesus's testimony" in Revelation invites John's audiences to affirm or disavow Jesus's relationship to God, including the claim that they share the heavenly throne and the implications of this relation. As this

---

12. Gail R. O'Day, "Narrative Mode and Theological Claim: A Study in the Fourth Gospel," *JBL* 105 (1986): 657–68. See also Lynn R. Huber, "Revealing Christ in Revelation," in *Narrative Mode and Theological Claim in Johannine Literature: Essays in Honor of Gail R. O'Day*, ed. Lynn R. Huber, Susan E. Hylen, and William M. Wright IV, BSNA 30 (Atlanta: SBL Press, 2021), 95–108.

introduction claims, this entire revelation makes visible Jesus Christ and his testimony. While some readers might take a quick glance at Revelation and say, "It's about the end of the world" or "It's about the Beast, also known as the antichrist," Revelation claims to be about Jesus Christ and the audience's present and future relationship to him.

Despite John's privileging of Jesus as the subject of the revelation, readers often come to the text to find out "what must soon take place" (v. 1). The word "soon" (τάχος) can be translated as "quickly," and Christians throughout history often hear this in reference to their own historical context, reading Revelation as a description of events soon happening in their own lifetimes. The best-selling Left Behind book and movie series provides one of the most popular modern examples of this phenomenon, populating Revelation's narrative with twentieth-century characters, including an intrepid reporter, college student, airline pilot, and flight attendant.[13] Even though interpreters tend to highlight this way of reading Revelation as a modern phenomenon, versions of it have been around for centuries. In the third century, for example, Hippolytus of Rome read Revelation as predicting the coming of Christ and the last judgment in 500 CE (*Comm. Dan.* 2.4-6). Later, in the eleventh century, Joachim of Fiore aligned Revelation's images with the events of his day, and some of his followers seemingly identified him with the angel described in Revelation 10:1-2.[14] One thing readers of Revelation across time have in common is the instinct to ask, "How soon is soon?"

Were Revelation simply about predicting what happens in the year of the most recent interpreter of the text, whether that year is 500 or 2500, those events could not be described as "soon" or "quickly" from John's perspective. Rather, "soon" suggests the things to be experienced by audiences once the veil is lifted. Once the book's audiences see and hear through the lenses John provides, there is no turning back; there is no unseeing. Reading or hearing the book causes those invested in the text to see and experience things differently, so the revelation gives its audiences a glimpse of how they will start to interpret the world around them. Another way of thinking about this change of impression, as Barbara Rossing explains, is that biblical prophecy, which is one way that Revelation describes itself (1:3), is about a "timely warning" and not a prediction

---

13. Tim LaHaye and Jerry B. Jenkins, *Left Behind: A Novel of the Earth's Last Days* (Wheaton, IL: Tyndale, 1995).

14. As referenced in Judith L. Kovacs and Christopher Rowland, *Revelation: The Apocalypse of Jesus Christ* (Malden, MA: Blackwell, 2004), 118.

of the future. A timely warning shows what might happen, but it does so with the intention of changing the actions and attitudes of those hearing it: "The future is not yet determined. There is hope that judgment can be averted."[15]

Following the introduction of this "apocalypse" comes a more traditional ancient letter opening. John identifies himself as the one writing to seven assemblies (ἐκκλησίαι) of the faithful in the Roman province of Asia (see "Translation Matters: ἐκκλησία"). These communities will soon be named (v. 11), but John begins with their collective identity. John offers the communities a salutation, "Grace to you and peace," like those used in other early letters by the followers of Jesus (e.g., 1 Thess 1:1; Rom 1:7; 1 Cor 1:3; Eph 1:2; Phil 1:2). By employing a traditional letter opening, John bridges the divide between the heavenly world, introduced in the opening verses, and the earthly world of his audiences.

John again attributes the message he brings to divine origins—God, the seven spirits before the throne, and Christ. Some Christian scholars read this trio as a reference to the Trinity,[16] but Revelation does not offer a clear picture of how these entities relate to one another. The reference to the trio does present a complex vision of the heavenly realm and suggests God works collaboratively, although God's distinctiveness generally persists throughout the book. There are some moments where God's and Christ's roles blur (e.g., 5:13), but for the most part, Revelation presents God as working through Christ as his Messiah.

John's references to God and Christ in these verses gesture to their unique identities, which John develops more fully in later chapters. The characterization of God's temporal expanse, "the one who is and who was and who is to come," appears throughout Revelation (4:8; 11:17; 16:5). Echoing the description of God as "I am" in the Greek translation (the Septuagint) of Exodus as well as the Hebrew version's characterization of the divine identity as "I will be what I will be" (Exod 3:14), this description of God's timelessness provides one way that John contrasts heavenly and earthly powers (3:6; 13:5; 17:10-11). The Roman Empire and especially its first emperor, Augustus, were often lauded as changing the course of time. One of the most telling examples of this was when, in 9 CE, the *koinon* (provincial council) of Asia adjusted the provincial calen-

---

15. Barbara R. Rossing, *The Rapture Exposed: The Message of Hope in the Book of Revelation*, 2nd ed. (New York: Basic Books, 2004), 89.

16. E.g., Gregory K. Beale, *The Book of Revelation: A Commentary on the Greek Text* (Grand Rapids: Eerdmans, 1999), 189.

dar to align with the birthday of Augustus, proclaiming in an inscription, "We could justly consider that day to be equal to the beginning of all things. He restored the form of all things to usefulness, if not to their natural state, since it had deteriorated and suffered misfortune. He gave a new appearance to the whole world."[17] In contrast, John positions the God of Israel as beyond and encompassing all time.

The introduction of Jesus as "the faithful witness, the firstborn of the dead, and the ruler of the kings of the earth" likewise introduces threads interwoven throughout the book. "Faithful witness" emphasizes again the testimony of Jesus communicated throughout Revelation (v. 2). The second facet of Jesus's identity here, that he is "the firstborn of the dead," comprises a part of this testimony and is the first of several paradoxical ways John depicts Christ. Christ is one who has died but who is now born or living. That fact that he is *first*born implies that others will follow him through death and into birth or life after death, an idea realized at the end of Revelation (20:4-6). Finally, by proclaiming Christ as "ruler of the kings of the earth" (v. 5), John anticipates a major theme of the narrative in which the Lamb is exalted above and victorious over earthly powers (chaps. 5 and 19).

Situated between God and Christ in this introduction is a reference to the seven spirits who reside before God's throne (v. 4). John's audiences will see these spirits briefly when he describes the heavenly throne room (4:5). Although this imagery is not as fully developed as Revelation's depictions of God and Christ, the reference hints at a heavenly realm inhabited by multiple beings who work together, something we see in other Jewish traditions. In Proverbs 8:22, for instance, a personified Wisdom, sometimes called *Chokhmah* or Sophia (names derived, respectively, from transliterations of the Hebrew and Greek terms for wisdom), appears with God at creation. Some early Jesus followers may have interpreted his references to "the spirit" in relation to personified Wisdom,[18] and some early readers may have thought of these seven spirits in feminine terms as well, even though the Greek word for "spirit," πνεῦμα, is a neuter noun (the Hebrew word for spirit, רוח, is feminine).

17. As quoted in Steven J. Friesen, *Imperial Cults and the Apocalypse of John: Reading Revelation in the Ruins* (Oxford: Oxford University Press, 2001), 33.

18. In her work on Christian origins, Schüssler Fiorenza maintains that Sophia, embodied by Jesus, was part of the original Jesus followers' beliefs. See *In Memory of Her: A Feminist Theological Reconstruction of Christian Origins* (New York: Crossroad, 1983), 133–34.

The idea that God works within a complex and collaborative system resonates with some feminist theological thinking. Theologian Laurel Schneider argues for the importance of acknowledging the multiplicity of the divine since that multiplicity is both part of the biblical tradition and an invitation to embrace different ways of being in the world.[19] The most famous allusion to God as collaborative and, in Christian interpretation, multiple, appears in the opening chapter of Genesis, when God says, "Let *us* make humankind in *our* image, according to *our* likeness" (1:26). English translations of other references to the plurality of God (e.g., Gen 11:7; Pss 29:1; 82:1) tend to "monotheize" or downplay this plurality, as Amy-Jill Levine and Marc Zvi Brettler note.[20] Like Genesis 1, Revelation's vision assumes a rich and complex understanding of the divine that is consonant with other ancient views. Most everyone at the time believed in a multiplicity of divine beings—just as there was a continuum of masculine to feminine, so there was a continuum of divine to human, and beings could move up and down the ladder through apotheosis, i.e., being made a god, or by choosing to take on humanity (cf. Phil 2:6-8). Even though this idea is not easily squared with later philosophical visions of God as singular and impersonal, this complexity allows feminists to consider multiple ways of approaching and engaging the divine, even beyond those presented in the text.

These verses begin to create a sense of communal identity for Revelation's geographically scattered recipients, those in the seven communities of Asia Minor to which the book is addressed. Using the first-person plural, "us," John offers a doxology that assumes a bond between and among himself and those hearing Revelation read aloud:[21] "To him who loves *us* and freed *us* from *our* sins by his blood" (v. 5b). Together, the community offers Christ glory and dominion or power. The disparate communities are united in their worship of Christ. These communities will also be called throughout the narrative to construct a shared sense of identity, and, here, John introduces one of the first images of this community. They are the ones "made . . . to be a kingdom, priests serving his God and Father" (v. 6).

19. Laurel Schneider, *Beyond Monotheism: A Theology of Multiplicity* (London: Routledge, 2007), passim.

20. Amy-Jill Levine and Marc Zvi Brettler, *The Bible With and Without Jesus: How Jews and Christians Read the Same Stories Differently* (New York: HarperOne, 2020), 88–92.

21. Carey, *Elusive Apocalypse*, 118.

The imagery of those who are faithful as a kind of kingdom (βασιλεία) will appear most fully in the final chapters of Revelation, where the faithful are imaged not simply as a kingdom but as kings seated on thrones and judging alongside Christ (20:4). John's promise of kingship raises a concern for feminist interpreters of Revelation, as it seemingly reinscribes a kyriarchal system of power. As discussed in the introduction, *"kyriarchy"* describes political systems of domination that use multiple kinds of hierarchies, not just gender hierarchies, to organize society (see p. lxxi).[22] As we will see in subsequent chapters, Revelation challenges the legitimacy of kingdoms or kyriarchal systems that compete with the kingdom of God. John's use of kingdom imagery and language, including ascribing "dominion" to Christ, however, suggests replacing one type of kyriarchy such as the Roman Empire, with another, the empire of God and Christ. We return to the question of whether Revelation reinforces kyriarchal systems throughout this commentary. Here, it seems that John may be engaging in just such a move.

The idea of being made a kingdom is nuanced by the description of this as a kingdom of priests or a priestly kingdom. This imagery comes directly from Exodus, when God, through Moses, calls the Israelites to be "for me a priestly kingdom and a holy nation" (Exod 19:6). Being a priestly kingdom was an identity to which all Israelites were called by God, even though some families were selected to perform the specific tasks associated with the religious cult.[23] Revelation similarly envisions the role of priest as including all of God's people (cf. 1 Pet 2:9) and highlights God's faithfulness to his followers by noting that they have been "made" (ἐποίησεν), an aorist verb, into this priestly kingdom. The community already shares this identity, even if they do not fully realize it, and even though it will be more fully realized in the future when evil is subdued and Christ returns. Living into this identity, learning its expectations, and acting accordingly is one of John's goals for his audiences.

John's audiences may have heard in this image an allusion to the priestly roles in the imperial cults present in the urban centers of first-century Asia Minor as well as the reference to Exodus. In addition to the various priests who worked tending to and serving the myriad gods and their temples, elite women and men could be appointed as priests of local imperial cults or even as high priests of provincial imperial cults (these were regionally organized cults with centers in Pergamum,

---

22. Elisabeth Schüssler Fiorenza, *Empowering Memory and Movement: Thinking and Working across Borders* (Minneapolis: Augsburg Fortress, 2014), 108.

23. Koester, *Revelation*, 228; Levine and Brettler, *Bible With and Without Jesus*, 139.

Smyrna, and Ephesus).[24] This role was not simply symbolic; it involved participating in festivals, attending games and competitions, and offering sacrifices to or on behalf of imperial family members. An inscription from Aphrodisias, a city in Asia Minor, notes that a female priest "sacrificed throughout all the years on behalf of the health of the emperors."[25] As Steven J. Friesen explains, people in priestly roles were "entrusted with the task of expressing the province's reverence for imperial authority."[26] Similarly, John understands the faithful as united in expressing reverence for the authority of God and Christ. The doxology he offers to Christ on behalf of "us" in verse 5 gestures to the worship that Revelation calls the faithful to offer God and Christ.

Before the audiences have time to imagine other possible responsibilities associated with being a kingdom of priests, John commands, "Look!" This imperative begins a short refrain that combines verses from Zechariah and Daniel: "He is coming with the clouds; every eye will see him, even those who pierced him; and on his account all the tribes of the earth will wail" (v. 7). Drawn from Daniel 7:13-14, the announcement of one coming on the clouds appears in the Gospels to describe a coming "Son of Humanity," a Messiah anointed by God (Matt 24:30; 26:46; Mark 13:26; Luke 21:27). While the Gospels are ambiguous about identifying this Son of Humanity directly with Jesus, the inclusion of "pierced," language from Zechariah 12:10, implies that Jesus is the Son of Humanity, since Jesus is "pierced" at the crucifixion (John 19:34). In this way, Revelation presents a specific interpretation of Israel's traditions that reads Jesus into the texts. The prophetic texts were read and continue to be read quite differently by other Jews, an important consideration for feminist Christian readers given the church's history of faulting Jews who do not read the prophets in the same way.[27]

This mention of piercing is not John's only reference to Jesus's crucifixion. Later, the text refers to the "great city . . . where also their Lord was crucified" (11:8). The crucifixion is one of the few parts of Jesus's

24. Steven J. Friesen, "High Priestesses of Asia and Emancipatory Interpretation," in *Walk in the Ways of Wisdom: Essays in Honor of Elisabeth Schüssler Fiorenza*, ed. Shelly Matthews, Cynthia Briggs Kittredge, and Melanie Johnson-Debaufre (Harrisburg, PA: Trinity Press International, 2003), 137.

25. As quoted in S. R. F. Price, *Rituals and Power: The Roman Imperial Cult in Asia Minor* (Cambridge: Cambridge University Press, 1984), 211.

26. Steven J. Friesen, *Twice Neokoros: Ephesus, Asia, and the Cult of the Flavian Imperial Family* (Leiden: Brill, 1993), 81.

27. Levine and Brettler, *Bible With and Without Jesus*, 43–66.

biography, along with a possible allusion to his birth (12:5), that Revelation references. John focuses on the crucifixion as *the* defining moment of Jesus's life, and here, he directs his audience's gaze to the cross. With the command to "look" along with the claim that "every eye will see him," he places his audiences at the foot of the cross, looking up to see that the pierced body of Jesus is the Son of Humanity.

At the conclusion of both the doxology (v. 5) and his call to view the pierced Messiah, John prompts the audiences to respond positively by including the congregational affirmation "amen," a transliteration of the Hebrew term meaning "so be it" (e.g., Neh 8:6; 1 Chr 16:36). He calls his audiences to confirm that they too see that the one who was pierced is the Messiah who has made them into a kingdom of priests. This affirmation that the one to whom glory and power are given is the one whose side is pierced signals that John's understanding of "kingdom" does not simply replicate Rome's kyriarchal system.[28] Instead, Revelation challenges this vision by lifting to the throne one characterized by weakness, a victim of violence. This idea is more explicit in John's description of the Lamb in God's throne room (Rev 5).

TRANSLATION MATTERS: ἰδού

The word "apocalypse" implies making something visible, and when John describes his visionary experience, he sometimes includes a singular imperative form of the verb "to see," ἰδού (4:1, 2; 5:5; 6:2, 5, 8; 7:9; 12:3; 14:1, 14; 19:11).[29] This command appears three times in the first four seals as John calls hearers to "Look!" at the horses that come when called by the living creatures (6:2, 5, 8). A number of these instances involve John using a Greek phrase, καὶ εἶδον καὶ ἰδού, that sounds awkward when translated literally into English, "and I looked and look!" The KJV captures the idea of the text while smoothing out the redundant use of "look" by translating the phrase as "and I saw and behold." The NRSV, however, smooths out the Greek to a much simpler: "I looked . . . !" The exclamation point at the end of the phrase supposedly signals a command, but the rhetorical impact of the imperative is diminished by failing to include the word "look." The command is essentially erased from the NRSV.

---

28. Cf. Stephen D. Moore, "Mimicry and Monstrosity," in *Untold Tales from the Book of Revelation: Sex and Gender, Empire and Ecology*, ed. Stephen D. Moore (Atlanta: SBL, 2014), 22.

29. In some cases, ἰδού is used by the risen Christ or another character within the text (1:7, 18; 2:10, 22; 3:9, 20; 9:12; 11:14; 16:15; 21:3, 5; 22:7, 12).

The command to "Look!" is central to how the book of Revelation communicates. Through it, John summons audiences to share in *his* vision, how *he* sees things. He demands that they—and so we—move through the narrative according to his direction and guidance. He shows just what he wants, and he does not allow his audiences a chance to snoop around on their own or to draw their own conclusions. While we might say the same about other texts, John's commands force the issue.

As interpreters of Revelation, we heed the call to respond to John's command to "Look!" with him. As feminists, however, we refuse to let John limit where we look. We think it is appropriate for us to look at characters in the text, such as the Lamb and Babylon, from different angles and with different concerns than the ones John promotes. As we noted in the introduction, we will look at the world John described with interpreters who are women, who are feminists, or who are scholars of color as well as Jewish and Christian scholars. We will "Look!" but we will decide whether we think John's vision is sufficient or empowering.

Introducing himself in verse 9, John attempts to bond with Revelation's audiences by referencing their common struggle (see "Translation Matters: θλῖψις"). He is their brother, and he shares their experience of persecution (θλῖψις) and their patient endurance (ὑπομονή). By referencing this shared experience, John signals that he and his message are trustworthy; at the same time, he inadvertently raises a question about his authorial reliability.[30] John suggests he experiences persecution but remains silent about any details. Even though traditions about John's exile and persecution became part of church teaching (e.g., Clement, *The Rich Man's Salvation* 42; Tertullian, *Praescr.* 36.3), questions swirl around his reason for being on Patmos and the nature of the "persecution" he experienced.

Perhaps because he assumes that his audiences can fill in the gaps about his experience of persecution, John finds it unnecessary to provide specifics. All he offers is that he is on the island of Patmos "because of the word of God and the testimony of Jesus" (v. 9). The question of why John was on Patmos is not simply an intellectual curiosity; for some readers, the belief that John writes from a place of exile and an experience of adversity makes Revelation's depictions of vengeance and visions of bloodshed understandable (e.g., 19:3, 17-19). Emerging out of a direct ex-

30. Carey, *Elusive Apocalypse*, 116.

perience of anguish and oppression, the text paves the way for catharsis and the transformation of "rage into consciousness."[31] Revelation is not a text for every time and place. It is addressed to and meant for the oppressed. If removed from this context Revelation can be used to justify violence based on a perceived sense of persecution or threat,[32] as was the case in some justifications of the Crusades.[33] In a similar way, Revelation's imagery, divorced from a sense of the book's original rhetorical purpose, can stoke fear and chaos. In March 2021, for instance, a member of the United States House of Representatives compared "vaccine passports," evidence that one has received the COVID-19 vaccine, to the "mark of the Beast" in Revelation 13:17-18 in an apparent effort to discourage US citizens from getting the potentially life-saving shots.[34] Readings of Revelation like this certainly did not help public health efforts.

Yet, as other scholars contend, while John and his audiences did not necessarily experience empire-initiated persecution, they likely sustained a range of maltreatment—from social exclusion to physical threats—as well as dealt with the effects of the Jewish war.[35] John himself was almost certainly not boiled in oil, as Tertullian would later contend (*Praescr.* 36.3); however, there remains a sense that this text reflects the perspective of someone who sees his world in terms of conflict and who uses this backdrop for his message.

31. Pablo Richard, "Reading the *Apocalypse*: Resistance, Hope, and Liberation in Central America," in *From Every People and Nation: The Book of Revelation in Intercultural Perspective*, ed. David Rhoads (Minneapolis: Fortress, 2005), 150.

32. Wendy Mayer, "Heirs of Roman Persecution: Common Threads in Discursive Strategies across Late Antiquity," in *Heirs of Roman Persecution: Studies on a Christian and Para-Christian Discourse in Late Antiquity*, ed. Éric Fournier and Wendy Mayer (Abingdon: Routledge, 2019), 332.

33. Miriam Rita Tessera, "Philip Count of Flanders and Hildegard of Bingen: Crusading against the Saracens or Crusading against Deadly Sin?," in *Gendering the Crusades*, ed. Susan B. Edgington and Sarah Lambert (New York: Columbia University Press, 2002), 83–84.

34. Alexandra Hutzler, "Marjorie Taylor Greene Rebukes Vaccine Passports as 'Biden's Mark of the Beast,'" *Newsweek*, March 30, 2021, https://www.newsweek.com /marjorie-taylor-greene-rebukes-vaccine-passports-bidens-mark-beast-1579880.

35. Sarah Emanuel, *Humor, Resistance, and Jewish Cultural Persistence in the Book of Revelation: Roasting Rome* (Cambridge: Cambridge University Press, 2020), 41; Hidalgo, *Revelation in Aztlán*, 82–83; Shanell T. Smith, *The Woman Babylon and the Marks of Empire: Reading Revelation with a Postcolonial Womanist Hermeneutics of Ambiveilence* (Minneapolis: Augsburg Fortress, 2014), 111–17.

TRANSLATION MATTERS: θλῖψις

The noun θλῖψις appears only five times in Revelation, but the NRSV translates it in multiple ways. When John compares his experience to that of his audiences (Rev 1:9), the NRSV translates θλῖψις as "persecution." In 2:9-10, where it is used twice, θλῖψις becomes the "affliction" of imprisonment. In 2:22, the Son of Humanity uses the term, translated as "distress," to threaten a teacher in Thyatira. The word θλῖψις is "ordeal" when it refers to the experience of those who wash their robes in the blood of the Lamb (7:14). Elsewhere in the New Testament, the NRSV continues to render θλῖψις in inconsistent ways, using "anguish" in reference to birthing pains (John 16:21) and "distress" to characterize the experience of widows and orphans (Jas 1:27). While these translations all reference negative experiences, they differ in how they envision the source of and reason for the affliction. While distress and anguish may suggest negative experiences stemming from natural causes, "persecution" implies an outside force causing that affliction. As Candida Moss writes, "persecution" suggests "that a certain group is being *unfairly* targeted for attack and condemnation, usually because of blind hatred."[36] Even though the English translation implies such, John's use of θλῖψις does not necessarily imply this to be the case.

Moss's definition suggests that persecution can be perspectival. While Jesus followers may have seen themselves as unfairly targeted, those around them might have considered actions against them as warranted punishment. Suetonius, for example, recounts how Christians were treated as part of Nero's (54–68 CE) attempt to "clean up" Rome: "During his reign many abuses were severely punished and put down . . . Punishment [*afflicti*] was inflicted on the Christians, a class of [people] given to a new and mischievous superstition. He put an end to the diversions of the chariot drivers, who from immunity of long standing claimed the right of ranging at large and amusing themselves by cheating and robbing the people" (*Nero* 16.2). For Suetonius, punishing Jesus followers fell in the same category as stopping other forms of crime. Later historians accused Nero of killing Christians as punishment for a fire that consumed a significant section of Rome. The question of whether this was persecution or punishment is more ambiguous. The historian Tacitus reports that while some had pity on the Christians for this treatment, especially since some suspected that Nero set the fire himself, the Christians still deserved punishment because of their "hatred against mankind" (*Ann.* 15.44).

As discussed in the introduction, there has been a long history of reading Revelation as a response to the persecution of Christians by the Roman Empire. Some early Christian authors even depict John as the victim of torture at the hands of governmental authorities, likely Domitian. The third-century author Tertullian noted, for example, that John's time on Patmos came after having

---

36. Candida Moss, *The Myth of Persecution: How Early Christians Invented a Story of Martyrdom* (New York: HarperOne, 2013), 164; emphasis added.

been "plunged, unhurt, into boiling oil" (*Praescr.* 36.3).[37] Despite this tradition, the only evidence for John being persecuted is what he describes in the text. Similarly, what we know about his audience's experience of persecution comes from Revelation, and it is unclear how widespread any conflict or sense of exclusion was. And yet, Revelation is heavy with a sense of impending violence and death, and θλῖψις is on the horizon for audience members simply because of their allegiance to God and the Lamb.

Seeing and Hearing the Son of Humanity (1:12-20)

John prefaces his visionary experience by explaining that he was "in [the] spirit on the Lord's day" (v. 10). The NRSV includes a "the" before the word "spirit," which Christian readers could easily interpret as meaning the Holy Spirit. The NIV capitalizes "Spirit" to underscore this point, even though Revelation was written prior to Christian teaching on the Trinity. The Greek does not include the pronoun "the" and could read as either "I was in *a* spirit" or "I was in spirit." When John refers elsewhere to being "in spirit," he is taken to otherworldly locales, including heaven (4:1), the wilderness (17:3), and a high mountain (21:10). Whatever John means, the state of being in a spirit implies a lack of agency and lends further credence to his claim that God is the source behind Revelation. As he did when emphasizing his shared experience with his audiences, again John tries to gain their trust.

John's experience in the spirit begins when a voice, like a trumpet, commands him to write what he sees in a book and send it to seven communities in Asia Minor. The number seven alludes to the day on which God rested after creating the world (Gen 2:2); here, it conveys a sense of completeness. John's statement that he writes to seven communities has long been read as indicating that Revelation addresses the whole of Christianity (Victorinus, *Commentary on the Apocalypse* 1). John offers no reason for selecting the seven communities he names—Ephesus, Smyrna, Pergamum, Thyatira, Sardis, Philadelphia, and Laodicea (v. 11)—and not others, such as Colossae (Col 1:2) or Hierapolis (Col 4:13); however, given his familiarity with the situations of the communities he addresses (Rev 2–3), he seems to know them well. Or at least that is the impression John wants to give since there is no evidence of whether these seven communities saw themselves reflected in the text.

37. Ian Boxall, *Patmos in the Reception History of the Apocalypse* (Oxford: Oxford University Press, 2013), 33.

¹²Then I turned to see whose voice it was that spoke to me, and on turning I saw seven golden lampstands, ¹³and in the midst of the lampstands I saw one like the Son of Man, clothed with a long robe and with a golden sash across his chest. ¹⁴His head and his hair were white as white wool, white as snow; his eyes were like a flame of fire, ¹⁵his feet were like burnished bronze, refined as in a furnace, and his voice was like the sound of many waters. ¹⁶In his right hand he held seven stars, and from his mouth came a sharp, two-edged sword, and his face was like the sun shining with full force.

¹⁷When I saw him, I fell at his feet as though dead. But he placed his right hand on me, saying, "Do not be afraid; I am the first and the last, ¹⁸and the living one. I was dead, and see, I am alive forever and ever; and I have the keys of Death and of Hades. ¹⁹Now write what you have seen, what is, and what is to take place after this. ²⁰As for the mystery of the seven stars that you saw in my right hand, and the seven golden lampstands: the seven stars are the angels of the seven churches, and the seven lampstands are the seven churches."

Revelation and Mind-Altering Substances

When first encountering Revelation, students sometimes ask whether "being in the spirit" implies that John was under the influence of a mind-altering substance. These questions are often offered in jest, but numerous religious traditions, ancient and modern, use drugs or other practices such as fasting or physical exertion to induce visions or access spiritual knowledge. The Temple of Apollo at Delphi was famous for the oracles given by priestesses who may have been under the influence of trance-inducing fumes (Strabo, *Geogr.* 9.3.5; Plutarch, *Mor.* 435B).[38] Similar sites existed in Asia Minor, including Claros, where a priest would prophesy after drinking from a mysterious spring (Tacitus, *Ann.* 2.54). Apocalyptic texts similarly mention ingesting specific substances or adhering to special diets before experiencing visions (4 Ezra 9:23-29; 12:51; 14:38-48).[39] Because John does not

38. Despite accounts of having discovered the source of trance-inducing fumes on site, there continues to be a debate over whether these were the cause of the priestesses' oracles. See Daryn Lehoux, "Drugs and the Delphic Oracle," *CW* 101 (2007): 41–56.

39. Vicente Dobroruka, "Chemically-Induced Visions in the Fourth Book of Ezra in Light of Comparative Persian Material," *JSQ* 13 (2006): 1–26.

explain how he came to be "in spirit," we do not know whether his experience included ritual practices to induce visions.

Scholars of Revelation generally avoid discussing the impetus for John's visionary state, instead highlighting John's role as an author who draws on other literary traditions. This seems to reflect Euro-American and masculinist bias for rational ways of knowing. Even though he does not broach drug use, Fidon R. Mwombeki, a biblical scholar and pastor from Tanzania, explains that one of the strengths African readers bring to Revelation is belief in revelations through dreams and visions. Mwombeki asks, "Is it more difficult to understand [the text] as a real revelation than trying to find explanations for a composition that someone invented?"[40] From our perspective, acknowledging the possibility that Revelation emerged from visionary experience does not require foregoing explorations of the text as a "composition that someone invented," as Mwombeki describes it. These are not mutually exclusive approaches. John may have been influenced by some substance or practice that gave him visions, which he then transcribed into a form that reflects the signs of literary composition. To rule out such a possibility reflects a narrow vision of religious experience.

Following the command to write, John attempts to identify the source of the voice and immediately sees seven golden lampstands (v. 12) that he will equate with the communities to which he addresses Revelation. Amid the lampstands appears the command's source, traditionally described as "one like the Son of Man [υἱὸν ἀνθρώπου]" (see "Translation Matters: υἱὸν ἀνθρώπου"). Although "Son of Man" or, more accurately, "Son of Humanity" can be a poetic way of referring to a person (e.g., Ezek 2:1, 3, 6), this figure's eyes like flames and burnished bronze feet (vv. 13-15) indicate he is not the typical "man on the street" from Sardis. Rather, Revelation draws on earlier traditions that describe "one like a Son of Man" as a heavenly mediator (e.g., 1 En. 46, 48, 62, 69–70; 4 Ezra 13:3) and one who comes upon the clouds of heaven (Dan 7:13-14). Given the earlier pairing of the one "coming with the clouds" with the one who was pierced (Rev 1:7), John's reference to "one like the Son of Humanity" points to Jesus.

Revelation's audiences would be accustomed to seeing depictions of both gods and emperors unclothed, the nudity of the latter reflecting

40. Fidon R. Mwombeki, "The Book of Revelation in Africa," *WW* 15 (1995): 149.

their proximity to the divine. Art historian Larissa Bonfante explains that gods could "afford to be naked" as their power ensured no one would molest or diminish them.[41] Nudity in the classical world could function, therefore, as a way of asserting one's power. The Son of Humanity, in contrast, appears cloaked in a "long robe" with only his feet and face visible (vv. 13-16). Ezekiel, likewise, seems hesitant to describe the divine "loins," referring more generally to the gleaming areas above, below, and around them (1:27). These more modest depictions of the divine body should not, however, be mistaken as shame regarding the power of the divine penis. Clothing something draws attention to what is covered, as Paul notes in 1 Corinthians 12:23. In the case of Ezekiel, and perhaps here in Revelation, covering the Son's genitals might be a way of emphasizing divine power and protecting human eyes.

Ironically, John emphasizes the Son's masculine power by focusing the audience's attention elsewhere (vv. 14-15). His feet are burnished bronze, suggesting the strength of something tempered by flames. This image echoes Ezekiel's vision of the likeness of the divine with legs like fire (Ezek 1:27). The attributes John associates with the Son of Humanity's head echo prophetic depictions of God. Like Daniel's representation of the divine, called the "Ancient of Days," the Son has hair like wool (7:9). The white color suggests age, wisdom, and purity. John's description of hair like wool also evokes ancient descriptions of African, especially Egyptian and Ethiopian, hair (e.g., Herodotus, *Persian Wars* 2.104). Wooly hair was often contrasted with the straight hair of the Scythians, a population from north of the Black Sea, as a way of indicating the "extreme boundaries of the ancient world."[42] Theologian Dwight N. Hopkins points to this imagery, along with the figure's bronze feet, which can be imagined as dark brown, as an affirmation of divine Blackness and a liberative resource for Black theology. Most important, Hopkins's reading draws attention to the fact that Revelation's Son of Humanity was not a White European, as Jesus has often been depicted in art.[43]

Claims that the Son's eyes are like flames of fire and that his face shines like the sun anticipate the association between fire and light and the throne of God that appears in 4:5 and 21:23. These features also evoke radiating heat and so allude to the ancient connection between heat and maleness.

41. Larissa Bonfante, "Nudity as a Costume in Classical Art," *AJA* 93 (1989): 561.

42. Gay L. Byron, *Symbolic Blackness and Ethnic Difference in Early Christian Literature* (London: Routledge, 2002), 32.

43. Dwight N. Hopkins, *Down, Up, and Over: Slave Religion and Black Theology* (Minneapolis: Fortress, 2000), 263.

For example, Galen, the noted physician from Pergamum (d. ca. 210 CE), maintained that testicles were a source of heat. Although the Son's genitals are obscured, the association with fire and heat underscores his power and strength. Hence, the masculine epitaph, "*Son* of Humanity," rings true.

One of the most interesting characteristics of this vision is the two-edged sword that extends from the Son's mouth. Recognizing the absurdity of a mouth sword, scholars often interpret the image as metaphor for judgment.[44] That this sword appears later to "strike down" others and make war (2:16; 19:15) suggests that it functions as a kind of phallic symbol, a sign of the Son's masculine power and ability to penetrate and dominate. Such signs are crucial to masculinity in John's context. John's audiences need not see the Son's genitals to know that he embodies the ancient masculine ideal since he wields a tool proving his masculine identity.[45]

Despite his prominent sword and covered loins, the Son of Humanity's biological sex is not clearly defined since John describes him as having breasts bound with a golden sash (v. 13). The NRSV translates μαστοί (whence the familiar term mastectomy), commonly used for a woman's breasts (Ezek 16:7 [LXX]; Luke 11:27; 23:29), as "chest" even though there is a word (στῆθος) used to refer to a man's chest (e.g., Luke 18:13).[46] In fact, the term in Revelation is plural; the Son of Humanity has breasts and not *a* breast, even though translations like the NRSV render this as a singular, essentially smoothing out the shape of the Son of Humanity. This translation reflects several assumptions about sex, gender, and bodies, including the notion that men have "chests" and women have "breasts" which traditionally signal fertility and desirability. Breasts are "cultural genitals," physical characteristics that culturally indicate one's assigned sex.[47] Bodies vary wildly, however, and do not always correspond to cultural assumptions about what male and female bodies "should" look like.

44. David L. Barr, "Doing Violence: Moral Issues in Reading John's Apocalypse," in *Reading the Book of Revelation: A Resource for Students*, ed. David L. Barr (Atlanta: SBL, 2003), 97–108; Greg Carey, "Revelation's Violence Problem: Mapping Essential Questions," *PRSt* 42 (2015): 295–306; Susan E. Hylen, "Metaphor Matters: Violence and Ethics in Revelation," *CBQ* 73 (2011): 777–96.

45. Jonathan Walters, "Invading the Roman Body: Manliness and Impenetrability in Roman Thought," in *Roman Sexualities*, ed. Judith P. Hallett and Marilyn B. Skinner (Princeton: Princeton University Press, 1997), 29–43.

46. Jesse Rainbow, "Male μαστοί in Revelation 1:13," *JSNT* 30 (December 2007): 249–53.

47. Meredith Heller, *Queering Drag: Redefining the Discourse of Gender-Bending* (Bloomington: Indiana University Press, 2020), 152.

Ironically, the tendency to hide the Son of Humanity's breasts emphasizes the character's complex sex and gender identity. His breasts can be read as an example of hypermasculinity. Stephen D. Moore notes that some male bodybuilders develop significant breasts due to steroid use. Breasts reveal the bodybuilder's attempt to heighten his manliness, signaled by large muscles and a hard body, even though steroid use leads to low sperm count and shrunken testicles.[48] Perhaps the Son's breasts signal that he is trying a bit too hard to come across as a "manly man." Perhaps the Son of Humanity, instead, is a man identified female at birth who binds his breast as he waits for gender confirmation surgery.[49] Maybe the golden sash facilitates a sense of gender euphoria, a sense of relief and empowerment that comes when his body finally aligns with his identity as the Son of Humanity.

Another way modern interpreters might think about Revelation's Son of Humanity is that John depicts him like a drag performer. The word "like" in the phrase "one *like* the Son of Humanity" points to how the one in the long robe performs masculinity. Like drag kings who bind their breasts and pack their trousers, the Son's masculinity is exaggerated and performed.[50] Thus, the imagery hints at the fact that identities, including gender and sex, consist of repeated practices that are culturally determined to be "male," "female," "masculine," or "feminine," as philosopher Judith Butler famously outlines.[51] An individual is interpreted by others as male because his appearance, actions, and habits conform to how the culture in which he lives expects males to perform. The Son of Humanity embodies and performs masculinity, even though this performance might not reflect "his" sex or gender identity. The fact that his performance seems like artifice—a phallic sword coming from his mouth seems like extreme camp—emphasizes that anyone can either conform to cultural gender expectations or disrupt and subvert these expectations. Although this introduction to the risen Christ is as the one like the

---

48. Stephen D. Moore, "The Beatific Vision as a Posing Exhibition: Revelation's Hypermasculine Deity," *JSNT* 60 (1995): 52–53.

49. For a discussion about gender confirmation surgery from a trans perspective, see Mercedes Allen, "Trans-ing Gender: The Surgical Option," in *Gender Outlaws: The Next Generation*, ed. Kate Bornstein and S. Bear Bergman (Berkeley: Seal Press, 2010), 101–5.

50. Judith Halberstam and Del LaGrace Volcano, *The Drag King Book* (London: Serpent's Tail, 1999), 16.

51. Judith Butler, *Undoing Gender* (New York: Routledge, 2004), 10.

Son of Humanity, when we move through John's visionary experience, Christ will appear more gender fluid. Thus, we learn that a related kind of gender ambiguity is expected of those who follow him as well.

Our focus on gender here aligns with Revelation's overarching rhetorical goals and does not simply reflect that this is a feminist commentary. As we begin to see in the next two chapters, Revelation focuses on shaping how audiences relate themselves to God, Christ, one another, and the imperial culture. John wants his audiences to embody the faithfulness of Christ, who is *the* "faithful witness" (v. 5). Projects like John's necessarily engage a culture's expectations about gender and sex, since they involve calling others to inhabit an ideal form of personhood and since most cultures envision human ideals in gendered terms even if they disagree over the number of genders (i.e., Native American and Polynesian cultures typically include gender identities beyond the categories of male and female) and how gender is performed.[52]

John falls down as though he were dead upon seeing the Son of Humanity. Falling down is an appropriate response when standing in the presence of the divine (e.g., Ezek 1:28), and it signals the divine figure's dominance over a mere human. The Son encourages John not to fear, even though the consolation he offers reinforces the view that John's reaction was fitting. Personally, we think this understanding of the human in relation to the divine, what theologians call "theological anthropology," could use some rethinking. The Son introduces an idea found throughout Revelation, that the faithful should be obedient and subservient to the divine. This includes John's characterization of the faithful as being enslaved to God (e.g., 7:3; see pp. 102–5). Despite John's predilection for this understanding, there are other ways of casting humanity in relation to God that are more empowering, especially for women. Some of these might include thinking about humans as intentional worshipers before the throne (e.g., 7:9-12), instead of being more passive doers of obeisance, or as those who are able to "come out of the great ordeal" (7:14).

The Son of Humanity describes himself in terms that evoke God, "I am the first and the last and the living one," and he highlights his power over death, "I was dead, and see, I am alive forever and ever" (vv. 17-18). In addition, the Son claims possession of "the keys of Death and Hades." Basically, the Son manages everyone's fate. Such descriptions

---

52. Susan Stryker, *Transgender History: The Roots of Today's Revolution*, 2nd ed. (Berkeley: Seal Press, 2017), 15.

point to the fact that John wants his audiences to respond to the Son as though he is the manliest man of all men, even though there are signs suggesting his gender is more complicated. Christ will appear gender fluid in subsequent chapters, especially when introduced in the throne room (chap. 5), and yet, this figure remains King of kings.

TRANSLATION MATTERS: υἱὸν ἀνθρώπου

The first vision of the risen Christ in Revelation is as υἱὸν ἀνθρώπου, a phrase traditionally rendered in masculine terms as "Son of Man." Even though this epithet is familiar to many, multiple scholars have suggested gender-neutral versions, including "human being"[53] and "child of humanity."[54]

Gender-neutral language typically signals the desire for all people, regardless of gender, to see themselves included and, therefore, affirmed. Despite this impulse toward gender equity, such translations hide gender biases within the text that need to be addressed, and they may cause us to miss the occasions when authors exploit gendered thinking to make a theological point. In the case of Revelation 1:12-20, for instance, John depicts this υἱὸν ἀνθρώπου in an almost stereotypically masculine way. The character's burnished bronze feet imply hardness, a physical quality associated specifically with males in antiquity. According to medical guides, women—in contrast to men—were porous and soft (e.g., Hippocrates, *Mul.* 1.1). Other masculine traits include a voice that is loud and strong, like the sound of many waters, and a sword, a stereotypical phallic symbol, protrudes from the mouth of this υἱὸν ἀνθρώπου (v. 6).

The depiction of υἱὸν ἀνθρώπου in masculine terms continues in chapters 2–3. In the letters, the υἱὸν ἀνθρώπου proclaims to know what is happening in each community (2:2, 3, 9, 13, 19; 3:1, 8, 15) and so suggests that he is omniscient. The description of his standing amid seven golden lampstands, representing the seven communities, reinforces this idea. Thus, we retain the use of the term "Son," which we capitalize since it is employed as a title in the text. Since, however, the second half of the title, ἀνθρώπου, is a more general reference to the human race, we choose to use "Son of Humanity." In fact, even in this vision of Christ, we see the character is not gendered consistently and that Christ embodies masculine and feminine characteristics. Even though John may emphasize Christ as a son, in several ways he embodies the range of genders implied in the term "humanity."

53. Koester, *Revelation*, 245.
54. Blount, *Revelation*, 40.

Revelation 2–3

To the Victor

Despite the sword that awkwardly emerges from his mouth (1:16), the Son of Humanity, the risen Christ, dictates a letter or message to each of the seven assemblies (ἐκκλησία) (see "Translation Matters: ἐκκλησία"). In these messages, which extend over Revelation 2–3, Christ assesses the situation and performance of each community while encouraging individual community members to become victors or conquerors (so NRSV translation of ὁ νικῶν; see below "Translation Matters: ὁ νικῶν"). This victor imagery draws on a culture of competition and athleticism popular throughout the cities of Asia Minor (and other parts of the Greek-speaking Roman Empire).[1] Impressive bath-gymnasium complexes, stadiums for racing, and amphitheaters for games, the remains of which can still be seen today, dominated the landscape. Ephesus, for one, had four gymnasiums by the second century CE, and Pergamum may have had five by the mid-first century.[2] Public spaces, likewise, were filled with monuments celebrating victors and decorated with images of prizes, especially crowns and palm branches. Athletics and the culture of competition were essential to civic identity in Revelation's world.

---

1. Zahra Newby, *Greek Athletics in the Roman World: Victory and Virtue* (Oxford: Oxford University Press, 2005), 10.

2. E. Norman Gardiner, *Athletics in the Ancient World* (Mineola, NY: Dover, 2002), 79.

²:¹"To the angel of the church in Ephesus write: These are the words of him who holds the seven stars in his right hand, who walks among the seven golden lampstands:

²"I know your works, your toil and your patient endurance. I know that you cannot tolerate evildoers; you have tested those who claim to be apostles but are not, and have found them to be false. ³I also know that you are enduring patiently and bearing up for the sake of my name, and that you have not grown weary. ⁴But I have this against you, that you have abandoned the love you had at first. ⁵Remember then from what you have fallen; repent, and do the works you did at first. If not, I will come to you and remove your lampstand from its place, unless you repent. ⁶Yet this is to your credit: you hate the works of the Nicolaitans, which I also hate. ⁷Let anyone who has an ear listen to what the Spirit is saying to the churches. To everyone who conquers, I will give permission to eat from the tree of life that is in the paradise of God.

⁸"And to the angel of the church in Smyrna write: These are the words of the first and the last, who was dead and came to life:

⁹"I know your affliction and your poverty, even though you are rich. I know the slander on the part of those who say that they are Jews and are not, but are a synagogue of Satan. ¹⁰Do not fear what you are about to suffer. Beware, the devil is about to throw some of you into prison so that you may be tested, and for ten days you will have affliction. Be faithful until death, and I will give you the crown of life. ¹¹Let anyone who has an ear listen to what the Spirit is saying to the churches. Whoever conquers will not be harmed by the second death.

¹²"And to the angel of the church in Pergamum write: These are the words of him who has the sharp two-edged sword:

¹³"I know where you are living, where Satan's throne is. Yet you are holding fast to my name, and you did not deny your faith in me even in the days of Antipas my witness, my faithful one, who was killed among you, where Satan lives. ¹⁴But I have a few things against you: you have some there who hold to the teaching of Balaam, who taught Balak to put a stumbling block before the people of Israel, so that they would eat food sacrificed to idols and practice fornication. ¹⁵So you also have some who hold to the teaching of the Nicolaitans. ¹⁶Repent then. If not, I will come to you soon and make war against them with the sword of my mouth. ¹⁷Let anyone who has an ear listen to what the Spirit is saying to the churches. To everyone who conquers I will give some of the hidden manna, and I will give a white stone, and on the white stone is written a new name that no one knows except the one who receives it.

¹⁸"And to the angel of the church in Thyatira write: These are the words of the Son of God, who has eyes like a flame of fire, and whose feet are like burnished bronze:

¹⁹"I know your works—your love, faith, service, and patient endurance. I know that your last works are greater

than the first. [20]But I have this against you: you tolerate that woman Jezebel, who calls herself a prophet and is teaching and beguiling my servants to practice fornication and to eat food sacrificed to idols. [21]I gave her time to repent, but she refuses to repent of her fornication. [22]Beware, I am throwing her on a bed, and those who commit adultery with her I am throwing into great distress, unless they repent of her doings; [23]and I will strike her children dead. And all the churches will know that I am the one who searches minds and hearts, and I will give to each of you as your works deserve. [24]But to the rest of you in Thyatira, who do not hold this teaching, who have not learned what some call 'the deep things of Satan,' to you I say, I do not lay on you any other burden; [25]only hold fast to what you have until I come. [26]To everyone who conquers and continues to do my works to the end,

I will give authority over the
 nations;
[27]to rule them with an iron rod,
 as when clay pots are
 shattered—

[28]even as I also received authority from my Father. To the one who conquers I will also give the morning star. [29]Let anyone who has an ear listen to what the Spirit is saying to the churches.

[3:1]"And to the angel of the church in Sardis write: These are the words of him who has the seven spirits of God and the seven stars:

"I know your works; you have a name of being alive, but you are dead. [2]Wake up, and strengthen what remains and is on the point of death, for I have not found your works perfect in the sight of my God. [3]Remember then what you received and heard; obey it, and repent. If you do not wake up, I will come like a thief, and you will not know at what hour I will come to you. [4]Yet you have still a few persons in Sardis who have not soiled their clothes; they will walk with me, dressed in white, for they are worthy. [5]If you conquer, you will be clothed like them in white robes, and I will not blot your name out of the book of life; I will confess your name before my Father and before his angels. [6]Let anyone who has an ear listen to what the Spirit is saying to the churches.

[7]"And to the angel of the church in
 Philadelphia write:
These are the words of the holy
 one, the true one,
 who has the key of David,
 who opens and no one will
  shut, who shuts and no
  one opens;

[8]"I know your works. Look, I have set before you an open door, which no one is able to shut. I know that you have but little power, and yet you have kept my word and have not denied my name. [9]I will make those of the synagogue of Satan who say that they are Jews and are not, but are lying—I will make them come and bow down before your feet, and they will learn that I have loved you. [10]Because you have kept my word of patient endurance, I will keep you from the hour of trial that is coming on the whole world to test the inhabitants of the earth. [11]I am coming soon; hold fast to what you have, so that no one may seize your crown.

[12]If you conquer, I will make you a pillar in the temple of my God; you will never go out of it. I will write on you the name of my God, and the name of the city of my God, the new Jerusalem that comes down from my God out of heaven, and my own new name. [13]Let anyone who has an ear listen to what the Spirit is saying to the churches.

[14]"And to the angel of the church in Laodicea write: The words of the Amen, the faithful and true witness, the origin of God's creation:

[15]"I know your works; you are neither cold nor hot. I wish that you were either cold or hot. [16]So, because you are lukewarm, and neither cold nor hot, I am about to spit you out of my mouth. [17]For you say, 'I am rich, I have prospered, and I need nothing.' You do not realize that you are wretched, pitiable, poor, blind, and naked. [18]Therefore I counsel you to buy from me gold refined by fire so that you may be rich; and white robes to clothe you and to keep the shame of your nakedness from being seen; and salve to anoint your eyes so that you may see. [19]I reprove and discipline those whom I love. Be earnest, therefore, and repent. [20]Listen! I am standing at the door, knocking; if you hear my voice and open the door, I will come in to you and eat with you, and you with me. [21]To the one who conquers I will give a place with me on my throne, just as I myself conquered and sat down with my Father on his throne. [22]Let anyone who has an ear listen to what the Spirit is saying to the churches."

The imagery and language of the letters assumes audience familiarity with this culture of competition and athleticism, a culture that specifically served to shape elite male identity. Within the gymnasium walls, boys were shaped into men, and men were reminded of what it meant to be at the top of their game, to be ideal men. The recognition that athletics in the ancient world served primarily as part of shaping male identity does not mean Asia Minor lacked female athletes. Gymnasiums were "boys' clubs," but there is some evidence for girls' training in the gymnasium and winning athletic competitions. In the first century, a certain Hedea, for example, "won contests in both foot-racing and lyre playing" at a competition in Delphi, Greece.[3] Still, ancient athletic culture emerged out of the classical Greek tradition of training warriors through a gymnasium discipline or curriculum (παιδεία), and it continued to be a tradition associated with cultivating masculinity. By echoing this culture, John

3. Katherine Bain, *Women's Socioeconomic Status and Religious Leadership in Asia Minor: In the First Two Centuries C.E.* (Minneapolis: Augsburg Fortress, 2014), 38.

similarly nurtures a kind of masculinity among his audience members. This does not mean that John believed his book would be read or heard only by male-identified audience members. Indeed, he was aware of the gender diversity within early communities of Jesus followers and that some members would have been enslaved or formerly enslaved. (He identifies, in fact, a rival teacher with a traditionally female name in 2:20.) Despite this, John draws on cultural assumptions about ideal masculinity as he depicts the Son of Humanity calling hearers to become the "victor."

As feminist readers, we find John's use of a generic male identity to shape his narrative unsurprising, but it makes us both weary and wary. Women and femmes, people of all genders who embrace the "traits, mannerisms, or appearances usually associated with femininity,"[4] are familiar with translating masculinist expectations to fit our experiences. Working in academia, for example, requires navigating professional structures and expectations designed during a time when most professors were men with wives at home. Attending professional conferences and evening events does not easily align with the realities of caring for children, aged parents, and sick partners, responsibilities often shouldered by women. Given this, we adjust our roles as scholars and family members around the gendered expectations of the past. Similarly, hearers of Revelation who were not free men would likely have to translate what they heard in the letters to fit their realities. A young married woman living in her husband's family home or an enslaved person working for an elite family would hear the call to be a victor and embody that call differently from the men for whom the role was created.

TRANSLATION MATTERS: ἐκκλησία

In Revelation 2–3, the Son of Humanity refers to seven communities of Jesus followers in Asia Minor using the term ἐκκλησία. Along with most other English Bibles, the NRSV translates this word as "church." This translation reflects the fact that the Greek term ἐκκλησία provides the root for English words for Christian institutions, including "ecclesiastic" and "ecclesiastical." Some medieval manuscript illustrators depicted these communities as actual church buildings. For example, a fourteenth-century French manuscript signifies the congregations

4. Susan Stryker, *Transgender History: The Roots of Today's Revolution*, 2nd ed. (Berkeley: Seal Press, 2017), 23.

with brightly colored gothic-style buildings, each with an angel standing in the portal.[5] These images are misleading, however, since the term refers to a group or assembly of people.

Even though Jesus followers comprised the seven communities in Revelation, ἐκκλησία did not carry connotations of a specifically Christian or even religious identity in the first century. Before Revelation's penning, the Greek term, which can be translated into English as "assembly" or "association," conveyed mainly political and civic meanings. In Greek literature dating back to the fifth century BCE, ἐκκλησία described a city's political association, a group of men who made decisions for the community.[6] The playwright Aristophanes (d. 386 BCE) underscores the gendered identity of this civic assembly by referencing the "absurdity of the idea" that women would have a place in the ἐκκλησία.[7] Eventually, the term came to describe a broader range of civic groups, including neighborhood and trade associations, which could include women but which were still focused on solidifying communal bonds and developing civic identities. To those ends, associations might support political candidates, fund monuments, and even attend public games or the theater as a group. In addition, association gatherings typically included some ritual worship, such as sacrifices in honor of patron deities or imperial cult figures, even though ἐκκλησία did not imply a specific religious identity.[8] In other words, there might be religious activities conducted as part of an assembly, but it was not necessarily a religious organization.

In the Septuagint (LXX), the Greek translation of the Hebrew Bible, ἐκκλησία often translates references to the "assembly" or "congregation" (קָהָל) of Israel (e.g., Deut 9:10; 23:1-4; 31:30). (The Greek word συναγωγή, the basis of the English "synagogue," is also used to translate the Hebrew word for "assembly."[9]) Here, again, ἐκκλησία references a community with a complex identity—social, political, and religious—and not only a gathering of people for worship. Authors of the New Testament, including Paul and Luke, use ἐκκλησία to describe communities of Jesus followers (e.g., Acts 5:11; 8:1-3; 1 Cor 1:2; 2 Cor 1:1; Gal 1:22), drawing a connection to the ancient Israelite assembly.[10] When John uses ἐκκλησία he similarly implies continuity between the Israelite community described in the Jewish Scriptures and the congregations he addresses in this letter.

5. "The Cloisters Apocalypse" (Normandy, France, ca. 1330), f. 4 r., 68.174, The Cloisters Collection, https://www.metmuseum.org/art/collection/search/471869.

6. Paul Trebilco, "Why Did the Early Christians Call Themselves ἡ Ἐκκλησία?," *NTS* 57 (2011): 440–60.

7. Barbara Levick, "Women and Law," in *A Companion to Women in the Ancient World*, ed. Sharon L. James and Sheila Dillon (West Sussex: John Wiley & Sons, 2012), 98.

8. For more on ancient associations, see Philip A. Harland, "Honouring the Emperor or Assailing the Beast: Participation in Civic Life among Associations (Jewish, Christian and Other) in Asia Minor and the Apocalypse of John," *JSNT* 77 (2000): 99–121.

9. Trebilco, "Early Christians Call Themselves ἡ Ἐκκλησία?," 449.

10. Trebilco, "Early Christians Call Themselves ἡ Ἐκκλησία?," 443.

The social and political origins of ἐκκλησία should remind Christian feminists that religious assemblies are not simply religious; instead, these communities serve communal, political, and cultural purposes. Even though some people argue that individual communities should not take political stands, the complex relationship between the church and community has been around since John and others first used the term ἐκκλησία. Of course, the political and social power of the modern ἐκκλησία can be used for positive or negative ends, to achieve justice and equity or in ways that create prejudice and bias. Hosting community organizing efforts, such as phone banking for legislation that protects the rights of women, trans people, and gays and lesbians; providing transportation to the polls and advocating for those whose voting rights have been limited; providing water, food, toiletries, and respite from the elements for those who are houseless; offering educational opportunities: these are just some of the ways our communities can evoke the ancient notion of ἐκκλησία.

The Son of Humanity's Messages to the Seven Communities

Since the seven messages allude to the lived experiences of these communities of early Jesus followers, readers of Revelation have long been interested in how the physical remains of the cities illuminate the letters and vice versa. Some Christian believers even tour the excavated remains of the ancient cities, wanting a connection to Revelation and its first hearers. My aunt Lois traveled to Turkey in the late 1960s with this hope, and fifty years later, I receive emails promising me the same kind of experience—"pilgrim tours" offering a chance to walk "where the apostles walked."[11] I am similarly interested in how the built culture of the ancient world can help us understand how early audiences might have heard and responded to Revelation.[12] Sometimes, however, this focus on the *realia*, the actual stuff, of the ancient world can overshadow the meaning of the text, as mentioned below; however, knowledge of the material world surrounding John's audience members can help us imagine how early readers might have engaged the text. At the same time, remembering the historical distance between ourselves and ancient audiences is equally essential. We may feel a connection to the past and

11. Pilgrim Tours, "Turkey Tours and Cruises," https://www.pilgrimtours.com/turkey-tours/.

12. Lynn R. Huber, "Making Men in Rev 2–3: Reading the Seven Messages in the Bath-Gymnasiums of Asia Minor," in *Stones, Bones, and the Sacred: Essays on Material Culture and Ancient Religion in Honor of Dennis E. Smith*, ed. Alan H. Cadwallader (Atlanta: SBL Press, 2016), 101–28.

early followers of Christ, but we have no idea whether they would have sensed a parallel connection. We simply cannot know all the ways our experiences are connected. We can only imagine and try not to impose our perspectives on ancient audiences.

Reading the messages from the Christ to the seven communities in Asia Minor is a lot like reading other people's mail or eavesdropping when someone is on the phone nearby. We hear only one half of the conversation, and we cannot fully understand the context for what is said. We do not know what the earliest audiences thought of John's descriptions of their experiences. Did they think his take on Thyatira, which paints a negative portrait of another teacher, was fair? Would the Jesus followers in Philadelphia have agreed that they had "little power" (3:8) or appreciated hearing it mentioned? Did the leaders in these assemblies find John's advice helpful or a hindrance? Reactions to the messages likely varied, and thinking through the possibilities can be a useful tool for imagining the diversity of the earliest communities.

Revelation scholars differ in describing these seven "letters," which is the most common way of describing the messages dictated by Christ. Since John echoes various genres in constructing these communications, there are other ways to think about and, therefore, describe the messages. For example, David E. Aune observes that the "thus says" or "these are the words of" (τάδε λέγει) formula employed by John echoes imperial edicts or decrees, emphasizing an opposition between Christ and imperial figures who are a "pale and diabolical imitation of God."[13] Both issue decrees, but the faithful follower of Christ can follow only one. David A. deSilva, however, argues that the letters function as oracles or divine messages, such as those delivered by the prophets of the Hebrew Bible (e.g., Isa 1:24; 3:16; Jer 2:5; Ezek 2:4) or the priests of other Greek and Roman deities. The idea of an oracle, a spoken pronouncement, captures that "John intends for his audience members to hear Christ speaking to them" and, more specifically, commanding them.[14] The variety of labels for these passages indicates that they perform multiple functions as letters. They present John's audiences with authoritative instructions akin to edicts and oracles, and they hold the communities accountable for their actions.

13. David E. Aune, *Revelation*, WBC 52 A-C (Dallas: Word Books, 1998), 129.
14. David A. deSilva, *Seeing Things John's Way: The Rhetoric of the Book of Revelation* (Louisville: Westminster John Knox, 2009), 179.

Although the identities of the seven assemblies dominate these two chapters, once John enters the heavenly throne room at the beginning of Revelation 4, their distinctions fade into the background as John's concern shifts to the saints more generally. This change in focus leads some interpreters to speculate about the connection between the seven messages and the rest of the narrative. Were the correspondences initially part of another text and separated from the rest of Revelation? Or were the individual messages once seven individual introductions intended for the specific communities identified in each message? For instance, was the message to Ephesus intended only for the Jesus followers in that city? Despite these questions, there is no physical evidence that the messages were ever disconnected from each other or the full text. On the contrary, the earliest manuscripts of Revelation include chapters 2–3 with the rest of the narrative, and the images introduced in these chapters appear throughout the rest of the text, especially in the final chapters. All of this suggests the messages were part of the original text. Christ's intimate knowledge of each community becomes everyone's business as the entire text, including all seven letters, is read aloud to each community. This type of collective instruction, highlighted by the uniformity of the messages, cultivates a shared identity among the audiences. Each community is made vulnerable before the others, and they are implicitly encouraged to learn from one another's successes and mistakes.

Each message begins with an introductory phrase: "To the angel of the assembly [ἐκκλησία] in Ephesus [or other city], write . . ." Addressing community angels evokes traditions in which nations had specific angelic guardians (e.g., Dan 10:13, 20-21; 12:1) or where individuals had angels watching over them (e.g., Tobit 2:14-16).[15] Each community has its liaison to the divine. Despite evoking this angelic hierarchy, the unmistakable voice of authority is that of the one like the Son of Humanity, whose words are prefaced with τάδε λέγει, "these are the words of him" in the NRSV, and followed by an introduction to Christ using imagery from the vision of 1:12-20. For example, to Smyrna, Christ begins, "These are the words of the first and the last, who was dead and came to life" (2:8); to Thyatira, he claims, "These are the words of the Son of God, who has eyes like a flame of fire, and whose feet are like burnished bronze" (2:18). These references tie the reports to the surrounding narrative and underscore the divine authority of the letter giver.

15. Craig R. Koester, *Revelation: A New Translation with Introduction and Commentary*, AYB 38A (New Haven: Yale University Press, 2014), 248.

Christ follows the introductions with an assessment of each community using the phrase "I know." He *knows* the affliction and poverty Smyrna experienced (2:9); he *knows* that the community of Pergamum lives where Satan's throne is located (2:13); he *knows* that the community at Thyatira has done works of love, faith, service, and patient endurance (2:19); he *knows* the works in Sardis, Philadelphia, and Laodicea (3:1, 8, 15). In this way, the messages resemble a coach's postgame talk. Good plays and strong efforts are affirmed, and skills needing improvement are noted. Audience members living in Smyrna and Philadelphia garner mostly praise, while those in Ephesus, Pergamum, Thyatira, and Sardis get mixed reports. The people of Laodicea probably cringe as they hear their report aloud since Christ offers them only criticism. After providing these status reports, Christ wraps up with exhortations for the community members, described as messages from the spirit of God and promises of reward to those who are victors. (These last two elements are sometimes flipped.)

One of the main functions of these messages is asserting Christ's presence in and authority over the communities. By repeating "I *know* your . . . ," "I *know* that you . . . ," and "I *know* what you are doing" (2:2, 3, 9, 13, 17, 19; 3:1, 8, 15, 17), Christ asserts his ability to see all things within the assemblies. At times, the claims are reminiscent of a parent or guardian supervising children who should know better than to cause trouble: when things go quiet in another room, the parent calls out, "I *know* what you are doing!" The sense of surveillance is palpable, as it is a way of exercising control even when the seer is not physically present, an idea described by French philosopher Michel Foucault.[16] The Son of Humanity's "knowing" can be frightening or reassuring, depending on the community and the people in it.

This experience of being watched creates a gendered power dynamic between Christ and the communities. Fixing one's gaze on another was a way of controlling or exerting force. This power imbalance was highly gendered in the ancient world, positioning the seer as an active masculine subject and the seen as a passive feminine object. The Roman scholar Varro argued that the Latin word for sight, *visus*, came from *vis*, the word for "force," and compared seeing to sexual assault (*On the Latin*

---

16. Michel Foucault, *Discipline & Punish: The Birth of the Prison* (New York: Pantheon Books, 1977), 200–201. See also Harry O. Maier, "Staging the Gaze: Early Christian Apocalypses and Narrative Self-Representation," *HTR* 90 (1997): 143.

Language 6.80).[17] Although the evidence for Varro's linguistic theory is questionable, his observation reflected common ancient thinking about sight. Seeing or gazing was akin to penetrating the other. Hence, John's depiction of Christ as one who sees what happens in these communities positions him as the masculine viewer.

Modern feminist scholars likewise recognize the power involved with seeing and watching, especially when the one doing the seeing is a man. In the 1970s, feminist film theorist Laura Mulvey explored the "male gaze," how Hollywood movies invite audiences to adopt the role of the active masculine viewer of the passive feminine image.[18] In some movies, this dynamic is central to the plot, as in Alfred Hitchcock's classic *Rear Window* (1954), where the protagonist, confined to his apartment because of an injury, spends most of the film viewing others in his apartment complex through a telescopic camera lens, including a woman referred to only as "Miss Torso."[19] Revelation, arguably, does something similar with both the commands to "Look!" Revelation effectively places us, those who hear or read the text, in the masculine role where we both envision and assess the actions of those in the seven assemblies. Even though the individuals within these communities are long gone, Mulvey's insight should prompt us to ask how we relate to those ancient people. Do we gawk at their foibles and faults from a position of superiority, or do we empathize and acknowledge their humanity? Do we catch members of the seven communities gazing back at us?

Even as Christ's dominant gaze effectively feminizes the communities, *individuals* in the communities are encouraged to "man up." To this end, Christ employs second-person singular pronouns and verbs in the messages. For example, he knows "your [σου, singular]" works and that "you [singular] are enduring patiently" (ὑπομονὴν ἔχεις, 2:2-3). Similarly, the references to the victor, ὁ νικῶν, are all singular; each person is called to be a victor. This tension between gender expectations appears throughout Revelation.

Returning to the idea that John draws on the competitive athletic culture of first-century Asia Minor, it can be helpful to imagine John casting Christ in the role of a gymnasiarch, the head of an ancient gymnasium.

17. David Fredrick, "Introduction: Invisible Rome," in *The Roman Gaze: Vision, Power, and the Body*, ed. David Fredrick (Baltimore: Johns Hopkins University Press, 2002), 1–30.

18. Laura Mulvey, "Visual Pleasure and Narrative Cinema," *Screen* 16 (1975): 6–18.

19. Alfred Hitchcock et al., *Rear Window* (Alfred J. Hitchcock Productions, 1954).

The individuals who inhabited this role financed the gymnasium,[20] leaving most of the day-to-day training to appointed leaders and trainers; however, they leveraged their social and financial status to sustain a system that created ideal men and, therefore, a perfect community.[21] There were guidelines, a gymnasium law or code of conduct, that outlined proper behavior inside and outside the gymnasium walls to facilitate these goals. A monument from Beroia, Macedonia, for example, explained that athletes must be obedient to this law and to the gymnasium leaders who enact it or be subject to discipline by the gymnasiarch (*SEG* 27-261.B.5-10).[22] In many ways, John's vision of Christ resembles a gymnasiarch who may not be setting up the daily exercises for those in his care, but through both the promise of reward and threat of discipline, he pushes others to reach the goal set out for them—victory.

TRANSLATION MATTERS: ὁ νικῶν

Each message from the Son of Humanity ends with a promise to ὁ νικῶν. The term describes someone victorious, although there are many ways an individual can experience victory. The NRSV translates ὁ νικῶν through the lens of military victory, such as "everyone who conquers" or "whoever conquers." This translation aligns with Revelation's use of militaristic imagery elsewhere in the text to characterize the experience of those faithful to the Lamb (e.g., 13:10). In addition, John uses military imagery to depict Christ as he defeats his foes later in the text (19:11-21). Furthermore, as the narrative of Revelation unfolds, the idea of conquest predominates.[23] John contests the authority of Roman imperial power, but he also envisions the empire's destruction and replacement with a kingdom centered around God and the Lamb. Conquering, therefore, is an integral part of Revelation's story; however, victory language conveys not only the idea of military conquest but also other ways of being victorious, such as athletic victory.

20. For a discussion of the presence of women gymnasiarchs in Asia Minor, see Paul Trebilco, *Jewish Communities in Asia Minor* (Cambridge: Cambridge University Press, 1991), 118.

21. Onno van Nijf, "Athletics and Paideia: Festivals and Physical Education in the World of Second Sophistic," in *Paideia: The World of the Second Sophistic*, ed. Barbara E. Borg, Millenium Studies 2 (Berlin: De Gruyter, 2004), 207–8.

22. For an English translation, see Roger S. Bagnall and Peter Derow, eds., *The Hellenistic Period: Historical Sources in Translation*, new ed. (Malden, MA: John Wiley & Sons, 2004), 135.

23. Stephen D. Moore, *Empire and Apocalypse: Postcolonialism and the New Testament* (Sheffield: Sheffield Phoenix, 2006), 114.

Privileging the idea of athletic victory allows us to see the ways that ideologies of competition and agonistic culture appear in contexts that, on the surface, seem more benign than war, such as sports and gym culture. I use "seem more benign" here because the gymnasium and battlefield were related in the ancient world. In the classical Greek gymnasium tradition (ca. fifth and fourth centuries BCE) that shaped the practices of Asia Minor, athletics were a form of training for combat. Evoking that classical period, a character from a dialogue by Lucian explains that young men receive athletic training because they are expected "to become stout guardians of our city, and that we shall live in freedom through them, conquering our foes if they attack us and keeping our neighbours in dread of us, so that most of them will cower at our feet and pay tribute" (Lucian, *Athletics* 30).[24] Even though the explicit connection between military training and sport had diminished by the first century CE, the two share a connection. The athlete is always preparing for competition, whether the outcome is a prize and bragging rights or the spoils of war. The language of "the victor" allows us to think about the multiple kinds of victory and how they are intertwined.[25]

Training the Victor for the Fight

The image of the victor implies that the faithful have undergone, or should have undergone, rigorous training, a theme threaded throughout the letters. The very first letter introduces this when Christ recognizes the "works . . . toil and . . . patient endurance [ὑπομονή]" of Jesus followers in Ephesus (2:2). Moments later, he commends their ability to "bear up" and "not grow weary" (2:3). The community members of Thyatira and Philadelphia similarly possess patient endurance (ὑπομονή) according to Christ (2:19; 3:10). The importance of this characteristic, which John himself claims (1:9), is captured in a eulogy by Dio Chrysostom for the boxer Melancomas, who could fight a whole day in the heat. Dio explains that this type of endurance, ὑπομονή, was worth more than any prize (*1 Melanc.* 10-11). The victors from Ephesus who exhibit ὑπομονή will, however, receive a prize—the opportunity to eat from the tree of life in Paradise.

Not all the "athletes" addressed by Christ are so diligent in their training from his perspective. Most notably, he criticizes the Laodiceans for being "lukewarm," a reference to their lackluster performance. Scholars

24. Newby, *Greek Athletics in the Roman World*, 145–49.

25. For more on the athletic context of ὁ νικῶν in Revelation, see Mark Wilson, *The Victor Sayings in the Book of Revelation* (Eugene, OR: Wipf and Stock, 2007).

regularly suggest this is a reference to the city's water in contrast to the nearby Hierapolis, a city famous for its geothermal springs.[26] While this may be a dig for not having the naturally warm water of Hierapolis or for having poor-tasting water (the city had fine drinking water drawn from multiple sources),[27] in the letter's context "lukewarm" metaphorically represents the Laodicean's lack of intensity or strength. This becomes clear when Christ intones, "I wish that you were either cold or hot" (3:15 cf. 19:8). The fact that he mentions "cold or hot" three times in three sentences emphasizes that he wants intensity or strength from the Laodiceans. In contrast to being hot or cold, lukewarmness implies dilution, weakness, and being "wishy-washy."

Sometimes concern about water temperature is about more than water temperature. The characterization of the Laodiceans' lack of intensity, their "temperature," implicitly criticizes their gender performance. Ancient theorists associated the binaries of the gender continuum with temperature. Hot and cold are, respectively, masculine and feminine characteristics. As mentioned earlier, Galen of Pergamum taught that testicles were a source of heat. Thus, if an individual needed to beef up their masculinity, he needed to apply remedies, such as exercise, that increased one's heat.[28] We might be surprised that Christ wants the audience to choose between hot *or* cold since the latter is a feminine characteristic. This metaphor, however, is about blurring the boundaries of gender, and mentioning both hot *and* cold together highlights the idea of lukewarmness as a mixture. In some sense, being neither hot nor cold was even more threatening than being cold. Consequently, Christ, unable to tolerate such obvious feebleness in the Laodiceans, dramatically (or perhaps melodramatically) claims that he is about to spit or vomit them out of his mouth (3:16).

Christ's aversion to those who are lukewarm echoes the bias against "soft" men in Paul's list of those who will not inherit the kingdom of God (1 Cor 6:9).[29] Men should be hot and hard according to ancient perspectives on gender, so male individuals lacking these qualities are not "real"

---

26. E.g., Craig S. Keener, *Revelation* (Grand Rapids: Zondervan, 2000), 158; Brian K. Blount, *Revelation: A Commentary* (Louisville: Westminster John Knox, 2009), 80.

27. Koester, *Revelation*, 337.

28. Maud W. Gleason, *Making Men: Sophists and Self-Presentation in Ancient Rome* (Princeton: Princeton University Press, 1995), 94–95.

29. The NRSV translates the Greek μαλακός, "soft" or "effeminate," as "male prostitutes," though no economic exchange is implied in this gendered slur.

men. This impression reflects the ancient Roman view that people should remain within their appointed places on the gender scale (see p. lxxii).

A similar impulse to keep people in clearly defined gender categories occurs today among English speakers unsympathetic to those who use they/them or other pronouns that signal a person's nonbinary gender identity.[30] While those who insist on binary pronouns appeal to grammatical clarity as justification (failing to recognize how language usage changes over time), it seems more likely an issue of discomfort with what seems like gender uncertainty. Nevertheless, this discomfort potentially harms. The Trevor Project, a US nonprofit focused on suicide among LGBTQIA+ youth, reports that the experience of having one's chosen pronouns recognized by people in their lives dramatically reduces the likelihood that nonbinary or trans youth will attempt suicide. Youth whose pronouns are respected "[attempt] suicide at half the rate of those who did not."[31] While we do not know precisely why Christ saw the Laodicean Jesus followers as lukewarm, his accusation has a gendered nuance. Christ appears as a kind of gender bully and not a helpful model for Christians who affirm the variety of gender within God's creation.

Lack of heat is not the only fault Christ finds among the Laodiceans. He accuses the community members of thinking they have everything they need when they lack everything. They are "wretched, pitiable, poor, blind, and naked" (3:17), traits indicating deficiency, whether of well-being, virtue, honor, or material goods. They do not possess the virtues required for manhood, let alone for being an ideal Jesus follower. Not only do the community members want for these things, but they fail to recognize their deficiencies. Christ then presents the Laodiceans with a metaphorical shopping list of things they need to "buy" from him to correct their shortfalls—refined gold, white clothes, and eye salve. These items allude to their need to become faithful followers of Christ:

30. Being "nonbinary," which is sometimes called "enby" (pronounced like the letters n and b), means identifying beyond or outside of the binary male and female gender categories. The ways of being nonbinary are varied. Some nonbinary people describe this as being both genders, while others will describe themselves as "gender fluid" with a gender identity that shifts depending on situation, context, feeling, etc. For an example of those not willing to use they/them pronouns, see Anemona Hartocollis, "Gender Pronouns Can Be Tricky on Campus: Harvard Is Making Them Stick," *The New York Times*, February 19, 2020, sec. U.S., https://www.nytimes.com/2020/02/19/us/gender-pronouns-college.html.

31. "The Trevor Project National Survey on LGBTQ Youth Mental Health 2020," https://www.thetrevorproject.org/survey-2020/.

gold suggests the pure gold of the New Jerusalem where the faithful will reside (21:18); white clothes are given to those who experience violence and even death because of their faithfulness to God and Christ (6:11; 7:13-14). The imagery of eye salve, which may refer to a product manufactured near Laodicea,[32] indicates that the community members are having trouble "seeing," something implied by their lack of self-awareness. Perhaps Revelation itself, which makes visible the world in which Laodiceans live and the reign of God, is the salve Christ offers.

Critique, in the case of the Laodiceans, leads to Christ issuing a warning in the guise of a statement of fact: "I reprove and discipline [παιδεύω] those whom I love" (3:19). The reference to discipline evokes the code of conduct associated with gymnasiums, as Beroia mentioned above. A similar threat appears in the report to Sardis, where Christ orders audience members to "wake up" two separate times and instructs them to strengthen what they have remaining (3:1-6). The tone of this report suggests that the people in Sardis are drowsy athletes whose efforts are wanting. Given this dire situation, Christ threatens to wake them up the hard way by coming like "a thief in the night" (3:4). In both cases, Christ will act to bring these communities in line.

Despite moments of negative discipline, Christ consistently promises those in the seven communities rewards or prizes to incentivize them. This is another way the letters echo the surrounding athletic culture. Ancient athletes competed for crowns, palms, and even monetary awards, prizes that signaled the honor that victory brought athletes and their communities (Lucian, *Athletics* 15).[33] Similarly, the rewards promised by Christ are symbolic recognitions of the victor's faithfulness. For example, he promises the victor in Ephesus a chance to eat from the tree of life (2:7), which suggests their inclusion in the New Jerusalem (22:2). Christ offers the victor of Sardis a white robe, and he will "confess" or speak their name before God (3:5) when the dead are judged (20:11-15). Noting that the victor in Philadelphia already has a crown, the ancient athlete's quintessential prize, Christ explains that the victor here will become a pillar within God's temple (3:12). John highlights the stability and endurance of the pillar, a symbol of masculine strength, by noting, "you will never go out of [the temple]." (Compare this with the image of lukewarm water in Laodicea.) While it was common practice in ancient Asia Minor

---

32. Koester, *Revelation*, 339.
33. Newby, *Greek Athletics in the Roman World*, 247.

to inscribe temple pillars with honorifics and civic monuments with the names of athletic victors, here the victor receives the honor of having God's name, along with the names of the New Jerusalem and Christ, inscribed upon them.[34] This will not be the only time followers of God and Christ bear the names of the divine (14:1; 22:4).

Identifying the Victor's Opponents

The image of victor assumes an opponent or opponents. In the message to the assembly in Smyrna, the Son of Humanity characterizes this reality in terms of θλίψις or "affliction" (2:9 [2x]), since the community in that city is, from John's perspective, overwhelmed by adversaries who are slandering them (see "Translation Matters: θλίψις"). These adversaries, whom John describes as "those who say they are Jews and are not," are associated with Satan (2:9), who will appear throughout Revelation as *the* opponent to God and the faithful. Later, John will offer a fuller depiction of Satan, whom he casts as the archenemy of God and Christ and who is embodied in various political powers and institutions (12:18–13:1). Here, however, Christ only begins to introduce this opponent. In the message to Pergamum that follows the one to Smyrna, the city is named as both the site of "Satan's throne" and "where Satan lives" (2:13-14). Even though some interpreters read "Satan's throne" as a reference to a massive altar to Zeus and Athena that sat on an acropolis overlooking the city,[35] the presence of evil forces that oppose God is more diffuse and insidious than this gigantic altar. The altar is a symptom of the presence of evil. More revealing of evil's existence in Pergamum is the death of Antipas, presumably killed for being Christ's "faithful one" (2:13). This competition has life-and-death consequences, which makes training vital.

Christ's identification of two "synagogue[s] of Satan," which he also characterizes as "those who say they are Jews and are not" (2:9; 3:9), as opponents of the Jesus followers in Revelation's audiences are some of this book's most dangerous passages. As one might imagine, interpreters from a variety of contexts have deployed this association for antisemitic ends: Louis Farrakhan, leader of the Nation of Islam, has often referenced

---

34. Robert M. Royalty Jr., "Etched or Sketched? Inscriptions and Erasures in the Messages to Sardis and Philadelphia (Rev. 3.1-13)," *JSNT* 27 (2005): 447–63, esp. 453.

35. See Steven J. Friesen, "Satan's Throne, Imperial Cults and the Social Settings of Revelation," *JSNT* 27 (2005): 351–73.

the "synagogue of Satan" in explicitly anti-Jewish speeches;[36] a spokesperson for Gab, a far-right social media network, posted a screenshot of Revelation 3:9 on Twitter when activists called for the network's shutdown in the wake of the deadly shootings at the Tree of Life Synagogue in Pittsburgh, Pennsylvania, in 2018 (the shooter had posted John 8:44 as part of his antisemitic message on Gab);[37] and, more recently, harassing letters were sent to synagogues in the United States calling Jews part of the "synagogue of Satan" on the seventy-fifth anniversary of the liberation of Birkenau-Auschwitz.[38] Revelation 2:9 and 3:9 are, sadly, "go-to" verses for antisemitic hate.

Despite the appropriation of these verses by antisemitic bigots, pinpointing the identity of the individuals behind John's slurs is complicated. How one reads these verses hinges on whether the reader understands "synagogue" as a reference to a community of Jews *outside* the Jesus movement"[39] or as an example of John's sarcasm pointed at those *inside* the movement.[40] In either case, John challenges neighboring communities' legitimate claim to Jewish identity, suggesting that these communities are "synagogues," in scare quotes, and not faithful Jewish communities.[41]

Reading "synagogue of Satan" as a reference to Jews who are not Jesus followers often supposes that John's vitriol responds to Jewish hostility toward Jesus followers. Scholars imagine that Jewish communities in Smyrna and Philadelphia were threatened by those in the assemblies associated with John. Adela Yarbro Collins supposes that John's congregations struggled with other Jewish communities in a fight for status,

36. Anti-Defamation League, "Farrakhan: In His Own Words," January 12, 2013, https://www.adl.org/resources/backgrounder/farrakhan-his-own-words.

37. Molly Boigon, "Is Gab's Leadership as Antisemitic as Its Users?," *The Forward*, January 14, 2021, https://forward.com/news/462140/is-gabs-leadership-as-antisemitic-as-its-users/.

38. Souad Mekhennet, "As Anti-Semitic Incidents Rise in U.S., Group Launches New Online Tracking Tool," *The Washington Post*, February 1, 2020, sec. National Security, https://www.washingtonpost.com/national-security/as-anti-semitic-incidents-rise-in-us-group-launches-new-online-tracking-tool/2020/02/01/71bc33bc-4452-11ea-b503-2b077c436617_story.html.

39. David Frankfurter, "Jews or Not? Reconstructing the 'Other' in Rev 2:9 and 3:9," *HTR* 94 (2001): 403.

40. Steven J. Friesen, "Sarcasm in Revelation 2–3: Churches, Christians, True Jews, and Satanic Synagogues," in *The Reality of Apocalypse: Rhetoric and Politics in the Book of Revelation*, ed. David L. Barr (Atlanta: SBL, 2006), 127–44.

41. Friesen, "Sarcasm in Revelation 2–3," 138.

which was in short supply.[42] While Roman authorities afforded the Jewish communities of Asia Minor some autonomy, the Jesus followers' resistance to Roman religion and practices could have been seen as a threat. To illustrate this, Yarbro Collins draws upon a story of martyrdom from the second century in which the Jews of Smyrna publicly accuse the bishop Polycarp (d. second century CE) of teaching others not to sacrifice to the Roman gods (*Mart. Pol.* 12). The accusation serves to obscure the fact that the Jews themselves did not typically participate in Roman religions. Given the fear that the cities of Asia Minor possessed a limited capacity for tolerating nonconformist groups, the different groups sought to distinguish themselves from one another as the true heirs of Israel. Thus, they engaged in the type of boundary drawing we see in Revelation 2:9 and 3:9, where John literally demonizes the other by associating them with Satan.

Among the charges leveraged against the "synagogue of Satan" in Smyrna is slander (2:9). The language of slander echoes Jesus's polemic in the Gospel of John when he associates lies with Satan and, therefore, the Jews with whom he quarrels (8:44, 55). Whether the members of this group *are* slandering the community John addresses is uncertain, of course. We simply do not have the evidence to determine that. John, however, implies that these individuals' claims are causing real harm to the community and possibly their imprisonment. The fact that the accusation of Jewish opposition to the Jesus movement continues to be spread by later Christian authors, such as the person who penned *Martyrdom of Polycarp*, suggests that John is potentially the one guilty of slander.

Boundary drawing and demonization of the other has a precedent in the ancient Jewish world. The Jewish author of a text called *The War Scroll* characterizes Jews who lived in the ascetic community at Qumran, near the Dead Sea, as the "Sons of Light" in contrast to those who lived outside the community, which the author characterized as the "Sons of Darkness" and the "army of Belial," i.e., Satan (1QM; see also 1QS 5).[43] Disagreement over doctrine and practice leads one group to dismiss another's claims to a presumably shared identity. Likewise, the Gospel of John includes Jesus accusing Jews in Jerusalem of being "from your father the devil" (8:44). Yarbro Collins underscores the importance of recognizing that this kind of boundary-drawing polemic occurs in a context very different from modern Christianity in Europe and the United States;

---

42. Adela Yarbro Collins, "Vilification and Self-Definition in the Book of Revelation," *HTR* 79 (1986): 313.

43. Frankfurter, "Jews or Not?," 408.

rather, it happens in a world where Jesus followers were "an extreme minority in a precarious position."[44] Elaine Pagels, however, notes that, "In the process, they shaped in ways that were to become incalculably consequential, the self-understanding of Christians in relation to Jews for two millennia."[45] Whatever John intended by labeling others as "synagogue of Satan," the phrase contributed to a growing sense that early Jesus followers were not Jewish and that Jews were their opponents. Furthermore, while it is possible that John used "synagogue of Satan" to vilify Jewish groups in response to their antagonism, the only evidence for this kind of antagonism is found in early Christian sources, like the Gospel of John. There are no independent or unbiased sources from the first century that suggest Jews were able to hand over Jesus followers to authorities or that they were eager to do so.[46]

Another perspective on these verses suggests that the "synagogue of Satan" refers to gentile Jesus followers who claimed Jewish identity or associated themselves with Judaism. This understanding of the text offers a quite literal reading of the phrase "and are *not*" in the description "those who say they are Jews and are not" (2:9; 3:9). Since John assumes his audience members know why these groups should not be considered legitimately Jewish, he offers very little explanation for the claim. Noting that John's conflicts with other communities and teachers tend to be over issues described as "fornication," a possible allusion to assimilation to the dominant culture, and the eating of food sacrificed to Roman gods (2:14, 20), David Frankfurter argues John's conflict with the "so-called synagogues" probably revolves around observing Jewish purity practices.[47] Perhaps members of these groups were like some of the Jesus followers described in Paul's letters, open to eating food sacrificed to Roman gods (1 Cor 10:19-26) and tolerant of familial and sexual relationships that John understood as contradictory to Jewish teaching.[48] For instance, in 1 Corinthians even Paul balks at the community's tolerance of someone "living with his father's wife," presumably a stepmother (1 Cor 5:1-2). The reference to "synagogue of Satan" could point to an early conflict among Jesus followers over how to be faithful to Jewish tradition and identity.

44. Yarbro Collins, "Vilification and Self-Definition," 320.
45. Elaine Pagels, *The Origin of Satan* (New York: Vintage Books, 1995), 111.
46. Frankfurter, "Jews or Not?," 406.
47. Frankfurter, "Jews or Not?," 419.
48. Frankfurter, "Jews or Not?," 411. See also Elaine Pagels, *Revelations: Visions, Prophecy, and Politics in the Book of Revelation* (New York: Penguin, 2012), 60.

Whether John uses the language of "synagogue of Satan" to challenge a Jewish community's identity or a gentile community's appropriation of Jewish identity remains a mystery. Perhaps there is another referent unimagined by modern readers. Even though sarcasm is "seldom ambiguous," as biblical scholar Steven Friesen points out,[49] the temporal distance between us and John makes interpreting sarcasm and polemic difficult. No matter how one reads the group targeted by these slurs, however, the fact that John's demonization of his opponents intersects with a long history of Christian anti-Judaism, whether the "correct" reading of the text or not, is something that cannot be ignored. The apparent demonization of Jews within Christian sacred texts has legitimated viewing Jews as less than human and, therefore, worthy of harm and annihilation. Given this, Christian interpreters of Revelation must acknowledge the harm this imagery has done historically and condemn its continued use. Even if these texts are explainable as part of a conflict that happened at a time when Jesus followers were in the minority, they continue to have impact today and Christians, especially clergy and those who teach about the Bible, must actively educate others about their problematic nature. Uses of these verses, moreover, in ways that foment antisemitic attitudes or that justify hate crimes against Jewish people and places of worship must be swiftly condemned.

TRANSLATION MATTERS: συναγωγή

The Greek term συναγωγή, transliterated into English as "synagogue," literally means a gathering of people or a coming together. In classical Greek texts, it describes any sort of gathering. For example, in his history of the Peloponnesian war, Thucydides (ca. 460–400 BCE) used the word for the gathering of the Spartan army (2.18.3). In the Greek translation of the Hebrew Bible, the Septuagint, it translates a word for "community" (קהל), although it can reference other kinds of gatherings, including defeated Assyrians (Ezek 32:22) and even the gathered waters of the sky at creation (Gen 1:9). Still, in the first century CE, it is used primarily to reference a Jewish gathering or the place where such a communal gathering took place.

John's use of συναγωγή to describe those communities he deems as errant, while using ἐκκλησία to characterize those addressed by Christ, has contributed to an insidious form of othering. Given the authority assigned to Revelation as part of Christian Scripture, the dichotomy John draws between "church" and "synagogue" has contributed to a sense that there was a clear division between Jew and Christian in the earliest centuries of the Christian movement. In fact,

---

49. Friesen, "Sarcasm in Revelation 2–3," 132.

English translations need not render συναγωγή as "synagogue," despite the clear connection between the two terms. The NRSV translates συναγωγή as "assembly" in James 2:2, when the author describes diverse treatment of the obviously rich and poor in a συναγωγή of Jesus followers. Given this, we wonder how people's perspectives might have been different had translations like the NRSV, KJV, NIV, and NASB, all of which translate συναγωγή in Revelation 2:9 and 3:9 as "synagogue," simply chosen to use "assembly" in these verses as well.

Building Walls and Drawing Boundaries

Unlike the modern impulse to lessen hurt feelings by asserting that "everyone's a winner" for participating or showing up, not everyone is a victor in the eyes of Revelation's Christ. Given this, he encourages the seven communities to draw strict boundaries between themselves and those he casts as dangerous. Again, this approach resembles the formative processes in a gymnasium, where both physical walls and codes of conduct demarcated insiders from outsiders. Returning to the gymnasium law posted in Beroia is again instructive, as it similarly created boundaries. Specifically, it forbade enslaved people, sex-workers, those who drank to excess, and various "others" from entering the gymnasium.[50] These categories of people fell outside the bounds of ideal masculinity and threatened the manly virtue of those involved in the training of the gymnasium. The person who drinks too much, for example, does not exhibit the virtue of self-control, and sex-workers ostensibly risk the ability of those in the gymnasium to maintain that essential virtue. Note that this kind of boundary drawing presumes that outsiders are the threat. In this manner, Christ praises the community in Ephesus for maintaining boundaries and reinforces that separation by characterizing others as "evildoers," including those who falsely claim the title of "apostles." Just as the community members are tested, so they have tested these others and found them wanting. Moreover, John characterizes appropriate boundary drawing as a gendered act. Those who draw and maintain boundaries are masculinized, while those who do not are clearly portrayed in feminine terms.

Christ identifies a few local groups and teachers as especially dangerous. He commends the Ephesians for hating the works of the Nicolaitans (2:6), a mysterious group known primarily from Revelation. Another threat to communal identity is the teaching associated with "Balaam" (2:14-15). Balaam alludes to a seer mentioned in the Hebrew Bible, best known for the story of his talking donkey (Num 22). Balaam colludes

50. Bagnall and Derow, *Hellenistic Period*, 135.

with King Balak of Moab to curse the Israelites, and, later, Moses holds him responsible for encouraging Israel's women to participate in illicit sex and Baal worship (Num 31:16). By invoking this tradition, John casts a negative light on teachings that he sees as coming from outside the community, teachings that lead Jesus followers astray (cf. 2 Pet 2:15). The slur implicitly compares the faithful in Pergamum to the ancient Israelite women and reflects a popular ancient assumption that women as well as young boys are particularly susceptible to the smooth-talking teachers peddling dangerous ideas. In fact, early Christians were accused of this very thing (Tatian, *Or. Graec.* 33)!

The charges John levels against those following Balaam point to what he understands as the key problem in the cities of Asia Minor: assimilation to the values and practices of the dominant culture. "Eating food sacrificed to idols" (εἰδωλόθυτος) refers either to the practice of procuring meat from markets where meat sacrificed to Greek and Roman gods would be sold (Pliny, *Ep.* 10.96.10) or to sacrificing meat to a god before serving it at a banquet (2:14; 2:20; see below "Translation Matters: εἴδωλον"). As Paul's correspondence with the Corinthian assemblies reveals, some early gentile followers of Jesus had no problem with the practice of eating the leftovers from a Roman sacrifice, given that "there is no God but one" (1 Cor 8.4). Others, however, thought eating this meat was tantamount to participating in the worship of another god. Paul suggests that while the meat was fine to eat, assembly members should abstain lest their eating disturb others in the community: "if food is a cause of their falling, I will never eat meat, so that I may not cause one of them to fall" (1 Cor 8:13). John, in contrast, sees the issue as clear cut—those who eat meat sacrificed to Greek and Roman gods are unfaithful and worthy of exclusion.

Not so long ago, the question of whether eating a particular food signals acceptance of the institution behind that food's production became a live issue on the campus where I teach, Elon University. Students, faculty, and staff were divided over the on-campus presence of a popular restaurant known for both chicken sandwiches and their founder's support of Christian anti-LGBTQIA+ organizations. The conflict made national headlines[51] as student organizations debated whether a campus with a commitment to including and supporting those within the LGBTQIA+

---

51. Tyler Kingkade, "Chick-Fil-A Voted Out by Elon University Students, Booted from Other Campuses in North Carolina," *Huffington Post*, October 16, 2012, https://www.huffpost.com/entry/chick-fil-a-elon-university_n_1971376.

community should allow this company to do business on campus. Since the company was contracted by a third-party vendor, the issue became whether the restaurant's presence on campus was tacit approval of its owner's views. Students angry that people were calling for the removal of their favorite campus restaurant consumed sandwiches in venues where they could be seen by gay students and their allies. This aggressive consumption made LGBTQIA+ students as well as faculty and staff feel like outsiders. On the other side, those who wanted the restaurant removed labeled those who ate the sandwiches, even if offered freely at an event, as intolerant. Eating chicken sandwiches became a litmus test for dividing insiders from outsiders, a kind of practice that Christ advocates in these messages. If you eat food sacrificed to other gods, you are unequivocally an outsider.

Along with the charges related to eating illicit food, the messages use the language of fornication (πορνεία), a term for illicit sex, to label outsiders. Christ's accusations of fornication likely signal disapproval of sexual practices that John associates with the dominant culture, even though the text is not specific about what those practices entailed. Later, John uses the image of the "virgin," an unmarried and presumably sexually inactive girl, to depict those who follow God and the Lamb (14:4). This imagery encourages Revelation's audiences to think, and act, in ways that challenge Roman expectations about what it means to be a man, including male sexual prowess and a willingness to create heirs and citizens. Given John's valorization of virginity, which we discuss when addressing Revelation 14, it is conceivable that John envisions any kind of sex as illicit. This approach would align him with those in Corinth who thought, "It is well for a man not to touch a woman" (1 Cor 7:1), and later Christian authors, like Jerome (ca. 347–420), who advocated celibacy (e.g., Jerome, *Jov.* 1).

By pairing the accusation of fornication with the eating of meat sacrificed to other gods, John echoes a prophetic tradition in which illicit sex, specifically adultery, serves as a metaphor for disloyalty to God. The prophets frequently criticize what they see as the people's proclivity for religious infidelity by depicting Israel or Jerusalem as God's adulterous wife (e.g., Jer 2:1–3:5). Ezekiel offers the most integrated picture of these ideas by depicting Jerusalem as an adulterous wife who acts like a sex-worker in her self-fashioned religious shrines (Ezek 16:15-18).[52] Scholars who highlight this understanding of fornication often downplay the

---

52. See Mary E. Shields, "Multiple Exposures: Body Rhetoric and Gender Characterization in Ezekiel 16," *JFSR* 14 (1998): 5–18.

possibility that John could be referring to sexual acts.[53] While John may imply that the sexual practices of the people in Pergamum and Thyatira are unacceptable, the imagery also insinuates that community members are being unfaithful to God in some direct way. Perhaps their actions entail attending a local religious festival where they offer incense in honor of the emperor or even eat the ancient equivalent of a chicken sandwich. For John, there is no difference.

The accusation of fornication foregrounds the feminized identity of the seven assemblies. To some extent in the Roman world, it was socially acceptable for men, including married men, to have sex with multiple partners, including sex-workers and enslaved people in their households of any gender. Women and girls were not afforded the same freedom, although they were imagined as being more sexually motivated than men. Expressing a popular trope, the first-century author Valerius Maximus explained that women used to be "content with a single marriage," for which they were rewarded the "crown of chastity" (e.g., Valerius Maximus, *Memorable Doings and Sayings* 2.1.3); however, "modern" women were prone to infidelity. Given this assumption, Roman law, initiated under Augustus, aimed at curtailing women's supposed tendency toward adultery.[54] Thus, "fornication" was associated with women, and John's use of πορνεύω to characterize the communities of Asia Minor suggests that they are acting like women, which belies the calling to become victors.

Christ's comments on "fornication" include an extended condemnation of a teacher he calls "Jezebel" (2:20).[55] Jezebel could be the only real woman mentioned in Revelation, although Sarah Emanuel notes the possibility that John might be using a woman's name to discredit a male teacher.[56] This points to how John first masks and then undercuts Jezebel's identity. The name alludes to a Phoenician princess who became queen of Israel through her marriage to King Ahab (1 Kgs 16:29-31). While Ahab initially erected a temple and altar to Baal in Samaria, the Deuteronomic historian blamed Jezebel for killing Israel's prophets and

---

53. E.g., Elisabeth Schüssler Fiorenza, *Revelation: Vision of a Just World* (Minneapolis: Fortress, 1991), 14.

54. Catharine Edwards, *The Politics of Immorality in Ancient Rome* (Cambridge: Cambridge University Press, 2002), 36–42.

55. Pamela Thimmes, "Women Reading Women in the Apocalypse: Reading Scenario 1, the Letter to Thyatira (Rev. 2.18-29)," *CurBR* 2 (2003): 128–44. On the ways that "Jezebel" has been reinterpreted, see Tina Pippin, "Jezebel Re-Vamped," *Semeia* 69–70 (1995): 221–33.

56. Sarah Emanuel, *Humor, Resistance, and Jewish Cultural Persistence in the Book of Revelation: Roasting Rome* (Cambridge: Cambridge University Press, 2020), 116.

subsidizing the prophets of Baal (1 Kgs 18:12-19). By naming the Thyatiran teacher "Jezebel," John references these traditions by implying that she opposes the prophets of God, perhaps including John, in favor of other gods. Next, John delegitimizes her by suggesting that she is not a prophet; she simply *"calls* herself a prophet." Christ then accuses this teacher of the same wrongs as those who hold to the teaching of Balak and Balaam, namely, "fornication and [eating] food sacrificed to idols" (Rev 2:20). By associating this teacher with Jezebel, a non-Israelite figure, Revelation portrays her as an outsider and pariah. And yet, it is possible and even likely that "Jezebel" has a closer connection to the community in Thyatira than does John.

Perhaps Jezebel shares Paul's perspective about eating meat sacrificed to the gods: "We are no worse off if we do not eat [idol meat], and no better off if we do" (1 Cor 8:8). Still, in John's Revelation, Christ threatens her and her associates, those who "commit adultery with her," with sexual and physical violence. He will cause them all "great distress," even striking her children dead. Christ singles out Jezebel for a specific punishment: he will throw her on a bed, which, given the message's gendered imagery, suggests rape. Seeking to draw boundaries, John crosses a line for many feminist interpreters. He will cross this line again in Revelation 17 when he depicts the rape and dismemberment of Babylon depicted as a woman.

Jezebel and her "children" are not the only members of Revelation's audiences threatened by Christ. He notes that the Nicolaitans have gotten a foothold in Pergamum, and he commands the community members to repent. Failure to do so will lead to Christ coming to "make war against *them"* (2:16). In a violent twist, Christ threatens community members from Pergamum, not the Nicolaitans, for their association with another group. The threat points to how serious John is about maintaining group identity, and the image of the Son of Humanity as a violent bully remains unsettling.

Revelation's Prostitution Imagery

Echoing earlier Jewish prophetic traditions, such as Isaiah, Ezekiel, and Hosea, Revelation uses the language and imagery of sex-work and/or sexual impropriety in a metaphorical way. Along with the noun πορνεία (2:21; 9:21; 14:8; 17:2, 4; 18:3; 19:2) and the verb πορνεύω (2:14, 20; 17:2; 18:3, 9), which the NRSV translates as "fornication" and "to fornicate," John uses the term πόρνη (17:1, 5, 15; 19:2), which the NRSV translates as "whore" but which can be translated in a less stigmatizing way as "sex-worker" (see "Translation Matters: πόρνη").

Scholars often claim that this cluster of terms and its prophetic predecessors refer to religious infidelity or "idolatry," as the religions of the ancient Mediterranean have often been labeled.[57] Ezekiel 16, for example, uses this metaphor for Jerusalem. The prophet emphasizes how God, in taking Jerusalem as his wife, is loving and generous, only to have the city degrade "herself" sexually by building lofty shrines to other gods and opening "her" legs to anyone who passed by (Ezek 16:25).

The terms "fornication" and "prostitution" convey a range of ideas and therefore should not be read only as a code for misguided and thus "unfaithful" worship. The prophets sometimes use the imagery to characterize the greed and boundless ambition of cities other than Jerusalem. Nahum describes Nineveh, the capital of the Assyrian Empire, as a "gracefully alluring" sex-worker who "enslaves nations through her debaucheries" (Nah 3:4). Isaiah likewise characterizes Tyre as a sex-worker because of the city's unbridled quest for wealth (Isa 23). In these texts, the language of fornication or, more precisely, sex-work suggests a shameless quest for power and wealth as well as a willingness to degrade oneself for advancement.

Revelation uses the imagery of fornication to represent "unfaithful" worship, including the misuse of religious titles, such as Lord and Savior. "Fornication" appears in conjunction with both eating meat offered to the gods, often called "idols" (e.g., Rev 2:20), and blasphemy (17:3). There is an element of financial critique in the sex-working imagery of Revelation 17–18, and with each usage, the imagery accrues new connotations given its literary context. Thus, readers should avoid simply treating it as a code but to explore the various cultural associations John evokes when using the imagery.

Finally, this imagery perpetuates dangerous biases against sex-workers, especially prostitutes. The imagery clearly associates sex-workers, envisioned exclusively as women, with evil, sinfulness, self-debasement, and greed. The imagery fails to recognize that some have little choice in terms of profession, whether because of being controlled or enslaved by another or financial reasons, and that sex-workers, regardless of their gender, meet a demand from mostly male consumers. Unfortunately, Revelation's perspective is shared by many today. A sex-worker, identified as Veronica,

---

57. E.g., Gregory K. Beale, *The Book of Revelation: A Commentary on the Greek Text* (Grand Rapids: Eerdmans, 1999), 250.

in a study of sex-workers' responses to prostitution in the Bible, explains, "[Sex-workers are] blamed for everything, for whatever is going on: serial killers, drugs, crime, bad neighborhoods, drug problems, moral decay of the family, husbands cheating on their wives . . . we're blamed for everything."[58] This is the setting in Revelation 17–18, when John witnesses the "judgment of the Great Prostitute."

Jezebel and Sexual Violence

John's message concerning Jezebel suggests sexual violence. This violence is implied in his threat to "throw her on a bed" and reinforced by the chapter's other depiction of sexuality and gendered violence, including the description of Jezebel's followers as adulterers (invoking the long-standing association in the Hebrew prophets between idolatry and adultery) as well as references to *porneia* in the letter to Pergamum. A reading attuned to sexual violence and rape culture in ancient and modern texts and worlds also draws out other important details. I suggest a reading that positions John as the perpetrator of sexual violence and Jezebel as victim/survivor.

John introduces Jezebel in 2:20. He writes, "But I have this against you: you tolerate that woman Jezebel." John introduces her via the traffic in women: Jezebel is not a subject but rather an object (of discussion, of scorn) to be exchanged between men. The "Jezebel question" is a question about masculinity. As Lynn Huber notes, Jezebel may not be the woman's name; the name comes from a Phoenician princess who married King Ahab and is widely reviled in the Deuteronomistic History. From this perspective, identifying the victim/survivor as "Jezebel" is a way of undermining her credibility. (Interestingly, the Hebrew Bible's Jezebel, though she does many terrible things—at least according to the narrators—never commits adultery. In modern usage, however, "Jezebel" has come to mean a promiscuous, loose, or slutty woman; it sometimes takes on racial valences, as Patricia Hill Collins has discussed in *Black Feminist Thought*.[59]) John accuses Jezebel of sexual transgressions (she "is teaching and beguiling

---

58. Avaren Ipsen, *Sex Working and the Bible* (London: Routledge, 2014), 180.

59. Patricia Hill Collins, *Black Feminist Thought: Knowledge, Consciousness, and the Politics of Empowerment*, 2nd ed. (New York: Routledge, 2000), 81–84. Cf. Febbie Dickerson's study, *Luke, Widows, Judges, and Stereotypes*, Womanist Readings of Scripture (Lanham,

my servants to practice fornication"); his response is to threaten to rape her. The use of sexual violence as a punishment for the uncooperative woman is typical of narratives of sexual and domestic violence; John, like many perpetrators, believes this response to be "appropriate." "I will give to each of you as your works deserve" (v. 23) underscores the idea that sexual assault survivors and others "get what they deserve."

Perhaps sensitive to the charge that his actions are excessive, John tries to moderate his position in verse 21: "I gave her time to repent, but she refuses to repent of her fornication." At first glance, this move seems to diverge from the common rape-culture script of, "It was consensual but then she changed her mind." It contains, however, the same fundamental assumption that the male perpetrator knows how the female survivor ought to feel about what has happened. John's demand that Jezebel repent is a classic script of male power.

As a perpetrator, John moves to isolate Jezebel from her community; he promises to kill her children, to punish her followers, and to separate her from the rest of the community. This is a common strategy used by perpetrators to groom potential victims, as researchers such as David Lisak and Paul Miller have shown.[60] There is also a repeated—and problematic—issue of isolating the survivor from the community. As I have argued elsewhere, the survivor who refuses to follow specific scripts in describing her experience is frequently represented as difficult.[61] She also becomes, in Sara Ahmed's terms, an "unhappy object," insofar as she refuses to follow a narrative of violence and restoration that ultimately shores up the community's own sense of itself.[62] Jezebel attracts bad feelings, from John and from the implied readers. Furthermore, these feelings threaten to transfer to others, such as her community, and to contaminate them as well. A response that takes seriously sexual violence in the text must acknowledge and respond to all of these factors.

Rhiannon Graybill

MD: Lexington Books/Fortress Academic, 2019), who reads Luke 18:1-8 in conversation with Mammy, Jezebel, and Sapphire.

60. David Lisak and Paul M. Miller, "Repeat Rape and Multiple Offending among Undetected Rapists," *Violence and Victims* 17 (2002): 73–84.

61. Rhiannon Graybill, Meredith Minister, and Beatrice Lawrence, "Sexual Violence in and around the Classroom," *Teaching Theology & Religion* 20 (2017): 70–88.

62. Sara Ahmed, *The Promise of Happiness* (Durham, NC: Duke University Press, 2010), passim.

The Son of Humanity's letters to the seven communities are rich enough to warrant their own commentary. They evoke the lived experiences and material world of Revelation's first audiences while drawing hard boundaries between the seven communities and their close neighbors, characterized as "idolaters" and collaborators with Satan. Tying these elements together is John's metaphorical use of training and discipline imagery in which Christ as gymnasiarch pushes individuals within the communities toward the goal of becoming victors. Even though this is metaphorical training, John implies that there are real-world physical consequences to this competition. In addition to embodying faithfulness by drawing strict boundaries between themselves and others, John casts as part of the competition the social pressure faced by audience members (e.g., the slander mentioned in 2:9 and the temptation to eat meat sacrificed to other gods mentioned in 2:14 and 20) and even the physical violence experienced (2:13). Eventually, John will make clear that being a victor requires a willingness to die like Christ, the ultimate victor. This makes, moreover, the image of the victor somewhat ironic, as the death of Christ is not the noble death of a gladiator. It is, instead, the death of a slaughtered Lamb (5:6).

By lifting up the athletic imagery in the letters, it becomes possible to see how they engage assumptions about what it meant to be a "winner" in Revelation's world and how this was intertwined with ancient gender expectations. Again, John would have likely realized that his audiences included many who were not men or who could not become ideal men, such as women, girls, boys, enslaved males who were not allowed to become fully men, males who were perhaps "soft" or "lukewarm," and others who challenged traditional gender norms. Likewise, he will redefine being victorious in a way that challenges the masculine ideal. Still, John's idea of what it means to be faithful is so woven into his gendered ways of thinking in these letters that it is incredibly difficult, if not impossible, to separate being a faithful follower of Christ from being a good and successful man. Consequently, Christ appears to push hearers into the mold of ideal manhood, threatening to discipline those who do not, or maybe cannot, endure, hold fast, stay alert, bear up, and be either hot or cold. Of course, women, queer men, nonbinary individuals, and others who are "not men" endured, much like the Lamb "endured" by standing despite being slaughtered. In fact, we know that "not men" often endure more because of the hypermasculine reality shaped by authoritative authors such as John. As feminist Christian readers of Revelation we have our work cut out for us as we try to disentangle masculinist ways of thinking from ideas of Christian faithfulness and try to find new models.

Perhaps, taking a page from John, we look to athletes for inspiration. However, unlike John we can imagine a more diverse set of victors, such as Simone Biles, the US gymnast who prioritized her own mental wellness over competing for another gold medal despite social pressure, or Caster Semenya, the South African runner who continues to train and to persist in her efforts to race, even though officials in the racing world do not recognize her as a woman because of her natural testosterone levels. These are models of endurance for those of us outside of the traditional masculine ideal. Of course, these models do not provide the ironic impact that Revelation offers when depicting the victor as one who is slaughtered; however, perhaps that ironic twist is only really necessary for those audience members who can actually aspire to being a traditional victor.

The connection between athletics and masculinity should prompt readers to think about how modern athletics similarly extol the vision of the ideal male. This is evidenced by the pay disparity between male and female athletes. In September 2021, the US Women's National Soccer Team (USWNT) successfully negotiated with the US Soccer Federation to be paid equally to their male counterparts,[63] a remarkable thing given the rarity of pay equality in sports. Big revenue sports, especially in the United States, also privilege *White* male identity and not just males. Black players in the National Football League, for example, are more likely to be fined for "excessive celebration" and to be perceived negatively by the public for doing so than White players who celebrate on the field.[64] Likewise, in Europe, Black and Brown professional football (or soccer) players have faced racist slurs and harassment both on and off the field.[65] Even when particular sports are dominated by athletes of color, the structures surrounding athletics privilege being an elite White male, that is the ideal "victor" in modern culture.[66]

63. Abigail Johnson Hess, "U.S. Soccer Federation Announces Men's and Women's National Teams Will Be Offered the Same Contract," CNBC, September 15, 2021, https://www.cnbc.com/2021/09/15/us-soccer-federation-to-offer-men-and-women -players-same-contract.html.

64. Marcia W. Mount Shoop, *Touchdowns for Jesus and Other Signs of Apocalypse: Lifting the Veil on Big-Time Sports* (Eugene, OR: Cascade Books, 2014), 41.

65. Guy Davies, "Racism in Soccer an 'Epidemic' That Mirrors Disturbing Trends in Europe: Advocates," ABC News, February 1, 2020, https://abcnews.go.com/Sports /racism-soccer-epidemic-mirrors-disturbing-trends-europe-advocates/story?id =67850877.

66. Shoop, *Touchdowns for Jesus*, 45–46.

Revelation 4–5

Who Sits upon the Throne?

Immediately following the Son of Humanity's messages to the seven communities, John sees a door open in heaven. John's entry through this door marks the beginning of Revelation's primary vision, which lasts until the conclusion of the book. Once in heaven, John witnesses the sensory-overwhelming spectacle of the throne room as well as the tumultuous events of the world below. From this vantage point nothing looks like it once did.

John's heavenly perch will offer a glimpse of all that happens on earth, although in these two chapters he focuses on the activities and inhabitants of the throne room. Here John experiences the theological and christological heart of Revelation, a vision that shines a light on the centrality of the reign of God and Christ. Even though things in the throne room will look very different from things on earth and will challenge earthly expectations about power, Revelation's depictions of the throne room, including the hymns sung in this space, appear to transpose the earthly kyriarchy into a heavenly key. Given this, Lynne St. Clair Darden argues that John's mind was so colonized by the oppressive political systems around him that he offered here a "blurred copy" of Roman imperial cults.[1] While John certainly brings aspects of the dominant culture and

---

1. Lynne St. Clair Darden, *Scripturalizing Revelation: An African American Postcolonial Reading of Empire*, SemeiaSt 80 (Atlanta: SBL Press, 2015), 134.

its understanding of power into his vision, there are places in these chapters that invite readers to think about power in different ways. John's abstract imaging of the One Who Sits upon the Throne and his vision of the slaughtered Lamb, which challenges expectations and resists easy gender identification, can inspire us to resist the power structures that privilege masculine strength and fortitude. Together these two chapters bid feminist Christians to think about how we envision power and God's work in the world.

Looking with John (4:1-6a)

Just as Revelation begins with an act of unveiling, so the opening verse of chapter 4 evokes an image of things revealed: "After this I looked, and look,[2] there in heaven a door stood open" (v. 1). The door's openness visually signals God's invitation to know the things of heaven, including the divine. Through the command "look!" (see "Translation Matters: ἰδού"), which audiences hear as the text is read aloud (1:3), John invites the faithful to accompany him as he looks around this heavenly space. These elements, both the open door and the call to "look," encourage audience members to experience for themselves the theological claims made through the sounds and sights of this space.[3] By bringing hearers with him, John creates for them an experience usually reserved for prophets and seers (Ezek 1:2; Isa 6:1-7; see also 1 En. 14:25–15:2), and his description echoes these earlier visions. Since these things and spaces are not typically seen by the person on the ground, almost everything in this space is described through comparison, as mentioned in the introduction (see p. lxxxvi). There is a rainbow that looks *like* an emerald and something *like* a sea of glass (vv. 3, 6). What John witnesses in the throne room is not of the earth and must be characterized through approximation.

John and his audiences see, first and foremost, "a throne, with one seated on the throne" (v. 2). (Again, hearers are prompted to "look!" at the throne, although the NRSV does not translate the command.) They quickly realize that the throne is the space's focal point, something emphasized through the repeated use of the word "around" (κυκλόθεν) in reference to the throne (vv. 3, 4, 6).

---

2. This translation varies from the NRSV by adding the word "look" to acknowledge the presence of the command ἰδού in the Greek text.

3. Robyn J. Whitaker, *Ekphrasis, Vision, and Persuasion in the Book of Revelation*, WUNT 2.410 (Tübingen: Mohr Siebeck, 2015), 106.

⁴:¹After this I looked, and there in heaven a door stood open! And the first voice, which I had heard speaking to me like a trumpet, said, "Come up here, and I will show you what must take place after this." ²At once I was in the spirit, and there in heaven stood a throne, with one seated on the throne! ³And the one seated there looks like jasper and carnelian, and around the throne is a rainbow that looks like an emerald. ⁴Around the throne are twenty-four thrones, and seated on the thrones are twenty-four elders, dressed in white robes, with golden crowns on their heads. ⁵Coming from the throne are flashes of lightning, and rumblings and peals of thunder, and in front of the throne burn seven flaming torches, which are the seven spirits of God; ⁶and in front of the throne there is something like a sea of glass, like crystal.

Before the throne are seven flaming torches, which are the "seven spirits of God" (v. 5). Although the Greek term for "torches" (λαμπάδες) differs from that translated as "lampstands" (λυχνίαι) in earlier chapters, the language evokes the torches seen by Ezekiel in the throne room (Ezek 1:13 [LXX]) and suggests a comparison to the lights around the Son of Humanity in Revelation 1:12 and 2:1. At the end of the earlier vision, John learns that the lampstands are the seven communities or churches addressed in chapters 2–3 (1:20). Thus, through the logic of apocalyptic imagery and the miracle of a heavenly journey, John sees representations of the faithful communities he addressed earlier as torches before God's throne. Such proximity signals both access to the divine as well as God's ability to monitor the communities. This can have either positive or negative valances, depending on the interpreter's perspective. Still, the centrality of God's throne both in heaven and among the faithful on earth is evident.

Something like a sea of glass or crystal reflects God's power as well as the light from the torches before the throne (v. 6; see also 15:2). A similar "sea," a round bronze basin that held over forty-seven tons of water, once stood before the holy of holies of the Jerusalem temple (1 Kgs 7:23; 2 Chr 4:2-5; Jer 52:17). The presence of the sea in the vicinity of God symbolizes the divine's control over chaos by recalling the creation story of Genesis 1 when God separates the chaotic waters of the deep to make a space for creation (1:1-7). This is emphasized by John's characterization of the sea as being like crystal, something essentially "frozen" in place. For audience members who thought of the sea as tumultuous and dangerous, including those who made their living on the sea, this imagery might be especially meaningful. God controls the dangers that threaten their lives and livelihood. The imagery of a tamed sea also seems mournful, however, since churning swells epitomize the ocean. The rainbow that encircles the throne (4:3) likewise evokes Genesis by recalling God's promise never again to destroy all flesh through water (Gen 9:11-17). This allusion to the flood has repercussions throughout the narrative: John never forecasts the complete destruction of life at God's hands; however, Revelation vividly represents God's judgment through other means, including fire, hail, and plagues (cf. 2 Pet 3:7). God has stilled the water, but divine fury might be unleashed on the earth and humanity at any moment. In fact, this calm sea and stashed-away rainbow downplay the destruction that will eventually come from the throne room later in the book.

All these things focus the audience members' attention on the throne and who sits upon it—God. "The one who sits on the throne," which we represent as One Who Sits upon the Throne since the description effectively serves as a title in Revelation, serves as John's primary way of describing God (4:2, 3, 4, 9, 10; 5:1, 7, 13; 6:16; 7:10, 15; 11:16; 19:4; 20:11; 21:5). The imagery recollects depictions of the enthroned God in earlier biblical traditions, including poetic and prophetic texts where God appears as ruler and judge (e.g., Pss 9:7; 11:4; 45:6; 47:8; 89:14, 29, 36, 44; Dan 7:9-10). The thunder, flashes of lightning, and earthquake-like rumblings that come from this throne recall Ezekiel's vision (1:1-28), which highlights God's otherworldly power and presence. By drawing on these traditions, John "speaks of the God who is already known through Scriptures."[4] The God of Revelation is clearly the same deity that is proclaimed by the prophets and worshiped through the language of the Psalms.

The One Who Sits upon the Throne likewise recalls depictions of the god Zeus, also known as Jupiter by the Romans, who was similarly associated with thunder and who would have been visually familiar to Revelation's hearers. One of the most famous ancient representations of Zeus, popularly understood as the king of the gods and the heavens, was a colossal statue of the god enthroned. The statue, located in a temple in Olympia in Greece and approximately three-and-a-half stories high, was considered one of the seven wonders of the ancient world (*Paus.*

---

4. Craig Koester, *Revelation: A New Translation with Introduction and Commentary*, AYB 38A (New Haven: Yale University Press, 2014), 367.

5.11.9). Portraits of emperors on coins and in statuary were fashioned in the guise of the enthroned Zeus,[5] including a statue of Augustus in a temple at Caesarea in ancient Judea (Josephus, *J.W.* 1.21.7).[6] A similarly colossal statue of either Domitian or Titus, who reigned from 79 to 81 CE, was housed in the imperial temple at Ephesus, where some in John's audiences would have seen it from time to time.[7] The visual similarity between imperial portraits and representations of Zeus drew a clear line between the god and the emperors' claims to divinity. Given the significance of this kind of imagery, Revelation's vision of God upon the throne potentially reads as mimicking imperial posturing, even if John meant to affirm the One Who Sits upon the Throne's dominance over Zeus and those who would be Zeus. How powerful and impressive is the One Who Sits upon the Throne if his throne is secondhand?

Even though the image of enthronement verges on depicting the divine embodied in human form, like depictions of Zeus and other enthroned deities, John complicates this by emphasizing God's otherworldly appearance: he "looks like jasper and carnelian" (v. 3). Carnelian, a reddish-orange stone, was, as Jorunn Økland observes, often used in the Roman world for *intaglios* (engraved gemstones) depicting gods and other important figures.[8] Here, John flips the practice by suggesting that the divine itself appears as the gemstone.

The description of God through references to precious stones offers a striking comparison to Ezekiel's vision of the divine as "something that seemed like a human form" with "loins" that appear as amber with fire and splendor below (1:26-28). For Ezekiel the divine is simultaneously embodied and unbodied or not bound by a body, a phenomenon that can be described as "transcendent anthropomorphism."[9] The obscured

5. Laszlo Gallusz, *The Throne Motif in the Book of Revelation* (London: Bloomsbury, 2013), 86–87.

6. Stephen D. Moore, ed., *Untold Tales from the Book of Revelation: Sex and Gender, Empire and Ecology* (Atlanta: SBL, 2014), 92.

7. Steven J. Friesen explains why the statue, the head and forearm of which are in a museum in Selçuk, Turkey, is most likely Titus and not Domitian in *Imperial Cults and the Apocalypse of John: Reading Revelation in the Ruins* (Oxford: Oxford University Press, 2001), 50.

8. Jorunn Økland, "Carnelian and Caryatids: Stone and Statuary in the Heavenly Sanctuary," in *Constructions of Space III: Biblical Spatiality and the Sacred*, ed. Jorunn Økland, J. Cornelius de Vos, and Karen J. Wenell (London: Bloomsbury, 2016), 206.

9. Wesley Williams, "A Body Unlike Bodies: Transcendent Anthropomorphism in Ancient Semitic Tradition and Early Islam," *JAOS* 129 (2009): 19–44.

genitalia of the Ezekiel imagery raises the question of whether the God of these visions possesses reproductive anatomy or is more like the male companion of the famous Barbie doll, Ken, with a sexless, plastic crotch.[10] Perhaps, the divine's genitalia departs from traditional ways of categorizing bodies as male and female, like the 1.7 percent of people born intersex (a more common phenomenon than albinism).[11] Revelation, in contrast, obscures the entire body of the divine (even though John will see God's hand in 5:1). The artist Myrtice West captures this in her painting "Thou Art Worthy, O Lord, to Receive Glory and Honor and Power" (fig. 1), representing literally the description of the divine as a kind of gemstone positioned under a rainbow. John's hearers and West's viewers are reminded that this God is not human, nor is God like Greek and Roman gods who look (and sometimes act) very human.

Revelation's resistance to anthropomorphizing God[12] obviously does not stop interpreters from developing their own images of "the one seated upon the throne," which usually render the divine as White and male. This imagery, which sometimes overlaps with images of Christ enthroned, often appears in apses and above church portals as well as in illustrated versions of the book of Revelation, such as the black-and-white block print version produced by the German artist Albrecht Dürer.[13] There are some notable exceptions, such as Ethiopian illuminated manuscripts of Revelation, which disrupt the depiction of God as White by rendering the divine as a Black man sitting upon a throne.[14] Finding representations of this scene that avoid gendering God, however, are harder to come by, a notable example being the West painting.[15]

<hr>

10. Angels, played by Matt Damon and Ben Affleck, in the popular movie *Dogma* were similarly depicted as sexless, signaled by their revealing crotches like Ken. See Kevin Smith, *Dogma* (Lions Gate Films, 1999).

11. Anne Fausto-Sterling, *Sexing the Body: Gender Politics and the Construction of Sexuality* (New York: Basic Books, 2000), 51–53.

12. Whitaker, *Ekphrasis, Vision, and Persuasion*, 108.

13. Natasha O'Hear and Anthony O'Hear, *Picturing the Apocalypse: The Book of Revelation in the Arts over Two Millennia* (Oxford: Oxford University Press, 2015), 35.

14. E.g., "አብቀለምሲስ, 'The Revelation of St. John'" (Ethiopia, 1730 1700), f. 19r, Or 533, British Library, https://www.bl.uk/manuscripts/FullDisplay.aspx?ref=Or_533.

15. Another exception is Robert Roberg, *John Sees God (John Sees a Lamb)*, Mixed Media, 1992. A picture of this piece, which is owned by the artist, can be found in Nancy Grubb, *Revelations: Art of the Apocalypse* (New York: Abbeville, 1997), 40. In this piece, the divine appears as a bright pink figure adorned with rhinestones and a sunburst face.

Feminist Christians have long challenged the tendency to depict or refer to God as male as a default. This is not, as theologian Sallie McFague pointed out, just a language problem. The language and images used to describe or depict God shape how divine-human relationships are envisioned and even how society is structured. Thinking of God as "God the Father" helps give rise to patriarchal thinking and power structures.[16] Similarly, womanist scholar JoAnne Marie Terrell notes that internalized racism emerges from "imbibing cultural projections of whiteness and maleness as the standard of the holy."[17] Depictions that resist the vision of a White male God by imagining God otherwise, such as the popular t-shirt that reads, "I Met God and She's Black," remind us that God is not bound by human categories and point to the power that comes with associating the deity with specific gender and racial identities. In this way, the evocative description of the divine as jasper and carnelian can invite interpreters into conversations about the possibilities for thinking of the divine beyond human social categories.

While the depiction of God apart from a human body can subvert patriarchal assumptions about power, envisioning the divine as human can affirm the reality of human embodiment. This is one of the main claims of the incarnation, the Christian affirmation that God "became flesh and dwelt among us" (John 1:14). Theological thinking that imagines God embodied in ways not aligned traditionally with the expectations of the dominant culture, in a body that is disabled, queer, intersex, trans, fat, Brown or Black, can subvert White and masculinist theologies.[18] As we will see shortly, Revelation invites this more radical imagining of the divine through the vision of the slaughtered Lamb.

The One Who Sits upon the Throne (4:6b-11)

God's court in the throne room court includes twenty-four elders seated upon their own thrones (v. 4) as well as four "living creatures"

---

16. Sallie McFague, *Metaphorical Theology: Models of God in Religious Language* (Minneapolis: Fortress, 1982), 9–10.

17. JoAnne Marie Terrell, "Our Mothers' Gardens: Discrete Sources of Reflection on the Cross in Womanist Christology," in *I Found God in Me: A Womanist Biblical Hermeneutics Reader*, ed. Mitzi J. Smith (Eugene, OR: Cascade Books, 2015), 97.

18. Heike Peckruhn, "Embodied Knowing: Body, Epistemology, Context, and Hermeneutics," in *What Is Constructive Theology? Histories, Methodologies, and Perspectives*, ed. Marion Grau and Jason Wyman (London: T&T Clark, 2020), 79–80.

Rev 4:6b-11

⁶Around the throne, and on each side of the throne, are four living creatures, full of eyes in front and behind: ⁷the first living creature like a lion, the second living creature like an ox, the third living creature with a face like a human face, and the fourth living creature like a flying eagle. ⁸And the four living creatures, each of them with six wings, are full of eyes all around and inside. Day and night without ceasing they sing,
"Holy, holy, holy,
    the Lord God the Almighty,
        who was and is and is to
            come."

⁹And whenever the living creatures give glory and honor and thanks to the one who is seated on the throne, who lives forever and ever, ¹⁰the twenty-four elders fall before the one who is seated on the throne and worship the one who lives forever and ever; they cast their crowns before the throne, singing,
¹¹"You are worthy, our Lord and
        God,
    to receive glory and honor and
        power,
for you created all things,
    and by your will they existed
        and were created."

each with six wings covered in eyes (4:6, 8). References to God's royal court appear elsewhere in biblical traditions (e.g., 1 Kgs 22:19; Job 1:6; Pss 82:1; 89:7; Isa 24:23; Dan 7:9-10), but John's inspiration for the four living creatures clearly comes from the book of Ezekiel, where a similar group of four creatures attends God's throne. In Ezekiel's depiction, each creature has four different faces of a human, lion, ox, and eagle and only four wings, and they move in unison with the spirit of God (Ezek 1:10-12). John untangles these complex creatures into four distinct beings, even though they remain fantastic in appearance, signaling that the space around the heavenly throne is unlike any earthly reality.

Envisioned within a world where Roman imperial power was signaled visually in imagery used throughout the empire, the throne room of Revelation mirrors some ancient assumptions about courts. The presence of courtiers alongside of a ruler signaled, for example, a ruler's power and prestige. In this vein, high Roman officials traditionally were accompanied by ceremonial bodyguards, called lictors, carrying bundles of rods (called fasces and leading to the term "fascism") symbolizing the official's authority. Augustus had twelve lictors, and Domitian doubled the number to twenty-four. Too many courtiers, however, risked conveying negative connotations, such as a ruler's insecurity and excess. Such was the case with Nero who purportedly had five thousand young men trained to applaud for him, a kind of "cheerleading squad," according to Stephen D. Moore, when he tried his hand at playing the harp (Suetonius, *Nero* 20.3).[19] In Revelation's court, the number of elders around the throne, twenty-four, suggests completeness and perfection. There are neither too few nor too many attending the One Who Sits upon the Throne. Twenty-four calls to mind the hours of the day as well as alluding to the twelve tribes of Israel doubled. The Gospels similarly evoke Israel with the number of twelve (Matt 10:1-6; Mark 6:7-13; Luke 9:1-6; see also Acts 1:15-26), implying that Jesus's closest disciples represent the fullness of the twelve tribes. Consequently, many interpreters read Revelation's twenty-four elders as signaling a combination of the twelve tribes and the twelve disciples, even though it remains unclear whether John was familiar with gospel traditions about the disciples. Still, twenty-four suggests that these elders are "representatives of God's people" before the throne.[20] Despite this relatively fixed number of individuals within the throne room, those who worship the One Who Sits upon the Throne will increase in number as the narrative unfolds and eventually the heavenly choir will grow to include "every creature in heaven and on earth and under the earth and in the sea, and all that is in them" (5:13). This expansion suggests John may be trying to outdo the Roman imperial court.

The depiction of the elders around the throne encompasses both religious and political imagery, reflecting the fact that there was little or no distinction between political and religious realms in the ancient world. The title "elder," πρεσβύτερος in Greek and the root of the word "presbyter," appears in the Greek translation of the Hebrew Bible in reference to the leaders of the tribes of Israel (e.g., Judg 11:7-11), reinforcing that these figures are representatives of God's people before the throne.[21] Dressed in white, a color associated with worship and the upper classes,[22] the elders occupy thrones and wear crowns, symbolizing political power. By prostrating themselves before God's throne, however, the elders relativize the political power of all others in relation to the One Who Sits upon the Throne. They simultaneously give voice to this reality through the hymn coming from their lips, "You [God] are worthy . . . to receive glory and honor and power" (4:11).

---

19. Moore, *Untold Tales*, 84–85.

20. Koester, *Revelation*, 360.

21. Koester, *Revelation*, 362.

22. Kelly Olson, *Masculinity and Dress in Roman Antiquity* (Abingdon: Routledge, 2017), 113.

One of the distinctive aspects of Revelation among the writings of the New Testament is its depiction of worship. As John moves through the narrative, he repeatedly hears and recounts the stanzas of hymns sung by the inhabitants of heaven (7:9-17; 11:15-18; 14:2-3; 15:2-4; 19:1-8). Occasionally, John mentions the presence of harps or the sound of harps (5:8; 14:2; 15:2). These hymns echo the praise of God described in the Psalms and the Prophets. Notably, the four living creatures begin their hymn in the throne room with what is known as the *trisagion*, "Holy, holy, holy" (4:8), an affirmation that appears in the throne room scene of Isaiah 6 as well. Some of these choruses may sound familiar to modern Christians, since they have inspired popular hymns, like "Holy, Holy, Holy" and "Crown Him with Many Crowns," and have found their way into the lectionary.[23] These appropriations bring the praise and acclamation of the heavenly throne room into modern earthly contexts, making good on Revelation's claim that the One Who Sits upon the Throne is the one "who was and is and is to come" (4:8). The God of Revelation is still worshiped today in churches around the globe.

The never-ending worship of the One Who Sits upon the Throne models for John's audiences right worship in contrast to the kinds of worship that occurred in the cities of Asia Minor, where choirs were employed to offer hymns as part of the imperial cults. An altar found in Pergamum, for instance, names almost forty men who served as members of a choir dedicated to "the god Augustus and the goddess of Rome."[24] These kinds of choirs were widespread and performed at temples as well as civic events, such as religious processions, festivals, and athletic games. In their songs, choir members ascribed titles and characteristics to emperors that emphasized the rulers' power and even cosmic significance. Imperial figures were "the greatest," the source of the people's "salvation," and even enjoined to live forever: "May it please our Augustuses to live forever!"[25] Revelation's hymns correct these attributions. While in Asia Minor emperors were often described as *autokratōr*, suggesting that they were ruled by no one else,[26] the heavenly choruses of Revelation affirm that the One Who Sits upon the Throne is *pantokratōr* (παντοκράτωρ), the

23. Gail R. O'Day, "Teaching and Preaching the Book of Revelation," *WW* 25 (2005): 246–47.

24. Friesen, *Imperial Cults*, 108.

25. As quoted in David E. Aune, "The Influence of Roman Imperial Court Ceremonial on the Apocalypse of John," *BR* 28 (1983): 17.

26. Koester, *Revelation*, 220.

"Almighty," who rules not only himself but over all things (4:8; see also 1:8; 11:17; 15:3; 16:7; 19:6; 21:22). Additionally, the living creatures who offer Revelation's hymn do not simply request that God live forever if it pleases him, as in the imperial hymn; they assert and celebrate God's eternal nature as the one "who was and is and is to come" (see also 1:8). Even more important, the hymns affirm God's creative capacity. This is noted, like with the *trisagion*, three times: "you *created* all things, and by your will *they existed* and *were created*" (4:11). Even this avowal of God's role in creation sets right the belief that Augustus should be understood as "the beginning of all things," a claim made by the provincial council of Asia when they recalibrated the provincial calendar to align with the emperor's birthday.[27] Throughout these hymns Revelation's early audiences heard both affirmations of God's creative power and marked criticism of imperial claims to that power. While some in John's audiences may be tempted to accept the claims of Rome or other imperial manifestations, John reminds all who hear and read Revelation that the one who occupies the heavenly throne, the God of Israel, Genesis, and the Psalms, is the source of all power and creation.

Even as they correct the forms of worship surrounding his audiences in real life, these throne room scenes simultaneously replicate the assumptions undergirding imperial worship. For instance, the depiction of the elders bowing before the throne evokes the ancient Persian court custom of *proskynesis*, in which subordinates show deference to the one who rules over or dominates them by prostrating themselves.[28] The power disparity is embodied in a literal way. Given these similarities, critical readers of Revelation must ask, as Darden articulates, "How could John, who was so *against* empire, mimic empire?"[29] Darden answers this question by suggesting that as someone living within a culture that embraced imperial ways of thinking, realizing these through the imperial cults, John might not see how his fundamental ways of thinking have been shaped by his cultural context. That is, even while criticizing the Roman Empire, he fails to recognize that the problem is kyriarchal thinking more generally. Margaret Aymer offers another helpful way of describing what happens in Revelation 4, characterizing Revelation's perspective "alter-empire." In contrast to the system around him, John presents his audiences with a vision of God's kingdom as "an empire stronger than Rome, more enduring

27. As quoted in Friesen, *Imperial Cults*, 33.
28. Darden, *Scripturalizing Revelation*, 136, 148–50.
29. Darden, *Scripturalizing Revelation*, 137.

than Rome, more all-encompassing than Rome."[30] Instead of rethinking empire, for the most part John simply relocates the empire's seat of power, revealing it to be in heaven instead of across the Mediterranean. The main difference, however, will appear in Revelation 5, as John witnesses the paradoxical way in which God works in the world.

Figure 1: Myrtice West, *Thou Art Worthy, O Lord, to Receive Glory and Honor and Power,* oil on cloth, 47x35, United States, c. 1980. Used with permission from Rollin Riggs.

Signifying on Empire

The critical analysis of the images of the imperial cult in the heavenly throne room scenes (chaps. 4 and 5) in the book of Revelation framed by the postcolonial concept of cultural hybridity unveils the complex cultural negotiations involved in the construction of a Christian identity. John the Seer's virulent signifying on empire (that is, his anti-imperial rhetoric) aptly demonstrates that he is well aware of the oppressive nature of Roman imperialism on the lives

30. Margaret P. Aymer, "Empire, Alter-Empire, and the Twenty-First Century," *USQR* 59 (2005): 145.

of Christians in the province of Asia. This is made clear by his fierce, nonaccommodating stance toward participation in the imperial cult, a ritualistic religio-political system that justifies an imperialist worldview. John's anti-imperial stance is, however, a contradiction because he simply re-presents and reenacts imperial policy/propaganda in the heavenly throne room scenes. And so, ironically, John reinscribes imperial processes and practices in his articulation of the new Jerusalem. Seemingly, no matter how determined the Seer is to disconnect from the cultural manipulations of empire, his hybridity prohibits him from doing that. His signifying on empire remains fixed on the persistent cycles of war, conquest, and revolt, paralleled by cycles of worship, ritual, and mythmaking. Thus, the images he conjures in the heavenly throne room scenes both allude to and signify on the ritualistic practices of conquest performed by various power structures of the ancient past, including Babylon and Persia as well as the axis of power in his own day, the Roman Empire of the first century. How could John, who was so against empire, mimic empire?

John's colonized construction as "almost the same but not quite like" has resulted in the production of a resistance strategy that is a blurred copy of the hegemonic tactics of the Roman Empire. Since domination is not simply a system of military control but is a systematic cultural penetration that subjugates psychologically as well as intellectually, John mimics the ideological assumptions and methods of constructing empire because, to a certain degree, he is a member of a society that embraced participation in the cultic rituals of empire. Imperial cult ritual performance caused participants to connect with imperial ideological codes that, in turn, modified their behavior. In addition, I suggest that John's denial of his own ambivalent, hybrid construction, his repression or nonrealization of his own fragmentation, his own double consciousness, may be the cause for his contradictory stance toward empire.

Lynne St. Clair Darden

Anticipating the Lion (5:1-5)

Amid the activity of the throne room, John suddenly notices a scroll with seven seals in the right hand of the One Who Sits upon the Throne (5:1). Some English translations describe the sealed object as a book (e.g., KJV, NASB), since John uses βιβλίον, a word eventually used to describe a bound collection of pages (i.e., a codex). At the time John wrote, however, βιβλίον referred mainly to papyrus scrolls, and visualizing this object as

⁵:¹Then I saw in the right hand of the one seated on the throne a scroll written on the inside and on the back, sealed with seven seals; ²and I saw a mighty angel proclaiming with a loud voice, "Who is worthy to open the scroll and break its seals?" ³And no one in heaven or on earth or under the earth was able to open the scroll or to look into it. ⁴And I began to weep bitterly because no one was found worthy to open the scroll or look into it. ⁵Then one of the elders said to me, "Do not weep. See, the Lion of the tribe of Judah, the Root of David, has conquered, so that he can open the scroll and its seven seals."

a scroll allows us to imagine how the opening of each seal leads to the scroll's complete unfurling later in the text. Further, thinking about this as a scroll helps us understand how compelling it is that this object has writing "inside and on the back," since scrolls typically only had writing on one side. Imagine how difficult it would be to flip over a long, unwieldly scroll to read writing on the backside. The imagery suggests the contents of the scroll are so abundant and significant that they cannot be confined to a single side. The fact that this meaning-full text is secured with seven seals, keeping it closed, makes the object mysterious and incredibly captivating.

The inaccessibility of the scroll's contents piques John's interest, and so the narrative's focus shifts quickly from the scroll to the identity of someone "worthy" of opening such an amazing thing (5:2). A double mention of the fact that no one is worthy heightens the tension around the opening of the scroll and prompts John to weep bitterly (vv. 3-4). With the build-up emphasizing the importance of the one who will open the scroll, Revelation's audiences recognize the pivotal moment when one of the twenty-four elders reassures John, along with them, that someone *is* worthy. The elder prompts John, along with his audiences, to "See!" the one who will open the scroll, even though at this moment the audiences only *hear* about the worthy one—"the Lion of the tribe of Judah, the root of David" (v. 5).

The elder's announcement that "the Lion" will open the sealed scroll reassures John and the faithful that someone strong and courageous will suddenly appear. The depiction of John as unable to control his emotions and as unable to open the seals himself positions him as a feminized figure in need of a hero to sweep in to save the day. A lion will fit this bill. Lions appear in biblical stories and other myths as a way of highlighting the strength, physical or spiritual, of heroic men, such as Samson,

Daniel, and Hercules (Judg 14:6; Dan 6:16-28; Euripides, *Heracl.* 360). Given this connection, audience members might anticipate a strong man like Hercules, a son of Zeus who was often depicted wearing the skin of the slayed Nemean lion, arriving on the scene. Some Roman emperors, including Nero and later Commodus, depicted themselves in this hero's guise as a way of asserting their virility (Suetonius, *Nero* 53).[31] Perhaps some hearers expect to see the Son of Humanity from John's earlier vision (1:12-20) now clad as a lion and approaching the heavenly throne to solve the puzzle of the scroll. Surely, one worthy to open the scroll held by the One Who Sits upon the Throne needs to embody masculine power, an idea underscored by the elder's description of the Lion as having "conquered [ἐνίκησεν] *so that* he can open the scroll and its seven seals" (5:5; emphasis added).[32] This language of conquering recalls the promises made to the victorious, the "conquerors," throughout chapters 2–3, and it points to the Lion as a model of victory for the faithful (see "Translation Matters: ὁ νικῶν").

Furthermore, the specification "Lion *of Judah*" signals that the figure who will open the scroll is not just a victor; rather, this is *the* victor—Christ, the Messiah. In Genesis, Judah, the ancestor of David, is described by his father Jacob as a lion who will become ruler: "Judah is a lion's whelp. . . . He crouches down, he stretches out like a lion, like a lioness—who dares rouse him up? The scepter shall not depart from Judah, nor the ruler's staff from between his feet, until tribute comes to him; and the obedience of the peoples is his" (49:9-10). This Lion, who is a descendent or "root" of David, is coming not just to open the scroll, but he will share the throne as judge and ruler (cf., 4 Ezra 11:37; 12:31-32).[33] Given this, it is possible that Revelation's early audiences hearing the narrative for the first time anticipate the Son of Humanity to reappear and open the scroll. As Gail R. O'Day notes elsewhere, however, Revelation "intends to discomfit the Christian community about its perceptions of God,"[34] a reality that happens in the next moment.

31. For a discussion of Heracles on coins circulating in Smyrna during the first and second century CE, see C. P. Jones, "Heracles at Smyrna," *American Journal of Numismatics Second Series* 2 (1990): 65–76.

32. The words "so that" are not included in the Greek text but capture the meaning of the aorist infinitive verb ἀνοῖξαι or "to open."

33. Koester, *Revelation*, 375.

34. Gail R. O'Day, "Revelation," in *Theological Bible Commentary*, ed. Gail R. O'Day and David L. Petersen (Louisville: Westminster John Knox, 2009), 474.

Viewing the Genderqueer Lamb (5:6-14)

John and his audiences anticipate the coming of a masculine hero when they *hear* about the "Lion of Judah." What they then *see* challenges this expectation. It is a surprise.[35] Peering through the four living creatures and the elders that surround the throne, John sees that the Lion is "a Lamb standing as if it had been slaughtered" (v. 6). The diminutive "little lamb" (ἀρνίον), instead of terms associated with an older lamb or sheep (ἀμνός, πρόβατον), highlights the vulnerability of this animal, especially in contrast to a lion. The paradoxical nature of the Lion that is a "little Lamb" is made more explicit by the description of the Lamb standing "between" the throne and the four living creatures. The Greek here suggests that the Lamb is "in the middle" or "in the midst" (ἐν μέσῳ) of the throne. The small, vulnerable animal is encircled by a massive structure, which is surrounded by four monstrous creatures and twenty-four more thrones. We can imagine audiences asking incredulously, "*This* is the one who conquered? *This* is the one who is supposed to open God's scroll?"

The elder promises the ideal masculine figure, which in the ancient Roman world meant a man who was impenetrable and capable of penetrating others. Instead, the Lion appears as a Lamb wounded and penetrated. Described earlier as "pierced" (1:7), the saints will call to attention the Lamb's blood (5:9), conjuring the Lamb's body as an open wound. According to ancient logic, this passive and penetrated body is feminized. It is "not man." Drawing on a similar understanding of gender, medieval depictions of Christ's side wound look suspiciously labia-like, emphasizing the feminized body of the crucified and wounded Christ.[36]

The reference to being slaughtered clearly connects the Lamb to Jesus's crucifixion, although without explicit reference to the cross. As mentioned in the introduction, this Lamb imagery evokes the depiction of Jesus in the Gospel of John, where the crucifixion occurs on the day lambs were slaughtered in preparation for the Passover (John 19:31). Despite this connection, Revelation avoids depicting the life and experiences of Jesus from a historical or earthly perspective; instead, the paradoxical image of the conquering Lion who is a slaughtered Lamb is how the

35. Loren L. Johns, *The Lamb Christology of the Apocalypse of John: An Investigation into Its Origins and Rhetorical Force* (Eugene, OR: Wipf and Stock, 2014), 162.

36. Caroline Walker Bynum, *Christian Materiality: An Essay on Religion in Late Medieval Europe* (Brooklyn, NY: Zone Books, 2015), 196–200.

Rev 5:6-14

⁶Then I saw between the throne and the four living creatures and among the elders a Lamb standing as if it had been slaughtered, having seven horns and seven eyes, which are the seven spirits of God sent out into all the earth. ⁷He went and took the scroll from the right hand of the one who was seated on the throne. ⁸When he had taken the scroll, the four living creatures and the twenty-four elders fell before the Lamb, each holding a harp and golden bowls full of incense, which are the prayers of the saints. ⁹They sing a new song:

> "You are worthy to take the scroll
>   and to open its seals,
> for you were slaughtered and by
>   your blood you ransomed
>   for God
>   saints from every tribe and
>   language and people
>   and nation;
> ¹⁰you have made them to be
>   a kingdom and priests
>   serving our God,
>   and they will reign on earth."

crucified Christ appears under the bright lights of the heavenly throne room. At the same time, the vision evokes the violence of ancient Roman spectacles, like gladiatorial games, where criminals were victims of state violence. Again, the earlier reference to "those who pierced him" (1:7) captures the public and communal nature of Roman punishment.[37] That this crucified Christ appears in animal form, Lion and Lamb, evokes the use of animals in these ancient punishments, when sometimes beasts were used to make executions into entertainments, thereby dehumanizing those being killed. Apuleius describes criminals being fed a banquet before death, as a way of feeding the beasts to which they were thrown (*Metam.* 4.13). Ironically, for Revelation, it is the one treated as a beast through capital punishment who challenges the imperial system by being the one worthy to open the scroll.

The fact that the slaughtered Lamb is presented to John and his audience members as something to be seen, for the elder commands all who hear him to "See!" (5:5), underscores this body as a demasculinized or feminized object. Just as Romans of the first century gazed upon the penetrated bleeding bodies of those unable to protect themselves and prove their manliness in Roman amphitheaters, so the throngs of heaven visually dominate and penetrate with their eyes the body of the Lamb before them. As Christopher A. Frilingos suggests, the Lamb, despite

37. Maia Kotrosits, "Seeing Is Feeling: Revelation's Enthroned Lamb and Ancient Visual Affects," *BibInt* 22 (2014): 490.

[11]Then I looked, and I heard the voice of many angels surrounding the throne and the living creatures and the elders; they numbered myriads of myriads and thousands of thousands, [12]singing with full voice,

> "Worthy is the Lamb that was slaughtered
> to receive power and wealth and wisdom and might
> and honor and glory and blessing!"

[13]Then I heard every creature in heaven and on earth and under the earth and in the sea, and all that is in them, singing,

> "To the one seated on the throne
> and to the Lamb
> be blessing and honor and glory and might
> forever and ever!"

[14]And the four living creatures said, "Amen!" And the elders fell down and worshiped.

having multiple horns, eyes, and crowns, all of which are markers of power, "struggle[s] to overcome its apparent impotence."[38] From where John stands, the Lamb seemingly fails in this struggle.

While the Lamb is slaughtered, this is not a vision of the Lamb as sacrificial animal; there is no altar for sacrifice in sight (although an altar will appear in 6:9). Rather, the language of slaughter (σφάζω), a term used in 1 John to describe the murder of Abel by Cain (3:12), implies the Lamb has experienced a violent death and not a ritual slaughter.[39] This distinction is important, since sometimes Revelation's language sounds like Christ's death "pays for" human sin (e.g., 5:9), a concept known as the atonement. This model of salvation seems to imply that "Satan was owed his due for crimes God's people had committed against God and each other," as Brian K. Blount explains,[40] which contradicts Revelation's insistence that God is the One Who Sits upon the Throne and whose angels roundly defeat Satan and his minions (12:7-12; 20:1-3, 10). Instead of atonement, this imagery evokes the Passover, when lambs were slaughtered in Egypt so that the Israelites could mark their doorposts with blood, ensuring them life and, eventually, liberation from

38. Christopher A. Frilingos, "Sexing the Lamb," in *New Testament Masculinities*, ed. Stephen D. Moore and Janice Capel Anderson (Atlanta: SBL, 2003), 308.

39. Robyn Whitaker, "Victim to Victor: The Appeal of Apocalyptic Hope," *Religions* 11 (September 2020): 4.

40. Brian K. Blount, *Can I Get a Witness? Reading Revelation through African American Culture* (Louisville: Westminster John Knox, 2005), 71.

enslavement (Exod 12). As the living-creatures and elders proclaim (5:9), the Lamb's blood "similarly functions to liberate people."[41]

Furthermore, as the allusion to the Passover suggests, the Lamb's failed masculinity is only part of the picture. This is not a "bait and switch" scenario, with the slaughtered Lamb being a subpar replacement for the Lion. The slaughtered Lamb *is* the conquering Lion. Christ is both Lion and Lamb, simultaneously conqueror and slaughtered, although the text will privilege the title "Lamb." This image confirms John's earlier paradoxical descriptions of Christ as "the firstborn of the dead" (1:5) and as one who lives, even though dead (1:18). As Robyn J. Whitaker aptly notes, the Lamb is "the ultimate victim turned victor." [42] This turns traditional gender expectations on their head, as the feminized figure of the Lamb inhabits the role of the masculine victor.

Returning to the idea of the gaze, even though Revelation puts the slaughtered Lamb on display for John and his audiences, the Lamb's *seven* eyes complicates this. Not only does seven suggest the perfection of the Lamb's vision, but these eyes are also the seven spirits that God sends "out into all the earth" (5:6). The Lamb is like a spiritual drone with the ability to stare right back at those who gaze upon his wounds. Perhaps this all-seeing Lamb even looked into the eyes of those who slaughtered him. While violence was done to this one, who is characterized in animalistic terms, maybe this ability to see others reveals *their* animalistic ways. Perhaps, Revelation's unveiling of the Lamb exerts affective power over those in the book's early audiences who participated in or attended Roman spectacles where others were put to death for resisting the self-aggrandizing claims of empire and/or asserting the reign of God.[43]

Even though it appears before the throne wounded and penetrated, the Lamb is not entirely passive. Instead, the Lamb immediately goes and takes the scroll from God's right hand (v. 7). Elsewhere John depicts God as "allowing" things to happen (e.g., 6:4; 13:7), and the Greek term λαμβάνω,[44] which the NRSV renders as "took," can be translated in terms of either taking or receiving. The Lamb, however, makes the first move toward the scroll, going to get it from God, revealing that the Lamb acts with volition. The Lamb's action evokes an immediate response from the

---

41. Whitaker, "Victim to Victor," 5.

42. Whitaker, "Victim to Victor," 2.

43. Kotrosits, "Seeing Is Feeling," 489–91.

44. This is a perfect-tense form of the verb λαμβάνω.

living creatures and the elders, who now fall in worship before the Lamb (5:8). This shift to include the Lamb as an object of worship with God points to a shared power and symbiotic relationship between the two. As John's audiences see in the next chapter, the Lamb acts on behalf of God.

Because of the Lamb's status as one who is worthy to open God's scroll, a new song is introduced in heaven in which both God and Lamb receive praise (v. 9). This song, which unfolds in three parts (vv. 9-10, 12, 13), does not replace earlier songs, since God reigns eternal and is "who was and is and is to come" (1:8; 4:8). Rather, the new song builds on the continuing praise offered to the One Who Sits upon the Throne. As the song changes and grows, so the number of participants in the chorus expands. By the end of the song in 5:13, John envisions "*every* creature in heaven and on earth and under the earth and in the sea, and all that is in them" praising both God and the Lamb.

The new song commences by linking the Lamb's ability to open the scroll with having been slaughtered and consequently being able to "ransom," the Greek verb ἀγοράζω, "for God saints from every tribe and language and people and nation" (v. 9). Again, this should not be thought of in terms of the Lamb's death serving to pay a debt for sin or to rectify a cosmic debt.[45] In contrast, Whitaker compares the Lamb's ransoming of the saints to the liberation of prisoners of war.[46] By conquering, the Lamb has the power to free those who have been held captive. This reading is appealing since it sheds a positive light on the Lamb. However, ἀγοράζω, evokes the idea of exchange in the marketplace (ἀγορά), suggesting "purchase" as a translation. This language anticipates the later depiction of the faithful as those enslaved by God and the Lamb (e.g., 7:3), a troubling metaphor that John uses throughout the text (see "Translation Matters: δοῦλος"). Nevertheless, the elders' affirmation that those purchased or ransomed are made "a kingdom and priests to God" (5:10) suggests the text does not valorize enslavement here. Through the actions of the Lamb, those who are faithful rule alongside of the Lamb. Unfortunately, the translators of the NRSV cast this in terms of the enslavement metaphor by adding the word "serving" to verse 10 when it is not in the Greek. Instead, as noted in the final clause of the stanza, the saints will reign on earth. This becomes reality toward the end of Revelation, during the millennium (20:4-6).

45. Blount, *Can I Get a Witness?*, 71.
46. Whitaker, "Victim to Victor," 6.

The second two stanzas of the hymn, voiced by myriads of angels accompanying the living creatures and elders, offer further acclamations of the Lamb's power, might, honor, and glory, and even include the claim that the Lamb deserves wealth (5:12-13). As we saw previously, this language aligns with the kyriarchal language of the Roman Empire, positioning the Lamb as a kind of lord, king, and even master. This evokes the alter-empire that Aymer names.[47] The ones who praise the Lamb with a unified voice, however, begin their song with a reminder that the Lamb is slaughtered (v. 12). Everything said about the Lamb is filtered through this very specific and shattered lens. In fact, while John uses a variety of images to depict Christ throughout Revelation, including the one like a Son of Humanity (1:12-20) and the Rider on a White Horse (19:11-16), he defaults to the Lamb throughout the narrative (5:8, 12, 13; 6:1, 16; 7:9-10, 14, 17; 8:1; 12:11; 13:8, 11; 14:1, 4, 10; 15:3; 17:14; 19:7, 9; 21:9, 14, 22, 23; 22:1, 3).

The four living creatures affirm the claims made by those worshiping the Lamb with an "Amen," which the elders punctuate by falling down to worship (5:14). Feminist and queer interpreters might join in the celebration since this throne room scene places at the center a genderqueer figure. More precisely, in this vision a genderqueer Lamb shares the throne with the One Who Sits upon the Throne and becomes an object of worship. Not only does the conquering Lion who is a slaughtered Lamb encompass both obviously masculine and feminine traits, the fact that these traits cannot be so easily pinpointed challenges the fixity of gender. In this way, the Lamb's existence "queers" or troubles conventional ideas about gender, including the claim that it is binary. Transgender activist and scholar Kate Bornstein talks about being a "gender outlaw," someone whose mere presence challenges conventional assumptions about gender, sex, and sexual identity as well as traditional expectations around desire and revulsion.[48] The Lamb, with a body defined by its experience of violence, might seem at first glance to be frightening or revolting, but it is a body that is welcomed in throne room and embraced by the throne itself. As such the Lamb likewise troubles expectations around gender, power, and worth. The Lamb is a heavenly gender outlaw, a status that will have effects for those who follow the Lamb on the earth (14:1-4; see pp. 207–16).

47. Aymer, "Empire, Alter-Empire."

48. Kate Bornstein, "Gender Terror, Gender Rage," in *The Transgender Studies Reader*, ed. Susan Stryker and Stephen Whittle (New York: Routledge, 2006), 237.

The centering of the genderqueer body within the heavenly throne room is revolutionary and liberative. Those in the ancient world who challenged gender expectations or whose bodies exhibited differences in sexual development were often considered monstrous, sometimes treated as "entertainments" or "prodigies," disruptions in the natural order (Pliny the Elder, *Nat.* 7.34).[49] This could lead to a violent end as a way of ritually "making things right."[50] Things have changed little, according to contemporary poet and activist Alok Vaid-Menon, who is gender nonconforming: "they will say that we / are ugly. they will say we are imposters, frauds, / predators, mistakes. mostly, they will say that we / are ugly . . . sometimes they will not say, so they will spit, / point, grope, laugh instead."[51] By giving glory and honor to the genderqueer Lamb, the throngs of heaven subvert what "they say" and dignify the one who is often victimized. Again, the Lamb stands as "the ultimate victim turned victor."[52]

A genderqueer Lamb sharing the throne with God does not mean John embraces a progressive, feminist perspective throughout the rest of the narrative (even though we might wish for that). The Seer continues to use language that reeks of misogyny by associating women with filth (14:4; 17:4-5) and employs imagery that seemingly valorizes masculine power (e.g., 19:11-16). He will also describe the coming New Jerusalem as an exclusive space, unwelcoming to those described as "abominations" and "fornicators" (21:27; 22:15), designations often deployed against those who defy traditional gender categories and sexual norms. On the one hand, we can explain this dichotomy by asserting that Revelation is a product of its historical context and that upsetting ancient gender norms is not necessarily John's primary task. On the other hand, upsetting gender norms *is* Revelation's primary task, since John sets about to unsettle traditional notions of power, and gender and power are inseparable. Challenging traditional views of power necessarily means disrupting traditional perspectives on gender. John's seeming reticence

49. See also the discussion of the monstrous in Diana M. Swancutt, "*Still* before Sexuality: 'Greek' Androgyny, the Roman Imperial Politics of Masculinity and the Roman Invention of the *Tribas*," in *Mapping Gender in Ancient Religious Discourses,* ed. Todd Penner and Caroline Vander Stichele, BibInt 84 (Boston: Brill, 2007), 11–61.

50. Anthony Corbeill, *Sexing the World: Grammatical Gender and Biological Sex in Ancient Rome* (Princeton: Princeton University Press, 2015), 151–53, 162.

51. Alok Vaid-Menon, "They Will Say," *Femme in Public* (self-published, 2017), 4.

52. Whitaker, "Victim to Victor," 2.

to embrace this leaves Revelation teetering between replicating kyriarchy and completely revisioning the systems in which the narrative is embedded. Hence, Revelation can be characterized as *alter*-empire and not *anti*-empire.[53]

Given John's ambivalence about empire, feminist interpreters invested in Revelation being part of the Christian canon must find ways of deploying John's visions in ways that are feminist, antiracist, and accepting of gender and sexual diversity. Among other things, this should include thinking about how we envision power, exploring visions of the divine that eschew traditional notions of a White man sitting upon a throne, and inviting alternative notions of power. For example, what happens if we take seriously the vision of God as the kind of gemstone, like carnelian, onto which images of imperial figures and other gods are typically inscribed? The divine as envisioned by John emerges from the processes of nature, while others are manufactured by human hands. Moreover, imagine the power of thinking about the divine sharing a throne with someone who presents as radically genderqueer, like the slaughtered Lamb. Centering the body of those who refuse to conform to sex and gender expectations provides a kind of salvation to all, not just "gender outlaws," but to all humans, as our opportunities are filtered through the gender binary. These things may not have been on John's mind when he invited us into the throne room, but now we're here, we should make the most of our time inside the door.

53. Aymer, "Empire, Alter-Empire."

Revelation 6

Revelation Unsealed

Among all the scenes in Revelation, the opening of the seven seals offers some of the text's most poignant glimpses into the harsh reality of life on earth for Revelation's audiences. The events brought forth by the seals provide a sense of how things on the ground appear from the perspective of the throne room. This offers a heavenly "reality check" that, unsurprisingly, contradicts the view perpetuated by the Roman Empire. According to imperial propaganda Augustus's reign ushered in a "golden age," and subsequent emperors were similarly touted for their greatness. The poet Statius, in this manner, described Domitian as the "hope of mankind" (*Silvae* 4.2.15), and Martial celebrated the dedication of a temple to the Flavians proclaiming that "thus the lofty ornament of the Flavian race [will] endure together with sun and stars and Roman daylight" (*Epigr.* 9.1).[1] (Ironically, the temple was eventually struck by lightning, and an inscription on a statue of Domitian was damaged in the storm [Suetonius, *Dom.* 15].) The parallel to contemporary politicians, including a recent US president with a penchant for self-praise, is noteworthy. Against the backdrop of imperial aggrandizement, Revelation's seals unfurl.

---

1. Brenda Longfellow, *Roman Imperialism and Civic Patronage: Form, Meaning, and Ideology in Monumental Fountain Complexes* (Cambridge: Cambridge University Press, 2011), 58.

While the Roman imperial backdrop shapes John's rhetoric throughout Revelation, interpreters disagree over whether the events ushered in by opening the seals describe current events for Revelation's audiences or anticipate future events. Are the seals descriptive or predictive? The fact that the text begins with the claim that it reveals "what must soon take place" (1:1) suggests a future orientation to Revelation as a whole, including the seals, whereas the messages to the seven assemblies ground the narrative within the current affairs of John's audience members. An either/or way of reading is too simplistic for anything found in the pages of Revelation, including the seals; rather, the meaning-full text lends itself to a both/and approach. With an eye on the present and another on the future, the Seer's recounting of the seals reveals the realities that come with imperial or kyriarchal systems, including war, conquest, economic disparity, disease, and death. Accompanying these realities is a momentum that ensures the seals are simultaneously predictions of what will emerge in time. As Catherine Keller aptly notes, "Description slides into prediction."[2] The seals are the current reality for Revelation's audiences, but they are on the horizon as well. Moreover, just as John saw the manifestations of the seals in his own time, we continue to see similar phenomena today. The persistence of kyriarchy lends Revelation an air of predictiveness.

Unleashing the Riders (6:1-8)

In popular culture, the horses and riders that appear with the opening of the first four seals appear as ciphers for the coming of evil and chaos. An ironic bumper sticker from the 2004 US presidential election depicts George W. Bush, Dick Cheney, Karl Rove, and John Ashcroft with the caption "Don't Change Horsemen in the Middle of an Apocalypse." By suggesting that the United States was in the middle of an "apocalypse," the sticker criticized the Bush administration as a kind of disaster and, consequently, mocked those who would vote again for these supposed horsemen. A more recent example of the political appropriation of this imagery appeared in North Carolina in the form of a billboard that de-picted four US Congresspeople, all women of color, as the horsemen

2. Catherine Keller, *Apocalypse Now and Then: A Feminist Guide to the End of the World* (Boston: Beacon, 1996), 54–55.

6:1Then I saw the Lamb open one of the seven seals, and I heard one of the four living creatures call out, as with a voice of thunder, "Come!" 2I looked, and there was a white horse! Its rider had a bow; a crown was given to him, and he came out conquering and to conquer.

3When he opened the second seal, I heard the second living creature call out, "Come!" 4And out came another horse, bright red; its rider was permitted to take peace from the earth, so that people would slaughter one another; and he was given a great sword.

5When he opened the third seal, I heard the third living creature call out, "Come!" I looked, and there was a black horse! Its rider held a pair of scales in his hand, 6and I heard what seemed to be a voice in the midst of the four living creatures saying, "A quart of wheat for a day's pay, and three quarts of barley for a day's pay, but do not damage the olive oil and the wine!"

7When he opened the fourth seal, I heard the voice of the fourth living creature call out, "Come!" 8I looked and there was a pale green horse! Its rider's name was Death, and Hades followed with him; they were given authority over a fourth of the earth, to kill with sword, famine, and pestilence, and by the wild animals of the earth.

because of their criticism of Donald J. Trump.[3] In both cases, the imagery of the riders suggests a looming threat, and neither usage realizes that in Revelation the four horses and their riders are agents of heaven who act at the behest of God and the Lamb. The fact that interpreters so easily associate the "four horsemen" with supposedly bad actors points to Revelation's perplexing and paradoxical depictions of God and Christ's work in the world.

For all the disorder the riders bring to earth, the opening of the first four seals occurs quite systematically. John recounts the Lamb opening a seal, and then one of the four living creatures calls out, "Come!" and a rider appears immediately on a horse, each a distinct color—white, red, black, and "pale green." The imagery draws on Zechariah's description of divinely appointed agents, associated with the winds, that patrol the earth in chariots drawn by multicolored horses (Zech 1:7-11, 6:1-8). Like Zechariah's horses, Revelation's horses appear ready to act on behalf of

3. Morgan Gstalter, "North Carolina Gun Shop Puts up '4 Horsemen' Billboard to Slam Progressive Congresswomen," *The Hill*, July 30, 2019, https://thehill.com/home news/house/455320-north-carolina-gun-shop-puts-up-4-horsemen-billboard-to-slam -progressive.

the divine. Their emergence with the opening of the seals implies the timeliness of the moment.

With the first seal (6:2), John again draws attention to what he sees by using the command ἰδού ("look" or "behold"; not translated in the NRSV) to prompt his audiences to envision the first horse and rider along with him (see "Translation Matters: ἰδού"). As the command to "Look!" suggests, the rider on the white horse, bedecked with a crown and armed with a bow, is something to behold. Interpreters have long puzzled over whether this rider offers a vision of Christ (e.g., Irenaeus, *Haer.* 4.21.3), since, later, he will appear on a white horse (19:11), or as something more nefarious.[4] The image is threatening, as the rider is armed and comes "conquering and to conquer," suggesting he is a warrior. His bow connects the rider to some of Rome's opponents, including the Parthians with whom the Romans fought along the border of Asia Minor and who were known for using bows in combat.[5] The Romans saw the Parthians as persistent threats and naturally "predatory" (Strabo, *Geog.* 11.13.6). In this way, John's imagery reveals Roman anxiety about the "other" who must be held at bay to protect the imperial expanse, contrary to the confident posturing of imperial propaganda.

Still, the fact that this rider comes on a *white* horse, wearing a crown and conquering—the same language John uses in Revelation 2–3 to characterize being faithful and in reference to the Lion of Judah (5:5)—makes him seem like a Christ figure (see "Translation Matters: ὁ νικῶν"). Since Revelation's hearers have not yet witnessed the Rider of Revelation 19, the identity of this rider is ambiguous. Therefore, some interpreters suggest that this first rider represents an "antichrist," someone who misleads people by looking like something he is not.[6] Although Revelation never includes the term "antichrist," a term used in 1 John to describe individuals who have left the community and who do not confess Jesus is God (2:18-22; 4:3), perhaps John envisions Christ's return heralded by false messiahs. This motif appears in the Synoptic Gospels (e.g., Mark 13:21-22). Later, when John depicts the Beast from the sea, a figure who embodies the power of Satan on earth, he will bear some resemblance to the image of Christ as Lamb (12:18–13:4). These types of resemblances point to the necessity of developing discernment, as good and evil actors

4. Mathias Rissi, "The Rider on the White Horse: A Study of Revelation 6:1-8," *Int* 18 (October 1964): 407–18.

5. Craig R. Koester, *Revelation: A New Translation with Introduction and Commentary,* AYB 38A (New Haven: Yale University Press, 2014), 394.

6. Rissi, "Rider on the White Horse," 417–18.

can be easily confused. As feminist interpreters know, a "hermeneutics of suspicion" is not just for texts.[7]

When the Lamb opens the second seal, a living creature calls out, "Come!" and a bright red horse and its rider appear (6:3). Brandishing a great sword, this second rider is "permitted to take peace from the earth, so that people would slaughter one another" (v. 4). This is what happens in the rider's wake. As such, this imagery challenges the claims made by and on behalf of Roman emperors. Strabo claimed of Augustus, "Never have the Romans and their allies thrived in such peace and plenty" (*Geog.* 6.4.2). Nero, according to Seneca the Younger, saw himself, personally, as a peacemaker, proclaiming that "with me the sword is hidden, nay, is sheathed" (*On Mercy* 1.1.4), even though the Jewish revolt against Rome began at the end of his reign (Josephus, *J.W.* 2.14.4). Domitian, likewise, emphasized his role in bringing peace by issuing coins adorned with Pax, the female personification of peace, setting fire to a pile of weapons.[8]

Some in Revelation's audiences may have embraced the vision of Roman peace spread by the empire and even felt a sense of security under imperial rule. This perspective appears in artwork adorning a processional way to an imperial temple, called a *sebasteion*, in Aphrodisias, near Laodicea. Commissioned by citizens of Aphrodisias, the decoration consists of reliefs depicting conquering emperors "securing" peace over land and sea, sometimes literally depicted as an emperor standing over a bound "barbarian," and representations of the emperors violently subduing nations personified as women. Among these is Emperor Claudius "defeating" Britannia (fig. 2).[9] From a modern perspective, the imagery is startling in its violence and reminds us that one person's peace is another person's terror. Similarly, Revelation's depiction of this rider, which comes after the conqueror on a white horse, encourages audiences to recognize that empire brings conflict and domination, not peace.

The third horse bears a rider who carries scales used for trade signaling adversity and uncertainty related to economics and the marketplace (v. 5). A voice from amid the living creatures explains this vision: "A quart of

7. Elisabeth Schüssler Fiorenza, *Bread Not Stone: The Challenge of Feminist Biblical Interpretation*, 2nd ed. (Boston: Beacon, 1995), 15–17.

8. *Sestertius with Head of Domitian*, 85, Coin, 85, 34.1415, Boston MFA: Ancient Greece and Rome, https://collections.mfa.org/objects/162166/sestertius-with-head -of-domitian.

9. R. R. R. Smith, "The Imperial Reliefs from the Sebasteion at Aphrodisias," *JRS* 77 (1987): 88–138.

wheat for a day's pay [a denarius], and three quarts of barley for a day's pay, but do not damage the olive oil and the wine" (v. 6). The amounts concern a daily ration, but the prices are "eight to sixteen times higher than usual."[10] These prices reflect the economic inflation and scarcity that occur during war or extreme shortage periods. Once again, this imagery counters the messaging of imperial Rome. From the perspective of those in power, Roman rule led to abundance and prosperity. For example, the appearance of Ceres, the goddess of wheat and fertility, on coins throughout the provinces, along with corresponding images of the emperors and their wives, reminded consumers that the abundance of the marketplace was a product of imperial efforts and benevolence.[11]

Roman rule meant abundance for some in the provinces, likely including some among John's audiences. Classicist Barbara Levick explains that the cities of Asia Minor supported niche markets for specific goods, such as linen or marble, that were exported to Rome or to the empire's frontiers, where the military forces were relocating.[12] Production efforts were focused on meeting imperial rather than local needs, including the need for staples destined for export like wine and olive oil. The rider carrying scales embodies concern over a growing economic divide and so warns Revelation's audiences that the increasing signs of wealth they see around them are indicators of economic distress for most.

The fourth and final horse and rider are the culmination of the first three, conquest, war, and economic disparity. Unlike the other seals, the fourth living creature names the rider who comes on a "pale green" horse. This rider is the personification of Death, who happens to be accompanied by Hades, a reference to both the Greek god who ruled the underworld and an embodiment of that place. Together, with the power of the "sword, famine, and pestilence, and by the wild animals of the earth" (v. 8), Death and Hades kill a quarter of the earth's population. These numbers remind audience members that the underworld seems insatiable in its appetite for life (Isa 5:14; Hab 2:5; Prov 1:12). The presence of Hades with Death also suggests a sudden and violent end. The god

10. Koester, *Revelation*, 396.

11. Harry O. Maier, *Picturing Paul in Empire: Imperial Image, Text and Persuasion in Colossians, Ephesians and the Pastoral Epistles* (London: T&T Clark, 2013), 113–15; Barbette Stanley Spaeth, "The Goddess Ceres in the *Ara Pacis Augustae* and the Carthage Relief," *AJA* 98 (1994): 92–93.

12. Barbara Levick, "The Roman Economy: Trade in Asia Minor and the Niche Market," *GR* 51 (2004): 180–98.

Hades was known in ancient mythology for abducting Persephone, also known as Proserpina, the daughter of the goddess Demeter, also known as Ceres, and taking her into the underworld (*Hymn to Demeter* 40–70). The scene was familiar in funerary art during the Roman Empire, invoking the range of emotions associated with losing someone, especially a daughter, because of untimely death.[13] Given the possible mythological allusion, the reference to Hades sounds especially threatening to women and girls sitting in Revelation's earliest audiences.

Seen as describing the situation experienced by John's audiences, the picture revealed by the first four seals is grim. Moreover, it explicitly contradicts the claims of Rome and its supporters—that imperial rule brings peace, abundance, and security. The seals' alternative message underscores how those in power often spin narratives to their advantage with little consideration of how their perspectives align with the experiences of the powerless. Even if some think conquest brings about positive change, those conquered mourn the loss of lands, tradition, and self-determination. Likewise, while imperial powers may claim peace because there are no active "hot wars," the family member who has a loved one living far from home and protecting a contested border may have a different perspective. These horses and riders reveal to John's audiences some of the realities unfolding around them, but they are not unique to this setting.

That the Lamb's actions unleash these disasters might be puzzling; however, John's point is that as the source of all power, God and the Lamb control distress as well as bliss. This raises the question of how to respond. Do we, like the friend Elihu in the book of Job, double down on asserting God's greatness and on the goodness of God's actions (e.g., Job 34:10-12)? While we understand the impulse to respond in this way, since the idea of a benevolent deity is comforting, we resist this view. Even if God does not will the events accompanying the horse and riders into existence,[14] they effectively bear the divine "seal of approval." Do we suggest that the first four seals entail John ascribing to God the ills that stem from systemic realities, such as inequity and poverty? Yes, this tends to be one of the ways we think about these passages and talk about them with our students. We ask our students why John would make this claim. What did he gain from placing these events under the

---

13. Paul Zanker and Bjorn C. Ewald, *Living with Myths: The Imagery of Roman Sarcophagi*, trans. Julia Slater (Oxford: Oxford University Press, 2012), 384–85.

14. Elisabeth Schüssler Fiorenza, *Revelation: Vision of a Just World* (Minneapolis: Fortress, 1991), 63.

control of God and the Lamb? Do we lament along with those experiencing the wrath of the riders? Yes, completely. We stand with those living through conflict, poverty, and illness, and we do our best to ease their pain and work for economic justice. Do we see the distress coming from the throne room and allow ourselves to be angry with God and the Lamb for allowing these things to happen? Again, yes. The all-powerful one who sits on the throne does not get a pass when it comes to bearing responsibility for the earth's harsh realities.

Figure 2: Sebasteion Relief of Claudius and Britannia, Aphrodisias, Turkey, first century CE. Photo courtesy of New York University Excavations at Aphrodisias (G. Petruccioli).

"How Long?" (6:9-11)

The narrative current that John's audiences follow through the first four seals shifts dramatically when the Lamb opens the fifth. Now, John's attention turns to the souls of those "who had been slaughtered for the word of God and for the testimony they had given" (v. 9). These souls have not been taken to or by Hades, who just appeared alongside Death; instead, these souls appear unexpectedly under the heavenly altar.

On the one hand, this glimpse under the altar reveals the destructive momentum of empire, extending the energy that came in the opening of the previous seal. This includes the prediction that many faithful will die for their witness to the reign of God and the Lamb, a possible surprise for some in Revelation's audiences who believe that being good citizens ensures their safety and comfort. For others, this is old news. There was a long history of those faithful to God dying on account of their commitments and identities. Many in John's audiences surely recalled the massive loss of life due to the Jewish war against Rome. Josephus reports over a million casualties overall (*J.W.* 6.3.9). Some likely recalled that some of Jesus's followers were put to death by Nero after the fire in Rome in 64 CE (Tacitus, *Ann.* 15.44; see p. 16). Still, John anticipates more will be added to the count (v. 11).

On the other hand, even though the image of the fifth seal predicts that those who are faithful will die, it simultaneously promises them life. Elsewhere in Revelation, the term translated here as "souls" (ψυχή) can refer more generally to life or things that are living (e.g., 12:11; 16:3). Even though those under the altar have been slaughtered, which implies death, they continue to be alive. This paradox is underscored by the language of "slaughter," which connects their lives to the Lamb, who stood though slaughtered (5:6, 9, 12). They share his fate as ones living through and despite death. As souls who continue to live, those under the altar should not be envisioned as sacrificial victims. Sacrifices, in fact, would be on top of an altar and not underneath. The location of the souls under the altar suggests, in contrast, the ancient practice of dedicating votives, often small terracotta items, to the gods in appreciation of their favor or mercy; many were in the shape of a body part—a foot, uterus, arm, etc.—that the gods had healed. These gifts might be buried in and around the temple and its altar.[15] In a similar way, those killed because

---

15. Beate Dignas, *Economy of the Sacred in Hellenistic and Roman Asia Minor* (Oxford: Oxford University Press, 2002), 20.

⁹When he opened the fifth seal, I saw under the altar the souls of those who had been slaughtered for the word of God and for the testimony they had given; ¹⁰they cried out with a loud voice, "Sovereign Lord, holy and true, how long will it be before you judge and avenge our blood on the inhabi- tants of the earth?" ¹¹They were each given a white robe and told to rest a little longer, until the number would be complete both of their fellow servants and of their brothers and sisters, who were soon to be killed as they them- selves had been killed.

of their testimony are stored under this altar as part of God's property or holdings. They are, in a sense, evidence of divine care.

Despite being slaughtered, the souls maintain an attitude of resistance to the dominant culture. Speaking with a singular voice, they appeal to God as "sovereign" (δεσπότης, whence the English "despot"), a title that emphasizes God's power over all others, especially earthly emperors who claim the title (e.g., Philo, *Flacc.* 4.23). The souls assert God's sovereignty while they petition the divine to act on their behalf, asking for vengeance: "they cried out '. . . how long will it be before you judge and avenge our blood on the inhabitants of the earth?'" (v. 10). For some Christians, this request might seem un-Christlike: Would not Christ advocate forgiveness instead of vengeance?[16] Given this, some interpreters nuance the call for vengeance by noting that the word translated as "avenge" (ἐκδικέω) is related to the term for justice (δίκη),[17] an idea that is more palatable to modern readers. Later, however, a multitude in heaven, which presum- ably includes the souls under the altar, celebrates the fact that God "has avenged [ἐκδικέω] . . . the blood of the saints" by destroying the city Babylon (19:2). God will grant the request for vengeance, even though the slaughtered must wait "until the number would be complete of [those] . . . who were soon to be killed as they themselves had been killed" (v. 11). This is a case of vengeance, or justice, deferred.

Feminist Bible scholar Elisabeth Schüssler Fiorenza suggests that the discomfort some Christians have with the language of vengeance corre- sponds to their distance from oppression.[18] Those familiar with violence and injustice may hear in this seal a parallel to their own experiences.

16. Schüssler Fiorenza, *Revelation: Vision of a Just World,* 64.

17. Koester, *Revelation,* 399–400.

18. Schüssler Fiorenza, *Revelation: Vision of a Just World,* 64.

Thus, writing in the 1980s, theologian Alan Boesak read the experience of Black South Africans living under apartheid as a reiteration of the cry from under the altar:

> From the earliest days of colonial rule, whole communities have been slaughtered to secure the continuation of white power. . . . During recent years there has hardly been a place where the police and the army have not wantonly murdered our children, piling atrocity upon atrocity for the sake of the preservation of apartheid and white privilege. And as they go from funeral to funeral, burying yet another victim of law and order or yet another killed by government-protected death squads, the cry continues to rise to heaven: "How long, Lord?" How long before this illegitimate power is removed? How long before the blood of our children is avenged?[19]

In contrast, many who are more distant from oppression are inclined to say, "rest a little longer" (v. 11), since responding to the cry would mean putting our own comfort in jeopardy. One must only look at the responses of White Christians in the United States to the continued exonerations of police officers and others who have shot Black men, supposedly in self-defense. We express outrage on social media, saying, "That's not who we are," but do nothing to rectify things. We don't act on behalf of the cries from those calling out, "How long?"

"#blacksoulsmatter"

The souls under the altar of Revelation 6:9-11 find themselves frozen in a historical future; these are they who had been, who will be, and who are being slain,[20] existentially stuck between the cry of "how long" and the state of "rest."[21] One wonders what is worse, being a victim of imperial violence and its state-sanctioned slaughter, or bearing defenseless witness to it while future deaths are fulfilled. Because some scholars argue that the persecution of John's audience was limited or nonexistent at the time of

---

19. Allan Aubrey Boesak, *Comfort and Protest* (Philadelphia: Westminster John Knox, 1987), 73.

20. That is, τάς ψυχάς τῶν ἐσφαγμένων (6:9), οἱ μέλλοντες ἀποκτέννεσθαι, and ἕως πληρωθῶσιν—the ongoing fulfillment of the victims of slaughter (6:11).

21. Interpreters have a choice of how to translate ἵνα αναπαύσονται. Nestle-Aland presents the phrase as an intransitive future middle indicative, "so that they will rest (a little while longer)," and footnotes the subjunctive variant ἵνα αναπαύσωνται, "so that they might rest."

Revelation's circulation, the precarious situation of the souls is often minimized, allowing the assumption of apocalyptic hyperbole, as in "it wasn't really that bad" or "it didn't really happen."[22]

Reading 6:9-11 through the lens of the HerStory of the #blacklivesmatter movement offers the souls a different hearing.[23] Through this lens we agree with scholars who note that the giving of white robes signified a divine recognition of the souls as victims of imperial tribulation. White robes can also be seen, however, as consolation prizes, given in place of the souls' plea for the Lamb to judge and avenge their blood (κρίνεις καὶ ἐκδικεῖς τὸ αἷμα ἡμῶν . . .) (6:10). The robes function like pacifiers that bring neither peace nor justice—kind of like a first-century version of the twenty-first-century hashtag.

The #blacklivesmatter hashtag is "a call to action for Black people after 17-year-old Trayvon Martin was post-humously [*sic*] placed on trial for his own murder and the killer, George Zimmerman, was not held accountable for the crime he committed."[24] It is a sign that signifies victims of state-sanctioned slaughters by police officers unjustly enforcing the pax Americana, civilians with all-too-easy access to guns, and the violent deaths of women and people of color, including trans persons, immigrants, and other precariously marginalized people. The cry that #blacklivesmatter is intoned with a loud voice for Trayvon Martin, and its harmonics make the lives of Emmet Till, Eleanor Bumpers, Fred Hampton, and Amadou Diallo, along with those of other unknown and unnamed victims, audible.

The roll of those yet to be killed is not complete, so #blacklivesmatter becomes: #EricGarner, #TamirRice, #JordanDavis, #PhilandoCastile, #FreddieGray, #AltonSterling, and at the time of this writing, #Emantic(EJ)BradfordJr.[25] #Sayhername becomes: #SandraBland,

22. See, for example, Leonard L. Thompson, *The Book of Revelation: Apocalypse and Empire* (New York: Oxford University Press, 1990).

23. See https://blacklivesmatter.com/herstory/. For more about the Black Lives Matter movement, see Patrisse Khan-Cullors and Asha Bandele, *When They Call You a Terrorist: A Black Lives Matter Memoir* (New York: St. Martin's Press, 2018); Keeanga-Yamahtta Taylor, *From #Blacklivesmatter to Black Liberation* (Chicago: Haymarket Books, 2016); Kelly Brown Douglas, *Stand Your Ground: Black Bodies and the Justice of God* (Maryknoll, NY: Orbis Books, 2015).

24. https://blacklivesmatter.com/herstory/.

25. Mihir Zaveri, "Black Man Killed by Officer in Alabama Mall Shooting Was Not the Gunman, Police Now Say," *The New York Times*, November 24, 2018, https://www.nytimes.com/2018/11/24/us/alabama-mall-shooting.html.

#RekiaBoyd, #ShantelDavis, #TanishaAnderson, #BettieJones, #TieraThomas, and #KorrynGaines.[26] White/hashtag robes are also given to the #CharlestonNine of Mother Emanuel A.M.E. Church in Charleston, South Carolina, who invited a man with a gun to join their Bible study, and to the shooting victims of #PulseNightclub in Orlando, Florida, who were partying on a random "Latin night." Their deaths haunt us with a historical-future realization that these events could take place on any ordinary day, in any church/synagogue/school, or at any nightclub across the country (as subsequent deaths and mass shootings continue to demonstrate). Each of these fallen lives are themselves a call for the churches that are at Ferguson, Detroit, Oakland, the Bronx, Charleston, Baltimore, Baton Rouge, and all Others who have an ear to hear what the Spirit is saying to us in this context. Instead of resting until the number of those who are to be slaughtered is complete, "we name the dead in the name of the living."[27]

The act of opening the fifth seal allowed the souls to be heard, very much like we are now aware of the cries of slaughtered African Americans and other precariously marginalized people not truly heard until the death of Trayvon Martin. It is arguable if their voices are being heard today, particularly the voices of trans persons of color. They were, however, each given a hashtag. By the time this commentary is published more hashtags will be given and the souls, frozen in their historical future, will still be crying out, "How long?"

Eric Thomas

The Great Day of Wrath (6:12-17)

The opening of the sixth seal draws John's attention back to the earth, which he and his audiences still view from a cosmic perspective. The unsealing brings cataclysmic events associated with the end of time in other ancient texts—earthquake, the sun turning black, the moon becoming like blood, and stars falling from the sky (e.g., Joel 2:31; Mark 13:24-25). Adding to the drama of these events, the sky vanishes as it rolls up like

26. Kate Abbey-Lambertz, "These 15 Black Women Were Killed during Police Encounters: Their Lives Matter, Too," *Huffington Post*, February 13, 2015, https://www.huffingtonpost.com/2015/02/13/black-womens-lives-matter-police-shootings_n_6644276.html.

27. Christopher J. Lebron, *The Making of Black Lives Matter: A Brief History of an Idea* (New York: Oxford University Press, 2017), ix.

¹²When he opened the sixth seal, I looked, and there came a great earthquake; the sun became black as sackcloth, the full moon became like blood, ¹³and the stars of the sky fell to the earth as the fig tree drops its winter fruit when shaken by a gale. ¹⁴The sky vanished like a scroll rolling itself up, and every mountain and island was removed from its place. ¹⁵Then the kings of the earth and the magnates and the generals and the rich and the powerful, and everyone, slave and free, hid in the caves and among the rocks of the mountains, ¹⁶calling to the mountains and rocks, "Fall on us and hide us from the face of the one seated on the throne and from the wrath of the Lamb; ¹⁷for the great day of their wrath has come, and who is able to stand?"

a scroll. The imagery, beautiful and terrifying, is particularly striking as this "scroll" closes just as the seals on the heavenly scroll are almost all open. Along with the sky rolling up, *every* mountain and island is unmoored (v. 14). Everything is out of place. The sixth seal threatens to turn creation back to the original watery void of Genesis 1:1, although the rainbow around the throne (Rev 4:3) reminds hearers of God's promise not again to destroy the world by flood (Gen 9:14-15).

The seal ends with John glimpsing the human response to these apocalyptic events. All the people of earth cry out for a strange kind of mercy: asking the mountains and rocks to fall on them so that they are hidden "from the face of the one seated on the throne and from the wrath of the Lamb" (v. 16). The listing of various classes and statuses of people who cry out—"the magnates and the generals and the rich and the powerful, and everyone, slave and free"—ensures that John's audiences know the breadth of the seal's impact. The notable exclusion of the poor from the list of people impacted may make this apocalyptic destruction appear as a type of equalizing event, uplifting the poor and bringing down the rich (cf. Luke 1:52-53). As many of us know firsthand or have seen through the media, however, cataclysmic events rarely, if ever, impact humans equally or bring justice. When disaster strikes, kings, magnates, and the free have a distinct advantage over the enslaved, impoverished, and otherwise disempowered. Gender, race, class, ability, and age all contribute to making a person more or less vulnerable in the face of a disaster and more or less equipped to rebuild after disaster strikes. While everyone may cry out for the mountains to hide them, some have more to fear.

The people experiencing the sixth seal interpret their experience as "the great day of their [God and the Lamb] wrath" and consequently ask, "who is able to stand?" (v. 17). Other biblical texts similarly anticipate this day, when God's judgment is revealed, and humans cry out in distress. Joel queries, "Truly the day of the Lord is great; terrible indeed—who can endure it?" (2:11), and Nahum asks, "Who can stand before his indignation? Who can endure the heat of his anger? His wrath is poured out like fire, and by him the rocks are broken in pieces" (1:6). Like their prophetic predecessors, the people on the earth respond to calamity by holding God and the Lamb accountable through their questioning. We believe these are good models for feminist engagement with Revelation and the Bible more generally.

Revelation 7

Who Can Stand?

Who can stand? At first, it seems that the question asked at the conclusion of the sixth seal will remain unanswered (6:17). Audience members are left wondering whether the Lamb will open the seventh seal as several angels, four at the corners of the earth and one ascending from the sun, draw his attention (7:2). Soon we realize things have paused so that the question can be answered in a fashion characteristic of Revelation with both oral and visual responses. John *hears* 144,000 from the twelve tribes of Israel and then *sees* that this group is an innumerable multitude standing before the throne and before the Lamb. As with the image of the Lamb "standing as if it had been slaughtered" (5:6), the identity of the 144,000 is characterized by paradox—they are both identifiable and innumerable, from the people of Israel and from every nation, tribes, peoples, and languages. Even though John's vision of this group is layered, the image of the faithful as enslaved, an idea that challenges assumptions about power in the ancient world, is one that modern readers must interrogate. This imagery flows throughout Revelation, but it is most visible here as the 144,000 receive seals bearing the name of the master (7:3).

TRANSLATION MATTERS: δοῦλος

The term δοῦλος, which appears throughout Revelation, is translated by the NRSV in two different ways: "slave" and "servant." When John uses the term to refer to enslaved people in contrast to those who are free, the NRSV translates δοῦλος as "slave" (6:15; 13:16; 19:18); however, when John uses δοῦλος to characterize those who are faithful to God, the NRSV reads "servant" (1:1; 2:20; 7:3; 10:18; 15:3; 19:2, 5; 22:3, 6). This second usage frequently occurs since John presents δοῦλος as a metaphorical identity his hearers should adopt in relation to God. In Revelation 7 and 14, John elaborates on the metaphor of the faithful as enslaved persons by encouraging his audience members to see themselves as "owned" by God (14:4), even to the point of having God's name stamped on their foreheads (7:3; 14:1). Likewise, John characterizes himself as a slave, a conduit through which God's word is revealed (1:1).

Even though the NRSV's use of "servant" and "slave" helps readers distinguish between metaphorical and literal uses of δοῦλος, "servant" is a problematic euphemism. By possibly alluding to someone who might be employed and not enslaved or someone who is allowed to maintain a sense of personhood, "servant" sidesteps the fact that Revelation assumes the presence of systems of enslavement that were oppressive and diminished human lives. Given this, the use of servant "minimizes," according to womanist biblical scholar Clarice J. Martin, "the full psychological weight of the institution of slavery itself."[1] Moreover, the euphemism occurs almost exclusively in translations of the Bible and not in translations of other ancient Greek writings, indicating it is a tactic for distancing the Bible and Christianity from the practice of enslaving humans.[2] Ostensibly, readers can ignore Christianity's culpability if texts like Revelation do not appear to refer to enslavement. In fact, very little has been written about enslavement in Revelation.[3]

In addition, the use of "servant" in place of "slave" for δοῦλος perpetuates a common myth that enslavement in the ancient world was in some ways less oppressive than more modern forms of the institution, namely, slavery in the pre–Civil War United States. This misconception comes up frequently in my classes, as students repeat what elders, who are reluctant or unwilling to address the New Testament's role in perpetuating enslavement, teach them. While there are differences between the ancient Mediterranean and modern American systems of enslavement, in both contexts enslaved humans experienced coercion

---

1. Clarice J. Martin, "Womanist Interpretations of the New Testament: The Quest for Holistic and Inclusive Translation and Interpretation," *JFSR* 6 (1990): 46.

2. Martin, "Womanist Interpretations of the New Testament," 45.

3. Notable exceptions focus on Rev 18:3. See Craig R. Koester, "Roman Slave Trade and the Critique of Babylon in Revelation 18," *CBQ* 70 (2008): 766–86; Murray Vasser, "Bodies and Souls: The Case for Reading Revelation 18.13 as a Critique of the Slave Trade," *NTS* 64 (2018): 397–409.

and a kind of "social death."[4] Natal connections, including connections to lands and families of origin, were erased, ensuring that the enslaved were a "social nonperson."[5] Translating δοῦλος in a way that clouds this reality functions as a double erasure of ancient slaves.

Furthermore, many contemporary scholars addressing issues around slavery advocate using "enslaved" when talking about individuals who have been born or taken into bondage. The importance of this shift in language is explained thoughtfully by the US National Park Service: " 'Enslaved' . . . demonstrates the condition of the individual within the class and economic system of the dominant society, and less of an internalized, or intellectual condition."[6] Using "enslaved" acknowledges that a complex system contributes to the enslavement of a person, and it is not something innate or a status one chooses. The language signals that humans enslave other humans.

Sealing the Faithful (7:1-3)

Four powerful angels stand at the corners of the earth, preventing the winds from blowing over its surface. The different "moods" exhibited by winds easily led ancient poets and authors to personify winds and associate them with divine figures active in the heavens. In Greek and Roman myth, breezes were depicted as nymphs with billowing capes, and intense winds were gods, like Boreas, whom sailors needed to appease for safe passage across the ocean.[7] Communities used ritual practices to harness the power of the wind in war and erected shrines to thank the winds for their benevolence.[8] The famous Roman general Scipio even dedicated a temple to the winds after his fleet survived a

4. Orlando Patterson, *Slavery and Social Death* (Cambridge, MA: Harvard University Press, 1982), 5.

5. Patterson, *Slavery and Social Death*, 5.

6. National Park Service, "Language of Slavery—Underground Railroad (U.S. National Park Service)," October 13, 2021, https://www.nps.gov/subjects/underground railroad/language-of-slavery.htm. The use of "enslaved" is becoming the scholarly norm. See, for example, Bernadette J. Brooten, "Introduction," in *Beyond Slavery: Overcoming Its Religious and Sexual Legacies*, ed. Bernadette J. Brooten with Jacqueline L. Hazelton (New York: Palgrave Macmillan, 2010), 1–29.

7. Barbette Stanley Spaeth, "The Goddess Ceres in the *Ara Pacis Augustae* and the Carthage Relief," *AJA* 98 (1994): 77; Sandra Blakely, "Maritime Risk and Ritual Responses: Sailing with the Gods in the Ancient Mediterranean," in *The Sea in History—The Ancient World*, ed. Philip de Souza, Pascal Arnaud, and Christian Buchet (Suffolk: Boydell and Brewer, 2017), 365.

8. Blakely, "Maritime Risk and Ritual Responses," 368–69.

Rev 7:1-3

7:1After this I saw four angels standing at the four corners of the earth, holding back the four winds of the earth so that no wind could blow on earth or sea or against any tree. 2I saw another angel ascending from the rising of the sun, having the seal of the living God, and he called with a loud voice to the four angels who had been given power to damage earth and sea, 3saying, "Do not damage the earth or the sea or the trees, until we have marked the servants of our God with a seal on their foreheads."

storm when defeating Carthage in Corsica in 259 BCE (Ovid, *Fasti* 6.191-95). The God of Israel, like Canaanite deities, was known for using the wind as a tool, like when he "hurled a great wind upon the sea" when Jonah tried to flee from his presence (Jonah 1:1-4; see also Jer 49:36).

In earlier biblical texts, the *four* winds, which represent the cardinal points of a compass, do God's bidding and are crucial in gathering God's people at the end of time (e.g., Dan 7:2; 8:8; 11:4; Zech 2:6; 6:5). For example, in Ezekiel's final vision, the four winds "breathe" on the dry bones reconstituting all of Israel (Ezek 37:9). Similarly, in the gospel traditions, the four winds signify places from which the elect will be gathered (Mark 13:27; Matt 24:31). By depicting the angels holding back these winds, John suggests that the final gathering is coming but that there is still time to join the ranks of the faithful. The act creates a literal calm but simultaneously generates a sense of anxiety. This is a moment of divine restraint, although audience members may feel nervous about how long this will last. Ascending from the rising sun, a poetic way of referencing the east, a fifth angel commands the others to continue holding back the winds, "Do not damage the earth or the sea or the trees" (v. 3).

Some interpreters read this command as a divine message of ecological concern. T-shirts, cards, and other items emblazoned with the King James Version of this verse, "Hurt not the earth, neither the seas nor the trees," are marketed online and in Christian bookstores to ecologically minded believers. A popular rendition by the artist Mary Engelbreit depicts a girl wearing an old-fashioned dress, a black bow in her blonde hair, holding a globe of the earth close to her heart. Next to her in a stylized font is the text of Revelation 7:3.9 The message is clear, *love* the earth and

---

9. Mary Engelbreit, *Hurt Not the Earth*, n.d., illustration, https://www.maryengelbreit.com/products/hurt-not-the-earth-fine-print.

do not harm it. Revelation's relationship to the environment is complicated, however, despite this easily excisable bit. Events directed by the heavenly throne room lead to disastrous environmental consequences, including the sea becoming blood (8:3; 16:3) and a portion of the sun and stars darkening (8:12). Ultimately, John envisions a healed natural world (22:2), but not before it is destroyed.

The angel offers the reason for the earth's reprieve, explaining that "we," presumably God's angels, mark "the servants [slaves] of our God with a seal on their foreheads" (v. 3). The image of a divinely commissioned figure marking the foreheads of God's followers appears in Ezekiel as well. All those without the mark or sign (σημεῖον in the LXX) are "cut down" (Ezek 9:3-6). This connection implies that sealing here provides divine protection, an idea that appeals to those who count themselves among the faithful. Charles Johnson and the Revivers, a southern gospel band from the 1980s, sang assuredly, "I know I've been sealed / To the day of redemption / Soon Jesus will come / And he'll take me away."[10] Being sealed can offer a much-needed sense of comfort or confidence. In some parts of Revelation, the benefits of being sealed are apparent, like when scorpions from the abyss are allowed to torture the unsealed but not the sealed (9:4).[11]

Even though the assurance of protection that comes with being sealed can be necessary at times, the connection between the two feeds into a perception that the people of God do not or should not experience abuse, violence, oppression, or disaster, but that is not the case. Bad things *do* happen to "good" people, and experiencing hardship does not point to a person's lack of faith or moral failure. In Revelation, quite the opposite is true, as the faithful experience abuse and death because of their faithfulness. As the Seer reported from the throne room after the opening of the sixth seal, the faithful can "look forward to" being slaughtered and joining those already under the heavenly altar (6:9-11). As we know from the experience of Christians across time and the globe, the "seal" of Christianity does not mean one is immune to oppression, violence, and abuse.

10. Charles Johnson, Darrell Luster, and Ricky Luster, "I Know I've Been Sealed," *There Is a Guarantee in Jesus* (Gloryland Records, 1986).

11. Elisabeth Schüssler Fiorenza, *Revelation: Vision of a Just World* (Minneapolis: Fortress, 1991), 66.

Early Christians used the language of "sealing" to describe baptism.[12] While John does not explicitly reference baptism here or elsewhere in Revelation, thinking about this perspective on sealing is instructive. In the popular second-century text *The Shepherd of Hermas*, the water of baptism is described as a seal that protects the bearer from death (Herm. *Sim.* 9.16.4). Likewise, in an early Christian story, an unmarried girl named Thecla asks Paul for the seal to be protected from temptation. Since Paul makes her wait, Thecla takes matters into her own hands and baptizes herself by jumping into a pit of water as she is about to face the beasts in the arena (*Acts of Paul and Thecla* 25, 34). Even though she has the seal, there are still beasts and torture for her to face. The water of baptism does not wash away hardship; instead, the seal empowers Thecla as she faces the torments before her. Similarly, the seal about to be applied to the foreheads of God's people can be read as a way of preparing them for the struggle John believes they will face.

John's description of an angel carrying a seal or signet ring (the word σφραγίς can mean both) brings to mind the idea of God claiming or marking ownership. A seal is, quite literally, a physical manifestation of a king's authority (e.g., Esther 8:8) and a tool for delineating what belongs to him. Upon hearing about the presence of an angel carrying God's seal (v. 2), which happens before the act of sealing is mentioned, John's audience members must realize that something, or in this case someone, will be marked as belonging to God.[13] Thus, when the angel wielding the seal commands the other angels not to damage the earth, sea, or trees "until we have marked the servants [lit. "slaves"] of our God with a seal on their foreheads," it becomes clear that these people are being marked as God's property. As the author of 2 Timothy notes, God's seal signals that, "The Lord knows those who are his" (2 Tim 2:19).[14]

Ancient enslavement often included marking the bodies of the enslaved as property. The pervasiveness of the practice made it fodder

12. Karl Olav Sandnes, "Seal and Baptism in Early Christianity," in *Ablution, Initiation, and Baptism: Late Antiquity, Early Judaism, and Early Christianity*, ed. David Hellholm et al. (Berlin: De Gruyter, 2011), 1441–81. For a modern reading of Rev 7 that approaches sealing as baptism, see Gail R. O'Day, "Revelation," in *Theological Bible Commentary*, ed. Gail R. O'Day and David L. Petersen (Louisville: Westminster John Knox, 2009), 478.

13. Peter S. Perry, "The People of God in the Book of Revelation," in *The Oxford Handbook of the Book of Revelation*, ed. Craig R. Koester (New York: Oxford University Press, 2020), 330–33.

14. The NRSV translates σφραγίς here as "inscription."

for ancient comedy. In one of his plays, Plautus depicts one enslaved person referring to another as a "man of letters" (*litteratus*), presumably alluding to his having been marked or tattooed as part of being enslaved (*Casina* 401).[15] Similarly, in *Satyricon*, Petronius describes characters trying to disguise themselves as slaves with fake branding consisting of large letters "scrawled" on their foreheads (103).[16] Less permanent forms of marking, such as placards hung around an individual's neck and collars, were employed in some contexts. Further, as Jennifer A. Glancy explains, enslaved bodies were often visually identifiable through coarse and scant clothing and the scars sustained from physical abuse.[17] Simply put, part of being enslaved included bearing on one's person signs of that status. Even though John never describes the moment of sealing these people, the marks on their foreheads, the names of God and the Lamb, will be visible when John encounters this group later in the narrative (14:1).

John is not the only biblical author who uses enslavement imagery to characterize faithful followers of God. The gospel traditions include parables in which Jesus uses the image of the enslaved person to describe the follower of God (e.g., Matt 18:23-35), and Paul uses the imagery as well, suggesting that the faithful were "bought with a price" (1 Cor 7:23; see also Romans 6:15-23). Both Paul and John use enslavement imagery to characterize their relationship with the divine (e.g., Rom 1:1; 1 Cor 3:5; Gal 1:10; Rev 1:1). (The fact that Paul and other New Testament authors suggest the enslaved should embrace and not resist their enslavement is another highly complex issue [e.g., 1 Cor 7:21 and Eph 6:5-8].) These metaphorical uses of enslavement draw on traditions from within the Hebrew Bible, including those that describe Israelite patriarchs and kings, such as Moses (e.g., 1 Chr 6:49) and David (e.g., 2 Sam 3:18; 1 Kgs 11:13), as slaves (עבד) of God.[18] More notable for understanding Revelation are prophetic depictions of Israel in terms of being enslaved by God. In Isaiah, God speaks to Israel, "You are my servant [עבד, "slave"], I have chosen you and not cast you off" (Isa 41:9; see also Isa 42:1, 19; Jer

---

15. C. P. Jones, "Stigma: Tattooing and Branding in Graeco-Roman Antiquity," *JRS* 77 (1987): 148.

16. Jennifer A. Glancy, *Slavery in Early Christianity* (Oxford: Oxford University Press, 2002), 13.

17. Glancy, *Slavery in Early Christianity*, 29.

18. Page duBois, *Slavery: Antiquity and Its Legacy* (New York: Oxford University Press, 2009), 66.

2:14).[19] The Israelites' status as God's slaves is linked to their liberation from Egypt, which is why there is a prohibition against the enslavement of other Israelites (Lev 25:38-39). They have been freed by God so that God alone is their master, albeit "a merciful and compassionate master, who will not abandon his slaves."[20]

The biblical tradition of using enslavement imagery as a positive way of characterizing the relationship between the individual and the divine differs from the common ancient trope in which the free individual resists metaphorical enslavement. For authors within Greek and Roman philosophical traditions, enslavement provided an apt tool for talking about freedom and the individual's ability to "master" the various parts of himself. Plato, for instance, warned about being enslaved by the "godless and disgusting" parts of oneself, such as greed (Plato, *Rep.* 9.590),[21] and Cicero argued that an individual could not truly be a free man if he was enslaved by passions (*Parad.* 5.33).[22] Some Jewish philosophical authors similarly deployed enslavement imagery to warn against the soul being controlled by passions and vice. In the treatise *Every Good Man Is Free*, Philo explained, "Slavery then is applied in one sense to bodies, in another to souls; bodies have men for their masters, souls their vices and passions" (3.17). In other words, just as men enslave "bodies," so vices and passions can enslave souls, which is something to avoid. These authors were, in fact, primarily concerned with *men's* freedom, a bias that appears when Cicero describes how a free man might become enslaved by a controlling woman. "Such a fellow," the statesman noted, "deserves to be called not only a slave but a very vile slave" (*Parad.* 5.36).[23] Elite male authors who had little chance of being enslaved found enslavement a useful metaphor, especially since they encouraged their peers to inhabit a metaphorical role, that of lord, which aligned with the social status of being a free man.

John's use of enslavement imagery reflects his own privileged position and assumption that Revelation's audience members are likewise free men. For the metaphor of enslavement to be rhetorically effective as a tool for shaping an audience's self-understanding, those in the audience must be free to *adopt* the identity of an enslaved person. As Elizabeth A. Castelli

19. In these instances, the NRSV translates עבד as "servant" rather than "slave."

20. Catherine Hezser, *Jewish Slavery in Antiquity* (Oxford: Oxford University Press, 2006), 328–29.

21. duBois, *Slavery*, 57.

22. duBois, *Slavery*, 63.

23. duBois, *Slavery*, 63.

notes about Paul's use of slavery imagery in Romans, the metaphorical use of enslavement is not *about* literal slavery or those who are enslaved; rather, it uses the idea of being enslaved to make a theological point.[24] In this case, John commends adopting the identity as a way of acknowledging one's relationship to God as "master." The four living creatures anticipated this by lauding the One Who Sits upon the Throne as the most powerful lord or master (κύριος) in the universe (4:11). John prompts hearers to recognize God's lordship through this imagery, lest they unwittingly find themselves enslaved by other forces, namely, the Beast (e.g., 13:16-17).

By commending the identity of enslavement, John encourages audience members to resist the Roman vision of the ideal free man who ultimately controls his own body. In the Roman context, the enslaved person completely lacked honor and had the legal status of an object. Even though enslaved people could acquire freedom and even become quite powerful once manumitted,[25] the "thingness" of the enslaved person was a defining characteristic of Roman slavery.[26] John, like some other Jewish thinkers in the first century (e.g., Philo, *Spec. Laws* 2.69, 83), will reject this depersonalization of the enslaved human in 18:13; however, adopting the metaphorical status of someone enslaved by God involves rejecting the ancient assumption that the individual should exercise complete control over himself. We can imagine that the response to this metaphor among Revelation's audience members would have varied depending on their status as free, freed, or enslaved.[27]

Unlike some other New Testament authors, John does not exhort, "slaves, obey your master" (1 Pet 2:18). Still, the metaphorical use of enslavement imagery does "depend on and ultimately reinscribe the ancient social relations of a slave system."[28] The positive use of enslavement imagery assumes familiarity with the structure of slavery and does not criticize or condemn the system. John's use of enslavement imagery, while not an explicit endorsement of the oppressive system, is a tacit acceptance. Furthermore, the authority granted to Revelation and other

24. Elizabeth A. Castelli, "Romans," in *Searching the Scriptures: A Feminist Commentary*, ed. Elisabeth Schüssler Fiorenza with Ann Brock and Shelly Matthews (New York: Crossroad, 1994), 294; Glancy, *Slavery in Early Christianity*, 98.

25. Pedro López Barja de Quiroga, "Freedmen Social Mobility in Roman Italy," *Historia: Zeitschrift Für Alte Geschichte* 44 (1995): 328.

26. Patterson, *Slavery and Social Death*, 32.

27. Castelli, "Romans," 294.

28. Glancy, *Slavery in Early Christianity*, 98.

biblical texts that employ this imagery preserves ancient hierarchies of domination.[29] Even though it may not have been John's intention, his writing contributes to the normalization of enslavement in Christian contexts. Recognizing this demands that Christians, especially White Christians whose predecessors have benefitted from systems of slavery, work toward a real undoing of harm. This undoing includes fighting for reparations for the descendants of enslaved people and for an overhaul of a justice system that is far from just.

Additionally, interpreters of Revelation's enslavement imagery must recognize the continued reality of enslavement and the persistence of human trafficking. Even though interpreters in the twenty-first century typically envision enslavement as a thing of the past, the International Labour Organization estimates that as many as 21 million people today may be victims of forced labor, most of whom are women and girls.[30] Identifying with this imagery ignores the reality of contemporary enslavement, erroneously casting slavery as an entirely symbolic identity. At the same time, taking this imagery seriously can be a tool for highlighting our solidarity with those who experience being trafficked and enslaved. As Alec Hill has noted, biblical enslavement imagery can be a way of reminding ourselves that we, those who come to the text with social privilege, are not the center of the universe, that we are not God, and that we need to care for others.[31]

Hearing the Number of Those Sealed (7:4-8)

Even though Revelation's audiences never witness the angel actively sealing the slaves of God, they hear with John the number of those sealed—144,000 made up of twelve thousand "out of every tribe of the people [υἱοί, lit. sons] of Israel" (v. 4). The naming of each group and their numbering happens in a deliberate manner: "From the tribe of Judah twelve thousand sealed, from the tribe of Reuben twelve thousand, from the tribe of Gad twelve thousand," and so on (vv. 5-8). This

29. Ellen M. Barry, "From Plantations to Prisons: African American Women Prisoners in the United States," in *Beyond Slavery: Overcoming Its Religious and Sexual Legacies*, ed. Bernadette J. Brooten with Jacqueline L. Hazelton (New York: Palgrave Macmillan, 2010), 75–88.

30. See International Labour Organization, https://www.ilo.org/global/topics/forced -labour/lang--en/index.htm.

31. Alec Hill, "The Most Troubling Parable: Why Does Jesus Say We Are Like Slaves?," *Christianity Today* 58 (2014): 76–79.

Rev 7:4-8

⁴And I heard the number of those who were sealed, one hundred forty-four thousand, sealed out of every tribe of the people of Israel:

⁵From the tribe of Judah twelve thousand sealed,

from the tribe of Reuben twelve thousand,

from the tribe of Gad twelve thousand,

⁶from the tribe of Asher twelve thousand,

from the tribe of Naphtali twelve thousand,

from the tribe of Manasseh twelve thousand,

⁷from the tribe of Simeon twelve thousand,

from the tribe of Levi twelve thousand,

from the tribe of Issachar twelve thousand,

⁸from the tribe of Zebulun twelve thousand,

from the tribe of Joseph twelve thousand,

from the tribe of Benjamin twelve thousand sealed.

way of counting the 144,000 in groups resembles Jewish traditions that avoid actual counting of the people who are like the sands of the sea and too numerous to count or be numbered (Hos 1:10). Given this context, the "counting" here is not John limiting the faithful to a paltry 144,000. Instead, the use of twelve and one thousand, both of which suggest wholeness, points to the completeness of this group. In spite of this, Revelation's twelve tribes do not align neatly with listings of the tribes found in earlier Scripture (e.g., Gen 35:23-26; Exod 1:2-4; Num 1:5-15). John begins with the tribe of Judah rather than Reuben, and he omits the tribe of Dan but includes Manasseh. Judah's preeminent placement recollects the Lion of Judah in Revelation 5:5. John may have omitted Dan because the tribe was sometimes associated with worshiping "idols" (Judg 18; 1 Kgs 12:25-33).[32] More important, this imagery describes the act of making whole what had long been scattered and dispersed. Like other authors of both biblical and extrabiblical texts, John envisions the reunion of the twelve tribes of Israel as an eschatological hope (e.g., Isa 11:11-16; 27:12-13; Ezek 37:15-28; 2 Bar 78; 4 Ezra 13:40-47).[33] Other New Testament writings also anticipate a unified Israel; for example, the

32. Brian K. Blount, *Revelation: A Commentary* (Louisville: Westminster John Knox, 2009), 147–48.

33. Richard Bauckham, "The Book of Revelation as a Christian War Scroll," *Neot* 22 (1988): 17–40.

Gospel of Matthew depicts Jesus telling the twelve apostles that they will sit upon thrones at "the renewal of all things . . . judging the twelve tribes of Israel" (19:28; cf. Luke 22:30). In Revelation, the twelve tribes are not brought together to be judged, as in Matthew; rather, they come together as those protected by and in service to God. Eventually, they will constitute the New Jerusalem, alongside the apostles, and not be subject to them (21:12-14).

For Jews living at Qumran, a community destroyed by the Romans during the first Judean war with Rome (66–73 CE), this regathering of the twelve tribes would happen as part of an end-time battle between "sons of light" and "sons of darkness" (1QM 3:14; 5:1-2). A common way of reading Revelation's numbering of the 144,000 draws on the Qumran tradition, suggesting it offers an example of military census-taking.[34] The roll call functions as an assessment of Israel's military preparedness for a holy war (Num 1:20-46). This reading complements John's earlier call for the faithful to be victors or conquerors, although he offers no discussion of the 144,000 being trained in the same way that he depicted the need to endure and become victors in Revelation 2–3. Moreover, John does not forecast human participation in battle, only the armies of heaven (19:14).

Even though Revelation's image of the 144,000 draws on Jewish depictions of a reconstituted Israel, Christian readers have long read the image as referring to followers of Jesus more generally, sometimes to the exclusion of the Jewish people. If Christian interpreters do take seriously the group's connection to Israel, the group is read as comprised of Jewish converts to Christianity (e.g., Irenaeus, *Haer.* 5.30.2). The authors of the popular Left Behind series of books go one step further in "Christianizing" this Jewish group, depicting the 144,000 as both converts *and* evangelists who explain how Scripture points to the coming reign of Christ.[35] More common are Christian groups reading themselves as the 144,000. Jehovah's Witnesses believe the 144,000 constitute a select group of Witnesses co-ruling in heaven with Jesus.[36] Latter-day Saints similarly see the 144,000 as referring to an elite group of the LDS priesthood, although they do not necessarily read the number literally. The fact that Christian sects identify so closely with this image points to the tendency among Christians in general toward supersessionism. Supersessionism is Christian coloniza-

34. Bauckham, "Revelation as a Christian War Scroll," 22.

35. Tim LaHaye and Jerry B. Jenkins, *Apollyon: The Destroyer Is Unleashed* (Wheaton, IL: Tyndale, 2000), 47–49.

36. Carolyn R. Wah, "An Introduction to Research and Analysis of Jehovah's Witnesses: A View from the Watchtower," *RRelRes* 43 (2001): 161–74.

tion of Jewish identity and tradition, a type of cultural appropriation and erasure of a distinctive Jewish identity. Unfortunately, John's vision of the faithful easily feeds this type of reading, as we will see below.

Seeing the Innumerable Crowd (7:9-17)

Just as John *hears* about the Lion of the tribe Judah in 5:5 and then *sees* the slaughtered Lamb in 5:6, John *hears* the number of the 144,000 in 7:4-8 and then *sees* in 7:9 something that complicates what he has heard. The NRSV again downplays the visual language, but the Greek literally translates as "After these things I looked, and Look! a great multitude" (v. 9). John's audiences see with him the "great multitude that no one could count." In contrast to the 144,000, which is whole but bounded, the image of the great multitude is expansive, including people "from every nation, from all tribes and peoples and languages." John uses a variety of similar phrases elsewhere (10:11; 11:9; 13:7; cf. 17:15), but this is one of the few instances where the list begins with the word "nation" (ἔθνος; cf. 14:6). Because "nations" can refer specifically to gentiles (11:2), its place at the beginning of this list points to the inclusion of gentiles within this vision of the faithful. Just as the Lion and the Lamb metaphorically represent the risen Christ, the 144,000 and the innumerable multitude offer two pictures of those who stand before God's throne. When Christian readers approach this, the tendency is to highlight the 144,000 being swallowed up by the diverse multitude. In fact, my own past reading of this imagery has verged on this kind of effacing of the 144,000's Jewish identity.[37]

Even though the 144,000 and the multitude are linked through John's act of hearing and seeing, the former incorporates the latter and not vice versa.[38] The 144,000 may seem like a finite entity, but its wholeness allows for the inclusion of the innumerable crowd. John makes this clear in 14:1, when those standing before the throne, like the multitude here, are described as the 144,000 and *not* as the "great multitude that no one could count" (7:9). This is heavenly math, which does not abide the limits of earthly math. Similarly, the twelve tribes of Israel, along with the twelve apostles (the number suggesting that the apostles are modeled on the tribes of Israel), will comprise the very structure of the New Jerusalem when it appears at the end of the narrative (21:21). This idea

---

37. Lynn R. Huber, *Thinking and Seeing with Women in Revelation*, LNTS 475 (London: Bloomsbury, 2013), 44.

38. Sarah Emanuel, *Humor, Resistance, and Jewish Cultural Persistence in the Book of Revelation: Roasting Rome* (Cambridge: Cambridge University Press, 2020), 23–24.

Rev 7:9-17

⁹After this I looked, and there was a great multitude that no one could count, from every nation, from all tribes and peoples and languages, standing before the throne and before the Lamb, robed in white, with palm branches in their hands. ¹⁰They cried out in a loud voice, saying,

> "Salvation belongs to our God
> who is seated on the
> throne, and to the Lamb!"

¹¹And all the angels stood around the throne and around the elders and the four living creatures, and they fell on their faces before the throne and worshiped God, ¹²singing,

> "Amen! Blessing and glory and
> wisdom
> and thanksgiving and honor
> and power and might
> be to our God forever and ever!
> Amen."

¹³Then one of the elders addressed me, saying, "Who are these, robed in white, and where have they come from?" ¹⁴I said to him, "Sir, you are the

is somewhat akin to Paul's description in Romans of the relationship between Jewish and gentile Jesus followers. There, the Jews are likened to a tree on which gentile branches are grafted. This is not a cause for gentile boasting, as they are being supported by the root that is Judaism. Instead, gentiles are called to stand in awe of the tree and its strength (Rom 11:17-20). This vision aligns with other Jewish eschatological traditions, including Isaiah's depiction of Israel as "a light to the nations" (Isa 42:6; 49:6). Israel serves as a beacon drawing people of the nations to God. John's final description of the New Jerusalem will reaffirm this idea by depicting the "nations" bringing glory and honor into the heavenly city (21:12, 14). For John, the heavenly Jerusalem brings together Israel and those faithful to the Lamb (21:27). As Sarah Emanuel observes, the inclusion of gentiles in Revelation's New Jerusalem is a product of the book's Jewishness.[39]

In August 2017, in Charlottesville, Virginia, about three hours from where I work, Neo-Nazis and other far-right adherents marched through town carrying ornamental torches and flags decorated with symbols of White supremacy. The event, a rally called "Unite the Right," was partly a reaction to calls to remove a statue of Confederate General Robert E. Lee (since taken down). Among the most audible rallying cries heard that night was "Jews will not replace us." This antisemitic sentiment has a long history and reflects the White supremacist belief that Jews

---

39. Emanuel, *Humor, Resistance, and Jewish Cultural Persistence*, 24.

one that knows." Then he said to me,
"These are they who have come out
of the great ordeal; they have washed
their robes and made them white in the
blood of the Lamb.
   [15]For this reason they are before
      the throne of God,
   and worship him day and night
      within his temple,
   and the one who is seated on
      the throne will shelter
      them.

[16]They will hunger no more, and
   thirst no more;
   the sun will not strike them,
   nor any scorching heat;
[17]for the Lamb at the center of
   the throne will be their
   shepherd,
   and he will guide them to
      springs of the water of
      life,
   and God will wipe away every
      tear from their eyes."

are part of an "organized plan to wreak havoc on 'White Christian' civilization in Europe and North America by flooding these continents with non-Christians and people of color."[40] Accusing a historically oppressed minority group of such nefarious plans is absurd and evil. This sort of thinking foments hate and violent acts, such as the shootings at the Tree of Life Synagogue outside Pittsburgh, Pennsylvania; the Chabad Center in San Diego, California; and a synagogue in Halle, Germany.[41] The destructive intentions clearly reside with White supremacists and not with those who find themselves their targets.

Even though Revelation was written by a Jewish author who presented himself as faithful to the God of Israel and as an heir to the prophets, read in predominantly Christian contexts, its images are easily distorted to support supersessionist thinking, the erroneous notion that Christianity replaces and nullifies Judaism. The Revised Common Lectionary, used by numerous mainline Christian churches, even skips 7:1-8, the sealing of the 144,000 from the twelve tribes of Israel, including only the image of the multi-ethnic, multi-lingual multitude in vv. 9-17, erasing the image of a complete Israel from the text as read in the Christian Church. As Greg Carey points out, this move may reflect John's belief that "those who follow the Lamb constitute the New Israel," an eschatological or future

40. Roberta Kaplan and Deborah Lipstadt, "Three Years Later, Charlottesville's Legacy of Neo-Nazi Hate Still Festers," CNN, August 12, 2020, https://www.cnn .com/2020/08/11/opinions/charlottesville-three-years-later-hate-festers-lipstadt -kaplan/index.html.
41. Kaplan and Lipstadt, "Three Years Later."

Israel; however, John makes this move from within Judaism. As Carey notes, this does not mitigate the "anti-Jewish potential" of this passage, making it essential that "Christians confess their place in the trajectory of God's covenant with Israel."[42]

In Charlottesville, after the rally of White supremacists, a group of Christian clergy, including my friend and colleague Jeffrey C. Pugh, embodied their connection to the Jewish people and others. Joining arms with Jews, Muslims, Buddhists, and atheists, they stood and sang "This Little Light of Mine" to drown out the Neo-Nazi chants. Reflecting on the experience, Pugh describes those linking arms as a "raggedy band."[43] Even though Pugh claims he's "not a hero, not a brave person,"[44] at that moment, he was part of a new multitude standing alongside the 144,000. This twenty-first-century multitude embraces the belief that being from "every nation, from all tribes and peoples and languages" includes standing in solidarity with people of different religious traditions, including those who do not recognize the Lamb as *the* one upon the throne. The willingness to confront those who use Christian Scripture to justify narratives of anti-Judaism as well as Islamophobia and other forms of religious and ethnic hate is to live as part of the innumerable multitude.

A brief exchange between one of the elders and John in 7:13 underscores the importance of the multitude's identity. The elder asks John about those dressed in white, only to have John remind the elder, whom John addresses as "my lord" (κύριος) or "sir" (so NRSV), that he is probably better suited to answer questions about the group (v. 13). This quick conversation provides an opportunity for John and his audiences to learn about the identity of the crowd in tandem and effectively begins to destabilize the authority of John as a Seer,[45] a theme that appears again in Revelation 10.

The description of the great multitude as those "standing before the throne and before the Lamb, robed in white, with palm branches in their hands" (v. 9b) echoes the paradoxical identity of the Lamb, who

---

42. Greg Carey, "Revelation 7:9-17" in *Feasting on the Word: Year C; Preaching the Revised Common Lectionary*, ed. David L. Bartlett and Barbara Brown Taylor, vol. 2 (Louisville: Westminster John Knox, 2009), 439–43.

43. Jeffrey C. Pugh, "Fear on Display in Charlottesville," *Roanoke Times*, August 16, 2017, https://roanoke.com/opinion/commentary/pugh-fear-on-display-in -charlottesville/article_4e8adc62-2a5d-54a2-a65d-cf1bc9dec6c0.html.

44. Pugh, "Fear on Display."

45. Peter S. Perry, *The Rhetoric of Digressions: Revelation 7:1-17 and 10:1–11:13 and Ancient Communication*, WUNT 2.268 (Tübingen: Mohr Siebeck, 2009), 217.

was both victim and victor.[46] Those characterized as enslaved in verse 3 and then sealed wear the white promised to the faithful in Sardis who had been found worthy (3:4). They appear as victors, holding palm branches that were traditional prizes given out in athletic competitions and subsequently used to symbolize victory on tombs and honorific statues.[47] While seemingly contradictory, the blending of imagery related to enslavement and athletic victory has an ancient parallel in the popular image of the gladiator. Even though gladiators were often enslaved, a status considered lacking in honor, their willingness to face death head-on meant that many were lauded as heroic.[48] The early Christian writer Tertullian (d. ca. 220 CE), who was perturbed by the spectacle of gladiatorial games, commented on the irony, noting that gladiators suffered ignominy and loss of rights while they were simultaneously esteemed and "deemed worthy of merit" (*Spect.* 22).[49] The gladiator, as historian Carlin Barton explains, could even be deployed as a "paradigm of the 'good man,' the soldier/philosopher who through his consistent and unflinching fierceness in the face of death and his complete collusion (and even pleasure) in his own powerlessness couples his slavery with honor."[50] The coupling of "unflinching fierceness" with powerlessness could easily describe Revelation's slaughtered Lamb (5:5-6) and those depicted here before the throne and the Lamb.

Like the ancient gladiator, those standing before the Lamb are both dishonored and honored in the face of a violent death, which Revelation describes as the "great ordeal" (v. 14). This language harks back to John's description of the persecution he shares with his audiences (1:9). Both "ordeal" and "persecution" translate the same Greek term (θλῖψις), which conveys the sense of being afflicted by something external (see "Translation Matters: θλῖψις"). The description of the "great ordeal" implies that Revelation's audience members see themselves or their future identity in the image of the multitude. John encourages them to see themselves as going through this ordeal (1:9). Convinced that his audiences are

46. Robyn Whitaker, "Victim to Victor: The Appeal of Apocalyptic Hope," *Religions* 11 (September 2020): 1–11.

47. Zahra Newby, *Greek Athletics in the Roman World: Victory and Virtue* (Oxford: Oxford University Press, 2005), 172.

48. Carlin A. Barton, *The Sorrows of the Ancient Romans: The Gladiator and the Monster* (Princeton: Princeton University Press, 2020), 11–15.

49. Barton, *Sorrows of the Ancient Romans*, 12.

50. Barton, *Sorrows of the Ancient Romans*, 18.

currently experiencing or will soon experience oppression and even violent death, John offers this paradoxical model of being faithful. While enslaved, they will go through the great ordeal and come through standing, like the Lamb. The elder's description of the crowd's garments as having been washed and made white in the "blood of the Lamb" points to the strange nature of their experience (v. 14), since a thing that stains, blood, washes their garments and makes them clean. The blood of a violent death might bring shame, but the Lamb's own death transforms that dishonor into honor or victory. In fact, the gladiator's paradoxical kind of honor continued to provide a way of thinking about Christian identity as martyrdom became an even more real possibility.[51]

Despite experiencing the great ordeal, the multitude's primary activity, according to Revelation, is worshiping God and the Lamb (vv. 10, 15). As Peter Perry observes, this is "the first group of human beings to explicitly praise God and the Lamb."[52] They have not replaced God with the Lamb. Instead, they attribute their salvation (σωτηρία) to God and the Lamb together (v. 10). This stands in contrast to the claim made in Roman rhetoric that imperial rule, including the likes of Julius Caesar and Augustus, brings the peace and security of salvation.[53] Eventually, those who stand before the throne will become a part of a new creation, a New Jerusalem. Now, however, the members of the multitude need a space of salvation to endure until this is realized. Here, they affirm their hope in God and the Lamb's ability to create this space. The proclamation of the multitude is readily affirmed by the inhabitants of heaven with an "Amen!" and a short hymn (vv. 11-12).

The chapter ends with a short poetic section (vv. 15-17) that echoes some of the promises made to Israel in prophetic traditions (e.g., Isa 25:8), gesturing toward the benefits of the gentile multitude being included in the 144,000. The verses envision God's temple and throne room as a safe space for those who belong to God. The One Who Sits upon the Throne "shelters" (σκηνόω) the faithful, an image repeated in 21:3 when John witnesses the descent of the New Jerusalem where God "dwells" (σκηνόω) with them. The language recalls the Israelites' time in the wil-

---

51. L. Stephanie Cobb, *Dying to Be Men: Gender and Language in Early Christian Martyr Texts* (New York: Columbia University Press, 2008), 48–55.

52. Perry, *Rhetoric of Digressions*, 215.

53. Stanley E. Porter, "Paul Confronts Caesar with the Good News," in *Empire in the New Testament*, ed. Stanley E. Porter and Cynthia Long Westfall (Eugene, OR: Wipf and Stock, 2011), 171–73; Schüssler Fiorenza, *Revelation: Vision of a Just World*, 68.

derness when God's presence camped among the people in an ornate tent or tabernacle (σκηνή; Exod 25:9 LXX). It also echoes the opening chapter of the Fourth Gospel, which describes the Word becoming flesh and dwelling (σκηνόω) among humans (1:14). By dwelling alongside the divine, the multitude becomes part of the divine household or family, just like gladiators, and other enslaved people, who became part of a new family cohort (*familiae*) when separated from their natal families.[54] Even though these families might not have been chosen, members often cared for one another and even memorialized those who had "fought the good fight." In the monument for "Victor, the left-handed," for example, the gladiator's non-natal family members defend the honor of Victor physically and by giving Victor the last word: "Doom killed me, not the liar Pinnas. No longer let him boast. I had fellow gladiator, Plyneikes, who killed Pinnas and avenged me."[55] These family members had one another's backs, even after death. Likewise, the "gladiators" of Revelation are under the care of their family, headed by God and the Lamb. The latter serve together as their shepherd (another kind of master) who "will guide them to springs of the water of life, [where] God will wipe away every tear from their eyes" (7:17 cf. 21:4).

54. Christian Marek, *In the Land of a Thousand Gods: A History of Asia Minor in the Ancient World*, trans. Steven Rendall (Princeton: Princeton University Press, 2016), 504.

55. As quoted in Alison Futrell, *The Roman Games: A Sourcebook*, Blackwell Sourcebooks in Ancient History (Malden, MA: Blackwell, 2006), 149.

Revelation 8–9

Sounding the Alarm

In popular culture, "apocalypse" signals cataclysmic destruction, ecological disaster, and zombies—humans that become shells of their former selves. It is easy to see where these associations come from when we read about the trumpet blasts unleashing a series of natural disasters and violent attacks against earth's inhabitants in Revelation 8–9. The events caused by these blasts feel eerily familiar. Reading about "something like a great mountain burning with fire" (8:8) as the world experiences unprecedented wildfires can be overwhelming.[1] Likewise, hearing John's announcement that "many died from the water" (8:11) while reading headlines about inaccessible and contaminated water throughout the world, including ongoing stories about poisoned tap water in Flint,

---

1. In 2020, for example, 44.5 million acres of Australia and over 5 million acres of the west coast of the United States burned. Nick Baker, "One Year since Australia's Devastating Wildfires, Anger Grows at Climate Change 'Inaction,'" NBC News, February 4, 2021, https://www.nbcnews.com/science/environment/one-year-australia -s-devastating-wildfires-anger-grows-climate-change-n1256714; Blacki Migliozzi et al., "Record Wildfires on the West Coast Are Capping a Disastrous Decade," *The New York Times*, September 24, 2020, https://www.nytimes.com/interactive/2020/09/24 /climate/fires-worst-year-california-oregon-washington.html; see also Catherine Keller, *Facing Apocalypse: Climate, Democracy, and Other Last Chances* (Maryknoll, NY: Orbis Books, 2021), 54.

Michigan, seems too spot on.[2] Some might be tempted to avoid the real apocalypses around us by staying inside and watching apocalyptic stories on TV or at the theater; however, we do so at our peril. At the age of sixteen, Swedish activist Greta Thunberg prophetically voiced to the United Nations, "How dare you continue to look away and come here saying that you're doing enough, when the politics and solutions needed are still nowhere in sight?"[3] Similarly, even though we may want to stop our ears from the trumpet blasts or refuse to look at the things John saw, the destruction they bring is part of the message, and we simply cannot ignore them. Like John, Thunberg associates lack of response with evil, telling UN representatives that "failing to act" means "you would be evil." Thunberg, however, expresses hope in people's ability to change, adding, "And that I refuse to believe."[4] John, in contrast, seems more ambivalent about people's proclivity to repent, although he continues throughout these chapters to sound the alarm that change is necessary.

The Sound of Silence (8:1-6)

Now that John has answered the sixth seal's question of who can stand by introducing the 144,000 victors before the Lamb, the narrative circles back to the opening of the seventh seal. When the Lamb opens this final seal, the unexpected happens: The tumult of heaven, the singing and thundering and clanging of crowns, stops while silence takes over for "about half an hour." John W. Marshall describes this as "the sabbatical seal," connecting the rest that comes with this seal to the practices of observing the sabbath on the seventh day and allowing fields to lay fallow (not be cultivated) every seven years.[5] For some who experience the narrative, the silence must be a relief. Amid everything that has unfolded

2. Lucy Tompkins, "Millions More People Got Access to Water: Can They Drink It?," *The New York Times*, December 2, 2021, sec. World, https://www.nytimes.com /2021/12/02/world/clean-water-to-drink.html.

3. Greta Thunberg, "Transcript: Greta Thunberg's Speech at the U.N. Climate Action Summit," NPR.org, September 23, 2019, https://www.npr.org/2019/09 /23/763452863/transcript-greta-thunbergs-speech-at-the-u-n-climate-action-summit. See Keller, *Facing Apocalypse*, 9–10.

4. Thunberg, "Greta Thunberg's Speech."

5. John W. Marshall, "Who's on the Throne? Revelation in the Long Year," in *Heavenly Realms and Earthly Realities in Late Antique Religions*, ed. Ra'anan S. Boustan and Annette Yoshiko Reed (Cambridge: Cambridge University Press, 2004), 132.

8:1When the Lamb opened the seventh seal, there was silence in heaven for about half an hour. 2And I saw the seven angels who stand before God, and seven trumpets were given to them.

3Another angel with a golden censer came and stood at the altar; he was given a great quantity of incense to offer with the prayers of all the saints on the golden altar that is before the throne. 4And the smoke of the incense, with the prayers of the saints, rose before God from the hand of the angel. 5Then the angel took the censer and filled it with fire from the altar and threw it on the earth; and there were peals of thunder, rumblings, flashes of lightning, and an earthquake.

6Now the seven angels who had the seven trumpets made ready to blow them.

upon the earth and all the activity of heaven, there is space to listen, breathe, and pause. For others, the silence might come across as eerie. The length of this silence—it lasts *about* half an hour—is undetermined, unlike other precise time references in this text (e.g., 11:3, 9; 12:6; 13:5; 17:12; 20:2-3). The open-ended nature of "about half an hour" creates a sense of unknowing about what is on the horizon.

This "half-ish" hour of quiet reminds us of all the silences, intentional and unintentional, we experience. Silences can be painful when they involve broken friendships, differences of opinion, and failures to right past wrongs. Nevertheless, painful silences can also be necessary pauses. Gathered groups acknowledge the loss of life or a shared tragedy with a "moment of silence." When we sit with a friend or loved one undergoing a health crisis, loss, breakdown, breakup, or financial hardship, we may remain quiet because our words are insufficient. These moments provide space to connect with others in a way that would be impossible if we formulated words or processed the sounds of speech. Perhaps John offers his audience members a moment to experience one another apart from the tumult around them. This chance to sit in silence provides everyone a much-needed opportunity to catch their collective breath before experiencing the events just on the horizon.

Eventually the silence in heaven will be shattered with trumpet blasts, but first there is a time of worship. However, having been given a "great quantity" of incense, an angel before the heavenly throne offers it to God along with the prayers of the saints (see "Translation Matters: ἅγιοι").

Earlier, John described the twenty-four elders holding golden bowls of incense, which were metaphorically equated with these same prayers (5:8). In both cases, the praises and requests of the faithful find their way to God via the smoke of incense offered in worship. The imagery evokes the words of Psalm 141, "Let my prayer be counted as incense before you" (v. 2), and may remind audiences across time of their own experiences of incense-filled worship. In this way, Revelation's text invites its many audiences to fully experience and even embody this journey through the heavenly narrative.

The smoke of the incense rising from the angel's hand to God in 8:4 provides a striking counterpoint to the angel's next act—throwing the censer, filled with fire, to the earth (v. 5). The linking of upward and downward movement creates a visual connection between heaven and earth. What happens in one place impacts the other. The result of throwing fire from the altar to earth includes the same manifestations of power that come from the heavenly throne (4:5)—"thunder, rumblings, flashes of lightning, and an earthquake" (8:5). Since the prayers of the saints have just drifted before the divine throne, this visual display of heavenly power could be read as a response, although whether this "answer to prayer" is positive or negative depends on whether audience members count themselves among the saints or not.

TRANSLATION MATTERS: ἅγιοι

One of the terms John uses to describe the faithful in Revelation's narrative is ἅγιοι, which the NRSV translates as "saints" (5:8; 8:3-4; 11:18; 13:7; 14:12; 16:6; 17:6; 18:20, 24; 19:8; 20:9). When modern readers encounter the "saints" in this narrative, they may think of the images of saints displayed in stained glass or on an altar in their local church. These saints are moral exemplars and performers of miracles, such as Saint Catherine or Saint Francis or the more recently canonized Oscar Romero. Saints such as these serve as conduits between the faithful on earth and God, intervening on behalf of those who pray to them or honor them in some way. The belief that these individuals are still accessible to the living through prayer and acts of devotion reflects Christian belief in the "communion of the saints," an idea affirmed in the Apostles' Creed. While Revelation's saints eventually come to be associated with these important historical church figures, Revelation predates this history, and the term "saints" signals an identity that all in Revelation's audiences can and should, according to John, embrace.

The term "saints" could be rendered more literally as "holy ones," a designation that suggests a state of purity (e.g., Lev 19); however, in this text, being a holy one relates to the relationship between the individual and God and the Lamb. It is, according to Peter S. Perry, "a status conferred by the relationship with God."[6] This relationship should not be imagined as the kind of "personal relationship with Jesus" that some modern Christians describe, although it certainly does not exclude that. Instead, this relationship is about a commitment to following God and the Lamb, eschewing possible attachments to institutions and persons who deign to replace God. Still, the designation "saint" does not presume that a person is particularly good or exceptional or endowed with miraculous powers.

As Revelation's narrative progresses and the conflict between the Beast and the Lamb intensifies, John makes more references to the "saints," and in the second half of the book he will reference "the blood of the saints" (16:6; 17:6; 18:24). The trajectory of sainthood, according to John, becomes apparent. Even though the association between saints and dying on account of one's religious commitment becomes more common after the book of Revelation, John anticipates this idea by implying that these individuals shed blood because of their faithfulness.[7] In Revelation, the concepts of "saint" and "witness" (μάρτυς), or martyr, overlap and point to the eventual connotations of both terms (see "Translation Matters: μάρτυς").

Sounding the Trumpets (8:7-13)

As mentioned in the introduction, Revelation includes several "buoys," numbers and patterns, that provide the audiences a sense of direction as they move through the narrative. By introducing seven angels who are given seven trumpets in 8:1, John prepares listeners to experience seven trumpet blasts, just as the reference to seven seals on the scroll held by God anticipated the systematic opening of the seals (Rev 6). Likewise, the description of seven angels with bowls of plague will lead to the pouring out of these bowls (Rev 15–16). The sequential nature of these events contributes to the sense that the narrative and time more generally move forward and toward an end. The parallels between these sequences, however, simultaneously create a sense of time as cyclical, implying that history repeats itself. Things happening now have happened in the past and will happen again. Despite this, these sequences are often interrupted or postponed, suggesting that God's time exists apart from and above the order of human events.

6. Peter S. Perry, "The People of God in the Book of Revelation," in *The Oxford Handbook of the Book of Revelation*, ed. Craig R. Koester (New York: Oxford University Press, 2020), 333.

7. For a discussion of the tradition of martyrdom that Revelation anticipates, see Stephanie L. Cobb, *Dying to Be Men: Gender and Language in Early Christian Martyr Texts* (New York: Columbia University Press, 2008), passim.

[7]The first angel blew his trumpet, and there came hail and fire, mixed with blood, and they were hurled to the earth, and a third of the earth was burned up, and a third of the trees were burned up, and all green grass was burned up.

[8]The second angel blew his trumpet, and something like a great mountain, burning with fire, was thrown into the sea. [9]A third of the sea became blood, a third of the living creatures in the sea died, and a third of the ships were destroyed.

[10]The third angel blew his trumpet, and a great star fell from heaven, blazing like a torch, and it fell on a third of the rivers and on the springs of water.

[11]The name of the star is Wormwood. A third of the waters became wormwood, and many died from the water, because it was made bitter.

[12]The fourth angel blew his trumpet, and a third of the sun was struck, and a third of the moon, and a third of the stars, so that a third of their light was darkened; a third of the day was kept from shining, and likewise the night.

[13]Then I looked, and I heard an eagle crying with a loud voice as it flew in midheaven, "Woe, woe, woe to the inhabitants of the earth, at the blasts of the other trumpets that the three angels are about to blow!"

As with the first four seals, the first four trumpets constitute a distinct unit within the seven. These four episodes are of comparable length, beginning with the numbering of the angel and trumpet (e.g., "The first angel blew his trumpet"). Each of the first four trumpet blasts is recounted systematically: The angel blows the trumpet, and there is a description of the trumpet's specific effects, measured as thirds. The first trumpet brings "hail and fire, mixed with blood," that burns one-third of the earth, including trees and grass (8:7); the second trumpet results in a third of the sea becoming like blood, killing a third of all sea creatures and destroying a third of all ships (8:9); the third trumpet unleashes a star identified as "Wormwood" (the herb used to make the powerful hallucination-inducing liqueur absinthe [Cf. Jer 9:15])[8] that falls from heaven making a third of the rivers, springs, and all other waters bitter (8:10-11); and the fourth trumpet extinguishes a third of the sun, moon, and stars, so that day and night are a third darker (8:12).

The cyclical nature of the apocalyptic narrative accentuates the parallels between the trumpets and other biblical plagues, including the ones

8. Wormwood has several medicinal uses, both in the ancient and modern contexts; however, in larger doses it can be fatal. See David Eric Brussell, "Medicinal Plants of Mt. Pelion, Greece," *Economic Botany* 58 (2004): S181.

leading to Israel's exodus out of Egypt (Exod 7–11). Later in the narrative, when John observes angels pouring bowls of torment upon the earth, he will evoke the Egyptian ordeals more explicitly (Rev 15–16). The trumpets similarly evoke prophetic descriptions of the events heralding the coming judgment and wrath of God. Among these is the prophet Joel who calls for a trumpet blast as a warning that the "Day of the LORD," which brings earthquakes and darkness, is coming (2:1-2; see also Zeph 1:14-17). Likewise, in the Gospels, Jesus warns that cosmic and ecological events, like falling stars, earthquakes, and famines, will precede the coming of the Son of Humanity (Matt 24:29; Mark 13:24-25; Luke 21:11). The notion that cataclysmic events signal coming divine judgment or wrath appears in Greek and Roman traditions as well. For instance, Artemidorus, who lived in Ephesus during the second century CE, explained it was "inauspicious to see stars falling down upon the earth. For they prophesy the death of many men: large stars, the death of important men."[9]

One way of understanding the trumpets is to highlight how the portioning of the destruction into thirds implies limit.[10] The harm is real, but there is some element of restraint. This is not a case of God "wiping out" all living things, as with the flood in Genesis (6:7). This approach, however, fails to recognize that seeing the destruction in thirds reflects John's distance from the earth. Because John witnesses this destruction from heaven, he fails to see and explain how cataclysmic events impact individuals and groups differently. This distance is one of the flaws of the apocalyptic worldview. Natural disasters and environmental calamities do not affect people equally, even people within the same country, city, or household. According to the World Health Organization, women are generally more vulnerable to the detrimental effects of climate change than men, although those vulnerabilities differ from culture to culture. For example, most respondents to a survey on the impact of drought conducted in Ninh Tuan, Viet Nam, agreed that women were impacted more by drought than men because women gathered water for the household, and droughts meant increasingly long distances to available sources.[11] In addition, women and girls in various contexts "are more prone to nutritional deficiencies," especially in the wake of climate change, because

9. *Onirocritica* 2.36 as quoted in Craig R. Koester, *Revelation: A New Translation with Introduction and Commentary*, AYB 38A (New Haven: Yale University Press, 2014), 449.

10. Gail R. O'Day, "Revelation," in *Theological Bible Commentary*, ed. Gail R. O'Day and David L. Petersen (Louisville: Westminster John Knox, 2009), 475.

11. World Health Organization, "Gender, Climate Change and Health," 14, https://www.who.int/publications/i/item/9789241508186.

of pregnancy and breastfeeding and cultural hierarchies impacting food distribution within households.[12] These disparities are just the tip of the (quickly melting) iceberg, but these details highlight the problem with taking only the bird's-eye view of disaster offered in apocalyptic texts.

Amid the destruction caused by the trumpets, an eagle flies through mid-heaven, the space between heaven and earth. A bird's presence can be a hopeful sign, as can its absence (Gen 8:12). Birds can, however, also warn of danger. Such is the case here. The eagle's message, which mimics the sound of an eagle through the repetition of the Greek word "οὐαί" or "woe" (a case of onomatopoeia), makes known the three remaining trumpet blasts. Romans believed that birds, given their proximity to the heavens, revealed messages from the divine through their flight patterns, calls, and other behaviors. Romans interpreted these messages through the practice of divination or "taking the auspices" at critical times, including before important military campaigns.[13] The mythical founders of Rome, Romulus and Remus, even settled a dispute on where to locate the city based on the number of vultures seen by each brother (Plutarch, *Rom.* 9.4-7). Thus, this eagle communicates through a means that should be intelligible "to the inhabitants of the earth" (8:13), one of the ways that Revelation describes those who follow the Beast and not the Lamb (13:8). Despite the eagle's cry, however, the earth's inhabitants fail to repent and follow God and the Lamb (9:20-21). The image of a majestic bird warning humans of the need to change their ways is striking since birds are susceptible to environmental change and therefore " 'winged sentinels' of environmental degradation."[14]

> ### *"Alas"—Not "Woe" for the Earth*[15]
>
> In addition to the Exodus story, several other theological considerations are also important for navigating the middle chapters of Revelation. The most important is that God does not curse the world, nor does God sentence the earth to destruction.

---

12. World Health Organization, "Gender, Climate Change and Health," 17.

13. Jeremy Mynott, *Birds in the Ancient World: Winged Words* (Oxford: Oxford University Press, 2018), 249–66.

14. Barry Yeoman, "What Do Birds Do for Us?," *Audubon*, April 8, 2013, https://www.audubon.org/news/what-do-birds-do-us.

15. Barbara R. Rossing, *The Rapture Exposed: The Message of Hope in the Book of Revelation*, 2nd ed. (New York: Basic Books, 2004), 128–29.

After the fourth trumpet, an eagle flies through the air crying out "Woe" with a loud voice. . . . This is only one of the many declarations of woe in Revelation. These "woes" sound terrifying, coming as they do in the midst of the plagues. Dispensationalists use the "woe" verses to explain that God has sentenced the world to awful destruction.

But "woe" is not really a helpful translation for the Greek word. Its sense is rather one of lament—like a mourner keening in grief, wailing out repeated cries of "Oh, oh, oh" at the death of a loved one. Spanish Bibles simply translate the sound as "Ay, ay, ay." I would translate the word as "Alas." The meaning of the Greek word *ouai* is first of all a cry of pain, like the word "ouch" in English. It can mean "woe," but it can also express deep lamentation of mourning, as in the laments of the merchants and kings over Rome in chapter 18. . . .

It is as if God is crying "ouch" or "alas" on behalf of the suffering world: "Alas for the inhabitants of the earth." It is a subtle but significant shift in direction because "Alas" conveys God's sympathy in a way that "woe" does not.

Barbara Rossing

The Trumpets Continue (9:1-21)

While the earth, sea, and sky are primary targets of the first four trumpets, the mayhem unleashed by the fifth and sixth targets the "inhabitants of the earth" (8:13). John characterizes the earth's inhabitants specifically as those who do not have God's seal (9:4). Later in Revelation, this group will gloat over the death of God's witnesses (11:10) and worship the Beast (13:8, 12, 14; 17:2, 8). As a result, this group functions as an "other" against which Revelation's audience members are to define themselves.[16] Thus, the fifth and sixth trumpets reveal to John's audiences the consequences of failing to align with God and the Lamb.

Whereas the destruction of the first four trumpets came from the heavens, now the trumpets unleash destructive forces from the earth. The planet turns on its inhabitants. John signals this shift by mentioning a star that has fallen from heaven to earth with a key that opens the shaft to "the bottomless pit," a translation of the Greek word ἄβυσσος which can be rendered literally as "abyss" (9:1-2). The connection between stars and heavenly beings appears elsewhere in Scripture (Judg 5:20; Job 38:7; Dan 8:10). Here, the image of a fallen star points to Satan, the prototypical

---

16. Greg Carey, *Elusive Apocalypse: Reading Authority in the Revelation to John* (Macon, GA: Mercer University Press, 1999), 162.

9:1And the fifth angel blew his trumpet, and I saw a star that had fallen from heaven to earth, and he was given the key to the shaft of the bottomless pit; 2he opened the shaft of the bottomless pit, and from the shaft rose smoke like the smoke of a great furnace, and the sun and the air were darkened with the smoke from the shaft. 3Then from the smoke came locusts on the earth, and they were given authority like the authority of scorpions of the earth. 4They were told not to damage the grass of the earth or any green growth or any tree, but only those people who do not have the seal of God on their foreheads. 5They were allowed to torture them for five months, but not to kill them, and their torture was like the torture of a scorpion when it stings someone. 6And in those days people will seek death but will not find it; they will long to die, but death will flee from them.

7In appearance the locusts were like horses equipped for battle. On their heads were what looked like crowns of gold; their faces were like human faces, 8their hair like women's hair, and their teeth like lions' teeth; 9they had scales like iron breastplates, and the noise of their wings was like the noise of many chariots with horses rushing into battle. 10They have tails like scorpions, with stingers, and in their tails is their power to harm people for five months. 11They have as king over

fallen angel (Rev 12:9; see Luke 10:18; 1 En. 86:1). The thought of this occurrence, a fallen star who will unleash the horror of the underworld, might make Revelation's audience members think of comets, which were often interpreted by Romans as omens. For example, Augustus interpreted Hayley's comet as a sign that the deceased Julius Caesar had become a god and that this was a good omen for his reign (Pliny the Elder, *Nat.* 2.93-94). Revelation flips this script, reading the celestial event as a sign of foreboding.

Reverence for the underworld gods was part of the landscape of ancient Asia Minor. Not far from Laodicea, in the city of Hierapolis, a temple called a *ploutonion* was built with a shaft leading to what was believed to be an entrance to the underworld. This was one of three such temples in the Lykos valley, where there was obvious geothermal activity. Even today, from a distance Hierapolis looks like a mountain of snow year-round because of the limestone deposits left from the city's active hot springs. Priests at the *ploutonion* took birds, bulls, and other animals down the shaft and to the mouth of a cave, where they were left

them the angel of the bottomless pit; his name in Hebrew is Abaddon, and in Greek he is called Apollyon.

[12]The first woe has passed. There are still two woes to come.

[13]Then the sixth angel blew his trumpet, and I heard a voice from the four horns of the golden altar before God, [14]saying to the sixth angel who had the trumpet, "Release the four angels who are bound at the great river Euphrates." [15]So the four angels were released, who had been held ready for the hour, the day, the month, and the year, to kill a third of humankind. [16]The number of the troops of cavalry was two hundred million; I heard their number. [17]And this was how I saw the horses in my vision: the riders wore breastplates the color of fire and of sapphire and of sulfur; the heads of the horses were like lions' heads, and fire and smoke and sulfur came out of their mouths. [18]By these three plagues a third of humankind was killed, by the fire and smoke and sulfur coming out of their mouths. [19]For the power of the horses is in their mouths and in their tails; their tails are like serpents, having heads; and with them they inflict harm.

[20]The rest of humankind, who were not killed by these plagues, did not repent of the works of their hands or give up worshiping demons and idols of gold and silver and bronze and stone and wood, which cannot see or hear or walk. [21]And they did not repent of their murders or their sorceries or their fornication or their thefts.

as sacrifices to the subterranean gods.[17] Animal victims of the human desire to appease the gods would be overcome by the carbon dioxide and other gasses that came up from the ground. Strabo described the place as being "full of vapour so misty and dense that one can scarcely see the ground" (*Geogr.* 13.4.14). Likewise, in Revelation the "smoke" from the abyss appears ominous, even blocking out the sun and filling the air (9:2). It seems fitting for such obvious air pollution to come from the realm of death, given its harmful effects on humans and other living things.

Instead of sacrificial victims being taken down into the abyss, John witnesses locusts coming up from underground, appearing as "horses equipped for battle" with "iron breastplates" (v. 9). These well-equipped locusts reflect John's familiarity with the book of Joel, where the prophet

17. Francesco D'Andria, "Nature and Cult in the *Ploutonion* of Hierapolis before and after the Colony," in *Landscape and History in the Lykos Valley: Laodikeia and Hierapolis in Phrygia*, ed. Celal Şimşek and Francesco D'Andria (Newcastle upon Tyne: Cambridge Scholars Publishing, 2017), 207–40.

depicts invading armies as swarming locusts and the environmental devastation they bring. Joel blends the concepts of human and insect so thoroughly that the troops he describes are entirely monstrous. As Kevin Chau notes, the complex imagery, which also evokes meteorological events, alludes to the practice of destroying crops by ancient armies and to war's toll on the natural world.[18] Despite his depiction of these events, Joel seems uncertain as to the source of the destruction, vacillating between attributing it to a powerful God and to the warrior-locusts (e.g., Joel 1:15). Amid the destruction being wrought, however, the people are instructed to return or turn back to God multiple times because "he is gracious and merciful, slow to anger, and abounding in steadfast love, and relents from punishing" (2:13). God, as voiced by Joel, eventually reassures the animals of the field that they need not fear and humans that they will recoup their losses (2:22, 25). In Joel, it almost seems as though God actually responds to the call to repentance. In Revelation, no one repents.

Revelation's locusts are a monstrous blend of animal parts, lions' teeth, scorpion stingers, and wings (9:8-9; see also Joel 1:6). It is almost as if the sacrificial animals of the *ploutonion* have emerged from the underworld to take their revenge on the humans who offered them as sacrifices. Unlike typical locusts who feed on plant matter (Joel 1:10-12), these are told *not* to harm plants or the earth. Instead, they are instructed to use their scorpion stingers to torture humans who do not have the seal of God on their foreheads (vv. 4-5, 10). At the same time, their human-like faces suggest that they manifest in and through humanity. As in Joel, the imagery blends human and insect to describe monstrous forces. Among their other characteristics, the locusts appear with "hair like women's hair" (v. 8), reflecting a tendency to dehumanize all who are "non-men" and to feminize the dangerous. Untamed women's hair could be seen as threatening and as a sign of female unpredictability, something images of Medusa's snake-bedecked head reminded people throughout the ancient Mediterranean.[19] With their human hair and faces, these locusts teeter on the boundary of

18. Kevin Chau, "Conceptual Blending in Joel 2:1-11: God's Apocalyptic Storm-Locusts-Warriors," in *T&T Clark Handbook of Asian American Biblical Hermeneutics,* ed. Uriah Y. Kim and Seung Ai Yang (London: T&T Clark, 2019), 277. See also Julia M. O'Brien, "Joel," in *Theological Bible Commentary,* ed. O'Day and Petersen, 265–66.

19. Molly Myerowitz Levine, "The Gendered Grammar of Ancient Mediterranean Hair," in *Off with Her Head! The Denial of Women's Identity in Myth, Religion, and Culture,* ed. Howard Eilberg-Schwartz and Wendy Doniger (Berkeley: University of California Press, 1995), 76–130.

human and unhuman. For some this indicates they are demonic, while others see them as a horrible divine army that enforces God's will.[20] Their human visages suggest, however, that they can be read as something more nefarious, as humans that Satan has turned against themselves.

In addition to the star that releases them from the pit, a "king," the angel of the bottomless pit, rules over the monstrous locusts (v. 11). The kingly imagery makes clear that the locusts are agents of political power. John connects this angel to the Roman emperors who associated themselves with Apollo, such as Augustus and Nero, using wordplay.[21] While his "name in Hebrew is Abaddon," a destructive force associated with Sheol and death (e.g., Job 26:6; 28:22; 38:12; Ps 88:11), John transliterates this into Greek as Apollyon (9:11). Apollyon is not the name of a deity in Greek; rather, John crafts the name by drawing an aural connection between the name of the god Apollo and the Greek verb "to destroy" (ἀπόλλυμι). The name mocks a god popular among emperors, including Augustus who even wore a laurel crown to visually present himself as the sun god and built a temple to the deity on the Palatine Hill above the Roman forum. Through these efforts Augustus presented himself as one who destroyed evil and ushered in a new golden age marked by peace.[22] John, however, turns this idea inside out by implying that Apollo, along with those who emulate the god, is a thinly disguised Satan. "Destroyer" clearly stands in opposition to God as the "one who created all things" (4:11), while his locust-minions bring those who follow him to the point of yearning for destruction through months of torture (9:6). The vision of the fifth trumpet indicates that the experience of those who follow the Beast and do not bear God's seal is, put simply, hell on earth.

Immediately after the sixth angel blows their trumpet, a voice comes from the four "horns," a decorative element on the corners of the heavenly altar (v. 13). The altar commands the angel to release four other angels who have been "bound," like Satan will eventually be bound (20:2), at the Euphrates. The fact that they were being held at a supposedly far-off

20. Heather Macumber argues the latter, although she offers a thorough discussion of those who read the image as demonic. See *Recovering the Monstrous in Revelation* (Lanham, MD: Lexington Books/Fortress, 2021), 126–33.

21. Elisabeth Schüssler Fiorenza, *Revelation: Vision of a Just World* (Minneapolis: Fortress, 1991), 71.

22. David A. Sánchez, *From Patmos to the Barrio: Subverting Imperial Myths* (Minneapolis: Fortress, 2008), 19–22; John F. Miller, *Apollo, Augustus, and the Poets* (Cambridge: Cambridge University Press, 2009), 23.

location, presumably to keep them from enacting the horrors they unleash at this "very hour and day and month and year" (v. 15), indicates
that these are not good or benevolent beings. The idea that fallen angels
are being kept imprisoned until the end appears in other writings from
around this time, including 2 Peter 2:4 and Jude 6.[23] The angels do not
work alone; rather, a massive cavalry, numbering 200 million, assists in
the massacre. So powerful is this force that John hears their number before
seeing them (9:16), just as he heard about the Lion before seeing the Lamb
(5:5-6) and heard the number of the 144,000 from the tribes of Israel before
seeing an innumerable multinational crowd (7:5-9). The calvary appears
fearsome, wearing breastplates "of fire and of sapphire and of sulfur"
and seated upon horses with heads like lions, breathing fire, smoke, and
sulfur (9:17). The sulfur connects these to the abyss that was opened by
the one fallen from heaven (v. 1), again blending supernatural forces of
evil with human prowess. Within the context of Revelation, these forces
could take many forms, ranging from imperial armies to the poverty that
forced workers to the mines. Breathing fire and wielding serpent-like tails,
these forces destroy a third of humanity (v. 19).

With the fifth and sixth trumpets, John offers a complex layer atop the
apocalyptic destruction unleashed in the first four trumpets. These latter trumpet blasts come from heaven, but the actions they initiate have
an earthly source. The disasters described in Revelation, according to
biblical scholar Micah Kiel, evidence Rome's negative impact upon the
environment. Mines and other large-scale industries with major environmental impacts sustained the Roman imperial system, producing the
metals necessary to make coins essential for the Roman economy and
to support the architectural projects associated with imperial rule. The
aqueduct systems of cities like Sardis, Ephesus, and Smyrna required
massive amounts of lead.[24] Similarly, imperial spread led to deforestation in the provinces, since wood was used to construct the multistory
buildings necessary to support urbanization and to heat the massive
bathing complexes central to Roman social and political culture.[25] The
connection between environmental degradation and imperial power is
not simply a modern observation; ancient authors connected the dots

---

23. Koester, *Revelation*, 466.

24. Sing C. Chew, *World Ecological Degradation: Accumulation, Urbanization, and Deforestation, 3000 BC–AD 2000* (Lanham, MD: AltaMira Press, 2001), 87.

25. Micah D. Kiel, *Apocalyptic Ecology: The Book of Revelation, the Earth, and the Future* (Collegeville, MN: Liturgical Press, 2017), 65; Chew, *World Ecological Degradation*, 93.

between Rome and phenomena such as the collapse of mountains and the presence of poisoned air.[26] One example noted by Kiel is the ancient poet Lucretius, who spoke mournfully about how the mines took the lives of those who had no choice but to work in them:[27] "Do you not see or hear in how short a time they are accustomed to perish, how their vital force fails, who are held fast in such work as this by the great constraint of necessity?" (*The Nature of Things* 6.810-15).

Just as many in the ancient world were "constrained" to do work that would eventually kill them, people today are likewise exploited by industries that harm the natural world. Environmental degradation walks hand in hand with racism and classism. In both cities and rural communities in the United States, there is a "long history of noxious and hazardous facilities being located within or close to minority and low-income communities," according to author Dorceta E. Taylor.[28] Taylor notes a 1987 study conducted by the United Church of Christ that found that "race was the strongest predictor of location of the commercial hazardous waste facilities . . . [and] that three out of five Black and Hispanic residents lived in communities with uncontrolled toxic waste sites."[29] Industries that exploit the environment exploit the communities that surround their facilities, especially Black and Latinx communities, and rely on the fact that many cannot afford to, or simply do not want to, relocate. There is little or no corporate motivation to contribute to a community's development, to invest in education, health care, and social services, since those things might make people in the community more mobile. There is a symbiotic relationship between environmental and human oppressions that John evokes and names as evil in his depiction of these final two trumpets.

John characterizes the response to this destruction by those who survive as a refusal to repent and a doubling-down on the worship of gods other than God. The text describes this as the worship of "demons and idols," effectively diminishing the religious practices of those who do not worship the God of Israel (9:20; see "Translation Matters: εἴδωλον"). Turning to one's gods amid the devastation described in these chapters makes sense. John, however, casts this as a negative thing, associating it with several stereotyped "sins" embraced by humankind, such as murder,

26. Kiel, *Apocalyptic Ecology*, 66.

27. Kiel, *Apocalyptic Ecology*, 65.

28. Dorceta E. Taylor, *Toxic Communities: Environmental Racism, Industrial Pollution, and Residential Mobility* (New York: NYU Press, 2014), 1.

29. Taylor, *Toxic Communities*, 36.

sorcery, fornication, and theft (9:21). What if, however, this resistance to repentance and acknowledging God isn't willful sinfulness? Maybe it has something to do with the inability to even comprehend the coming destruction? Ingrid Esther Lilly notes that climate scientists and others working on behalf of the environment embrace increasingly drastic or apocalyptic imagery to motivate people toward action, since many have become almost numb to the scientists' warnings. The climate crisis, according to Lilly, is a cliff toward which humanity, imagined as a mountain bike rider, is careening.[30] Or perhaps the insistence that the events of the first five seals are "acts of God" creates not just a sense that God is in charge, but that humans have little or no ability to change. If a third of the water, a third of the light, a third of humanity are *destined* by God to be destroyed, human efforts at change seem pointless. Despite all this, human abuse of the natural environment and environmental racism are things for which humans need to repent, and Christians must repent for the way apocalyptic rhetoric has contributed to the sense that we can do nothing in the face of environmental disaster. Repentance without change, furthermore, is meaningless, and it is necessary for Christians to pinpoint the things that have drawn our attention away from care for God's creation and realign our perspective.

The prophets of the Hebrew Bible associated the sound of the trumpet blast with the coming of God's judgment (e.g., Joel 2:1; Jer 4:5, 19, 21; 6:1, 17; 51:27). Romans similarly used trumpets to signal cataclysmic and cosmic events. Ovid spoke of "fear-inspiring trumpets and horns heard in the sky" when Julius Caesar was murdered and deified (*Metam.* 15.784). The connection between the sound of trumpets or horns with wrath and woe reflects a long history of the instrument's use in battle. The trumpet sound, which Romans generally thought of as harsh (especially compared to stringed instruments like harps), indicated that what was to come would be unpleasant or even dire.[31] This suggests that the repeated trumpet blasts of Revelation 8–9 are John's attempt at offering his audience members an obvious wake-up call. Even though John describes the inhabitants of the earth resisting the notion of repentance at their peril, Revelation itself signals John's hope that people's perspectives and attitudes can be changed. Thus, despite the destruction depicted in these chapters, underneath it all is a sliver of hope.

---

30. Ingrid Esther Lilly, "The Planet's Apocalypse: The Rhetoric of Climate Change," in *Apocalypses in Context: Apocalyptic Currents through History*, ed. Kelly J. Murphy and Justin Jeffcoat Schedtler (Minneapolis: Fortress, 2016), 369.

31. John Ziolkowski, "The Invention of the Tuba (Trumpet)," *CW* 92 (1999): 367–73.

TRANSLATION MATTERS: εἴδωλον, εἴδωλα

In Revelation's description of the inhabitants of the earth's failure to repent, John uses εἴδωλα, which the NRSV translates as "idols" (9:20). Earlier in the text, John describes the practice of "eating idol meat" (εἰδωλόθυτος; 2:14, 20). Later he satirizes Roman worship of an εἰκών (13:14), a word that the NRSV translates as "image" but which could easily be translated as "icon" in English. By using these related terms, John participates in the ancient Jewish and early Christian critique of other ancient religions, a critique that has justified Christian violence toward countless people throughout history, including other Christians, who incorporate images and statues in their worship practices.

In the Septuagint, εἴδωλα typically describes gods worshiped in religions distinct from the worship of the God of Israel and features regularly in prophetic critiques of the Israelites, who are imagined as eagerly wanting to worship these gods (e.g., Hos 13:2). Set within the context of polemic, Hebrew Bible authors offer a decidedly simple view of these physical gods, deriding them as human creations, ineffectual, and unable to speak (e.g., Hab 2:18; Isa 37:19; Jer 14:22). They make clear that this type of worship, worship of other deities, stands at odds with the worship of God. In Leviticus, God commands, "Do not turn to idols [εἰδώλοις] or make cast images for yourselves: I am the LORD your God" (19:4; see also, Exod 20:4; Deut 5:8).

Despite the association between εἴδωλα and worship in these critiques, in ancient Greek sources εἴδωλον refers more generally to an image. For instance, it can connote a statue of a person (e.g., Herodotus, *Hist.* 1.51.5) or even a phantom (e.g., Plutarch, *Caes.* 27.4). Greek speakers used a variety of other words, including εἰκών, to refer to the images and objects that played a central role in ancient Greek and Roman religions.[32] As Revelation describes, these objects of worship were made of gold, silver, bronze, stone, or wood.

For many in the ancient world, the statues found in temples and shrines were actual embodiments of the deities. As such they were bathed and clothed and processed through cities on special occasions; they were touched and kissed and offered food, just as one would offer the gift of food to someone of a higher status.[33] At the same time some Greeks and Romans, philosophers in particular, understood these physical manifestations as material representations of nonmaterial gods (e.g., Plato, *Leg.* 931a). Given the prevalence and importance of physical depictions of the divine in the ancient world, some were suspicious of the Jewish prohibition against images. Thus, the satirist Juvenal mocked Jews for worshiping "the clouds and spirit of the sky" (*Sat.* 14.97). In other words, worshiping what John and others describe as "idols" and "icons" was the norm and understood as a part of being pious and good.

Building upon the critique of other religious traditions in the prophets, John associates the worship of εἴδωλα with the worship of demons (δαιμόνια), which can

---

32. Philip Kiernan, *Roman Cult Images: The Lives and Worship of Idols from the Iron Age to Late Antiquity* (Cambridge: Cambridge University Press, 2020), 5.

33. Kiernan, *Roman Cult Images*, 204–7, 213, 220.

refer simply to other gods (e.g., Acts 17:18) or, in the context of Jesus followers, to evil spirits (e.g., Matt 9:33-34; 12:24-28). As such, John's use of "idols," along with later references to images or icons, is part of Revelation's overall criticism of any worship not directed at the God that John and his followers believe sits upon the throne of heaven. For John, all other worship, including the worship of imperial figures, is worship of Satan.

John's contempt for the religious practices of those around him anticipates later Christian polemic against the use of images in worship. Reading through nineteenth-century missionary publications, for example, Brian K. Pennington shows that Christian missionaries to India under British rule imagined Hindu "idol" worship as leading to moral depravity, cruelty, and violence, a basis for justifying British colonial rule.[34] Contributing to this type of religious and cultural oppression is part of the text's harmful legacy.

One of the ironies of this is, of course, that John's audiences feared social pressure and persecution at the hands of others for their own failure to conform to the dominant religious practices of their day. As a result, early Jesus followers were sometimes characterized as atheists and seen as depraved (Eusebius, *Hist. eccl.* 4.13.1-7). Although John's polemic can be understood as a minority religion's attempt at distinguishing itself from the majority practice, which treated Jews and Jesus followers as religiously deviant, the power that Christianity now wields makes it incumbent upon those in the tradition to recognize and respect religious difference. This includes acknowledging how the critique of "idols" and "icons," even when used to encourage the followers of God to return to hold tight to their religious practices, has harmed others and diminished their lives.

---

34. Brian K. Pennington, *Was Hinduism Invented? Britons, Indians, and the Colonial Construction of Religion* (Oxford: Oxford University Press, 2005), 96–100.

Revelation 10

A Queer Prophetic Digression

A mighty angel "coming down from" heaven disrupts the destruction of the first six trumpets and captures John's attention at the beginning of chapter 10 (v. 1). With this descent, the narrative's perspective shifts from heavenly to earthly things. This marks a change in John's role, moving him from visionary to prophet (vv. 8-11). Because of these changes in perspective and focus, Revelation 10 serves as a digression within the narrative, even though it does a lot of work in the text.[1]

First, the digression provides John's audiences a necessary break from the destruction of the first six trumpets, which came shortly after the devastations of the seven seals. Even though earth and its inhabitants have experienced significant horrors within the narrative, the heavenly envoy assures John's audiences that they have not been abandoned by the heavenly realm. The connection between heaven and earth remains, and the faithful on the planet have not been cut off. In addition, this digression, which depicts John receiving a scroll from heaven that reinvigorates his prophetic message, repeats the opening notice that Revelation's source is divine and not simply the words of mortal John. The authority of Revelation's message comes from above. Second, the digression in this chapter helps listeners understand John and, consequently, the identity

---

1. Peter S. Perry, *The Rhetoric of Digressions: Revelation 7:1-17 and 10:1–11:13 and Ancient Communication*, WUNT 2.268 (Tübingen: Mohr Siebeck, 2009), 236–37.

that they are called to adopt. More than other places in the narrative, Revelation 10 focuses on John's role as a prophet who serves as a vessel through which the divine communicates. Here, John awkwardly depicts himself as a character in his own story. Moreover, he depicts himself in a way that complicates his gender, presenting himself as a model of a queer kind of faithfulness.

The adjective "queer," sometimes used as shorthand for the identities signaled by LGBTQIA+, describes things, actions, and ways of being that challenge traditional categorizations and expectations, especially those related to gender, sex, and sexuality. Resisting the norms of gender, including assumptions about the characteristics and affects women and men are "supposed" to embody, is what I mean when using "queer" in relation to John. There is also the sense that the queer disrupts expectations in a way that forces us to see things, understand, and act differently.[2] In addition, "queer" can be used as a verb to describe a mode of inquiry. Theologian Kent L. Brintnall describes this in the following way: "To queer means to question, to interrogate, to trouble: it signifies a process by which the familiar, the dominant, the coherent are rendered strange, marginal, unstable. Scholars use the term this way when investigating the unacknowledged strangeness—especially in relation to gender and sexuality—of religious and theological discourses."[3] This kind of reading is consistent with feminist interpretation as it too aims at challenging oppressive perspectives on gender, sex, and sexuality. In the following, I "queer" John as a prophet to shed light on how Revelation recasts traditional forms of masculinity in its depiction of what it means to be faithful.

John and the Mighty Angel (10:1-7)

A "mighty angel," literally and figuratively, dominates the first half of the chapter. The language of might (ἰσχυρός) to describe the angel prompts audiences to think of this figure in masculine terms. Some medieval commentators associated this specific angel with powerful men in history, such as Justin I, a former peasant turned emperor (ca. 450–527 CE).[4] The angel's appearance, in addition, bears some similarities to the

2. Kent L. Brintnall, "Queer Studies and Religion," *CRR* 1 (2013): 52. See also Joseph A. Marchal, *Appalling Bodies: Queer Figures before and after Paul's Letters* (New York: Oxford University Press, 2019), 5–6.

3. Brintnall, "Queer Studies and Religion," 53.

4. Judith L. Kovacs and Christopher Rowland, *Revelation: The Apocalypse of Jesus Christ* (Malden, MA: Blackwell, 2004), 118.

¹⁰:¹And I saw another mighty angel coming down from heaven, wrapped in a cloud, with a rainbow over his head; his face was like the sun, and his legs like pillars of fire. ²He held a little scroll open in his hand. Setting his right foot on the sea and his left foot on the land, ³he gave a great shout, like a lion roaring. And when he shouted, the seven thunders sounded. ⁴And when the seven thunders had sounded, I was about to write, but I heard a voice from heaven saying, "Seal up what the seven thunders have said, and do not write it down." ⁵Then the angel whom I saw standing on the sea and the land
raised his right hand to heaven
⁶and swore by him who lives
forever and ever,
who created heaven and what is in it, the earth and what is in it, and the sea and what is in it: "There will be no more delay, ⁷but in the days when the seventh angel is to blow his trumpet, the mystery of God will be fulfilled, as he announced to his servants the prophets."

Son of Humanity described in 1:12-16. Like the earlier character, the angel has a face that shines like the sun, and his legs are pillars of fire (10:1). The Son of Humanity's legs were like burnished bronze refined in a furnace, implying some kind of fire (1:15). The association of the angel's garment with clouds likewise echoes John's earlier description of the Son of Humanity "coming with the clouds" (1:7), and the rainbow over the angel's head draws a visual connection between this scene and the heavenly throne (4:3). Moreover, the image of the angel bridging sea and land with his stride (a scene that looks very similar to an image of Augustus from the *sebasteion* in Aphrodisias) points to his magnitude and authority.

The angel's voice confirms his manly guise. Just as in modern contexts, ancient people assigned gender to certain types of voices and speaking styles. In a speech to the men of Tarsus, Dio Chrysostom queried: "Supposing certain people should as a community be so afflicted that all the males got female voices and that no male, whether young or old, could say anything [in a manly] fashion, would that not seem a grievous experience?" (*1 Tars.* 38).⁵ Men were encouraged to cultivate, through practice and exercises, a loud voice, pushing their full breath through the neck and throat.⁶ A soft and breathy voice, the kind of voice we might

5. Maud W. Gleason, *Making Men: Sophists and Self-Presentation in Ancient Rome* (Princeton: Princeton University Press, 1995), 82.

6. Gleason, *Making Men*, 92.

associate with Marilyn Monroe, was a sure sign that a male lacked the self-control needed to be a true man.[7] The mighty angel of Revelation 10, however, need not fear the "grievous experience" of having a "female-voice," since a shout like a lion's roar (v. 3) puts him in the company of the messianic Lion announced in the throne room (5:5). Further, that voice is so powerful that it prompts a response from the "the seven thunders" (10:3-4), likely the thunders associated with God's throne and through which the divine communicates (4:5; see also Exod 20:18-19). The angel's voice signals an almost stereotypically "butch" persona. This is a queer identity, adopted by some lesbians and gay men, in which an individual acts, speaks, and appears in ways that culturally emphasize their masculinity.[8] So convincing is the angel's "butch swagger" that even the thunders respond to his voice.

After the manly call and response between the angel and thunders, John inserts himself into the narrative as a character who both interrupts and is interrupted. Upon hearing the thunders sound, John jumps at the chance to write down the message of their "sounding" for his audiences: "I was about to write" (ἤμελλον γράφειν), but his plans are aborted. Just as John picks up his pen, a voice from heaven squashes John's impulse by insisting that the message be sealed up and that John stop writing. The negative command "do not write" offers a stark contrast to the earlier command to "write …what you see" (1:11). John, it seems, has acted out of turn. He has misunderstood his role in this instance of communication. This is a moment of confusion, John's confusion, about who has the power to control and share heavenly information.

John's depiction of control being exercised over his attempt to convey the message, the command, "do not write it down" (10:4), heightens the digression's gendered power dynamic. John is now part of a hierarchical relationship in which he is to submit to the will of hypermasculine heavenly powers. This hierarchy is righted when the mighty angel takes back control of the narrative by raising his right hand and swearing that "there will be no more delay" (v. 7). The angel effectively shushes John in the narrative that John writes! By doing this, the angel controls when and how the message of God's "mystery" will be revealed (v. 8; see "Translation Matters: μυστήριον"). As a result, John depicts himself

---

7. Gleason, *Making Men*, 83.

8. Susan Stryker, *Transgender History: The Roots of Today's Revolution*, 2nd ed. (Berkeley: Seal Press, 2017), 23.

as "put in his place," or effectively feminized within the ancient under-standing of gender, a queer kind of experience.

As feminist readers, we might sympathize with John for being quieted in this way. There is a long history of women being told not to speak in one way or another. The "shushing" of women and femmes, those whose traits and mannerisms are aligned with femininity,[9] famously appears in Paul's letter to the Corinthians where the apostle asserts that they should be silent and subordinate (e.g., 1 Cor 14:34; see also 1 Tim 2:12). The presence of women actively involved in his congregations, even holding leadership positions, suggests that many women did not take this too seriously (e.g., Rom 16:1-16). More recently, attempts at quieting women politicians, like US Senators Kamala Harris (now US vice president) and Elizabeth Warren, have led to feminist outrage and organizing.[10] Still, John's being told to shut up does not entirely compare. Even though John attributes his vision to God, decentering his importance to some extent, his voice looms large throughout Revelation. Maybe we should take consolation, however, in knowing that John is not always correct and that he occasionally needs to be shut down and disempowered.

The mighty angel's claim that the "mystery of God" will be fulfilled (10: 7) reminds audiences that this narrative is an apocalypse, an unveil-ing of things that have been hidden or covered, i.e., mysterious things (1:1). This mystery, in contrast, is not just the revelations offered by John. Rather, the angel affirms that God's mystery was "announced to his servants the prophets" (10:7). While John may count himself among the prophets, since he characterizes the words of Revelation as prophecy (1:3), the use of the past tense, "announced," stresses that the angel refers to John's predecessors, the prophets of Israel and other godly messen-gers. They are the ones who announced, from Revelation's perspective, the soon-to-be revealed mystery that will be fulfilled. This claim affirms the continuing significance of the biblical prophetic tradition. Again, this is a reminder that John presents his vision within the currents of Jewish tradition and teaching, even if Revelation eventually becomes part of a different stream.

9. Stryker, *Transgender History*, 23.

10. Paul Kane and Ed O'Keefe, "Republicans Vote to Rebuke Elizabeth Warren, Saying She Impugned Sessions's Character," *The Washington Post*, February 8, 2017, https://www.washingtonpost.com/news/powerpost/wp/2017/02/07/republicans-vote-to-rebuke-elizabeth-warren-for-impugning-sessionss-character/.

TRANSLATION MATTERS: μυστήριον

Μυστήριον, often translated as "mystery," occurs several times in Revelation (1:20; 10:7; 17:5, 7). The language of mystery appears in other Jewish apocalyptic texts, including Daniel. In this text, mystery (μυστήριον in the LXX and רז in the Hebrew) refers to both the dream given to King Nebuchadnezzar that must be interpreted and the interpretation God gives to Daniel in a vision (2:18-19). A mystery is both the unknown and that made known by God. Elsewhere in the writings of the New Testament, the term tends to denote things and teachings associated with God or Christ. The Gospels depict Jesus telling his followers that they will "know the mysteries [μυστήρια] of the kingdom of heaven" (Matt 13:11) or, in Mark and Luke, the "kingdom of God" (Mark 4:11; Luke 8:10). Paul, likewise, describes the message of Christ that he preaches as a mystery of God (e.g., 1 Cor 2:1, 7; 4:1) and the author of 1 Timothy suggests that the "mystery of our religion is great" before proceeding to offer an early Christian creed (3:16).

Some ancient Greek religions, which continued to be popular in the Roman period, revolved around initiates learning mysterious teachings and undergoing secret rituals. The most famous of these "great mysteries" were the Eleusinian mysteries, a tradition memorializing Hades's kidnapping of Persephone, and the Samothracian mysteries, rituals conducted in a temple complex atop a peak on the island of Samothrace. Plutarch compares the initiation rites of the mysteries to dying and then finding oneself in an open meadow, a kind of heaven, where there is freedom, including freedom from ignorance (*Mor.* 15.178).[11] Ironically, while the Greek word for mystery comes from the word for "to close" (μύω, or the infinitive μυεῖν),[12] the rites of mystery traditions lay bare the meaning of life and death to the initiated. Sarah Iles Johnston notes that elites in the Roman imperial period sometimes participated in a kind of "grand tour" to visit the locations of different mystery religions, to be initiated into as many as possible.[13]

Given the importance of these traditions in the ancient Mediterranean, John's use of μυστήριον in Revelation potentially evokes all these meanings, as his audience members would likely have had a range of religious experiences and backgrounds. Some may have been initiates into the mysteries at one point in time, coming to the Jesus movement, which initiated adherents through baptism (e.g., Acts 2:38-39; 10:48; 19:1-5), as another mystery religion.

With the proliferation of mystery traditions around him, John uses μυστήρια in an ambivalent way. Mystery does not always connote something given or fulfilled by God, as it does in Revelation 10:7. The fact that "Mystery" is emblazoned on the forehead of Babylon (17:5), providing a mystery that needs interpreting by John's angelic guide (17:7), suggests that not all mysteries are created equal.

---

11. Yulia Ustinova, "To Live in Joy and Die with Hope: Experiential Aspects of Ancient Greek Mystery Rites," *BICS* 56 (2013): 108, 116.

12. Sarah Iles Johnston, "Mysteries," in *Ancient Religions*, ed. Sarah Iles Johnston (Cambridge: Harvard University Press, 2007), 99.

13. Johnston, "Mysteries," 107.

While it is necessary for John's audiences to understand the mystery behind Babylon, the title "Mystery" points to something that John presents as evil. Hearers, with the guidance of revelation from God and communicated through John, must be able to discern between mysteries that are divinely given and those being sold by bad actors.

The fact that Babylon, who will be characterized as a sex-worker, bears the name "Mystery," moreover, points to an ancient association between some mystery traditions, especially the cults of Dionysus (god of wine) and Cybele (a mother goddess), and being "non-man" (see p. lxxii). Both traditions were associated with the "East" or what is now Turkey, and one way of highlighting their "foreignness," especially during the Roman period, was by depicting the cults' adherents as non-men and excessive in their behavior. In his play *The Bacchae*, Euripides depicts the story of how Dionysus's female followers were swept up by the god into a violent kind of ecstasy, tearing cattle apart piece by piece with their bare hands (730–770). In the case of Cybele, her male priests, called *galli*, were known for the practice of self-castration as well as a tendency toward frenzy (Livy, *Ab urbe cond.* 11.63, 65). As Jacob Latham observes, the focus on the "exotic" and fanatical actions of the *galli* by Romans served as a way of defining, negatively, ideal masculinity.[14] The practices of mystery cultists like the *galli* were treated with disdain by many Roman elites, including Dionysius of Halicarnassus (d. ca. 7 BCE) who famously described them as "fabulous clap-trap" (*Rom. Ant.* 2.19.4).[15] This negative association between mystery religions and gender performance may be one reason why John identifies Babylon as Mystery, but his use of it in relation to God also points to the fact that his own religious grounding stands outside of the Roman norm.

John the Submissive Prophet (10:8-11)

After being put in his place by the voice from heaven, John reaffirms his status as a prophet although he highlights his submissive or feminized role in relation to the divine. The scene parallels the story of the prophet Ezekiel, who preceded John in communicating God's mystery: "He said to me, O mortal [lit. "son of humanity"], eat what is offered to you; eat this scroll, and go, speak to the house of Israel. So I opened my mouth, and he gave me the scroll to eat. He said to me, mortal, eat this scroll that I give you and fill your stomach with it. Then I ate it; and in my mouth it was as sweet as honey" (Ezek 3:1-3). The explicit echoing

14. Jacob Latham, " 'Fabulous Clap-Trap': Roman Masculinity, the Cult of Magna Mater, and Literary Constructions of the *galli* at Rome from the Late Republic to Late Antiquity," *JR* 92 (2012): 102.

15. Latham, "Fabulous Clap-Trap," 101. While originally from Halicarnassus, a city in Asia Minor, Dionysius studied and worked in Rome and wrote the influential *Roman Antiquities* in which he makes this characterization.

[8]Then the voice that I had heard from heaven spoke to me again, saying, "Go, take the scroll that is open in the hand of the angel who is standing on the sea and on the land." [9]So I went to the angel and told him to give me the little scroll; and he said to me, "Take it, and eat; it will be bitter to your stomach, but sweet as honey in your mouth." [10]So I took the little scroll from the hand of the angel and ate it; it was sweet as honey in my mouth, but when I had eaten it, my stomach was made bitter.

[11]Then they said to me, "You must prophesy again about many peoples and nations and languages and kings."

of this earlier tradition underscores for audiences that John is not the first prophet, even though he will imply that he is the last (22:18-19).

In *Are We Not Men?*, Rhiannon Graybill uses the language of "unmanning" to describe how the prophetic figure of Ezekiel is demasculinized in a way that allows him to become open and receptive to the message of God. The term "unmanning" comes from the journals of a nineteenth-century German judge who experienced a nervous breakdown before being called by God as a prophet. Graybill explains that the judge, Daniel Paul Schreber, believed he must be feminized to be penetrated by God and God's message.[16] Graybill finds this a helpful way for understanding Ezekiel's prophetic mission and identifies a number of ways that he too is unmanned, or feminized, by God. Among the things that unman Ezekiel is being penetrated by the divine scroll (2:9-3:3), which John re-creates here.

John's unmanning, something hinted at in the previous verses, is made explicit when a voice from heaven and the mighty angel command him to take and eat the "little scroll" the mighty angel holds. As with Ezekiel before him, John's very body receives an object of divine origin, although in contrast to the earlier tradition John does not receive the scroll directly from God. Still, the mighty angel looks enough like the Son of Humanity to be his proxy. Unlike before, when John presumptively set out to write, now he willingly and without question does what he is told—taking, eating, and ingesting the scroll. Viewed through the lens of ancient assumptions about gender and sex, where receptivity is understood generally as a feminine characteristic,[17] John takes on the role of

16. Rhiannon Graybill, *Are We Not Men? Unstable Masculinity in the Hebrew Prophets* (New York: Oxford University Press, 2016), 16.

17. Deborah Kamen and Sarah Levin-Richardson, "Lusty Ladies in the Roman Imaginary," in *Ancient Sex*, ed. Ruby Blondell and Kirk Ormand (Columbus: Ohio State University Press, 2015), 231–52.

someone who is intentionally receptive or a "bottom," to use language often employed in gay and other queer sexual relationships.[18] (In fact, all who are faithful to God are effectively bottoms.) The scroll is phallic in shape but feminine, perhaps even vaginal, in its comparison to honey. The sticky and sweet substance traditionally evokes thoughts of sex and sexuality, including in the Song of Songs where the female lover's lips "distill nectar" and under her tongue is "milk and honey" (Song 4:11).[19] In the Roman context, being a receptive sexual actor in this way, through oral sex, was a stigmatized role. Accusations of performing *fellatio*, a Latin term Roman authors used, becomes a conventional way of slandering opponents.[20] In this way, by taking a kind of queer scroll into his mouth, John confirms his queerness and that of his message.

Revelation is not literally depicting oral sex; however, the analogy aids in recognizing the power dynamics of this scene. Thinking about how the gendered performance between the mighty angel and John recollects a sexual relationship helps us see the hierarchy at play in these verses and sheds light on how John depicts himself as a faithful prophet. Even though the dominant culture values the one who speaks with a masculine voice and acts with authority, in this scene John is quieted and takes on the receptive role, a kind of queer identity. Again, we are not making any claims about John's sexual identity. Modern notions of sexual identity are anachronistic, since first-century ideas about gender and sex were quite different from our own. Even the terms of "homosexuality" and "heterosexuality" are a relatively recent (and Western) invention, emerging only during the eighteenth and nineteenth centuries.[21] Our point is that in this digression, John begins to show us what it means to be a faithful follower of the Lamb, that ambiguously gendered figure who shares the throne with God.

In this chapter, Revelation shows John in a power dynamic that may have been unsettling to some, especially those who might want to hear that their God works through powerful leaders. By showing himself in a way that may diminish his masculinity in the eyes of his audiences, John emphasizes both God's ultimate power (e.g., God is the only true "top" in the cosmic hierarchy) and the belief that God works through

18. Graybill, *Are We Not Men?*, 105.

19. Graybill, *Are We Not Men?*, 102–3.

20. Craig A. Williams, *Roman Homosexuality*, 2nd ed. (Oxford: Oxford University Press, 2010), 218–19.

21. Williams, *Roman Homosexuality*, 6–7.

things that are a "scandal," an idea similar to Paul's teaching about the cross (1 Cor 1:23). Given this, I wonder if the resistance that some early Christians had to the book of Revelation being counted as Scripture (see p. lxxxvii) might be on account of John's self-presentation. Were those in the cities of Roman Asia Minor reluctant to listen to a message to a self-depicted "bottom"? This is speculation, but the fact that some modern Christians refuse to listen to and learn from "queer" teachers and preachers, evidenced by church policies around ordination, suggests the possibility. Here, moreover, an expansive understanding of queer is helpful, since even those of us in the LGBTQIA+ community should ask whether there are other "queer" or non-normative identities, especially intersectional identities, that we fail to acknowledge. That is, is the authority of LGBTQIA+ people with multiple minoritized identities, such as race, class, ability, recognized in the same way as White, middle-class gays and lesbians?

Despite its sweet taste, the scroll that John ingests leaves his stomach bitter. This bodily sensation indicates that the message John as prophet will share is harsh, just as Ezekiel offered words of judgment (Ezek 5:8). This message, according to both the angel and the voice from heaven, pertains to "many peoples and nations and languages and kings" (10:11). John used a similar phrase to describe the multiethnic and multilingual crowd that stands before the throne of God (7:9). Here, however, the addition of "kings" signals that this prophecy specifically implicates those in power, those who embrace and perform masculinity on the world stage.

Revelation 11

The Power of Witness

Coined years earlier by Black feminist activist Tarana Burke, "#MeToo" went viral in 2017 as women (mostly) began using the hashtag to acknowledge their experiences of sexual harassment and assault. Revelations about famous and powerful men (again, mostly, but not entirely) who were serial abusers, including actors, directors, political figures, coaches, doctors, professors, and religious leaders, fueled the "#MeToo" responses online and in print. This brought renewed attention to the magnitude of the problem of sexual violence, and the "#MeToo" hashtag spawned additional versions, including #NiUnaMenos (Argentina), #ArewaMeToo (Nigeria), and #ChurchToo. The result of these testimonies included the arrest, prosecution, and punishment of a few perpetrators, and public conversations created some space for survivors to deal with their pain and outrage.[1]

The #MeToo movement revealed, in addition, the danger of witnessing as the claims of many survivors were met with disbelief, mockery, and further harassment. One of the most notable witnesses of the #MeToo movement was Dr. Christine Blasey Ford, who testified that Supreme

1. For an early recounting of the "me too" movement, see Carly Gieseler, *The Voices of #MeToo: From Grassroots Activism to a Viral Roar* (Lanham, MD: Rowman & Littlefield, 2019). See also Shanell T. Smith, *Touched: For Survivors of Sexual Assault Like Me Who Have Been Hurt by Church Folk and for Those Who Will Care* (Minneapolis: Fortress, 2020).

Court nominee Brett Kavanaugh sexually assaulted her. Her witness was met with public scrutiny and her credibility attacked publicly; ultimately, Kavanaugh was appointed to a lifetime seat on the highest court in the United States.[2] Discussions of the #MeToo movement were highly gendered and focused primarily on cisgender, White women, and in cases where men witnessed to their experiences of sexual abuse, their gender and sexual identities were challenged. For instance, when actor Terry Crews revealed that a Hollywood executive had groped him, rapper 50 Cent mocked him online, implying he wasn't a man for being assaulted.[3] Witnessing, especially to the violence of patriarchy, often brings with it further repression and even more violence. Sometimes that takes the form of erasure. Even though almost half (47 percent) of all trans and gender nonconforming individuals experience sexual assault at some point in their lives (the percentage is even higher for those who are Native American, Black, Middle Eastern, or multiracial), their #MeToo stories and experiences receive comparably little attention.[4]

The power and peril of witness are important themes in Revelation 11, and gender plays a role in how John depicts the Two Witnesses[5] at the center of this vision. John presents these two nameless witnesses as models of what it means to be an ideal Jesus follower, which he foresees as including victimization. The Two Witnesses are depicted as vulnerable and feminized, echoing the "unmanning" of John in Revelation 10. Despite this, John promises the possibility of a "remanning" of the Witnesses, as their lives parallel the first and "faithful witness," Jesus Christ (1:5). Thus, the Two Witnesses provide a model for John's audience members.

2. See Peter Baker, "Christine Blasey Ford's Credibility under New Attack by Senate Republicans," *The New York Times*, October 3, 2018, https://nyti.ms/2OAmJUw.

3. For example, "50 Cent Mocks Terry Crews over Sexual Assault Claims," *BBC News*, June 27, 2018, sec. Newsbeat, https://www.bbc.com/news/newsbeat-44625597.

4. S. E. James et al., "Executive Summary of the Report of the 2015 U.S. Transgender Survey" (Washington, DC: National Center for Transgender Equality, 2016), https://transequality.org/sites/default/files/docs/usts/USTS-Executive-Summary-Dec17.pdf. See also V. Jo Hsu, "(Trans)forming #MeToo: Toward a Networked Response to Gender Violence," *Women's Studies in Communication* 42 (July 3, 2019): 269–86.

5. I capitalize "Two Witnesses," since these unnamed figures function collectively as a character.

Imagining the Temple (11:1-2)

John sets the scene for the Two Witnesses by continuing to draw on the story of Ezekiel, the prototype for John's prophetic ministry, as seen in the last chapter. Here, John's inspiration comes from the final chapters of the prophetic book. Writing after the destruction of the temple by the Babylonians in the sixth century BCE, Ezekiel builds a visionary temple for his audience by orally describing, and thereby constructing conceptually, how an angelic figure measures the temple walls, gates, courts, furniture, and surrounding areas. The specific measurements and references to decorative motifs make this imagined space feel real (Ezek 40–42).[6] This visionary temple promises the prophet's audience a new temple and continuing access to the divine (43:1-5). Like Ezekiel, John's prophetic vision comes in the wake of the Jerusalem temple's destruction, albeit by the Romans. John, however, resists taking his audiences on a visionary tour of a future temple. Although a voice instructs him to measure the temple and its altar and worshipers, and he even receives a measuring rod (11:1), John fails to follow through with the task. This lack of interest in the physical details of the temple reveals that this imagery is more about who his audience members are called to be than about the former or any future temple.

Even though John appears disinterested in the physical structure of the Jerusalem temple, it seems likely that the space and its destruction would have loomed large in the memories of many of Revelation's audience members. Prior to its destruction, the temple connected Jews throughout the empire to their ancestral home and to the hope of a future home for all who had been dispersed (Isa 2:1-5). Annual offerings sent to Jerusalem nurtured this connection, as did the occasional pilgrimages and the stories told by returned pilgrims.[7]

6. The language of "imagined space" originates with Edward Said's work on the imagined geographies of colonial and postcolonial thinking. See Edward W. Said, *Orientalism* (New York: Knopf Doubleday, [1978] 2014). The idea of using this to think about Revelation 11 was introduced to me through the work of my former student Erin Palmer. See Erin Palmer, "Imagining Spaces: The Function of Imagined Space in Ezekiel and Revelation" (Undergraduate Honors Thesis, Elon University, 2013).

7. Jonathan Trotter, *The Jerusalem Temple in Diaspora: Jewish Practice and Thought during the Second Temple Period* (Leiden: Brill, 2019), 13–15, 106–10. See also Rivka Ulmer, "The Jerusalem Temple in *Pesiqta Rabbati*: From Creation to Apocalypse," *Hebr. Stud.* 51 (2010): 242.

Rev 11:1-2

^{11:1}Then I was given a measuring rod like a staff, and I was told, "Come and measure the temple of God and the altar and those who worship there, ²but do not measure the court outside the temple; leave that out, for it is given over to the nations, and they will trample over the holy city for forty-two months."

Given the cultural importance of the temple for conceptualizing Jewish identity, temple imagery appears throughout Revelation's narrative.[8] At this point in his account, John has already mentioned several things associated with the temple, including the altar (6:9; 8:3-5; 9:13), incense (8:3-4), pillars (3:12), and worshipers (7:15). Later, he will mention seeing the temple (ναός) itself open in heaven (11:19) and angels moving in and out of the temple space (14:15, 17; 15:5, 8; 16:1, 17). At this point, however, John's focus turns to the idea of the temple as a way of characterizing the faithful.

The command to include the altar (θυσσιαστήριον) when measuring the temple evokes the altar imagery that appears earlier in Revelation. The first reference to the altar occurs in John's description of the fifth seal, where he observes the altar in the throne room, where it shelters the souls slaughtered for their faithfulness to the word of God (6:9). In that space, John hears the souls calling out to God and the divine offering a response. The altar functions as a place of refuge for the faithful and as a place of connection between them and God. The idea that the altar serves as the site where God and the faithful connect appears again after the seventh seal when an angel with a censor stands before the altar offering up the saints' prayers to God (8:3). In Revelation, the altar represents the ancient idea of the temple as an important point of contact between the divine and human.

Given Revelation's use of altar imagery to connect the faithful with God, it is not surprising that the voice commands John to measure the altar *and* then "those who worship there" (11:1; NRSV). The English word "there" gives the sense that John might be referencing those who worship at the altar; however, "there" translates two words in Greek that literally read as "in it" (ἐν αὐτῷ). "In it" suggests that the voice commands John

---

8. Jacqueline M. Hidalgo, *Revelation in Aztlán: Scriptures, Utopias, and the Chicano Movement* (New York: Palgrave Macmillan, 2016), 87.

to measure those in the temple (and not those at it), evoking the idea of the temple as a space that contains and has boundaries. The idea of measuring those who worship *in* the temple connotes the construction of an insider group, a community characterized by worshiping (προσκυνέω) God. Elsewhere in the text this kind of worship includes, specifically, bowing before the throne to acknowledge God's greatness and authority (4:10; 5:14; 7:11).

In addition to the command to measure, the voice instructs John *not* to measure the court *outside* (ἔξωθεν), emphasizing "leave that out [ἔξωθεν]" (11:2). The voice explains that this "outside" area has been "given over to the nations," a description that seemingly alludes to the court of the gentiles, the so-called nations, in the historical temple in Jerusalem (Josephus, *J.W.* 5.193-94).[9] This court was the largest part of the first-century structure and provided non-Jews proximity to the worship of Israel's God, thereby physically alluding to the prophetic hope that salvation would extend to all people (e.g., Isa 60:2, 11). Despite this hope, Revelation describes the nations trampling over the "holy city," an image that is hard not to hear as a reference to the war with Rome. In the opening lines of the final volume of *The Jewish War*, Josephus, who lived through the war, describes the Roman emperor Vespasian ordering the razing of both the temple and the city of Jerusalem itself since nothing remained to slaughter or plunder (7.1.1).

Whether or not John wants his audiences to think of the siege of Jerusalem by the Romans, the temple imagery of 11:1-2 distinguishes between those who worship God and those who reject such worship. The "nations" destroy a central place providing access to the divine. John's concern here is not with the original temple in Jerusalem, nor is he concerned with rebuilding a future temple. Instead, like the coming image of the New Jerusalem in Revelation 21–22, where the temple's absence is noted (21:22), the temple communicates more about a people than a place.[10] The temple provides an image through which John again draws boundaries and reinforces communal identity. There are those inside the temple who worship and who should be measured and those outside who should not be measured.

---

9. Gregory Stevenson, *Power and Place: Temple and Identity in the Book of Revelation* (Berlin: De Gruyter, 2001), 132. See also Byron R. McCane, "Simply Irresistible: Augustus, Herod, and the Empire," *JBL* 127 (2008): 732.

10. In reference to the New Jerusalem as a community image, see Robert H. Gundry, "The New Jerusalem: People as Place, Not Place for People," *NovT* 29 (1987): 254–64.

Despite its brevity, Revelation's temple image demonstrates how building community involves boundary setting and exclusion. Even when we create community around something positive, like worship, we do so at the expense of others. Being part of a social group means conforming to the expectations of that group, whether those expectations are based on a particular identity, practice, or set of beliefs, and failure to do so means some kind of exclusion. As queer theologian Kent L. Brintnall writes, "Every social order requires a queer, and efforts to move the queer into the heart of the social order do not eliminate queerness; they displace it."[11] Even a community that focuses attention on those who have been excluded historically, whether because of sexuality, gender, race, religion, ability, or age, excludes others, especially when those others challenge the very existence of those now at the center. As feminists, we may aspire to create inclusive and welcoming communities, but our commitment to supporting women, girls, femmes, and others who have been oppressed by patriarchy and kyriarchy means that those who do not share those commitments must be left out.

John, likewise, envisions a community that leaves out those who do not worship God. At times, John suggests this exclusion is based on others' refusal to repent (e.g., 9:20). He assigns blame to those who are left outside. Nevertheless, John explicitly addresses Revelation to Jesus followers in these seven cities of Asia Minor, those who count themselves as insiders. In other words, John's insider and outsider rhetoric is not an attempt to convince those outside of the communities to join. Instead, Revelation highlights boundaries between them and "gentiles" to keep Jesus followers inside the fold. By using temple imagery to characterize Jesus followers in contrast to the "nations" or gentiles, John anticipates early Christian appropriation of Jewish identity in which the label "gentile" or "nations" means those outside the church and not, specifically, those who are not Jewish. "Gentile" becomes a way of saying "not us" and "not Christian." Christians today, however, need to remember that this way of using "gentile" puts Christians in the places of Jews and erases their identity. Exclusion, therefore, too easily slides into erasure, something we must vigilantly avoid.

11. Kent L. Brintnall, "Who Weeps for the Sodomite?," in *Sexual Disorientations: Queer Temporalities, Affects, Theologies*, ed. Kent L. Brintnall, Joseph A. Marcahl, and Stephen D. Moore (New York: Fordham University Press, 2018), 152.

TRANSLATION MATTERS: μάρτυς

Today the word "martyr," a transliteration of the Greek noun μάρτυς, conjures the faces and stories of people across time and space whose deaths are remembered as being for a cause bigger than their own interests. These are individuals who risk death in their commitment to a cause, such as religious or political freedom. Harvey Milk, the first openly gay person elected to office in California, is often considered a martyr since he was gunned down because he fought for the rights of gays and lesbians. The six women and three men who died at Mother Emanuel AME (African Methodist Episcopal) church in Charleston, South Carolina, one June evening in 2015 are considered martyrs because they extended hospitality to the man who would murder them. They invited him to join them for Bible study, even though he was a stranger, not knowing he was a White supremacist planning to use their deaths to begin a race war.

At the time Revelation was written, μάρτυς simply described anyone who was a witness to an event. It implied seeing and speaking, not dying. In the Greek translation of Exodus, God commands the Israelites not to act as a "malicious witness" (μάρτυς) in the context of a lawsuit (23:1). According to Numbers, a single μάρτυς is not sufficient in cases of murders; multiple witnesses are needed to put a murderer to death (35:30; see also Deut 17:6). The term can be used more metaphorically, as when God describes calling the people of Israel as witnesses in a "trial" being held by the nations. They will be witnesses to God's identity as the one God (Isa 43:10; see also Isa 44:8). The term can also be used in religious settings. Matthew, for example, describes bringing witnesses when there is a conflict within the community of Jesus followers (18:16).

In Revelation, John adds another layer of meaning to the word μάρτυς by explicitly associating the idea of being a μάρτυς with death. Jesus is a witness as the "firstborn of the dead" (1:5), and the One Like a Son of Humanity identifies Antipas who "was put to death" in Pergamum as "my witness, my faithful one" (2:13). John will later describe a Great Prostitute who drinks the blood of witnesses (17:6), implying that they have been killed violently. And, in Revelation 20 we see those who have been beheaded because of their "testimony" (μαρτυρία) as witnesses (20:4; see also 6:9; 12:11, 17). Being a witness or witnessing is so closely linked to dying in the text that μάρτυς eventually becomes equated with death. This meaning begins to grow during the first half of the third and fourth centuries CE, when Christians became the target of Roman persecution under Decius (ca. 250 CE) and then Diocletian (ca. 303 CE).[12]

---

12. The number of Christians who were put to death is impossible to know. Although Christian tradition suggests there was widespread loss of life during the third and early fourth centuries, only a handful of the martyr accounts that circulated in the ancient world are historically reliable. For a discussion of this, see Candida Moss, *The Myth of Persecution: How Early Christians Invented a Story of Martyrdom* (New York: HarperOne, 2013), 16.

Within this context of persecution, Christians used stories of death, which typically included some attention to lives as well, to construct and convey what it meant to be a faithful Christian. In so doing, authors necessarily used the gender categories and expectations given to them by the culture in which they lived. They worked within the common understanding of what it meant to be an ideal human, which meant being a man, and showed how Jesus followers put to death as treasonous were noble and virtuous. In other words, even though their lives and deaths did not fit neatly into Roman notions of ideal masculinity, as L. Stephanie Cobb writes, "Through martyrdom, then, Christians were literally dying to be men."[13] Female martyrs, however, were simultaneously called to be ideal women. Thus, the martyr Perpetua, after envisioning herself as a male gladiator ready for battle, pins her hair up, demonstrating that she is simultaneously an honorable woman (*Passion of Perpetua* 20). Revelation's use of μάρτυς, including the depiction of the Two Witnesses, anticipates these later martyrdom accounts, including negotiations of ancient gender categories and expectations.

Witnessing to Faithful Masculinity (11:3-13)

Unlike other characters in Revelation whose appearances receive significant attention from John, such as the One Like a Son of Humanity and the coming Woman Clothed in the Sun, the Witnesses are described simply as being draped in sackcloth, indicative of grief or mourning (e.g., Matt 11:21). The lack of specificity allows for much speculation about the Witnesses' identities. Interpreters sometimes align them with biblical characters who are expected to return to earth at the end of time. Enoch and Elijah are popular candidates since Scripture claims they were taken from the earth by God instead of dying at the end of their lives.[14] Hildegard of Bingen, for example, taught that Enoch and Elijah would return to the earth during a time when the church's faith was in doubt and that they would call believers back to lives of virtue (*Scivias* 3.11.10, 30). Other popular candidates among medieval interpreters were St. Francis of Assisi (d. 1226), famous for his love of animals and for embracing a life of poverty, and Peter John Olivi (d. 1298), a prolific Franciscan monk venerated by many. William Blake suggested that the Two Witnesses were John Wesley (d. 1791) and George Whitfield (d.

---

13. L. Stephanie Cobb, *Dying to Be Men: Gender and Language in Early Christian Martyr Texts* (New York: Columbia University Press, 2008), 15.

14. In Gen 5:21-24, Enoch walks with God and is taken by God at his death. God also takes Elijah, the prophet, although he does so with a chariot, according to 2 Kgs 2:11-12. The prophet Malachi reports that Elijah will return on the day of the Lord (4:5) and 4 Ezra 6:26 explains that those who have not died will return at the end.

[3]"And I will grant my two witnesses authority to prophesy for one thousand two hundred sixty days, wearing sackcloth."

[4]These are the two olive trees and the two lampstands that stand before the Lord of the earth. [5]And if anyone wants to harm them, fire pours from their mouths and consumes their foes; anyone who wants to harm them must be killed in this manner. [6]They have authority to shut the sky, so that no rain may fall during the days of the prophesying, and they have authority over the waters to turn them into blood, and to strike the earth with every kind of plague, as often as they desire.

[7]When they have finished their testimony, the beast that comes up from the bottomless pit will make war on them and conquer them and kill them, [8]and their dead bodies will lie in the street of the great city that is prophetically called Sodom and Egypt, where also their Lord was crucified. [9]For three and a half days members of the peoples and tribes and languages and

1770), founders of Methodism.[15] More recently, the two leaders of Heaven's Gate, an apocalyptic religious movement that believed UFOs were coming to take their eternal souls to the "Next Level," identified themselves as the Two Witnesses of Revelation. They went by the names "Bo and Peep" and "Ti and Do" and died by suicide in 1997 in preparation for leaving earth.[16] In each of these cases, the Witnesses are thought to serve as heralds of a quickly approaching end. Associating the Two Witnesses with specific persons links the text to the historical moment of the interpreter, even though the tendency to make these connections runs counter to John's generic depiction of the Witnesses. Despite this, the fact that interpreters have found Revelation's depictions of the Two Witnesses malleable enough to fit the identities of individuals across time points to the effectiveness of the imagery.

John models the Witnesses after a description of two figures envisioned by Zechariah, a connection signaled when he describes them as "the two olive trees and the two lampstands that stand before the Lord of the earth" (Rev 11:4).[17] Zechariah makes clear the identity of the two

15. Judith L. Kovacs and Christopher Rowland, *Revelation: The Apocalypse of Jesus Christ* (Malden, MA: Blackwell, 2004), 127–30.

16. Benjamin E. Zeller, *Heaven's Gate: America's UFO Religion* (New York: NYU Press, 2014), 28.

17. The prophet Zechariah, like John in Rev 10, receives a bit of rebuke from an interpreting angel, who seems to think the prophet should know the meaning of his vision (Zech 4:4, 13). See Bart B. Bruehler, "Seeing through the עיכים of Zechariah: Understanding Zechariah 4," *CBQ* 63 (2001): 440.

Rev 11:3-13 (cont.)

nations will gaze at their dead bodies and refuse to let them be placed in a tomb; [10]and the inhabitants of the earth will gloat over them and celebrate and exchange presents, because these two prophets had been a torment to the inhabitants of the earth.

[11]But after the three and a half days, the breath of life from God entered them, and they stood on their feet, and those who saw them were terrified. [12]Then they heard a loud voice from heaven saying to them, "Come up here!" And they went up to heaven in a cloud while their enemies watched them. [13]At that moment there was a great earthquake, and a tenth of the city fell; seven thousand people were killed in the earthquake, and the rest were terrified and gave glory to the God of heaven.

figures, associating the presence of olive trees with the oil that is used to anoint individuals as God's chosen messengers or messiahs (Zech 4:1-14). In the prophetic text, their proximity to lamps implies that they draw people to God, like moths to a light. In Zechariah, the two likely signify Joshua and Zerubbabel, who are instrumental in the rebuilding of the temple after its destruction by Babylon.[18] While Revelation's audiences may not be familiar with all the layers of allusion here, the images of lamps and olive trees, a source for oil, suggest, at the least, that the Witnesses offer light to others. The connection to Zechariah, especially after a description of a temple, might imply that John presents the Witnesses as instrumental in bringing together the people of God.

The task of the Two Witnesses is straightforward; they have come to prophesy, and they will do so for 1,260 days, or three and half years (v. 3). Revelation's audiences hear none of their prophesying and testifying despite this long period of time (v. 7). Instead, their testimony resembles that of Jesus, as presented in Revelation—it is an embodied experience—a humiliating and public death, which is simultaneously a death of honor and victory. Before addressing their witness, it is important to note that John depicts the Two Witnesses as powerful and authoritative. The two possess superhuman and super-destructive powers that they can leverage if anyone tries to harm them (v. 6). John sources these powers from the stories of prophets and heroes.[19] Like Moses, the two can turn water into

18. Bruehler, "Seeing through the עיכים of Zechariah," 442–43.

19. Craig R. Koester, *Revelation: A New Translation with Introduction and Commentary,* AYB 38A (New Haven: Yale University Press, 2014), 497.

blood and strike the earth with plague (e.g., Exod 7:14-25); like Elijah they can stop the rain (1 Kgs 17:1; 18:1). While the words of the prophet Jeremiah were compared to fire (Jer 5:14; 20:9), these two can bring forth actual fire from their mouths to "consume" their foes (v. 5). The Two Witnesses wield powers that could easily be ascribed to the conquering Lion of Judah announced in the throne room (5:5). Yet, just as John never reports their testimony, neither does he ever mention the two unleashing their might.

TRANSLATION MATTERS: ἐξοθσία

The Greek text uses ἐξουσία twice in verse 6 to describe the powers of the Witnesses. The NRSV includes the English term "authority" in verse 3, suggesting that they have the "authority to prophesy," even though the Greek does not use ἐξουσία in that verse. The idea of being authorized, however, is implied by the voice speaking in verse 3 who says, roughly, "I will give [δώσω] to my two witnesses and they will prophesy." This is a place where John's Greek is simply unclear and English translators must try to make sense of the meaning.

Despite their power and authority (ἐξουσία), the Beast "that comes up from the bottomless pit [ἄβυσσος]" conquers and kills the Two Witnesses (v. 7). The reference to the abyss indicates that their conqueror, whom John describes in more detail in Revelation 13, is a manifestation of Satan, like both the fallen star and the angel who rules over the abyss (9:1-11). The Witnesses have been seemingly defeated by evil. The language of conquering (νικάω) recalls Revelation 2–3, where Christ called those in the seven churches to be conquerors or victors (ὁ νικῶν) and *not* the conquered (see "Translation Matters: ὁ νικῶν"). However, a central irony of Revelation, revealed in the image of the conquering Lion who is a slaughtered Lamb (5:5-6), is that conquering includes being conquered.

Describing the Witnesses' death as being conquered suggests a kind of "unmanning," just as John was unmanned in the previous chapter.[20] Even though they possess the authority and power of prophets, they still succumb to a foe. Moreover, the Witnesses are humiliated in death by having their dead bodies lie untended for everyone, "members of the peoples and tribes and languages and nations," to gaze upon (11:9). The "peoples," along with those in Revelation's audiences who see along with

---

20. Rhiannon Graybill, *Are We Not Men? Unstable Masculinity in the Hebrew Prophets* (New York: Oxford University Press, 2016), 16.

John, exercise power over the Two Witnesses through looking, placing the two in the role of a dishonored "non-man." This genderqueer positionality is, arguably, central to their witness, since it is an identity shared with the Lamb who stands slaughtered for all to see in the midst of the heavenly throne room. This is an embodied and envisioned testimony.

Refusing to bury the Witnesses' bodies, the "earth's inhabitants" gloat and celebrate over their deaths and even exchange gifts in response. The striking callousness echoes the crowds rooting for death in the gladiatorial games or crowds today egging on bullies who abuse others. YouTube seems to be a repository for heart-wrenching videos chronicling parents who cheer as their children get into physical altercations. For Roman moral thinkers, such as Seneca, this type of behavior indicated a serious character flaw and a lack honor (e.g., Seneca, *Ep.* 7.5). The inability of the crowd to control its own desire for blood and violence reveals a lack of virtue and, hence, their unmanliness. Ironically, the shameful and unmanly death of the Two Witnesses lays bare the shame and unmanliness of those influenced by the Beast, who, as we see in chapter 13, is hypermasculine. In some sense, the death of the Witnesses reveals for John's audiences the fragility of traditional masculinity and the folly of following the Beast.

Death at the hands of another, whether in war or in the arena, was not necessarily dishonorable in Revelation's world. A defeated gladiator, for example, could die a noble, manly death by embracing his fate without fear. In so doing, he (most gladiators were male, even though there were exceptions) exhibited control over the passions and bodily desires, including the desire to live. Moreover, Romans perceived the acceptance of death as a more noble path than enslavement.[21] Thus, the mother described in 4 Maccabees embodies ideal manhood, even though she dies: "O mother, soldier of God in the cause of religion, elder and woman! By steadfastness you have conquered even a tyrant, and in word and deed you have proved more powerful than a man" (16:14).[22] The Witnesses, however, are robbed of a noble death, as they are left in the streets, before the eyes of all, and thereby lose their manhood, just as Hector's body was feminized, penetrated by the swords of his foes, after being defeated by Achilles (*Iliad* 22).

---

21. Carlin A. Barton, *The Sorrows of the Ancient Romans: The Gladiator and the Monster* (Princeton: Princeton University Press, 2020), 11–30.

22. For a discussion of masculinity in 4 Maccabees, see Stephen D. Moore and Janice Capel Anderson, "Taking It Like a Man: Masculinity in 4 Maccabees," *JBL* 117 (1998): 249–73.

Just as John measures a temple that evokes the Jerusalem temple but is not the literal temple, so he situates the Witnesses within a Jerusalem that is not the literal Jerusalem. Upon their death, they lay dead "in the street of the great city that is prophetically called Sodom and Egypt, where also their Lord was crucified" (v. 8). Rome was *the* great city that ruled the world of Revelation's audience members and, consequently, materializes whenever John mentions "the great city," which he metaphorically describes as "Babylon" throughout the narrative (16:19; 17:18; 18:10, 16, 18, 19, 21). The "spiritual" names that John ascribes to this city signal that this is not a single a city, but a *kind* of city or political entity.[23] Just as the temple in 11:1-2 is not the Jerusalem temple and the Two Witnesses are not identifiable individuals, so this great city appears in various forms—Babylon, Rome, Egypt (which isn't even a city), and Sodom. Wherever God's people must witness bodily, experiencing violence and death at the hands of the Beast from the abyss, there stands the great city. Such was the case for those who could not find hospitality in Sodom (Gen 18–19)[24] and for the Israelites enslaved in Egypt. The seven cities where Revelation's audiences live likewise function as outposts of the great city as places where the followers of Jesus must endure (e.g., 2:2, 19; 3:10). The connection between the great city and Jesus's crucifixion signals Jerusalem, albeit not Jerusalem in general. This is Jerusalem as controlled by Roman powers. Perhaps, John's move to associate Jerusalem with Sodom, Egypt, and Rome serves as criticism of those who ruled the city, namely the Romans, implying their corruption.

The connection between the great city where the Witnesses die and come to life and Jerusalem explicitly connects their deaths with the "firstborn of the dead" (1:5). Like Jesus, their bodies testify to the reality of resurrection; when "the breath of life from God entered them" the two "stood on their feet" (11:11). The breath of life enlivens the body, including their feet; this is not a spiritual or metaphorical rebirth. John further emphasizes the connection to Jesus's death and resurrection by noting that this happens after three and a half days (v. 9), alluding to Jesus's

---

23. Even though the Greek reads that these cities are "spiritually" called Sodom and Egypt, the NRSV alters the language to "prophetically."

24. There is a long history of associating the destruction of Sodom with sexual sin (e.g., Jude 7), despite biblical traditions that associate Sodom's sin with pride and failure to take care of the poor and needy (e.g., Ezek 16:49). Revelation, however, does not associate the city with sexual sin.

three days in the tomb (e.g., Luke 24:7).[25] While terrifying for those who witness this event firsthand, the image promises those in Revelation's audiences that they have nothing to fear amid the cosmic conflict John reveals. The Witnesses' ascent into heaven on a cloud, moreover, parallels the ascension of Christ described in Acts: "he was lifted up, and a cloud took him out of their sight" (1:9) as well as evoking the descent of the Son of Humanity in clouds earlier in Revelation (1:7). It is on account of their death that the Two Witnesses faithfully witness to the testimony of Jesus.

The Two Witnesses function as part of a revisioning of masculinity that John performs throughout the narrative, beginning with the Son of Humanity and continuing through the end of the text. In this revisioning John negotiates for his listeners how to be a faithful Jesus follower, one of the saints, or someone at the top of a new gender hierarchy while potentially disassociating from the structures that ensure masculinity for their fellow Ephesians, Laodiceans, etc. The Two Witnesses' unmanning and subsequent remanning through resurrection potentially endorses a kind of toxic masculinity. As Brintnall observes, "It may very well be that the doctrine of the resurrection . . . has played the largest role in maintaining the illusion of masculinity necessary for the patriarchal denigration of women and womanish men."[26] That is, with the resurrection even the male body that has been feminized through violence and death regains its virility. The man conquers the ultimate enemy, death, by standing erect on his own two feet. This insinuates that being feminized is not enough to be faithful, not enough to procure a ticket on the cloud heading to the heavens. Thus, even while John continues to challenge traditional visions of masculinity the narrative of resurrection seemingly reasserts the gender status quo.

The Sound of the Seventh Trumpet (11:14-19)

After announcing the passing of the second woe, likely an earthquake that occurs when the Two Witnesses ascend into heaven (11:12), and the

---

25. The fact that three and a half is not the same as three is worth noting. This discrepancy reflects John's use of seven throughout the narrative, and three and a half is half of seven. Three and a half, likewise, alludes to the time that the Beast exercises authority (13:5) and to the time that the Woman Clothed in the Sun is in the desert, "a time, times, and half a time" (12:4; cf. Dan 7:25). See Koester, *Revelation*, 502.

26. Kent L. Brintnall, *Ecce Homo: The Male-Body-in-Pain as Redemptive Figure* (Chicago: University of Chicago Press, 2011), 62.

¹⁴The second woe has passed. The third woe is coming very soon.

¹⁵Then the seventh angel blew his
trumpet, and there were loud
voices in heaven, saying,
"The kingdom of the world has
become the kingdom of our
Lord
and of his Messiah,
and he will reign forever and ever."
¹⁶Then the twenty-four elders who sit
on their thrones before God fell on their
faces and worshiped God, ¹⁷saying,
"We give you thanks, Lord God
Almighty,
who are and who were,
for you have taken your great
power
and begun to reign.
¹⁸The nations raged,
but your wrath has come,
and the time for judging the
dead,
for rewarding your servants, the
prophets
and saints and all who fear
your name,
both small and great,
and for destroying those who
destroy the earth."
¹⁹Then God's temple in heaven was
opened, and the ark of his covenant
was seen within his temple; and there
were flashes of lightning, rumblings,
peals of thunder, an earthquake, and
heavy hail.

coming of a third (see also 9:12), the seventh angel reappears to blow a trumpet (11:14-15). The angel standing on the sea and the land had earlier announced the blast (10:7). These markers help Revelation's audiences keep their bearings as they experience John's visions, but they also unsettle things in the narrative, appearing unexpectedly at times. This trumpet takes audiences back into the heavenly throne room where the twenty-four elders praise the Lord God Almighty (11:16-18) and God's temple is opened in heaven with "the ark of his covenant" made visible (v. 19).

The two-part hymn in this chapter seems similar to earlier hymns. It comes, however, at a crucial point in the narrative. The first part of the hymn (v. 15), sung by voices in heaven, articulates the worldview that will unfold over the course of the next two chapters: a kingdom of the world, ruled by Satan and his earthly agents, which God and his Messiah, Jesus, have made their own. The next verses, which offer the twenty-four elders' response to this announcement, affirm this locus of power. God is "the one who is and the one who was" (the Greek uses singular verbs, while the NRSV uses plural to conform to the following clause), and he, along with Christ, has taken power and begun to reign (v. 16). They will make things right through their judgment. Moreover, the language of the hymn responds to the deferred masculinity of the Witnesses by asserting the power of the One Who Sits upon the Throne. Sitting on the heavenly throne means being at the top of the gender scale as the one who is "the Almighty," literally the all-powerful one (παντοκράτορ; v. 17). The Two Witnesses may be resurrected, but they remain subordinate to God.

Since this chapter opens with John measuring a temple that recalls the memory of the Jerusalem temple, it makes sense to interpret this temple in the same vein. This vision reveals the temple's heavenly location, beyond the ravages of time and history. The presence of the ark of God's covenant, the ceremonial box that held the covenant made between God and Moses on behalf of the Israelites (Exod 25:16, 21), highlights that this is not an earthy temple, since the ark had long been missing. John sees and reveals that this symbol of the relationship between God and God's people resides in heaven, likely with God.

Despite the memories evoked by the reference to a temple that has been destroyed, John highlights hope. This hope is true not only for the Witnesses, who are taken into heaven in a cloud (11:12), it is true for the temple as well. Even though the physical Jerusalem temple was destroyed, John sees a version in heaven (v. 19). Lightning, hail, and thundering show this as a place of power and a place of God's revelation. Just as God's revelation on Sinai was accompanied by thunder and lightning (Exod 19:16-19), so too God reveals to the people in John's audiences that the divine presence continues to reside in the temple of heaven.

Even though the violence and humiliation experienced by the Two Witnesses challenge traditional narratives about masculinity, the violence they endure remains a problem. The Witnesses should not have to be murdered, abused, and humiliated to experience life with God. God's grace can be experienced without first experiencing abuse. Along these lines, Shanell Smith, when discussing sexual abuse in Christian congregations, declares that God is not the "author of . . . sexual assault."[27] Revelation may depict a God who demands faithfulness through harm and even torture and who appears both to threaten and instigate sexual assault (2:22; 17:16-17), but these claims reflect a human perspective. In fact, the claim that God requires abuse or that an act that demeans and harms is God's will is one of the ways the Beast, who appears in Revelation 13, usurps God's authority. These are among the Beast's blasphemous claims. What John, Revelation's human author, does get

27. Smith, *Touched*, 104.

right is the likelihood of experiencing abuse in systems that privilege domination, especially for people who do not fit neatly into gender binaries. At the same time, the stories of male survivors of sexual abuse shared during the #MeToo movement witness to the reality that even those with masculine power can experience victimization at the hands of others. The promise of resurrection in Revelation can offer and, again, the #MeToo phenomenon, remind us that there are possibilities for life even after our abusers have gloated over our pain. The online "trolls" who mock the stories of abuse recounted by assault survivors do not have the last word.

At the same time, it is important to acknowledge that the call to witness—to put personal pain out in the world for others to see, hear, engage, and even judge, is a difficult call to heed. Even though Revelation's idea of being a witness is not explicitly a call to share stories of abuse, recounting these experiences can be understood as part of a testimony against evil in the world. Just as John envisions being a witness as part of being faithful, so, as Rhiannon Graybill observes, "In the present moment there is a criticism of survivors who fail to narrate their experiences properly (even as this demand is itself grounded in the imperative to 'tell your story'). The invitation to share stories can also become an imperative, and/or a compulsion."[28] However, such divestment of power may be transformative for those who are invested culturally with masculine power, especially cisgender heterosexual White men, but for those who occupy a less privileged place being *compelled* to witness can be dangerous to body and spirit. Thus, it is imperative for individual readers of Revelation to recognize that John's vision of witness is born out of his historical context and that there are fruitful conversations to be had on how followers of Christ can witness in the present moment.

---

28. Rhiannon Graybill, "Fuzzy, Messy, Icky: The Edges of Consent in Hebrew Bible Rape Narratives and Rape Culture," *BCT* 15 (2019): 20, https://www.bibleandcriticaltheory.com/issues/vol-15-no-2-2019-bible-and-critical-theory/fuzzy-messy-icky-the-edges-of-consent-in-hebrew-bible-rape-narratives-and-rape-culture/.

Revelation 12:1-17

Revelation of the Goddess

The description of the Woman Clothed in the Sun in Revelation 12 provides a rare glimpse of goddess imagery within the New Testament.[1] In a book dominated by attention to masculinity, as we have seen throughout, an image that draws on traditions related to the feminine and the female divine seems to promise a change of pace. Understandably, many Christian women have embraced the Woman Clothed in the Sun as a source of authority. Feminist Christian author and peace activist Joyce Hollyday proclaims: "What an image of the glory and power of womanhood we have in the Bible's last book! Women as *portent*, an indication of things momentous and marvelous about to occur. . . . [T]he Woman Clothed with the Sun invites us forward, beckoning us toward the courage that she possesses. She will be there at the end, welcoming us into the light of her glory."[2] There is little doubt that women have found and continue to find inspiration in this shining goddess figure, although the text offers a more ambivalent portrayal of the Woman's role in God's reign.

---

1. Other references include mention of Artemis in Acts 19 and the allusion to Aphrodite in the name Epaphroditus, one of Paul's colleagues in Phil 2:25.

2. Joyce Hollyday, *Clothed with the Sun: Biblical Women, Social Justice, and Us* (Louisville: Westminster John Knox, 1994), xi.

In 1978 the groundbreaking feminist scholar Carol P. Christ, who passed away in 2021,[3] addressed the "Great Goddess Re-Emerging" conference with a clear explanation of "why women need the goddess." Christ offered multiple reasons, including both the psychological and political power of symbols, for why women should seek out images of female divinity.[4] Other feminists have been more cautious in recommending that women seek out goddess images since not all goddesses are created equal. Highlighting this, Rita Gross answered her own question about whether goddesses are inherently feminist with the response, "It depends."[5] Goddesses can be feminist or empowering if they "promote the humanity of women," but not all goddesses fit that bill.[6] More often than not, goddesses serve the needs of the patriarchal contexts from which they emerge. In such a manner, some feminist interpreters emphasize that the Woman Clothed in the Sun serves primarily as a vessel for John's patriarchal impulses.[7] Not only does she lack a name and much of a voice (save for crying out), but John also defines her primarily as the mother of a male child. Given this, can she really, paraphrasing Hollyday, "beckon us toward courage"?

The Woman Clothed in the Sun (12:1-6)

The Woman Clothed in the Sun is one of two "portents," literally "signs" (σημεῖα), that appear in heaven at the beginning of this chapter. The other is a Great Red Dragon who pursues and opposes her. Like the many "signs" in the Fourth Gospel (e.g., 2:11, 23; 3:2; 4:54; 6:2, 14; 11:47; 12:37; 20:30), these point to something meaningful beyond themselves and help audiences understand how God works in the world. Signs facilitate

3. Xochitl Alvizo, "In Memoriam: A Collective Tribute to Carol Patrice Christ 1945–2021," *Feminism and Religion,* July 15, 2021, https://feminismandreligion .com/2021/07/15/in-memoriam-a-collective-tribute-to-carol-patrice-christ-1945 -2021/.

4. Carol P. Christ, "Why Women Need the Goddess," in *Womanspirit Rising: A Feminist Reader in Religion,* ed. Carol P. Christ and Judith Plaskow (San Francisco: Harper and Row, 1979), 277.

5. Rita Gross, "Is the Goddess a Feminist?," in *Is the Goddess a Feminist? The Politics of South Asian Goddesses,* ed. Alf Hiltebeitel and Kathleen M. Erndl (New York: NYU Press, 2000), 104.

6. Gross, "Is the Goddess a Feminist?," 106.

7. E.g., Tina Pippin, "The Heroine and the Whore: Fantasy and the Female in the Apocalypse of John," *Semeia* 60 (1992): 71–73; Marla J. Selvidge, "Powerful and Powerless Women in the Apocalypse," *Neot* 26 (1992): 161–63.

[12:1]A great portent appeared in heaven: a woman clothed with the sun, with the moon under her feet, and on her head a crown of twelve stars. [2]She was pregnant and was crying out in birth pangs, in the agony of giving birth. [3]Then another portent appeared in heaven: a great red dragon, with seven heads and ten horns, and seven diadems on his heads. [4]His tail swept down a third of the stars of heaven and threw them to the earth. Then the dragon stood before the woman who was about to bear a child, so that he might devour her child as soon as it was born. [5]And she gave birth to a son, a male child, who is to rule all the nations with a rod of iron. But her child was snatched away and taken to God and to his throne; [6]and the woman fled into the wilderness, where she has a place prepared by God, so that there she can be nourished for one thousand two hundred sixty days.

understanding and belief.[8] Already, it seems the Woman is not important in her own right, serving more as a rhetorical tool or pedagogical aid.

As a visual sign, the Woman's appearance is striking. She wears the lights of the sky—the sun and stars, befitting her presence in heaven. Her feet rest on the moon (v. 1). The imagery resembles the iconography of Isis,[9] one of the most popular deities in the first-century Mediterranean world. An account of a vision of Isis from a second-century novel by Apuleius depicts the goddess hovering above the sea, wearing fine linen garments, a crown resembling a moon, and a cloak adorned with stars (Apuleius, *Metam.* 11.3-4). In the vision, Isis claims the mantles "mother of the universe, mistress of all the elements . . . queen of the dead, and foremost of heavenly beings" (Apuleius, *Metam.* 11.5). She describes herself as the embodiment of all gods and goddesses, identifying with Artemis, Aphrodite, Juno, Ceres, and the list goes on. This kind of overlapping and blending of divine identities was characteristic of ancient Mediterranean religion, where gods traveled with their devotees across the sea and via land routes.[10] John's appropriation of this goddess imagery is nothing out of the ordinary.

8. Gail R. O'Day and Susan Hylen, *John* (Louisville: Westminster John Knox, 2006), 59.

9. Adela Yarbro Collins, "Feminine Symbolism in the Book of Revelation," *BibInt* 1 (1993): 20–33.

10. Fritz Graf, "What Is Ancient Mediterranean Religion?," in *Ancient Religions*, ed. Sarah Iles Johnston (Cambridge, MA: Harvard University Press, 2007), 10.

Famous for her mercy and the gift of salvation, Isis counted among her devotees those in the highest echelons of the empire, especially during the Flavian dynasty (69–96 CE), when Revelation was written. During his reign (81–96 CE), Domitian rebuilt a shrine to Isis in Rome that had been destroyed by fire (Dio Cassius 66.24). To commemorate this and to ensure people were aware of his support of the goddess, even though he was not necessarily initiated as a member of her cult, Domitian issued coins depicting Isis and her consort Serapis (associated with Osiris) along with his own image.[11] Depictions of Isis often emphasized her role as mother to the god Horus. Statuettes and charms depicting her nursing Horus, an image type called "Isis Lactans," were popular in the ancient world and anticipated later depictions of Mary nursing Jesus ("Maria Lactans.")[12] This might be one reason why Isis was prevalent among Roman elites since the goddess aligned with an imperial emphasis on the importance of reproduction. Since the strength of the empire depended on population, Roman law incentivized having multiple children: men with three or more children received priority for government appointments, while women with three children were released from needing a male tutor or legal guardian to approve financial decisions.[13]

John evokes the reproductive aspect of his goddess image by stressing that the Woman Clothed in the Sun is both pregnant and in the process of giving birth (v. 2). Like Isis, the Woman is a divine mother. Even though John resists Roman political structures and dominance, John replicates patriarchal ideas about women, including the close association between a woman's worth and reproduction.[14] The assumption that a woman who is childfree is defective in some way is seen throughout biblical traditions about "barren" women, such as Sarah, Rebekah, Rachel, Elizabeth, and others (Gen 11:30; 25:21; 29:31; Luke 1:7). Notably, in biblical texts it is always the woman who is identified as unable to conceive, and therefore defective, and not her male partner. Candida R. Moss and Joel S. Baden observe that the bias against child-free women persists, even when it

11. Laurent Bricault, "The '*Gens Isiaca*' in Graeco-Roman Coinage," *The Numismatic Chronicle (1966–)* 175 (2015): 83–102; Sarolta A. Takács, *Isis and Sarapis in the Roman World* (Leiden: Brill, 2015), 19, 100–103.

12. Christopher A. Faraone, *The Transformation of Greek Amulets in Roman Imperial Times* (Philadelphia: University of Pennsylvania Press, 2018), 167.

13. Judith Evans Grubbs, *Women and the Law in the Roman Empire: A Sourcebook on Marriage, Divorce and Widowhood* (London: Routledge, 2002), 84.

14. Pippin, "Heroine and the Whore," 71.

comes to some of the world's most influential and powerful women, such as the former chancellor of Germany Angela Merkel. During Merkel's first campaign, the German media questioned her capacity to lead because of her being childfree.[15] Conversely, biblical images that reduce women's identity to being *only* a mother, such as we see in Revelation 12, similarly contribute to the distrust and cultural disparagement of childfree women and undermine the multifaceted abilities of mothers.[16]

Isis's popularity and prominence suggest that John purposely evokes her as part of his alter-imperial rhetoric, his assertion of the superiority of God's reign over that of Rome.[17] The Woman Clothed in the Sun is *not* Isis; instead, she is John's way of "throwing shade" at Isis and other goddesses and those who worship these deities. Relegating Isis's moon crown, one of the goddess's most notable attributes, to a position beneath the feet of the Woman puts Isis in "her place." Isis may be powerful, especially in Roman politics, but the Woman Clothed in the Sun is part of God's realm. The use of the Woman to critique a prominent goddess is one way John uses her image to support an agenda focused on challenging the dominant power structure. Still, this erasure of one "woman" by another "woman," an erasure contrived by a man, feels familiar. John fails to invite solidarity among women in his vision of God's reign.

John continues to diminish one of the Roman world's most famous mother goddesses and ancient mother goddesses more generally by focusing on the Woman's pain. In one verse, John references the pain of the Woman's pregnancy three times: "She was pregnant and was *crying out* in *birthpangs*, in the *agony* of giving birth" (v. 2; my emphasis). The focus on the Woman's pain evokes the Genesis story, where the intensity and pain of giving birth can be associated with being cast out of Paradise (Gen 3:16). The pain, it seems, is a result of having been tricked into disobeying God. The references to pain also reflect ancient Roman assumptions about the nature of childbirth, where women were often "victims of their motherhood" (Pliny the Younger, "To Velius Cerealis," *Ep.* 4.21.2-3).[18] Inscriptions on funerary monuments for women who

15. Candida R. Moss and Joel S. Baden, *Reconceiving Infertility: Biblical Perspectives on Procreation and Childlessness* (Princeton: Princeton University Press, 2015), 1.

16. Moss and Baden, *Reconceiving Infertility*, 14.

17. Margaret P. Aymer, "Empire, Alter-Empire, and the Twenty-First Century," *USQR* 59 (2005): 145.

18. Maureen Carroll, *Infancy and Earliest Childhood in the Roman World: "A Fragment of Time"* (Oxford: Oxford University Press, 2018), 57.

died in childbirth testify to the difficult births of ancient women. One memorial dedicated to an enslaved woman named Candida described labor as "torturous" (*CIL* 3.2267).[19] Another describes the "fury" of the infant over four days of labor.[20] Some in Revelation's audiences, especially those who may have gone through childbirth, might have felt for and with the Woman. Others, however, especially those with a negative assessment of women, might hear the Woman's cries as proof that women lack strength and self-control, essential masculine virtues in the Roman world. In other words, both giving birth and her agony highlight the Woman as a "non-man." From a modern perspective, however, the fact that the Woman gives birth while in the presence of a dragon who wants to devour her child underscores her power and resilience (12:4-5).

Because of her role as mother and the characterization of her child as the Messiah (see below), many interpreters associate the Woman of Revelation 12 with Mary. As a result, traces of the Woman's description appear in visual representations of the mother of Jesus. Among these are images of La Virgen de Guadalupe, which are based on a vision experienced by Cuauhtlatoatzin, a Nahuatl[21] man who took the name Juan Diego, evocative of John himself, in the sixteenth century. When La Virgen first revealed herself to Cuauhtlatoatzin as an Aztec princess, speaking in Nahuatl, the sun shone behind her, connecting her to an indigenous goddess.[22] When La Virgen's image miraculously materialized on Juan Diego's cloak, however, it resembled Mary, adorned in the guise of the Woman Clothed in the Sun with a star-covered veil, rays of the sun shining behind her, and a sliver of the moon beneath her feet. The cloak's imagery arguably reflects an encounter between indigenous religious experience and the colonizing efforts of the Spanish mission, which has been variously interpreted as the "Christianization" of an indigenous sun goddess or as a sign of God's acceptance of the indigenous people

19. Carroll, *Infancy and Earliest Childhood*, 61.

20. Carroll, *Infancy and Earliest Childhood*, 61. The original inscription is recorded in Georgius Kaibel, *Epigrammata Graeca* (Berlin, 1878), 218.

21. "Nahuatl" refers to indigenous peoples of Central Mexico at the time of the Spanish conquest of the Aztec Empire in 1519 as well as to the language they spoke. See Jeanette Rodriguez, *Our Lady of Guadalupe: Faith and Empowerment among Mexican-American Women* (Austin: University of Texas Press, 2010), 2.

22. Rodriguez, *Our Lady of Guadalupe*, 40.

despite Spanish prejudice.[23] Despite the historical distance, these interpretations of La Virgen raise the possibility that Revelation's imagery might have been similarly received as a validation of Isis traditions and not simply as an example of John's use of Isis to criticize the worship of mother goddesses.[24] Could ancient goddess devotees have understood the Woman Clothed in the Sun as the mother goddess infiltrating or subverting the Jesus followers' narrative? Perhaps. The goddess works in mysterious ways.

The connection between Revelation's Woman and Mary has become so culturally embedded that it is almost impossible for modern readers to disentangle them. The association appears early in Christian tradition; Oecumenius's sixth-century commentary offers one of the earliest attestations.[25] As a portent, however, the Woman Clothed in the Sun points to something beyond Mary. By adorning her with a crown of twelve stars, John connects the Woman and Israel's twelve tribes. The personification of Israel or the city Zion, as the heart of Israel, appears throughout Scripture. Often, this imagery casts Israel as a mother. Isaiah, for instance, explicitly depicts Zion as a woman in labor, although in this case, she delivers her son *before* labor pains come (66:7). Zion also nurses her children in Isaiah, although God characterizes himself as the mother of Jerusalem in this exact text (66:11-13).[26] Evoking this tradition, for John, the Woman can also be understood as Israel, the symbolic "mother" of the Messiah. John mentions the Beast making war on her "other children" who "hold the testimony of Jesus" (12:17),[27] a description which raises the idea that Jesus followers are a collective with a shared identity and anticipates later personifications of the church.

The Woman Clothed in the Sun is not the only sign or portent in heaven. The Great Red Dragon, who threatens the Woman and her future child, is similarly labeled (v. 3). The tension between the two figures is palpable as the Dragon stands before the woman and threatens her offspring. A gold-leafed illumination from the Bamberg Apocalypse (ca.

23. Ondina E. González and Justo L. González, *Christianity in Latin America: A History* (New York: Cambridge University Press, 2008), 58–60.

24. For a discussion of *La Virgen* in relation to Revelation, see David A. Sánchez, *From Patmos to the Barrio: Subverting Imperial Myths* (Minneapolis: Fortress, 2008).

25. Judith L. Kovacs and Christopher Rowland, *Revelation: The Apocalypse of Jesus Christ* (Malden, MA: Blackwell, 2004), 137.

26. Christl M. Maier, *Daughter Zion, Mother Zion: Gender, Space and the Sacred in Ancient Israel* (Minneapolis: Fortress, 2008), 203.

27. E.g., Brian K. Blount, *Revelation: A Commentary* (Louisville: Westminster John Knox, 2009), 232.

1010) captures this, the seven-headed creature glaring upward at the Woman and her child (fig. 3). John reveals the Dragon's identity as an embodiment of Satan in verse 9, but the description of the Great Dragon's tail sweeping down a third of the stars, throwing them to earth, makes his destructive nature obvious. The reference to his multiple heads, horns, and crowns, imagery that appears again in Revelation 13 and 17, indicates that this Dragon exercises great power.

The conflict between the Woman and Dragon is an example of what scholars call the "combat myth," a popular type of ancient story describing a cosmological battle between good and evil. Originating in ancient Near Eastern stories of creation, combat myths recount how a male hero, birthed by a divine mother, defeats the forces of chaos, represented by a monster or dragon, to restore order to creation.[28] One version of the myth featured Isis and her nemesis Typhon or Set, who was often depicted as a snake-like monster; Plutarch associates him with the color red (*Is. Os.* 22). Other ancient accounts of the combat myth revolved around the birth of twins Apollo and Artemis. In one version, the dragon Python pursued their mother Leto at the behest of the goddess Hera since their father was Hera's notoriously unfaithful husband, Zeus. A four-day-old Apollo avenges his mother by killing Python with arrows in this version.[29]

The far-reaching nature of the combat myth made it a popular source for political propaganda. Augustus, most notably, was depicted as a new Apollo, and images of Leto and Apollo defeating Python even adorned the military breastplate he wears in one of his most famous statues (now part of the Vatican's Roman art collection), *Augustus of Prima Porta.* Augustus wanted his subjects to envision him defeating threatening enemies to restore peace and order to the empire, just as Apollo defeated Python.[30] This version of the myth would have been familiar to some in Revelation's audiences; Artemis, Apollo's twin sister, was the patron deity of Ephesus, one of the cities referenced in the seven messages (2:1). Reenactments of the dramatic birth of Artemis and Apollo may have even played a part in Ephesian civic rituals.[31] John's vision presents an alternative version of the cosmic conflict in which the hero is now the child of the Woman Clothed in the Sun (v. 5).

28. Yarbro Collins, "Feminine Symbolism," 23.

29. Sánchez, *From Patmos to the Barrio*, 15–16.

30. Sánchez, *From Patmos to the Barrio*, 19–22.

31. David L. Balch, "Cult Statues of Augustus' Temple of Apollo on the Palatine in Rome, Artemis'/Diana's Birthday in Ephesus, and Revelation 12:1-5a," in *Contested Spaces: Houses and Temples in Roman Antiquity and the New Testament*, ed. David L. Balch and Annette Weissenrieder, WUNT 285 (Tübingen: Mohr Siebeck, 2012), 414.

Like versions of the combat myth that elevate Apollo over Artemis, John notes that the Woman's child is male by using both "son" (υἱός) and "male" (ἄρσην) in his description (v. 5). The emphasis on the child's maleness made very clear in the Bamberg illumination in which the child's penis is prominently displayed (fig. 3), raises the question, perhaps inadvertently, of whether there could be a female Messiah. For Revelation, the Messiah is associated with masculinity, as he will "rule all the nations with a rod of iron" (v. 5). John draws on the Greek translation of Psalm 2, which describes God's Messiah, the "anointed one" (χριστός or "christ"), as one who will "rule" (ποιμαίνω). In Revelation 12, ποιμαίνω is rendered "rule," even though the NRSV translates it as "shepherd" elsewhere (Luke 17:7; John 21:16; Acts 20:28; 1 Cor 9:7; Rev 7:17). The messianic child will be the Lamb, but here he is characterized as a shepherd with a staff made of iron. The phallic symbolism of the rod/staff brings attention to the maleness of this child and his power as Messiah. Again, we see that Revelation's concern here is not necessarily the Woman herself, but the Woman who gives birth to a son, who will supposedly become a man.

Some interpreters align Revelation 12 with the life of Jesus and suggest that being "snatched away" (ἁρπάζω) refers to his death and ascension into heaven (Acts 1:6-11). Brian K. Blount argues that the force of the verb ἁρπάζω implies the idea of crucifixion.[32] Another way of reading this being taken into heaven is as an adoption narrative. Adoption was a reality in the ancient world, especially for families with power and wealth but no male heirs. Augustus, for example, adopted his daughter's sons to secure a successor. A massive altar honoring the emperor in Rome, the *Ara Pacis*, memorializes the adoption by depicting the children in a religious procession led by Augustus. Even though Augustus's adopted children died before him, the imagery conveys the cultural importance of children, mainly sons, as the ones who continue the work of their fathers.[33] In this vein, some second-century Christians, including a group referred to as "Ebionites," believed that God adopted Jesus of Nazareth to become Christ. Unfortunately, we do not know whether they used Revelation's narrative as part of their justification for this belief since we only hear about them secondhand through their detractors (Irenaeus, *Haer.* 1.26.1-2). Nevertheless, it's possible to imagine that they thought of Jesus as continuing or maintaining the work of his divine father. In the case of Revelation, the messianic son will continue God's battle against the Dragon.

---

32. Blount, *Revelation*, 231.
33. Kathleen Lamp, "The *Ara Pacis Augustae*: Visual Rhetoric in Augustus' Principate," *Rhetoric Society Quarterly* 39 (2009): 15–17.

The image of the Woman's child being taken from her reverberates in countless similar stories of family separation, including recent accounts of a "zero-tolerance" immigration policy at the US and Mexico border that took children coming with families across the border into custody while deporting or incarcerating their parents. While the United States has made efforts to reunite families, in May 2021, almost a thousand families remained separated, and the progress for reuniting those torn apart continues to be slow.[34] At one point, the whereabouts of many children's parents remained unknown.[35] This is not the only case of children being "snatched" from parents in order to punish parents or protect children from other "dragons" such as a parent's drug addiction or mental illness, a situation of domestic abuse, or incarceration. Removing children from their parents and especially removing infants from their mothers have long been understood as harmful to both child and mother; such separation can have the same type of emotional and psychological impact on a mother as the death of a child.[36] Revelation's depiction of the Woman and the Male Child who is taken evokes the violence of these acts of separation. While we might agree that being saved from the Great Red Dragon is a good thing, this Woman reminds us that even women who may resemble a goddess may have a child taken from them at the same time they battle against forces of evil, poverty, racism, and other forms of institutional violence. Along these lines, Sharon Jacob and Jennifer T. Kaalund compare the experience of the Woman Clothed in the Sun with Black enslaved wet nurses in the antebellum United States. Like the Woman, these women were often not allowed to care for their own children as they were forced to care for those of their enslavers. She is not allowed to "protect or provide" for her child, although she is eventually able to care for other children, even though they may not be those she has birthed.[37] John, unfortunately, fails to offer any resolution to the

34. Miriam Jordan, "Migrants Separated from Their Children Will Be Allowed into U.S.," *The New York Times*, May 3, 2021, sec. U.S., https://www.nytimes.com /2021/05/03/us/migrant-family-separation.html.

35. Caitlin Dickerson, "Parents of 545 Children Separated at the Border Cannot Be Found," *The New York Times*, October 21, 2020, https://www.nytimes.com /2020/10/21/us/migrant-children-separated.html.

36. Wendy Marsh and Jen Leamon, "Babies Removed at Birth: What Professionals Can Learn From 'Women Like Me,'" *Child Abuse Review* 28 (January 1, 2019): 82–86.

37. Sharon Jacob and Jennifer T. Kaalund, "Flowing from Breast to Breast: An Examination of Dis/Placed Motherhood in African American and Indian Wet Nurses," in *Womanist Interpretations of the Bible: Expanding the Discourse*, ed. Gay L. Byron and Vanessa Lovelace (Atlanta: SBL Press, 2016), 230.

Woman's story. There is no happy reunion between mother and son. To me, this demands that Christian feminists advocate for parents like the Woman who have had their children taken or who live with that fear. It also means we should work to create social structures that support parents and care-givers in their roles as nurturers.

Defeat of the Dragon (12:7-12)

The cosmic conflict that pits the Great Red Dragon against the Woman and her child escalates once he is taken to the throne. A full-scale war breaks out in heaven (v. 7), and its description comprises two sections. The first half of 12:7-12 focuses on the defeat of the Great Red Dragon, while the second half offers a hymn, sung by an anonymous heavenly voice, that celebrates and interprets this defeat for hearers. In this latter section, John connects cosmic evil with the evil manifested in humans and political systems.

In contrast to the unnamed Woman, John assigns the Dragon a series of names and titles: "that ancient serpent, who is called the Devil and Satan, the deceiver of the whole world" (v. 9). The "ancient serpent" connects the Woman's antagonist with the serpent from the Garden of Eden (Gen 3:1-5). By drawing this connection to Genesis, Revelation offers an early example of reading Satan into the Genesis story.[38] Contrary to popular belief, the serpent who converses with Eve is not identified as Satan or a personification of evil in that story. Despite this, in making the connection to the Garden story, John emphasizes the persistence of evil across time. This enemy, according to John, has been with humanity since the beginning. Moreover, the antagonism between this Dragon and the Woman Clothed in the Sun enacts the enmity the Lord God predicts will emerge between the serpent and its offspring and Eve and her offspring (Gen 3:15).

By identifying this cosmic Dragon as Satan, whom he also names as the Devil, John puts a mythological spin on earlier biblical traditions that depict Satan as the archenemy of God. Even though John draws heavily on Hebrew Bible traditions throughout his vision, this understanding of Satan reflects perspectives that develop most fully in the writings of Jesus followers, including the authors of the Gospels.[39] In the early chapters of Luke and Matthew, Satan appears as an almost human-like interlocutor

---

38. Elaine Pagels, "The Social History of Satan, Part Three: John of Patmos and Ignatius of Antioch; Contrasting Visions of 'God's People,'" *HTR* 99 (2006): 487–505.

39. For a history of the development in Satan, see Elaine Pagels, *The Origin of Satan* (New York: Vintage Books, 1995).

Rev 12:7-12

[7]And war broke out in heaven; Michael and his angels fought against the dragon. The dragon and his angels fought back, [8]but they were defeated, and there was no longer any place for them in heaven. [9]The great dragon was thrown down, that ancient serpent, who is called the Devil and Satan, the deceiver of the whole world—he was thrown down to the earth, and his angels were thrown down with him.

[10]Then I heard a loud voice in
heaven, proclaiming,
"Now have come the salvation
and the power
and the kingdom of our God
and the authority of his Messiah,
for the accuser of our comrades
has been thrown down,
who accuses them day and
night before our God.
[11]But they have conquered him by
the blood of the Lamb
and by the world of their
testimony,
for they did not cling to life even in
the face of death.
[12]Rejoice then, you heavens
and those who dwell in them!
But woe to the earth and the sea,
for the devil has come down to
you with great wrath,
because he knows that his
time is short!"

and Jesus's moral sparring partner (Luke 4:1-13; Matt 4:1-11). This understanding of Satan is a far cry from the monstrous figure witnessed by John in Revelation, although the author or the Gospel of John depicts a more nefarious Satan figure who essentially possesses Judas, leading him to betray Jesus (John 13:2, 27-30; see also Luke 22:3).[40] Likewise, the Gospel of Mark depicts Jesus engaged in a kind of spiritual warfare with Satan, whom Jesus characterizes as a "strongman," and his demonic minions, who fear Jesus and his intentions (e.g., Mark 1:24; 3:22-30).

John heightens the tension between Satan and God by revealing the cosmic context of their conflict and by evoking the combat myth described above. At the same time, in this chapter, he decenters Christ's role in the conflict by depicting Satan and his forces fighting, literally "making war" (πολεμέω), against Michael and his fellow angelic combatants. The only named angel in Revelation, Michael was traditionally the angelic overseer and protector of the people of Israel (e.g., Dan 12:1-2). This fact aligns with the understanding of the Woman Clothed in the Sun as a personification of Israel or Zion. Instead of depicting the defeat of Satan at the hands of the Woman's child, as one might expect following the

40. Pagels, *Origin of Satan*, 105.

combat myth, Michael and his angels defeat the Dragon and his angels (12:7). The child's failure to act or do anything, especially in contrast to a four-day-old Apollo avenging his mother, suggests a delay before he fully grows into the power of that "iron rod" (v. 5).

Ultimately, the Dragon and his forces are thrown from heaven to earth by divine forces, just as the stars mentioned in verse 4. This "demotion" recalls traditions found in other Jewish apocalypses that describe rebellious angels expelled from heaven. The apocalypses associated with Enoch date this event to the time immediately preceding the flood (Gen 6), as the angels' rebellious actions contribute to the evil that the flood supposedly remedies (e.g., 1 En. 10; 2 En. 29). Revelation then promises an end to the ancient conflict. A voice from heaven announces, "Now have come the salvation and power and the kingdom of our God" (v. 10). The heavens are called to rejoice over this victory. There is, however, a catch. This defeat in the cosmic or heavenly realm has not yet occurred on earth. The final defeat of the Dragon and his forces on earth must wait (20:7-10).

The hymn offered in 12:10-12 presents a complex explanation of the Dragon's defeat by associating Michael's victory with the authority of the Messiah and his followers. The hymn begins with the affirmation that the accuser, Satan, has been thrown down (v. 10). The language of accusation (κατηγορέω) draws on some Hebrew Bible traditions that use the language of "the satan" to describe a heavenly court figure who was oppositional or prosecutorial (e.g., Zech 3:1-2; Job 1:6-12).[41] Here, the voice from heaven reveals that Satan accuses the faithful, described literally as "brothers" (ἀδελφοί) or "comrades" in the NRSV, seemingly before the throne of God (see "Translation Matters: ἀδελφός, ἀδελφοί"). Those accusations, however, will no longer be heard, as Satan no longer has a place in heaven.[42]

Michael and his angels do most of the work battling Satan and his cosmic forces of evil, yet those whom Satan accuses participate in this victory. They may have been accused, "but *they* conquered [αὐτοὶ ἐνίκησαν] him by the blood of the Lamb and by the word of their testimony; for they did not cling to life even in the face of death" (12:11). Here John extends the paradox at the heart of Revelation, the idea that the Lamb conquers through his death, to include the faithful, the saints. They, too, conquer, as they were called to do in chapters 2–3, and they do so *by* the Lamb's blood and through their own willingness to die. The preposition "by," which can also be translated as "through" (διά), implies that the Lamb's

---

41. For multiple examples of κατηγορέω used in a legal context, see the writings of Demosthenes, a lawyer and statesperson of the fourth century BCE.

42. Blount, *Revelation*, 237.

blood contributes to the victory of those who follow the Lamb, perhaps by inspiring those who do not "cling to life." The willingness to die, it appears, is the word of their testimony (μαρτυρία) (see "Translation Matters: μάρτυς"). Just as the Two Witnesses in chapter 11 embodied their testimony, so too will all those described as "brothers."

TRANSLATION MATTERS: ἀδελφός, ἀδελφοί

Revelation 12:10-12, a hymn sung by a voice from heaven to celebrate the victory of the forces of heaven and the faithful over Satan, describes the faithful using a word that the NRSV translates as "comrades" (ἀδελφοί). "Comrades," which the NRSV also uses in 19:10, presumably intends to offer a gender-inclusive translation since the term typically is translated as "brothers." Even though his audiences indeed included more than just faithful men, John assumes masculine identity as normative (see p. 53). At times, this assumption plays a role in the text's meaning, as evident in the messages to the seven communities (Rev 2–3), which use language and imagery that evokes the male-dominated athletic culture of Asia Minor. In the hymn, gender is less important to the meaning of the text; however, the familial language John uses for those faithful to God is lost with the term "comrades." This points to one of the downsides of replacing gendered language with more gender-neutral terms; some of the textual meaning is lost.

John only occasionally uses the language of "brother" (ἀδελφός), although other New Testament authors use it frequently to describe the faithful. Four of the five times John uses the term are self-referential. For example, John describes himself as his audience's brother in 1:9, and angels will refer to John and his brothers, both those who "hold the testimony of Jesus" and the prophets (19:10; 22:9). Here in chapter 12, the self-referential aspect is the use of "our." Even though the voice from heaven utters a plural pronoun, "our brothers" creates a familial relationship between John and the audience members hearing the narrative. The implication is that the faithful, past, present, and future, comprise a family unit.

Familial language is not without its problems. Families often replicate the hierarchies associated with kyriarchy, privileging men over women and children, certain forms of labor over others, and often the able-bodied over the disabled or elderly. Moreover, the terms "brother" and "sister" reflect a gender binary that has become problematic as individuals increasingly describe themselves as nonbinary, gender fluid, genderqueer, and the like. Consequently, "comrades," although it might sound a bit like something from the Soviet era, might be a better way of thinking about how members of faithful communities relate to one another, since it evokes notions of equality and shared labor. Still, we use the language of "brother" when talking about the places where John uses ἀδελφός to shed light on his gendered thinking. We encourage our readers, however, to consider whether using terms like "comrade" or "friend" instead of familial language might change the way we think about relationships within Christian communities and might shift our assumptions about the gender expressions of those with whom we worship.

TRANSLATION MATTERS: ἔρημος

The geography of Revelation includes several symbolic spaces, including a place described as ἔρημος, which the NRSV translates as "wilderness" (12:6, 14; 17:3). The term can also be translated as "desert," suggesting that this wilderness is a place of emptiness or a barren landscape.

Even though ἔρημος appears only three times in Revelation, it plays a prominent role throughout Scripture. Probably the most notable usage of the term appears in the Septuagint version of Exodus, which describes the Israelites' forty years in the ἔρημος after they escape from Egypt. In these accounts, the wilderness is an ambivalent space, a place that the Israelites associated with hunger (Exod 16:3) and a place where God fed his people (16:32). Likewise, in New Testament writings, and even early Christian hagiographies, the wilderness or desert serves as a place where the faithful encounter both God and Satan (e.g., Mark 4:1) and where identities are revealed. It is in the ἔρημος that John the Baptist proclaims Jesus as the one who comes to baptize in the Holy Spirit (Matt 3:1-11).

In an exploration of the desert imagery in the lives of early Christian saints, Peter Anthony Mena, drawing on the work of Gloria Anzaldúa, describes ἔρημος as a borderland or frontier where identity and space mutually influence and shape each other.[43] Such is the case in Revelation, where the wilderness is neither good nor bad.[44] For the Woman Clothed in the Sun, this space is prepared by God (12:6), although it is also a place where her mettle is tested as she continues to be pursued by evil (12:13). The other reference to ἔρημος in Revelation occurs in Revelation 17 when John is taken there to witness the judgment of Babylon, who is depicted as the Great Prostitute (v. 3). In this case, Babylon does not reside in the wilderness; rather, she sits on many waters (v. 1) and on seven mountains (v. 9). The wilderness, however, will become her identity when she is made "desolate" (ἐρημόω) by the kings of the earth, an image of sexual violence (v. 16).

Solidarity in the Wilderness (12:13-17)

The final section of Revelation 12 returns to the Woman Clothed in the Sun. Moments *before* the heavenly battle between Michael and the Dragon, she flees into the wilderness (ἔρημος) to a place prepared by God (v. 6; see "Translation Matters: ἔρημος"). In a temporal glitch, however, John also describes the Dragon pursuing the Woman into the wilderness *after* the battle in heaven (v. 13). This discrepancy should remind us that

43. Peter Anthony Mena, *Place and Identity in the Lives of Antony, Paul, and Mary of Egypt: Desert as Borderland*, Religion and Spatial Studies (Cham, Switzerland: Palgrave Macmillan, 2019), 17.

44. Heather Macumber, *Recovering the Monstrous in Revelation* (Lanham, MD: Lexington Books/Fortress, 2021), 112.

¹³So when the dragon saw that he had been thrown down to the earth, he pursued the woman who had given birth to the male child. ¹⁴But the woman was given the two wings of the great eagle, so that she could fly from the serpent into the wilderness, to her place where she is nourished for a time, and times, and half a time. ¹⁵Then from his mouth the serpent poured water like a river after the woman, to sweep her away with the flood. ¹⁶But the earth came to the help of the woman; it opened its mouth and swallowed the river that the dragon had poured from his mouth. ¹⁷Then the dragon was angry with the woman, and went off to make war on the rest of her children, those who keep the commandments of God and hold the testimony of Jesus.

Revelation's narrative rarely moves in a straightforward and linear way. It also sheds light on John's ambivalent depiction of feminine power and agency. That is, even though the Woman's appearance promises audience members an image of feminine strength or women's empowerment, John uses the Woman to "(re)produce his hegemonic ideas," as Jacob and Kaalund observe.⁴⁵ John's depiction of the Woman Clothed in the Sun potentially attests to the power of the goddess; however, John simply will not allow the character to reach her full capacity because he works with a limited understanding of what it means to be a woman.

The Woman's time in the wilderness evokes the Israelites' time of wandering after their escape from Egypt, aligning with her identity as a symbol of Israel (Exod 16:1). God nourishes the Woman for "one thousand two hundred sixty days," just as he provided food for Israel while in the wilderness (Exod 16:12). When, however, the Woman reappears after the battle and is pursued by the Dragon, now described as a serpent, her help comes from a source who gives her "the two wings of the great eagle" and nourishes her (v. 14). The unnamed source may be divine, but the text cryptically avoids specifying its origin. Even though the Woman is given the wings, suggesting rescue she does fly with the wings on her own. The Woman truly plays a role in her own salvation. The giving of wings evokes Isaiah's promise that "those who wait for the LORD . . . mount up with wings like eagles" (40:31), and thus John may even believe that the Woman earns her wings through faithfulness. New Testament scholar Love L. Sechrest proposes that John draws on

45. Jacob and Kaalund, "Flowing from Breast to Breast," 228.

imagery from Exodus, which characterizes God bearing the Israelites on his eagle wings (19:4).[46] With this intertextual connection, the Woman appears as an embodiment of the divine. Her home in the wilderness may be prepared by God, but she saves herself by moving there. Furthermore, wings were commonly associated not only with Isis but also with the popular goddess Nike, the personification of victory, and so the image would signal to some in Revelation's audiences the Woman's role in the victory over the Dragon.[47]

In the wilderness, the Woman Clothed in the Sun encounters an ally in the guise of another powerful female-identified figure, another goddess. The dragon's attempt to drown the Woman by spewing a river at her (12:15) is thwarted by the earth, γῆ, who swallows the water (v. 16). The earth, γῆ, was regularly depicted as a goddess named Gaia; by describing the "earth" as having a mouth, John evokes the anthropomorphized goddess.[48] Mary Ann Beavis suggests that by including the name of the great Earth Mother goddess John slips up and makes an unintentional reference to a pagan deity that belies his rejection of all that challenge God and the Lamb.[49] Whether John intended to reference Gaia or not, these verses include traces of feminine power and point to the possibility of solidarity between women.

Finally, even though John seems focused on the Male Child, as he is the source of the conflict between the two portents, we learn later in the chapter that she has other children, "those who keep the commandments of God and hold the testimony of Jesus" (v. 17). This reference has led some Christian interpreters to understand the Woman Clothed in the Sun as a representation of the church (cf., the "elect lady" in 2 John 1), the faithful Jesus followers constituting her children. Medieval visionary Hildegard of Bingen made the most of this idea by describing a woman,

46. Love L. Sechrest, "Antitypes, Stereotypes, and Antetypes: Jezebel, the Sun Woman, and Contemporary Black Women," in *Womanist Interpretations of the Bible: Expanding the Discourse*, ed. Gay L. Byron and Vanessa Lovelace (Atlanta: SBL Press, 2016), 123.

47. Sometimes Isis could take on the attributes of Nike, including her wings. See Drusus Pollini, "A Bronze Statuette of Isis-Fortuna Panthea: A Syncretistic Goddess of Prosperity and Good Fortune," *Latomus* 4 (2003): 875–82.

48. Steven J. Friesen, *Imperial Cults and the Apocalypse of John: Reading Revelation in the Ruins* (Oxford: Oxford University Press, 2001), 186.

49. Mary Ann Beavis, "Jezebel Speaks: Naming the Goddesses in the Book of Revelation," in *A Feminist Companion to the Apocalypse of John*, ed. Amy-Jill Levine with Maria Mayo Robbins, FCNTECW 13 (London: T&T Clark, 2009), 141–42.

like the one in Revelation 12, wearing a crown and clothed in splendor but composed almost entirely of a womb that is "pierced like a net" and through which she gives birth, e.g., the baptism of people into the church (*Scivias*, 2.3.vision).[50]

Feminist interpreters vary in how they interpret the Woman Clothed in the Sun and so reflect both the variety of perspectives and the richness of the imagery itself. Adela Yarbro Collins, for example, maintains that the Woman represents Israel and highlights the woman's "exalted" nature. She is "a cosmic queen who has power over the rhythm of night and day and over human destiny."[51] Hollyday presents the woman as a model for Christian women and an emanation of the divine.[52] Other feminist interpreters highlight the more ambivalent nature of the chapter's feminine imagery: the Woman Clothed in the Sun is defined solely in relation to male characters, such as her child, and she is portrayed as unable to care for herself. Tina Pippin observes that the woman really "does not get enough credit" and that as a goddess she is "subdued, tamed, and under control."[53]

Sechrest emphasizes the importance of embracing the unnamed woman at the center of Revelation's narrative. Acknowledging that the Woman Clothed in the Sun might appear passive, Sechrest encourages readers not to shame a woman in distress, a woman on the margins who chooses to accept assistance from others. Instead of engaging in a kind of criticism that perpetuates "the American myth of rugged individualism,"[54] we need to recognize the intellectual and ethical agency of accepting help from God, from the anonymous donor giving wings, and from Gaia. Moreover, the Woman Clothed in the Sun ultimately chooses to retreat to the wilderness, where the Dragon will battle with her children (v. 17). She chooses the possibility of conflict over some form of security.[55] In this way, the woman of Revelation 12 is, according to Sechrest, like the "Civil Rights mothers and #BlackLivesMatter daughters."[56] As a portent whose actions and motivations have been

50. Lynn R. Huber, *Thinking and Seeing with Women in Revelation*, LNTS 475 (London: Bloomsbury, 2013), 102.

51. Yarbro Collins, "Feminine Symbolism," 22.

52. Hollyday, *Clothed with the Sun*, xi.

53. Tina Pippin, *Death and Desire: The Rhetoric of Gender in the Apocalypse of John* (Louisville: Westminster John Knox, 1992), 76.

54. Sechrest, "Antitypes, Stereotypes, and Antetypes," 123.

55. Sechrest, "Antitypes, Stereotypes, and Antetypes," 124–25, 132.

56. Sechrest, "Antitypes, Stereotypes, and Antetypes," 133.

dissected for meaning across centuries, the Woman Clothed in the Sun provides readers an opportunity to think about the ways all those who give birth, along with women and femmes, resist, creatively and in solidarity, other dragons throughout history and across the globe.

"Clothed with the Sun: Resisting the Imperial Divine"

What kind of God snatches a newborn baby from his laboring mother and sends the mother far away into the wilderness? And how does the woman respond? Is this banished and bereaved mother passively grateful to a God of power and might, whose strong arm saves her child from a dragon, brings down the Beastly ravages of Evil, and keeps her safe from harm? Or is this woman, clothed as she is with the sun, blazing with anger at yet another patriarchal manifestation of deadly desire for imperial power?

In our time, as in every age, empire violently and relentlessly snatches up human life, using the dangers of the hydra-headed dragon and the presumed righteousness of the powerful as justifications for the ruthless pursuit of privilege and control. Granted, the author of Revelation may have intended this narrative to be anti-imperial. White Western Christianity has, however, appropriated the duality of good and evil that this text invokes time and again in its historical alliances with the forces of conquest, colonization, slavery, White racism, neocolonialism, and neoliberal capitalism. Imperial to the core, White Western Christianity has identified itself with the messianic child who was to rule the nations with a rod of iron and its military might with the serpent-slaying armies of Michael. Even after the modern collapse of Christendom, this dualism of White Western goodness over and against different and darker "others" persists.

In the past fifty years alone, how many mothers' children have been suddenly snatched up or slowly destroyed in the name of conquering the race- and class-coded dragons of communism, terrorism, illegal immigration, drug use, and street crime? How many mothers have wandered the wilderness in their grief, gathering authority from their anger and strength from their solidarity? How many mothers have clothed themselves with the sun and cried out from the wilderness to protest the role of empire in their children's demise? Let us call to mind the voices of mothers in late twentieth-century Latin America, whose children were tortured, murdered, and/or "disappeared" for their association with the subversive serpent of communism. In Argentina, the Mothers of the Disappeared refused to be silent in their demands for truth and justice for their children. In El Salvador, women such as Rufina Amaya and Exaltación Luna spoke the truth and demanded justice for their children's murders in massacres perpetrated by US-trained soldiers whose mission was total eradication of the communist threat. Let us also call to mind the more contemporary and close-to-home voices of African American mothers, whose children are threatened and too often destroyed by police brutality and mass incarceration, all in the racially charged name of upholding "law and order" over and against the "lawlessness" of "our inner cities." The mothers of children whose Black bodies have been sacrificed on the altar of law and order are gathering in strength as they protest police brutality and advocate for more just policing policies. These Mothers of the Movement—including Sybrina Fulton, mother of Trayvon Martin, and Geneva Reed-Veal, mother of Sandra Bland—have refused to let the idolatrous gods of racism have the last word about their children's lives. They refuse to let their children's deaths be justified or their characters tarnished by the imperial association of Black bodies with perpetual guilt.

Where does the woman clothed with the sun fit into this schema? Is she the favored White daughter of empire, who obediently offers her son for the sake of salvation? Unfortunately, she has been interpreted as such insofar as the Most Blessed Virgin Mary has been interpreted as the divinely empowered protectress of Christian imperialism. This imperial narrative is interrupted, however, if we identify the woman clothed with the sun as Mary of Nazareth, whose son's brutal execution was justified by his association with the serpents of anti-imperial subversion. This woman—scandalous, poor, and brown-skinned—refuses identification with empire. Her lot, and her son's lot, is cast with the marginalized. She therefore sings her songs of lament and praise in concert with the other wilderness women who weep like the rain and shine like the sun, refusing to comply with an imperial god who snatches up babies, demonizes his enemies, and slays anyone who gets in his way. Who among us will be bold enough to clothe ourselves with the sun and join them?

Elizabeth O'Donnell Gandolfo

Figure 3: "The Woman Clothed in the Sun and the Male Child." *Bamberg Apocalypse*, Reichnau, ca. 1010. Staatsbibliothek Bamberg, Msc.Bibl.140, v26. Photo: Gerald Raab. Available under the Creative Common License CC-BY-SA 4.0.

Revelation 12:18–13:18

Meeting the Beast at the Shore

One of the most famous images from Revelation's visual arsenal is a multiheaded creature who emerges out of the sea and receives authority and power from the Dragon, also known as Satan (12:18–13:2). This Beast, who bears some striking similarities to the Dragon, reveals how evil manifests upon the earth. Medieval illustrations occasionally represent this evil Beast literally, as a monster cobbled together with parts from a leopard, bear, and lion. Even though the Beast is no laughing matter, these images are sometimes cartoonish. Other visual portrayals emphasize the Beast's human nature, its heads representing oppressive powers, political figures, and even those perceived as religious opponents. Among the images I show students when I teach Revelation 13 is one with a head labeled clearly as Martin Luther, and another image depicts the Beast with the face of Hitler.[1] Interpreters of Revelation vacillate between using the Beast's heads as a polemical tool or as a form of critique. Scholars similarly debate whether the heads of this

---

1. For a discussion of this image and other depictions of the Beast in visual art, see Natasha O'Hear and Anthony O'Hear, *Picturing the Apocalypse: The Book of Revelation in the Arts over Two Millennia* (Oxford: Oxford University Press, 2015), 131–54. See also the collected images in Frances Carey, *The Apocalypse and the Shape of Things to Come* (London: British Museum Press, 1999); Nancy Grubb, *Revelations: Art of the Apocalypse* (New York: Abbeville, 1997).

Beast coincide with specific Roman emperors, like Nero and Domitian, or whether the Beast represents imperial power more generally. The former perspective results in charts that outline schemas for aligning the heads with emperors. One popular version of the NRSV includes this kind of chart alongside Revelation 17, where another version of the Dragon appears. It consists of no fewer than eight ways the heads could line up with first-century Roman emperors, although none of the scenarios works perfectly.[2] Mainly, the problem is that there are too many candidates for the heads. This reveals one of the main assumptions of Revelation—evil is pervasive. Like the mythical Hydra, a multiheaded monster that can regenerate heads even after they are cut off (Euripides, *Heracl.* 1275), the faces of the Beast always emerge in new situations and scenarios.

Phallic Humor in the Roman World[3]

Sometimes a horn is more than a horn. Reading Revelation's horn imagery alongside ancient Roman texts and material culture suggests that John deploys this phallic imagery for the sake of humor. Romans seem to have liked penis jokes. The god Priapus, depicted with a persistently erect, enormous penis, is the poster boy for this type of humor.[4] (The god lends his name to the medical condition priapism, which entails a painful erection that does not go away.) Not only were statues of the well-endowed god placed in gardens like obscene garden gnomes, but Priapus also adorned frescoed walls in domestic and public spaces. The humorous nature of his image served several functions, from warding off evil spirits who would "laugh" at the absurdly large penis to threatening would-be thieves with rape if they were caught. For instance, upon entering one of the brothels in Pompeii (a popular site on modern tours), visitors saw a painting of Priapus with two enormous penises pointing in opposite

2. Harold W. Attridge and Society of Biblical Literature, eds., *The HarperCollins Study Bible*, rev. ed. (San Francisco: HarperOne, 2006), 2107.

3. I presented a fuller version of this material at the 2020 Society of Biblical Literature Annual Meeting as part of a panel reviewing Sarah Emanuel, *Humor, Resistance, and Jewish Cultural Persistence in the Book of Revelation: Roasting Rome* (Cambridge: Cambridge University Press, 2020). Even though the ideas are my own, Emanuel's introduction of humor into conversations about Revelation inspired these observations.

4. Amy Richlin, *The Garden of Priapus: Sexuality and Aggression in Roman Humor*, rev. ed. (New York: Oxford University Press, 1992), xvii.

directions. The bi-phallic figure both promises punishment for those who might harm the individuals working in the brothel and serves as a humorous directional sign pointing toward the different cubicles designed for sexual activity.[5]

Another well-known Priapus fresco from Pompeii "points to" yet another function of phallic humor in the ancient world—signaling class boundaries. Visitors easily see the painting in the doorway to the House of the Vettii, one of the city's largest homes. Here Priapus holds a scale with which he weighs a large bag of coins against his massive phallus, balancing across one of the scale's pans. The bag weighs about the same amount as the god's penis, humorously suggesting that this is a wealthy household.[6] The visual joke alerts visitors to the household's wealth, making clear to everyone who passes by the family's high status within the community.[7] The message of the fresco might be colloquially rendered as, "Don't fuck with us."

The visibility of Priapus and phallic images more generally throughout Pompeii challenge the assumptions that human bodies are meant to be covered and that sex is shameful. In the ancient context, sexual humor is overt and often crass, functioning as a way of asserting dominance over the other. With the depiction of the many-horned Beast, John too uses phallic imagery and, quite likely, humor. The question is whether John does this to make fun of the Roman phallic obsession, especially given his tendency to redefine masculinity, or perhaps here he buys into the use of phallic humor, suggesting that the Beast is overcompensating and sexually out of control. Some might point out that the Lamb is also pretty "horny," although the seriousness with which John presents him as slaughtered makes any humorous intention in Revelation 5 less likely.

The Great Red Dragon and the Hybrid Beast (12:18–13:8)

The Great Red Dragon's appearance on the "sand of the seashore" at the end of Revelation 12 creates a sense of dread as the text is read aloud. Ancient sailors feared the sea's power and unpredictability. The remains of shipwrecks discovered by underwater archeologists, which

---

5. Sarah Levin-Richardson discusses several meanings for this image in *The Brothel of Pompeii: Sex, Class, and Gender at the Margins of Roman Society* (Cambridge: Cambridge University Press, 2019), 80.

6. Levin-Richardson, *Brothel of Pompeii*, 80.

7. Richlin, *Garden of Priapus*, 210–13.

¹⁸Then the dragon took his stand on the sand of the seashore. ¹³:¹And I saw a beast rising out of the sea, having ten horns and seven heads; and on its horns were ten diadems, and on its heads were blasphemous names. ²And the beast that I saw was like a leopard, its feet were like a bear's, and its mouth was like a lion's mouth. And the dragon gave it his power and his throne and great authority. ³One of its heads seemed to have received a death-blow, but its mortal wound had been healed. In amazement the whole earth followed the beast. ⁴They worshiped the dragon, for he had given his authority to the beast, and they worshiped the beast, saying, "Who is like the beast, and who can fight against it?"

⁵The beast was given a mouth uttering haughty and blasphemous words, and it was allowed to exercise authority for forty-two months. ⁶It opened its mouth to utter blasphemies against God, blaspheming his name and his dwelling, that is, those who dwell in heaven. ⁷Also it was allowed to make war on the saints and to conquer them. It was given authority over every tribe and people and language and nation, ⁸and all the inhabitants of the earth will worship it, everyone whose name has not been written from the foundation of the world in the book of life of the Lamb that was slaughtered.

include protective amulets and figurines of gods among the capsized cargo, reveal this fear was justified.[8] In biblical traditions, the sea is a monstrous thing, sometimes depicted as an actual monster, that only God can subdue (e.g., Ps 74:13; Isa 27:1; Job 41). In this vein, a Beast emerges from these depths to exercise the authority given by the Dragon (13:1). Besides evoking a sense of foreboding, these waters link Asia Minor to the rest of the Roman Empire and point to the Beast's association with Rome, the great ruling city that understood the Mediterranean as its own "vast harbor" (Cicero, *Prov. Cons.* 31). Even though there were land routes between Rome and Asia Minor, sea routes were used more commonly to trade high-value resources, such as grain and wine,[9] which John describes in 18:17-19. Despite the land distance between Asia Minor and Rome, the sea brought Rome to the province's shores.

8. Sandra Blakely, "Maritime Risk and Ritual Responses: Sailing with the Gods in the Ancient Mediterranean," in *The Sea in History—The Ancient World*, ed. Philip de Souza, Pascal Arnaud, and Christian Buchet (Suffolk: Boydell and Brewer, 2017), 362–79.

9. Phyllis Culham, "The Roman Empire and the Seas," in de Souza, Arnaud, and Buchet, *Sea in History*, 285.

John's depiction of the Beast draws explicitly on the book of Daniel, a rich source for many of Revelation's images. The ancient prophet describes a vision of the sea and four different creatures emerging from it: a lion, a bear, a leopard, and a beast with ten horns and iron teeth (Dan 7:1-7). While he disaggregates the beasts around the divine throne room in Ezekiel's vision, making the hybrid beasts into four separate living creatures (4:6; Ezek 1:5-11), John combines the creatures of Daniel's vision into what Heather Macumber describes as a "super-monster."[10] The fiercest parts of the beasts from Daniel appear in Revelation's Beast—feet like a bear, a mouth like a lion, and the overall appearance of a leopard (13:2). For Daniel, the multiple beasts that come out of the sea represent successive political powers, including the Babylonians, Medes, Persians, and Hellenistic kings, that had dominated God's people.[11] Like its predecessors, the Beast from the sea will similarly serve as a metaphorical depiction of political power, wearing multiple diadems, or crowns, upon its multiple horns (v. 1). This composite Beast appears as a culmination of its predecessors from Daniel, implying that these past imperial powers contribute to the existence of this Beast, the multifaceted and multiheaded Roman Empire.

As a culmination of Daniel's different beasts, the Beast that emerges from the Sea appears as a composite creature. Sometimes interpreters read being composite as an indication of the Beast's evil or flawed character. I have personally offered that reading of the Beast in the past. That misguided reading, however, flattens how "monsters," like the Creature from Mary Shelley's gothic novel *Frankenstein* (1818), function culturally.[12] While the Creature created in Dr. Frankenstein's lab might be startling to encounter, he is not inherently or necessarily evil. Rather, he reflects the responses of others upon seeing his difference. The monstrous Creature reveals the fears and concerns of the culture and its creators.

Similarly, being a composite creature in Revelation signals neither good nor evil.[13] Composite or hybrid creatures, such as the four living creatures, reside in the throne room (4:6), and the Lamb, with multiple horns and eyes, shares the throne with God (5:13). The Beast from the

10. Heather Macumber, "The Threat of Empire: Monstrous Hybridity in Revelation 13," *BibInt* 27 (2019): 121.

11. Craig R. Koester, *Revelation: A New Translation with Introduction and Commentary*, AYB 38A (New Haven: Yale University Press, 2014), 580.

12. Mary Shelley, *Frankenstein: The 1818 Text* (New York: Penguin, 2018).

13. Heather Macumber, *Recovering the Monstrous in Revelation* (Lanham, MD: Lexington Books/Fortress, 2021), 15–17.

sea is evil not on account of its composite character; it is evil because Satan grants it authority. Disconnecting the idea of hybridity from evil is crucial since the association fosters narratives of purity, including ethnic purity, that harm people who visibly embody hybridity. Even though there are growing numbers of people worldwide who explicitly identify as multiethnic, embracing their composite origins and experiences, the myth of ethnic purity continues to be pervasive as it privileges people in power. A feminist interpretation of the Beast must guard against perpetuating these oppressive patterns of thought.[14]

Hybridity signals resistance to easy classification and traditional categories.[15] The Beast of Revelation, for example, challenges modern boundaries drawn between political, religious, and social categories, exercising power in all these ways. As mentioned in the introduction to this chapter, the Beast's most notable characteristic is that it has multiple heads, horns, *and* diadems. This overloading of symbols of power reinforces the view that Revelation's Beast functions somewhat like the beasts in Daniel (7:1-7), as a depiction of earthly kingdoms or systems of political power. The heads, horns, and diadems are multiple since these systems are complex networks of authority with emperors at the top and then a cascade of governors, administrators, and local officials managing provincial and civic matters. Many of these civic leaders would have been local elites who did things like collect taxes and exercise the authority of Rome in the cities of Asia Minor.[16] Some of the members of John's audiences may have been connected directly to these networks via family members or social contacts, and this complex system of influence would have impacted the lives of all who heard Revelation first read aloud.

14. Juliana Menasce Horowitz and Abby Budiman, "Key Findings about Multiracial Identity in the U.S. as Harris Becomes Vice Presidential Nominee," *Pew Research Center* (blog), August 18, 2020, https://www.pewresearch.org/fact-tank/2020/08/18/key-findings-about-multiracial-identity-in-the-u-s-as-harris-becomes-vice-presidential-nominee/. Remi Adekoya, "Biracial Britain: Why Mixed-Race People Must Be Able to Decide Their Own Identity," *The Conversation*, February 11, 2021, https://theconversation.com/biracial-britain-why-mixed-race-people-must-be-able-to-decide-their-own-identity-154771.

15. Jeffrey Jerome Cohen, "Monster Culture (Seven Theses)," in *Monster Theory: Reading Culture*, ed. Jeffrey Jerome Cohen (Minneapolis: University of Minnesota Press, 1996), 6.

16. Christof Schuler, "Local Elites in the Greek East," in *The Oxford Handbook of Roman Epigraphy*, ed. Christer Bruun and Jonathan Edmondson (Oxford: Oxford University Press, 2015), 254.

Having seven heads means the Beast can be looking in seven different directions and may try to do so simultaneously. How does one anticipate the moves of such a creature? Additionally, one of its heads has a healed "death blow," suggesting a visible fatal wound (13:3). This creepy bit proves tantalizing for those who approach the image as a code to be cracked. For a long time, interpreters have related this zombie head to Nero (e.g., Victorinus, *Commentary on the Apocalypse* 17.16) since he reportedly cut his own throat, even though some ancient conspiracy theorists doubted whether that was indeed the case (Suetonius, *Nero* 49). Rumors were that Nero was waiting on the sidelines somewhere, likely Parthia, to come and retake control of Rome, and some even predicted that he might return from the dead to rule (Suetonius, *Nero* 57). Other possible ways of interpreting this head are that it refers to the assassination of Julius Caesar or that it represents Caligula, who miraculously recovered from severe illness (Suetonius, *Cal.* 14.2).[17] The fact that readers can align this head with a variety of different historical emperors makes clear that the heads of the Beast are not a code to be cracked. Instead, the Beast's heads paint a picture of multifaceted and seemingly ever-present power. The resuscitated head suggests that systems like the Beast do not expire easily. Further, the fact that at least a part of the Beast has been killed and now lives shows why some might easily mistake themselves for followers of the Lamb when they actually follow the Beast. The imagery, therefore, warns John's audience members to be discerning since appearances can be deceiving.

Having multiple heads is only one of the family traits shared by the Beast and the Great Red Dragon. Both boast multiple horns and diadems as well, although the Beast has three more diadems than his predecessor. As with the Lamb's horns in Revelation 5, the Beast's multiple horns reveal its power. Animal horns, like those grown by cattle and antelope, have evolved as one way for males within a species to signal and maintain dominance over others in a herd.[18] Because they display male dominance, horns can function as a phallic symbol—a representation of the erect penis and masculine power. Again, John echoes his prophetic predecessor Daniel, who portrays the Hellenistic king Antiochus IV, infamous for his persecution of the people of Judea (1 Macc 1:1-24), as a little horn who speaks arrogantly (Dan 7:8). Something little making a big noise,

17. Koester, *Revelation*, 570.

18. Donald R. Prothero and Robert M. Schoch, *Horns, Tusks, and Flippers: The Evolution of Hoofed Mammals* (Baltimore: Johns Hopkins University Press, 2002), 63.

suggesting an error in self-perception, is both humorous and a biting critique. John likewise mocks the Beast, who flaunts his power by wearing more horns, ten, than he has heads, seven (13:1). John implies that the Beast might be overcompensating for some lack (see Excursus: "Phallic Humor in the Roman World"). Again, multiple horns are a characteristic the Lamb and the Beast share. Power, for John, is not inherently wicked; whether power is good or evil depends entirely on the identity of the one wearing the horns. Likewise, this Beast's multiple "diadems" (διαδήματα) seem suspiciously like the crowns (στέφανοι) worn by the heavenly elders (4:4) and those promised to those who conquer (2:10; 3:10). The latter term (στέφανοι) describes a wreath-like crown made of leaves or gold, while the "diadem" traditionally was used for a royal crown. Despite this distinction, both types of crowns indicate the wearer's victory, power, glory, and honor,[19] and in Revelation 19, the Rider on the White Horse, another Christ image, will wear diadems (διαδήματα). The fact that characters associated with Satan and God wear similar items again demonstrates that John is not critical of power and authority in general; rather, he thinks power and authority are only rightly associated with God.

Even though monsters need not be evil, Revelation's Beast functions within the realm of satire, a form of humorous critique cultivated by the Romans. As a literary form, satire can be over the top or, as Sarah Emanuel puts it, "stuffed-to-the-gills."[20] Satire can use humor and mockery to take the powerful and prestigious down a notch, to point out the absurdity of those people and institutions that take themselves very seriously. While parts of Revelation, especially those focused on the One Who Sits upon the Throne and the Lamb, convey an air of reverence and solemnity, the depiction of the Beast seems almost like a comedic interlude. The Beast crawls up out of the sea and immediately appears as "too much" with its ten horns, seven heads, and ten diadems, not to mention being a combination of three different animal types (13:1-2).[21] The Beast looks likely to tip over since it is so top-heavy with heads, horns, and crowns. In this way, John presents his audiences with an

---

19. Gregory M. Stevenson, "Conceptual Background to Golden Crown Imagery in the Apocalypse of John (4:4, 10; 14:14)," *JBL* 114 (1995): 257–72.

20. Emanuel, *Humor, Resistance, and Jewish Cultural Persistence*, 87.

21. For a discussion of how excess relates to disgust, see Joseph A. Marchal, "The Disgusting Apostle and a Queer Affect between Epistles and Audiences," in *Reading with Feeling: Affect Theory and the Bible*, ed. Fiona C. Black and Jennifer L. Koosed (Atlanta: SBL Press, 2019), 123.

image of Roman power as bloated and ridiculous to cast doubt on the system that presents itself in terms that rival God.

John's mocking image of the Beast fails to mask his anger at the political system and imperial leaders who try to rival God. With "blasphemous names" on its heads and "blasphemous words" coming out of its multiple mouths, the Beast presents itself as God (vv. 1, 5; see also 17:3). This depiction points to the practices of the imperial cults of Asia Minor. As discussed in the introduction, associations between divinity and the emperors and their family members appeared throughout Rome's cities. People encountered references to the emperors and their kin as sons of God, divine, and saviors on coins and in civic spaces. For instance, a silver coin minted during the reign of Domitian depicts his wife, Domitia, on the front. His infant son, who died near the beginning of his father's reign, sits on a globe surrounded by seven stars on the back of the coin. The toddler exists in the heavenly realm. The inscription around the child describes him as Domitian's deified son (fig. 4). For Revelation, such claims of divinity, combined with the Beast's power and ability to survive attack (evidenced in the resuscitated head), are dangerous because they mislead the people of earth. Instead of following God and the Lamb, who rightfully share the heavenly throne, "the whole earth [follows] the Beast" (v. 3). Humans worship the Beast and emphasize its unique claim to power by asking, "Who is like the Beast?" (v. 4).

One answer to the question "Who is like the Beast?" is, ironically, the Lamb. Therein lies the problem. The similarities between the Beast and the Lamb imply that it is easy to mistake the Beast for the Lamb and to worship the Beast instead of the Lamb. Sometimes it seems easy to identify a Beast. Political figures who loudly proclaim to be the greatest, most powerful, or most brilliant and demand absolute adulation, while at the same time doing everything out of craven self-interest, clearly share the Beast's quest for popularity, as ethicist D. Stephen Long observed about Donald Trump's presidency, comparing the MAGA ("Make America Great Again") chants of Trump followers to the worshipers of the Beast proclaiming, "Who is like the beast, and who can fight against it" (v. 4).[22] When political figures are less vocal or incendiary, it becomes more difficult to discern whether they may be authorized by the Great Red Dragon. When a political or cultural leader appears benign, it is

---

22. D. Stephen Long, "Should We Call Donald Trump 'Antichrist'?," Opinion, ABC Religion & Ethics (Australian Broadcasting Corporation, June 8, 2020), https:// www.abc.net.au/religion/stephen-long-should-we-call-trump-antichrist/12335450.

easy to acquiesce and assume that they operate with the world's best interests in mind. Erin Runions suggests this is why we *need* narratives about the Beast or antichrist.[23] The blurry boundary between the Lamb and the Beast reminds us that we don't often recognize evil when we see it and that we should resist making decisions based on a sense of moral superiority, assuming that right and wrong are easily identified and untangled.[24] John might disagree with this view of things since he sees things as black and white. His vision reveals the difficulty, however, that sometimes occurs in discerning between systems aligned with good and those aligned with evil. The vision of the Beast calls into question whether there even exist such simple categorizations.

There remains a second part to the question posed by the people of the earth, "and who can fight against [the Beast]?" (v. 4). This too can be answered with the response, "the Lamb," even though this becomes fully evident only in Revelation's closing chapters. The risen Christ will appear as a rider on a white horse, and the Beast and his minions will be captured and "thrown alive into the lake of fire that burns with sulfur" (19:20). At this point in the narrative, however, John focuses on the Beast's ability to make war against the saints and to "conquer" them (13:7). This imagery connects to the pictures of affliction John paints elsewhere in the narrative, including the persecution experienced by John and his audience members (1:9), the death of Antipas (2:13), and the souls under the altar (6:9-11). These are all casualties in the Beast's war. One might say that the Beast is behind all of this; however, John simultaneously asserts God's control of the situation by claiming that the Beast was effectively given or effectively allowed, presumably by God, to make war and conquer the saints. Given John's assertion that God is all-powerful, the One Who Sits upon the Throne bears some responsibility for what happens to the saints.

John's use of "conquer" (νικάω) to describe the result of the Beast's war on the "saints" overflows with irony. The idea of conquering or being a victor has been recommended to those in John's audiences since the Son of Humanity directed the seven messages to their communities in

23. John does not use the term "antichrist," even though the character is often associated with the Beast of Revelation. The term appears in 1 John 2:18-22 and 2 John 7 where the author characterizes those who deny Christ as "antichrists" who lead believers astray.

24. Erin Runions, "Detranscendentalizing Decisionism: Political Theology after Gayatri Spivak," *JFSR* 25 (2009): 85.

Revelation 2–3. At the end of each message, the faithful were called to become the victor with the expectation that such an identity was possible. For instance, in the message to the Ephesians, Christ proclaims, "To the victor [τῷ νικῶντι[25]] I will give permission to eat from the tree of life" (2:7). Here, however, hearers see once more what the vision of the slaughtered Lamb implies (5:5-6): Being conquered is to conquer. Thus, being conquered by the Beast who makes war on them ensures the saints are ultimately victors.

The Beast, moreover, has the authority to make people worship him or at least all those "whose name has not been written from the foundation of the world in the book of life of the Lamb that was slaughtered" (13:8).[26] The idea of a book with the names of those to be delivered or protected appears in Daniel (12:1), one of John's favorite sources of inspiration. As in Daniel, this book will be opened at the resurrection, which John depicts later in Revelation. John explains there that those whose names are not inscribed in the book of life will be thrown into the lake of fire (20:15). The note that the names in the book have been written since "the foundation of the word," a reference to creation, sounds like the concept of predestination, the belief that select people are predetermined to be faithful while others are destined to travel a path leading to eternal death. While this idea recognizes that humans are born into conditions and systems that shape their options, it remains an immensely disempowering idea. Further, the idea potentially absolves individuals of responsibility for confronting systems that are oppressive and that deny God's reign. If everything is foreordained, why bother trying to create change? Revelation, however, addresses audience members who presumably see themselves having their names written in the book. Christ even promises the victor in Sardis that he "will not blot your name out of the book of life" (3:5). As such, this verse is not a theological treatise on a doctrine of predestination but a recognition that those who worship the Beast will reap a negative reward at the end and an affirmation that God knows those who resist worshiping the Beast.

25. The NRSV translates τῷ νικῶντι as "to everyone who conquers."

26. In the Greek text, "from the foundation of the world" directly follows the reference to the Lamb that was slaughtered, which might make it seem that John is saying the Lamb was slaughtered at creation. This, however, makes little sense in the context of Revelation. For a discussion of this translation issue, see Brian K. Blount, *Revelation: A Commentary* (Louisville: Westminster John Knox, 2009), 252.

Figure 4: Silver Denarius of Domitian depicting Domitia (obverse) and son (reverse), Rome, 82–83 CE. American Numismatics Society 1975.226.78. https://numismatics.org/collection/1975.226.78. American Numismatic Society, New York.

TRANSLATION MATTERS: βλασφημία

One of the characteristics of the Beast is his association with language that is blasphemous (βλασφημία) (13:1, 5; 17:3). The Beast, who also appears later as transportation for Babylon the Great, wears blasphemous names (13:1; 17:3) and actively "utter[s] blasphemies [βλασφημίας] against God, blaspheming [βλασφημῆσαι] his name and his dwelling, that is, those who dwell in heaven" (13:6). In these instances, blasphemy refers to denying God's reign by claiming the power and authority that belong only to God, including accepting worship as a god (13:4, 8). In this way, the accusation of blasphemy plays a part in John's attempt at helping audience members see the error of Roman imperial cults and propaganda. Those who follow the Beast, the people of earth, mimic the words of the Beast and likewise blaspheme against God after experiencing the wrath poured out in the bowls of plague (16:9, 11, 21). Given the horror they encounter on the receiving end of God's wrath, their accusations against God feel somewhat understandable. Honestly, who among us wouldn't respond to pain and sores so intense they make gnawing your tongue seem like a good idea with a few choice words (16:10)? Even though cursing God is not necessarily the same as blasphemy, claiming to be God or calling into question God's power, the line between the two seems faint.

The charge of blasphemy implies that there are things about God and other inhabitants of heaven we should never say. It suggests that some verbalized ideas are simply off-limits because they are offensive or disruptive. The Russian feminist punk band Pussy Riot challenged those limits in 2012 when they performed a piece titled "Punk Prayer" in Moscow's Cathedral of Christ the Savior. In the "prayer," the five artists in brightly colored balaclavas, their signature look, implored the Virgin Mary to "drive Putin away" and "become a feminist." As a result, three of the five band members were arrested and charged with "hooliganism motivated by religious hatred," eventually serving time for the act.[27] (The remaining two members were not identified.) The women were effectively charged with blasphemy, although it remains unclear which was deemed most offensive, decrying Vladimir Putin, who was running for office at the time, or challenging the Virgin Mary. Ironically, their call for divine powers to dismiss a would-be autocrat aligns neatly with Revelation's rhetoric. One person's blasphemy is another's praise chorus.

Feminists highlight the power of language and are often stereotyped as trying to limit people's speech when we advocate for gender-neutral language or speak out against using slurs. We are accused of trying to be "politically correct," which critics portray as being concerned only about surface-level issues. John too seems concerned with the power of language. Unlike the use of a slur, however, or a term that fails to capture that we're referring to people in general and not just men, blasphemy or cursing God does not harm God, especially if, as John asserts, God is all-powerful. One can argue, though, that blasphemy may mislead others. Participating in blasphemous claims, such as lauding a political leader as divinely inspired, might prop up those who are oppressive and even evil. Similarly, not speaking out against evil seems like another way of being blasphemous as feminists. That is part of Pussy Riot's purpose, to shed light on the "sins" of a church unwilling to ordain and support women, even as it lauds the Theotokos (Mother of God). Not to speak out, in that case, is blasphemy, as it allows people to think that such things are okay, that they are consistent with what we know about God. Perhaps, sometimes faithfulness requires a blasphemous, punk prayer.

A Warning Is Issued (13:9-10)

John makes the threat of the Beast's war against the saints real when, in Revelation 13:9-10, the text directly addresses Revelation's audiences, "Let anyone who has an ear listen." Listeners are reminded that they are part of the revelation unfolding before them. All humor falls to the wayside as the voice alerts hearers that "If you are to be taken captive into captivity you go" (v. 10a), an allusion to Jeremiah 15:2 and 43:11.[28] The language of captivity extends the battle imagery introduced in verse

27. Volha Kananovich, " 'Execute Not Pardon': The *Pussy Riot* Case, Political Speech, and Blasphemy in Russian Law," *Communication Law and Policy* 20 (October 2, 2015): 345. See also Elena Volkova, "Mater Nostra: The Anti-Blasphemy Message of the Feminist Punk Prayer," *Religion and Gender* 4 (2014): 202–8.

28. Blount, *Revelation*, 253–54.

Rev 13:9-10

⁹Let anyone who has an ear listen: with the sword you must be killed.
  ¹⁰If you are to be taken captive, into captivity you go;
  if you kill with the sword,
Here is a call for the endurance and faith of the saints.

7, suggesting that some may be taken as prisoners in the cosmic conflict between God and Satan. Prisoners of war in the Roman world became the enslaved labor force that sustained the empire and ensured its dominance. Given this, Craig Koester notes, "Romans sometimes marched their captives in the processions with which they celebrated their victories," highlighting Roman power and simultaneously humiliating the defeated.[29] Such a parade appears in relief on a triumphal arch dedicated to the Roman's defeat of Parthia (an area of modern Iran) still standing in the Forum in Rome, the Arch of Septimius Severus (dedicated in 203 CE). If you look closely at the relief, you can see the shackles on the prisoners of war.[30] One prisoner carries an infant, reminding the viewer that those taken into captivity include the young and old. What John envisions for those taken captive by the Beast is evident, since ancient captives were generally enslaved by their captors.

Corresponding to the statement about captivity is a more puzzling claim about the killing by the sword. The claim is puzzling because the poetic form suggests that the following two phrases should parallel the statement about captivity (i.e., "if you are killed by the sword, by the sword you will be killed"), but that's not quite the case. Instead, the doublet posits the faithful listener as one who first wields the sword and then dies by the sword (v. 10b).[31] The idea that someone in John's audiences might act violently as they resist the Beast seems out of step with other images of the faithful drawn by John, especially the souls of the slaughtered under the heavenly altar (6:9). At the same time, however, the lines convey the

29. Koester, *Revelation*, 575.

30. Keith Bradley, "On Captives under the Principate," *Phoenix* 58 (2004): 298–318.

31. Some ancient versions of Revelation offer a different reading: "If anyone is to be killed with the sword, with the sword he will be killed." This suggests the need to accept one's fate, even if that is death. For a discussion of these textual variants, see Mitchell G. Reddish, *Revelation*, Smyth and Helwys Bible Commentary (Macon, GA: Smyth & Helwys, 2001), 255.

paradoxical identity that John calls the faithful to inhabit, victims who are victors or the conquered who conquer.

In light of the reality that John anticipates for his audience members, John commends to them "endurance and faith" (v. 10). Some may hear this mandate as a call to stasis, to maintain the status quo. People in power often tell others to "endure" and "have faith" in the face of oppression, expecting that they will remain passive instead of demanding change. In Revelation, endurance and faith are envisioned as embodied actions and not inactive states. As Brian K. Blount puts it when talking about the idea of witnessing in Revelation, "[John] isn't interested in someone who just sits there and takes it; he is on the hunt for someone who will stand up and deliver."[32] Blount cites as an example of this kind of "endurance and faith" the Black Church itself, which has traditionally been a site of political activism and community development, even in the face of discrimination and persecution.[33]

Enacting the endurance and faith called for by John often entails finding new and creative ways of pushing against oppression. In Chile, a small feminist collective, La Tesis, introduced a song "Un Violador en Tu Camino" ("A Rapist in Your Path") at mass protests against rape and other forms of patriarchal oppression. In the song, which has been performed worldwide in solidarity with the women of Chile, singers resist victim-blaming, affirming that they are not responsible for their assaults. Further, the singers bravely condemn the police, judges, and presidents as rapists because of their complicity in a society that allows rape: "The rapist is you / It's the cops / The judges / The state / The president."[34] Obviously, by taking up the "sword" of this song, they risk potentially being killed by the sword. These activist singers have heard the call to endure and have faith, and in hearing, they are speaking out against sexual violence.

32. Brian K. Blount, *Can I Get a Witness? Reading Revelation through African American Culture* (Louisville: Westminster John Knox, 2005), 39.

33. David Marchese, "Rev. William Barber on Greed, Poverty and Evangelical Politics," *The New York Times*, December 28, 2020, sec. Magazine, https://www.nytimes.com/interactive/2020/12/28/magazine/william-barber-interview.html.

34. Thank you to Monica Rey for bringing this to my attention. See Charis McGowan, "Chilean Anti-Rape Anthem Becomes International Feminist Phenomenon," *The Guardian*, December 6, 2019, https://www.theguardian.com/world/2019/dec/06/chilean-anti-rape-anthem-becomes-international-feminist-phenomenon.

Hyping the Beast (13:11-18)

Political systems, such as the one embodied by the Beast, require what we now describe as a "public relations" or "strategic communications" infrastructure. The Roman Empire was no exception, with the sea routes facilitating communication and trade between the provincial cities and Rome's "great city." Ephesus was the entry point for Roman communications to other cities in Asia Minor and provinces further east, such as Galatia and Cappadocia.[35] One of the most impressive examples of this propaganda still appears on a wall of what used to be a temple to Rome and Augustus in Ankara, now the capital of Turkey. The *Res Gestae*, otherwise known as *The Deeds of the Divine Augustus*, the emperor's self-authored eulogy—or, put another way, his padded resumé for the job of deity—appears in both Latin and Greek to ensure that the people in the Asian province can understand it. The voice of the late Augustus proclaims all he accomplished for the empire: ending civil war, building infrastructure, restoring traditions, performing acts of generosity, etc., so that people who might never see Rome could read or hear of the emperor's greatness and be persuaded to honor and even worship him.[36] Like so many others that have come before and after, Revelation's audiences would be familiar with the grandiose claims of rulers vying for their loyalty and affection.

In 13:11-18, John glimpses a second beast who leverages this propaganda system to garner support for the Beast from the sea. Arising from the earth, this Second Beast seems to be a local "social influencer" or "hype-man" who rallies the support of friends and neighbors for the first Beast. That the Second Beast has only two horns implies that it is subordinate to the first. In a striking portrait of how oppressive systems work, the influencer gets the people of earth to worship the first Beast by using a combination of deception and force. The deception involves performing spectacular acts, such as bringing down fire from the sky and making an image of the Beast speak (vv. 13-14). In so doing, the second Beast manipulates the earth's inhabitants to create images of the first Beast and to worship them. Thus, the people, not recognizing their own

---

35. Paul Trebilco, *The Early Christians in Ephesus from Paul to Ignatius* (Grand Rapids: Eerdmans, 2007), 18.

36. The inscription was displayed in other cities of Asia Minor as well, including Pisidia Antioch and Apollonia ad Rhyndacum. See Alison E. Cooley, "Paratextual Readings of Imperial Discourse in the '*Res Gestae Divi Augusti*,'" *Cahiers Du Centre Gustave Glotz* 25 (2014): 215–30.

¹¹Then I saw another beast that rose out of the earth; it had two horns like a lamb and it spoke like a dragon. ¹²It exercises all the authority of the first beast on its behalf, and it makes the earth and its inhabitants worship the first beast, whose mortal wound had been healed. ¹³It performs great signs, even making fire come down from heaven to earth in the sight of all; ¹⁴and by the signs that it is allowed to perform on behalf of the beast, it deceives the inhabitants of earth, telling them to make an image for the beast that had been wounded by the sword and yet lived; ¹⁵and it was allowed to give breath to the image of the beast so that the image of the beast could even speak and cause those who would not worship the image of the beast to be killed. ¹⁶Also it causes all, both small and great, both rich and poor, both free and slave, to be marked on the right hand or the forehead, ¹⁷so that no one can buy or sell who does not have the mark, that is, the name of the beast or the number of its name. ¹⁸This calls for wisdom: let anyone with understanding calculate the number of the beast, for it is the number of a person. Its number is six hundred sixty-six.

suppression, contribute to it. We see this system play out with those who support political leaders with agendas that fail to benefit them, such as women and LGBTQIA+ voters who support politicians who ignore issues that impact them, like access to affordable health care, or who are openly sexist and abusive to women and LGBTQIA+ individuals.

The Second Beast, in addition, uses violence and economic systems to keep the first Beast in power. Those who fail to worship the Beast from the sea are allowed "to be killed" (v. 15). The language of the text is interesting since it is a passive construction that fails to identify who does this killing. In this way, the language of Revelation effectively captures the kind of deception and obfuscation employed by the second Beast. Speaking of obfuscation, the identities of the first Beast and second Beast blur together as John simply refers to both as "the beast." Thus, it is not entirely clear whether it is the first or second Beast that wields economic power by requiring those who buy and sell to be marked as a follower of the Beast (vv. 16-17).

The reference to a "mark of the Beast," which is both its name and number and controls one's access to economic exchange, has launched countless speculation and conspiracy theories. For those who read Revelation as a blueprint for the present and future, UPC symbols, Social Security numbers, and even COVID-19 vaccines have all been associated with this mark, causing real concern among some faithful Christian interpreters.[37] To understand this imagery, it is important to remember the previous reference to marking humans with a name. In that case John described the faithful as having been sealed (ἐσφραγισμένοι) on the forehead (7:3; see also 14:1), and here individuals are given a mark or brand (χάραγμα)[38] on the forehead and right hand (13:16). In both situations, the seal or mark identifies the individual as metaphorically owned by the one whose name they bear. Both images evoke enslavement (see pp. 102–3), but the distinction between sealing, which suggests a kind of royal signet, and marking, which can refer to any kind of marking or branding, points to John's understanding of a qualitative difference between the two "lords" or, more literally, enslavers.

The equation between the mark and the Beast's name and number indicates that this mark is about identity. Roman rulers used various "marks" to make their lordship visible, including the use of the abbreviation like SPQR to identify projects sponsored by the "Senate and People of Rome" (*Senatus Populusque Romanus*) and portraits of the emperors and their family members on coinage, such as the denarius bearing images of Domitian's wife and son (fig. 4). Participating in the first-century economy meant engaging with all of these "marks" and so much so that the individual was beholden to them, almost as if a person had to be stamped on the forehead and hand to buy or sell. John underscores that this enslavement to the Beast impacts everyone regardless of actual social status, noting, "It causes *all*, both small and great, both rich and poor, both free and slave, to be marked on the right hand or the forehead" (v. 17).

Even though the Beast controls the marketplace, John does not explicitly instruct his audience members to avoid it. This might be surprising since Christ praised the faithful in Ephesus for not tolerating evildoers (2:2). Rather, the marketplace likely provides the venue in which many of those "sealed" with the name of God and the Lamb will have to witness. Such is the case today as well. Revelation's repudiation of the mark of the Beast shows how Christians are called to actively resist the rampant consumerism that fosters unethical means of production and product distribution. In her book *Solidarity Ethics*, Christian social ethicist Rebecca

37. Eric M. Vanden Eykel, "No, the COVID-19 Vaccine Is Not Linked to the Mark of the Beast—But a First-Century Roman Tyrant Probably Is," *The Conversation*, April 7, 2021, https://theconversation.com/no-the-covid-19-vaccine-is-not-linked-to-the -mark-of-the-beast-but-a-first-century-roman-tyrant-probably-is-158288.

38. David E. Aune, *Revelation*, WBC 52 A–C (Dallas: Word Books, 1998), 721.

Todd Peters offers tangible strategies for Christians who do not reside in places with subsistence economies, including those likely reading this commentary, to leverage their money and purchasing power in socially responsible ways. These include considering how you allocate your income. If you have "disposable" income, you can support small and local businesses and producers of ethically made items. You might shift to a plant-based diet, since the production of livestock contributes even more to greenhouse gas emissions than transportation.[39] These are not easy shifts and I admit to not having made all of them; however, there are steps that can be taken in the right direction.

Finally, the number of the Beast, which people often voice or render as "666," has taken on a life of its own. Some people avoid the number when given a chance and balk when they see it on a receipt. There are even countless 666 jokes. "If 666 is the Beast, what is 667?" "The neighbor of the Beast." And, "What is 666 degrees?" "The temperature of roast Beast."[40]

The original text likely had the number written out entirely as "six-hundred and sixty-six" (v. 18), although some ancient scribes rendered the number as "six-hundred and sixteen."[41] In fact, maybe if people were forced to say "six-hundred and sixty-six" or "six-hundred and sixteen," the number would lose some of its cultural power. John's reference to calculating the number implies it is an example of "gematria," a type of calculation in which numerals and letters are interchanged. Since there is no set system for these kinds of calculations, however, the intended meaning is impossible to know. Writing in the second century, Irenaeus already noted that a variety of names and words were possible, such as *Lateinos* or Latin referring to the Roman Empire. In his opinion, this makes "casting about" for names a pointless task (*Haer.* 5.30.3).

Nevertheless, since John taunts his audiences by presenting a challenge, "This calls for wisdom: let anyone with understanding [literally 'a mind'] calculate the number of the beast," calculations continue. Among the most popular solutions among scholars is that the number refers to "Nero Caesar," albeit rendered in Hebrew when Revelation is written in

---

39. Rebecca Todd Peters, *Solidarity Ethics: Transformation in a Globalized World* (Minneapolis: Fortress, 2014), 95.

40. Elliott Oring, "Jokes on the Internet: Listing toward Lists," in *Folk Culture in the Digital Age: The Emergent Dynamics of Human Interaction*, ed. Trevor J. Blank (Boulder: University Press of Colorado, 2012), 105–6.

41. Aune, *Revelation*, 722.

Greek.[42] In other words, that remains a somewhat unsatisfying answer. The ongoing speculations show how easy it is to become focused on the one who is not God and who is not the Lamb. Those who sit and work through all the possible meanings of the number 666 find that the Beast can be anyone, and they potentially find themselves too busy to witness against the Beast and resist its claims.

42. Aune, *Revelation*, 770; Koester, *Revelation*, 597–98.

Revelation 14

Following the Lamb

When we come around the bend after encountering the Beast, John alerts us again, "Look!" (See "Translation Matters: ἰδού.") Even though the NRSV fails to include the command, the excitement is palpable when he announces that the Lamb is standing on Mount Zion. The location is awe-inspiring, the "axis mundi" where heaven meets earth. Adding to the thrill of the scene, John informs his audiences that surrounding the Lamb are the 144,000 who bear his name and follow him wherever he goes (v. 4).

When I read this passage, I can't help but think of a rock or pop concert. The Lamb is lit up in the center of the stage, and 144,000 of his biggest fans surge toward him.[1] Heads bob and bodies move in unison as the crowd sings the "new song" (v. 2). It is so loud John hears their voice as rushing water, thunder, and harps. Knowing the song and singing it with others who know it is part of being in the fandom, the family. The scene reminds me of the visceral experience of being at the show of a popular performer or band you love, connecting with both those on the stage and

---

1. The world's largest stadium in North Korea, the Rungrado 1st of May Stadium, has a capacity of 150,000 and is currently the only stadium in the world that could hold the 144,000. Rahul Venkat, "Biggest Stadium in the World: Venues in North Korea, India and the US in Top Three—Full List," Olympics.com, April 12, 2022, https://olympics .com/en/featured-news/largest-stadium-world-venue-capacity-spectator-seats.

the others in the crowd who have made an effort to get themselves there, sometimes at great cost. There is a powerful sense of community in these spaces. Being in the crowd when a beloved performer leads members of the audience in a call-and-response or when everyone starts moving in unison is a spiritual experience. Singing together the songs that are everyone's favorites makes strangers feel like old friends. I imagine that these are the feelings that John's vision of the Lamb on Mount Zion aims to capture. As a reader of Revelation, I want to be present to participate in communal admiration of the gender-bending Lamb.

Being at a great show is exhilarating. At the same time, standing on the floor with die-hard fans can be intimidating and frightening. Perhaps the song "everyone" knows is a "deep cut," that hidden track from the band's first album only a select few know, let alone know all the words. Knowing the song becomes a way of distinguishing between "true" fans and those who only recently started following. Even in this place of togetherness, exclusion looms for those who don't fit in or conform. Being by the stage or in "the pit" means losing control of your body at some shows. You are forced to move with the crowd, a scary experience when those around you are bigger or more powerful than you. In some cases, the force of the crowd is dangerous, especially if a performer fails to stop when things get out of control.[2] The thrill of the show can quickly turn into terror. Similarly frightening is how a crowd can be manipulated or even misled.

One reason the ancient theologian Tertullian warned Christians against attending "spectacles," such as gladiatorial games, was that the crowds could quickly become "frenzied" with "madness, anger, discord." He thought these feelings were counter to the Christian call to be "priests of peace" (*Spect.* 16). Interestingly, John does not describe the response of the 144,000 when a series of angels interrupt their worship to announce the judgment of those who worship the Beast and drink the wine of Babylon's fornication. We are not privy to the multitude's reaction when both the Son of Humanity and an angel descend to earth with sharp sickles to harvest, metaphorically, the people of earth (vv. 14-20). These actions lead to the kind of bloodshed typically associated with the spectacles Tertullian criticized, where masses of people and animals were slaughtered. I wonder, do the 144,000 fans of the Lamb roar in excitement over these events? Or, are they filled with fear and dread?

2. For example, "Crowd Surge at Travis Scott Concert Leaves at Least 8 Dead," *The New York Times*, November 6, 2021, https://www.nytimes.com/live/2021/11/06/us/houston-astroworld-festival.

Being One of the Lamb's Virgins (14:1-5)

The Lamb, who initially appeared "standing as if it had been slaughtered" (5:6), now stands (ἑστὸς) unequivocally and unqualified. The image of a mountain, which evokes height and strength, offers a striking contrast to the idea of being slaughtered, a position of weakness. Zion is where heaven and earth are connected and where God dwells and reigns (e.g., Ps 9:1; 50:2). This imagery evokes other apocalyptic traditions that anticipate the faithful gathering around the Messiah at Zion near the end of time (e.g., 4 Ezra 2:42-48), and here John shows the faithful crowding around the Lamb. The one who sat upon the throne with God (7:9-10) now appears close to their faithful worshippers.

When John introduced this crowd earlier, he depicted it as both an idealized Israel and a multinational group (7:4-9). Those identities conveyed the political and communal profile of those faithful to God and the Lamb, and now John offers a closer look at the character of the individuals who comprise this multitude. He does this by employing several overlapping metaphors to characterize the relationship between the 144,000 and the focus of their attention, the Lamb. In so doing, John picks up on the imagery of enslavement introduced in the earlier scene, observing that the 144,000 wear on their foreheads the name of the Lamb and "his Father's name" (14:1). This mark comes from the seal brandished by the angel and indicates that these 144,000 followers are the property of God and the Lamb (7:3).

John's specification that the seal on the foreheads of the 144,000 includes the names of the Lamb and his Father (πατήρ) highlights the close relationship between the two and alludes to the idea of the ancient household, traditionally led by a male head of household or father. Although modern readers may imagine a household primarily in terms of familial roles and relationships, the ancient household included those enslaved in the home as well.[3] In Colossians, for instance, the author delineates the different hierarchical relationships within the household—wife and husband, child and parent, enslaved and enslaver (or "slave" and "master" according to the NRSV; Col 3:18-22). The reference to God as the Lamb's Father evokes this kind of domestic hierarchy and stratification of power; however, even though the relationship between God and the

---

3. Richard P. Saller, "Symbols of Gender and Status Hierarchies in the Roman Household," in *Women and Slaves in Greco-Roman Culture*, ed. Sandra R. Joshel and Sheila Murnaghan (London: Routledge, 1998), 85–91.

14:1Then I looked, and there was the Lamb, standing on Mount Zion! And with him were one hundred forty-four thousand who had his name and his Father's name written on their foreheads. 2And I heard a voice from heaven like the sound of many waters and like the sound of loud thunder; the voice I heard was like the sound of harpists playing on their harps, 3and they sing a new song before the throne and before the four living creatures and before the elders. No one could learn that song except the one hundred forty-four thousand who have been redeemed from the earth. 4It is these who have not defiled themselves with women, for they are virgins; these follow the Lamb wherever he goes. They have been redeemed from humankind as first fruits for God and the Lamb, 5and in their mouth no lie was found; they are blameless.

Lamb is depicted as a parent-child relationship, John depicts the two as sharing authority and power (2:27; 3:21). This shared authority manifests in the fact that both of their names appear on the foreheads of the 144,000.

John continues to build upon the metaphorical depiction of the 144,000 as enslaved by describing them as "redeemed" or, literally, "purchased" (ἀγοράζω) from the earth. While the language of "redemption" carries a religious meaning in modern Christian thought, it brings up the idea of the ancient marketplace, the *agora* (ἀγορά). God and the Lamb *purchase* the 144,000, so they are no longer the property of the earth. Throughout Revelation, "earth" (γῆ) refers to a place distinct from heaven, the center of God's reign. Even though God's people will eventually rule over the earth with Christ (5:10; 20:4-6), at present the earth and its inhabitants are hostile toward God and those loyal to God. For instance, the "inhabitants of the earth" gloat over the death of the Two Witnesses (11:10), and the "whole earth" follows and worships the Beast (13:3, 8, 14). As part of the divine household, the 144,000 no longer belong to the earth where the Beast resides for the time being.

The language of being purchased triggers another metaphor for John, who describes the followers of the Lamb as produce sacrificed to God. They "have been redeemed from humankind as first fruits for God and the Lamb" (14:5). In Deuteronomy, Moses explains that the tradition of giving the first part of every harvest to God serves as a way of thanking the divine for divine faithfulness, not just in bringing about the harvest, but in leading the Israelites out of Egypt and into a new land "flowing with milk and honey" (26:9). By suggesting the 144,000 are first fruits, Revelation implies that they will be "harvested" and "sacrificed." They will face death because of their faithfulness to God and the Lamb. The multitude signals only the beginning of the harvest, however, which John will describe more fully later in the chapter (14:14-20).

Moreover, through the metaphor of first fruits, John introduces the idea that the 144,000 are blameless (ἄμωμος) since things sacrificed to God must be without blemish. The Greek term ἄμωμος, which is formed using a Greek alpha (α) to negate the noun μῶμος (blemish), introduces a rhetorical trope in verses 4-6. This is called *litotes*, and is when an author uses a negative construction to emphasize a positive claim (*Rhet. Her.* 4.38). When a person says, "You're *not* wrong," they, for example, underscore just how right you are. Or, if you say something is "*not* uncommon," you affirm the object referenced is actually quite common. Thus, when John notes that "in their mouth no lie was found," an allusion to Zephaniah's depiction of the people of Israel (3:13),[4] he emphasizes the multitude's truthfulness. In this way, John emphatically distances the multitude from the two Beasts, who are associated with deception and trickery (e.g., 13:14). Truth-telling, sometimes described as "frank" or "bold" speech, was seen as a virtue in the first-century world (*Rhet. Her.* 4.36).[5] This kind of speech trades in truth, even when conveying information that others do not want to hear or putting the speaker at risk. Speaking boldly is a characteristic of Jesus in the Gospel of John. He openly speaks of being the Messiah even when others want to kill him (John 7:26; see also John 11:14; 16:25, 29; 18:20). These followers of the Lamb are truth-tellers, and they will testify to the truth of God's reign and to the Lamb, a discourse that will put them at odds with the Beast.

Likewise, John affirms the multitude's blamelessness with the negative claim that these "have not defiled themselves with women" (14:4). The misogyny is glaring but common. Greek philosophers and physicians asserted that female bodies were naturally wetter and colder than male bodies and consequently more susceptible to impurity. Female bodies were more porous than male bodies and had a propensity to leak, making them messy and potentially dangerous to others. [6] The impurity of

---

4. Craig R. Koester, *Revelation: A New Translation with Introduction and Commentary*, AYB 38A (New Haven: Yale University Press, 2014), 611.

5. Gail R. O'Day, "Jesus as Friend in the Gospel of John," *Int* 58 (2004): 147.

6. Anne Carson, "Putting Her in Her Place: Woman, Dirt, and Desire," in *Before Sexuality: The Construction of Erotic Experience in the Ancient Greek World*, ed. David M. Halperin, John J. Winkler, and Froma I. Zeitlin (Princeton: Princeton University Press, 1990), 137, 153–54.

women's bodies was a topic among Roman authors as well. Pliny the Elder detailed the monstrous power of the menstruating body, warning readers to avoid sex when "that time of the month" coincided with an eclipse lest it prove fatal to a male partner. In addition, menstrual blood supposedly drove bees from a hive, killed plants, made linen being washed turn black, and gave copper cooking pots a wretched smell (*Nat.* 28.23). John's singling out sex with women as defiling reflects these sorts of assumptions. John remains tight-lipped, however, about sex with other "non-men," such as enslaved males or sex-workers. Sex between males was culturally acceptable and even expected in John's context so long as the penetrator was the individual culturally understood as the "man." (Ancient notions of sex generally assumed one person penetrated and the other was penetrator.[7]) John, however, ignores these kinds of experiences in his depiction of the 144,000 as those who are not defiled by women.

On the one hand, John's assertion that sex with women defiles men belies, moreover, the fact that in the first century, women, and not men, were more likely to bear the shame that came with illicit sexual activity. Under Augustan law, men in the Roman Empire could be legally punished for adultery with a married or single citizen woman, but there was a double standard between women and men, especially among elites.[8] For example, the ancient historian Suetonius matter-of-factly describes Augustus exiling his daughter Julia for adultery (*Aug.* 65). In contrast, the same author wrote off the emperor's own youthful sexual misdeeds as ploys for gathering information from the wives of political rivals (Suetonius, *Aug.* 69). On the other hand, this reference to the 144,000 being defiled by others points to John's vision of the multitude as virgins, imagery that calls to mind girls who have neither been married nor had sex. The notion that these faithful followers of the Lamb could be defiled (the verb ἐμολύθησαν is passive) points to their status as virgins (παρθένοι), a gender-bending image that mirrors that of the Lamb.

This description of the faithful as virgins (παρθένοι) has been a source of consternation for modern interpreters (see below, Hanna Stenström, "Christians Reading Revelation's 144,000 Male Virgins"). One commentator even

---

7. Craig A. Williams, *Roman Homosexuality*, 2nd ed. (Oxford: Oxford University Press, 2010), passim.

8. Suzanne Dixon, *The Roman Family* (Baltimore: Johns Hopkins University Press, 1992), 79.

describes it as "John's most puzzling sentence"[9]—a bold statement given Revelation's overall cryptic imagery. This puzzlement seemingly stems from: (1) the assumption that virginity and the related practice of celibacy seem like unattainable goals, even though those devoted to the monastic life might beg to differ; and (2) the fact that the term for "virgin" (παρθένος), although used with a masculine pronoun here, usually refers to young women or girls. The connection between παρθένος and girls is something rarely explored by Revelation commentators. Instead, most commentators, primarily male-identifying, connect the imagery to ancient holy war traditions in which soldiers refrained from sexual activity for a limited time (e.g., 1 Sam 21:4-5; 2 Sam 11:11-12).[10] This kind of limited celibacy may have been part of the practices adopted at Qumran, where ascetic community members understood themselves at war with forces of evil (e.g., 1 QM 7:3-6). Since this passage does not include other holy war imagery, however, the connection seems tenuous.[11] In addition, this reading does not take into account the most common way of understanding "virgin" in Revelation's world, as an unmarried, virginal teen girl or young woman.[12]

In modern English, "virgin" refers primarily to someone who has not had sex, and ancient authors similarly assumed that the virgin was sexually inexperienced. Medical theorists differed in opinion about when girls should lose their virginity, although they seemingly assumed it would happen at a young age. The first-century physician Soranus acknowledged that permanent virginity was not damaging to a girl or woman but noted that the age of fourteen, when a girl first starts to menstruate, was the ideal "time for defloration" (*Gyn.* 1.8.33). Preferably, this happened after the virgin was married. Some male authors thought death a better option for a girl who, for whatever reason, was no longer a virgin before

9. G. B. Caird, *A Commentary on the Revelation of St. John the Divine* (London: Black, 1984), 179. See Lynn R. Huber, "Sexually Explicit? Re-Reading Revelation's 144,000 Virgins as a Response to Roman Discourses," *Journal of Men, Masculinities and Spirituality* 2 (2008): 3–28, and Hanna Stenström, "Is Salvation Only for True Men? On Gendered Imagery in the Book of Revelation," in *Imagery in the Book of Revelation*, ed. Michael Labahn and Outi Lehtipuu (Leuven: Peeters, 2011), 183–98.

10. E.g., Gordon D. Fee, *Revelation*, New Covenant Commentary (Eugene, OR: Wipf and Stock, 2010), 192; Craig S. Keener, *Revelation* (Grand Rapids: Zondervan, 2000), 371.

11. David E. Aune, *Revelation*, WBC 52 A–C (Dallas: Word Books, 1998), 819.

12. On the importance of the *virgo*, the Latin equivalent to παρθένος, see Lauren Caldwell, *Roman Girlhood and the Fashioning of Femininity* (Cambridge: Cambridge University Press, 2015), 50–60.

marriage. Thus, the first-century chronicler Valerius Maximus lauds a Roman knight who killed his daughter and her teacher upon finding that the two had been sexually engaged, writing, "He held a too early funeral for her so he would not have to celebrate a shameful marriage" (Valerius Maximus 6.1.3).[13] In fact, families arranged marriages for freeborn girls when they were young (they could marry at the age of twelve) to avoid the possibility of pregnancy without a clear paternal obligation. Given the social importance of being a virgin at marriage, virgins or girls were even expected to protect themselves from the possibility of losing their virginity unwillingly (i.e., by sexual assault), by dressing modestly and traveling with a chaperone, according to classicist Lauren Caldwell.[14] A virgin assaulted while she was wearing the clothes of someone enslaved (i.e., something immodest and revealing) was considered partially responsible for her attack, according to ancient jurisprudence.[15] Sadly, victim-blaming and slut-shaming have long histories.

Ancient literature depicts a variety of ways of being a "virgin." In the New Testament, Mary is the quintessential παρθένος when she is engaged but not yet married to Joseph (Luke 1:27). When Mary learns she is pregnant, she is puzzled since she has "not yet known a man" (a phrase the NRSV renders as "virgin," Luke 1:34). In contrast, a second-century CE novel by Xenophon highlights a virgin's desire to wed and even have sex with the young man she falls in love with. The author, discussing how virgins processed through Ephesus to the shrine of the virgin goddess Artemis, described the character Anthia's body in ways that emphasize her youth and her attractiveness: She is "fourteen, her body . . . blooming with shapeliness" (*Ephesian Tale* 1.2.5). Upon seeing Habrocomes, whom she will marry, Anthia falls madly in love and even tries to get his attention by showing bits of skin (1.3.2). Even though the image of Anthia is crafted by a male author, the notion of a virgin's desire appears as well in the poems of a first-century BCE elite girl named Sulpicia. She describes "burning" for a lover she identifies as Cerinthus, with whom she shares "stolen raptures" ("Cerinthus' Birthday").[16] Sulpicia is, unsurprisingly, angered when she learns of Cerinthus's sexual entanglement with another ("Cerinthus Unfaithful"). While being a virgin in the ancient world might mean being unmarried and, supposedly, inexperienced sexually, it does not necessarily mean being passive and

---

13. As translated by Caldwell, *Roman Girlhood*, 45.
14. Caldwell, *Roman Girlhood*, 49.
15. Caldwell, *Roman Girlhood*, 55.
16. Caldwell, *Roman Girlhood*, 33.

passionless. Pointing to the importance of virgins in the Roman world was the practice of selecting six virgins as priestesses, the Vestal Virgins, who would live in the center of the Roman forum (see p. 250). Six, of course, is a paltry number compared to 144,000.

Despite the ancient understanding of "virgin," John uses the term metaphorically to characterize the 144,000, whom he marks as men. He signals this by using a masculine plural pronoun (οὗτοι), translated into English as "they," to reference the 144,000. The Greek is explicit and emphatic: "These men [οὗτοι] are the ones who have not defiled themselves with women, for they are virgins [παρθένοι]" (14:4). Given the cultural association between virginity and girlhood, this kind of characterization of a male figure as παρθένος is relatively rare.[17] Through this metaphor, however, John makes explicit that the Lamb, who defies gender categorization, should be the model for discipleship, emphasizing, "these men [οὗτοι] are the ones who follow the Lamb wherever he goes" (v. 4). They follow the Lamb even across gender boundaries. In fact, John's revelation of the faithful followers of Christ as virgins should be understood just as world-shaking as that of a Lion who is a Lamb.

Revelation's virgin imagery encourages audience members to see themselves in a way that challenges first-century perceptions of what constitutes ideal manhood. While Roman culture calls these men (οὗτοι) to be active, impenetrable, and strong, John encourages them to adopt a role associated more closely with vulnerability. Being a virgin requires strength to guard one's chastity. The virgin resides in a place of expectation, which can even, as evident in the poetry of Sulpicia, be tinged with desire. Most virgins knew that marriage of some sort was on the horizon, and their lives were structured in anticipation of that future union. The Roman philosopher Musonius Rufus, for instance, explores the question of whether daughters, like sons, should study philosophy. His answer is yes, since it will be beneficial to a girl's future as someone who manages a home and whose role is to support and defend her husband.[18] The virgin trains, in some sense, for life with her future partner; in the case of the 144,000 virgins the partner will be revealed as the Lamb in Revelation 19.

In addition, idealizing the Jesus follower as a sexually inexperienced and unmarried female potentially "queers" or troubles the ancient focus

---

17. For example, παρθένος is used in the Hellenistic Jewish novel *Joseph and Aseneth* to highlight the purity of Joseph and his ability to withstand advances (4:8; 8:1).

18. "Should Daughters Receive the Same Education as Sons?," trans. Cora E. Lutz, *Musonius Rufus: The Roman Socrates*, YCS 10 (New Haven: Yale University Press, 1947), 49.

on the family.[19] For elite Romans, marriage and having a family was essential to being a good citizen. The historian Dio Cassius conveys this through a speech he attributes to Augustus, where the emperor praises those men who have performed their duty by marrying and having children and questions the manliness of those who have failed to marry and start families. In this scene, Augustus asserts that being a good citizen requires making new citizens (*Hist. Rom.* 56.1-9). The historian's depiction of Augustus rings true since the emperor did institute laws incentivizing marrying and having children and penalizing citizens who divorced or committed adultery. (He did this despite his own's family's well-known difficulties with marriage.) For example, male citizens between twenty-five and sixty years of ages could not inherit if they were not married, and married men with children were prioritized for government appointments.[20] These laws were operative during the time Revelation was written and reaffirmed at different points during the imperial period, including during Domitian's reign (Suetonius, *Dom.* 8.3). Bearing children and being part of a family unit was equally important in non-elite families, where multiple sets of hands meant more economic and social security. Having children ensured, ideally, that a parent would be cared for as they aged. In addition, families were considered important sources of emotional support and generally regarded as contributing to a fulfilling life.[21] By upholding the image of the virgin, Revelation resists the dominant vision of what it meant to be a good person and citizen as well as challenging the popular vision of what it meant to live the good life. All of this is made relative to living in devotion to the Lamb, suggesting the possibility that early Jesus followers might eschew in a variety of ways the social and reproductive agenda of the Roman Empire.

John's depiction of faithfulness in terms of being a "virgin" possesses queer and even feminist potential. The imagery introduces the idea that girlhood is a model of faithfulness. Often hidden from the historical record, the social significance and strength of girls are often overlooked, and it is easy to overlook the fact that John chooses the image of a girl as one of the primary ways of being faithful to Christ. Even though he does not necessarily care about literal girls, feminist interpreters of Revelation might take this image and run with it, by looking at ways virgins were

19. Kent L. Brintnall, "Queer Studies and Religion," *CRR* 1 (2013): 53.

20. Judith Evans Grubbs, *Women and the Law in the Roman Empire: A Sourcebook on Marriage, Divorce and Widowhood* (London: Routledge, 2002), 84.

21. Dixon, *Roman Family*, 24–26.

depicted also as victors in the ancient world. Even though the ancient material culture associated with girls tends toward cultivating traditional feminine roles and virtues, such as motherhood and a pleasing appearance, there are scattered representations of ancient girls playing games together, like knucklebones and hoop rolling. In Piazza Armerina, Sicily, there is even a mosaic floor at a Roman Villa showing young women training and competing in athletic games. The mosaic, which is later than Revelation's time period (fourth century CE), is often described as the "bikini girls mosaic," after the girls' bikini-like outfits.[22] The fact that this nickname references the girls' clothing and not their athletic activity reflects the persistence of bias against girls. One girl even has a visible scar on her leg, however, suggesting a resilient athlete, especially since she holds a victory palm and dons a crown. There are similar glimpses of amazing girls within Christian literature, including a very dogged disciple of Paul named Thecla. Thecla's story comes to us through an early Christian novelization of her life in which she resists marriage, cuts her hair, dons masculine clothing, and even baptizes herself (*Acts of Paul and Thecla* 25, 34; see p. 102). Thecla exudes the energy of passionate youth and refuses to take no for an answer. She speaks boldly and is the kind of "virgin" who would certainly face down the Beast of Revelation.

By envisioning faithfulness to the Lamb as a kind of rejection of imperial "family values" Revelation can be read as an affirmation of those who forgo traditional notions of family. Even though the New Testament authors offer a more ambivalent picture of marriage and family (e.g., Mark 3:31-35; Luke 14:25-27; 1 Cor 7:8), some Christians look to the depiction of Adam and Eve and to the divine invitation of Genesis 1:28, "Be fruitful and multiply," as a blueprint for living.[23] In some modern Catholic teaching, having or "creating" children is how individuals live out being made in the image of God who is the original creator.[24] Procreation is

22. Katherine M. D. Dunbabin, *Mosaics of the Greek and Roman World* (Cambridge: Cambridge University Press, 1999), 133. The mosaic is located at Villa Romana del Casale in Piazza Armerina, which is a UNESCO world heritage site. For more information about the site, including images, see UNESCO World Heritage Convention, "Villa Romana del Casale," accessed December 26, 2021, https://whc.unesco.org/en/list/832/.

23. Amy DeRogatis, *Saving Sex: Sexuality and Salvation in American Evangelicalism* (New York: Oxford University Press, 2015), 93.

24. E.g., Richard M. Hogan and John M. LeVoir, *Covenant of Love: Pope John Paul II on Sexuality, Marriage, and Family in the Modern World, with a Commentary on* Familiaris Consortio (San Francisco: Ignatius Press, 1992), 71.

seen by some as one of the most sacred tasks. For those who are childless, whether intentionally or not, these visions of family can be devastating. In contrast, the image of the faithful as virgins decenters the importance of marriage, family, and sex. Obviously, this idea has been embraced by some who choose celibacy as a religious vocation, such as nuns and monks, but the idea might be similarly meaningful for Christians who are childless or who identify as asexual and/or "ace."[25] Scriptural inclusion of an orientation, asexuality, that has been historically dismissed[26] might help move churches toward acceptance and inclusion of a fuller range of ways of being in the world.

At the same time, even though resisting unjust political powers involves challenging their narrow definitions of gender, sexuality, and family, my experience teaches that stifling sexuality, even if we believe such stifling is what God wants, can be harmful. For instance, purity movements that teach girls and, to a lesser extent, boys that "true love waits"[27] can nurture a sexual shame so unshakable that it becomes difficult to embrace the possibility of pleasure even when married. Likewise, the emphasis on sexual purity can make it difficult for LGBTQIA+ youth to recognize and claim their sexual identities, since conversations about sexual identity are often discouraged. As Linda Kay Klein describes of her own experience being raised within evangelical purity culture, "Sex was such a shameful topic that we never got real talk on what we were and were not allowed to do. It was assumed that if no one ever talked to us about sex, it would just sort of go away until we needed it."[28] Conversation about what Revelation 14:1-4 might mean for modern Christians should attend to this history of harm, especially harm that has been done to girls and to those who are queer and trans.

25. Asexuality is *not* the same thing as celibacy. Rather, the term describes an identity in which a person does not generally experience sexual attraction. This does not, however, preclude a person from having romantic and sexual relationships. For an introduction to asexuality, see Anthony F. Bogaert, *Understanding Asexuality* (Landham, MD: Rowman & Littlefield, 2015).

26. Bogaert, *Understanding Asexuality*, 111–12.

27. "True Love Waits" is the name of a Christian movement in the United States that encourages teens to make a pledge to remain chaste until marriage. See DeRogatis, *Saving Sex*, 13.

28. Linda Kay Klein, *Pure: Inside the Evangelical Movement That Shamed a Generation of Young Women and How I Broke Free* (New York: Simon and Schuster, 2019), 77.

***Christians Reading Revelation's
144,000 Male Virgins***

Christian readers, including female feminist readers, who accept the invitation to see what John the prophet saw, the 144,000 together with the Lamb at Mount Zion singing a new song, will most probably feel great joy when they read Revelation 14. This is certainly a vision of ultimate liberation of those who are "redeemed" by God, although different Christian readers will understand "liberation" in different ways. Some will understand it as freedom from the Devil and from a godless world, others as freedom from death and sorrow, and still others as freedom from oppression and social, political, economic injustices.

Despite this type of interpretation, some female feminist readers—and perhaps also some female readers who hesitate to identify as feminists—will hear that the invitation is not for them. In 14:4, John the prophet tells us that the 144,000 "have not defiled themselves with women, for they are virgins." Women are forced into the role of "the Others," defiling, threatening, excluded from the Redeemed. The vision of ultimate liberation suddenly turns into a vision of the ultimate backlash. In fact, Revelation 14:4 is also a "text of terror" for Christian men who have, or at least want to have, a sex life. The challenge of Revelation 14:4 is actually summed up in a quotation from Ronald H. Preston and Anthony T. Hanson's commentary on Revelation published in 1949: "If taken literally it means that only male celibates can be saved!"

One reason to be concerned with Revelation 14:1-5, and Revelation as a whole, is that the peripheral and extreme text shows vividly what we find throughout the Christian tradition. It reminds Christian feminists of the pains, the paradoxes, and the ambivalence inherent in being a Christian feminist. Texts, practices, communities that are a source for faith and hope as well as places where we experience love are at the same time places where we are excluded, marginalized. They are a source for oppression as well as liberation.

Androcentrism is not just a biblical or, more generally, a Christian phenomenon. Feminist theory and research in various disciplines as well as feminist political reflection and activism have shown beyond doubt that "androcentrism" is fundamental in patriarchal societies. When we speak about "human beings" and "human existence," we are in the practice of talking about men, not women or women and men. Therefore, the construction of Christian identity in Revelation 14:1-5 is certainly extreme, but it is an extreme version of a way of thinking that is fundamental in what is considered normal in patriarchal cultures. Thereby, Revelation 14:1-5 is relevant also for feminist readers who are not Christians but live in a culture deeply influenced by Christianity.

Revelation 14:1-5 may certainly inspire reflections on constructions of Christian identity but also on constructions of identity in other contexts, including human identity, as a male identity. Hereby all feminists may be reminded of pains, paradoxes, and ambivalence, here inherent in living as a feminist in a patriarchal culture. Wherever we go, we may be involved in institutions, relations, contexts where we find so much that is valuable, where we can find meaning, love, hope—but

also experience exclusion and marginalization. We will often be invited to participate in male identities and even have to accept them since there are no real alternatives.

This mix of what we as feminist women find valuable and what we must liberate ourselves from is not an oddity we find in some verses in Revelation; it is a basic condition for living as a feminist woman in patriarchal societies— not only for those who belong to a religious tradition but for all of us. Therefore, feminist women and all others who struggle for gender justice have good reasons for reflecting on Revelation 14:1-5 and also creating new visions of liberation, as powerful as the old ones, but not defiled by androcentrism and gender injustice.

Hanna Stenström

Proclaiming the Eternal Gospel (14:6-13)

John's attention is drawn away from the virginal multitude by a series of three angels who fly through mid-heaven with an "eternal gospel." The word "gospel" (εὐαγγέλιον) literally means "good news," even though the following messages hardly seem like good news, at least from the perspective of those on the earth. The messages offer predictions of judgment and punishment for the fans of the Beast, who worship him and receive his mark (v. 11). The irony of describing these proclamations as good news makes it seem like John wants those in his audiences, who would likely envision themselves aligned with the 144,000, to relish in their good fortune: We've picked the right superstar to follow! The two verses that follow the angels' proclamations, however, presumably addressed to followers of the Lamb, offer an important reminder that following the Lamb is not the easy path (vv. 12-13).

⁶Then I saw another angel flying in midheaven, with an eternal gospel to proclaim to those who live on the earth—to every nation and tribe and language and people. ⁷He said in a loud voice, "Fear God and give him glory, for the hour of his judgment has come; and worship him who made heaven and earth, the sea and the springs of water."

⁸Then another angel, a second, followed, saying, "Fallen, fallen is Babylon the great! She has made all nations drink of the wine of the wrath of her fornication."

⁹Then another angel, a third, followed them, crying with a loud voice, "Those who worship the beast and its image, and receive a mark on their foreheads or on their hands, ¹⁰they will also drink the wine of God's wrath, poured unmixed into the cup of his anger, and they will be tormented with fire and sulfur in the presence of the holy angels and in the presence of the Lamb. ¹¹And the smoke of their torment goes up forever and ever. There is no rest day or night for those who worship the beast and its image and for anyone who receives the mark of its name."

¹²Here is a call for the endurance of the saints, those who keep the commandments of God and hold fast to the faith of Jesus.

¹³And I heard a voice from heaven saying, "Write this: Blessed are the dead who from now on die in the Lord." "Yes," says the Spirit, "they will rest from their labors, for their deeds follow them."

The first angel issues a command to fear and worship God, along with announcing the arrival of "the hour of judgment" (vv. 6-7). The proclamation is directed specifically to "those who live [τοὺς καθημένους, literally, 'sit'] *on* the earth [ἐπὶ τῆς γῆς]" (v. 6). This reference makes clear that the angel is describing those who do not follow the Lamb, since those who follow are "redeemed *from* the earth" (ἀπὸ τῆς γῆς) and "*from* humankind" (ἀπὸ τῶν ἀνθρώπων)" (vv. 3-4). At the same time, since Revelation addresses communities of the faithful, these angelic edicts are not actually for the "earth sitters." Rather, they indirectly affirm those among John's audiences who are faithful to the Lamb and, perhaps, help keep them in line.

The second angel proclaims the fall of "Babylon the great" (v. 8). In the first century CE, Babylon was far from the "great" city it had been at its height in the seventh and sixth centuries BCE; the once-great empire had since been conquered by multiple imperial regimes. Rather, the name "Babylon" evoked Israel's past oppressor, which had laid siege to Jerusalem, destroyed its temple, and forced many into exile in 586 BCE (1 Kgs 24). After the Romans similarly took Jerusalem and destroyed the second temple in 70 CE, "Babylon" became a way of villainizing Rome (e.g., 1 Pet 5:13; 4 Ezra 15:43-46). This use of "Babylon" as a label bears a similarity to calling someone a "Nazi" today. The label provokes and elides distinctions between historically distant realities. By calling Rome "Babylon," John hopes his audiences will automatically assume the worst about Rome without thinking. This kind of shortcut is an effective polemical tool because no one wants to be the person slow to decry the evil other, whether Nazi Germany or Babylon. Further, this kind of labelling does nothing to honor the memories of those oppressed by Nazis or Babylon, as it focuses attention only on the current situation. So John arguably has little or no real interest in remembering the destruction and pain caused by the historical Babylon; he is only concerned with utilizing that story to mobilize those living in the present, the followers of the Lamb.

Here, John first personifies the city of Babylon as a woman, an idea that he develops in much detail later (Rev 17–18). The image reflects the tradition of gendering cities as feminine and depicting them as women and, specifically, as goddesses that appear throughout the Mediterranean. These personifications overlapped with depictions of the goddess Tyche, who was associated with the fate and fortunes of cities. Statues and images of Tyche typically show her holding a cornucopia, symbolizing plenty, or a ship's rudder with which she steers a city's course.[29] In contrast to these comforting city representations, using the feminine pronoun "she" (ἤ), the angel accuses Babylon of making nations drunk on "the wine of the wrath of her fornication [πορνεία]" (14:8). The reference to fornication, or culturally unacceptable sexual practices, alludes to the later characterization of Babylon as a sex-worker to the "kings of the earth" and as the "mother of prostitutes" (17:2, 5). Instead of being a guide, Babylon causes nations to become drunk, i.e., lose focus and good judgment. Claims that Babylon is full of wrath and engages in "fornication" draw on ancient assumptions that women were prone to excess and lacked self-control. In keeping with this motif, John witnesses Babylon herself drunk on the blood of the saints and the witnesses to Jesus (17:6). While Babylon intoxicates the nations with fornication, her drink of choice is the violence she enacts against God's faithful followers.

Babylon's cup of fornication is quickly replaced with the cup of God's anger (14:9-10), which contains a much stronger vintage. The angel warns that this cup of anger contains contents that are "unmixed," a reference

---

29. Ronald Mellor, *ΘΕΑ ΡΩΜΗ: The Worship of the Goddess Roma in the Greek World* (Göttingen: Vandenhoeck & Ruprecht, 1975), 153.

to the ancient practice of mixing water into wine to dilute it.[30] John insists that the potency of God's wrath exceeds that of any competitors, including empires like Babylon. Hence, John further describes God's wrath on those who follow the Beast in terms of torment with fire and sulfur.[31] Anticipating his description of the fate of the "Great Prostitute," John writes, "And the smoke of their torment goes up forever and ever" (v. 11; 19:3).

While Babylon's fall draws on stereotypical feminine behaviors, John encourages his audiences to practice endurance (ὑπομονή), a characteristic typically associated with athleticism and masculinity in the ancient world (see p. 37). This might seem strange, since John just characterized the faithful as virgins (v. 4). John does not, however, define endurance entirely in physical terms; instead, Revelation describes endurance as "keep[ing] the commandments of God and . . . the faith of Jesus" (v. 12).[32] Jesus's faith, which is mentioned only here in Revelation, is made evident in his willingness to die. This can be understood as his faith that God is trustworthy and just. Holding up this endurance as an ideal, a voice from heaven commands John to write a blessing on those who "die in the Lord." God's spirit affirms this, offering that they will "rest," an apparent euphemism for death, from their labors (v. 13).

This type of masculine ideal, a brave acceptance of death for the sake of remaining faithful, undergirds Jewish and Christian stories of martyrs, regardless of the faithful's gender. These accounts, which emerge after Revelation's penning, emphasize the manliness of the martyr as a way of idealizing the Jesus followers in contrast to those who oppress them.[33] Accounts of women and girls in the arena and thrown to the beasts sometimes visually depict them embodying masculinity, appearing in a vision as a gladiator (Perpetua) or adopting the dress of a man (Thecla). These cases "[present] an even stronger case for the superiority of Christianity,"[34] since girls and women, according to ancient logic, had much more to overcome as they faced their opponents. John's vision here of the faithful as virgins who both endure and follow the Lamb into

---

30. Patrick Faas, *Around the Roman Table: Food and Feasting in Ancient Rome* (Chicago: University of Chicago Press, 2005), 91.

31. Brian K. Blount, *Revelation: A Commentary* (Louisville: Westminster John Knox, 2009), 275.

32. Even though the NRSV translation has two verbs, "keep" and "hold fast," in the Greek it is only a single verb (τηρέω) that can be translated either way.

33. L. Stephanie Cobb, *Dying to Be Men: Gender and Language in Early Christian Martyr Texts* (New York: Columbia University Press, 2008), 60–62.

34. Cobb, *Dying to Be Men*, 92.

death anticipates this. The faithful are like faithful girls who willingly follow the one they adore and worship into death.

A Bloody Flow (14:14-20)

John builds on the preceding proclamations with two visions of harvest, metaphors for judgment. The visions expand on Joel 3:13: "Put in the sickle, for the harvest is ripe. Go in, tread, for the wine press is full. The vats overflow, for their wickedness is great."[35] Depicting both a reaping of wheat, representing the faithful saints being taken from the earth by the Son of Humanity, and a harvest of grapes, representing the fate of the unfaithful, these scenes are a culmination of chapters 12–14, which present the cosmic conflict between God and Satan along with those who are faithful to God and the Lamb and those who follow the Beast.

The Son of Humanity, last seen at the beginning of this journey (Rev 2–3), now comes on a cloud, the ride of choice for messianic figures (e.g., Dan 7:13; Mark 13:26). Wearing a wreath-like crown (στέφανος) like a victorious athlete, he wields a sickle to "reap" those who are "fully ripe" (14:14-16). The ripe ones are those who follow the instructions outlined in Revelation 2–3 by resisting the Beast and his mark. They are "victors," like the Son of Humanity. The association between the faithful and a ripe crop continues the image of the 144,000 virgins as "first fruits" (v. 4).

Even though the text does not employ explicitly gendered language here, women's bodies and agricultural imagery were historically intertwined in the ancient Mediterranean.[36] In mythology the cycles of agricultural abundance and bareness were governed by Demeter, also known as Ceres (see p. 87). Demeter allowed new growth only at the times her virginal daughter Persephone, who the Romans called Proserpina, was released from the underworld by Hades who had abducted her. When Persephone was free from the subterranean realm of death, crops arose, blending the ideas of a life and death with virginity and marriage. John alludes to a similar set of associations by depicting the faithful virgins, free from the control of the Beast who comes from the underground realm, as an abundant crop to be harvested. Even though reaping sug-

---

35. David A. deSilva, *Seeing Things John's Way: The Rhetoric of the Book of Revelation* (Louisville: Westminster John Knox, 2009), 298.

36. Page duBois, *Sowing the Body: Psychoanalysis and Ancient Representations of Women* (Chicago: University of Chicago Press, 1991), 39–85.

¹⁴Then I looked, and there was a white cloud, and seated on the cloud was one like the Son of Man, with a golden crown on his head, and a sharp sickle in his hand! ¹⁵Another angel came out of the temple, calling with a loud voice to the one who sat on the cloud, "Use your sickle and reap, for the hour to reap has come, because the harvest of the earth is fully ripe." ¹⁶So the one who sat on the cloud swung his sickle over the earth, and the earth was reaped.

¹⁷Then another angel came out of the temple in heaven, and he too had a sharp sickle. ¹⁸Then another angel came out from the altar, the angel who has authority over fire, and he called with a loud voice to him who had the sharp sickle, "Use your sharp sickle and gather the clusters of the vine of the earth, for its grapes are ripe." ¹⁹So the angel swung his sickle over the earth and gathered the vintage of the earth, and he threw it into the great wine press of the wrath of God. ²⁰And the wine press was trodden outside the city, and blood flowed from the wine press, as high as a horse's bridle, for a distance of about two hundred miles.

gests the death of a crop, these faithful will eventually live with God as part of the new Jerusalem (21:4).

After watching Christ's harvest of the "fully ripe," John and his audience members witness another harvest, this one representing the fate of those who follow the Beast. An angel, and not Christ, collects the crop of grapes. The grape harvest recalls the red juice of the grapes, which recalls God's wine cup of wrath. The red liquid also invites thoughts of blood. This image takes a gruesome turn when John describes the "vintage of the earth," the followers of the Beast, tossed into the "great wine press of the wrath of God" (14:19). The metaphorical connection between wine and blood is made explicit and horrific when John describes a deluge of blood, enough to reach a horse's bridle, flowing from the winepress (v. 20). This massive amount of blood evokes memories of the ancient games, including gladiatorial and animal battles. In some of the biggest spectacles, which took place over days, thousands of animals were killed before the eyes of cheering audiences. (Hence Tertullian's disapproval as noted earlier.) Dio Cassius claims, for example, that at the inaugural games held by Titus in the Colosseum in Rome nine thousand animals were killed (66.25.1).

Even though the 144,000 virgins have faded into the background, the fact that copious amounts of blood follow their appearance seems significant. The bodies of teen girls are often associated with blood and even terror. In the classic American horror film *Carrie* (1976), the movie's titular protagonist is horrified by her own menstrual blood and later doused in a bucket of pig's blood at her school prom.[37] Blood and the color red are similarly prominent in the 2003 Korean movie *A Tale of Two Sisters*; the image used to promote the move depicts two girls in white blood-soaked dresses.[38] These movies, it seems, reveal both cultural fears about feminine power, symbolized in and through reproduction, and the ferocity of women's anger over patriarchal oppression. Does the blood spilled by God at the end of this chapter suggest the divine's identification with the virgins? What might we make of the Eucharist?

The connection between teen girls and blood, however, is not only modern. In a fragment of a medical text about diseases particular to girls (παρθένοι), one ancient theorist describes an affliction among girls who have not yet found a husband, meaning that they have not yet had sex: "Blood collects in the uterus, destined to run out, but when the mouth of the exit does not open up, more blood keeps being added . . . and then, left with nowhere to flow out, the blood springs up in its excess to the heart and the diaphragm. Now when these parts are filled, the heart becomes stupefied, then from the stupefaction numb, and finally from the numbness these women become deranged" (*Girls* 1).[39] Because they remain virgins past their prime, they are overwhelmed with blood, which serves as a justification for early marriage and the subsequent "defloration" of girls. (No wonder teen girls and women are angry.) Perhaps this massive flow signals a collective loss of "innocence." The virgins who follow the Lamb, ostensibly Revelation's audience members, are made aware of how God's wrath is made manifest.

Despite the connections between girls and blood, in John's vision the virgins remain somewhat removed from the effusive flow of blood. Their white robes, although washed in the Lamb's blood, remain pure (7:9, 13-14). Is this because they aren't really virgins and are men co-opting the role of girls? Are the 144,000 "virgins" without the horror and the mess? While this may be the case, I want feminist readers of Revelation to take seriously the possibility that John envisions the ideal follower of the Lamb taking on the persona or character of the teen girl or young woman, with all her desire and eagerness. How, if we envisioned faithfulness in this way, would the church and the world look?

37. Brian De Palma, *Carrie* (Red Bank Films, 1976).
38. Jee-woon Kim, *A Tale of Two Sisters* (B.O.M. Film Productions, 2003).
39. How this fragment, which also has been called "Diseases of Girls," relates to other medical writings associated with Hippocrates is unknown.

Revelation 15–16

Drowning in a Sea of Plague

When I started writing this chapter, I was "sheltering in place" in Kansas City, Missouri, as COVID-19 started spreading across the globe. It was March 2020 and according to the Johns Hopkins University Coronavirus Resource Center there were half a million known cases of the virus worldwide and over twenty-two thousand deaths.[1] Hospitals in the United States were at capacity, and in some cities the mortuaries were overwhelmed with bodies. At the height of the outbreak in New York City, there were "nearly 800 people dying per day, a rate five times as high as the city's normal pace of death," according to reporting in *The New York Times*.[2] In the spring of 2022, the United States surpassed every other country on the globe with one million deaths. Besides the sheer number of lives lost, other effects of COVID-19 included long-COVID, supply-chain breakdowns, lost jobs, learning loss in school-aged children, missed opportunities to make memories with loved ones, and the list goes on. The impacts of this modern "plague" are staggering.

1. Johns Hopkins Coronavirus Resource Center, "Johns Hopkins Coronavirus Resource Center," March 26, 2020, https://coronavirus.jhu.edu/.

2. Jeremy White et al., "How America Reached One Million Covid Deaths," *The New York Times*, May 13, 2022, https://www.nytimes.com/interactive/2022/05/13/us/covid-deaths-us-one-million.html.

The plagues poured out by angels in Revelation 15–16 result in similarly staggering effects, the extent of which is unprecedented within the narrative. The seven seals primarily described realities, such as economic disparity and war, that humans expect to happen as they live in society and upon the earth. The seven trumpets unleashed more destruction than the seals, causing major damage to the earth; however, the impact was limited. Now, there are no limits on the destruction wrought. Moreover, the pouring out of these plagues begins within the context of heavenly worship.

Beside the Sea of Glass (15:1-4)

John highlights the revelatory aspect of plagues as this chapter opens, describing the appearance of the seven angels who will deliver this third series of plagues as a "portent" (σημεῖον), just as the Woman Clothed in the Sun and the Great Red Dragon were portents (12:1, 3). By describing this portent as "great and amazing," John signals to his audiences that they are about to see and experience something unprecedented. "Great and amazing" (μέγα καὶ θαυμαστόν) refer to the size and scope of what is about to happen. In this context, the terms are not synonyms for "good" or "fortuitous." The impact and significance of this portent will be cast in terms like "just," "glory," and even "fear" (15:3-4). John further underscores its importance by explaining that "with [these plagues] the wrath of God is ended" (v. 1). Like the finale of a fireworks show, when the biggest and most powerful pyrotechnics are set off, these seven plagues leave your heart pounding and ears ringing.

Even before the angels pour their bowls out, the text reveals the identity of those who will survive the plagues—these are the victors who have conquered (τοὺς νικῶντας) the Beast, its image, and the number of its name (vv. 2-4). In this way, Revelation's audience members get a glimpse of who John calls them to be since they were called to be victors in the seven messages of Revelation 2–3 (see "Translation Matters: ὁ νικῶν"). The fact that they hold "harps of God" suggests conquering includes worshiping God. Their allegiance is oriented toward the heavenly throne in front of which sits the sea of glass (4:6).

The presence of the sea of glass places the victors in the heavenly throne room, which assumes a connection between being a victor and death. "Those who had been slaughtered for the word of God and for the testimony they had given" are the ones who ultimately end up in that

15:1Then I saw another portent in heaven, great and amazing: seven angels with seven plagues, which are the last, for with them the wrath of God is ended.

2And I saw what appeared to be a sea of glass mixed with fire, and those who had conquered the beast and its image and the number of its name, standing beside the sea of glass with harps of God in their hands. 3And they sing the song of Moses, the servant of God, and the song of the Lamb:

"Great and amazing are your
> deeds,
>> Lord God the Almighty!
Just and true are your ways,
>> King of the nations!
4Lord, who will not fear
>> and glorify your name?
For you alone are holy.
>> All nations will come
>> and worship before you,
for your judgments have been
>> revealed."

heavenly place. These victors may be *en route* to join their compatriots, who cry out for justice and vengeance, under the altar (6:9-11).[3]

John's vision of the victors beside the sea explicitly draws on the story in Exodus of the Israelites' flight from Egypt, although John reverses the order of events. The celebration of victory in Revelation comes before the outpouring of plagues. The story of God's faithfulness toward the Israelites, who had been enslaved in Egypt, was an important cultural touchstone for ancient Jews (as it continues to be for modern Jews in the celebration of Passover), and John, a Jewish author, draws on the story now as his vision intensifies and moves toward a climax. John's use of the exodus story as he launches into extended depictions of Babylon's judgment (Rev 17–18) and a coming New Jerusalem prepares audience members for understanding that they are being called to exit, albeit metaphorically, their current state. This will be made explicit when a voice from heaven calls those hearing Revelation to "come out" of Babylon (18:4). At this point in her commentary on the text, Elisabeth Schüssler Fiorenza helpfully reminds readers of the complexity of the apocalyptic narrative.[4]

While in Exodus the Israelites sing and celebrate by the Red Sea immediately after fleeing enslavement, an escape made possible through the ten plagues God instructs Moses to unleash on the Egyptians (Exod

---

3. Elisabeth Schüssler Fiorenza, *Revelation: Vision of a Just World* (Minneapolis: Fortress, 1991), 93.

4. Schüssler Fiorenza, *Revelation: Vision of a Just World*, 92.

15:1-18), in Revelation the song comes first. This casts the crowd as confident in God's consistency and faithfulness. Their God is the God that led the people out of Egypt, and they anticipate God acting again in their favor.

John identifies the victor's song as the "song of Moses . . . and the song of the Lamb" (v. 3), characterizing Moses as God's "servant" according to the NRSV (τοῦ δούλου τοῦ θεοῦ; see also Deut 34:5). This description connects Moses to the faithful in Revelation who are sealed as God's human property (7:3-8). The notion of the one who liberated Israel being called enslaved echoes the paradox embodied in the Lion who is simultaneously a slaughtered Lamb (5:4). Thus, John attributes this hymn to both Moses and the Lamb. This blurring of Moses and the Lamb in the context of Exodus imagery invites Revelation's audiences to see their experience as analogous to the ancient Israelites in Egypt. For John, life within the Roman Empire is akin to living within Egypt (see also Rev 11:8) and "the God of Revelation is the God of the exodus, who brought a nation out of the oppressive power of an empire into new life."[5]

The song sung by Moses, along with his siblings Miriam and Aaron and the Israelites, at the Red Sea is a victory song. The lyrics celebrate God's triumph over Pharaoh in clear terms. Most famously, the hymn begins, "he has triumphed gloriously; horse and rider he has thrown into the sea" (Exod 15:1). Similarly, the hymn in Revelation 15:3-4 celebrates a divine triumph, although, again, this is anticipatory. It is not until Revelation 19:18 that John describes the horse and riders who have been defeated. At the same time, the song in Revelation echoes a song Moses teaches the Israelites immediately before his death, when the Israelites enter the land "flowing with milk and honey." God teaches the song to Moses, who will, in turn, teach it to the Israelites "as a witness" (Deut 31:19-21). That is, the hymn will remind the Israelites that God is faithful and just, even when they are tempted to turn toward other gods. It is a reminder that "there is no god besides me" (Deut 32:39).[6] The possibility that John might evoke this song suggests a recognition that his audiences

5. Gail R. O'Day, "Revelation," in *Theological Bible Commentary*, ed. Gail R. O'Day and David L. Petersen (Louisville: Westminster John Knox, 2009), 475.

6. Jan A. du Rand, "The Song of the Lamb Because of the Victory of the Lamb," *Neot* 29 (1995): 204.

too might be tempted to turn to the comfort and familiarity of Babylon or Rome, especially when they hear of the plagues soon to be poured out.

The song in Revelation is much shorter than either taught by Moses, and its content is tightly focused. The song pivots around a question drawn from Jeremiah, "Who would not fear you, O King of the nations?" (10:7). In Revelation, the affirmation that God is "King of the nations" frames the reworded question, "Lord, who will not glorify and fear your name?" (Rev 15:3-4). Some ancient versions of Revelation use "King of ages" instead of "King of nations," although the latter clearly parallels the claim made in verse 4 that the nations will worship God. The King James Version translates the phrase "King of saints," which misses the point that this hymn is an affirmation of God's universal significance.[7] All the nations will come to glorify the God who led his people out of Egypt and who will lead the faithful out of Rome.

The main question of the hymn is two parts asking who will *not* glorify and fear God's name. The negative formulation (οὐ μή) appears in the Greek and is not simply an awkward translation. It is another example of understatement, using a negative to emphasize something positive (see p. 209). It plays up how unlikely or ludicrous it would be for someone *not* to glorify and fear God's name. Ironically, however, immediately after experiencing the bowls of plague, people will curse God, which seems to suggest a lack of fear and respect (16:9, 11, 21). Still, in answer to the question the victors announce, "All nations will come and worship before you" (15:4), which comes to fruition at the end of Revelation. The kings of the earth and their people will eventually bring into the New Jerusalem their glory and honor (19:24-26).

A Glimpse into the Temple of Heaven (15:5–16:1)

John continues to draw upon imagery from Israel's past as he describes the seven angels with their bowls of plague coming out of "the temple of the tent of witness" (15:5). This structure appears to be the tent or tabernacle around which the Israelites gathered during their forty years in the desert after the exodus from Egypt. The tent was the place of God's meeting with the Israelites (Num 17:4), and later tradition suggested it

---

7. Brian K. Blount, *Revelation: A Commentary* (Louisville: Westminster John Knox, 2009), 288.

⁵After this I looked, and the temple of the tent of witness in heaven was opened, ⁶and out of the temple came the seven angels with the seven plagues, robed in pure bright linen, with golden sashes across their chests. ⁷Then one of the four living creatures gave the seven angels seven golden bowls full of the wrath of God, who lives forever and ever; ⁸and the temple was filled with smoke from the glory of God and from his power, and no one could enter the temple until the seven plagues of the seven angels were ended.

¹⁶:¹Then I heard a loud voice from the temple telling the seven angels, "Go and pour out on the earth the seven bowls of the wrath of God."

was a copy or sketch or model of the heavenly sanctuary (e.g., Wis 9:8; Heb 8:1-6). John and his audiences see, it appears, the original. This vision, along with the divine voice commanding the plagues to be released in 16:1, underscores that the plagues ultimately come from God.

The peek into the heavenly temple makes clear that the pouring of the bowls of plague is a liturgical event.[8] The angels, dressed in white with gold sashes, are clothed for worship. The "bowls" they hold are φιάλας, shallow dishes used to pour out libations during sacrifices. Ryan Leif Hansen notes, in addition, that the verb "pour out" (ἐκχέω) evokes the image of priests pouring out the blood of sacrifice at the altar in the temple (e.g., Lev 4:6-7, 17-18, 25, 30).[9] Thus, the pouring out of the plague bowls is a kind of worship. As John explains, moreover, the smoke that fills this sacred space signals the presence of God, divine glory and power (15:8). The ritualistic feel of these verses extends into the description of the bowls being poured out in the following verses (16:1-21). More than the seals and the trumpets, John's narration of these events employs an explicit linguistic structure. After the initial command to pour out the bowls of plague (16:1), John describes each angel pouring their bowls, followed by an announcement of the plague's impact using the Greek καὶ ἐγένετο or, literally, "and it happened."[10]

As noted above, the effects of these plagues are much more intense than those of the seals and trumpets. While there were limits to the

8. Ryan Leif Hansen, *Silence and Praise: Rhetorical Cosmology and Political Theology in the Book of Revelation* (Minneapolis: Augsburg Fortress, 2014), 134.

9. Hansen, *Silence and Praise*, 134.

10. David E. Aune, *Revelation*, WBC 52 A–C (Dallas: Word Books, 1998), 868.

damage done by the trumpets, the bowls of plague bring complete devastation. This depiction of the plagues coming out of acts of worship challenges, arguably, many modern perceptions of what worship entails. These events, which include massive loss of life and destruction of the natural environment, seem not to glorify God or communicate God's goodness. Plagues, pandemics, and climate change seem like things that dishonor God and call into question God's fairness and mercy. These are the things that lead many away from their religion and make us lose faith. Yet the victors before the sea of glass proclaim, "Great and amazing are your deeds, / Lord God the Almighty! / Just and true are your ways, / King of the nations!" (Rev 15:3). Reconciling the victors' certainty of God's justice with the devastation wrought is a challenge.

Pouring out the First Five Plagues (16:2-11)

The first plague is poured upon the earth (γῆ), although only those who have "the mark of the beast and who worshiped its image" experience its effects. Throughout Revelation "earth" generally refers to the physical world and its inhabitants. The earth is home to creatures that praise God and the Lamb (e.g., 5:13) as well as those who gloat over the death of God's faithful witnesses (11:10). While the earth includes all types and this plague falls upon the whole earth, only those who have the mark of the Beast and who worship the Beast experience its impact, a "foul and painful sore" (16:2). The sore, which parallels the plague of festering boils in Exodus (Exod 9:8-12), functions as a tool of judgment, as it marks and identifies those who worship the Beast and, by default, not God and the Lamb.

The inclination to read visible sores and disease as a sign of God's judgment has a long and troubling history to which Revelation directly contributes. In fourteenth-century Italy, Gabriele de' Mussis, a chronicler of the Black Death, drew connections between "angels hurling vials of poison into the sea" and the spread of the bubonic plague.[11] Even though many blamed Jews for poisoning wells (leading to the torture and murder of countless innocent people),[12] medieval clerics and theologians

11. Gabriele de Mussis, *Historia de Morbo*, in *The Black Death*, trans. and ed. Rosemary Horrox (Manchester: Manchester University Press, 1994), 16.

12. Dan Freedman, "Why Were Jews Blamed for the Black Death?," *Moment Magazine*, March 31, 2020, https://momentmag.com/why-were-jews-blamed-for-the-black -death/; see also Horrox, *Black Death*, passim.

²So the first angel went and poured his bowl on the earth, and a foul and painful sore came on those who had the mark of the beast and who worshiped its image.

³The second angel poured his bowl into the sea, and it became like the blood of a corpse, and every living thing in the sea died.

⁴The third angel poured his bowl into the rivers and the springs of water, and they became blood. ⁵And I heard the angel of the waters say,

"You are just, O Holy One, who
    are and were
  for you have judged these
    things;
⁶because they shed the blood of
    saints and prophets,
  you have given them blood to
    drink.

catalogued the kinds of sins for which the plague was likely judgment. Among these were sins associated with sex and gender, such as women wearing provocative clothing, men wearing feminine clothing, adultery, and clerics failing to remain chaste.[13] In the 1980s, similar associations were made between supposedly "deviant" sexual practices and God's judgment when gay men first exhibited signs of what was called GRID or "gay-related immune deficiency." As Thomas Long notes, evangelical Christian leaders had already begun to talk about homosexuality as a plague or disease, so it was an easy conceptual move to interpret HIV and AIDS, a symptom of which were the lesions called Karposi sarcoma, as God's punishment.[14] This, of course, had very real consequences, as the boundary between fear of contagion and moral outrage was fluid. In the early years of the disease, an AIDS diagnosis was not just a physical death sentence but also a social death, as family, friends, employers, communities, and religious communities turned their backs on those who became ill.

While we like to think we know more than people back in the "dark ages," whether we use that phrase to mean medieval Europe or the 1980s, it is still common to moralize disease and disability. When possible connections emerged between COVID-19 and Chinese markets where

13. These explanations come out of various medieval primary sources collected in Horrox, *Black Death*, 131–34.

14. Thomas L. Long, *AIDS and American Apocalypticism: The Cultural Semiotics of an Epidemic* (Albany: SUNY Press, 2012), 2. See also Anthony M. Petro, *After the Wrath of God: AIDS, Sexuality, and American Religion* (Oxford: Oxford University Press, 2015).

It is what they deserve!"
[7]And I heard the altar respond,
    "Yes, O Lord God, the Almighty,
        your judgments are true and
            just!"
    [8]The fourth angel poured his bowl on the sun, and it was allowed to scorch people with fire; [9]they were scorched by the fierce heat, but they cursed the name of God, who had authority over these plagues, and they did not repent and give him glory.

    [10]The fifth angel poured his bowl on the throne of the beast, and its kingdom was plunged into darkness; people gnawed their tongues in agony, [11]and cursed the God of heaven because of their pains and sores, and they did not repent of their deeds.

fresh meat and live fish and animals are sold, many people in the West quickly resorted to racist claims about the "weird" foods eaten in Asian countries. The implication was that the racialized other, presumed to be backward and morally suspect, was to blame.[15] Sadly, in the US, this led to an uptick in acts of violence against Asian people. Moralization of disease happened in small ways as well, as people scrutinized over whether an infected person had properly masked, been vaccinated, or followed isolation protocols. There has been public shaming of so-called "super-spreaders."[16] I admit that I have personally rushed to judge others' decisions about COVID out of concern for my high-risk spouse.

Even though Revelation has fed into the logic behind the moralization of disease, assigning the origin of the plagues to God simultaneously works against such logic. According to John, plague, AIDS, and COVID are not the result of an individual's or group's actions, they come from God; and God is big enough to shoulder that blame. At the same time, as Elana Gomel observes in an exploration of literary representations of pandemic, it is easy to "[fall] prey to yet another millennial seduction, rewriting a meaningless biological accident as an omen of utopia."[17]

15. Barry Sautman, "Big Thunder, Little Rain: The Yellow Peril Framing of the Pandemic Campaign against China," *Chinese Journal of International Law*, October 2, 2021, https://doi.org/10.1093/chinesejil/jmab023.

16. D. T. Max, "The Public-Shaming Pandemic," *The New Yorker*, September 21, 2020, https://www.newyorker.com/magazine/2020/09/28/the-public-shaming -pandemic.

17. Elana Gomel, "The Plague of Utopias: Pestilence and the Apocalyptic Body," *Twentieth Century Literature* 46 (2000): 418.

Diseases emerge and spread, despite our best efforts and scientific research, and attributing them to a divine plan can make it difficult to see the ways we can and should reach out to others with compassion. Instead, these visions should prompt the followers of God and the Lamb to find ways of lessening the agony experienced by those at the receiving end of these bowls. There are examples of this that can be lifted up, including the work of the Metropolitan Community Church in San Francisco, where during the height of the AIDS crisis the pastor and staff performed up to four funerals a week, honoring the lives of those who succumbed to the disease, instead of moralizing their deaths.[18]

The second and third plagues turn water sources, including the sea, streams, and rivers, into blood. These plagues evoke the first plague from Exodus, when the Nile and all water in Egypt turns to blood (Exod 7:14-25). Water, essential to human life and potentially dangerous, becomes blood, but not just any kind of blood: the "blood of a corpse" (16:3). A liquid associated with life becomes a marker of death in this gruesome image. After the third bowl plague, "the angel of the waters," John's reworking of the Greek and Roman tradition of each river or stream having its own god, offers a short hymn affirming the justice of God's plagues, casting it in terms of *lex talionis*, where the punishment fits the crime: "you have judged these things; because they shed the blood of saints and prophets, you have given them blood to drink" (v. 6). The location of the verse, within the context of the third bowl, makes sense since all waters have just been turned to blood. The referent to "these things," however, sounds odd. We typically imagine people as the object of judgment, yet this phrasing indicates that bodies of water are the subject of God's wrath because they are complicit in the oppression of God's people.

Perhaps the two plagues poured out on the waters offer a critique of the ways Romans used them to advance and support the empire. This point is made more explicit elsewhere, as the first Beast emerges out of the sea and Babylon sits on many waters (13:1; 17:1). Later, after the destruction of Babylon, a symbol for Rome, those who mourn the city's death will be merchants, mariners, and all people involved in the shipping trade (18:11-19). Rome's imperial power depended on the sea. Likewise, the empire's ability to transport and control fresh water was celebrated in inscriptions on the aqueducts that served urban areas. In

---

18. Lynne Gerber, "AIDS and the Blessings of Staying: The Ministry of Reverend Jim Mitulski," *The Revealer* (blog), June 3, 2021, https://therevealer.org/aids-and-the-blessings-of-staying-the-ministry-of-reverend-jim-mitulski/.

the cities of Asia Minor, monumental fountains and baths provided the wealthy and politically powerful a way to gain the favor of their communities and fashion themselves as extensions of Roman benevolence. In Ephesus, for example, C. Sextilius Pollio, a wealthy citizen, funded a major aqueduct. His name was inscribed where the structure crossed over a major highway, like a billboard advertising his generosity. Later, his family would build a monumental fountain in the heart of the city, right across from an imperial temple.[19] While providing water for the community is an admirable thing, the Romans' celebration of their ability to control the natural world and to seemingly supply the basic needs of the people fails to recognize God's role as creator and provider.

In response to the angel's hymn, "the altar" echoes, "your judgments are true and just" (16:7). While I personally like to imagine that the heavenly altar has a mouth and talks, like an object from an animated film, it is more likely a case of metonymy.[20] Metonymy is a rhetorical trope in which part of a thing stands in for the whole. In this case, "the altar" refers to those who are under the throne, the souls of the slaughtered faithful (6:19). Those who have lost their lives on account of their witness approve of God's justice. As Greg Carey has observed, John conveniently uses voices of authority to shut down possible objections to depictions of God's vengeance.[21] Who would challenge the martyrs under the altar?

The fourth and fifth plagues are similar in structure, an angel pours their bowl and then the effects fall like dominoes. Each plague ends with people cursing the name of God, or literally blaspheming (βλασφημέω, 16:9, 11). This fact harks back to the song by the sea of glass, where victors asked, "Lord, who will not fear and glorify your name?" (15:4). Now we know the answer to this question. These two plagues are like opposite sides of a coin. In the fourth, the angel pours out plague on the sun, leading to fierce heat that scorches people (16:8-9). The fifth plague parallels the ninth in Exodus, which was "a darkness that can be felt" (Exod 10:21). Plunged into a similar darkness, the recipients of

---

19. Betsey A. Robinson, "Fountains as Reservoirs of Myth and Memory," in *Myths on the Map: The Storied Landscapes of Ancient Greece*, ed. Greta Hawes (Oxford: Oxford University Press, 2017), 178–203; Fikret Yegül and Diane Favro, *Roman Architecture and Urbanism: From the Origins to Late Antiquity* (Cambridge: Cambridge University Press, 2019), 163.

20. Craig R. Koester, *Revelation: A New Translation with Introduction and Commentary*, AYB 38A (New Haven: Yale University Press, 2014), 648.

21. Greg Carey, *Elusive Apocalypse: Reading Authority in the Revelation to John* (Macon, GA: Mercer University Press, 1999), 132.

the fifth bowl plague gnaw their tongues in agony, leading to even more pain and sores (16:10-11). Excessive light and overwhelming darkness emphasize the full sweep of these plagues. Not only are all people on earth impacted, they are impacted in every possible way. Still, the people of earth do not repent, do not turn to glorify God.

Pouring Out the Final Plagues of God's Judgment (16:12-21)

The sixth and seventh bowl plagues expand upon the idea that God's judgment will fall on those who hold allegiance to the Beast and prepare Revelation's audiences for the coming battle between the armies of heaven and the kings of the earth (19:19) and the fall of Babylon (Rev 17–18), respectively.

Conjuring the plague of frogs from the Exodus story (Exod 8:3), the sixth bowl plague warns audience members of a battle that will take place "on the great day of God the Almighty" (16:14). Other Jewish texts similarly anticipate a future battle of cosmic proportions between God and those opposed to God's people (e.g., Ezek 38–39; Zech 14:1-3). Here, Revelation's audiences are made aware of how foul and demonic spirits are preparing for this day, even though the plague from heaven paves the way for this strategizing, drying up the Euphrates to facilitate rallying the troops. John's conviction that God is all-powerful puts the divine in the awkward position of facilitating the efforts of the evil forces the Lamb will eventually have to defeat.

John's mention of the "kings from the east" associates those opposed to God with a foreign other. The connection between these kings and the Euphrates solidifies their "foreignness" since the river was beyond the eastern edge of the Roman Empire (Strabo, *Geog.* 16.1.28) and ran through the heart of Babylon.[22] Some modern premillennial interpreters (see pp. 313–15) who read Revelation as a blueprint for the end times interpret this as an indication that armies from Asia, including China and Japan, will be among those manipulated by the demonic spirits to go to war with the Lamb.[23] Here, John's language fuels racist logic, a logic that must be condemned.

These evil spirits use signs, miracles like those performed by Moses before Pharaoh (e.g., Exod 10:2), to convince "the kings of the whole

---

22. Koester, *Revelation*, 657.
23. Hal Lindsey, *The Late Great Planet Earth* (Grand Rapids: Zondervan, 1970), 81–87.

Rev 16:12-21

¹²The sixth angel poured his bowl on the great river Euphrates, and its water was dried up in order to prepare the way for the kings from the east. ¹³And I saw three foul spirits like frogs coming from the mouth of the dragon, from the mouth of the beast, and from the mouth of the false prophet. ¹⁴These are demonic spirits, performing signs, who go abroad to the kings of the whole world, to assemble them for battle on the great day of God the Almighty. ¹⁵("See, I am coming like a thief! Blessed is the one who stays awake and is clothed, not going about naked and exposed to shame.") ¹⁶And they assembled them at the place that in Hebrew is called Harmagedon.

¹⁷The seventh angel poured his bowl into the air, and a loud voice came out of the temple, from the throne, saying, "It is done!" ¹⁸And there came flashes of lightning, rumblings, peals of thunder, and a violent earthquake, such as had not occurred since people were upon the

world" to assemble for a great battle. The kings gather at a place that Revelation calls "Harmagedon" (commonly spelled "Armageddon"; 16:16). The word likely refers to Megiddo, a place where a few significant battles occurred in Israel's history, including one led by Deborah (e.g., Judg 5:19). John may have added the Hebrew term *"har,"* meaning "mountain," to Megiddo to construct this place name. According to Zechariah 12:11, Megiddo is a place where people mourned the god Haddad-Rimon, an allusion to a Canaanite or Nabatean dying-and-rising god. Zechariah proclaims that the people of Jerusalem will, near the end of time, mourn like those who wept in Megiddo.

The results of the final bowl of plague include an earthquake "such as had not occurred since people were upon the earth" (16:18). Most of the cities John addressed experienced earthquakes,[24] and imperial figures took the opportunity to demonstrate their generosity through major rebuilding efforts. For example, in 17 CE, after a major earthquake in the Lydian region of Asia Minor, Tiberius offered the city ten million sesterces and lifted taxes for five years. Philadelphia was likewise exempted from taxation (Tacitus, *Ann.* 2.47). Monuments, inscriptions, and even coins advertised this generosity across the empire. One such coin, depicting Tiberius, read "CIVITATIBUS ASIAE RESTITUTIS" or "The cities of Asia have been restored."[25] Here, however, it is the "great city" that will

24. James S. Murray, "The Urban Earthquake Imagery and Divine Judgment in John's Apocalypse," *NovT* 47 (2005): 145.

25. Murray, "Urban Earthquake Imagery," 154.

earth, so violent was that earthquake. ¹⁹The great city was split into three parts, and the cities of the nations fell. God remembered great Babylon and gave her the wine-cup of the fury of his wrath. ²⁰And every island fled away, and no mountains were to be found; ²¹and huge hailstones, each weighing about a hundred pounds, dropped from heaven on people, until they cursed God for the plague of the hail, so fearful was that plague.

experience the effects of the earthquake. The city that once rebuilt those impacted by earthquakes will be "split into three parts," and, as a result, the cities of earth will fall (v. 19).

The central focus of the earthquake is the "great city," Babylon, which we discuss in more depth over the next two chapters. Suffice it to say here that Babylon serves in Revelation as a way of signifying Rome, the political and symbolical center of an empire that controls other lands through military, economic, and social power. The image of Babylon's fall leading to the fall of cities in other nations points to Rome's interconnected reach (v. 19). John depicts Rome/Babylon as deserving of God's wrath, and in the next two chapters Revelation's audiences will witness what that looks like.

The final bowl of plague appears with a heavenly voice announcing, "It is done!" followed by lightning strikes and peals of thunder (vv. 17-18). Readers might be tempted to connect this pronouncement to Jesus's last words in the Gospel of John, "It is finished" (19:30), even though the Gospel and Revelation use different terms, τετέλεσται and γέγονεν, respectively. Still, the question "What does the death of Jesus have to do with the seventh bowl?" is relevant. For that matter, we should ask what the death of Jesus has to do with all the plagues released in Revelation, given the centrality of the slaughtered Lamb to John's overall vision. Admittedly, at first glance it is difficult to square the idea of the Lamb, an image of passive resistance and vulnerability, with these depictions of God's judgment.

The Lamb appears only briefly in Revelation 15–16, sharing billing with Moses as the victors stand before the sea of glass and sing their co-written song (15:3). This reference to the victors, which should evoke the idea of the victim made victor, and the subsequent description of Moses as one enslaved by God, reminds audience members that Revelation's vision of faithfulness subverts traditional assumptions about power and victory. The Lamb, who is simultaneously the Lion, is the model of this subversion. With this in mind, if we look back at the bowl plagues and ask ourselves, "Where's the Lamb?" we should look not in the heavenly temple but upon the earth. My conviction is that the Lamb resides where people gnaw their tongues, stumble in darkness, search for water, and even curse God. Maybe this is wishful thinking, but the only way I can reconcile the unfathomable destruction of the plagues with Revelation's vision of the Lamb is by imagining him present among those with suffer. In their midst, the Lamb cultivates the healing that comes with the New Jerusalem (22:2).

Revelation 17

The Judgment of Babylon the Great Prostitute

Alerted to Babylon's fall earlier in the narrative (14:8; 16:19), John is now invited by one of the plague angels to witness the gruesome details of God's judgment upon Babylon the Great Prostitute (17:1; see "Translation Matters: πόρνη"). And the details *are* gruesome. Revelation's reworking of a traditional metaphorical connection between cities and women is so effective that it is challenging to see Babylon, a thinly veiled allusion to Rome, as anything other than a woman. John twice characterizes "her" as a woman (γυνή) before sharing the name "Babylon" (vv. 3-4). John waits until after describing her rape and murder to clarify that Babylon is the "great city" (v. 18).[1] The text is, as Tina Pippin observes, "the ultimate misogynist fantasy."[2] Given this, the depiction of Babylon as a sex-worker in Revelation 17 overshadows for many the fact that this chapter, along with Revelation 18, entails one of the New Testament's most pointed

---

1. Caroline Vander Stichele, "Re-Membering the Whore: The Fate of Babylon According to Revelation 17.16," in *A Feminist Companion to the Apocalypse of John*, ed. Amy-Jill Levine with Maria Mayo Robbins, FCNTECW 13 (London: T&T Clark, 2009), 108.

2. Tina Pippin, "The Heroine and the Whore: Fantasy and the Female in the Apocalypse of John," *Semeia* 60 (1992): 75.

critiques of empire, including its structures of power and economics. The tension between Revelation's misogynistic depiction of Babylon as Great Prostitute and that of Babylon as an oppressive imperial city makes this section of Revelation one of the most complex parts of the book.

Reading Revelation 17 as feminists, in my opinion, requires intentionally putting aside the impulse to give the text either a thumbs up or thumbs down, labeling it as liberating or oppressive.[3] Even though interpretations of these chapters sometimes get cast in this binary way, most feminist readers acknowledge the text's competing claims and approach it as an invitation to go about "the business of creating [our] own apocalyptic tales."[4] Even if it is the last book in the Bible, Revelation is not the final word; rather, Scripture authors or authorizes conversation, including critical discussions about why specific images and ideas are untenable and harmful.[5] In this case, John's representation of the Prostitute invites interpreters to think about how a misguided focus on issues of sex and perceived immorality can derail political and economic critiques of systems and empires. The image of the Prostitute, arguably a queer figure, can also prompt individuals who similarly identify as queer, such as myself, to think about the allure of assimilating to the expectations of empire.[6] I resist trying to redeem or save this text, highlighting its complexity to equip feminist readers with tools for developing their own perspectives on the imagery.

TRANSLATION MATTERS: πόρνη

The image of Babylon as "Whore," the word the NRSV uses to translate πόρνη, has a life apart from the book of Revelation. An online search using the terms "whore" and "Babylon" yields results numbering in the millions, including links to medieval manuscripts and early printed Bibles, the plays of Shakespeare, TV shows, musical references, and countless online forums debating the image's mean-

---

3. Susan E. Hylen, "The Power and Problem of Revelation 18: The Rhetorical Function of Gender," in *Pregnant Passion: Gender, Sex, and Violence in the Bible*, ed. Cheryl A. Kirk-Duggan (Atlanta: SBL, 2003), 205.

4. Pippin, "Heroine and the Whore," 82.

5. Angela N. Parker, *If God Still Breathes, Why Can't I? Black Lives Matter and Biblical Authority* (Grand Rapids: Eerdmans, 2021), 41–42.

6. Lynn R. Huber, "Gazing at the Whore: Reading Revelation Queerly," in *Bible Trouble: Queer Reading at the Boundaries of Biblical Scholarship*, ed. Teresa J. Hornsby and Ken Stone (Atlanta: SBL, 2011), 301–20.

ing.[7] This image of Babylon as the Whore, sometimes mistakenly described as the Whore *of* Babylon, has become crystallized historical memory. Yet the question of whether πόρνη should be translated as "whore" remains up for debate. Not all English translations of Revelation use the term. The English Standard and New International Versions, for example, render πόρνη as "prostitute," a word that lacks at least some of the stigma conveyed by "whore."

Kate Lister, a historian of sex and sexuality, notes that the English word "whore" has been used almost exclusively in a derogatory sense and has not been "tied to a profession" unless used to shame an individual within that profession, i.e., sex-work.[8] While "whore" first appeared in writing during the twelfth century, Shakespeare popularized the term, according to Lister.[9] In the fourth act of the play that bears his name, Othello repeatedly accuses his wife Desdemona, who he has been misled to believe is unfaithful, of being a whore. Finally, Othello presses Desdemona to accept the label, demanding, "Why, what art thou?" She resists, but her maid Emilia narrates the harm done: "my lord hath so bewhored her. / Thrown such despite and heavy terms upon her, / As true hearts cannot bear" (Shakespeare, *Othello*, act 4, scene 2). Intended to belittle and even destroy the one to whom it is applied, "whore" is a heavy term indeed.

Πόρνη, in contrast, was not necessarily a slur in the first century. Even in the writings of the New Testament, it could be used to refer to someone employed as a sex-worker, even though that role was understood in negative terms. In the Gospel of Matthew, for example, sex-workers are paired with tax collectors as two groups of people who will enter the kingdom of God, even though some might assume that they are not worthy of such an honor (21:31-32; see also Heb 11:31; Jas 2:25). Here πόρναι, the plural of πόρνη, is not used to shame and demean, even though sex-workers were often characterized as dishonorable, shameful, and dirty in the ancient context (negative characteristics that were *not* applied to male clients).[10] Even though "sex-worker" is a better translation for πόρνη in Revelation, "whore" does capture how John draws on and heightens the negative stereotypes in his depiction of Babylon. This is because Babylon is not a literal sex-worker; rather, John's depiction of Babylon is meant to shame a city, envisioned as a woman, who challenges the ultimate authority, God. Πόρνη here presumes that sex-work and sex-workers are shameful,[11] so it serves as John's tool for shaming

7. For an introduction to Babylon in art, see Natasha O'Hear, "Images of Babylon: A Visual History of the Whore in Late Medieval and Early Modern Art; From the Margins," in *From the Margins 2: Women of the New Testament and Their Afterlives*, ed. Christine E. Joynes and Christopher C. Rowland (Sheffield: Sheffield Phoenix, 2009), 311–33.

8. Kate Lister, *A Curious History of Sex* (London: Unbound, 2020), 9–11.

9. Lister, *Curious History of Sex*, 9–11.

10. Catharine Edwards, "Unspeakable Professions: Public Performance and Prostitution in Ancient Rome," in *Roman Sexualities*, ed. Judith P. Hallet and Marilyn B. Skinner (Princeton: Princeton University Press, 1997), 66–95.

11. Avaren Ipsen, *Sex Working and the Bible* (London: Routledge, 2014), 169.

Babylon or Rome. John's explicit references to Babylon as a woman (17:4, 6, 7, 18; 18:7) and as a πόρνη are meant to put "her" in her place on the cosmic hierarchy, far beneath God. Furthermore, John seemingly wants his audience members to hate Babylon, like some of the earth's rulers will (17:16), and eventually distance themselves from "her" (18:4). "Whore" is offensive, disturbing, and abusive, but as a translation of πόρνη it captures the hateful tenor of this narrative.

Despite the accuracy of this translation, I choose to limit my use of the slur unless quoting the work of someone else or explaining, as I do here, issues of translation. Throughout the commentary I try to use "sex-worker," when referencing people apart from Babylon, although I do retain "the Great Prostitute" as a title for Babylon. This is a shift for me, as I have previously used the language of "whore" in my work. I am changing, however, to be a better ally to sex-workers and others who have been on the receiving end of similar slurs.[12] Even though some sex-workers claim the language of "whore," just as some in the LGBTQIA+ community, myself included, embrace the language of "queer," that is *their* prerogative. It is not my place, as someone from outside of that community, to appropriate or try to rehabilitate that slur. Claiming language demonstrates one's power over those who insult and oppress, but that power can only be claimed by the people from whom it has been taken.

An Amazing Woman: Babylon the Great (17:1-8)

Despite being forewarned that he would witness her judgment, John's first glimpse at the Great Prostitute amazes him. The Greek emphasizes this reaction, literally reading, "And I *wondered*, seeing her, with a great *wonder*" (v. 6). The angel then accentuates John's wonder by asking, "Why are you *wondering*?" (v. 7). The language of wonder (θαυμάζω) suggests that John is left astounded and speechless. In the Gospels, "wonder" describes the disciples' reaction to events like a fig tree withering at Jesus's command (e.g., Matt 21:20) and Jesus's conversation with a woman at a well (John 4:27). "Wonder" can even suggest desire. In the story of Judith, this same language describes how others react to Judith when she makes herself look alluring to seduce and assassinate, by beheading, an enemy general, Holofernes (10:19). Given her capacity to amaze, it is easy for Revelation's audiences to become so engrossed by the Great Prostitute that it is difficult to see what she represents. In one illustrated medieval commentary on Revelation, the face of Babylon is rubbed out, literally erased (fig. 5). Perhaps her visage was too powerful for one monastic reader.

12. Sex Workers Outreach Project, "How to Be an Ally to Sex Workers," 2019, https://swopusa.org/wp-content/uploads/2019/02/How_to_be_an_ally_draft_2.pdf.

17:1Then one of the seven angels who had the seven bowls came and said to me, "Come, I will show you the judgment of the great whore who is seated on many waters, 2with whom the kings of the earth have committed fornication, and with the wine of whose fornication the inhabitants of the earth have become drunk." 3So he carried me away in the spirit into a wilderness, and I saw a woman sitting on a scarlet beast that was full of blasphemous names, and it had seven heads and ten horns. 4The woman was clothed in purple and scarlet, and adorned with gold and jewels and pearls, holding in her hand a golden cup full of abominations and the impurities of her fornication; 5and on her forehead was written a name, a mystery: "Babylon the great, mother of whores and of earth's abominations." 6And I saw that the woman was drunk with the blood of the saints and the blood of the witnesses to Jesus.

When I saw her, I was greatly amazed. 7But the angel said to me, "Why are you so amazed? I will tell you the mystery of the woman, and of the beast with seven heads and ten horns that carries her. 8The beast that you saw was, and is not, and is about to ascend from the bottomless pit and go to destruction. And the inhabitants of the earth, whose names have not been written in the book of life from the foundation of the world, will be amazed when they see the beast, because it was and is not and is to come.

Similarly drawing attention to the Great Prostitute is the angel's description of her as *a* mystery or as Mystery, which could be her name (μυστήριον; 17:5). The designation suggests that this is an image with abundant meaning, like the Woman Clothed in Sun and the Great Red Dragon, who are both described as "portents" or "signs" (σημεῖον; 12:1, 3). Like being a portent, being a mystery implies that there is more to Babylon than what meets the eye. Likewise, since she is a "mystery," understanding her requires special knowledge and interpretation. Full knowledge of Babylon's significance requires "a mind that has wisdom" (17:9). Given this, the angel from the plagues who accompanies John in this chapter provides him with a necessary explanation.

The suspense that Revelation builds around the image of the Great Prostitute belies the fact that her identity appears obvious. The text identifies her as "Babylon," which seems like a clear allusion to Rome since both are ruling cities of almost mythic proportions. Roman authors marveled over the ancient capital's impressive size and strength. Strabo, for one, listed for posterity the measurements of Babylon's massive city walls (385 stadia in length and thirty-two feet thick), the width of the

Figure 5: Beatus of Liébana, "The Great Prostitute," *Commentary on the Apocalypse*, Liebana, Spain, ca. 945. The Morgan Library & Museum. MS M.644, fol. 194v. Purchased by J.P. Morgan (1867–1943) in 1919. Photographic credit: The Morgan Library & Museum, New York. Used with permission from the Morgan Library & Museum.

river that ran through it (a stadium), and the construction of the city's famous hanging gardens (quadrangular with cube-like foundations), just as John will later describe the New Jerusalem (Strabo, *Geog.* 16.1.5; Rev 21:15-21).[13] John's audiences would also be familiar with Babylon on account of biblical traditions that characterize the city, often personified as a woman, as the quintessential evil imperial city (e.g., Jer 50:10-46).

With Babylon no longer a significant player on the first-century political stage, John uses the name of the past political power to envision a "new Babylon," which is clearly Rome. John is not the only Jewish author to draw the connection since the two imperial cities share the infamous distinction of having conquered Jerusalem and destroyed the temple (e.g., 4 Ezra 3:1-2, 28-31; 15:43-46, 60; 16:1; 1 Pet 5:13)—Babylon in the sixth century BCE and Rome in 70 CE. Mishna Ta'anit 4:6 even pinpoints these events to the same date, the ninth of the Jewish month of Av or Tisha b'Av. Revelation further connects Babylon to Rome by describing the Great Prostitute as sitting on seven mountains (v. 9), an allusion to the seven hills of Rome (Varro, *Ling.* 6.24), and as "the great city that rules over the kings of the earth" (17:18).

Even though Babylon is Rome, the label "mystery" insinuates there is more to the Great Prostitute than this simple equation. Her being a mystery implies that while an audience member might think they recognize Babylon as Rome, they don't fully know or understand her from the perspective of the heavenly throne room. In fact, some scholars argue that Revelation's image of Babylon refers to Jerusalem and not Rome. This way of interpreting the "great city" in Revelation emphasizes John's reliance on prophetic traditions that use fornication or adultery language to criticize Jerusalem for unfaithfulness to God and to blame the people of Israel for the destruction of the temple by the Babylonians.[14] While John's description of Babylon as sitting on waters that are "multitudes and nations and languages" (v. 15) and as "the great city that rules over the kings of the earth" (v. 18) as well as the association between Babylon and the "blood of the saints" (v. 6) fits Rome better than first-century Jerusalem, Babylon can mean multiple things. Symbolic language is inherently multivalent and invites audience members to explore a range of possible connections. By using "Babylon" instead of "Rome," Revelation

---

13. Andrew Scheil, *Babylon under Western Eyes: A Study of Allusion and Myth* (Toronto: University of Toronto Press, 2016), 20.

14. For a discussion of this, see G. Biguzzi, "Is the Babylon of Revelation Rome or Jerusalem?," *Bib* 87 (2006): 371–86.

encourages discussion about the various ways that Babylon manifests in the world. Still, many of the book's earliest interpreters saw the connection between Babylon and Rome (e.g., Victorinus, *Commentary on the Apocalypse* 17.9) or a future manifestation of Rome (e.g., Andrew of Caesarea, *Commentary on the Apocalypse,* chap. 53) and that seems to be the most obvious referent within the first century.

Part of the mystery of Babylon pertains to John's depiction of her as a sex-worker (πόρνη), which the NRSV renders as "whore" (see "Translation Matters: πόρνη"). Even though the word πόρνη is not necessarily a slur in the ancient world, John constructs his image of Babylon/Rome by drawing on negative stereotypes and biases associated with sex-workers, which makes the NRSV use of "whore" a startlingly accurate translation. Sex-work or prostitution was legal and widespread at the time Revelation was written and not something hidden. Anyone who has visited Pompeii knows that purpose-built brothels could be in areas generally thought of as "respectable" since there is a *lupanare* a few blocks from Pompeii's main forum. There was little attempt at "zoning shame," as classicist Thomas A. J. McGinn puts it.[15] While it was culturally acceptable for men to purchase sex and visit brothels or other locations where sex could be procured, sex-workers themselves, many of whom were enslaved, were socially *infames,* lacking in honor or reputation.[16] A Roman-era slave collar found near a temple in modern Tunisia identified the wearer as "*Adultera meretrix,*" which could be read as "I am a slutty prostitute," reflecting the stigma sex-workers carried with them.[17] Likewise, John identifies Babylon/Rome as "mother of sex-workers and of earth's abominations" (17:5), evoking the ancient (and modern) double standard that stigmatizes sex-workers and not those "kings of the earth" who participate in the economy of prostitution.

At first glance, especially since she is associated with kings, it is easy to mistake Babylon for an elite escort or wealthy courtesan, like the *hetairai* (ἑταίραι) famously depicted on ancient Greek pottery.[18] Revelation's sex-

---

15. Thomas A. J. McGinn, "Zoning Shame in the Roman City," in *Prostitutes and Courtesans in the Ancient World,* ed. Christopher A. Faraone and Laura K. McClure (Madison: University of Wisconsin Press, 2006), 161–76.

16. Edwards, "Unspeakable Professions," 76.

17. As quoted in Jennifer Trimble, "The Zoninus Collar and the Archaeology of Roman Slavery," *AJA* 120 (July 2016): 457.

18. Marina Fischer, "Ancient Greek Prostitutes and the Textile Industry in Attic Vase-Painting ca. 550–450 B.C.E.," *CW* 106 (2013): 220–22. For a reading of Babylon as a courtesan, see Hanna Roose, "The Fall of the 'Great Harlot' and the Fate of the Aging Prostitute: An Iconographic Approach to Revelation 18," in *Picturing the New*

worker wears scarlet and purple, colors traditionally associated with emperors and elites (v. 4). These colors were so popular among the upper classes, especially women, that Julius Caesar tried to limit wearing purple to the ruling classes (Suetonius, *Jul.* 43).[19] While the colors she wears suggest Babylon/Rome is an imperial lady, her accessories, gold *and* jewels *and* pearls, are excessive from a Roman point of view. As Plutarch observed, "When women wear rouge, perfume, and gold and purple, they are considered too showily dressed" (*Mor.* 693B). She may appear wealthy and powerful, and she may even have access, like Rome, to these things; however, the Great Prostitute lacks the modesty and self-control that should come with being a ruler. Thus, John's depiction of her implies she is a fraud. She pretends to be "high class" but overshoots the mark to reveal her true nature—the overdressed and overaccessorized Babylon is a lower class sex-worker, a brothel worker or a "street-walker." As mentioned above, the label across her forehead identifies her as an enslaved person, an ordinary reality for many sex-workers who were trafficked.[20] Ironically, while John valorizes enslavement for the followers of the Lamb, here enslavement is counted against Babylon since she is beholden to the Beast and not the Lamb.

One of the central stereotypes related to sex-workers that John uses in his image of the Great Prostitute is the idea that sex-workers are dirty. He evokes disgust and loathing toward Babylon by associating her with "impurities," literally unclean things (ἀκάθαρτα), and "abominations" (βδέλυγμα), a term used twice in two verses (vv. 4-5).[21] The latter alludes to filthy or nauseating things. The medical author Hippocrates, for instance, used similar language to describe discharge from an anal fistula (*Fist.* 1). The connection between sex-work and filth is found throughout Roman texts and traditions. The satirist Juvenal described a brothel as "reeking of ancient blankets" (*Sat.* 6.120), and elite Romans sometimes used the term *stabulum* (stables or animal stalls) to describe brothels as well as low-income housing reflecting a clear class bias.[22] These connections reflect a

---

Testament: Studies in Ancient Visual Images, ed. Annette Weissenrieder Friederike Wendt, and Petra von Gemünden (Tübingen: Mohr Siebeck, 2005), 228–52.

19. Kelly Olson, *Dress and the Roman Woman: Self-Presentation and Society* (London: Routledge, 2008), 12.

20. Jennifer A. Glancy and Stephen D. Moore, "How Typical a Roman Prostitute Is Revelation's 'Great Whore'?," *JBL* 130 (2011): 551–69.

21. Stephen D. Moore, "Retching on Rome: Vomitous Loathing and Visceral Disgust in Affect Theory and the Apocalypse of John," *BibInt* 22 (2014): 503–28.

22. Thomas A. J. McGinn, *The Economy of Prostitution in the Roman World: A Study of Social History and the Brothel* (Ann Arbor: University of Michigan Press, 2004), 18–19.

metaphorical equation between cleanliness and morality and between dirt and immorality. She holds a gold cup *full* of filth, symbolizing her failure to recognize the value of things, such as gold. According to the text, the fact that these filthy things result from "her fornication" implies that she herself is filthy or immoral. Her actions yield unclean things. Clearly, the description of Babylon the Prostitute as "Great" (vv. 1, 5) is ironic unless it refers to the depth of her iniquity from John's perspective.

This vision of Rome as the Great Prostitute challenges the image the city projected by imperial propaganda, an image of Rome as protector of traditional morality and feminine purity. Indicative of this vision was the cult of Vesta, the goddess of the hearth, whose temple was in the heart of the imperial forum. Vesta's eternal flame was kept alight by virginal priestesses, the Vestal Virgins, who lived out their thirty-year commitment to the goddess in a home next to the temple. Living at its center and present at all significant public events and religious rites, the Vestals embodied Roman purity and integrity.[23] According to Pliny the Elder, for example, a Vestal could effectively stop, through prayer, a freedom-seeking enslaved person within the city walls as though she were controlling her own actions (*Nat.* 28.3). So connected to the city's well-being were the Vestals that a priestess would be buried alive if her virginity was suspect, as that signaled a threat to the city's integrity.[24] Simply put, Rome's well-being was unabashedly linked to the preservation of female virginity. The association between Rome and moral purity was not limited to the symbolism embodied in the Vestals; emperors also presented themselves as protectors of morality. Augustus established laws that incentivized marriage for citizens and penalized divorce and adultery (see p. 210), and he tried to model traditional morality and "family values" by requiring that his daughter and granddaughters learn to spin wool, a domestic skill associated with chastity and ideal womanhood (Suetonius, *Aug.* 64). Domitian, likewise, celebrated domesticity by decorating a portion of the forum with images of Roman matrons spinning and weaving.[25] The official portrait of Rome was a far cry from Babylon as the Great Prostitute depicted by John.

Revelation's sex-work imagery echoes prophetic traditions that use sexual infidelity and sex-work as metaphors for religious misdirection,

---

23. Robin Lorsch Wildfang, *Rome's Vestal Virgins* (London: Routledge, 2006), 22–28.

24. Wildfang, *Rome's Vestal Virgins*, 85.

25. Eve D'Ambra, *Private Lives, Imperial Virtues: The Frieze of the Forum Transitorium in Rome* (Princeton: Princeton University Press, 1993), 50–51.

often described as "idolatry" (see "Revelation's Use of Prostitution Imagery"). The description of Babylon riding on a Beast "full of blasphemous names" confirms this function (v. 3; see "Translation Matters: βλασφημία"). Rome's power and influence depend on a system that, according to John, misuses religious titles and demands allegiance be given to false gods, the emperors, and their families, who were celebrated through the imperial cult system. In addition to condemning Rome for wanton behavior, John indicts Rome for violence against the people of God, which he describes as being "drunk with the blood of the saints and the blood of the witnesses to Jesus" (v. 6). The metaphorical depiction of blood as wine paints the city not only as a violent actor but also as vampiric. The Great Prostitute is insatiable and will require more victims to feed her thirst. Therefore, John implies, she must be stopped.

John's description of Rome's thirst for blood is striking since in Asia Minor there was not the same kind of war against Rome as in Judea. The Roman military was present at the borders of the province, but ancient sources from Asia Minor do not depict Roman rule as especially threatening or oppressive.[26] Given this, the portrayal of Babylon's taste for blood, especially the blood of those faithful to God and the Lamb (v. 6), likely alludes to events that are somewhat removed from the day-to-day life of the people in Revelation's communities, such as the war in Jerusalem and the execution of Christians in Rome by Nero in 64 CE (Tacitus, *Ann.* 15.44; see pp. lxvi and 16). John reveals this aspect of Rome to his audiences precisely because they do not experience the empire as an immediate threat. John "magnifies the threat of imperial violence," according to Craig Koester, "in order to disclose the *character* of the empire."[27]

The fear that Babylon's past violence against the saints and witnesses might eventually impact the people in Revelation's audiences undergirds John's depiction of her as a mother and, specifically, as "mother of [sexworkers]" (v. 5). Her violent tendencies and penchant for fornication reproduce. This imagery evokes how imperial cities replicate themselves in the towns and cities of the provinces and colonies they control.[28] Even

26. Christian Marek, *In the Land of a Thousand Gods: A History of Asia Minor in the Ancient World*, trans. Steven Rendall (Princeton: Princeton University Press, 2016), 382.

27. Craig R. Koester, *Revelation: A New Translation with Introduction and Commentary*, AYB 38A (New Haven: Yale University Press, 2014), 688.

28. Stephanie Buckhanon Crowder, "A Mother-Whore Is Still a Mother: Revelation 17–18 and African American Motherhood," in *Parenting as Spiritual Practice and Source for Theology: Mothering Matters*, ed. Claire Bischoff, Elizabeth O'Donnell Gandolfo, and Annie Hardison-Moody (Cham, Switzerland: Springer International, 2017), 163.

though there was only one Rome, the cities of the Roman Empire sometimes highlighted their connection to it through architecture, tributes to
the emperors, and even temples to the personified city of Rome, Roma.
The imagery suggests this kind of spread of imperial power to cities such
as those addressed in the messages of Revelation 2–3.

While John depicts the Woman Clothed in the Sun giving birth and having children (12:2-4, 13-17) and John characterizes Jezebel as a metaphorical
mother (2:23), the Great Prostitute is the only figure that John explicitly
labels with the term "mother" (μήτηρ). Stephanie Buckhanon Crowder
notes that feminist interpreters often fail to discuss this identification as
they focus on the Prostitute's association with sex. As Crowder insists,
however, in the title of an essay on Revelation 17, "A Mother-Whore Is
Still a Mother."[29] Motherhood and the responsibilities of clothing, feeding,
and caring for family members are why some turn to sex-work. Babylon
may be a sex-worker because she is a mother and not a mother because
she is a sex-worker. In other words, one way of looking at Revelation's
use of sex-worker imagery to characterize Babylon is to challenge John's
insinuation that her aims are entirely self-serving (18:7). Crowder's analysis highlights the tendency among Revelation's interpreters to ignore
Babylon's identity as a mother and the possible connection between that
identity and her work. This can further biases against sex-workers and
erase the difficult decisions all parents must make about how to provide
and care for their children.

Revealing Babylon's Mystery (17:9-15)

In response to John's amazement, the plague angel elaborates upon
the "mystery" of the Great Prostitute and the Beast in these verses. The
conversation comes across as somewhat pedantic or, to use a popular
expression, "mansplaining," since the imagery of the Beast seems relatively straightforward. The angel notes, "you saw X," and then offers a
direct interpretation of the imagery's symbolism (17:8, 12, 15, 16). This
angelus interpres, "interpreting angel," is a literary device common in
apocalyptic literature that teaches audiences how to understand the text's
imagery by depicting a seer or narrator receiving similar instruction.[30]

If the Beast looks familiar, it is because it is a manifestation of the Great
Red Dragon that John saw in heaven (12:3) and then on the seashore (12:18).

---

29. Crowder, "Mother-Whore Is Still a Mother," 153.

30. Robyn J. Whitaker, *Ekphrasis, Vision, and Persuasion in the Book of Revelation*,
WUNT 2.410 (Tübingen: Mohr Siebeck, 2015), 63.

9"This calls for a mind that has wisdom: the seven heads are seven mountains on which the woman is seated; also, they are seven kings, 10of whom five have fallen, one is living, and the other has not yet come; and when he comes, he must remain only a little while. 11As for the beast that was and is not, it is an eighth but it belongs to the seven, and it goes to destruction. 12And the ten horns that you saw are ten kings who have not yet received a kingdom, but they are to receive authority as kings for one hour, together with the beast. 13These are united in yielding their power and authority to the beast; 14they will make war on the Lamb, and the Lamb will conquer them, for he is Lord of lords, and King of kings, and those with him are called and chosen and faithful."

15And he said to me, "The waters that you saw, where the whore is seated, are peoples and multitudes and nations and languages.

Both figures have seven heads and ten horns. Now, the angel explains that the seven heads are mountains, which explicitly recall the famous seven hills of Rome (e.g., Pliny, *Nat.* 3.66; Virgil, *Aen.* 6.780-785). The image of the goddess Roma seated on the seven hills even adorned coins minted during the reign of Vespasian (69–79 CE).[31] The thought of Rome atop "mountains" summons, in addition, the many high places throughout the empire from which political figures ruled. Positioned upon a high plateau, the temples and palaces of Pergamum loomed over the commercial streets and residences of the main city. In Ephesus, a temple dedicated to the imperial cult of the Flavians, including Domitian, overlooks the city's main commercial areas. The mountains of the Beast, its heads, provide Babylon with a perfect vantage point from which to entice and control the inhabitants of the earth. From these high places, imperial figures and their provincial representatives and supporters can literally look down on the people in the streets, although these vantage points are certainly not as privileged as the one occupied by the One Who Sits upon the Throne.

The angel notes that the seven heads that are mountains simultaneously represent seven kings. The idea that a head is a king makes metaphorical sense since head imagery is often used to denote a ruler or leader (e.g., Dan 7:6). The imagery of seven kings echoes the mythic history of Rome, which was ruled by seven kings (at least according to tradition) after the city's founding by Romulus (Livy, *Hist. Rom.* 1.1-60).[32]

31. David E. Aune, *Revelation*, WBC 52 A–C (Dallas: Word Books, 1998), 919–21.
32. Koester, *Revelation*, 678.

The angel's careful interpretation of the Beast's characteristics makes this text sound like a code, and interpreters often try to make direct connections between the heads and specific Roman emperors, as discussed in relation to Revelation 13 (see pp. 185–86). The "key" used in these attempts is the angel's claim that "five [kings] have fallen, one is living, and the other has not yet come" (17:10). "One is living" is often taken as a reference to the emperor reigning at the time Revelation was written; however, not knowing that emperor's identity makes it difficult to figure out the connections. It is also not clear whether one should start counting the heads with Julius Caesar or Augustus and whether emperors whose reigns were less than a year should be included in the accounting. One commentator, David E. Aune, offers at least nine ways the heads could be assigned, pointing to the problematic nature of such attempts.[33] The interpretive acrobatics that this type of alignment involves, in other words, suggest the text is not identifying specific figures. Instead, the three-part description of these kings' temporal reigns, which emphasizes the temporality of these figures, aligns with the earlier description of the Beast as the one who "was and is not and is to come" (v. 8). In contrast to the eternal nature of God, the one "who is and who was and who is to come" (1:4; 4:8), the Beast and related kings are finite and, therefore, clearly not divine. Kings and emperors come and go, but God's reign is forever. The description of the horns as kings-in-waiting, since they have not yet received their kingdoms, alludes to the persistent spread of empire. The Beast may look complete with its seven heads since the number seven often suggests wholeness or completion; however, imperial power is characterized by expansion and growth. The description of the city seated upon waters, which symbolize "peoples and multitudes and nations and languages" (17:15; see also v. 1), similarly refers to Rome's imperial reach. This reach was famously facilitated by Rome's command over the Mediterranean, a focus of Revelation 18 (vv. 11-20).

Despite empire's penchant for growth, the angel's explanation promises that the Beast is destined eventually for destruction. The Beast will come from the "bottomless pit," literally "the abyss" (ἄβυσσος), and go back to destruction (17:8, 11), anticipating the eventual and final defeat of evil by God (20:10). Likewise, the angel notes the future defeat of the kings of the earth who will be conquered by the Lamb (17:14). The description of the Lamb as "Lord of lords and King of kings" asserts his

33. Aune, *Revelation*, 947.

power over these heads of the Beast and foreshadows the Lamb's appearance as a rider on a white horse with the same titles inscribed upon his thigh (19:16). In that chapter, John will witness the demise of these kings and their armies.

The most provocative thing about this chapter is the relationship between the Great Prostitute and the Beast. Shanell T. Smith implies that the former can be interpreted as "riding" the Beast like a sex-worker servicing a client.[34] The issue of who controls this situation, however, remains unclear. On the one hand, the use of "prostitute" language to characterize Babylon implies that she seeks out this relationship for financial reasons and for power. Likewise, the reference to "her fornication" represents Babylon as the initiator of relationships with the kings of the earth (v. 4). John seemingly wants his audiences to blame Rome. On the other hand, the kings are the ones who commit fornication with Babylon, according to 17:2. And, as Michelle Fletcher points out, nowhere in the text does Babylon actively seduce the kings.[35] Despite John's replication of the double standard that stigmatizes sex-workers and not their johns (see above), the relationship between the Beast's heads and the Great Prostitute is, quite likely, mutually beneficial. Provincial rulers and elites benefitted in tangible ways from Rome's favor. Under the emperor Vespasian, for example, the gymnasiarchs and teachers of Pergamum were exempt from paying imperial taxes and the requirement they house Roman troops. The result was that the emperor was granted titles or, as John would call them, "blasphemous names," such as "Benefactor of the World" and "Benefactor and Savior of All Mankind."[36] Likewise, Rome and its emperors profited from the allegiances of local kings, officials, and elites in the provinces since local leaders could facilitate imperial success abroad. Revelation's image of the Great Prostitute and Beast illustrates what seems to be an effective imperial system.

Even though John's depiction of the relationship between Babylon and the Beast may suggest a symbiotic connection between imperial

34. Shanell T. Smith, *The Woman Babylon and the Marks of Empire: Reading Revelation with a Postcolonial Womanist Hermeneutics of Ambiveilence* (Minneapolis: Augsburg Fortress, 2014), 143.

35. Michelle Fletcher, "Flesh for Franken-Whore: Reading Babylon's Body in Revelation 17," in *The Body in Biblical, Christian and Jewish Texts*, ed. Joan E. Taylor (London: Bloomsbury, 2014), 155.

36. David Magie, *Roman Rule in Asia Minor: To the End of the Third Century after Christ* (Princeton: Princeton University Press, 1950), 572.

and provincial powers, the imagery fails to recognize the power imbalance that comes with colonization. Likewise, John mischaracterizes the relationship between a sex-worker and their clients. Even though some sex-workers, even in the ancient world, chose the profession, they are still part of a system that can easily lead to exploitation and physical harm. Furthermore, John's use of sex-work imagery to denounce empire fails to recognize that sex-workers are easily victimized by empire. In her reading of Revelation 7, for instance, Jean K. Kim highlights how imperial and colonializing powers depend on the sexual labor of the colonized, as brothels and other establishments where sex can be procured regularly appear alongside military bases in foreign, especially colonized, contexts.[37] This is true not only in the modern world, where red-light districts accompany US military bases in foreign locations, but also in the Roman world, where soldiers were banned from marrying while they served.[38] Even legionnaires who could serve as long as twenty-five years were not allowed to marry. This reality led soldiers to find companions among local populations, potentially leaving these behind and with few options for the future once the soldier's term of service was over. Simply put, John's use of this imagery to criticize empire ignores the fact that sex-workers are some of the most vulnerable within imperial systems.

The Rape of the Great City (17:16-18)

Babylon's judgment is cast in the future, as it will be the Beast's horns, those kings who do not yet have a kingdom, who will eventually act out God's vengeance on her. The reason for their change in heart is not entirely clear. Perhaps, they come to see the true identity behind the clothes and accessories and don't like what they see. Perhaps, they don't want to be underneath the Great Prostitute, the "bottom" to her "top." Within the framework of ancient sexuality, which equated manliness with control, power, and penetration, men who were penetrated by others (whatever their gender) were seen as passive or womanly, a negative thing in the first-century world. Paul, in fact, includes "soft" or "passive" men (μαλακοί) in his list of those who will not inherit the kingdom of God, one of the biblical texts that the LGBTQIA+ community has come

---

37. Jean K. Kim, " 'Uncovering Her Wickedness': An Inter(Con)Textual Reading of Revelation 17 from a Postcolonial Feminist Perspective," *JSNT* 73 (1999): 67.

38. Kim, "Uncovering Her Wickedness," 68.

¹⁶And the ten horns that you saw, they and the beast will hate the whore; they will make her desolate and naked; they will devour her flesh and burn her up with fire. ¹⁷For God has put it into their hearts to carry out his purpose by agreeing to give their kingdom to the beast, until the words of God will be fulfilled. ¹⁸The woman you know is the great city that rules over the kings of the earth."

to describe as a "clobber passage" (1 Cor 9:6; see p. lxxii).[39] In some sense, Babylon's judgment comes as a result of the kings' perceived need to preserve their masculinity. Ironically, the gender and sex protocols perpetuated by Rome become the city's undoing.

The plague angel offers another reason for the horns' hatred of the Great Prostitute, attributing their change in attitude to divine interference: "God has put it in their hearts to carry out his purpose" (17:17). The idea that God can control the hearts and minds of his opponents stretches back to Exodus when God "hardens" the heart of Pharaoh (Exod 9:12). In Exodus, this initially leads to Pharaoh's refusal to heed the plagues sent to force his hand and release the enslaved Israelites but eventually results in the liberation of God's people. Here, as well, God's control of the horns leads first to their allegiance to the Beast and then to enacting God's judgment on Babylon. In this way, John promises his audiences that the mood will shift.

Given the connection between horns and phalluses (see pp. 191–92), we should not be surprised when the horns turn on Babylon. The horns engage in divinely sanctioned rape. Acting as God's surrogate phallus, the horns enact divine hate upon her "body." "Body" is in quotation marks here since the text clarifies that the Prostitute is not an actual woman in 17:15. Instead, "she" is an entity who rests upon waters that are "peoples and multitudes and nations and languages." The Great Prostitute is a political entity, and yet, through this symbolic vision, Revelation forces audiences to *imagine and envision* the violation of a woman's body. The horns' actions leave her body "desolate and naked" (v. 16), a description recollecting the brutality of physical and sexual assault.

39. The NRSV translates μαλακοί as "male prostitutes," even though the term is not specifically associated with sex-work. For a discussion of this vice list, see Joseph A. Marchal, *Appalling Bodies: Queer Figures before and after Paul's Letters* (New York: Oxford University Press, 2019), 167–68.

The language of being made desolate (ἐρημόω) implies that Babylon has become a desert. Elsewhere in the New Testament, ἐρημόω refers to the place where John the Baptist does his baptizing, and it the place where Jesus goes to fast for forty days before embarking on his mission (e.g., Matt 3:1; 4:1; Mark 1:3, 12; Luke 3:2; 4:1; see p. 177). This imagery also draws on traditional imagery equating women's bodies with earth. While ancient in its origins, this imagery continues to appear in descriptions of women's bodies as something to be "plowed" through sex and the earth as something that can be "raped" by acts of environmental violence or war.[40] Here, the Great Prostitute is not only "plowed" and "raped"; she is burned and devoured.

This part of Revelation, like so much of the text, is steeped in irony since rape appears throughout Rome's founding myths and pervades Greek and Roman mythology. In addition to the claim that Rome's founder, Romulus, may have been the product of Mars raping the Vestal Virgin named Rhea Silvia, the early city is populated when the men of the city abduct and rape the Sabine women (e.g., Livy, *Hist. Rom.* 1.9), and the rape of a woman named Lucretia was told as part of Rome's becoming a Republic (e.g., Dionysius of Halicarnassus, *Ant. Rom.* 4.64; Livy, *Hist. Rom.* 1.57-58). Rome's history, as Celene Lillie writes, is a history of rape.[41] Even though the divine rape of the Great Prostitute is indirect, God's participation in the act places him in the company of the same deities, such as Zeus and Mars, that John seeks to distance him from in Revelation 4. This, however, is not the first time God has been involved in sexual violence. In Ezekiel, God himself describes stripping a personified Jerusalem naked before her lovers and delivering her "into their hands" so that they can "break down [her] lofty places" and eventually incite a mob to stone her and cut her into pieces (Ezek 16:35-41). God does this to punish Jerusalem, whom he labels a "prostitute," and thereby satisfies "his" jealousy and fury. In addition, the prophets of the Hebrew Bible sometimes depict foreign cities, like Nineveh and Tyre, as sex-workers whom God will punish and shame (e.g., Nah 3:1-7; Isa 23:15-17).[42] In these cases, as in Revelation's depiction of Babylon,

---

40. Page duBois, *Sowing the Body: Psychoanalysis and Ancient Representations of Women* (Chicago: University of Chicago Press, 1991), 65–85.

41. Celene Lillie, *The Rape of Eve: The Transformation of Roman Ideology in Three Early Christian Retellings of Genesis* (Minneapolis: Fortress, 2017), 21.

42. Vander Stichele, "Re-Membering the Whore," 111.

there is no sense that the "woman" should be faithful to God, but divine punishment comes, nonetheless.

God's recounting of his actions against Jerusalem in Ezekiel is stomach-turning, just as the accounts of the shaming of feminized foreign cities are stomach-turning. There is no way of redeeming these stories, and the God depicted in these accounts is a horrifying projection of toxic masculinity. It is important to remember that John's depiction of God is *not* God; it is *John's depiction.*[43]

The Great Prostitute's fate rings too familiar to feminist readers. Surekha Nelavala admits that "when I first consciously read the text of Revelation 17:16, it was not possible for me to stay objective and pass on to the next verse. . . . My mind was filled with so many stories of women in similar situations which I have heard reported and read about in the newspapers."[44] Sex-workers, regardless of their gender or sexuality, are susceptible to exploitation violence. Sometimes these come from the hands of the lone individual who preys on sex-workers or people that he has sexualized (the gender here is intentional), such as the eight Asian women who were shot while working at a spa outside of Atlanta.[45] More often, violence comes at the hands of those who traffic sex-workers. In addition to physical violence, there is institutional (e.g., the disproportionate punishment of sex-workers versus "johns"), emotional, and even spiritual violence. Avaren Ipsen, the author of a book that explores how sex-workers read biblical depictions of sex-workers, explains that religious people proffer some of the most virulent hate sex-workers receive. They seem emboldened, according to Ispen, by the biblical text's negative depiction of sex-work.[46] Of course, some religious individuals support and empower current and former sex-workers, such as Rev. Becca Stephens, founder of the Magdalene Project and Thistle Farms, both of which offer support services to women survivors of trafficking and those seeking work after prostitution.[47]

43. Thank you to Elon University student Hannah Allen for reminding me of this when we talked about this text.

44. Surekha Nelavala, " 'Babylon the Great Mother of Whores' (Rev 17:5): A Postcolonial Feminist Perspective," *ExpTim* 121 (2009): 62.

45. Marlene Lenthang, "Atlanta Shooting and the Legacy of Misogyny and Racism against Asian Women," ABC News, March 21, 2021, https://abcnews.go.com/US /atlanta-shooting-legacy-misogyny-racism-asian-women/story?id=76533776.

46. Ipsen, *Sex Working and the Bible*, 181.

47. Thank you to Amy-Jill Levine for bringing this organization to my attention. See "Our Mission," Thistle Farms, https://thistlefarms.org/pages/our-mission.

In light of this sexualized violence, Christian feminists ask how and why this scene became part of our tradition's collection of sacred texts and how we should respond. Informed by womanist and postcolonial thought, Shanell T. Smith models how to engage the image of the woman Babylon in her "hermeneutics of ambiveilence" (see p. liv). She asks fellow interpreters to come to the text with commitments to taking women's experiences seriously and reflect honestly on what it shows us about our worlds and ourselves.[48] Smith sees in the image a reminder of how the bodies of enslaved Black women experienced physical and sexual violence at the hands of White enslavers, male and female. Simultaneously, the image reminds Smith that she benefits from systems of domination as someone educated and economically privileged.[49]

When I look at Babylon, I also recognize someone who, like those in the LGBTQIA+ community, is shamed and then brutalized because of her non-normative sexuality and gender performance. More than twenty-five years after the rape and murder of Brandon Teena, a young transgender man from the American Midwest, LGBTQIA+ individuals still experience threats of violence. In 2018, for example, almost 19 percent of the hate crimes perpetrated in the United States were motivated by anti-LGBTQIA+ bias, and the number of these crimes, which include rape and murder, had risen from the year before.[50] I look at Babylon and see some fear behind her bravado. Still, Babylon's wealth and her willingness to engage the "kings of the earth," i.e., wealth and power, remind me of the growing affluence of gays and lesbians, especially those who are White and educated, such as myself. Some of us in the LGBTQIA+ community, mainly those who are White and upper class, have been courted by big businesses and political brokers. They try to seek our attention for money and votes.[51] Babylon's fate reminds me that these "friends" might just be the ones who turn on us when it works to their advantage.

48. Smith, *Woman Babylon*, 67–69.

49. Smith, *Woman Babylon*, 178–79.

50. Tim Fitzsimons, "Nearly 1 in 5 Hate Crimes Motivated by Anti-LGBTQ Bias, FBI Finds," NBC News, November 12, 2019, https://www.nbcnews.com/feature/nbc-out/nearly-1-5-hate-crimes-motivated-anti-lgbtq-bias-fbi-n1080891.

51. Huber, "Gazing at the Whore," 317.

Excerpt from
The Woman Babylon
and the Marks of Empire

Reading the woman Babylon's text includes a reading of myself and the pain and trauma associated with my existence, and I sympathize with her. The manner in which she is horridly used, abused, and killed captures and reflects the historical black experience of American slavery. The negative connotations associated with her name that continue to survive remind me of the racist underpinnings of imperial ideology that remain in effect today. However, the woman Babylon's characterization as a victim of empire is only half of her ambivalent nature. As a *privileged* African American woman, I also resonate with what lies on the other side of the woman Babylon's veil: her association with, and participation in, empire. It is, therefore, difficult to employ the interpretive process of my ancestors, that is, to ignore the texts that further perpetuate slave ideology and embrace—albeit with adaption—the texts that give hope, when it comes to the "text" of the woman Babylon. I cannot tear her apart like the Beast and the kings (17:16), and pick and choose which aspects of her I will embrace, nor do I want to. The woman Babylon—in all her suffering and involvement in empire—functions as a mirror and I behold an image of myself.[52]

Shanell T. Smith

52. Smith, *Woman Babylon*, 166–67. Excerpt used with permission.

Revelation 18

The Judgment of the Great City

After witnessing the horror of the Great Prostitute's demise, John experiences another vision of the "great city" that signifies Rome. In this second look at Babylon, John sees more clearly and in further detail the city's political, social, and economic entanglements, including the extent of imperial reach and excess. As a result, Revelation 18 offers one of the New Testament's most sustained and multifaceted critiques of "empire," a term used to describe political systems that control others (usually distant) through political, military, economic, religious, and social domination.[1] Even though John shifts focus to emphasize Babylon as a city in this section, the image of Babylon as a woman, specifically a sex-worker, lingers. Language of how Babylon "seduces" her clients, and the negative valuation of sex-work are replicated along with the text's political and economic critique. "Sex sells," as they say, and the sexualized depiction of Babylon as the Great Prostitute seemingly helps John sell this criticism of the imperial and colonizing powers.

1. See the discussion in Davina C. Lopez, "Victory and Visibility: Revelation's Imperial Textures and Monumental Logics," in *An Introduction to Empire in the New Testament*, ed. Adam Winn (Atlanta: SBL Press, 2016), 273–95. The study of empire is most closely associated with postcolonial theory, especially as articulated by scholars such as Edward Said and Gaytri Spivak.

Coming Out of "Her" (18:1-8)

Just as the prophet Isaiah pronounces, "Fallen, fallen is Babylon" (Isa 21:9), the angel from heaven pronounces the city's destruction as a done deal, a completed action (18:2). The city is *fallen*; the Greek verb ἔπεσεν is aorist, that is, past tense and not a present or future verb. Despite this certainty, the new Babylon, Rome, was still standing during John's lifetime. The city was arguably at the height of its power. Given this, we might wonder how John could even fathom the possibility of the city's decline, let alone its demise. John's confidence in the city's fall comes from his familiarity with and faith in the prophetic traditions shaping his worldview. These texts burst at the seams with accounts of fallen imperial cities and superpowers of which Babylon is the most notable. Since only God's reign persists eternally, Babylon, Rome, or whatever imperial city follows will eventually fall and come to an end. Acknowledging the cycle of imperial rise and fall is part of aligning oneself with the Jewish scriptural traditions and an affirmation of God's sovereignty.[2]

In this depiction of Babylon as city, John does not dwell on its past glory. There's little need since Babylon was well known for its gardens, majestic walls, and beautiful canals (Pliny the Elder, *Nat.* 6.30). Instead, John highlights the city's ruin, detailing how a once majestic city has become a "dwelling place of demons" or a "haunt" (18:2). Again, this language echoes the words of a prophetic predecessor, specifically Jeremiah, who claimed Babylon would become uninhabited and a haunt for jackals (Jer 51:37 [28:37 LXX]). The word that the NRSV renders as "haunt" often describes a "prison" (φυλακή), an image that emphasizes how the city continues to contain what remains within its walls. The city walls that protected its inhabitants and wealth by encircling them are now the tools of imprisonment. Within empire, what was intended to provide a sense of safety and even freedom ultimately becomes stifling and oppressive.[3]

What remains in the fallen city are birds, beasts, and demons, things that suggest wildness and that typically reside outside a city's walls. The city, in some sense, has been turned inside out: what used to be kept outside has taken over the inside.

2. David L. Petersen, *The Prophetic Literature: An Introduction* (Louisville: Westminster John Knox, 2002), 37–39.

3. For a discussion of ancient Roman prisons, see Mark Letteney and Matthew D. C. Larsen, "A Roman Military Prison at Lambaesis," *SLA* 5 (2021): 65–102.

18:1After this I saw another angel coming down from heaven, having great authority; and the earth was made bright with his splendor. 2He called out with a mighty voice,

> "Fallen, fallen is Babylon the great!
> It has become a dwelling place
>   of demons,
> a haunt of every foul spirit,
>   a haunt of every foul bird,
>   a haunt of every foul and
>   hateful beast.
> 3For all the nations have drunk
> of the wine of the wrath of her
>   fornication,
> and the kings of the earth have
>   committed fornication with
>   her,
> and the merchants of the earth
>   have grown rich from
>   the power of her luxury."

4Then I heard another voice from
>   heaven saying,
> "Come out of her, my people,
>   so that you do not take part in
>   her sins,

The description of the things inhabiting Babylon as unclean (ἀκάθαρτος) associates them, moreover, with the impurities (ἀκάθαρτα) of the Great Prostitute's fornication (17:4). They have taken over Babylon *because of*—a connection signaled by the conjunction "for" (ὅτι)—the city's interactions with the nations and kings and merchants of the earth. John's explanation of Babylon's demise reveals a complex symbiotic relationship between the city and earth's nations, kings, and merchants (18:3). Still, the kings of the earth seemingly benefit from fornication with her, and the merchants of the earth get rich from the "power of her luxury." The word translated as "luxury" (στρῆνος) is uncommon but conveys a sense of excess, arrogance, and lack of control.[4] The merchants of the earth take advantage of this for their own gain.

Following his vision of the plague angel, John hears an unidentified voice further narrating the judgment of Babylon (v. 4). Since this voice comes from heaven and addresses Revelation's audience members as "my people," it seems reasonable to assume the voice communicates the will of the divine. Luis Menéndez-Antuña explains that the language of "my people . . . situates the audience within the frame of the covenant."[5] John prompts those hearing Revelation read aloud to remember they are

4. Craig R. Koester, *Revelation: A New Translation with Introduction and Commentary*, AYB 38A (New Haven: Yale University Press, 2014), 699

5. Luis Menéndez-Antuña, *Thinking Sex with the Great Whore: Deviant Sexualities and Empire in the Book of Revelation* (Abingdon: Routledge, 2018), 70.

Rev 18:1-8 (cont.)

and so that you do not share in her plagues;	so give her a like measure of torment and grief.
⁵for her sins are heaped high as heaven, and God has remembered her iniquities.	Since in her heart she says, 'I rule as a queen; I am no widow, and I will never see grief,'
⁶Render to her as she herself has rendered, and repay her double for her deeds; mix a double draught for her in the cup she mixed.	⁸therefore her plagues will come in a single day— pestilence and mourning and famine— and she will be burned with fire; for mighty is the Lord God who judges her."
⁷As she glorified herself and lived luxuriously,	

God's people, the people God brought out of Egypt, and the ones who wept for God by the rivers of Babylon (Ps 137). The voice also sounds like Christ,[6] since, like the Son of Humanity in Revelation 2–3, this voice issues a call for the book's audiences to act. In those early messages, the call was to "listen to what the Spirit is saying to the churches" (e.g., 2:11) and be the victor. Now, this voice explains part of what being a victor entails—coming out of *her*.

The feminine pronoun in the command to "come out of her [αὐτῆς]" functions as a double entendre: Αὐτή could be translated into English as "it," emphasizing Babylon as a city, but it can be "her" evoking Babylon as a woman, an image that dominated the last chapter. The double entendre works, furthermore, because of the conventional association between women and cities in the ancient Mediterranean. Both were envisioned as containers: Just as a city had walls to contain inhabitants, so ancient physicians defined women's bodies as having uteruses designed to "contain" children and vaginas that functioned as receptacles (Galen, *On the Usefulness of the Parts of the Body* 14.6). As containers, women and cities could also be entered and exited. Audience members hear this as a command both to exit from Babylon as they would a city and to "pull

6. Adela Yarbro Collins, "Revelation 18: Taunt-Song or Dirge?," in *L'Apocalypse johannique et l'Apocalyptique dans le Nouveau Testament*, ed. Jan Lambrecht (Leuven: Leuven University Press, 1980), 193.

out" sexually from "her," Babylon the Great Prostitute. John thereby casts a political-religious resolution in sexual terms.

John returns to the feminized image of Babylon in verse 7 of this section. He uses the ancient rhetorical technique of *prosopopoeia*, when an author imagines a thing or person speaking, to paint a picture of Babylon as a luxury-loving queen: "I rule as queen; I am no widow, and I will never see grief" (v. 7).[7] While it is possible to imagine this as a portrayal of Babylon pumping herself up through self-affirmations, the speech reveals the personified city's lack of self-awareness. The text's audiences know that she is not a queen, for the plague angel described her as a sex-worker (17:1, 5). Likewise, Babylon's rejection of widowhood and grief implies she has not been and never will be married, marriage being the expected trajectory for respectable ancient women. This almost gleeful disavowal of widowhood signals, in addition, Babylon's vanity and love of luxury since she will not be expected to wear the more modest dress expected of a woman in mourning for her husband.[8] Babylon's supposed affirmations sound a lot like the taglines uttered by cable television "housewives": "Life in Babylon is a game and *I* make the rules" or "I'm a Babylon girl, no one can knock *me* down!"[9] Like modern TV audiences, ancient Romans enjoyed stories about wayward wives. The writings of authors like Apuleius and Juvenal recounted the stories of scandalous women, such as Eppia the senator's wife who ran off with gladiators and Saufeia whom Juvenal seemingly credits with the invention of "twerking" (*Sat.* 6.320; see also Apuleius, *Metam.* 9). These stories were not only for entertainment; they supposedly offered proof that society was in a state of decline. It seems that John offers up his depiction of Babylon in a similar vein.

The innuendo in the command to "come out of her" aligns, moreover, with John's use of female imagery throughout the narrative, according to feminist biblical scholar Tina Pippin. Pippin argues that John tries to correct the audience's desire for the Great Prostitute, imagined as seductive and available, by directing them toward the virginal and pure Bride, an image of the New Jerusalem (21:1-10). Instead of screwing around

---

7. Ezekiel also uses *prosopopoeia* depicting the feminized Tyre bragging, "I am perfect in beauty" (27:3).

8. On the dress of Roman widows, see Kelly Olson, *Dress and the Roman Woman: Self-Presentation and Society* (London: Routledge, 2008), 42.

9. See, for instance, "Every 'Housewives' Tagline EVER!," Bravo TV Official Site, June 6, 2013, https://www.bravotv.com/the-real-housewives-of-beverly-hills/photos/every-housewives-tagline-ever.

with Babylon, Revelation's audience members are called to "thrust into the New Jerusalem."[10] By naming the innuendo that John may or may not use intentionally, Pippin uncovers the heterosexist assumptions that structure the final chapters of this book. This book clearly takes on a male viewpoint with little concern for women's perspectives. This is the case even though queer women may read themselves, or ourselves, into the narrative as those who also desire women.[11] Reading Revelation as a woman or as a man who does not desire women sexually requires continually positioning yourself in unnatural positions so you can see things the way John sees them. This is not unusual since so many ancient narratives were written with patriarchal perspectives, but when images of desire are central to the text's rhetorical aims, as is the case here, the accommodations to perspective are even more difficult to make.

In 18:4-5 the heavenly voice uses a series of traditional metaphors to characterize Babylon's sins and to emphasize her corruption, an apparent effort to encourage audience members to "come out." Her sins are contagious plagues, heaped up objects, and debts she needs to pay. In 17:4-5, John explicitly associated Babylon the sex-worker with dirt and unclean things, a common ancient stereotype. The heavenly voice expands on this idea by warning hearers that Babylon's sins are plagues that can be shared or spread (18:4). Paul, similarly, envisions sex-workers as potentially contagious, encouraging the Corinthians not to have sex with a sex-worker because that makes them "one body with her" and, therefore, susceptible to her supposed sin or dishonor (1 Cor 6:16-18). The idea that association with Babylon spreads impurity and iniquity echoes prophetic writings, such as those by Ezra and Nehemiah, that identify the presence of non-Israelite wives as potentially defiling to the land because they practice other religious traditions. According to the ancient logic of these prophets, this kind of permanent moral defilement could be solved only through the nullification of marriages and the expulsion of those believed to be foreign (e.g., Ezra 9–10; Neh 13:23-28).[12]

---

10. Tina Pippin, *Death and Desire: The Rhetoric of Gender in the Apocalypse of John* (Louisville: Westminster John Knox, 1992), 83. See also Tina Pippin and J. Michael Clark, "Revelation/Apocalypse," in *The Queer Bible Commentary*, ed. Deryn Guest et al. (London: SCM Press, 2006), 753–68.

11. Lynn R. Huber, "Gazing at the Whore: Reading Revelation Queerly," in *Bible Trouble: Queer Reading at the Boundaries of Biblical Scholarship*, ed. Teresa J. Hornsby and Ken Stone (Atlanta: SBL, 2011), 301–20.

12. Jonathan Klawans, "Idolatry, Incest, and Impurity: Moral Defilement in Ancient Judaism," *JSJ* 29 (1998): 401–2.

John operates with a similar logic when it comes to Babylon, although instead of expelling those who are foreign, audience members are called to come out of the "foreign woman."

Contagion is not the only way of envisioning and understanding sin. Hebrew Bible authors sometimes imagined sin as a burden a person bears or carries (e.g., Lev 24:15) or as a debt "remembered" by the one who is owed and for which an individual must pay (e.g., Ezek 18:22).[13] Evoking these metaphors in 18:4, the voice describes Babylon as having so many she is unable to carry them; rather, they are "heaped high as heaven." The word translated as "heaped," ἐκολλήθσαν, suggests things joined or glued together. I imagine a rickety tower of sins taped and tied together and threatening to collapse onto those associated with the city. Additionally, Babylon has "iniquities" (ἀδικήματα), literally unrighteous deeds, which God "remembers." The imagery suggests a divine accounting book with multiple entries for the city's numerous wrongdoings. Each way of envisioning sin—contagion, burden, debt—conveys different ideas about how one becomes sinful. By including these multiple types of sin, John emphasizes the depths and range of Babylon's immorality, thereby heightening the sense of danger that comes with associating with the city. One thing that unites these varied depictions of Babylon's sin is that they assign wrongdoing to a city, a political and economic system, and not to individuals. Babylon's sins impact those in and around the city, but they begin with the city at the heart of the imperial system. Revelation's recognition of systemic sin should prompt us to think about the systems in which we participate, interrogating for how they harm us and our neighbors and, potentially, push others into situations where we also harm others.

Even if we recognize why coming out of Babylon is necessary, the question of how one removes themselves from a city or system like this, practically speaking, remains unclear. How does an individual or community "come out of" a system that controls so much that surrounds them? Almost every aspect of the cities where John's audiences lived would have had intersected with Roman presence or the religious practices that John characterized as blasphemous: Many jobs would have required membership in guilds or associations that supported civic and imperial cults; public buildings, such as baths and gymnasiums, would have been financed by the wealthy who benefited from trade

---

13. For a discussion of how sin is imagined metaphorically in the Hebrew Bible, see Joseph Lam, *Patterns of Sin in the Hebrew Bible: Metaphor, Culture, and the Making of a Religious Concept* (New York: Oxford University Press, 2015).

with Rome; festivals and athletic events would include some recognition of Roman presence and patronage. One could not disentangle from the web of Roman imperialism, whether that web was spun by the Romans themselves or locals who saw imperial favor as an economic, political, or social necessity.

Does John want audience members to leave the cities in which they live and flee to the desert, like the Woman Clothed in the Sun and some later Christian monastics would do? Again, perhaps. But literally fleeing Roman cities would have been impossible for many in John's early audiences. Moreover, as Juan José Barreda Toscano explains, escaping Rome involves more than just moving out of the great city's range of influence: "The city is powerful (*great*). It has influenced everyone at every level with its ideologies and has engraved onto their bodies stories that will be difficult to leave behind (degradation, illness, sexual abuse, daily mistreatment, mutilation)."[14] The great city shapes how people think, act, and relate to one another. The city moves with and even within people. Given this, "coming out of Babylon" requires a kind of detachment or "disidentification," as Menéndez-Antuña puts it.[15]

For many modern readers, especially those living within the United States or other wealthy nations, disidentification begins with recognizing how we are entangled within the modern manifestations of Babylon. This can be difficult since people of privilege, "first world citizens," are taught to think they deserve or have earned the privilege they possess. As Christian ethicist Rebecca Todd Peters explains, "Privilege is often invisible to the people who possess it. Like the air that we breathe, most people don't think about how the world works unless it does not work for them."[16] Further, when a person lacks privilege in parts of their life, it can be difficult to see or acknowledge other areas where they do hold privilege. Perhaps our cloudy vision comes from drinking Babylon's wine. Only once we've started to understand how we have been part of Babylon can we begin to see ourselves as "my people" and distance ourselves from the prison the city has become.

14. Juan José Barreda Toscano, " 'Come Out of Her, My People': The Hope of Those Who Suffer Because of Corruption (Revelation 18:1–19:10)," *Journal of Latin American Theology* 12 (2017): 78.

15. Menéndez-Antuña, *Thinking Sex with the Great Whore*, 72.

16. Rebecca Todd Peters, *Solidarity Ethics: Transformation in a Globalized World* (Minneapolis: Fortress, 2014), 71.

Distancing oneself from Babylon is not enough from Revelation's perspective, and the voice from heaven issues a three-part call to repay the city for her evil deeds. Now that the audiences are no longer engaged in the city, penetrating the Great Prostitute sexually or being protected by her walls and her values, they are called to enact God's punishment of the city.[17] The divine seeks to shape the audience's reaction to Babylon in the same way that God influenced the Beast's horns (17:17). Things escalate, however, when the voice follows the command to repay Babylon with multiple references to doubling (διπλόω) the retribution: "repay [διπλώσατε] her double [τὰ διπλᾶ] for her deeds; mix a double [διπλοῦν] draught for her in the cup she mixed" (18:6). Even though John paints Babylon as especially sinful and violent toward God's people, the idea that the city's punishment should exceed the crime is troubling. Biblical scholar Brian K. Blount outlines the problem: "According to the scriptural tradition upon which John so heavily depends, the principle of lex talionis directs that a punishment's measure shall equal the measure of the crime (Exod 21:23-25; Lev 24:17-20; Deut 19:21). The law effectively prohibited angry and vengeful victims from excessive acts of retribution."[18] Now, however, God seemingly authorizes an excessive and unjust response to Babylon. Blount addresses this disparity by suggesting a shift in audience from the people in Revelation's audiences to the horns, who are kings, mentioned above. He suggests that God is calling those complicit in Babylon's evil ways, who mourn over the city in verses 9-20, to turn on their accomplice in this harsh way.[19]

Unfortunately, Revelation's call to punish Babylon has sometimes been interpreted literally. As Erin Runions recounts, prisoners at Abu Ghraib were forced to listen to "loud and constant repetitions of Boney M's version of the song 'Rivers of Babylon,'" a song that quotes Psalm 137, "By the rivers of Babylon / There we sat down / Yeah we wept / When we remembered Zion."[20] The soundtrack reveals a seemingly intentional connection between biblical condemnations of ancient Babylon and the

17. Some interpreters read these commands as generic and not addressed to the book's audiences. See a discussion of this in Susan M. Elliott, "Who Is Addressed in Revelation 18:6-7?," *BR* 40 (1995): 98–113.

18. Blount, *Revelation*, 329. There are, however, some prophetic precedents for this kind of doubling (e.g., Jer 16:18).

19. Blount, *Revelation*, 330.

20. As quoted in Erin Runions, *The Babylon Complex: Theopolitical Fantasies of War, Sex, and Sovereignty* (New York: Fordham University Press, 2014), 149.

torture of modern Iraqis by American soldiers. The dehumanizing treatment of Iraqis at the hands of their captors was publicized after "souvenir" photos were leaked. Runions notes that this kind of interpretation is literal, albeit transposed from the past into the interpreters' present.[21] In contrast, the intense retribution called for in this text should be understood in terms of John's paradoxical understanding of conquering and being a victor. Repaying Babylon does not mean engaging in violence and oppressing others; however, it might very well mean working to destroy the systems and institutions that Babylon symbolizes. The "burning" of Babylon (18:8) involves the complete dismantling of the ideologies that allow oppressive empires to thrive, including sexism, racism, ableism, religious and class bias, homophobia, transphobia, and xenophobia.

Narrating the Great City's Demise (18:9-24)

The voice from heaven falls silent, and groups within Babylon, kings and merchants and seafarers, lament the city's fall. The text signals a shift in speaker with heaven's final assessment over Babylon's judgment, "for mighty is the Lord God who judges her" (v. 8), and by introducing the kings of the earth. Some scholars suggest that the laments or dirges uttered in these verses come from the heavenly voice who mimics the city's elites just as it does Babylon "herself" in verse 7.[22] Whether these laments come from the voice or are John's report of what he hears from groups of people on the ground, these mournful lyrics are not meant to garner sympathy for Babylon from Revelation's audience members.[23] Rather, the laments echo Ezekiel's depictions of the fate of those economically invested in Tyre, another city that earned God's wrath, and provide evidence against those complicit in Babylon's sins.

It is not a surprise that the first lament comes from the kings of the earth (vv. 9-10) since John highlighted their relationship to Babylon in the previous chapter. While they were once *very* close to Babylon, having been her partner in fornication (v. 3; 17:2), now they watch her torment from "far off" (ἀπὸ μακρόθεν, v. 10). The merchants and shipmasters similarly stand "far off" (ἀπὸ μακρόθεν) as they watch the city burn (vv. 15, 17-18). This kind of reaction, putting distance between oneself and an accomplice who is now being punished, rings familiar (e.g., Jer 18:16).

<hr>

21. Runions, *Babylon Complex*, 154–55.
22. E.g., Koester, *Revelation*, 715.
23. Yarbro Collins, "Revelation 18," 195.

⁹And the kings of the earth, who committed fornication and lived in luxury with her, will weep and wail over her when they see the smoke of her burning; ¹⁰they will stand far off, in fear of her torment, and say,

> "Alas, alas, the great city,
> > Babylon, the mighty city!
> For in one hour your judgment
> > has come."

¹¹And the merchants of the earth weep and mourn for her, since no one buys their cargo anymore, ¹²cargo of gold, silver, jewels and pearls, fine linen, purple, silk and scarlet, all kinds of scented wood, all articles of ivory, all articles of costly wood, bronze, iron, and marble, ¹³cinnamon, olive oil, choice flour and wheat, cattle and sheep, horses and chariots, slaves— and human lives.

¹⁴"The fruit for which your soul longed
> has gone from you,
and all your dainties and your splendor
> are lost to you,
> never to be found again!"

¹⁵The merchants of these wares, who gained wealth from her, will stand far off, in fear of her torment, weeping and mourning aloud,

> ¹⁶"Alas, alas, the great city,
> > clothed in fine linen,
> > > in purple and scarlet,
> > adorned with gold,
> > > with jewels, and with
> > > > pearls!
> ¹⁷For in one hour all this wealth
> > has been laid waste!"

And all shipmasters and seafarers, sailors and all whose trade is on

Watching as a former partner takes the punishment and experiences torment for crimes you both committed and benefitted from can feel more abhorrent than admitting your own fault. Given this, the extreme grief of the kings and others sounds contrived.

The lengthiest lament is voiced by the "merchants of the earth," who offer a detailed list of all the goods lost because of God's judgment of Babylon (vv. 11-13). Many are luxury items or, as John calls them, "dainties" (λιπαρά, v. 14), including gold, silver, jewels, costly fabrics, and marble. Besides pointing to Rome's enormous wealth, these items reveal the reach of imperial power. The tiled floors and covered walls of wealthy Roman homes and imperial buildings functioned as "'material map[s]' of the empire" since the marbles were sourced from and associated with specific locations throughout Asia Minor, Greece, Egypt, and other regions.[24] The

---

24. Ben Russell, *The Economics of the Roman Stone Trade* (Oxford: Oxford University Press, 2013), 14.

Rev 18:9-24 (cont.)

the sea, stood far off [18]and cried out
as they saw the smoke of her burning,
  "What city was like the great city?"
[19]And they threw dust on their heads,
as they wept and mourned, crying out,
  "Alas, alas, the great city,
    where all who had ships at sea
    grew rich by her wealth!
  For in one hour she has been laid
    waste."
  [20]Rejoice over her, O heaven, you
saints and apostles and prophets!
For God has given judgment for you
against her.
  [21]Then a mighty angel took up a
stone like a great millstone and threw
it into the sea, saying,
  "With such violence Babylon the
    great city
  will be thrown down,
  and will be found no more;

[22]and the sound of harpists and
    minstrels and of flutists and
    trumpeters
  will be heard in you no more;
and an artisan of any trade
  will be found in you no more;
and the sound of the millstone
  will be heard in you no more;
[23]and the light of a lamp
  will shine in you no more;
and the voice of bridegroom and
    bride
  will be heard in you no more;
for your merchants were the
    magnates of the earth,
  and all nations were deceived
    by your sorcery.
[24]And in you was found the blood
    of prophets and of saints,
  and of all who have been
    slaughtered on earth."

Roman Empire maintained a trade network that brought wealth to the provinces but also depended on exploitation. For instance, marble quarries in Asia Minor contributed to local economies and relied on the labor of enslaved and imprisoned people.[25]

The merchants' laments are not necessarily a criticism of luxury goods or owning luxury items. The cargos named are not inherently evil; some, such as gold and jewels, even appear in the heavenly throne room and the coming New Jerusalem (e.g., 4:3-6; 21:11-21). This, in fact, is the point. These luxuries should be used in ways that honor God, which includes not exploiting God's creation, including human lives. We might draw a contemporary connection with diamonds sold to finance wars in Angola, the Central African Republic, the Democratic Republic of Congo,

25. J. Nelson Kraybill, *Imperial Cult and Commerce in John's Apocalypse* (Sheffield: Sheffield Academic, 1996), 106.

and Sierra Leone. The reality of "blood diamonds," which contribute a relatively small percentage of all the new diamonds sold, really came to public consciousness in the early 2000s, when movies like *Blood Diamond* (2006) shed light on the experiences of people forced to work by local militias. Mine owners reap maximum profit selling to the commercial markets that supply the diamonds wealthier people throughout the world buy as engagement rings, tennis bracelets, and earrings.[26] These things are not inherently evil, since they are part of God's creation; however, the system of exploitation and violence surrounding their procurement *is* evil.

Even though John associates Rome with luxury, some Romans similarly decried extravagance. Often, as with John, the Roman critique of luxury is a negative commentary on *women's* supposed penchant for fancy clothes, jewelry, and elaborate cosmetics. Classicist Kelly Olson explains that many Romans saw feminine adornment as a waste of time and resources, an indication of women's frivolity.[27] The poet Propertius, for example, accused Cynthia, an older woman and object of his affection, of spending "idle hours trying to improve your looks" and of "eagerly adorn[ing] your breast with . . . gems as a girl determined to meet a new lover looking her best" (*Elegies* 1.15.6). The love of luxury goods among men could mark them as effeminate and lacking self-control, an important masculine virtue. The rhetorician Quintilian hypothesizes that "to wear clothes like a woman's" is arguably a sign "of an effeminate and unmanly character" (*Inst.* 5.9.14). Despite this, Olson argues that some elite Roman men, including Julius Caesar, effectively presented themselves as "dandies," what some today might call "metrosexual," well dressed and flamboyant.[28] Simply put, luxury was acceptable for some, but not for all. Similarly, for John, luxury items are appropriate for heaven, but not for those on earth who deign to play God.

In addition to luxury goods, the merchants mourn the loss of staples, such as wine, olive oil, flour, and wheat. Rome's survival depended on trade with the provinces, as the city was unable to produce enough food to feed itself and those living in its environs. Nor did the emperor

26. Global Witness, "The Truth about Diamonds: Diamonds and Conflict," November 2006, https://cdn.globalwitness.org/archive/files/import/the_truth_about _diamonds.pdf.

27. Olson, *Dress and the Roman Woman*, 85.

28. Kelly Olson, "Masculinity, Appearance, and Sexuality: Dandies in Roman Antiquity," *JHS* 23 (2014): 182–205.

have a fleet to transport products to the Italian peninsula. Rome depended on people in the provinces wanting to make a profit to supply the city's needs and feed its appetite for luxury goods. Consequently, Rome secured land and sea trade routes through its military power, and the capital dispatched agents and administrators to provincial cities to safeguard its citizens and interests, political, social, and economic. Even though the system benefited merchants and seafarers from the provinces, it was primarily designed to meet the needs of Rome and Romans.[29] The laments offered over Babylon's demise in Revelation 18 can be read as a taunt or criticism of those who participate in these networks and depend on Rome for their own wealth. In some sense, Revelation's criticism of those who participate in the Roman economy parallels modern calls to boycott big businesses that manufacture in countries with histories of human rights abuses.

Among the cargo listed, after the animals, are "slaves—and human lives" (v. 13). The Greek reads literally, "bodies, also human souls." The translation of "bodies" (σώματα) as "slaves" in the NRSV reflects the fact that the term for someone who sold people into enslavement in the ancient Greek was "body merchant" (σωματέμπρος).[30] Revelation's distinction between these bodies and human lives, literally "souls" (ψυχαῖς), evokes an ancient assumption that the enslaved were not fully souled. For instance, Aristotle argued that "natural" slaves—as opposed to those who are not naturally predisposed to slavery (e.g., people who sold themselves to pay a debt)—had incomplete souls and lacked an ability to reason for themselves (*Pol.* 1.1254-55).[31] Some ancient thinkers, like Philo, rejected this idea (*Spec. Laws* 2.69, 83);[32] however, those who would profit off slavery obviously benefitted from this dehumanization of enslaved people. As Clarice J. Martin argues, John pushes back on this ancient understanding of enslavement with this reference to "human souls," a reference linked to "bodies" via the conjunction "and." The enslaved are humans with souls, even though Rome treats them as mere soulless

---

29. Kraybill, *Imperial Cult and Commerce*, 107.

30. Koester, *Revelation*, 705.

31. Clarice J. Martin, "Polishing the Unclouded Mirror: A Womanist Reading of *Revelation* 18:13," in *From Every People and Nation: The Book of Revelation in Intercultural Perspective*, ed. David Rhoads (Minneapolis: Fortress, 2005), 89–90.

32. Catherine Hezser, *Jewish Slavery in Antiquity* (Oxford: Oxford University Press, 2006), 58–59.

cargo. Revelation's critique of empire is not simply an economic one; it also protests Rome's use of slavery to dominate and oppress.[33]

The wails of the kings, merchants, and shippers might evoke a kind of *schadenfreude* among Revelation's audiences. It is easy to "stand far off" (vv. 10, 15, 17) and feel secure that *they* are getting their due because of *their* involvement with an oppressive system. If we adopt this perspective, however, we replicate the attitude of the kings, merchants, and shippers toward Babylon. Instead, for many of us living in the United States or Europe, Revelation pushes us to examine how we are implicated in the economics of empire. Are we supporting corporations, companies, and countries that ignore human rights abuses, fail to pay living wages, and perpetuate environmental degradation? Additionally, who are we working with and for, and how do the practices of these companies and institutions impact others? For some of us, it might be necessary to rethink how and where we do business. Of course, boycotting and divesting are not always viable options for everyone for a variety of reasons, and such efforts can potentially do more harm to wage employees than to their employers. There are no simple solutions.

The question of being implicated in empire, moreover, isn't simply a question for the rich and powerful, as John's inclusion of "all whose trade is on the sea" suggests (v. 17). Having grown up in Oregon, a state that "timber built," I sometimes hear in the laments of Revelation 18 the voices of loggers, truckers, mill workers, builders, and small-town politicians after the collapse of the lumber industry in the 1980s. Many, my dad included, lost their jobs when mills closed because of a national economic recession, changing international markets, and efforts to protect species endangered by the harvesting of large stands of old-growth trees.[34] The industry was, arguably, complicit in the "sins" of empire, but many depended on it for their livelihoods. The people most impacted by its fall were not powerful and wealthy. This is something John misses: The laments of kings, merchants, and shipmasters may seem hollow, but they cover up the cries of those lower down the "food chain," the individuals and families who live check-to-check. While we might think that John's call for vengeance against Babylon's oppressive system puts him on the side of the working class and the poor, his focus

33. Martin, "Polishing the Unclouded Mirror," 105.

34. Terra Rae Miner, "The State That Timber Built," *Oregon Humanities*, April 8, 2012, https://oregonhumanities.org/rll/magazine/here-spring-2012/the-state-that-timber-built/.

on the experiences of the powerful can erase those who would truly be hurt by the fall of Babylon.

If anyone in Revelation's audiences is confused about how they should react to Babylon's demise, 18:20 makes it clear: "Rejoice over her, O heaven, you saints and apostles and prophets! For God has given judgment for you against her." The plural "you" (ὑμεῖς) means that Revelation's audiences are prompted to hear themselves included in this command. The destruction of Babylon is part of God's justice for those who have been oppressed by the great city and experienced its violence. They are to rejoice over the fate of the city that is drunk on the blood of God's people (e.g., 17:6). Again, the text's meaning lands differently depending on the audience member's experience. For those who have experienced state-sponsored violence, the promise of Babylon's destruction might mean rejoicing in the possibility of life that comes with the destruction of a government or regime, things that the city symbolizes. For others, however, the call to rejoice over the ruin of an actual city, home to guilty and innocent alike, elicits disgust and shame as we remember the bombing of Hiroshima and Nagasaki.

The laments of those mourning over Babylon seemingly offer insufficient proof of the city's destruction; thus, an angel puts a kind of symbolic exclamation point on God's judgment by throwing a millstone into the sea (18:21). As Craig Koester observes, the symbol of a millstone seems apt for a city that consumed grain from abroad. Likewise, what once signaled prosperity and facilitated Rome's exploitation of other lands, the sea, now envelopes the millstone. The one who created the sea, God (10:6; 14:7), ultimately controls it, not those who exploit it for gain.[35]

The angel interprets the symbolic act of the millstone with a refrain that parallels the opening verses of this chapter by highlighting the emptiness of the city, again envisioned as a container. The angel emphasizes the destruction and the resulting absence of life through the repetition of a negative phrase, οὐ μή, which the NRSV translates as "no more," before a series of items that signal the flourishing of life. Among the things present *no more* in the city are music, the sounds of work and of processing grain, the voices of the newly married, and the light of a lamp (18:23). The suggestion that the city remains dark will serve as a contrast when John sees a new city, Jerusalem, enlightened by God and the Lamb (21:23). Moreover, the angel offers a final reminder of Babylon's

---

35. Koester, *Revelation*, 723.

current state by noting that the city does contain at least one thing: "the blood of prophets and of saints, and of all who have been slaughtered on earth" (18:24). Babylon's judgment is not based entirely on the city's love of luxury and economic oppression of others; rather, things lead to an environment incompatible with following God and the Lamb. These systems require ultimate loyalty, something the faithful cannot offer.

Revelation 19

Here Comes the Bride and Bridegroom

"Catfights," altercations and conflicts between women, are popular TV and social media fodder. The English expression, which has been around since at least the end of the nineteenth century, compares women to animals and trivializes their disagreements.[1] Its use points to the fact that fights between women, whether pop stars or politicians, are typically for the pleasure of others, often men. Pitting women against each other is not only done for entertainment, but it also serves as an effective patriarchal political strategy preventing women from organizing, gaining power, and making change. To paraphrase bell hooks slightly, "Female bonding [is] not possible within patriarchy; it [is] an act of treason."[2]

Ancient authors (and their modern translators) similarly depict women in conflict and competition with one another. Sarah and Hagar are the primary examples, even though the power imbalance between Sarah as the enslaver and Hagar as the enslaved makes this an unfair competition.

1. Kayleen Schaefer, *Text Me When You Get Home: The Evolution and Triumph of Modern Female Friendship* (New York: Penguin, 2018), 29–30.

2. bell hooks, *Feminism Is for Everybody: Passionate Politics* (London: Pluto Press, 2000), 14.

Despite this, the NRSV translators heighten the sense of competition by claiming that Hagar feels "contempt" for Sarah, although a better translation by the Jewish Publication Society suggests that Sarah is "lowered in [Hagar's] esteem" (Gen 16:4). Still, the author of Genesis similarly portrays sisters Leah and Rachel in conflict over a man, Jacob, and children (Gen 30:1). Even though this author, like others, recounts disputes between men—Cain and Abel and Jacob and Esau come to mind—the paucity of women who engage positively with other women in these texts accentuates conflicts between women. Even in cases where women do not interact with one another in the narrative, the notion of competition lingers over their portrayals, as in the case of Esther and Vashti. Even sacred texts hook their audiences with the promise of women "throwing down."

The assumption that women are poised against each other and not inclined to work together provides a rhetorical foundation for Revelation's final chapters, which depict the Great Prostitute and the Bride, metaphorical representations of two cities, as opposing ideas. This ancient rhetorical technique, which Barbara Rossing describes as the "two-woman *topos*," uses women to highlight the distinction between options, such as following the Beast versus following the Lamb.[3] In this kind of scenario, there is no possibility that the women might find common ground or come together since they are imagined as opposing forces. Such is the case in the hymn that opens Revelation 19: One woman, the Prostitute, fades into the background, while the other woman, a Bride, appears on the scene. To add insult to injury, the focus of the chapter moves quickly from Bride to Bridegroom and from catfight to a full-on battle between the armies of heaven and the nations led by an almost hypermasculine rider on a white horse.

Although much has been written about them, the images of the Great Prostitute and the Bride will continue to be important sites for feminist engagement with the book of Revelation, since they draw on and reinforce cultural assumptions about gender that impact the lives of real women. Thus, even though they are rhetorical constructions designed for audiences to "think with" and not literal or historical women, how interpreters engage these "women" have real-life impacts.

---

3. Barbara R. Rossing, *The Choice between Two Cities: Whore, Bride, and Empire in the Apocalypse* (Harrisburg, PA: Trinity Press International, 1999), passim.

TRANSLATION MATTERS: γάμος

The Greek word that the NRSV translates as "marriage," γάμος, can refer to both a wedding ceremony and the marital relationship that continues after the wedding. In the New Testament, the term typically refers to a wedding event, including the famous wedding at Cana where Jesus turns water into wine (John 2:1). Likewise, in both Matthew and Luke γάμος describes a banquet held in conjunction with a wedding. In these cases, the wedding symbolizes the kingdom of heaven (Matt 22:1-14; 25:1-13; Luke 12:35-36). In all these instances, wedding imagery conveys a sense of hope, newness, and even abundance.

Revelation, in contrast, is the only New Testament book where the NRSV translates γάμος as "marriage." The translation is puzzling since there are other words that signal the idea of marriage that John does not use. In 1 Peter, for example, the author uses "life together" (συνοικέω) to describe a marriage between a husband and wife (3:7). In addition, other parts of the text imply γάμος specifically references a wedding. John's reference to the Lamb's wife preparing herself (see "Translation Matters: γυνή") and his description of her garment are key, since the bride's costume was central to weddings in the ancient world. Furthermore, the idea of a "wedding" invokes the ideas of newness and beginning, which are themes that John picks up in later descriptions of the *new* Jerusalem as a Bride (21:2, 5).

TRANSLATION MATTERS: γυνή and νύμφη

By announcing a wedding in verse 7, John prompts his audience members to envision the actors traditionally associated with a wedding, the bride and groom. Instead of using the common term for a bride, νύμφη, John uses γυνή, which can be translated as "woman" or "wife." Despite this, the NRSV translators opt to translate γυνή with the English term "bride." As with γάμος, the decision behind this translation choice is unclear, although it does evoke the idea of the γάμος as a wedding. The translators' use of "bride" aligns 19:7 with Revelation 21 (vv. 2, 9), where John actually uses the word νύμφη. The NRSV translators are not the first to "correct" 19:7, making it consistent with Revelation 21. The scribe behind Codex Sinaiticus (one of the fourth-century manuscripts of the New Testament) used νύμφη in 19:7 instead of γυνή.

John's use of "woman" in 19:7 instead of "bride" reflects the ancient assumption that all free, elite females were expected to marry. Being a woman implied having been a girl or virgin (παρθένος) and a bride (νύμφη). The latter was a liminal role marking the transition from girl to woman and from virgin to wife. At least in some cases, the bride carried items during her wedding signifying her transition into the role of wife, including a spindle and distaff, tools for spinning wool (Pliny, *Nat.* 8.194).

Even though John uses "woman" in 19:7 to describe the bridal role, this woman might challenge some modern reader's assumptions about womanhood. In the Roman world, brides, especially those in the upper classes, might be better characterized as girls. The legal marriage age for girls was twelve, and marriage in the early teens, around the onset of menstruation, was the norm.[4] Funerary inscriptions, which often included the age at marriage, offer evidence of this. One tombstone, for example, outside of the city of Rome laments the death of a young woman who was married at fourteen and died at twenty-one. Her husband describes her as "my happiness" and lauds her chastity.[5] Thus, when John does employ the word νύμφη, bride, ancient audiences probably thought of a young woman or girl embarking on a new life as someone's wife.

The use of "woman" in this verse brings into relief the other times Revelation uses the word γυνή. For a text that characterizes its audience members in masculine terms, as seen in Revelation 2–3, the noun appears quite frequently. In several instances the term carries a negative valance. For example, John uses γυνή to describe both the prophet Jezebel (2:20) and Babylon (17:3-4, 6-7, 9, 18). He also describes the locusts from the abyss as having hair like "women's hair" (9:8) and associates women with impurity (14:4). At the same time, John uses the term in reference to the Woman Clothed in the Sun, who gives birth to the Messiah (12:1, 4, 6, 13-17). For all these uses, negative or positive, John uses γυνή only one time in reference to a real person, who may or may not be a woman (see p. 49).[6] The disparity between how many times John uses γυνή, around eighteen or nineteen times, and the one time he possibly references a woman reinforces that John uses women to "think with" and is not concerned with the lives and experiences of women and femmes. For some readers this is reason to lessen or qualify Revelation's role in Christian contexts. Personally, I take John's apparent lack of interest in women as a challenge to explore the ways women and other "not men" may have heard John's vision in the past and to lift up the ways women and minoritized interpreters have understood the book across time.

One Woman's Demise and Another's Celebration (19:1-8)

Revelation references the burning of Babylon multiple times (14:11; 17:16; 18:8, 9, 18), so the appearance of smoke from the city aflame should not be surprising. People who live near places where wildfires are increasingly common know the ominous feeling that comes with seeing smoke

---

4. Lauren Caldwell, *Roman Girlhood and the Fashioning of Femininity* (Cambridge: Cambridge University Press, 2015), 1–7.

5. As quoted in Caldwell, *Roman Girlhood*.

6. Sarah Emanuel, *Humor, Resistance, and Jewish Cultural Persistence in the Book of Revelation: Roasting Rome* (Cambridge: Cambridge University Press, 2020), 116.

19:1After this I heard what seemed to be the loud voice of a great multitude in heaven, saying,

"Hallelujah!
Salvation and glory and power to
our God,
2for his judgments are true and
just;
he has judged the great whore
who corrupted the earth with
her fornication,
and he has avenged on her the
blood of his servants."
3Once more they said,

"Hallelujah!
The smoke goes up from her
forever and ever."
4And the twenty-four elders and the four living creatures fell down and worshiped God who is seated on the throne, saying,
"Amen. Hallelujah!"
5And from the throne came a
voice saying,
"Praise our God,
all you servants,
and all who fear him,
small and great."

fill the air. Thus, this hymn might strike an off note for modern audiences, as the multitude of heaven *celebrates* at the sight of this smoke. Things become even more unsettling when we realize that they are celebrating the immolation of "the Great Prostitute" (τὴν πόρνην τὴν μεγάλην), proclaiming that "the smoke goes up from *her* [αὐτῆς] forever and ever" (19:2-3).

The image of a burning woman is startling. It is even more startling when we realize there is ancient precedent for the ritual murder of women and girls perceived as sexually suspect. The priestly codes of Leviticus note that a priest's daughter who has become a sex-worker "shall be burned to death" (21:9). This is because, according to the text, she profanes not only herself but also her father. The Romans similarly practiced ritual murder when a Vestal Virgin, one of the most sacred priestly roles in the Roman Empire, was believed to no longer meet the virginity job requirement (see p. 250).[7] In the case of the Vestal, she was buried alive, since her impurity disqualified her from tending the sacred flame of Vesta, goddess of the hearth (Cicero, *Leg.* 2.29). A Vestal's loss of virginity left the city in danger, since it compromised her ability to intercede on the city's behalf.[8] As an image of Rome, Babylon the Great

---

7. Ariadne Staples, *From Good Goddess to Vestal Virgins: Sex and Category in Roman Religion* (London: Routledge, 1998), 137.

8. Robin Lorsch Wildfang, *Rome's Vestal Virgins* (London: Routledge, 2006), 91.

Rev 19:1-8 (cont.)

⁶Then I heard what seemed to be the voice of a great multitude, like the sound of many waters and like the sound of mighty thunderpeals, crying out,

> "Hallelujah!
> For the Lord our God
>   the Almighty reigns.
> ⁷Let us rejoice and exult
>   and give him the glory,
> for the marriage of the Lamb has come,
>   and his bride has made herself ready;
> ⁸to her it has been granted to be clothed
>   with fine linen, bright and pure"—

for the fine linen is the righteous deeds of the saints.

Prostitute can be read as a parody of the Vestals, destroyed by the very fire she was called to maintain. Both traditions assume that the woman's body belongs to others, her father or Roman society, respectively, and must be destroyed lest the body bring dishonor or even danger to the owners. Likewise, according to similar logic, Babylon's "body" poses a threat to those who follow God and the Lamb, necessitating destruction.

The verses preceding the celebration of the Great Prostitute's demise frame this event as an indication that God's actions are true, just, and worthy of praise. This assessment is linked to Babylon's corruption of the earth through fornication and the shedding of the blood of the saints (see also 17:6; 18:24). Because she sinned in these ways, the multitude of heaven describes her death as divine vengeance (ἐκδικέω). Even though Revelation includes plenty of justice and judgment language, vengeance is only mentioned one other time, when the souls call out from the altar: "how long will it be before you judge and avenge our blood on the inhabitants of the earth?" (6:10). In Revelation 6, these souls are told to wait and given a white robe as evidence of their faithfulness. This second reference to vengeance suggests that the wait is over as God's judgment of Babylon avenges the faithful. God keeps promises.

The affirmation of God's reign in verse 6 provides an occasion for proclaiming the start of a royal wedding (γάμος) in verse 7 (see above, "Translation Matters: γάμος"), and the voice of the great multitude invites Revelation's audiences to rejoice at the announcement. The quick transition from celebrating the demise of the Great Prostitute to exulting over a wedding and the Bride's readiness underscores that these two things are linked, like flip sides of a coin. The Great Prostitute's destruction allows for the emergence of the Lamb's Bride.[9] One "woman" must be destroyed to make room for another, returning to the idea that women must compete for attention and even space.

The heavenly multitude announces the wedding of the Lamb, but the focus rests on the Bride and her readiness and preparation (v. 7; see "Translation Matters: γυνή"). Just as modern weddings often have been considered the bride's "big day" (something complicated by the growing number of weddings with two brides or two grooms), so ancient weddings were perceived as being about the wife-to-be. Elite male authors, our primary source for information about ancient weddings, depict the wedding as *the* culminating event in the life of a free girl. As classicist Lauren Caldwell explains, "An unmarried girl's life was organized around this goal."[10] Unlike elite Roman boys who had a rite of passage marking their entrance into manhood prior to marriage (the donning of a traditional garment called the *toga virilis*), the wedding functioned as a rite of passage for girls.[11] This event, which mainly entailed the bride being led to the home of her new husband's family, marked her transition from virgin to wife.[12] Given the importance of this event for young girls, the appearance of a bride who becomes a wife should not be surprising after John's reference to unmarried girls or virgins (παρθένοι) in Revelation 14:4.

Marrying was an expectation for free Roman citizens, although there were limitations on who could marry. For instance, soldiers could not marry while in the service and those in the senatorial classes could not marry people who had been previously enslaved.[13] Roman law also did not allow the enslaved and formerly enslaved to marry. Of course, people in these classes did form partnerships that looked much like legal marriages, but these relationships are described as "concubinage."[14] Although the language of concubine denotes sex-work or being a mistress to a married man (often a royal figure) when used in modern contexts, that is not the case when talking about the ancient world. Rather, according

---

9. Robert M. Royalty Jr., *The Streets of Heaven: The Ideology of Wealth in the Apocalypse of John* (Macon, GA: Mercer University Press, 1998), 212.

10. Caldwell, *Roman Girlhood*, 134.

11. Caldwell, *Roman Girlhood*, 137–39.

12. Lynn R. Huber, *Like a Bride Adorned: Reading Metaphor in John's Apocalypse* (New York: T&T Clark, 2007), 128–29.

13. Beryl Rawson, "Roman Concubinage and Other de Facto Marriages," *TAPA* 104 (1974): 282.

14. Caldwell, *Roman Girlhood*, 115.

to historian Beryl Rawson, concubinage was a *"de facto* marriage."[15] The partners have a marriage-like relationship, even though it was not defined as such under Roman law.

Given the circumscribed nature of legal marriage in the Roman world, Revelation's wedding imagery draws on an experience out of reach for some in John's audiences. This was not only the case in the ancient context, as the privileges associated with legal marriage have a long history of being extended only to some because of race, mental ability, or sexuality. As someone unable to legally wed my spouse until 2015, after the US Supreme Court decision *Obergefell v. Hodges* and ten years after we started living in a domestic partnership, I can imagine the dissonance some in Revelation's early audiences might have felt hearing marriage offered up as an ideal. Marriage is not the only way of living a good, happy, or ethical life, and Revelation is not advocating that individuals marry. Still, whenever I read about the Lamb's wedding I recognize that histories of exclusion are one thing that shape audiences' experience of Revelation's metaphorical language and imagery. Given my relatively privileged status, I must be unaware of other places in the text where hearers and readers feel exclusion and erasure. This, for me, is a call to engage the interpretations of those who come from a wide variety of experiences.

The focus of the wedding announcement rests on the Bride's preparation and attire, which parallels the importance of bridal adornment in ancient weddings. Depictions of weddings in art, although more common in Greek than Roman contexts, and discussions of wedding traditions highlighted the young woman's "adornment," the time before the wedding when she dressed and had her hair fixed by attendants who were, most likely, enslaved people.[16] When the multitude in heaven announces that the Lamb's Bride has "made herself ready" (v. 7), John's audiences might envision just such a scene (21:2). John's emphasis on the Bride's appearance correlates to the two-woman *topos*, noted above, which employed physical attributes and clothing imagery to contrast the two ways or options represented by each woman.[17] Clothing communicates something about a person's identity, an idea that is doubly true in a narrative where clothed figures are designed to persuade an audience. Just as the Great Prostitute's clothing and physical attributes,

15. Rawson, "Roman Concubinage."

16. Karen K. Hersch, *The Roman Wedding: Ritual and Meaning in Antiquity* (Cambridge: Cambridge University Press, 2010), 69, 73.

17. Rossing, *Choice between Two Cities*, 38.

such as her cup full of abominations (17:4), signaled her distance from the divine, the Bride's dress points to her proximity to God and the Lamb and will reveal her identity as the community of the faithful.

When they hear that the future wife of the Lamb wears "fine linen" (19:8-9, 2x), audience members might recall the fabric is listed among the cargo mourned by the merchants of Babylon (18:12). The repetition could be a coincidence; however, it reminds us that John does not necessarily see the luxury items imported by Rome as inherently evil.[18] John, instead, disapproves of how valuable objects are used by Babylon to honor the Beast and Satan, when these things should be used to honor the reign of God as creator. Just as the heavenly throne room is adorned with gold and gems, so the Lamb's Bride should be adorned in the most valuable material. This luxury item also alludes to Ezekiel's description of God clothing his bride in "fine linen" and "rich fabric" (16:10). In Ezekiel, the bride is a feminized representation of Jerusalem, and Revelation's audiences will soon learn that this Bride is a new Jerusalem (21:2, 9). The reference to linen also connects this Bride to the image of the faithful followers of God and the Lamb as priests (1:6; 20:6) since priestly garments were made of linen (Lev 16:4). This points to the identity of the Bride as a metaphor for the collective community of the faithful, an idea that becomes clearer in the final line of 19:8.

Albeit pithy, John's portrayal of the Bride's garment as "bright and pure" communicates essential aspects of "her" character (v. 8). First, the garment's brightness, literally "shining" (λαμπρός), indicates the figure's proximity to God, given the association between God and light throughout the text. Flashes of light come from the divine throne, before which are seven flaming torches (4:5), and in heavenly Jerusalem there will be no sun or moon since God's glory is bright enough. Similarly, the Lamb serves as the city's lamp (21:23). The Bride of the Lamb reflects, it seems, the light of her groom.[19] Second, John's reference to the bridal garment's purity or cleanliness (καθαρός) draws a clear contrast between the Bride and the Great Prostitute, who was associated with abominations (βδελυγμάτα) and impurities (ἀκάθαρτα) (17:4). The Greek word for "impurities," unclean things, is a plural noun formed from the negation of the word for purity. The verbal similarity, ironically, emphasizes a major conceptual distinction, making it easy for John's audiences to recognize which "woman"

---

18. Royalty, *Streets of Heaven*, 213.
19. Huber, *Like a Bride Adorned*, 156.

they should side with. Even though the Great Prostitute and Bride never actually meet within the text, John puts them in competition.

John's description of the bridal garment's purity contributes to the critique of Roman morality that John began in Revelation 14 and picked up again in his depiction of Rome as Great Prostitute in Revelation 17. Roman emperors presented themselves as moral exemplars. In his eulogy, for example, Augustus claimed he "handed myself down as a model of many things to future generations" (*Res gest. divi Aug.* 8.5). John, in contrast, depicts the personification of Rome as decidedly filthy as well as asserts that the Lamb's Bride is so pure she shines. The latter was a powerful claim in the first-century world where some people questioned the moral purity of Jesus followers. Tacitus, for example, noted that they were "loathed for their vices" (*Ann.* 15.44). Suetonius similarly reports general disdain for Christians, noting their embrace of a "new and mischievous superstition," a criticism referencing their refusal to participate in Roman religions (*Nero* 16). John, however, challenges these claims by envisioning the moral purity of the Jesus followers through the image of the Bride.

Most important, John's suggestion that the saints' righteous deeds constitute the fine linen of the bridal garment finally reveals that the Bride represents the faithful community who will be united with the Lamb. A Roman bride ideally used an upright loom to weave her own garment, called a *tunica recta*, as an indication of her readiness for the social role of wife.[20] Thus, by describing the Bride's garment as the saints' righteous deeds John positions Jesus's followers, collectively, as the Bride. The saints make the bridal garment because the saints are the Bride. *This* is one of Revelation's central revelations—*through* their actions, holding to the testimony of Jesus and resisting the demands of the Beast, the Jesus followers weave the wedding garment that binds them together and signals their faithfulness to the Lamb.

Just as John calls the individual to follow the genderqueer Lamb by becoming a victor who is a willing victim and a virgin, so he calls the collective community to be the Bride and become the Lamb's wife. Remembering that John envisions members of his audience in masculine terms, this communal identity is a queer one, resisting common gender expectations. Being a Jesus follower requires giving up control and power to the one who similarly appears powerless. The image flies in the face of

---

20. Kelly Olson, *Dress and the Roman Woman: Self-Presentation and Society* (London: Routledge, 2008), 21–22.

Roman notions of masculinity, even though it fails to challenge ancient assumptions about women or brides. As we will see in Revelation 21, Revelation's Bride is somewhat passive and reflects a circumscribed ancient understanding of women's roles in the family.

John's vision of the Lamb's partner highlights, through the image of the shining garment, that "she" mirrors her husband's values and views, an ideal commended by Plutarch (e.g., *Con. prae.* 7.14). While this can be read as though the Bride is simply a reflection of her husband, what if her shining garment actually contributes to the light associated with the Lamb? However that may be, even though they were often depicted as passive and subordinate, women and wives in the ancient world often took on more active and engaged roles in their households and communities. As Katherine Bain notes, given the age disparity between brides and grooms at marriage, "elite women often survived their older husbands to become widows,"[21] a position that could leave them with wealth and status to use at least to some extent as they chose. Even though their power to donate was more limited than for men of similar status, elite women contributed to their communities by financing building projects, distributing goods like grain, and sponsoring athletic competitions.[22] Their generosity resulted in these women being recognized with important communal roles and honorifics, including the title of "high priestess" within the imperial cults. Those women who are remembered via the extant inscriptions from the ancient world are, however, the most privileged, the proverbial "1 percent" at the top of the social and economic pyramid.[23] Surely, being part of the Lamb's Bride involves using privilege for good or even divesting oneself of privilege in the manner of the slaughtered Lamb.

Despite John's use of the Bride to denote the community envisioned as being made up of men, theologians have long associated being a "Bride of Christ" with women, namely, nuns or other women dedicated to a religious life.[24] Writing in the early third century, for example, Tertullian

21. Katherine Bain, *Women's Socioeconomic Status and Religious Leadership in Asia Minor: In the First Two Centuries C.E.* (Minneapolis: Augsburg Fortress, 2014), 96.

22. Bain, *Women's Socioeconomic Status*, 134–38.

23. Steven J. Friesen, "High Priestesses of Asia and Emancipatory Interpretation," in *Walk in the Ways of Wisdom: Essays in Honor of Elisabeth Schüssler Fiorenza*, ed. Shelly Matthews, Cynthia Briggs Kittredge, and Melanie Johnson-Debaufre (Harrisburg, PA: Trinity Press International, 2003), 149.

24. Elizabeth A. Clark, *Ascetic Piety and Women's Faith: Essays on Late Ancient Christianity* (Lewiston, NY: E. Mellen Press, 1986), 3–4. Even though Revelation's bridal imagery has often been applied to women, some medieval male mystics, including

recommended that female virgins who dedicated their lives to following Christ veil themselves, as they were the "espoused" of Christ (*Virg.* 16). Even though some girls and women may have found the role of Christ's Bride limiting since it necessitated chastity and other commitments, for others the opportunity to "marry" Christ provided a chance to pursue vocations other than being a wife and mother. Voicing this idea were medieval women mystics who read themselves into Revelation's bridal imagery. In the thirteenth century, Mechthild of Magdeburg, a poet and beguine envisioned the erotic possibilities after the wedding banquet, when the virgins who constitute the Bride "entertain themselves with [the Lamb] and devour [his] love's desire." She even anticipates "intimate sweetness and intense oneness" (*Flowing Light of the Godhead* 3.1; see p. xlviii). Another thirteenth-century beguine, Hadewijch of Brabant, saw herself in the bridal imagery of Revelation, swooning and being "embraced . . . with an unheard-of wonder" upon her encounter with the Bridegroom (*Visions* 10.70).[25] For Hadewijch the relationship between the Bride and the Bridegroom was sometimes queer, as she both received and was received by the divine: "In that abyss I saw myself swallowed up. Then I received the certainty of being received, in this form, in my Beloved, and my Beloved also in me" (12.172). For Hadewijch, being the Bride did not require being receptive or passive.[26]

Similarly, Gertrude Morgan, an artist and visionary who lived in New Orleans, Louisiana, in the 1980s, adopted Revelation's bridal imagery in ways that highlighted her power. A self-proclaimed bride of Christ who left her husband and donned white clothes to embody her role as Bride, the extremely prolific artist often represents herself as the Bride of Revelation. In her illustrations, many done in pen and crayon, Morgan avoids literalism by depicting the "Lamb" as a mustachioed man standing by her side (fig. 6). Similarly, Morgan typically resists depicting the kind of

---

the Cistercian abbot Bernard of Clairvaux and Carmelite friar John of the Cross, similarly described their soul as a bride longing for connection with the heavenly Bridegroom. See Shawn M. Krahmer, "The Virile Bride of Bernard of Clairvaux," *CH* 69 (2000): 304–27; John of the Cross, *John of the Cross: Selected Writings,* trans. Kieran Kavanaugh (Mahwah, NJ: Paulist Press, 1987).

25. Lynn R. Huber, *Thinking and Seeing with Women in Revelation,* LNTS 475 (London: Bloomsbury, 2013), 115–26.

26. Karma Lochrie, "Mystical Acts, Queer Tendencies," in *Constructing Medieval Sexuality,* ed. Karma Lochrie, Peggy McCracken, and James A. Schultz (Minneapolis: University of Minnesota Press, 1997), 180–200.

passivity associated with Revelation's Bride. In this image, for example, the Bride takes the lead before God's throne, her groom standing a step behind her. Morgan reminds us that readers have a role to play in the interpretive process, and she prompts us to think about what it means to actively embody the role of Christ's partner.[27] Even though she does not use the language of "feminist" to describe her textual interpretation, Morgan's art shows how she reads "her way," as biblical scholar Renita Weems puts it, through the imagery of the Bride.[28]

A Blessing on the Wedding Banquet (19:9-10)

The heavenly hymn concludes when an angel, presumably the same one that led or accompanied John to view Babylon's judgment (17:1), commands John to write out a blessing (v. 9). This extends the wedding imagery by issuing an invitation to the wedding's supper or banquet (δεῖπνον). The recipients of the invitation, along with the blessing, are audience members who were just envisioned as the Lamb's Bride. Revelation's audience members were commanded to come out of Babylon (18:4), and now they are invited to celebrate the community's union with the Lamb. Noting that John shifts quickly from bridal imagery to the idea of guests at a wedding, some scholars conclude that this invitation indicates the Bride is not a communal image. They assume one cannot be both bride and guest simultaneously.[29] This abrupt metaphorical pivot is, however, consistent with Revelation's tendency to reject linear, or "straight," narratives. Revelation regularly veers from one image to the next with little warning. One minute, John is taking dictation from the Son of Humanity as he addresses seven communities in Asia Minor; the next minute, he finds himself in the heavenly throne room (4:1-2). Revelation's shift from envisioning the saints collectively as a Bride to issuing an invitation to individuals to celebrate the wedding allows a distinction to be drawn between the faithful as a whole and those who make up the faithful, just as the messages from the Son of Humanity to

27. William A. Fagaly, *Tools of Her Ministry: The Art of Sister Gertrude Morgan* (New York: Rizzoli, 2004), 7.

28. Renita J. Weems, "Reading *Her Way* through the Struggle: African American Women and the Bible," in *Stony the Road We Trod: African American Biblical Interpretation*, ed. Cain Hope Felder (Minneapolis: Fortress, 1991), 57–77.

29. E.g., Rossing, *Choice between Two Cities*, 140.

⁹And the angel said to me, "Write this: Blessed are those who are invited to the marriage supper of the Lamb." And he said to me, "These are true words of God." ¹⁰Then I fell down at his feet to worship him, but he said to me, "You must not do that! I am a fellow servant with you and your comrades who hold the testimony of Jesus. Worship God! For the testimony of Jesus is the spirit of prophecy."

the seven communities also called individuals to inhabit the role of victor (see pp. 25, 36–37). The community weds the Lamb while individually the members of Revelation's audiences are invited to celebrate this union at the wedding supper or banquet.

Banquet imagery appears throughout biblical traditions, including places where the banquet marks a victory. In Isaiah, for instance, the prophet describes an opulent feast "of rich food, a feast of well-aged wines, of rich food filled with marrow, of well-aged wines strained clear" that God provides after besting ruthless nations and conquering death (Isa 25:3-6; see also Ps 23:5; Jer 31:12-14).[30] In the Gospels this kind of banqueting imagery conveys an eschatological hope, as Jesus promises that God will draw together people from across the earth to eat together in the kingdom of heaven (Matt 8:11; Luke 13:29) and that he will drink wine together with his followers in his Father's kingdom (Matt 26:29; Mark 14:25; Luke 22:18). Revelation's wedding banquet evokes both this sense of a victory celebration, given Babylon's destruction, and the promise of a future reunion with Christ. The latter idea will be developed further when John returns to wedding imagery in Revelation 21:1-4. Interestingly, however, John's future vision of the New Jerusalem does not include banquet imagery; instead, the banquet takes place before that, and the menu is far from appetizing.

John again appears as a character in the text he narrates when he falls to worship his angel guide (v. 10). As in 10:4, John receives a supernatural scolding from the angel, who informs him that they are fellow servants or slaves and brothers, although the NRSV uses the language

---

30. Phillip J. Long, *Jesus the Bridegroom: The Origin of the Eschatological Feast as a Wedding Banquet in the Synoptic Gospels* (Eugene, OR: Wipf and Stock, 2013), 43.

of "comrade" here (see "Translation Matters: ἀδελφός"). In this way the text reinforces that God and the Lamb are the only suitable subjects of worship and honor. Belief in spiritual beings, minor deities and *daimonia*, beings that could control a person's fate, was pervasive in the ancient Mediterranean, so the angel's affirmation that humans are on the same hierarchical level as supernatural beings might be an important reminder for some early hearers of the text.

Figure 6: Gertrude Morgan, *Rev. 19 Chap.*, crayon and pencil on paper, United States, ca. 1960. Collections of the Louisiana State Museum, 1981.106.009. Photo: Louisiana State Museum, New Orleans, LA. Used with permission from the Collections of the Louisiana State Museum.

The Blood-Soaked Bridegroom (19:11-16)

Moments after being corrected for worshiping an angel, John sees heaven open and commands his listeners to see along with him (see "Translation Matters: ἰδού"). Upon doing so, modern audiences might think they have drifted onto the set of a Disney movie, since they see a kingly rider on a white horse, someone who looks a lot like a "Prince Charming" come to

Rev 19:11-16

¹¹Then I saw heaven opened, and there was a white horse! Its rider is called Faithful and True, and in righteousness he judges and makes war. ¹²His eyes are like a flame of fire, and on his head are many diadems; and he has a name inscribed that no one knows but himself. ¹³He is clothed in a robe dipped in blood, and his name is called The Word of God. ¹⁴And the armies of heaven, wearing fine linen, white and pure, were following him on white horses. ¹⁵From his mouth comes a sharp sword with which to strike down the nations, and he will rule them with a rod of iron; he will tread the wine press of the fury of the wrath of God the Almighty. ¹⁶On his robe and on his thigh he has a name inscribed, "King of kings and Lord of lords."

marry the Bride. The imagery extends the wedding imagery of the hymn by borrowing directly from a psalm celebrating the marriage of a royal bridegroom (Ps 45). While the bridegroom in the psalm is depicted as "the most handsome of men," however, having "grace poured upon [his] lips" (45:2), the Bridegroom of Revelation 19 is far from Prince Charming. Soon it becomes clear that this rider offers yet another "complicated" understanding of what it means for Christ to be a victor.

Psalm 45, the inspiration for the opening of these verses, brings together wedding and warrior symbolism in a celebration of a king approaching marriage. The psalmist gushes over the appearance of a "mighty one," a king who is a victorious warrior, employing imagery that teeters toward double entendre: The rider has a sword girded to his thigh, he uses arrows to pierce the hearts of enemies, and he carries a scepter of equity (vv. 5-6).[31] The phallic imagery is abundant. After describing the rider's military victories, the psalmist turns to address a "daughter" who will be the object of the king's affection. Just as ancient Greek and Roman authors and artists emphasize the bride's preparation, so the psalmist describes her being "bedecked" with gold-woven robes in her chamber and being led to the king (v. 13). This results in the rider and his bride producing offspring, ensuring the rider's name is celebrated in all generations (v. 17). His legacy is assured through marriage.

While the psalmist promises the name of the king (who is ironically unnamed in the text) will endure, John reports that the name of Revelation's Bridegroom is known only by himself (19:12). This mysterious

---

31. Denise Dombkowski Hopkins, *Psalms, Books 2–3*, WCS 21 (Collegeville, MN: Liturgical Press, 2016), 28.

name connects the Bridegroom to God, whose name some ancient Jews thought of as ineffable (i.e., its pronunciation is unknown or unspeakable) or as a name that should not be spoken out of reverence for divine power.[32] The idea that a divine figure has a secret name likewise reflects a Roman belief that the gods had names they used only among themselves (Iamblichus, *De Myst.* 7.4).[33] This mysterious name points to the Bridegroom's power, as no one can control the one whose name remains a mystery. At the same time, John weaves names and titles throughout this description of the Bridegroom (vv. 11-16), making the Bridegroom simultaneously unknowable and knowable.

The titles ascribed to the rider on the white horse communicate key characteristics about the figure. When he first appears, audience members learn he is called "Faithful and True" (v. 11). John uses "faithful" (πιστός) and "true" (ἀληθινός) to describe Christ early in the narrative (1:5; 3:7, 14), and the followers of Christ are similarly called to be and called "faithful" (2:10; 17:4). The Bridegroom's fidelity is like that of the ideal spouse, signaled visually on ancient funerary monuments with a hand clasp (*dextrarum iunctio*).[34] In addition, "Faithful and True" emphasizes the Bridegroom's virtuous character in contrast to the Beast and Babylon, and their puppet-master Satan, characterized as deceptive and untrustworthy (e.g., 16:13; 17:2). Immediately after saying the Bridegroom's name is unknown, John reveals his name is the Word (ὁ λόγος) of God (19:13), an apparent allusion to the opening chapter of the Gospel of John (1:1). In the Gospel, as Gail R. O'Day argued, Jesus's identity as God's Word points to the fact that he reveals God and that encountering him is a revelatory event. Jesus prompts others to either accept or reject him as the one who makes God known.[35] Similarly, the revelation of the Bridegroom on the white horse prompts John's audiences to decide how they understand and will respond. Will they join their Bridegroom in the fight that lies ahead, or will they continue to associate themselves with Babylon, the Great Prostitute?

---

32. Thank you to Amy-Jill Levine for this observation. For a discussion of the different ways ancient Jews related to the divine name, see Nathanael Andrade, "The Jewish Tetragrammaton: Secrecy, Community, and Prestige among Greek-Writing Jews of the Early Roman Empire," *JSJ* 46 (2015): 198–223.

33. Andrade, "Jewish Tetragrammaton."

34. Hersch, *Roman Wedding*, 205–6.

35. Gail R. O'Day, "Narrative Mode and Theological Claim: A Study in the Fourth Gospel," *JBL* 105 (1986): 657–68.

In addition, like the kingly groom of Psalm 45, this Bridegroom presents as a kingly figure. He wears *many* (πολλά) diadems or crowns (19:12) and inscribed or written (γεγραμμένον) on his robe and thigh are the titles "King of kings and Lord of lords" (v. 16). In contrast to earthly figures claiming power and authority and adorned with blasphemous names (e.g., 13:1-4), this one is truly "ruler of the kings of the earth" (see 1:5; 17:4).

While the rider in the psalm appears wearing garments fragrant with myrrh (Ps 45:8), Revelation's "prince" shows up in a blood-soaked robe (Rev 19:13). The source of the blood is not identified and, even though the Son of Humanity "reaped" a bloody harvest earlier (14:17-20), at this point the Bridegroom has not engaged in the kind of violence that might lead to bloody robes.[36] Perhaps the blood comes from the Bridegroom himself, since under this robe is the slaughtered Lamb. Even though, as Brian K. Blount observes, "the Lamb's blood is spilled offstage,"[37] the idea of the Lamb as bloody "sticks" with the character throughout the narrative (1:5; 5:9; 7:14; 12:11).[38] Elsewhere in Revelation, the faithful wash their garments in the Lamb's blood, which makes these garments white (7:14). Blood was metaphorically depicted as a detergent for the washing away of sin.

The thought of red stains on white clothes strikes fear in the hearts of many people who menstruate or have menstruated, me included. Even though periods are natural and part of the "cycle of life," as explained in the pastel-colored pamphlets given out by parents, teachers, or school nurses, they have been a source of shame and something we are taught to hide. I can still feel the embarrassment and anxiety I experienced starting my period while I was wearing white pants, part of my middle-school marching band uniform, during a local parade. This shame stems from cultural disdain for women's bodies and their "leakiness," an idea that reflects ancient perspectives that understood women's bodies as more porous than men.[39] Perhaps this Bridegroom's bloody robe reveals a trans-

36. Greg Carey, "Revelation's Violence Problem: Mapping Essential Questions," *PRSt* 42 (2015): 299.

37. Brian K. Blount, *Revelation: A Commentary* (Louisville: Westminster John Knox, 2009), 352.

38. For a discussion of "stickiness," see Rhiannon Graybill, "Fuzzy, Messy, Icky: The Edges of Consent in Hebrew Bible Rape Narratives and Rape Culture," *BCT* 15 (2019): 3, https://www.bibleandcriticaltheory.com/issues/vol-15-no-2-2019-bible -and-critical-theory/fuzzy-messy-icky-the-edges-of-consent-in-hebrew-bible-rape -narratives-and-rape-culture/.

39. Candida R. Moss, "The Man with the Flow of Power: Porous Bodies in Mark 5:25-34," *JBL* 129 (2010): 507–19.

masculine identity (someone assigned female at birth but who identifies as a man),[40] suggesting familiarity with menstruating and the anxiety that comes with its unpredictability. In this case, the Bridegroom's refusal to let his leaky and bloody body stop him from engaging in battle encourages us to embrace "bleeding through [our] jeans" to quote spoken word artist Alix Olson.[41] The Bridegroom functions as a model of resisting period shame, something that leads some to hide tampons or pads when they go to the bathroom or even skip school because of "period poverty," that is, not having access to feminine hygiene products.[42]

Taking this bloody image even further, we might see the Bridegroom as embracing the power associated with menstrual blood in some Roman contexts. As mentioned earlier, Pliny the Elder reported that menstrual blood could destroy vermin, like beetles and caterpillars, but also crops as well. It could be an effective remedy, when applied to wool, when someone has been bitten by a rabid dog (*Nat.* 28.23; see p. 210). Maybe this transmasculine Messiah harnesses the superpower of menstrual blood to conquer those who refuse to acknowledge his authority and his manliness.

Bloody robes might also reveal experiences of sorrow and pain. The appearance of blood signals miscarriage and can be associated with endometriosis and fibroids. What would Christian hope look like if we imagined a heavenly Bridegroom familiar with these experiences? Personally, I imagine that such a Bridegroom's wrath might be aimed at those who defund reproductive health care in God's name or who fail to trust women's decisions about their health.[43]

At the same time, the Bridegroom's blood-soaked garment echoes prophetic descriptions of God as a warrior with "crimson" garments (e.g., Isa 63:1-3),[44] revealing a more traditional notion of power—the ability to shed another's blood. The imagery recalls the promise of the throne room, that there will be a messianic figure who conquers like a lion, a predator that tears and devours its prey (5:5). Revelation's narrative is not

40. For the definition of "transmasculine," see Susan Stryker, *Transgender History: The Roots of Today's Revolution*, 2nd ed. (Berkeley: Seal Press, 2017), 20.

41. Alix Olson, "Built Like That," *Built Like That* (Decatur, GA: Subtle Sister Productions, 2001).

42. Jennifer Weiss-Wolf, *Periods Gone Public: Taking a Stand for Menstrual Equity* (New York: Arcade, 2017).

43. For a discussion of reproductive justice from the perspective of a feminist Christian ethicist, see Rebecca Todd Peters, *Trust Women: A Progressive Christian Argument for Reproductive Justice* (Boston: Beacon, 2018).

44. David E. Aune, *Revelation*, WBC 52 A-C (Dallas: Word Books, 1998), 1048–49.

entirely linear, and John will soon describe the Bridegroom killing those who worship the Beast (19:20). The royal wedding segues into a blood bath, the original "Red Wedding."[45] In this vein, the Bridegroom revels in hypermasculinity, making war and dominating the nations by ruling them with a rod of iron (v. 15). This phallic symbol provides a striking contrast to the scepter of equity wielded by the rider in John's source (Ps 45:6), as it implies ruling with violence. The "male child" of Revelation 12 certainly has grown up (12:5), reminding us that male children are traditionally steeped in cultures of violence. Even parents who work to present alternatives for their children cannot entirely shield them from the influence of toxic masculinity; rather, communities and cultures must work together to shift gendered expectations around violence and power.

A Gruesome Wedding Banquet (19:17-21)

The earlier invitation to the wedding supper prepares Revelation's audiences to view a feast (19:9); however, John puts a gruesome spin on that imagery by having the guests, his audience members, hear an angel invite all the birds of mid-heaven to a banquet of flesh, mostly human. The angel makes sure the birds and Revelation's hearers are aware of the meal being offered, repeating the term for flesh (σάρξ) five times in a single verse (v. 18). The invitation, which emphasizes the range of people whose flesh will be consumed, precedes a description of the battle waged by the Bridegroom and his army who follow him against the Beast and the kings of the earth (v. 20). The banquet is announced, the Bridegroom "sources" the food, and the birds subsequently gorge themselves (v. 21). The thought of the birds being "gorged" (χορτάζω) on the humans' flesh (ἐκ τῶν σαρχῶν αὐτῶν) plays up the massiveness of this feast.

John's focus on the consumption of human flesh by birds is the stuff of nightmares and seems a lot like the inspiration for Alfred Hitchcock's 1963 horror movie, *The Birds*. The scene, which evokes Ezekiel 39:17-20, aims to arouse the audience's disgust and a disdain for those whose bodies provide the main course. Not only have they been defeated, but they are also denied a proper burial, left to have their flesh picked apart by birds. Similar references to enemies' bodies being left to birds and dogs are found elsewhere in biblical literature (e.g., 1 Sam 17:44, 46; Deut

---

45. "Red Wedding" refers to a massacre that takes place at a wedding in an episode of the popular television drama, *Game of Thrones*. David Nutter, "The Rains of the Castamere," *Game of Thrones* (HBO, June 2, 2013).

¹⁷Then I saw an angel standing in the sun, and with a loud voice he called to all the birds that fly in midheaven, "Come, gather for the great supper of God, ¹⁸to eat the flesh of kings, the flesh of captains, the flesh of the mighty, the flesh of horses and their riders—flesh of all, both free and slave, both small and great." ¹⁹Then I saw the beast and the kings of the earth with their armies gathered to make war against the rider on the horse and against his army. ²⁰And the beast was captured, and with it the false prophet who had performed in its presence the signs by which he deceived those who had received the mark of the beast and those who worshiped its image. These two were thrown alive into the lake of fire that burns with sulfur. ²¹And the rest were killed by the sword of the rider on the horse, the sword that came from his mouth; and all the birds were gorged with their flesh.

28:26).[46] The Bridegroom's enemies are humiliated, and Revelation's audience members are reminded that following the Beast leads to dire consequences. Still, the imagery, along with the earlier depiction of the Great Prostitute being burnt like a sacrifice, seems like overkill (pun intended). The excessiveness of the death and its particularly gruesome nature is disgusting and disgusts. That is, it certainly seems like John wants his audiences to react viscerally to *all the flesh* and be tempted to look away. And, that, it seems, is part of the point. Revelation's hearers might want to stop up their ears and cover their eyes, and modern interpreters might want to downplay the grossness of this imagery. As Yvonne Sherwood explains about disgusting images in the Hebrew Bible prophets, "Perhaps prophecy, far from seducing the ear with pretty images, sometimes actively courts its own rejection and defeat; perhaps it occasionally resorts to the kind of language which ensures that the eyes will be plastered over and the ears made heavy—in horror (Isa 6:10)."[47] In some sense, John, like prophets before him, insists that if his audiences want only things that delight and please, they need to look to the Beast, whose worship includes tricks and great signs (13:13-14). Followers of the slaughtered Lamb, who is simultaneously a slaughtering Lion, are forced to face the reality of death, decay, and disgust that potentially comes with their choice to follow the Lamb. Moreover, for modern Christian readers of Revelation, there is an ethical demand here to see and acknowledge the

46. Aune, *Revelation*, 1067–68.

47. Yvonne Sherwood, "Prophetic Scatology: Prophecy and the Art of Sensation," *Semeia* 82 (1998): 213.

horrors our tradition, following the Bridegroom, has wrought—crusades, inquisitions, enslavement, etc.

Between the invitation to the supper and the birds with full crops, John references briefly the capture of the Beast and the False Prophet (the second beast who promotes the worship of the first) and their being thrown alive into the lake of fire (19:20). It's as if John does not want to give too much attention to these characters, so he includes their capture as an afterthought. Similarly, he offers a short description of the Bridegroom killing "the rest," referring to the Beast's followers (v. 21). In contrast to the angel's extensive list of the types of flesh on the banquet menu, before the Bridegroom's sword those who follow the Beast are stripped of identity markers. They are effectively dehumanized.

Immediately after mentioning that the Bridegroom kills with his sword, John clarifies that this sword comes from his mouth. Even though the imagery was first mentioned in Revelation 1:16 and then again in 19:15, here it seems like a quick afterthought or qualification. As though John were to say, "The Bridegroom *kills* his enemies with a sword. But the sword comes out of his mouth, so maybe it isn't *that* bad of a killing." Perhaps John is wavering on his depiction of a genderqueer Messiah (see pp. 72–79), emphasizing first his masculine strength and aggression and then qualifying that depiction with a reminder that the Bridegroom is more complicated. The Bridegroom's phallic sword isn't quite what it seemed.

Many interpreters understandably want to distance this image of Christ from Revelation's depictions of violence and disentangle Revelation from justifications of war and killing.[48] In so doing, the tendency is to emphasize how the Bridegroom's sword comes from his *mouth*, suggesting that the Bridegroom "kills" through words of judgment. Barbara Rossing, for example, argues that this sword is "a reversal as unexpected as the substitution of a lamb for a lion" and that this reversal "undercut[s] violence by emphasizing Jesus' testimony and the word of God."[49] From this perspective, even though a surface reading of the text suggests it is full of violence, attention to its use of imagery and its privileging of the Lamb reveals the exact opposite. For Rossing, readings of Revelation that interpret its violence literally, such as readings by evangelical dispensa-

---

48. Some interpreters see Revelation's violence as justification for rejecting the text. For a discussion of this, see Susan E. Hylen, "Metaphor Matters: Violence and Ethics in Revelation," *CBQ* 73 (2011): 777–78.

49. Barbara R. Rossing, *The Rapture Exposed: The Message of Hope in the Book of Revelation*, 2nd ed. (New York: Basic Books, 2004), 120–21.

tionalist Christians who believe the Battle of Armageddon is on the near horizon, "hijack" the Lamb, a symbol of self-giving love and an example of "accepting the violence inflicted upon him in crucifixion."[50] Brian K. Blount likewise highlights Revelation's Lamb as modeling "non-violent resistance" in the face of evil.[51] Those who follow the Lamb to victory do so through their testimony, which can lead to death (e.g., 12:11). For Rossing, Blount, and many others, Revelation's depiction of violence is a recognition of violence and injustice in the world, and not a call to prepare for physical battle, despite John's vision of the coming armies of heaven (19:14).

At the same time, it is not possible to ignore that, as biblical scholar Greg Carey observes, Revelation "give[s] voice to the desire for violence on the part of its audience."[52] The text reveals that even within a movement centered around a victim of violence, the slaughtered Lamb, there is hope for vengeance against those who have been oppressors and a desire to envision violence against those understood as enemies. Revelation, Carey notes, displaces or redirects this desire for violent action by placing it clearly under God's purview and depicting it coming via the ultimate victim and, in this indirect way, through a sword of the mouth. At the same time, members of Revelation's audiences are encouraged to celebrate the violence of God and the Lamb in the book's many hymns,[53] as we saw at the beginning of Revelation 19, when Babylon's body is burned. John may not be calling the faithful to take up arms, but his vision encourages an attitude toward violence that is disturbing and wrong. This is especially problematic when the fortunes of Revelation's audience members shift, when those who follow the Lamb are no longer a despised minority but a group that exercises political and social power. In these contexts, reading Revelation should be done through a lens of repentance and as a reminder that the Lamb's armies defeat the powerful, kings and captains, regardless of their religious affiliations or cultural contexts. Perhaps the invitation to the wedding supper issued in 19:9 is more of a warning than a blessing: "Beware of becoming the main course at the wedding of the Lamb."

Finally, the imagery depicting Christ as one who acts violently reminds us of the importance of challenging the common and mistaken

---

50. Rossing, *Rapture Exposed*, 135.
51. Blount, *Revelation*, 29.
52. Carey, "Revelation's Violence Problem," 300.
53. Carey, "Revelation's Violence Problem," 301.

association of violence with the "God of the Old Testament" in contrast to a supposed loving Jesus. I have spent considerable time in Christian religious settings and have heard this trope over and over. I also hear it regularly from my students who have learned it in their churches and Sunday school classrooms. It reflects an anti-Jewish bias first by suggesting that Judaism equals the Old Testament and second by suggesting that Christianity is somehow more peace-loving and therefore advanced than Judaism. It also fails to account for the violence throughout Revelation.

Revelation 20

Millennial Hope?

These last few chapters of Revelation promise again and again God's victory over the evil forces and institutions that mimic the divine and "distort creation."[1] The destruction of Babylon in Revelation 17–18 foretells the end of imperial systems, epitomized in cities like Babylon and Rome, and the defeat of the Beast, False Prophet, and those kings and armies who do their bidding makes clear that those complicit in these systems have no future (19:19-21). Now, however, John sees the end to evil itself, although this end comes in stages rather than a single action. Still, the end of evil offers images of hope, including resurrection and a millennial reign, that have teased and tempted interpreters for centuries. Although light on details, this chapter has consistently invited speculation about the end of time that has had real impacts on the lives of Christians and those with whom they share the planet. Unfortunately, these encounters often replicate the kyriarchal and oppressive systems that supposedly come to an end with the binding of Satan. As a result, this chapter presents a challenge for feminist Christians. We are invited to imagine being in community with Christ and embracing the hope of resurrection while ensuring that we hold out this hope for others.

1. Gail R. O'Day, "Revelation," in *Theological Bible Commentary*, ed. Gail R. O'Day and David L. Petersen (Louisville: Westminster John Knox, 2009), 478.

A Brief Account of the Millennium (20:1-3)

The opening verses of chapter 20 make real heaven's victory over evil. John depicts this victory in spatial terms, as an angel comes *down* (καταβαίνω) from heaven to throw God's enemies into the bottomless pit or abyss (ἄβυσσος). Heaven and the abyss are as far apart as physically possible. The angel brings along the equipment necessary for the job, including a great chain and the key to the pit. The physicality of the imagery makes evil seem easy to control, as though one only needs to visit the local hardware store or purchase the proper equipment or borrow it from a neighbor. Earlier in the narrative, another angel, the fifth trumpet angel, possessed the key, although he used it to open the shaft to the abyss, which let loose blinding smoke and fearsome locusts ruled by Abaddon (9:1-11). Heavenly agents have the tools to restrain evil, even though those same tools can be used to unleash death and destruction.

The back and forth of allowing evil forces to act against humanity and the earth and subsequently subduing them continues in this chapter. In these first verses, the angel who descends from heaven quickly seizes, binds, locks up, *and* seals over the evil one for a thousand years (20:2-3). The repeated description of the angel's actions makes it sound as though, according to Brian K. Blount, "God's archenemy . . . is not coming out any time soon."[2] Still, almost as an afterthought, John notes that after the thousand years, Satan "must be let out for a little while" (v. 3). While a "little while" (μικρὸν χρόνον) is nothing compared to the thousand years (τὰ χίλια) when Satan will be locked away, the necessity of this furlough remains shrouded in mystery. Has Satan worked out a deal with God? Does that "ancient serpent" have some incriminating evidence from back in Eden? Whatever the exact reason for this "little season," as the KJV describes it, we should not imagine that the divine is ambivalent about ending evil. Instead, this is a realistic assessment that evil can and will appear again even when it seems like it has been completely buried.

Those Who Reign with Christ (20:4-6)

Satan's thousand-year imprisonment provides a respite for those faithful to the Lamb and an opportunity for interpreters to imagine a community unhindered by the evil forces of Satan. It is a time when

---

2. Brian K. Blount, *Revelation: A Commentary* (Louisville: Westminster John Knox, 2009), 361.

²⁰:¹Then I saw an angel coming down from heaven, holding in his hand the key to the bottomless pit and a great chain. ²He seized the dragon, that ancient serpent, who is the Devil and Satan, and bound him for a thousand years, ³and threw him into the pit, and locked and sealed it over him, so that he would deceive the nations no more, until the thousand years were ended. After that he must be let out for a little while.

⁴Then I saw thrones, and those seated on them were given authority to judge. I also saw the souls of those who had been beheaded for their testimony to Jesus and for the word of God. They had not worshiped the beast or its image and had not received its mark on their foreheads or their hands. They came to life and reigned with Christ a thousand years. ⁵(The rest of the dead did not come to life until the thousand years were ended.) This is the first resurrection. ⁶Blessed and holy are those who share in the first resurrection. Over these the second death has no power, but they will be priests of God and of Christ, and they will reign with him a thousand years.

the people of earth will be free from the deception of Satan and those who manifest his schemes in political and social systems. Interpreters describe this thousand-year period, which occurs before the coming of the final heavenly kingdom, as "the millennium," since the Latin word for thousand is *mille*. The idea of an interim period ruled by a messianic figure before a final judgment parallels other apocalyptic texts (e.g., 2 Bar. 39:7-40:3; 4 Ezra 7:28-29), although John's claim that this period is one thousand years is unique. Like others in the text, this number is symbolic, and it suggests perfection as ten cubed (10x10x10). This millennium should be perfection embodied in time.

Even though a thousand years is, obviously, a very long time, John's description of this period is brief and light on detail. John twice mentions, however, that these resurrected souls reign or will reign *with* Christ (20:4, 6). This emphasis reminds hearers that earlier in Revelation's narrative, John characterized the faithful as kings and priests that serve God (1:6); this reality will be visible during the millennium. The language of sitting on thrones echoes John's first vision of the throne room, where he witnessed the throne of God and the thrones on which the twenty-four elders were seated (4:2-4). Since the identity of those sitting on the thrones is not immediately apparent, John notes they are "the souls of those who had been beheaded for their testimony to Jesus and for the word of God" (v. 4).

The assurance of resurrection pervades these verses. Just as Christ is the "firstborn of the dead" (1:5), so those who follow him will "come to life" and be part of the "first resurrection" (20:4-5). According to the text, these resurrected ones are blessed and holy (v. 6). In offering this vision, John draws on biblical promises of life after death (Ezek 37; Dan 12:1-3) and echoes the hope of resurrection found in rabbinic Jewish teachings as well. The Amidah, a rabbinic prayer, affirms, "He sustains the living with kindness and revives the dead with great mercy, supports the falling, heals the sick, releases captives, and keeps faith with those who sleep in the dust."[3] Through resurrection God will fulfill divine promises to restore and renew God's people.[4]

The description of the resurrected as "souls" may sound as though John envisions resurrection as a spiritual reality and not as a bodily event. Throughout Revelation, however, the term translated as "soul" (ψυχή) is used more generally in reference to lives and even used to describe living things in the text, such as the "living creatures in the sea" (8:9; see also 16:3). When talking about Roman enslavement, John does speak in terms of bodies and souls (Rev 18:13), but for the most part, Revelation seems to avoid this kind of dualism. Instead, the souls of the beheaded can be understood in line with Jewish hopes in a bodily resurrection, a hope also articulated by Paul (1 Cor 15:35-58). Ancient and medieval Christians similarly imagined resurrection as physical, even envisioning dismembered bodies being reconstituted. A twelfth-century painting from a chapel in Rome, now in the Vatican Museums, captures this almost humorously; fish, birds, and land animals seem to regurgitate or bring up human body parts so these individuals can be made complete at the resurrection.[5] This depiction captures the hope of the resurrection, as the body will be re-membered and made whole.

In fact, these souls need to be re-membered since they are decapitated. Their description as beheaded conjures the Roman practice of capital punishment, which sometimes used this form of execution. The specific term used by John to describe this punishment, πελεκίζω, alludes, how-

3. As quoted in Jon D. Levenson, *Resurrection and the Restoration of Israel: The Ultimate Victory of the God of Life* (New Haven: Yale University Press, 2006), 3.

4. Levenson, *Resurrection and the Restoration of Israel*, 30.

5. Nicolaus and Johannes, *Last Judgment*, tempera on wood, late twelfth century, 40526, Vatican Museums, https://m.museivaticani.va/content/museivaticani-mobile/en/collezioni/musei/la-pinacoteca/sala-i---secolo-xii-xv/nicolo-e-giovanni--giudizio-finale.html.

ever, to the practice of using an axe for beheading, which was restricted by Roman law. Instead, decapitation was done by sword (Justinian, *Digest* 48.19.8.1). This detail suggests that John may be referring to capital punishment by Roman authorities more generally. The Greek word for axes, πελέκεις, was used to describe the *fasces* (Latin), a bundle of axes carried by Roman lictors or magistrates symbolizing their authority and power.[6] Being beheaded by axe (πελεκίζω) might be John's way of saying Roman power kills these souls. Another first-century Jewish author, Josephus, used the verb similarly (*Ant.* 15.8).

Despite depicting those on the thrones using capital punishment, Rome was not searching out and punishing Jesus followers at the time of Revelation's penning. John may have sensed this kind of persecution was on the horizon, as the correspondence between Pliny and Trajan implies (see p. lxxxi). Still, the imagery of the beheaded seems anachronistic. Revelation's emphasis on the conflict between Jesus followers and Rome belies that some in the book's audiences may have benefited from and welcomed Roman rule. This, perhaps, is the point. The idealization of future victims of capital punishment reveals John's conviction that opposition to Roman hegemony is the way of the Lamb. Thus, as Blount describes it, John offers his audiences "a delicious realization of poetic justice" by depicting those whom the empire will judge with authority to judge.[7]

While John notes that those seated on the thrones have been granted authority to judge, he never describes them acting on that authority. I tend to think this is because they know firsthand the horror of state-sponsored killing (despite John's apparent taste for vengeance). They refuse to give back what they have been given now that they reign. The brutality of Roman punishment made it into current headlines recently after a team of archeologists from Great Britain released a report on a Roman-era burial ground excavated between 2001 and 2010.[8] Among the graves were seventeen decapitated bodies, skulls placed neatly between the deceased people's feet.[9] The report's details include descriptions

---

6. David E. Aune, *Revelation*, WBC 52A-C (Dallas: Word Books, 1998), 1086–87.

7. Blount, *Revelation*, 364.

8. Jenny Gross, "Archaeologists Uncover Decapitated Bodies from Roman Britain," *The New York Times*, June 2, 2021, https://www.nytimes.com/2021/06/02/world/europe/roman-burials-decapitated.html.

9. Rob Wiseman, Benjamin Neil, and Francesca Mazzilli, "Extreme Justice: Decapitations and Prone Burials in Three Late Roman Cemeteries at Knobb's Farm, Cambridgeshire," *Britannia* 52 (November 2021): 150.

of how victims were decapitated from behind and evidence of bodily trauma, such as flaying.[10] These burials are a grim reminder of the violence deployed by Romans to maintain control and power. In an account of rhetorical controversies by Seneca the Elder, beheading is described as an appropriate punishment when the purpose is to create a sense of terror (*Controversiae* 9.2.8).[11] Perhaps Revelation's headless saints are reserving their judicial authority to indict those governments and government agents that continue to terrorize their citizens through violence. More important, Revelation's vision of the millennium promises life to those who have experienced death and not just any death but a culturally shameful death.

Promises of resurrection and life after death can sometimes seem like empty words to those left behind, especially when death comes too soon because of violence. The hope imbued within the idea of resurrection feels distant to me today, the day after a school shooting claiming twenty-one lives in Uvalde, Texas, and a week after ten people were shot and killed by a racist gunman in a grocery store in Buffalo, New York. Mass shootings are endemic to the United States, where guns, including automatic weapons, are accessible and legal to own.[12] In this context, many political leaders avoid dealing directly with the issue of gun violence and instead offer "thoughts and prayers" for the victims and their families. These platitudes make it difficult to hear and appreciate the hope of resurrection. Our children, parents, grandparents, friends, and neighbors should be alive here and now, not just there and then in a millennial kingdom. Justice deferred in this way seems like justice denied. Despite the meaningless words behind many offers of "thoughts and prayers," the promise of resurrection is *not* a call to give up working for change. Additionally, resurrection is not a call to adopt either/or thinking, the thought that we must choose between either justice now or justice later. Instead, the possibility of resurrection beckons us to embrace the impossible and both/and thinking: we can experience *both* justice in the present *and* a future resurrection. This vision of the souls reigning with

10. Wiseman, Neil, and Mazzilli, "Extreme Justice," 144.

11. Richard A. Bauman, *Crime and Punishment in Ancient Rome* (London: Routledge, 2002), 14.

12. Christopher B. Hays, "Gun Violence in America: A Theological Treatment for a Deadly Epidemic," in *God and Guns: The Bible against American Gun Culture*, ed. Christopher B. Hays and C. L. Crouch (Louisville: Westminster John Knox, 2021), 1–12.

Christ reminds Christians that our faith, as articulated in the Apostles' Creed, includes reconciliation with those in the "communion of saints." We will meet the beheaded and those killed by gun violence and must account for our role in responding to these injustices.

The lack of detailed description concerning the millennium has spawned speculation among Christian interpreters about the nature of this reign. In the early fifth century, Augustine already felt the need to correct those he described as "chiliasts," namely, those who focused on a literal reading of Revelation's description of the thousand-year reign. According to Augustine, chiliasts believed the millennium would be a time of the "most immoderate carnal feasts in which food and drink will be so plentiful that not only will they observe no limits of moderation but will also exceed all bounds even of incredulity" (*Civ.* 20.7). Augustine decried this view as a failure to understand the symbolic or allegorical nature of the text, explaining that the millennial kingdom exists already within the Christian Church and that the saints already reign with Christ (*Civ.* 20.9). Augustine's view, sometimes called *amillennial* since it eschews the idea of a literal thousand-year reign, remains the dominant perspective on the millennium in Catholic theology.[13]

Augustine's teaching, while influential, was not the end of the story regarding the millennium. In fact, the promise of a kingdom where the faithful, interpreted as Christians, reign has given rise to a steady stream of crusading, colonizing, and even communitarian movements in the name of Christ. In the 1960s, historian Norman Cohn cataloged many of the medieval European efforts at bringing about the millennium in the highly influential book *The Pursuit of the Millennium*. Among the "revolutionary millenarians" Cohn noted were egalitarian and peasant movements, such as the Taborites in what is now the Czech Republic, who advanced a philosophy of "nothing Mine nor Thine" or holding all possessions in common.[14] One of the most famous millennially motivated figures from the European continent, however, is not discussed by Cohn—Christopher Columbus.

13. For more on amillennial interpretations of Revelation, see Judith L. Kovacs and Christopher Rowland, *Revelation: The Apocalypse of Jesus Christ* (Malden, MA: Blackwell, 2004), 206–9.

14. Norman Cohn, *The Pursuit of the Millennium: Revolutionary Millenarians and Mystical Anarchists of the Middle Ages*, rev. ed. (Oxford: Oxford University Press, 1970), 217.

Sponsored by the Spanish monarchy, the Italian explorer Christopher Columbus was motivated by a desire to bring about Jesus's Second Coming and the millennial reign. Along with finding a passage to Jerusalem, Columbus characterized his voyage west as an effort to convert the peoples he encountered and acquire the funds sufficient for a crusade. In a 1493 letter to King Ferdinand and Queen Isabella about his first voyage, Columbus specifically mentions the "conquest of Jerusalem, for which purpose this enterprise was taken."[15] Writing in 1500, Columbus claimed being chosen by God to help bring about the millennium, explaining, "Of the new heaven and earth which our Lord made, as St. John wrote in the Apocalypse, after he had spoken it by the mouth of Isaiah, He made me the messenger thereof, and showed me where to go."[16] Moreover, near the end of his life, Columbus compiled *El Libro de las Profecías*, a book of writings about the end times and biblical prophecies, including references to writings of theologians such as Augustine and Nicholas of Lyra (a Franciscan who wrote a popular commentary on Revelation), documenting his millennial eagerness.[17] Columbus paved the way for others, like the sixteenth-century Spanish Friar Francisco de La Cruz, who saw Peru as ripe for enacting the millennial kingdom. Among the millennial ideas de La Cruz espoused were the "encomienda system," essentially the enslavement of indigenous people by the colonizers, and polygamy.[18] In fact, as Jacqueline M. Hidalgo, a contributor to the next chapter, explains in her book *Revelation in Aztlán*, John's vision of the New Jerusalem provided a kind of blueprint for missions in the so-called New World. In these missions, the Spanish tried to mold indigenous peoples into their subjects, often against their will and with disastrous consequences. Not only were significant parts of indigenous cultures repressed and lost, the lives of many were cut short due to violence and disease.[19] Simply put, the legacy

15. As quoted in Carol Delaney, "Columbus's Ultimate Goal: Jerusalem," *Comparative Studies in Society and History* 48 (2006): 266. For a more detailed discussion of how Christopher Columbus's apocalyptic views contributed to the colonization of the Americas, see Jacqueline M. Hidalgo, *Revelation in Aztlán: Scriptures, Utopias, and the Chicano Movement* (New York: Palgrave Macmillan, 2016), 106–9, and David A. Sánchez, *From Patmos to the Barrio: Subverting Imperial Myths* (Minneapolis: Fortress, 2008), 52–53.

16. Delaney, "Columbus's Ultimate Goal," 271–72. This same quote is noted by Hidalgo, *Revelation in Aztlán*, 106–7.

17. Delaney, "Columbus's Ultimate Goal," 272–73.

18. Kovacs and Rowland, *Revelation*, 212.

19. Hidalgo, *Revelation in Aztlán*, 109.

of Columbus, which includes the colonization of the Americas and subjugation of the lands' inhabitants, is the legacy of Revelation's millennium.

Millennial thinking did not end with the colonization of the Americas. It continues to have political and social impacts, especially within the United States, where evangelical Christianity has had considerable influence. Various thinkers have adopted the promise of a millennial kingdom on earth to different ends. Those often described as "postmillennial" see in Revelation 20 a call to create a "peaceable kingdom." Through good works, such as providing for the poor and hungry, postmillennialist thinkers of the nineteenth century, in particular, believed they could inaugurate the millennium and hasten Christ's return.[20] More popular in the twentieth century, however, has been "premillennial" theology (also sometimes called "dispensationalism"), which predicts that Christ's return and the rapture of the faithful, an idea derived from 1 Thessalonians 4:15-17, will take place before the millennium (hence "premillennial") and after or during a time of great tribulation and persecution for believers. Within this scenario, believers are called to stay faithful and bring others into the fold of Christianity as the Beast, also described as the Antichrist, exercises power over the earth; however, the faithful will be vindicated when they return to earth with Christ to rule over all things.[21]

While postmillennial thought aligns more closely to my values as a feminist and politically progressive Christian, I see the connections made by premillennialists. This comes, undoubtedly, from having been taught this way of reading the text as a child. My mom and aunt, along with friends and relatives, were avid consumers of premillennial media, such as Billy Graham's *Approaching Hoofbeats: The Four Horsemen of the Apocalypse* (1983), Hal Lindsey's *The Late Great Planet Earth* (1970), and the many works of Tim LaHaye, including the Left Behind novels LaHaye co-wrote with Jerry B. Jenkins in the 1990s and 2000s. Conversations about Armageddon and the end times were part of the background noise in my church and home, and I am not alone. According to LaHaye's 2016 obituary in *The New York Times*, more than 65 million copies of the Left Behind books sold worldwide and were "perhaps the most commercially

---

20. Matthew Avery Sutton, *American Apocalypse: A History of Modern Evangelicalism* (Cambridge, MA: Harvard University Press, 2014), 14.

21. For an introduction into the complexities of American premillennial thinking, see Sutton, *American Apocalypse*, 18–22.

successful Christian fiction in publishing history."[22] While acknowledging that their work is fictional, in *Kingdom Come: The Final Victory*, LaHaye and Jenkins offer very specific descriptions of what they imagine the millennial kingdom will be like. Their predictions include everyone speaking Hebrew and the absence of sexual urges among the faithful, presumably an allusion to the virgins in Revelation 14:4.[23] The kingdom envisioned, moreover, has a very clear hierarchy. As one character in the novel narrates to another, "The government now starts with the Christ and extends through His prince and king of Israel, David; the apostles, who are now judges over the twelve tribes; their princes; local judges under them; counselors; and finally, you foreigners [non-Jews]."[24] The millennial kingdom is clearly a kyriarchal kingdom with the Christian "Lord of lords" at the top of the chain.

Even though the Left Behind books are fiction, the authors espouse a theological perspective that has real-world consequences.[25] For a variety of reasons, including their embrace of mass media, premillennialists have been especially influential in the world of American politics, advocating for politically conservative causes, such as anti-abortion legislation, anti-LGBTQIA+ efforts (including conversion therapy), and pro-gun advocacy. Premillennial thought contributes most notably to US foreign policy toward Israel in which, as Barbara Rossing explains, Israel's significance is reduced to a "player in the dispensationalist Christian end-times drama."[26] Premillennial-inspired support of Israel against Palestine and other Middle Eastern countries places little or no value in the State of Israel itself; instead, conflict in the Middle East is reduced to a sign of Jesus's return, and the center stage for his appearance will be a rebuilt temple in Jerusalem.[27] Thus, when former president Donald Trump moved the US embassy from Tel Aviv to Jerusalem, many evan-

22. Robert D. McFadden, "Tim LaHaye Dies at 90: Fundamentalist Leader's Grisly Novels Sold Millions," *The New York Times*, July 25, 2016, https://www.nytimes .com/2016/07/26/books/tim-lahaye-a-christian-fundamentalist-leader-dies-at-90 .html.

23. Tim LaHaye and Jerry B. Jenkins, *Kingdom Come: The Final Victory* (Carol Stream, IL: Tyndale, 2007), 320, 33, 39.

24. LaHaye and Jenkins, *Kingdom Come*, 64.

25. Loren L. Johns, "Conceiving Violence: The Apocalypse of John and the Left Behind Series," *Direction* 34 (2005): 204.

26. Barbara R. Rossing, *The Rapture Exposed: The Message of Hope in the Book of Revelation*, 2nd ed. (New York: Basic Books, 2004), 48.

27. Rossing, *Rapture Exposed*, 48–49.

gelical Christians and some Orthodox Jews were united in seeing the move as a fulfillment of prophecy.[28] The Christians, however, also saw this as coming one step closer to Jesus's return and a Christian reign. Unfortunately, a full exploration of how premillennial thinking has shaped the US political landscape is beyond the purview of this commentary, but suffice it to say that Revelation's vision of the millennium shapes the lives of people today, especially in and through the United States, in ways that are impossible to overestimate, even if we are not always attuned to seeing them.[29]

John's vision of the millennium has inspired a variety of thinkers, including those who are committed to more equitable visions of the millennial kingdom. A notable example is the Shakers, formally the United Society of Believers in Christ's Second Coming. While this movement has only a handful of members today, they came to the American colonies from England, under the guidance of their leader Mother Ann Lee (1736–1784), to live out Revelation's vision of a celibate millennial community. Echoing Revelation 14 and 20, one of the movement's hymns proclaims, "On this mount his [the Lamb's] throne is fixed / Elders seated all around / . . . Children of the resurrection, Virgin souls with Christ arose . . . Follow him where e'er he goes."[30] The Shakers asserted the importance of gender equity even though they tended toward gender complementarity. They also rejected enslavement.[31] Even though there are only a handful of Shakers today, due partly to their celibate lifestyle, they are tangible evidence of how Revelation's vision challenges the structures and symbols of kyriarchy (see excursus, "Rebecca Cox Jackson, Interpreter of Revelation").[32]

28. Paul O'Donnell, "For Some, the US Embassy's Move to Jerusalem Fulfills Divine Prophecy," *Religion News Service*, May 14, 2018, https://religionnews.com /2018/05/14/some-christians-and-jews-hail-embassy-move-to-jerusalem-as-key -to-a-biblical-plan/.

29. For a recent introduction to these topics, see Jonathan D. Redding, *One Nation under Graham: Apocalyptic Rhetoric and American Exceptionalism* (Waco, TX: Baylor University Press, 2021).

30. Richard McNemar and Richard Treat, "The Lamb's Revelation," in *Millennial Praises: A Shaker Hymnal*, ed. Christian Goodwillie and Jane F. Crosthwaite (Amherst: University of Massachusetts Press, 2009), 135.

31. Rebecca Jackson, *Gifts of Power: The Writings of Rebecca Jackson, Black Visionary, Shaker Eldress*, ed. Jean McMahon Humez (Amherst: University of Massachusetts Press, 1987), 19.

32. One of the few remaining Shaker communities, Sabbath Day Lake, has an online presence at www.maineshakers.com.

Rebecca Cox Jackson, Interpreter of Revelation

Beginning her religious career as an African Methodist Episcopal preacher, Rebecca Cox Jackson (1795–1871) is most well known for starting a Shaker community in Philadelphia in 1851 along with her partner of over thirty years, Rebecca Perot. The two women were referred to as the "Two Rebeccas" and lived together as a couple, even though they embraced the Shaker doctrine of celibacy. After Jackson's death, Perot took the name Jackson and continued as a leader of the multiracial community they started together. Although we should not assume to imagine them as lesbian foremothers, as some feminist scholars have done,[33] the Two Rebeccas are an example of how individuals have constructed thriving familial relationships apart from the expectations of White heteronormativity. This is particularly astounding since they lived and worked during a time when the United States battled over the enslavement of Black people.

One of the distinctive parts of the Two Rebeccas' story is Jackson's experience of visions and revelations, many of which parallel and expand on the imagery of Revelation. As such, Jackson's writings are some of the earliest extant interpretations of Revelation by a Black woman.

Like the angels and elders that sometimes help John understand aspects of his visions, Jackson described being assisted in understanding the Bible, "from Genesis to Revelations," by a heavenly figure.[34] Even though this figure was male, her visions emphasize the role of women and the feminine within God's work. For instance, evoking Revelation 14, Jackson recounts a brief hymn given to her by a Saint wearing a white garment, "Holy, holy, is Mt. Zion and her daughters are holy too. Zion has brought forth sons and daughters to the glory of her God. Let us praise Him, for His glorious work in us. He has brought us to Mt. Zion, the City of the living God."[35] The City is also the Bride of the Lamb, and the Bride even appears to Jackson in a vision. Upon seeing the Bride, who was accompanied by her Groom, Jackson falls "to the floor, with my forehead leaning on the instep of Her right foot."[36] Unlike John, who is corrected for falling prostrate before an angel (19:10), Jackson is affirmed by

---

33. E.g., Lillian Faderman, *To Believe in Women: What Lesbians Have Done for America; A History* (Boston: Houghton Mifflin, 2000), 242.

34. Jackson, *Gifts of Power*, 146.

35. Jackson, *Gifts of Power*, 192.

36. Jackson, *Gifts of Power*, 169.

the Bride. The Bride—a divine figure worthy of veneration for Jackson—authorizes her as a spiritual teacher and prophet. Later in her journal, Jackson explains that John's vision of the new Jerusalem as Bride is a "clear view of the female spirit of Christ."[37] This Bride was present at the beginning of creation as the spirit breathed into Adam and is the place where humanity will be renewed through the chosen people who are part of the city and the spiritual children of the Lamb and his Bride. Even though Jackson's reading replicates a heterosexual idea of marriage, which makes sense given the time in which she was writing, for her the feminine divine is an important part of Revelation's vision of the end. In her visions, bridal imagery becomes a vehicle for asserting the importance of the feminine or female presence in God's plan. Far from the passive figure presented in John's text, Jackson's Bride is powerful and empowering, characteristics Jackson herself embodied.

A Final Judgment (20:7-15)

Released from prison, Satan immediately returns to his old tricks, deceiving the nations into one last battle against the followers of God (vv. 7-8). This points to the persistence of evil and the ease with which the nations fall prey to its machinations. Earlier, "the nations" were under the influence of Babylon, otherwise known as Rome (14:8; 17:15; 18:3), even though they will eventually come to worship God and the Lamb (15:4; 21:24, 26; 22:2). Now, however, the nations have one more bout of resistance, one more chance at asserting their will over that of the divine.

John associates the nations with the names "Gog and Magog," references from the book of Ezekiel. In that earlier tradition, Gog is the name of a prince from Magog (Ezek 38:2), but John follows a tradition depicting Gog and Magog primarily as places or nations (e.g., 3 En. 45:5). Even though Gog and Magog came to symbolize hostile nations in general,[38] Ezekiel depicts Gog as a tyrant in a way that may draw on myths about the seventh-century BCE Lydian ruler Gyges.[39] (Lydia was an ancient kingdom in Asia Minor.) One of the most famous accounts of Gyges is a story told in Plato's *Republic*, where Gyges, yet to be king, comes into

37. Jackson, *Gifts of Power*, 245; see also 248.

38. Craig R. Koester, *Revelation: A New Translation with Introduction and Commentary*, AYB 38A (New Haven: Yale University Press, 2014), 778.

39. Stephen L. Cook, *Ezekiel 38–48* (New Haven: Yale University Press, 2018), 74.

[7]When the thousand years are ended, Satan will be released from his prison [8]and will come out to deceive the nations at the four corners of the earth, Gog and Magog, in order to gather them for battle; they are as numerous as the sands of the sea. [9]They marched up over the breadth of the earth and surrounded the camp of the saints and the beloved city. And fire came down from heaven and consumed them. [10]And the devil who had deceived them was thrown into the lake of fire and sulfur, where the beast and the false prophet were, and they will be tormented day and night forever and ever.

[11]Then I saw a great white throne and the one who sat on it; the earth and the heaven fled from his presence, and no place was found for them. [12]And I saw the dead, great and small, standing before the throne, and books were opened. Also another book was opened, the book of life. And the dead were judged according to their works, as recorded in the books. [13]And the sea gave up the dead that were in it, Death and Hades gave up the dead that were in them, and all were judged according to what they had done. [14]Then Death and Hades were thrown into the lake of fire. This is the second death, the lake of fire; [15]and anyone whose name was not found written in the book of life was thrown into the lake of fire.

possession of a ring that grants him invisibility. With the ring, he seduces the king's wife, with whom he murders the king and then takes the kingdom for himself (*Rep.* 2.360). Gyges embodies the ease with which humans turn to injustice when there is possibility of escaping incrimination. Given how John depicts Gog as a place, it seems as though he may not be familiar with the possible reference to Gyges. Is John unfamiliar with the legend of the tyrant? Has the history of Gyges been forgotten by John, or has his story become so familiar that it can be easily overshadowed by the story of the defeat of Satan? Tyrants may seem, on the surface, interchangeable; however, to forget their names is to simultaneously forget those whom they have harmed and destroyed.

Despite the ancient tradition suggesting Gog refers to Gyges, interpreters have long drawn connections between these names and specific entities or countries. According to historian Paul Boyer, "With the rise of Islam, and specifically of the Ottoman Turks in the late thirteenth century, Gog came to be firmly identified with this aggressive and much-feared power."[40] Twentieth-century premillennialists tend to identify Gog and

---

40. Paul S. Boyer, *When Time Shall Be No More: Prophecy Belief in Modern American Culture* (Cambridge, MA: Harvard University Press, 1992), 153.

Magog with countries perceived as hostile to the United States, such as Russia.[41] At the time of the US invasion of Iraq, moreover, US President George W. Bush reportedly revealed to French President Jacques Chirac that he understood Gog and Magog as a reference to countries in the Middle East.[42] In contrast to these very specific readings, John associates these entities with forces coming from around the globe, literally from the "four corners of the earth" (20:8). Satan's appeal is universal. The description of these troops as being "as numerous as the sands of the sea" (v. 9) suggests a military campaign of unprecedented size and implies they are a foil of Abraham's descendants, the people of Israel (Gen 22:17).

The target of the nations' offensive is the camp of the saints, which John describes as "the beloved city" (v. 9). The language of the "beloved" (ἀγαπάω) evokes the wedding imagery of the previous chapter. The New International Version captures this notion, even though it is not the most literal translation: "They . . . surrounded the camp of God's people, the city he loves" (v. 9). The connection between the saints and the city anticipates the coming visions of the city, the heavenly Jerusalem, as Bride (21:1-4). The word here is not the same as the classical Greek term commonly used to describe a young male lover, who is the beloved, ἐρώμενος. At the same time, being "beloved" means being the object of another's attention and is a feminized role. The saints, as in Revelation 19:8, are collectively understood as Christ's beloved, and this beloved is threatened by troops that surround or encircle (κυκλεύω) the city.[43] Given this, it should not be surprising that fire from heaven thwarts the nations' advance (v. 9). In the ancient Roman context, war can be understood metaphorically as a sexual assault. Lead bullets used by Roman troops wielding slingshots often bore inscriptions conveying messages that one scholar describes as "nakedly phallic aggression against both male and female opponents."[44] Given this, one can read the divine protection of the beloved as preventing a possible sexual assault upon the city, a stark contrast to the fate of Babylon, whose rape and dismemberment appear at the conclusion of Revelation 17.

The fire deployed to protect the city gives way to a lake of fire into which the devil, or Satan, is cast. Undoubtedly, the Beast and the False

---

41. Boyer, *When Time Shall Be No More*, 154–62.

42. Sutton, *American Apocalypse*, 370.

43. The language of surrounding (κυκλεύω) is similar to that used in John's vision of the throne to describe the thrones and entities surrounding God's throne (4:3-4).

44. Craig A. Williams, *Roman Homosexuality*, 2nd ed. (Oxford: Oxford University Press, 2010), 21.

Prophet are ready with a "warm" welcome (v. 10). Moreover, punishment of evil agents appears in other Jewish apocalyptic texts. In 1 Enoch, for example, Enoch views a prison with pillars of fire where angels that have defied God will be held and punished for eternity (21:7-10; see also Jub. 5:6).

Revelation does not conclude with the eternal punishment of Satan. There is a recognition that humans too must be accountable for their actions and allegiances. Twice John notes that humans will be judged for what they have done (20:12, 13). The appearance of the divine throne, a thing so great that earth and heaven flee from its presence (v. 11), signals the enormity of this task, which includes judging all who have died, including "great and small" (v. 12). Even the sea gives up the dead in it so that everyone can come before the throne. Again, I am reminded of the painting of the Last Judgment from the Vatican Museums described above (see p. 308), where animals and fish help with the re-membering of humans.

This chapter closes with multiple references to the infamous lake of fire, an image that looms large in Christian depictions of hell. The lake, along with related images of rivers of fire, provides a backdrop for many early Christian "tours of hell." These tours, like the Apocalypse of Peter (second century CE) and the Apocalypse of Paul (fourth century CE), vividly describe the torments of hell as a way of making clear what types of behavior warrant punishment.[45] The anonymous authors of these visions eagerly describe hell as a place that tortures thieves, murderers, blasphemers, and those who defy gender norms and sexual roles. Women who adorn themselves are hung by their hair over boiling pits, and those who have children outside of marriage are attacked by fiery beams coming from the eyes of unborn children (Apoc. Pet. 24, 26). These scenes provide inspiration for Dante's *Inferno* and seemingly find new audiences through the taunts of modern anti-choice activists, homophobic protesters, and other radically conservative Christian activists who evoke the lake of fire and eternal torment in their hateful rhetoric.

In contrast to visions that linger on the pain and suffering of individuals, the description of judgment in Revelation 20 is surprisingly general. John seems uninterested in detailing the punishment of human individuals, although he makes clear that humans will be judged (v. 12).

---

45. Meghan R. Henning, *Hell Hath No Fury: Gender, Disability, and the Invention of Damned Bodies in Early Christian Literature* (New Haven: Yale University Press, 2021), 85.

Likewise, beyond not taking the mark of the Beast, John offers here little explanation of the criteria for judgment. In general, as Gail R. O'Day has noted, Revelation resists easily excised "lessons for good and faithful living."[46] While Revelation avoids didacticism, codes of conduct, and commandments, John still presents audience members an ethical vision. This vision must be experienced as a revelation, as an unveiling. Through the revelation, hearers are oriented in ways that should find their names written in the book of life. They are turned toward the heavenly throne room and toward the slaughtered Lamb whose enthronement challenges ancient assumptions about power and prestige. John calls his audience members to witness, like Christ, through what Blount in his book *Can I Get a Witness?* calls "engaged resistance."[47] This kind of witness is modeled by the Two Witnesses whose very presence challenges and exasperates evil systems and powers (11:7). This kind of witness takes many forms—taking a knee, walking out, sitting in, drumming, dancing, and praying in ways that draw attention to the need for justice, equity, and mercy.

The fact that the final judgment of humanity occurs after the millennial reign in John's vision of the final things at the end of time feels intentional. As mentioned above, millennial thinking leads easily to building empires and kyriarchies and to colonizing and conquest. Christians have replicated the kingdom of the Beast in the name of reigning alongside the Lamb. We do this at our own peril, however, since judgment looms on the horizon.

46. Gail R. O'Day, "Teaching and Preaching the Book of Revelation," *WW* 25 (2005): 249.

47. Brian K. Blount, *Can I Get a Witness? Reading Revelation through African American Culture* (Louisville: Westminster John Knox, 2005), 46.

Revelation 21–22:5

Unveiling the Bride

At a 1979 feminist conference on "The Personal and the Political," Black lesbian feminist Audre Lorde observed in her address how White feminists dominated the event. She noted what seemed to be a minimal effort on the part of the organizers to include the voices of Black, Brown, poor, non-European, and lesbian women. She asks, "And what does it mean in personal and political terms when even the two Black women who did present here were literally found at the last hour?"[1] Her talk would later be published in a now-famous essay, required reading in most feminist studies courses, titled "The Master's Tools Will Never Dismantle the Master's House." Dismantling oppressive systems, she argued, cannot be done with the tools, methods, and tactics employed by oppressors to construct these systems. Challenging empires and kyriarchies requires new tools. The same is surely true for rebuilding worlds, like the New Jerusalem.

The idea of locating and finding new tools can be daunting. Do we have to make them ourselves? Would I even recognize a new tool if I saw one? Our professions require us to use the "tools of the trade." Writing and publishing in biblical studies, for instance, requires careful reading of biblical texts in relation to their historical contexts or analysis of how

---

1. Audre Lorde, "The Master's Tools Will Never Dismantle the Master's House," in *Sister Outsider: Essays and Speeches* (Berkeley: Crossing Press, 2004), 110.

texts have been interpreted historically, so our traditional tools include things like translation, historical analysis, and literary analysis. Especially in biblical studies, these tools have been honed in workplaces that privilege White, Christian, straight, cis-male perspectives. The manuals that teach how to use these tools reflect those assumptions as well. So, what does an interpreter who exists outside that mold or who wants to decenter and dismantle those assumptions, metaphorically known as "the master's house," do? Angela N. Parker and Tina Pippin are two New Testament scholars who encourage "activist translation," translation that is "faithful" by being faithful to the embodied experiences of individuals and communities, especially those who have been harmed by these texts (see, for instance, "Translation Matters: πόρνη").[2] We can and should find ways of "retooling" our tools to use for change. Likewise, bringing new tools to the master's house includes using reading practices historically avoided, such as sass and chutzpah, recommended by Mitzi J. Smith and Adele Reinhartz, respectively (see pp. xlv–xlvi).[3] Deploying new tools also includes inviting to the table voices and perspectives that have been excluded, including those of women, people of color, and queer readers as well as creatively engaging the work of other fields of study. The task of finding and making new tools takes effort, but it is possible and worthwhile as we try to engage Revelation without sliding into what Lorde calls "tragic repetition."[4]

Speaking of old and new tools, one of the main feminist criticisms of the book of Revelation is that John uses "the master's tools" when building his vision of the heavenly reign. The fact that he uses the idea of a reign, replete with thrones and crowns and the language of courtly

---

2. Angela N. Parker, *If God Still Breathes, Why Can't I? Black Lives Matter and Biblical Authority* (Grand Rapids: Eerdmans, 2021), 83. Parker notes the importance of the work of two Hebrew Bible scholars on shaping her perspective, Randall Bailey and Wil Gafney. She cites as well Clarice J. Martin, "Womanist Interpretations of the New Testament: The Quest for Holistic and Inclusive Translation and Interpretation," *JFSR* 6 (1990): 41–61. However, she specifically engages the work of Tina Pippin, "Translation Happens: A Feminist Perspective on Translation Theories," in *Escaping Eden: New Feminist Perspectives on the Bible*, ed. Harold C. Washington, Susan Lochrie Graham, and Pamela Thimmes (New York: NYU Press, 1999), 163–76.

3. Mitzi J. Smith, *Womanist Sass and Talk Back: Social (In)Justice, Intersectionality, and Biblical Interpretation* (Eugene, OR: Cascade Books, 2018); Adele Reinhartz, "The Hermeneutics of Chutzpah: A Disquisition on the Value/s of 'Critical Investigation of the Bible,'" *JBL* 140 (2021): 8–30.

4. Lorde, "Master's Tools," 114.

praise, points to this. He seemingly tries to depict something new—
at least he keeps telling his audiences that everything is new—but he
uses old tropes and images. We have seen these throughout our journey
through Revelation: pitting women against each other, deploying slurs
and polemic, depicting justice through violence. John's reliance on these
old tools often undercuts his message. Imagine what he could have done
if John had access to some of the resources available in feminist toolkits.
Of course, just because John didn't have these tools doesn't mean we
can't bring them into our interpretations of the text.

Like a Bride Adorned (21:1-2)

While something new sounds like a good thing, especially given all the
damage that has been done to the earth in the earlier chapters, one might
wonder what happened to the first heaven and earth. John noticeably
avoids the adjective "old," as though he is trying not to sound ageist.
Likewise, the sea, a symbol of chaos and the place from where the Beast
emerged, is gone (21:1).

Although modern ideas about the apocalypse associate the phenomenon with destruction typical in apocalyptic literature and movies, Revelation does not include a specific vision of the earth and heaven being
destroyed. Even though it was subject to earthquakes and plagues, the
earth as a whole does not go up in flames, as some ancient Jewish thinkers and early Christians thought might happen (e.g., Josephus, *Ant.* 1.70;
2 Pet 3:10; Augustine, *Civ.* 20.16).[5] Rather, John mentions that the "first"
heaven and earth have gone away (ἀπῆλθαν, 21:1). The NRSV translation
of ἀπῆλθαν, an aorist verb, as "passed away" can be misleading since
some English speakers use this as a euphemism for death. Heaven and
earth have not, however, died; instead, earlier, they fled the scene (20:11).
Barbara Rossing argues that John here affirms that God's creation, earth
and heaven, are good and need not be destroyed, and yet he seemingly
needs for there to be an earth and heaven without the sinful presence of
empire.[6] By having the first heaven and earth go away, John creatively

5. David E. Aune, *Revelation*, WBC 52 A-C (Dallas: Word Books, 1998), 1117–18;
Craig R. Koester, *Revelation: A New Translation with Introduction and Commentary*, AYB
38A (New Haven: Yale University Press, 2014), 803.

6. Barbara R. Rossing, "For the Healing of the World: Reading *Revelation* Ecologically," in *From Every People and Nation: The Book of Revelation in Intercultural Perspective*,
ed. David Rhoads (Minneapolis: Fortress, 2005), 173.

Rev 21:1-2

²¹:¹Then I saw a new heaven and a new earth; for the first heaven and the first earth had passed away, and the sea was no more. ²And I saw the holy city, the new Jerusalem, coming down out of heaven from God, prepared as a bride adorned for her husband.

allows God to fulfill the promise, "For I am about to create new heavens and a new earth" (Isa 65:16; see also 66:22) without resorting to destroying the creation.

Amid this newness, a holy city—a new Jerusalem—comes down out of heaven from God. John is not the only apocalyptic thinker to envision a New Jerusalem. Especially after the destruction of the Jerusalem temple by the Romans in 70, there are multiple traditions that express hope in a renewed holy city (e.g., 4 Ezra 10:25-28; 2 Bar. 4:1-3). The earthly Jerusalem, the religious center of God's people, was damaged and dishonored by the evil manifest in Roman power and, before that, Babylon. Thus, the renewed city that descends from heaven is like no other; is it not, as Craig R. Koester notes, "built from the ground up."[7]

John highlights Jerusalem's newness by describing a vision of the city as Bride in two parallel visions, 21:2 and 21:9. Even though the second of these two visions is facilitated by one of the plague-pouring angels, hardly a good sign, wedding imagery signals beginnings. And, as discussed earlier, brides in the ancient world suggest youth (see pp. 283–84). John has already noted the presence of virgins (14:4), essentially brides-to-be, and celebrated the Bride's readiness to wed the Lamb by noting the garment "she" has created through "her" deeds, i.e., the righteous deeds of the saints (19:7-8). Even Revelation's opening word hints at the appearance of a bride since, as we have noted, the word ἀποκάλυψις ("apocalypse" in English) bears some similarity to the word describing the moment in an ancient wedding when the groom lifted the bride's veil, the ἀνακάλυψις or *anacalypsis*.[8] The Bride has been almost at the altar since the beginning of the book.

While earlier John highlighted the Bride's garments and preparation (19:7-8), here he witnesses the actual wedding, the descent of the city from heaven. In ancient Greek and Roman weddings, the bride processed

---

7. Koester, *Revelation*, 804.

8. John Howard Oakley and Rebecca H. Sinos, *The Wedding in Ancient Athens* (Madison: University of Wisconsin Press, 1993), 30.

or was led from her home to that of her groom. This event was such an important part of the wedding that the Latin term for wedding was even *ducere uxorum* or, literally, "to lead a wife."[9] The groom's physical presence was not even necessary for the wedding to be official. It could take place "by means of a letter, or a messenger, if [the bride] is afterwards conducted to [the groom's] house" (Justinian, *Edict.* 23.2.5). Here, the Bride's "coming down" from heaven (21:2, 10) evokes this kind of wedding procession since we do not see the Bridegroom or Lamb.

God among Mortals (21:3-10)

Even though John just mentioned seeing the New Jerusalem descend from heaven, a voice from the throne, God, commands John and his audiences to take a second look (see "Translation Matters: ἰδού"). In so doing, God announces that the New Jerusalem is "the home [σκηνή] of God . . . among mortals" (21:3). God will dwell with humanity. Thus, the New Jerusalem will be both people *as* place, communicated through the notion of the saints as the Lamb's Bride, and place *for* people.[10] Moreover, in these verses, God describes the facets of this dwelling together, focusing on the New Jerusalem as site of intimate connection: God is *with* humans, dwells *with* them, is their God, and will himself be *with* them. The repeated use of "with" or "among," which are the same preposition in Greek (μετά), underscores this as a place of divine and human togetherness and connection.

Even though John highlights the newness of the New Jerusalem, the relationship between God and his people in the New Jerusalem is not entirely new. John makes this explicit by using σκηνή, "tent," which the NRSV renders as "home," instead of the more common Greek word for "home" or "house," which is οἶκος. Σκηνή is the way the Greek version of Exodus translates the Hebrew term אהל, which describes the "tent of meeting" that housed God's presence with Israel in the desert (Exod 40:34-35). John reinforces this allusion by using a related verbal form, σκηνόω, which the NRSV renders as "dwell."[11] I often encourage my students to think of it as "camp" instead. God will camp among and

---

9. Lynn R. Huber, *Like a Bride Adorned: Reading Metaphor in John's Apocalypse* (New York: T&T Clark, 2007), 128.

10. See Robert H. Gundry, "The New Jerusalem: People as Place, Not Place for People," *NovT* 29 (1987): 254–64, although Gundry offers these readings of the New Jerusalem as mutually exclusive.

11. This is also the term used in the Gospel of John to describe the Word being made flesh to "dwell among us" (1:14).

³And I heard a loud voice from the throne saying,

> "See, the home of God is among mortals.
> He will dwell with them;
> they will be his peoples,
> and God himself will be with them;
> ⁴he will wipe every tear from their eyes.
> Death will be no more;
> mourning and crying and pain will be no more,
> for the first things have passed away."

⁵And the one who was seated on the throne said, "See, I am making all things new." Also he said, "Write this, for these words are trustworthy and true." ⁶Then he said to me, "It is done! I am the Alpha and the Omega, the beginning and the end. To the thirsty I will give water as a gift from the spring of the water of life. ⁷Those who conquer will inherit these things, and I will be their God and they will be my children. ⁸But as for the cowardly, the faithless, the polluted, the murderers, the fornicators, the sorcerers, the idolaters, and all liars, their place will be in the lake that burns with fire and sulfur, which is the second death."

⁹Then one of the seven angels who had the seven bowls full of the seven last plagues came and said to me, "Come, I will show you the bride, the wife of the Lamb." ¹⁰And in the spirit he carried me away to a great, high mountain and showed me the holy city Jerusalem coming down out of heaven from God.

with the people as God did after the escape from oppression in Egypt. In the modern world, where millions of people are forced to live in camp settings because of being displaced from houses due to war, natural disaster, lack of affordable housing, among other reasons, God camping with God's people is a powerful image.[12]

The divine voice continues to build the picture of the community's intimate life with God by echoing Isaiah's vision of God comforting a rebuilt and renewed Jerusalem: "Then the Lord GOD will wipe away the tears from all faces, and the disgrace of his people he will take away from all the earth, for the LORD has spoken" (Isa 25:8). The image of God physically wiping tears from peoples' eyes casts the divine as parent, lover, companion, or friend. This seems a striking contrast to John's initial vision of God as jasper and carnelian and as "the one who sits upon the throne" (4:3). In that

---

12. According to the United Nations Refugee Agency, 6.6 million people worldwide live in refugee camps. See "Refugee Camps Explained," April 6, 2021, https://www.unrefugees.org/news/refugee-camps-explained/.

earlier encounter John compared the divine to gemstones, including jasper and carnelian, and emphasized how the throne was surrounded by living creatures, thrones, elders, flashes of lightening, flames of fire, and even a sea of glass (4:3-6). In retrospect, that God seemed so distant, but now God will be nearby. In addition, God will ensure there is no longer a reason for tears, as the voice assures Revelation's hearers that death, mourning, and pain will be no more. Overall, the depiction of God dwelling or camping with humans is a picture of abundant life and radical care. When I read these verses, I want to lean in and soak up these promises. The voice from the throne encourages John to reassure his audiences that these words are "trustworthy and true" (21:5), since they may seem like too much, like impossible dreams. The voice even announces, "It is done" (21:6). These realities are enacted. Presumably, all that needs to happen are for the hearers of Revelation to "see" (ἰδού) that God "is making all things new."

The final promise here is God's offer of water to the thirsty, "a gift from the spring of the water of life" (21:6). The imagery recalls the story of Jesus and the Samaritan woman from John's Gospel. At the well, Jesus tells the woman about living water that will offer the one who drinks "a spring of water gushing up to eternal life" (John 4:14). In that story, the promise of eternal life-giving water prompts the woman to proclaim, "I know that Messiah is coming" (John 4:25).[13] Jesus responds to her that he is present. Jesus, according to the Gospel, is the water that gives life. And now, all the faithful have unprecedented access to this resource.

The water of life promised in both the Gospel of John and Revelation manifests in the practice of leaving water in the desert for immigrants into the United States. As they cross the border from Mexico into the United States, people must travel miles without access to water, a reality leading to certain death for many. In 2020, for example, Pima County Arizona recorded 227 migrant deaths in the desert.[14] Given this startling reality, humanitarian groups have begun strategically placing gallon jugs filled with water in this wilderness for migrants to drink. Scholar of religion Barbara Sostaita explains, these water bottles "point to life that persists despite walls and barriers."[15] Following the Lamb certainly includes making the New Jerusalem a reality for those among us who suffer.

13. Gail R. O'Day and Susan Hylen, *John* (Louisville: Westminster John Knox, 2006), 88.

14. As reported by Barbara Sostaita, "Waste Land: For Migrants, Water Bottles Are a Matter of Life and Death," *Bitch Media*, January 14, 2022, https://www.bitchmedia.org/article/waste-land-for-migrants-water-bottles-are-a-matter-of-life-and-death.

15. Sostaita, "Waste Land."

Demonstrating the fluidity with which one metaphor can give way to another, the bridal and dwelling imagery leads to child and inheritance symbolism in 21:7.[16] The verse echoes the promises to "the one who conquers" (ὁ νικῶν) in Revelation 2–3, promising that the conqueror will inherit all the things associated with the New Jerusalem. A literal translation of the text reads, "The one who conquers [ὁ νικῶν] will inherit these things and I will be his God and he will be my son" (21:7). The term "son" (υἱός) does not necessarily convey the sense of youthfulness that the NRSV conveys with "children," since one remains a son even when an adult. Still, the description of the faithful as both one who conquers, an image of strength and sufficiency, and son, a status that suggests being subordinate to a father, references the paradoxical masculinity recommended throughout the text. That the bridal New Jerusalem is associated with the ideas of being a conqueror and a son similarly conveys the gender instability that pervades Revelation. More important, the promise of inheritance is a reassurance that one will be cared for in the future. This might be a reassurance to those who fear that being faithful to the Lamb, a faithfulness that requires giving up gender and familial norms, might put earthly inheritance in jeopardy, especially since childless Roman citizens received only partial inheritances.[17] Despite possibly forfeiting inheritances from biological families, the faithful learn that they will receive an inheritance from God as part of the New Jerusalem (cf. 1 Pet 1:4).

Unfortunately, the newness and intimacy that John offers in the vision of God dwelling among humans is, seemingly, not for everyone. Multiple times in Revelation 21–22 John lists those he imagines will or should be excluded from the New Jerusalem. After describing God's tenderness toward those who dwell with God, John clarifies that "the cowardly, the faithless, the polluted, the murderers, the fornicators, the sorcerers, the idolaters, and all liars" are relegated to a place outside of New Jerusalem. He reinforces the exclusionary nature of the heavenly city with a similar list in 21:27 and again in 22:15 when John offers, "Outside are the dogs and sorcerers and fornicators and murderers and idolaters, and everyone who loves and practices falsehood."

The lists of the excluded, sometimes called "vice lists" since they name behaviors considered corrupt, do not necessarily reflect an author's robust ethical thinking about what constitutes living a life of faithfulness. Instead,

---

16. Even though the Greek ὁ νικῶν is singular, the NRSV translates it as a plural, "those who conquer" (v. 7).

17. Lauren Caldwell, *Roman Girlhood and the Fashioning of Femininity* (Cambridge: Cambridge University Press, 2015), 125n86.

vice lists, common in Greek and Roman rhetoric, are formulaic and generally reflect traditional prejudices. Ancient rhetoricians were even taught the topics that should be used in a vice list (e.g., origin, employment, mood, appearance, habits, financial status) as a way of discrediting the character of another.[18] These kinds of lists were so common, veritable "old tools," they easily became part of early Christian rhetoric. A quick flip through the pages of the New Testament reveals just how unoriginal they are (e.g., Matt 15:19; Mark 7:21-22; Rom 1:29-31; 1 Cor 5:10-11; 6:9-10; 2 Cor 6:9-10; 12:20-21; Gal 5:19-21; 1 Tim 1:9-10; 2 Tim 3:2-5; Titus 3:3). At times these lists explicitly reveal how they are intended to "other" certain groups of people. The author of 1 Peter writes, for instance, "you have already spent enough time in doing what the Gentiles like to do, living in licentiousness, passions, drunkenness, revels, carousing, and lawless idolatry" (1 Pet 4:3). Here, the use of "gentiles" reveals the author's ethnic biases, even though the audience members he is trying to persuade are most likely gentile themselves. This is akin to manipulating someone's internalized racism or homophobia.

Vice lists arguably say more about the person or people constructing the list, including their anxieties and prejudices, than they do about those groups who find themselves on the list. Early Jesus followers likely found themselves associated with those grouped together on ancient vice lists, since they were disparaged by others in the first and second centuries for their supposedly superstitious and degenerate behavior (e.g., Tacitus, *Ann.* 14.44; Pliny the Younger, *Ep.* 10.96.8).[19]

The groups of those included on John's lists—fornicators, idolators, polluted, faithless—are unsurprising in comparison to other early Christian vice lists and given what we have seen in Revelation as a whole. The groups align with Revelation's focus on faithfulness to God and the Lamb and John's use of dirt and fornication as metaphors for assimilation to the dominant culture. The inclusion of "sorcerers" among the excluded (21:8), for example, denigrates those who practice religions and therapies that John perceives as out of line with the worship of God.[20] It coheres with John's earlier denigration of "idol worship" (see pp. 133–34). By repeating these kinds of slurs, John, again, tries using old tools for constructing New Jerusalem.

18. Jennifer Wright Knust, *Abandoned to Lust: Sexual Slander and Ancient Christianity, Gender, Theory, and Religion* (New York: Columbia University Press, 2005), 21.

19. Knust, *Abandoned to Lust*, 119.

20. On the accusation of magic to other, see David Frankfurter, *Evil Incarnate: Rumors of Demonic Conspiracy and Satanic Abuse in History* (Princeton: Princeton University Press, 2018), 220.

Perhaps a surprising inclusion on the list is "dogs." John is not excluding canine companions from the New Jerusalem. Instead, he employs a common insult, even used by Jesus in the Gospels. In the story of the "Syrophoenician Woman," Jesus uses "dog" to mark the woman as "other" (Mark 7:27-28; see also Matt 7:6; 15:26-27).[21] The woman does not reject the label, but embraces it and uses it to call Jesus to account. Although Jesus uses it as an insult, "dog" was mostly used in connection with Cynics, those who practiced a philosophy of living according to nature and resisting cultural norms. In fact, the word "cynic" is based on the Greek word for "dog-like," κυνικός. At the time, the Cynics' rejection of social convention took extreme forms. Diogenes, an early Cynic, defecated, urinated, and even masturbated in public (Diogenes Laertius, *Lives* 6.2.34-35, 46). In a spirit of rejecting social acceptability, Diogenes even embraced the moniker "dog" when it was used to insult him (e.g., Diogenes Laertius, *Lives* 6.2.33).

Some modern biblical scholars fall back on old assumptions when they read the list of those who are left outside the New Jerusalem. This is especially notable when they explain John's use of "dog," as Eric A. Thomas has detailed in an essay on Revelation's future vision.[22] Even though he will note "dog" may refer to unclean outsiders more generally, commentator David E. Aune begins his discussion of the term in Revelation 22:15 by offering, "It may be that κύων, 'dog' (and perhaps οἱ πόρνοι, 'the fornicators,' as well . . .), is used more specifically here for male homosexuals, pederasts, or sodomites."[23] "Dog" can be used to reference sexual practices, especially anal sex (i.e., "doggy-style") in modern contexts, but nothing in Revelation connects being a dog with sex or gender. As Aune notes, John includes "fornicators" in this list, but John also mentions "sorcerers." Why choose one term to understand dog and not the other? The suggestion that "dog" *may* refer to gay males, even when couched in terms of possibility, reveals a heterosexual interpretive bias. It assumes that Revelation envisions a future world without gay men

21. Mitzi J. Smith, "Race, Gender, and the Politics of 'Sass': Reading Mark 7:24-30 through a Womanist Lens of Intersectionality and Inter(Con)Textuality," in *Womanist Interpretations of the Bible: Expanding the Discourse*, ed. Gay L. Byron and Vanessa Lovelace, 95–112 (Atlanta: Society of Biblical Literature, 2016).

22. Eric A. Thomas, "The Futures Outside: Apocalyptic Epilogue Unveiled as Africana Queer Prologue," in *Sexual Disorientations: Queer Temporalities, Affects, Theologies*, ed. Kent L. Brintnall, Joseph A. Marchal, and Stephen D. Moore (New York: Fordham University Press, 2018), 96.

23. Aune, *Revelation*, 1222; see also Craig S. Keener, *Revelation* (Grand Rapids: Zondervan, 2000), 515.

and can easily be used to justify the exclusion of those in the LGBTQIA+ community from Christian attempts at realizing the future city.[24]

The lists of folks restricted from the New Jerusalem and literally left to the lake of fire are impossible to ignore (21:8); however, there is no requirement that we agree with or endorse them. In his discussion of the new Jerusalem's "outside," Thomas, who offers a queer Africana reading of Revelation, explores the possibility of disidentifying with being outside. The concept of disidentification comes from the work of queer theorist José Esteban Muñoz, who offers it as one strategy marginalized individuals use in response to the categorizations and labels the dominant culture uses to exclude and ostracize. Disidentification is a survival strategy used by individuals in minoritized communities that involves recognizing oneself in the slurs and stereotypes and then using those as source of power, just like the Syrophoenician woman mentioned earlier. It is finding "identity-in-difference."[25] It is manifest, for example, when a high school girl unsure about her sexuality gets called "lesbian" in a pejorative way by a schoolmate and then embraces the identity with a powerful "Yes!" instead of feeling shame and embarrassment (like a young Lynn did back in the 1980s). Muñoz notes that this strategy is not for everyone and for all times; however, Thomas finds it an empowering strategy for dealing with John's hate. In some sense, disidentification is necessary precisely because we may not have the resources and mental space to develop new tools. Like, Parker and Pippin's understanding of translation (see p. 324), this is a strategy using existing tools differently.[26]

Thomas, moreover, shows us that we transform being outside into a place of power and revelation, just as John himself experienced revelation while on Patmos, outside the cities where members of his audiences lived.[27] Marginalized and minoritized readers, those relegated to the lake of fire by others, can revision *that place* as our own heavenly Jerusalem. Outside

---

24. The proposition that οἱ πόρνοι, "the fornicators," *may* refer to male prostitutes or pederasty, as opposed to individuals engaged in illicit sex more generally, is problematic since nothing in the text narrows the term in these ways. Even though neither prostitution nor pederasty is the same as homosexuality, Aune groups them all together without any distinctions or explanation of the complications surrounding sex and gender in Revelation's context. Likewise, Aune fails to mention that homosexuality is a modern category and not intrinsic to the ancient world. Aune, *Revelation*, 1223–24.

25. José Esteban Muñoz, *Disidentifications: Queers of Color and the Performance of Politics* (Minneapolis: University of Minnesota Press, 1999), 3–4, 6–7.

26. Thank you to Kent L. Brintnall for this observation.

27. Thomas, "Futures Outside," 98.

of the gated city, we will wipe away our own tears and those of all who have been called fornicators and dogs. My guess is that the slaughtered Lamb will be right alongside us. The Lamb seems like a "dog person."

The Radiant City (21:11-21)

Echoing the earlier encounter of the angel taking John to see the Great Prostitute (17:1), an angel shows John "the Bride, the wife of the Lamb" (21:9). Ironically, this textual parallel emphasizes the contrasting images of Prostitute and Bride. In 21:11-12, the Bride appears as a perfectly planned and opulent city that surpasses the beauty of any earthly city, including Rome. This impression is supported both through John's detailed description of the parts of the city and the angel's act of measuring the city, its gates, and its walls (21:15-18). Even with its imperial monuments and treasures taken as spoils of war, including items taken from the Jerusalem temple, Rome is no match for the New Jerusalem (see also Josephus, *J.W.* 7.158–62).

The difference between the New Jerusalem and Rome is reinforced by John's repeated references to the Bride Jerusalem's holiness and purity in contrast to Babylon's cup of impurities and abominations (17:4-5) and hunt for all that is foul (18:2). In contrast to Babylon's filth, New Jerusalem is depicted as clear crystal (21:11) and as made from pure gold that is like clear glass (v. 18). The city's street, likewise, is pure gold and transparent like glass (v. 21). The emphasis on transparency points to the city's purity but also its opulence, as clear glass was the most valuable kind of glass in the Roman world because of its rarity.[28]

The repeated use of the number twelve, evoking the tribes of Israel, the twelve apostles, the months of the year, and signs of the zodiac, points to the city's perfection and completeness. Similarly, the repeated reference to three gates when describing the gates on the north, south, east, and west (this means there are a total of twelve gates) confirms the city's perfection. The angel's use of a ruler to measure the city prompts audience members to see along with John how this city is a gigantic cube (vv. 15-16); its width, length, and height each equaling twelve thousand stadia, which the NRSV converts into 1,500 miles, which is more than half the width of the United States (ca. 2,800 miles) or Brazil (ca. 2,700 miles) and more than two times the length of Italy (ca. 740 miles). Even though John seemingly wants his audiences to envision the massive city, it is unfathomable.

---

28. K. T. Erim and Joyce Reynolds, "The Aphrodisias Copy of Diocletian's Edict on Maximum Prices," *JRS* 63 (1973): 99–110.

[11]It has the glory of God and a radiance like a very rare jewel, like jasper, clear as crystal. [12]It has a great, high wall with twelve gates, and at the gates twelve angels, and on the gates are inscribed the names of the twelve tribes of the Israelites; [13]on the east three gates, on the north three gates, on the south three gates, and on the west three gates. [14]And the wall of the city has twelve foundations, and on them are the twelve names of the twelve apostles of the Lamb.

[15]The angel who talked to me had a measuring rod of gold to measure the city and its gates and walls. [16]The city lies four-square, its length the same as its width; and he measured the city with his rod, fifteen hundred miles; its length and width and height are equal. [17]He also measured its wall, one hundred forty-four cubits by human measurement, which the angel was using. [18]The wall is built of jasper, while the city is pure gold, clear as glass. [19]The foundations of the wall of the city are adorned with every jewel; the first was jasper, the second sapphire, the third agate, the fourth emerald, [20]the fifth onyx, the sixth carnelian, the seventh chrysolite, the eighth beryl, the ninth topaz, the tenth chrysoprase, the eleventh jacinth, the twelfth amethyst. [21]And the twelve gates are twelve pearls, each of the gates is a single pearl, and the street of the city is pure gold, transparent as glass.

Oddly, the city's wall is only 144 cubits or about seventy-five yards.[29] The short length could be, according to Juan Hernández Jr., a reference to Ezekiel 40, where a similar measuring is performed by a heavenly figure to show the prophet how the Jerusalem temple would be rebuilt after the Babylonian exile. Among the measurements taken is the altar's edge, which might be what is referenced here.[30] Hernández also explains that at least one ancient scribe tried to "correct" this problem by changing the word "wall" to a word that could be understood as "edge" or "ledge," and so reminds us that Revelation's readers have long struggled to make literal sense of the text.[31]

Adorning the city walls are twelve kinds of gemstones, an allusion to the breastplate worn by the ancient Israelite high priest. God himself instructs Moses on how to construct the breastplate, explaining that the gems represent the twelve tribes of Israel. Therefore, when Aaron, who served as high priest during the exodus, entered the tent of meeting, he brought the

29. Juan Hernández Jr., "A Scribal Solution to a Problematic Measurement in the Apocalypse," *NTS* 56 (2010): 276.

30. Hernández, "Scribal Solution," 277–78.

31. Hernández, "Scribal Solution," 276–77.

people into God's presence: "So Aaron shall bear the names of the sons of Israel in the breastpiece of judgment on his heart when he goes into the holy place, for a continual remembrance before the LORD" (Exod 28:29). Covered with gems, the walls suggest that the entire city, which is adorned as the Lamb's bride, is simultaneously adorned as high priest.[32] The city embodies the promise that God's faithful will be a "kingdom of priests" (Rev 1:6).

The New Jerusalem's opulent appearance may seem ostentatious and even hypocritical, given the earlier critique of Rome's love of luxury and its participation in commerce (Rev 18).[33] Revelation, however, espouses a vision of the heavenly realm as the rightful place for wealth and abundance as befitting God's role as creator and ruler of all. The description of the New Jerusalem's opulence has precedents in Tobit 13:16-17, and it draws on Isaiah 60, which references multiple times how the nations will bring their wealth into the city (21:5, 6, 10, 13). According to John's vision, wealth is not a problem when it is in the city of God. In fact, according to ancient logic, the wealth of the New Jerusalem reflects the city's greatness and points to the character of its inhabitants. In a culture in which citizens demonstrated their goodness by making civic donations, the city's facades and statuary revealed the generosity of the city's patrons. In some sense, the jewels of the New Jerusalem reflect the fact that this city is adorned by the saints whose deeds construct its garment (19:8).

The Place of Encounter (21:22-27)

The faithful who comprise and inhabit the New Jerusalem are a kingdom of priests serving God (1:6). Now the audiences see again what such a kingdom looks like. John repeats the imagery of God dwelling with his people (21:3-4): as the bridal city, the faithful are perpetually in a state of encounter with God and the Lamb. John notes that the city has no need for a temple, since God and the Lamb effectively are the temple (v. 22). The community is the city, and the divine is the temple. Just as Ezekiel re-envisioned how God encountered the people after the destruction of the first Jerusalem temple by depicting the divine upon a wheeled and movable throne (Ezek 1), so John envisions the temple as direct encounter between God, the Lamb, and the faithful in response to the destruction of the Jerusalem temple by the Romans.

---

32. William W. Reader, "The Twelve Jewels of Revelation 21:19-20: Tradition History and Modern Interpretations," *JBL* 100 (1981): 433–57.

33. For a discussion of Revelation's use of wealth imagery, see Robert M. Royalty Jr., *The Streets of Heaven: The Ideology of Wealth in the Apocalypse of John* (Macon, GA: Mercer University Press, 1998).

²²I saw no temple in the city, for its temple is the Lord God the Almighty and the Lamb. ²³And the city has no need of sun or moon to shine on it, for the glory of God is its light, and its lamp is the Lamb. ²⁴The nations will walk by its light, and the kings of the earth will bring their glory into it. ²⁵Its gates will never be shut by day—and there will be no night there. ²⁶People will bring into it the glory and the honor of the nations. ²⁷But nothing unclean will enter it, nor anyone who practices abomination or falsehood, but only those who are written in the Lamb's book of life.

As a place of encounter between the divine, both God and the Lamb, and the faithful, the New Jerusalem is full of light and glory. Even though the city was described as having a "great, high wall" (21:12), that wall is only seventy-five yards in length, seemingly leaving the city open. John mentions that the gates of the city are never shut since there is no night in the city (v. 25). This place is continually open for encountering and walking in the light of the divine. The openness of the city is evidenced, moreover, in the ability of the nations and the kings of the earth, once envisioned as foes of the Lamb, to enter the city and bring into it their glory (vv. 24, 26). Even though John mentions multiple times those left outside of the city, the city itself invites others in. Moreover, it invites them in with their glory, that is, with the thing that makes them who they are. There is not a call to change their identities. This openness should prompt contemporary Christians to think seriously about how our visions of the New Jerusalem, our communities and churches, draw people in and whether and how we can welcome the glory of others on their own terms.

Between Good Places and No Places

Aztlán, the New Jerusalem, and the Utopian Imagination

What is Aztlán? Where—and when—is Aztlán? Since the late 1960s, varying Chican@ activists, artists, and intellectuals have mobilized Aztlán as an alternative political imagination and political theology in order to challenge and reframe the dominant US narrative of Manifest Destiny. Casting Aztlán as an ancient homeland or a future utopia, certain ethnic Mexican political activists sometimes just used Aztlán to designate the US Southwest in general because the land had once belonged to Mexico. Other activists asked, though, if Aztlán might be better understood as a spiritual inbreaking—a place that exists wherever Chican@s find themselves. Yet Chican@ critics also questioned the utility of this utopian imaginary. In this ongoing debate over its spatiality, its temporality, its membership, and its power, Aztlán provides an intriguing parallel to the manifold and multivalent interpretations of Revelation's New Jerusalem.

Publicly proclaimed at the First National Chicano Youth Liberation Conference in March 1969, El Plan Espiritual de Aztlán quickly became a "scriptural" document of the Chican@ civil rights movement, especially its nationalist edge. When declaring, "We are Aztlán," the document laid claim to Aztlán as more than just a place. Aztlán represented an alternative political economy and way of life that would enshrine self-determination for ethnic Mexicans.

While one might parallel Aztlán and the New Jerusalem as imaginaries that belonged specifically to minoritized populations living under imperial rule, Aztlán and the New Jerusalem are also historically intertwined imaginaries with some intersecting imperial histories. The imperial Aztec version of Aztlán may have portrayed the Aztecs as led from their homeland (Aztlán) to a destined site in the Valley of Mexico. The legend also promised that the Aztecs would someday return to Aztlán. When they encountered the myth of Aztlán, Spanish interpreters easily assimilated it to Eden and the New Jerusalem. Puritan visions and US Manifest Destiny also relied on Revelation and Exodus in constructing a divine mandate behind settler colonial conquest. As imperial imaginaries, both Aztlán and the New Jerusalem have often been figured in heteropatriarchal manners as submissive female landscapes (Aztlán as a nurturing woman and the New Jerusalem as a bride) populated with dominating male faithful.

Refusing the constraints of their imperialist, misogynistic, homophobic, and heteronormative interpretive legacies, feminist and queer critics have likewise reconfigured both the New Jerusalem and Aztlán. Marshaling the ambivalence of utopian vision, a world caught between the good and the nonexistent, Chicana feminist and lesbian artists and writers such as Gloria Anzaldúa and Cherríe Moraga transformed Aztlán, pressing at its capacity to exist as a borderlands imaginary that moves between worlds, constantly fluctuating and negotiating between contradictory desires, never fully existing and always being redrawn for the people who

> most need Aztlán to nourish their survival and flourishing. Given the New Jerusalem's inscription as a city caught between earth and heaven, landing at the end of the Christian Bible and pressing the reader beyond the bounds of the canon, the city may also be fittingly reinterpreted as a borderlands space.
>
> *Jacqueline M. Hidalgo*

Does John use the master's tools? Definitely. He uses problematic gendered imagery to make his rhetorical point when he could use some other way of signaling the option he hopes his audiences will embrace. He uses slurs and unfair categorizations to emphasize the purity and perfection of the heavenly community. At the same time, John does not use all the "old tools" available to him, even those things that we might want him to use. He seemingly disregards the prophetic critique of wealth and, therefore, replicates Roman economic ideals. Given this, the onus is on interpreters to decide whether we should occupy *this* house or find new and more just ways of creating community. Perhaps the problem rests with the idea of recreating a structure, something made of stone, even if they are precious stones.

Along with Eric A. Thomas, I want to envision the New Jerusalem by drawing on my experiences of when I have felt most included and alive, memories of when I sensed true community with the diverse people around me. One of those experiences of "New Jerusalem" occurred for me in October 2015, when, after months of planning, a diverse group of citizens in Burlington, North Carolina, successfully pulled off our community's first-ever Pride celebration, Alamance Pride. Before the event, our organizing committee had very real concerns about safety and community reaction. Our county, Alamance County, is one of the most conservative in the state of North Carolina. For example, a few years before our Pride, the US Department of Justice even sued the county sheriff's office alleging, "discriminatory policing and unconstitutional searches and seizures."[34] (The suit was eventually dropped.) More recently, local law enforcement pepper sprayed some attending a "get out the vote" rally near the county courthouse, and there have been ongoing

---

34. United States Department of Justice, "Justice Department Files Lawsuit against the Alamance County, North Carolina, Sheriff's Office," June 23, 2011, https://www.justice.gov/opa/pr/justice-department-files-lawsuit-against-alamance-county-north-carolina-sheriff-s-office.

clashes over a Confederate statue that stands outside the courthouse.[35] In this type of environment, our Pride board worried about protesters and potential acts of violence, along with more mundane fears about the weather forecast. The local newspaper endorsed the event, but letters to the editor decried the decision. The day of the event came—and about one thousand people from all over the county, including kids, senior citizens, and families of all kinds, danced with drag queens, enjoyed music, and supported the local LGBTQIA+ community.[36] My spouse and I organized the vendor booths, which were, as is typical at a community festival in the rural South, dominated by Christian churches. These churches were at this event because they wanted to let the community know that they are welcoming and that their vision of the New Jerusalem is characterized by inclusion and acceptance. There was only a handful of people outside the "wall" that day with signs protesting the event. As we were dismantling vendor booths, however, the face-painter told me how one of the protesters brought her children down to have their faces painted. As people like to say around here, "Y'all means all."[37]

The City Is a Garden (22:1-5)

The chapter begins with the angel with the measuring rod continuing to show John the New Jerusalem, although now the focus is less on structure and adornment and more on what can be found within the city. Central is the heavenly equivalent of a "greenway," a clear river "bright as crystal" running through the city's street, which is surrounded by the tree of life (vv. 1-2), an image that defies logic. The idea of rivers and lush areas in cities would be familiar to ancient audiences, since the Romans were well known for feats of engineering that allowed them to move large amounts of fresh water into cities for drinking, bathing, and pleasure. By depicting a river of life coming from the heavenly throne, John evokes the monumental fountains seen and even enjoyed by his audience

35. Emma Peaslee, "Lawsuits Filed after Police Use Pepper Spray at North Carolina March to the Polls," *NPR*, November 3, 2020, https://www.npr.org/2020/11/03/930912025/lawsuits-filed-after-police-use-pepper-spray-at-north-carolina-march-to-the-poll.

36. Isaac Groves, "Rainbow Not Rainout: Crowd Enjoys Gay Pride Event," *Burlington Times-News*, October 11, 2015.

37. This phrase has been adopted by the Southern Poverty Law Center as part of a campaign against legislation that discriminates against those in the LGBTQIA+ community. See Southern Poverty Law Center, "Y'all Means All," June 3, 2020, https://www.splcenter.org/news/2020/06/03/yall-means-all.

22:1Then the angel showed me the river of the water of life, bright as crystal, flowing from the throne of God and of the Lamb 2through the middle of the street of the city. On either side of the river is the tree of life with its twelve kinds of fruit, producing its fruit each month; and the leaves of the tree are for the healing of the nations. 3Nothing accursed will be found there any more. But the throne of God and of the Lamb will be in it, and his servants will worship him; 4they will see his face, and his name will be on their foreheads. 5And there will be no more night; they need no light of lamp or sun, for the Lord God will be their light, and they will reign forever and ever.

members and associates this life-giving liquid with God and the Lamb. Here is the source of the water promised in 21:6. Coming straight from God, the water is clear and bright, in contrast to the poisoned, bitter, and bloody waters described earlier in Revelation (9:11; 16:4). John, however, sees clean water as something coming directly from God. This imagery, according to Barbara Rossing, offers "a prophetic critique of our damage to ecosystems, of waters polluted by industrial and agricultural waste, of the denial of drinking water to those who cannot pay."[38] Moreover, the imagery affirms the importance of the natural world for God and the Lamb and points to their role in creating and sustaining the natural world.[39]

Included in the greenway stretching from the throne is the tree of life, which grows on both sides of the river and bears twelve different kinds of fruit (22:2). The combination of river and tree of life imagery suggests that the New Jerusalem is also a new Eden (Gen 2:9-10), conveying the sense that creation has been renewed and no longer bears the scars of environmental degradation that come with the growth of the empire. John draws this imagery from Ezekiel's vision of a rebuilt Jerusalem, where the water teems with fish and attracts abundant wildlife (Ezek 47:9-11). It seems likely that Revelation's audience members similarly imagine the different forms of life that come when fresh water flows.

John's note that the tree of life bears twelve fruits over the course of twelve months indicates that food scarcity is not an issue. For those in John's audiences living in poverty and those impacted negatively by the practice of focusing production on goods for export to Rome and other

38. Rossing, "For the Healing of the World," 179.
39. Rossing, "For the Healing of the World," 177–78.

provinces (see p. 86),[40] the imagery of available and abundant food must be appealing. Further, the idea that the tree of life growing in the center of the New Jerusalem offers "healing to the nations" confirms prophetic promises that those outside the community of the faithful, including those who have been deceived by the "wine" of empire (14:8), will become part of this new world (Isa 60:2, 11). This is a tension in Revelation, which depicts both the judgment of those who follow the Beast, including "the nations," and the reconciliation of these nations with God and the Lamb. Ultimately, it seems that John holds out hope that all people are included in God's heavenly city.

The contrast between this New Jerusalem and Babylon, which was described in terms of a desert or "wilderness," as the NRSV translates ἔρημος (17:3), is not subtle. John transforms the feminized version of Babylon, the Whore, into a desert or desolate space in imagery that suggests rape (17:16; see p. 258). He describes Babylon, an urban space, as a place of demons and all that is foul and hateful, spirit, beast, and bird (18:2). As Barbara Rossing observes, "the choice between [these] two cities" is obvious.[41]

Within this idyllic space, those who are faithful to God and the Lamb worship at the throne (22:3-4). Although brief, this imagery draws together multiple themes. First, the description of these faithful ones recalls Revelation 7, where they are "sealed" or marked like those who are enslaved with the name of God and the Lamb on their foreheads (7:3; see also 14:1 and "Translation Matters: δοῦλος"). The status of the faithful as those enslaved to God and the Lamb persists even into the New Jerusalem. At the same time, the faithful worship before the heavenly throne as kingly priests. Like God, these saints will reign "forever and ever" (22:5). We see again, as in 1:6 and in 20:4-6, the realization of God's promise to the Israelites that his people will be made a "priestly kingdom and a holy nation" (Exod 19:6). Combined with the imagery of enslavement, this is a paradoxical identity for audience members to embrace. Just as they are both victors and virgins, so they are simultaneously kingly priests and slaves. While the point John is making with this imagery is understandable, it is equally understandable that some in Revelation's audiences might decline entering the city since the idea

---

40. Barbara Levick, "The Roman Economy: Trade in Asia Minor and the Niche Market," *GR* 51 (2004): 180–98.

41. Barbara R. Rossing, *The Choice between Two Cities: Whore, Bride, and Empire in the Apocalypse* (Harrisburg, PA: Trinity Press International, 1999), passim.

of enslavement persists. Scripture's prolific use of enslavement language and imagery must be a topic of conversations among Christian congregations living in slavery's wake.

One of the most theologically intriguing parts of this passage is John's description of God and the Lamb using a singular masculine pronoun to reference both figures. This singular pronoun is evident even in the English translation: "But the throne of God *and* the Lamb will be in [the New Jerusalem], and *his* servants will worship *him*; they will see *his* face, and *his* name will be on their foreheads" (22:3-4; emphasis added). The reference to "his name" being on their foreheads belies the earlier reference to the faithful having "his [the Lamb's] name and his Father's name written on their foreheads" (14:1). Here, in the New Jerusalem, the boundary between God and the Lamb is blurred, and entities that were separate in the throne room (5:7) now share the same face. Even though the throne belongs to two, the faithful relate to them as one. As we noted in chapter 1, at points in Revelation the divine seems to be more of a multiplicity than a singular entity, an idea that resonates with some feminist theological thinking.[42] Here in the final chapters, God and the Lamb seem to merge into one. Moreover, the use of a masculine pronoun to describe the God-Lamb combination subsumes the queerness of the Lamb into a masculine framework. Unfortunately, this potentially undercuts the gender ambiguity of the Lion who appears as a slaughtered Lamb (see pp. 72–78). And yet, in verse 5, the language pushes back at this oneness in the image of the faithful reigning along with God and the Lamb. This inconsistent language sounds like hesitance on John's part to embrace the radical re-gendering of God and the Lamb he gestures to throughout the text. Personally, I take this as an opportunity to affirm for him the queerness of the divine.

These final visions of Revelation emphasize newness. John proclaims in 21:1, "Then I saw a new heaven and a new earth; for the first heaven and the first earth had passed away, and the sea was no more"; he next describes a lengthy and complex vision of a New Jerusalem. The new city characterized by the purity and faithfulness of those who follow God and the Lamb replaces the city or, really, all cities established by those who reject God and his work in and through the Lamb, the one who stands though slaughtered. This new city is comprised of those who

---

42. Laurel Schneider, *Beyond Monotheism: A Theology of Multiplicity* (London: Routledge, 2007), 19–26.

reject kyriarchal positions of power and who embrace instead the roles of virgin and bride and even enslaved. This is a city where those who have been deceived by Satan, including his earthly political and social manifestations, experience healing. This is a city where those who follow God and the Lamb, those who are the Bride, invite others to enter.

As we know from the coming of each new year, the old is hard to shake. Our past habits and affects are etched into our daily routine, and the things we had hoped to leave behind with the old year, whether they are financial, political, social, physical, or relational, are still present after we've watched the clock tick past midnight, sipped champagne, and kissed the ones we love. So, John brings the baggage of kyriarchal ways of thinking into his new vision. The fact that over the centuries Christians have deemed his text authoritative makes this baggage potentially dangerous. We are susceptible to repeating John's mistakes, especially since he anxiously threatens anyone who adds or takes away from the words of the book (22:18-19).

Revelation 22:6-21

Final Things?

This commentary began by comparing the experience of reading Revelation to navigating a river, and so the image of a river offers a fitting idea with which to end. John even suggests this idea, drawing his vision to a close by depicting a river flowing from the throne of God and the Lamb and through the New Jerusalem (vv. 1-2). Those hearing or reading the vision are invited to "take the water of life as a gift" (v. 17).

Even if they meander, rivers give the impression of being forward-moving. They begin with headwaters and seemingly run toward an end. The sense that a river is a contained and defined path is, however, somewhat misleading. Rivers pour into oceans, where their fresh waters mingle with salt water before being swallowed up into something bigger. Rivers can also end with deltas, where the water that was relatively contained by the river's bed fans out into multiple streams, pools, and wetlands. Deltas provide rich habitats for birds, animals, plants, fish, and other living things. Human life and river deltas are interconnected. Specifically, river deltas are essential sites of food production, especially rice.[1]

Revelation comes to an end much like a river becomes a delta. Rivulets of text fan out and pool up. There are divine proclamations, first-person

---

1. Thomas S. Bianchi, *Deltas and Humans: A Long Relationship Now Threatened by Global Change* (New York: Oxford University Press, 2016), 112–13.

⁶And he said to me, "These words are trustworthy and true, for the Lord, the God of the spirits of the prophets, has sent his angel to show his servants what must soon take place."

⁷"See, I am coming soon! Blessed is the one who keeps the words of the prophecy of the book."

⁸I, John, am the one who heard and saw these things. And when I heard and saw them, I fell down to worship at the feet of the angel who showed them to me; ⁹but he said to me, "You must not do that! I am a fellow servant with you and your comrades the prophets, and with those who keep the words of this book. Worship God!"

¹⁰And he said to me, "Do not seal up the words of the prophecy of this book, for the time is near. ¹¹Let the evildoer still do evil, and the filthy still be filthy, and the righteous still do right, and the holy still be holy."

¹²"See, I am coming soon; my reward is with me, to repay according to everyone's work. ¹³I am the Alpha and the Omega, the first and the last, the beginning and the end."

narrative, an angelic scolding, blessings, warnings, and affirming "Amens." These pools and trickles come from further upstream in the narrative. There are pieces of earlier text and parts that look and sound familiar. Instead of coming to a nice, neat close, John's story ends with multiple splashes, which is saying something when dealing with a text as unwieldy as Revelation.

Among the themes streaming through these closing verses are John's authority and the authority of the narrative. The verses diminish the former while building up the latter. Revelation 22:6 returns to the opening verses of Revelation, reminding John's audiences that the source of all that is written in the book is supposedly God, not John. God is the one who reveals "what must soon take place" (1:1; 22:6). A similar decentering of John's authority takes place in 22:8-9, when John himself relativizes his role in bringing this narrative to fruition. John reminds his hearers of his receptive role, something underscored when John received the scroll to eat (10:8-10). Two times he makes clear that he heard and saw these things, implying that he did not create them. John is a "fellow servant" or an enslaved person, like the angels who accompany him throughout the narrative, along with his prophetic brothers, ἀδελφοί, which the NRSV translates as "comrades" (see "Translation Matters: ἀδελφός"). John, the angels, and the prophets all work at the behest of God and the Lamb.

Although John depicts his narrative coming from a divinely inspired and managed visionary experience (1:9-11; 4:1; 17:1; 21:9), he is the author of Revelation, and his self-effacement allows him to underscore the

¹⁴Blessed are those who wash their robes, so that they will have the right to the tree of life and may enter the city by the gates. ¹⁵Outside are the dogs and sorcerers and fornicators and murderers and idolaters, and everyone who loves and practices falsehood.

¹⁶"It is I, Jesus, who sent my angel to you with this testimony for the churches. I am the root and the descendant of David, the bright morning star."

¹⁷The Spirit and the bride say, "Come,"

And let everyone who hears say, "Come."

And let everyone who is thirsty come. Let anyone who wishes take the water of life as a gift.

¹⁸I warn everyone who hears the words of the prophecy of this book: if anyone adds to them, God will add to that person the plagues described in this book; ¹⁹if anyone takes away from the words of the book of this prophecy, God will take away that person's share in the tree of life and in the holy city, which are described in this book.

²⁰The one who testifies to these things says, "Surely I am coming soon."

Amen. Come, Lord Jesus!

²¹The grace of the Lord Jesus be with all the saints. Amen.

extreme importance of his message. John's place in Christian history is secured by his being a conduit for God's message, effectively placing him in the company of prophetic luminaries such as Ezekiel, Isaiah, and Enoch. Thus, even while his audiences are informed of John's low status—he is an enslaved person and not the Alpha and Omega—they are reminded over and again to keep "the words of the prophecy" (vv. 7, 9, 10; see also 1:3) and act according to John's view of "what must soon take place" (1:1; 22:6). In fact, these final verses remind hearers and readers of what's at stake in shunning or heeding this message. Those who wash their robes, a metaphor for being willing to die like the Lamb (7:13-14), will be able to enter the New Jerusalem and experience the tree of life (22:14). Those who are filthy and stay filthy will end up outside. These are the dogs and their lot (see p. 332).

John's suggestion that only the clean can enter the opulent city seems at odds with the affirmations and invitations of verses 16-17. Jesus begins these by reminding audience members of his messianic role and describing himself as the "bright morning star" (v. 16). Even though "morning star" is sometimes understood as a title for Satan, also called Lucifer, based on the KJV's translation of Isaiah 14:12,² the imagery here alludes

2. Elaine Pagels, *The Origin of Satan* (New York: Vintage Books, 1995), 48.

to the planet Venus visible at dawn. As the "morning star," Jesus brings light after the darkness of night, an image of hope and beginnings.

In response to Jesus's proclamation, the Spirit and Bride in unison utter the invitation "come," after which John instructs those hearing the text to say "come." This command to "come," Ἔρχου, is a second-person singular, implying that the Spirit, Bride (which is the community of the faithful), and the audience summon Christ. These words echo the events described in the text, taking us back to Revelation 1:7, "Look! He is coming with the clouds." This is a conjuring of Jesus and the dawn since Christ is the morning star. Moreover, the call for the Bridegroom to appear is an inversion of the traditional Roman wedding in which the bride comes to the bridegroom. The Bride, however, expresses a desire for communion and consummation with the one she will wed, challenging the assumption that the bridal identity is entirely passive. This Bride, the collective image of the faithful, wants and seeks union with the divine groom. Thankfully, the Bridegroom confirms that he is, hopefully, coming soon (22:20). The promise of connection will be realized.

Just as Christ hears "come" addressed to him, Revelation's audience members may hear the multiple commands to "come" as a personal beckoning into the New Jerusalem. This invitation is underscored by a reminder that all are invited to come and drink the water of life that flows in the heavenly city, a promise made by God earlier (21:6). Despite John's description of those outside the city and the aspersions he casts on the filthy, these invitations present Revelation's audience members with both an invitation into the New Jerusalem and, I believe, an invitation to enter and engage the text. Set within these verses that have a liturgical ring, including call and response and affirmations, "come" is a call to engage in a kind of textual interpretation that is simultaneously worship. Hence, Gail O'Day explained,

> Revelation demands an exegetical practice that enables the interpreter to be drawn more and more deeply into the text, its view of God, and a world shaped by the awesome mystery of God. When exegesis enables the interpreter to enter into a text, it is as fully a religious practice as prayer or hymn singing, because it becomes an avenue to experience God and God's world in ever changing ways.[3]

3. Gail R. O'Day, "Teaching and Preaching the Book of Revelation," *WW* 25 (2005): 252.

Exegesis as worship demands recognition of how our interpretations potentially impact others and their relationship to the divine. We must ask whether our interpretations are life-giving. Specifically, we must ask whether our interpretations and interpretative practices support the flourishing of those whom the text has harmed. I hope this is true of this commentary, although I recognize that even best intentions sometimes continue to impede and exclude.

The invitation from the Bride and Spirit would be a lovely way to bring Revelation to an end, but John does not leave well enough alone. Instead, John offers a dire warning to anyone who would add or take away from the words of this book (22:18-19). The consequence for taking editorial license is being kept from the tree of life and, even more frightening, experiencing *all* the plagues described in the book. Given all that has come before in Revelation, this threat is daunting.

The proximity of the threat to words uttered by Christ might lead those hearing Revelation aloud (1:3) to believe they are from Christ. The use of the first-person pronoun, "I," sounds a lot like John at the beginning of Revelation, when he directly addresses his hearers (1:9). John is not the only voice in the text to use the first person—God does in 1:8—but the speaker of these threats refers to God in a way that suggests the divine one is not the speaker. In other words, even though the identity of the speaker of the threats remains unclear, we know that they have been penned by John, the author of Revelation. They are not unequivocally the words of God.

Why does it matter who speaks these words about adding and taking away from the text? It matters because these verses attempt to control and circumscribe how the book is interpreted, something that we reject as feminist interpreters. Despite his threats, we believe we can disagree with or challenge John, especially when he replicates the language and structures of kyriarchy. Again, we hear the call to "come" as an invitation to engage, interpret, and navigate this text. Moreover, the hope behind this commentary is that readers will similarly hear this invitation in and through these pages and that you will join us as we navigate these waters in new ways together.

Writing a feminist commentary requires reading for the feminist relevance in all parts of the text, not only parts where characters and images are explicitly gendered. It means taking seriously the notion that *everything* is a feminist issue. For the author of a feminist commentary on a text as detailed and wide-ranging as Revelation this can be difficult, especially since feminist interpretation has been preoccupied with, understandably, John's use of gendered images, including the Woman Clothed in the Sun, Babylon, and the Bride of the Lamb. These images are rhetorically important and, consequently, have significant afterlives apart from Revelation. These "women" continue to appear in visual and literary arts and in more modern media. Due in no small part to John's vision of the great city as a sex-worker, the idea of "Babylon" has become a pop culture trope signaling excess, wantonness, and debauchery.[4] The cultural significance of these images, which contributes to sexist and misogynistic thinking, must continue to be interrogated and unsettled by feminist interpreters. Yet, a feminist commentary hopefully uncovers how these easily excisable images are part of a textual network in which domination, oppression, and even sometimes liberation are interwoven. Attending to these more subtle or often overlooked aspects of the text is also important feminist work.

Finally, writing a feminist commentary on Revelation during a time when the world seems to be in a state of upheaval due to a pandemic, rampant gun violence, growing political and religious extremism, challenges to the rights of women and those in the LGBTQIA+ community, and unprecedented environmental degradation (just to name a few current realities) is daunting. The parallels between current events and John's visions sometimes seemed eerily close. Sometimes the resonances were so loud, it was necessary to take a step back and ask whether I was reading too much of my modern experience into the ancient text. Surely, some readers may think that is the case in some places, while in other places you may find connections and illuminations I undersold or missed. If anything, writing a feminist commentary on Revelation reminded me of the continuing relevance of this text, whether it is being engaged to understand how we came to this time and place or being used to call to account those who want to claim divine power for themselves and turn peoples' attention away from God and the Lamb. Even with all of its faults, Revelation still matters and feminist interpretation of the book is needed now more than ever.

4. See, for example, the allusions to Babylon the Great in both *Metropolis* (Universum Film, 1927) and *Babylon* (Paramount Pictures, 2022). Even though a century apart, both films find the reference to Revelation's image meaningful.

Works Cited

Ancient and Medieval Sources

"1QS." In *The Dead Sea Scrolls Translated*, edited by Florentino García Martínez and translated by Wilfred G. E. Watson, 3–19. 2nd ed. Leiden: Brill, 1996.

"2 Baruch." In *The Apocrypha and Pseudepigrapha of the Old Testament*, vol. 2: *Pseudepigrapha*, translated and edited by R. H. Charles, 481–526. Berkeley: Apocryphile Press, 2004. First published in 1913 by Clarendon Press.

"Acts of Paul and Thecla." In *The Apocryphal New Testament: A Collection of Apocryphal Christian Literature in an English Translation*, edited by J. K. Elliott, 364–74. Rev. ed. Oxford: Oxford University Press, 2005.

Andrew of Caesarea. *Commentary on the Apocalypse*. Translated by Eugenia Scarvelis Constantinou. The Fathers of the Church. Washington, DC: The Catholic University of America Press, 2011.

Apuleius. *Metamorphoses (The Golden Ass)*. 2 volumes. Edited and translated by J. Arthur Hanson. LCL. Cambridge, MA: Harvard University Press, 1989 and 1996.

Aristotle. *Minor Works: On Colours. On Things Heard. Physiognomics. On Plants. On Marvellous Things Heard. Mechanical Problems. On Indivisible Lines. The Situations and Names of Winds. On Melissus, Xenophanes, Gorgias.* Translated by W. S. Hett. LCL 307. Cambridge, MA: Harvard University Press, 1936.

Aristotle. *Poetics*. In *Aristotle, Longinus, Demetrius. Poetics. Longinus: On the Sublime. Demetrius: On Style*. Translated by Stephen Halliwell, W. Hamilton Fyfe, Doreen C. Innes, W. Rhys Roberts. Revised by Donald A. Russell. LCL 199. Cambridge, MA: Harvard University Press, 1995.

Augustine. *City of God*. Volume 6: Books 18.36-20. Translated by William Chase Greene. LCL 416. Cambridge, MA: Harvard University Press, 1960.

Augustus. "Res Gestae Divi Augusti." In *Res Gestae Divi Augusti: Text, Translation, and Commentary*, translated by Alison E. Cooley, 124–74. Cambridge: Cambridge University Press, 2009.

Cassius Dio. *Roman History*. 9 volumes. Translated by Earnest Cary with Herbert B. Foster. LCL. Cambridge, MA: Harvard University Press, 1924.

Catullus, Tibullus. *Catullus. Tibullus. Pervigilium Veneris*. Translated by F. W. Cornish, J. P. Postgate, J. W. Mackail. Revised by G. P. Goold. LCL 6. Cambridge, MA: Harvard University Press, 1913.

Cicero, M. Tullius. *On the Consular Provinces*. In *The Orations of Marcus Tullius Cicero*. Translated by C. D. Yonge, B. A. London. Covent Garden: George Bell & Sons, 1891.

Cicero, M. Tullius. *On the Laws*. In *On the Republic. On the Laws*. Translated by Clinton W. Keyes. LCL 213. Cambridge, MA: Harvard University Press, 1928.

Cicero, M. Tullius. *On the Orator: Book 3. On Fate. Stoic Paradoxes. Divisions of Oratory*. Translated by H. Rackham. LCL. Cambridge, MA: Harvard University Press, 1942.

Cicero, M. Tullius. *Rhetorica ad Herennium*. Translated by Harry Caplan. LCL 403. Cambridge, MA: Harvard University Press, 1954.

Clement of Alexandria. *The Exhortation to the Greeks. The Rich Man's Salvation. To the Newly Baptized*. Translated by G. W. Butterworth. LCL 92. Cambridge, MA: Harvard University Press, 1919.

"The Cloisters Apocalypse." Normandy, France, ca. 1330, f. 4 r., 68.174, The Cloisters Collection. https://www.metmuseum.org/art/collection/search/471869.

Demosthenes. *Orations*. 6 volumes. Translated by J. H. Vince et al. Cambridge, MA: Harvard University Press, 1926–1949.

de Mussis, Gabriele. *Historia de Morbo*. In *The Black Death*, translated and edited by Rosemary Horrox, 14–26. Manchester: Manchester University Press, 1994.

Dio Chrysostom. *Discourses 12–30*. Translated by J. W. Cohoon. LCL 339. Cambridge, MA: Harvard University Press, 1939.

Diodorus Siculus. *Library of History*, vol. 1: *Books 1–2.34*. Translated by C. H. Oldfather. LCL 279. Cambridge, MA: Harvard University Press, 1933.

Diogenes Laertius. *Lives of Eminent Philosophers*, vol. 2: *Books 6–10*. Translated by R. D. Hicks. LCL 185. Cambridge, MA: Harvard University Press, 1925.

Dionysius of Halicarnassus. *Roman Antiquities*. Multiple volumes. Translated by Earnest Cary. LCL. Cambridge, MA: Harvard University Press, 1937–1950.

Epiphanius. *Panarion of Epiphanius of Salamis, Books II and III. de Fide*. Translated by Frank Williams. Leiden: Brill, 2013.

Euripides. *Bacchae. Iphigenia at Aulis. Rhesus*. Edited and translated by David Kovacs. LCL 495. Cambridge, MA: Harvard University Press, 2003.

Euripides. *Suppliant Women. Electra. Heracles*. Edited and translated by David Kovacs. LCL 9. Cambridge, MA: Harvard University Press, 1998.

Eusebius. *The Church History of Eusebius*. Vol. 1 in *The Nicene and Post-Nicene Fathers*, series 2, edited by Philip Schaff and Henry Wace. New York: The Christian Literature Company, 1890.

Fell, Margaret. *Women's Speaking Justified, Proved and Allowed by the Scriptures*. London, 1667.

Galen. *On the Usefulness of the Parts of the Body*. In *Opera Omnia*. Edited by Karl Gottlob Kühn. Vol. 4. 20 vols. Lipsiae: C. Cnobloch, 1821–1833.

Gellius. *Attic Nights*. 3 volumes. Translated by J. C. Rolfe. LCL. Cambridge, MA: Harvard University Press, 1927.

"The Great Hymn to Osiris." In *Ancient Egyptian Literature: The New Kingdom*, vol. 2, edited by Miriam Lichtheim, 81–86. Berkeley: University of California Press, 2006.

Hadewijch. *Hadewijch: The Complete Works*. Translated and introduced by Columba Hart. The Classics of Western Spirituality. New York: Paulist Press, 1980.

Hermas. *The Shepherd*. In *The Apostolic Fathers*, vol. 2: *Epistle of Barnabas. Papias and Quadratus. Epistle to Diognetus. The Shepherd of Hermas*. Edited and translated by Bart D. Ehrman, 174–474. LCL 25. Cambridge, MA: Harvard University Press, 2003.

Herodotus. *The Persian Wars*, vol. 1: *Books 1–2*. Translated by A. D. Godley. LCL 117. Cambridge, MA: Harvard University Press, 1920.

Hildegard. *Scivias*. Translated by Columba Hart and Jane Bishop. The Classics of Western Spirituality. New York: Paulist Press, 1990.

Hippocrates. *Diseases of Women 1–2*. Edited and translated by Paul Potter. LCL 538. Cambridge, MA: Harvard University Press, 2018.

Hippocrates. *Girls*. In *Coan Prenotions. Anatomical and Minor Clinical Writings*. Edited and translated by Paul Potter. LCL 509. Cambridge, MA: Harvard University Press, 2010.

Hippocrates. *Places in Man. Glands. Fleshes. Prorrhetic 1–2. Physician. Use of Liquids. Ulcers. Haemorrhoids and Fistulas*. Edited and translated by Paul Potter. LCL 482. Cambridge, MA: Harvard University Press, 1995.

Hippolytus. "Commentary on Daniel." Vol. 5 in *The Ante-Nicene Fathers: Translations of the Writings of the Fathers Down to A.D. 325*, edited by Alexander Roberts and James Donaldson. Peabody, MA: Hendrickson, 1994.

Historia Augusta. Vol. 1. Translated by David Magie. LCL 139. Cambridge, MA: Harvard University Press, 1921.

Homer. *Iliad*, vol. 1: *Books 1–12*. Translated by A. T. Murray. Revised by William F. Wyatt. LCL 170. Cambridge, MA: Harvard University Press, 1924.

Horace. *The Odes of Horace*. Translated by Jeffrey H. Kaimowitz. Johns Hopkins New Translations from Antiquity. Baltimore, MD: John Hopkins University Press, 2008.

Hymn to Demeter. In *The Homeric Hymn to Demeter: Translation, Commentary, and Interpretive Essays*, translated by Helene P. Foley, 2–27. Princeton: Princeton University Press, 1994.

Irenaeus. *Against Heresies*. Vol. 1 in *The Nicene and Post-Nicene Fathers*, series 2, edited by Philip Schaff and Henry Wace. New York: The Christian Literature Company, 1890.

John of the Cross. *John of the Cross: Selected Writings*. Translated by Kieran Kavanaugh. Mahwah, NJ: Paulist Press, 1987.

Josephus. *Jewish Antiquities*, vol. 1: *Books 1–3*. Translated by H. St. J. Thackeray. LCL 242. Cambridge, MA: Harvard University Press, 1930.

Josephus. *The Jewish War*. 3 vols. Translated by H. St. J. Thackeray. LCL. Cambridge, MA: Harvard University Press, 1928.

Justin. *Dialogue with Trypho*. Vol. 1 of *The Ante-Nicene Fathers: Translations of the Writings of the Fathers Down to A.D. 325*. Edited by Alexander Roberts and James Donaldson. Peabody, MA: Hendrickson, 1994.

Justinian. *The Civil Law*. Translated by S. P. Scott. 17 vols. Cincinnati: Central Trust, 1932.

Juvenal. *Satires*. In *Juvenal and Persius*. Edited and translated by Susanna Morton Braund. LCL 91. Cambridge, MA: Harvard University Press, 2004.

Lucian. *Anacharsis or Athletics. Menippus or The Descent into Hades. On Funerals. A Professor of Public Speaking. Alexander the False Prophet. Essays in Portraiture. Essays in Portraiture Defended. The Goddesse of Surrye*. Translated by A. M. Harmon. LCL 162. Cambridge, MA: Harvard University Press, 1925.

Lucretius. *On the Nature of Things*. Translated by W. H. D. Rouse. Revised by Martin F. Smith. LCL 181. Cambridge, MA: Harvard University Press, 1924.

Luther, Martin. "Preface to the Revelation of St. John [I]." In *Luther's Works: Word and Sacrament I*, vol. 35, edited by E. Theodore Bachmann, 398–99. Philadelphia: Fortress, 1960.

Macrobius. *Saturnalia*, vol. 1: *Books 1–2*. Edited and translated by Robert A. Kaster. LCL 510. Cambridge, MA: Harvard University Press, 2011.

Martial. *Epigrams*, vol. 2: *Books 6–10*. Edited and translated by D. R. Shackleton Bailey. LCL 95. Cambridge, MA: Harvard University Press, 1993.

Martyrdom of Polycarp. In *The Apostolic Fathers*, vol. 1: *I Clement. II Clement. Ignatius. Polycarp. Didache*, edited and translated by Bart D. Ehrman, 366–401. LCL 24. Cambridge, MA: Harvard University Press, 2003.

Mechthild of Magdeburg. *The Flowing Light of the Godhead*. Translated and introduced by Frank Tobin. The Classics of Western Spirituality. New York: Paulist Press, 1998.

Nicolaus and Johannes. *Last Judgment*. Tempera on wood, late twelfth century, 40526, Vatican Museums. https://m.museivaticani.va/content/museivaticani-mobile/en/collezioni/musei/la-pinacoteca/sala-i---secolo-xii-xv/nicolo-e-giovanni--giudizio-finale.html.

Origen. *Commentary on the Gospel of John*. Vol. 9 of *The Ante-Nicene Fathers: Translations of the Writings of the Fathers Down to A.D. 325*. Edited by Alexander Roberts and James Donaldson. Peabody, MA: Hendrickson, 1994.

Ovid. *Metamorphoses*, vol. 1: *Books 1–8*. Translated by Frank Justus Miller. Revised by G. P. Goold. LCL 42. Cambridge, MA: Harvard University Press, 1916.

Passion of Perpetua and Felicity. In *The Passion of Perpetua and Felicity*, edited and translated by Thomas J. Heffernan, 125–35. Oxford: Oxford University Press, 2012.

Pausanias. *Description of Greece*, vol. 4: *Books 8.22-10: Arcadia, Boeotia, Phocis and Ozolian Locri*. Translated by W. H. S. Jones. LCL 297. Cambridge, MA: Harvard University Press, 1935.

Petronius, Seneca. *Satyricon. Apocolocyntosis*. Edited and translated by Gareth Schmeling. LCL 15. Cambridge, MA: Harvard University Press, 2020.

Philo. *Every Good Man Is Free. On the Contemplative Life. On the Eternity of the World. Against Flaccus. Apology for the Jews. On Providence*. Translated by F. H. Colson. LCL 363. Cambridge, MA: Harvard University Press, 1941.

Philo. *On the Decalogue. On the Special Laws, Books 1–3*. Translated by F. H. Colson. LCL 320. Cambridge, MA: Harvard University Press, 1937.

Plato. *Republic*, vol. 1: *Books 1–5*. Edited and translated by Chris Emlyn-Jones and William Preddy. LCL 237. Cambridge, MA: Harvard University Press, 2013.

Pliny the Elder. *Natural History*. 10 volumes. Translated by H. Rackham. LCL. Cambridge, MA: Harvard University Press, 1938.

Pliny the Younger. *Letters*, vol. 1: *Books 1–7*. Translated by Betty Radice. LCL 55. Cambridge, MA: Harvard University Press, 1969.

Pliny the Younger. *Letters*, vol. 2: *Books 8–10. Panegyricus*. Translated by Betty Radice. LCL 59. Cambridge, MA: Harvard University Press, 1969.

Plutarch. "Advice to the Bride and Groom," translated by Donald Russell. In *Plutarch's Advice to the Bride and Groom and A Consolation to His Wife*, edited by Sarah B. Pomeroy, 5–13. New York: Oxford University Press, 1999.

Plutarch. *Lives*, vol. 1: *Theseus and Romulus. Lycurgus and Numa. Solon and Publicola*. Translated by Bernadotte Perrin. LCL 46. Cambridge, MA: Harvard University Press, 1914.

Plutarch. *Moralia*. 15 volumes. Translated by Frank Cole Babbitt. LCL. Cambridge, MA: Harvard University Press, 1936.

Quintilian. *The Orator's Education*, vol. 2: *Books 3–5*. Edited and translated by Donald A. Russell. LCL 125. Cambridge, MA: Harvard University Press, 2002.

Seneca the Elder. *Controversiae in Declamations*, vol. 2: *Controversiae, Books 7–10. Suasoriae. Fragments*. Translated by Michael Winterbottom. LCL 464. Cambridge, MA: Harvard University Press, 1974.

Seneca the Younger. *Epistles*, vol. 1: *Epistles 1–65*. Translated by Richard M. Gummere. LCL 75. Cambridge, MA: Harvard University Press, 1917.

Statius. *Silvae*. Edited and translated by D. R. Shackleton Bailey. Revised by Christopher A. Parrott. LCL 206. Cambridge, MA: Harvard University Press, 2015.

Strabo. *Geography*. 8 volumes. Translated by Horace Leonard Jones. LCL. Cambridge, MA: Harvard University Press, 1929.

Suetonius. *Lives of the Caesars*, vol. 1: *Julius. Augustus. Tiberius. Gaius. Caligula*. Translated by J. C. Rolfe. Introduction by K. R. Bradley. LCL 31. Cambridge, MA: Harvard University Press, 1914.

Suetonius. *Lives of the Caesars*, vol. 2: *Claudius. Nero. Galba, Otho, and Vitellius. Vespasian. Titus, Domitian. Lives of Illustrious Men: Grammarians and Rhetoricians. Poets (Terence. Virgil. Horace. Tibullus. Persius. Lucan). Lives of Pliny the Elder and Passienus Crispus.* Translated by J. C. Rolfe. LCL 38. Cambridge, MA: Harvard University Press, 1914.

Sulpicia. "Cerinthus' Birthday" and "Cerinthus Unfaithful." In *Catullus, Tibullus. Catullus. Tibullus. Pervigilium Veneris*, translated by F. W. Cornish, J. P. Postgate, J. W. Mackail, 328–35. Revised by G. P. Goold. LCL 6. Cambridge, MA: Harvard University Press, 1913.

"Supplementum Epigraphicum Graecum Online." 2009. https://scholarlyeditions .brill.com/sego/.

Tacitus. *The Annals*. 3 vols. Translated by John Jackson. LCL. Cambridge, MA: Harvard University Press, 1937.

Tertullian, Minucius Felix. *Apology. De Spectaculis. Minucius Felix: Octavius.* Translated by T. R. Glover, Gerald H. Rendall. LCL 250. Cambridge, MA: Harvard University Press, 1931.

Tertullian. *Prescription against Heretics.* Vol. 3 in *The Ante-Nicene Fathers: Translation of the Writings of the Fathers Down to A.D. 325*, edited by Alexander Roberts and James Donaldson. Revised and chronologically arranged, with brief prefaces and occasional notes, by A. Cleveland Coxe. New York: Christian Literature, 1885.

Thucydides. *History of the Peloponnesian War*, vol. 1: *Books 1–2*. Translated by C. F. Smith. LCL 108. Cambridge, MA: Harvard University Press, 1919.

Valerius Maximus. *Memorable Doings and Sayings*, vol. 1: *Books 1–5*. Translated by D. R. Shackleton Bailey. LCL 492. Cambridge, MA: Harvard University Press, 2000.

Varro. *On Agriculture*. Translated by W. D. Hooper and Harrison Boyd Ash. LCL 283. Cambridge, MA: Harvard University Press, 1934.

Varro. *On the Latin Language*, vol. 1: *Books 5–7*. Translated by Roland G. Kent. LCL 333. Cambridge, MA: Harvard University Press, 1938.

Victorinus. *Commentary on the Apocalypse.* Vol. 7 in *The Ante-Nicene Fathers: Translations of the Writings of the Fathers Down to A.D. 325*, edited by Alexander Roberts and James Donaldson. Peabody, MA: Hendrickson, 1994.

Virgil. *Eclogues. Georgics. Aeneid: Books 1–6.* Translated by H. Rushton Fairclough. Revised by G. P. Goold. LCL 63. Cambridge, MA: Harvard University Press, 1916.

Vitruvius. *On Architecture.* 2 vols. Translated by Frank Granger. LCL. Cambridge, MA: Harvard University Press, 1931.

Xenophon. *Anthia and Habrocomes.* In Longus, Xenophon of Ephesus. *Daphnis and Chloe. Anthia and Habrocomes*, edited and translated by Jeffrey Henderson. LCL 69. Cambridge, MA: Harvard University Press, 2009.

Modern Sources

"50 Cent Mocks Terry Crews over Sexual Assault Claims." *BBC News*. June 27, 2018. Sec. Newsbeat. https://www.bbc.com/news/newsbeat-44625597.

Abbey-Lambertz, Kate. "These 15 Black Women Were Killed during Police Encounters: Their Lives Matter, Too." *Huffington Post*. February 13, 2015. https://www.huffingtonpost.com/2015/02/13/black-womens-lives-matter-police-shootings_n_6644276.html.

Adekoya, Remi. "Biracial Britain: Why Mixed-Race People Must Be Able to Decide Their Own Identity." *The Conversation*. February 11, 2021. https://theconversation.com/biracial-britain-why-mixed-race-people-must-be-able-to-decide-their-own-identity-154771.

Aguilar, Grace. *The Women of Israel*. London: R. Groombridge, 1845; New York: D. Appleton, 1872.

Ahmed, Sara. *Living a Feminist Life*. Durham, NC: Duke University Press, 2017.

Ahmed, Sara. *The Promise of Happiness*. Durham, NC: Duke University Press, 2010.

Ahmed, Sara. *What's the Use? On the Uses of Use*. Durham, NC: Duke University Press, 2019.

Allen, Mercedes. "Trans-ing Gender: The Surgical Option." In *Gender Outlaws: The Next Generation*, edited by Kate Bornstein and S. Bear Bergman, 101–5. Berkeley: Seal Press, 2010.

Alvizo, Xochitl. "In Memoriam: A Collective Tribute to Carol Patrice Christ 1945–2021." *Feminism and Religion*. July 15, 2021. https://feminismandreligion.com/2021/07/15/in-memoriam-a-collective-tribute-to-carol-patrice-christ-1945-2021/.

Anderson, Janice Capel, and Stephen D. Moore, eds. *Mark and Method: New Approaches in Biblical Studies*. 2nd ed. Minneapolis: Fortress, 2008.

Ando, Clifford. *Imperial Ideology and Provincial Loyalty in the Roman Empire*. Berkeley: University of California Press, 2000.

Andrade, Nathanael. "The Jewish Tetragrammaton: Secrecy, Community, and Prestige among Greek-Writing Jews of the Early Roman Empire." *JSJ* 46 (2015): 198–223.

Anti-Defamation League. "Farrakhan: In His Own Words." January 12, 2013. https://www.adl.org/education/resources/reports/nation-of-islam-farrakhan-in-his-own-words.

Aquino, María Pilar, and María José Rosado-Nunes, eds. *Feminist Intercultural Theology: Latina Explorations for a Just World*. Studies in Latino/a Catholicism. Maryknoll, NY: Orbis Books, 2007.

Aquino, María Pilar, Daisy L. Machado, and Jeanette Rodríguez, eds. *A Reader in Latina Feminist Theology*. Austin: University of Texas Press, 2002.

Ascough, Richard S., Philip A. Harland, and John S. Kloppenborg. *Associations in the Greco-Roman World: A Sourcebook*. Waco, TX: Baylor University Press, 2012.

Astell, Mary. *Some Reflections upon Marriage.* New York: Source Book Press, 1970. Reprint of the 1730 edition; earliest ed. 1700.

Attridge, Harold W., and Society of Biblical Literature, eds. *The HarperCollins Study Bible.* Rev. ed. San Francisco: HarperOne, 2006.

Aune, David E. "The Influence of Roman Imperial Court Ceremonial on the Apocalypse of John." *BR* 28 (1983): 1–26.

Aune, David E. *Revelation.* WBC 52 A–C Dallas: Word Books, 1998.

Aymer, Margaret P. "Empire, Alter-Empire, and the Twenty-First Century." *USQR* 59 (2005): 140–46.

Bach, Alice, ed. *Women in the Hebrew Bible: A Reader.* New York: Routledge, 1999.

Bagnall, Roger S., and Peter Derow, eds. *The Hellenistic Period: Historical Sources in Translation.* New ed. Malden, MA: John Wiley & Sons, 2004.

Bain, Katherine. *Women's Socioeconomic Status and Religious Leadership in Asia Minor: In the First Two Centuries C.E.* Minneapolis: Augsburg Fortress, 2014.

Baker, Nick. "One Year since Australia's Devastating Wildfires, Anger Grows at Climate Change 'Inaction.'" *NBC News.* February 4, 2021. https://www.nbcnews.com/science/environment/one-year-australia-s-devastating-wildfires-anger-grows-climate-change-n1256714.

Baker, Peter. "Christine Blasey Ford's Credibility under New Attack by Senate Republicans." *The New York Times.* October 3, 2018. https://nyti.ms/2OAmJUw.

Bal, Mieke. *Lethal Love: Feminist Literary Readings of Biblical Love Stories.* Bloomington: Indiana University Press, 1987.

Balch, David L. "Cult Statues of Augustus' Temple of Apollo on the Palatine in Rome, Artemis'/Diana's Birthday in Ephesus, and Revelation 12:1-5a." In *Contested Spaces: Houses and Temples in Roman Antiquity and the New Testament,* edited by David L. Balch and Annette Weissenrieder, 413–34. WUNT 285. Tübingen: Mohr Siebeck, 2012.

Barr, David L. "Doing Violence: Moral Issues in Reading John's Apocalypse." In *Reading the Book of Revelation: A Resource for Students,* edited by David L. Barr, 97–108. Atlanta: SBL, 2003.

Barreda Toscano, Juan José. "'Come Out of Her, My People': The Hope of Those Who Suffer Because of Corruption (Revelation 18:1–19:10)." *Journal of Latin American Theology* 12 (2017): 63–81.

Barry, Ellen M. "From Plantations to Prisons: African American Women Prisoners in the United States." In *Beyond Slavery: Overcoming Its Religious and Sexual Legacies,* edited by Bernadette J. Brooten with Jacqueline L. Hazelton, 75–88. New York: Palgrave Macmillan, 2010.

Barton, Bernadette. *Pray the Gay Away: The Extraordinary Lives of Bible Belt Gays.* New York: NYU Press, 2014.

Barton, Carlin A. *The Sorrows of the Ancient Romans: The Gladiator and the Monster.* Princeton: Princeton University Press, 2020.

Baskin, Judith R. "Women and Post-Biblical Commentary." In *The Torah: A Women's Commentary,* edited by Tamara Cohn Eskenazi and Andrea L. Weiss, xlix–lv. New York: URJ Press and Women of Reform Judaism, The Federation of Temple Sisterhoods, 2008.

Bauckham, Richard. "The Book of Revelation as a Christian War Scroll." *Neot* 22 (1988): 17–40.

Bauman, Richard A. *Crime and Punishment in Ancient Rome*. London: Routledge, 2002.

Baynes, Leslie A. "Revelation 5:1 and 10:2a, 8-10 in the Earliest Greek Tradition: A Response to Richard Bauckham." *JBL* 129 (2010): 801–16.

Beale, Gregory K. *The Book of Revelation: A Commentary on the Greek Text*. Grand Rapids: Eerdmans, 1999.

Beavis, Mary Ann. "Jezebel Speaks: Naming the Goddesses in the Book of Revelation." In *A Feminist Companion to the Apocalypse of John*, edited by Amy-Jill Levine with Maria Mayo Robbins, 131–46. FCNTECW 13. London: T&T Clark, 2009.

Beavis, Mary Ann, Irmtraud Fischer, Mercedes Navarro Puerto, and Adriana Valerio, eds. The Bible and Women: An Encyclopaedia of Exegesis and Cultural History. https://www.bibleandwomen.org.

Bianchi, Thomas S. *Deltas and Humans: A Long Relationship Now Threatened by Global Change*. New York: Oxford University Press, 2016.

Biguzzi, G. "Is the Babylon of Revelation Rome or Jerusalem?" *Bib* 87 (2006): 371–86.

Bird, Phyllis A. *Missing Persons and Mistaken Identities: Women and Gender in Ancient Israel*. Minneapolis: Fortress, 1997.

Blakely, Sandra. "Maritime Risk and Ritual Responses: Sailing with the Gods in the Ancient Mediterranean." In *The Sea in History—The Ancient World*, edited by Philip de Souza, Pascal Arnaud, and Christian Buchet, 362–79. Suffolk: Boydell and Brewer, 2017.

Blickenstaff, Marianne. *While the Bridegroom Is with Them: Marriage, Family, Gender and Violence in the Gospel of Matthew*. LNTS 292. London: Bloomsbury, 2005.

Blount, Brian K. *Can I Get a Witness? Reading Revelation through African American Culture*. Louisville: Westminster John Knox, 2005.

Blount, Brian K. *Revelation: A Commentary*. Louisville: Westminster John Knox, 2009.

Boesak, Allan Aubrey. *Comfort and Protest*. Philadelphia: Westminster John Knox, 1987.

Bogaert, Anthony F. *Understanding Asexuality*. Lanham, MD: Rowman & Littlefield, 2015.

Boigon, Molly. "Is Gab's Leadership as Antisemitic as Its Users?" *The Forward*. January 14, 2021. https://forward.com/news/462140/is-gabs-leadership -as-antisemitic-as-its-users/.

Bonfante, Larissa. "Nudity as a Costume in Classical Art." *AJA* 93 (1989): 543–70.

Boring, M. Eugene. *Revelation*. Louisville: John Knox, 1989.

Bornstein, Kate. "Gender Terror, Gender Rage." In *The Transgender Studies Reader*, edited by Susan Stryker and Stephen Whittle, 236–42. New York: Routledge, 2006.

Børresen, Kari Elisabeth, and Adriana Valerio, eds. *The High Middle Ages*. The Bible and Women: An Encyclopaedia of Exegesis and Cultural History. Atlanta: SBL Press, 2015.

Botha, Pieter J. J. *Orality and Literacy in Early Christianity*. Eugene, OR: Wipf and Stock, 2012.

Boxall, Ian. *Patmos in the Reception History of the Apocalypse*. Oxford: Oxford University Press, 2013.

Boyer, Paul S. *When Time Shall Be No More: Prophecy Belief in Modern American Culture*. Cambridge, MA: Harvard University Press, 1992.

Bradley, Keith. "On Captives under the Principate." *Phoenix* 58 (2004): 298–318.

Bresson, Alain. *The Making of the Ancient Greek Economy: Institutions, Markets, and Growth in the City-States*. Princeton: Princeton University Press, 2019.

Bricault, Laurent. "The '*Gens Isiaca*' in Graeco-Roman Coinage." *The Numismatic Chronicle (1966–)* 175 (2015): 83–102.

Briggs, Sheila. "Can an Enslaved God Liberate? Hermeneutical Reflections on Philippians 2:6-11." *Semeia* 47 (1989): 137–53.

Brintnall, Kent L. *Ecce Homo: The Male-Body-in-Pain as Redemptive Figure*. Chicago: University of Chicago Press, 2011.

Brintnall, Kent L. "Queer Studies and Religion." *CRR* 1 (2013): 51–61.

Brintnall, Kent L. "Who Weeps for the Sodomite?" In *Sexual Disorientations: Queer Temporalities, Affects, Theologies*, edited by Kent L. Brintnall, Joseph A. Marchal, and Stephen D. Moore, 145–60. New York: Fordham University Press, 2018.

Brooten, Bernadette J. "Introduction." In *Beyond Slavery: Overcoming Its Religious and Sexual Legacies*, edited by Bernadette J. Brooten with the editorial assistance of Jacqueline L. Hazelton, 1–29. New York: Palgrave Macmillan, 2010.

Brooten, Bernadette J. *Love Between Women: Early Christian Responses to Female Homoeroticism*. Chicago: University of Chicago Press, 1996.

Broucke, Pieter B. F. J. "Tyche and the Fortune of Cities in the Greek and Roman World." *Yale University Art Gallery Bulletin* (1994): 34–49.

Bruehler, Bart B. "Seeing through the עיכים of Zechariah: Understanding Zechariah 4." *CBQ* 63 (2001): 430–43.

Brussell, David Eric. "Medicinal Plants of Mt. Pelion, Greece." *Economic Botany* 58 (2004): S174–202.

Butler, Judith. *Undoing Gender*. New York: Routledge, 2004.

Bynum, Caroline Walker. *Christian Materiality: An Essay on Religion in Late Medieval Europe*. Brooklyn, NY: Zone Books, 2015.

Byron, Gay L. *Symbolic Blackness and Ethnic Difference in Early Christian Literature*. London: Routledge, 2002.

Caird, G. B. *A Commentary on the Revelation of St. John the Divine*. BNTC 19. London: Hendrickson, 1984.

Caldwell, Lauren. *Roman Girlhood and the Fashioning of Femininity*. Cambridge: Cambridge University Press, 2015.

Callahan, Allen Dwight. "Babylon Boycott: The Book of Revelation." *Int* 63 (January 2009): 48–54.

Callahan, Allen Dwight. "The Language of Apocalypse." *HTR* 88 (1995): 453–70.

Callahan, Allen Dwight, and Richard A. Horsley. "Slave Resistance in Classical Antiquity." *Semeia* 83–84 (1998): 133–51.

Cannon, Katie G. "The Emergence of Black Feminist Consciousness." In *Feminist Interpretation of the Bible*, edited by Letty M. Russell, 30–40. Philadelphia: Westminster, 1985.

Carey, Frances. *The Apocalypse and the Shape of Things to Come*. London: British Museum Press, 1999.

Carey, Greg. *Elusive Apocalypse: Reading Authority in the Revelation to John*. Macon, GA: Mercer University Press, 1999.

Carey, Greg. "Revelation 7:9-17." In *Feasting on the Word: Year C; Preaching the Revised Common Lectionary*, edited by David L. Bartlett and Barbara Brown Taylor, vol. 2:439–43. Louisville: Westminster John Knox, 2009.

Carey, Greg. "Revelation's Violence Problem: Mapping Essential Questions." *PRSt* 42 (2015): 295–306.

Carroll, Maureen. *Infancy and Earliest Childhood in the Roman World: "A Fragment of Time."* Oxford: Oxford University Press, 2018.

Carson, Anne. "Putting Her in Her Place: Woman, Dirt, and Desire." In *Before Sexuality: The Construction of Erotic Experience in the Ancient Greek World*, edited by David M. Halperin, John J. Winkler, and Froma I. Zeitlin, 135–70. Princeton: Princeton University Press, 1990.

Carter, Warren. "Matthaean Christology in Roman Imperial Key: Matthew 1.1." In *The Gospel of Matthew in Its Roman Imperial Context*, edited by John Riches and David C. Sim, 143–65. London: T&T Clark, 2005.

Carter, Warren. *The Roman Empire and the New Testament: An Essential Guide*. Nashville: Abingdon, 2006.

Castelli, Elizabeth. "*Les Belles Infidèles*/Fidelity or Feminism? The Meanings of Feminist Biblical Translation." In *Searching the Scriptures: A Feminist Introduction*, vol. 1, edited by Elisabeth Schüssler Fiorenza with the assistance of Shelly Matthews, 189–204. New York: Crossroad, 1993.

Castelli, Elizabeth A. "Romans." In *Searching the Scriptures: A Feminist Commentary*, vol. 2, edited by Elisabeth Schüssler Fiorenza with the assistance of Ann Brock and Shelly Matthews, 272–300. New York: Crossroad, 1994.

Chau, Kevin. "Conceptual Blending in Joel 2:1-11: God's Apocalyptic Storm-Locusts-Warriors." In *T&T Clark Handbook of Asian American Biblical Hermeneutics*, edited by Uriah Y. Kim and Seung Ai Yang, 273–83. London: T&T Clark, 2019.

Chew, Sing C. *World Ecological Degradation: Accumulation, Urbanization, and Deforestation, 3000 BC–AD 2000*. Lanham, MD: AltaMira Press, 2001.

Christ, Carol P. "Why Women Need the Goddess." In *Womanspirit Rising: A Feminist Reader in Religion*, edited by Carol P. Christ and Judith Plaskow, 273–87. San Francisco: Harper and Row, 1979.

Claassens, L. Juliana, and Carolyn J. Sharp, eds. *Feminist Frameworks and the Bible: Power, Ambiguity, and Intersectionality*. LHBOTS 630. London: Bloomsbury T&T Clark, 2017.

Claassens, L. Juliana, and Irmtraud Fischer, eds. *Prophecy and Gender in the Hebrew Bible*. The Bible and Women: An Encyclopaedia of Exegesis and Cultural History. Atlanta: SBL Press, 2021.

Clark, Elizabeth A. *Ascetic Piety and Women's Faith: Essays on Late Ancient Christianity*. Lewiston, NY: E. Mellen Press, 1986.

Cobb, L. Stephanie. *Divine Deliverance: Pain and Painlessness in Early Christian Martyr Texts*. Oakland: University of California Press, 2017.

Cobb, L. Stephanie. *Dying to Be Men: Gender and Language in Early Christian Martyr Texts*. New York: Columbia University Press, 2008.

Cohen, Jeffrey Jerome. "Monster Culture (Seven Theses)." In *Monster Theory: Reading Culture*, edited by Jeffrey Jerome Cohen, 3–25. Minneapolis: University of Minnesota Press, 1996.

Cohn, Norman. *The Pursuit of the Millennium: Revolutionary Millenarians and Mystical Anarchists of the Middle Ages*. Rev. ed. Oxford: Oxford University Press, 1970.

Collins, Patricia Hill. *Black Feminist Thought: Knowledge, Consciousness, and the Politics of Empowerment*. 2nd ed. New York: Routledge, 2000.

Consolino, Franca Ela, and Judith Herrin, eds. *The Early Middle Ages*. The Bible and Women: An Encyclopaedia of Exegesis and Cultural History. Atlanta: SBL Press, 2020.

Cook, Stephen L. *Ezekiel 38–48*. New Haven: Yale University Press, 2018.

Cooley, Alison E. "Paratextual Readings of Imperial Discourse in the 'Res Gestae Divi Augusti.'" *Cahiers Du Centre Gustave Glotz* 25 (2014): 215–30.

Corbeill, Anthony. *Sexing the World: Grammatical Gender and Biological Sex in Ancient Rome*. Princeton: Princeton University Press, 2015.

Cornwall, Susannah. "Introduction: Troubling Bodies?" In *Intersex, Theology, and the Bible: Troubling Bodies in Church, Text, and Society*, edited by Susannah Cornwall, 1–26. New York: Palgrave Macmillan, 2015.

Crenshaw, Kimberlé. "Mapping the Margins: Intersectionality, Identity Politics, and Violence against Women of Color." *Stanford Law Review* 43 (1991): 1241–99.

Crowder, Stephanie Buckhanon. "A Mother-Whore Is Still a Mother: Revelation 17–18 and African American Motherhood." In *Parenting as Spiritual Practice and Source for Theology: Mothering Matters*, edited by Claire Bischoff, Elizabeth O'Donnell Gandolfo, and Annie Hardison-Moody, 153–70. Cham, Switzerland: Springer International, 2017.

Culham, Phyllis. "The Roman Empire and the Seas." In *The Sea in History—The Ancient World*, edited by Philip de Souza, Pascal Arnaud, and Christian Buchet, 283–93. Suffolk: Boydell and Brewer, 2017.

Daly, Mary. *Beyond God the Father: A Philosophy of Women's Liberation.* Boston: Beacon, 1985.

D'Ambra, Eve. *Private Lives, Imperial Virtues: The Frieze of the Forum Transitorium in Rome.* Princeton: Princeton University Press, 1993.

D'Andria, Francesco. "Nature and Cult in the *Ploutonion* of Hierapolis before and after the Colony." In *Landscape and History in the Lykos Valley: Laodikeia and Hierapolis in Phrygia*, edited by Celal Şimşek and Francesco D'Andria, 207–40. Newcastle upon Tyne: Cambridge Scholars Publishing, 2017.

D'Angelo, Mary Rose. "Women Partners in the New Testament." *JFSR* 6 (1990): 65–86.

Darden, Lynne St. Clair. *Scripturalizing Revelation: An African American Postcolonial Reading of Empire.* SemeiaSt 80. Atlanta: SBL Press, 2015.

Davies, Guy. "Racism in Soccer an 'Epidemic' That Mirrors Disturbing Trends in Europe: Advocates." *ABC News.* February 1, 2020. https://abcnews.go.com/Sports/racism-soccer-epidemic-mirrors-disturbing-trends-europe-advocates/story?id=67850877.

Delaney, Carol. "Columbus's Ultimate Goal: Jerusalem." *Comparative Studies in Society and History* 48 (2006): 260–92.

De Palma, Brian. *Carrie.* Red Bank Films, 1976.

DeRogatis, Amy. *Saving Sex: Sexuality and Salvation in American Evangelicalism.* New York: Oxford University Press, 2015.

deSilva, David A. *Seeing Things John's Way: The Rhetoric of the Book of Revelation.* Louisville: Westminster John Knox, 2009.

DeYoung, Kevin. *What Does the Bible Really Teach about Homosexuality?* Wheaton, IL: Crossway, 2015.

Dickerson, Caitlin. "Parents of 545 Children Separated at the Border Cannot Be Found." *The New York Times.* October 21, 2020. https://www.nytimes.com/2020/10/21/us/migrant-children-separated.html.

Dickerson, Febbie. *Luke, Widows, Judges, and Stereotypes.* Womanist Readings of Scripture. Lanham, MD: Lexington Books/Fortress Academic, 2019.

Dignas, Beate. *Economy of the Sacred in Hellenistic and Roman Asia Minor.* Oxford: Oxford University Press, 2002.

Dinkler, Michal Beth. *Literary Theory and the New Testament.* AYBRL. New Haven: Yale University Press, 2019.

Dixon, Suzanne. *The Roman Family.* Baltimore: Johns Hopkins University Press, 1992.

Dobroruka, Vicente. "Chemically-Induced Visions in the Fourth Book of Ezra in Light of Comparative Persian Material." *JSQ* 13 (2006): 1–26.

Douglas, Kelly Brown. *Stand Your Ground: Black Bodies and the Justice of God.* Maryknoll, NY: Orbis Books, 2015.

Dube, Musa W., ed. *Postcolonial Feminist Interpretation of the Bible.* St. Louis: Chalice, 2000.

duBois, Page. *Slavery: Antiquity and Its Legacy.* New York: Oxford University Press, 2009.

duBois, Page. *Sowing the Body: Psychoanalysis and Ancient Representations of Women.* Chicago: University of Chicago Press, 1991.

Du Bois, W. E. B. *The Souls of Black Folk.* Oxford: Oxford University Press, 2007.

Dunbabin, Katherine M. D. *Mosaics of the Greek and Roman World.* Cambridge: Cambridge University Press, 1999.

du Rand, Jan A. "The Song of the Lamb Because of the Victory of the Lamb." *Neot* 29 (1995): 203–10.

Eagleton, Terry. *Ideology: An Introduction.* London: Verso, 2007.

Eagleton, Terry. *Literary Theory: An Introduction.* 3rd ed. Minneapolis: University of Minnesota Press, 2008.

Edwards, Catharine. *The Politics of Immorality in Ancient Rome.* Cambridge: Cambridge University Press, 2002.

Edwards, Catharine. "Unspeakable Professions: Public Performance and Prostitution in Ancient Rome." In *Roman Sexualities,* edited by Judith P. Hallet and Marilyn B. Skinner, 66–95. Princeton: Princeton University Press, 1997.

Edwards, David A. "Joseph Smith and the Book of Revelation." *Ensign* (December 2015).

Elkins, Kathleen Gallagher. *Mary, Mother of Martyrs: How Motherhood Became Self-Sacrifice in Early Christianity.* Indianapolis: Dog Ear, 2018.

Elliott, Susan M. "Who Is Addressed in Revelation 18:6-7?" *BR* 40 (1995): 98–113.

Emanuel, Sarah. *Humor, Resistance, and Jewish Cultural Persistence in the Book of Revelation: Roasting Rome.* Cambridge: Cambridge University Press, 2020.

Emmerson, Richard K. "Introduction: The Apocalypse in Medieval Culture." In *The Apocalypse in the Middle Ages,* edited by Richard K. Emmerson and Bernard McGinn, 293–332. Ithaca: Cornell University Press, 1992.

Engelbreit, Mary. *Hurt Not the Earth,* n.d., illustration. https://www.maryengelbreit.com/products/hurt-not-the-earth-fine-print.

Erim, K. T., and Joyce Reynolds. "The Aphrodisias Copy of Diocletian's Edict on Maximum Prices." *JRS* 63 (1973): 99–110.

Eskenazi, Tamara Cohn, and Andrea L. Weiss, eds. *The Torah: A Women's Commentary.* New York: URJ Press and Women of Reform Judaism, The Federation of Temple Sisterhoods, 2008.

Evans Grubbs, Judith. " 'Marriage More Shameful Than Adultery': Slave-Mistress Relationships, 'Mixed Marriages,' and Late Roman Law." *Phoenix* 47 (1993): 125–54.

Evans Grubbs, Judith. *Women and the Law in the Roman Empire: A Sourcebook on Marriage, Divorce and Widowhood.* London: Routledge, 2002.

Exum, J. Cheryl. "Second Thoughts about Secondary Characters: Women in Exodus 1.8–2.10." In *A Feminist Companion to Exodus to Deuteronomy,* edited by Athalya Brenner, 75–97. FCB 6. Sheffield: Sheffield Academic, 1994.

Exum, J. Cheryl, and David J. A. Clines, eds. *The New Literary Criticism and the Hebrew Bible*. Valley Forge, PA: Trinity Press International, 1993.

Faas, Patrick. *Around the Roman Table: Food and Feasting in Ancient Rome*. Chicago: University of Chicago Press, 2005.

Faderman, Lillian. *To Believe in Women: What Lesbians Have Done for America; A History*. Boston: Houghton Mifflin, 2000.

Fagaly, William A. *Tools of Her Ministry: The Art of Sister Gertrude Morgan*. New York: Rizzoli, 2004.

Faraone, Christopher A. *The Transformation of Greek Amulets in Roman Imperial Times*. Philadelphia: University of Pennsylvania Press, 2018.

Fausto-Sterling, Anne. *Sexing the Body: Gender Politics and the Construction of Sexuality*. New York: Basic Books, 2000.

Fee, Gordon D. *Revelation*. New Covenant Commentary. Eugene, OR: Wipf and Stock, 2010.

Feminist Biblical Interpretation: A Compendium of Critical Commentary on the Books of the Bible and Related Literature. Translated by Lisa E. Dahill, Everett R. Kalin, Nancy Lukens, Linda M. Maloney, Barbara Rumscheidt, Martin Rumscheidt, and Tina Steiner. Edited by Luise Schottroff and Marie-Theres Wacker. Grand Rapids: Eerdmans, 2012.

Fewell, Danna Nolan, and David M. Gunn. *Gender, Power, and Promise: The Subject of the Bible's First Story*. Nashville: Abingdon, 1993.

Fischer, Irmtraud, and Mercedes Navarro Puerto, with Andrea Taschl-Erber, eds. *Torah*. The Bible and Women: An Encyclopaedia of Exegesis and Cultural History. Atlanta: SBL, 2011.

Fischer, Marina. "Ancient Greek Prostitutes and the Textile Industry in Attic Vase-Painting ca. 550–450 B.C.E." *CW* 106 (2013): 220–22.

Fitzsimons, Tim. "Nearly 1 in 5 Hate Crimes Motivated by Anti-LGBTQ Bias, FBI Finds." NBC News. November 12, 2019. https://www.nbcnews.com /feature/nbc-out/nearly-1-5-hate-crimes-motivated-anti-lgbtq-bias-fbi -n1080891.

Fletcher, Michelle. "Flesh for Franken-Whore: Reading Babylon's Body in Revelation 17." In *The Body in Biblical, Christian and Jewish Texts*, edited by Joan E. Taylor, 144–64. London: Bloomsbury, 2014.

Fletcher, Michelle. *Reading Revelation as Pastiche: Imitating the Past*. London: Bloomsbury, 2017.

Foucault, Michel. *Discipline & Punish: The Birth of the Prison*. New York: Pantheon Books, 1977.

Frankfurter, David. *Evil Incarnate: Rumors of Demonic Conspiracy and Satanic Abuse in History*. Princeton: Princeton University Press, 2018.

Frankfurter, David. "Jews or Not? Reconstructing the 'Other' in Rev 2:9 and 3:9." *HTR* 94 (2001): 403–25.

Fredrick, David. "Introduction: Invisible Rome." In *The Roman Gaze: Vision, Power, and the Body*, edited by David Fredrick, 1–30. Baltimore: Johns Hopkins University Press, 2002.

Fredriksen, Paula. *From Jesus to Christ: The Origins of the New Testament Images of Jesus*. New Haven: Yale University Press, 2008.

Fredriksen, Paula. *Paul: The Pagan's Apostle*. New Haven: Yale University Press, 2017.

Freedman, Dan. "Why Were Jews Blamed for the Black Death?" *Moment Magazine*. March 31, 2020. https://momentmag.com/why-were-jews-blamed-for-the-black-death/.

Freeman, Elizabeth. *Time Binds: Queer Temporalities, Queer Histories*. Durham, NC: Duke University Press, 2010.

Friesen, Steven J. "High Priestesses of Asia and Emancipatory Interpretation." In *Walk in the Ways of Wisdom: Essays in Honor of Elisabeth Schüssler Fiorenza*, edited by Shelly Matthews, Cynthia Briggs Kittredge, and Melanie Johnson-Debaufre, 136–50. Harrisburg, PA: Trinity Press International, 2003.

Friesen, Steven J. *Imperial Cults and the Apocalypse of John: Reading Revelation in the Ruins*. Oxford: Oxford University Press, 2001.

Friesen, Steven J. "Poverty in Pauline Studies: Beyond the So-Called New Consensus." *JSNT* 26 (2004): 323–61.

Friesen, Steven J. "Sarcasm in Revelation 2–3: Churches, Christians, True Jews, and Satanic Synagogues." In *The Reality of Apocalypse: Rhetoric and Politics in the Book of Revelation*, edited by David L. Barr, 127–44. Atlanta: SBL, 2006.

Friesen, Steven J. "Satan's Throne, Imperial Cults and the Social Settings of Revelation." *JSNT* 27 (2005): 351–73.

Friesen, Steven J. *Twice Neokoros: Ephesus, Asia, and the Cult of the Flavian Imperial Family*. Leiden: Brill, 1993.

Frilingos, Christopher A. "Sexing the Lamb." In *New Testament Masculinities*, edited by Stephen D. Moore and Janice Capel Anderson, 297–317. Atlanta: SBL, 2003.

Frilingos, Christopher A. *Spectacles of Empire: Monsters, Martyrs, and the Book of Revelation*. Philadelphia: University of Pennsylvania Press, 2004.

Frymer-Kensky, Tikva. *Reading the Women of the Bible*. New York: Schocken Books, 2002.

Fuller, Robert C. *Naming the Antichrist: The History of an American Obsession*. Oxford: Oxford University Press, 1995.

Futrell, Alison. *The Roman Games: A Sourcebook*. Blackwell Sourcebooks in Ancient History. Malden, MA: Blackwell, 2006.

Gallagher, Edmon L., and John D. Meade. *The Biblical Canon Lists from Early Christianity: Texts and Analysis*. Oxford: Oxford University Press, 2017.

Gallusz, Laszlo. *The Throne Motif in the Book of Revelation*. London: Bloomsbury, 2013.

Gardiner, E. Norman. *Athletics in the Ancient World*. Mineola, NY: Dover, 2002.

Gerber, Lynne. "AIDS and the Blessings of Staying: The Ministry of Reverend Jim Mitulski." *The Revealer* (blog). June 3, 2021. https://therevealer.org/aids-and-the-blessings-of-staying-the-ministry-of-reverend-jim-mitulski/.

Getty-Sullivan, Mary Ann. *Women in the New Testament.* Collegeville, MN: Liturgical Press, 2001.

Gieseler, Carly. *The Voices of #MeToo: From Grassroots Activism to a Viral Roar.* Lanham, MD: Rowman & Littlefield, 2019.

Glancy, Jennifer A. *Slavery in Early Christianity.* Oxford: Oxford University Press, 2002.

Glancy, Jennifer A., and Stephen D. Moore. "How Typical a Roman Prostitute Is Revelation's 'Great Whore'?" *JBL* 130 (2011): 551–69.

Gleason, Maud W. *Making Men: Sophists and Self-Presentation in Ancient Rome.* Princeton: Princeton University Press, 1995.

Global Witness. "The Truth about Diamonds: Diamonds and Conflict." November 2006. https://cdn.globalwitness.org/archive/files/import/the_truth_about_diamonds.pdf.

Gomel, Elana. "The Plague of Utopias: Pestilence and the Apocalyptic Body." *Twentieth Century Literature* 46 (2000): 405–33.

Gonzalez, Michelle A. "Latina Feminist Theology: Past, Present, and Future." *JFSR* 25 (2009): 150–55.

González, Ondina E., and Justo L. González. *Christianity in Latin America: A History.* New York: Cambridge University Press, 2008.

Good, Deirdre J. "Reading Strategies for Biblical Passages on Same-Sex Relations." *Theology and Sexuality* 7 (1997): 70–82.

Goodwillie, Christian, and Jane F. Crosthwaite. *Millennial Praises: A Shaker Hymnal.* Amherst: University of Massachusetts Press, 2009.

Graf, Fritz. "What Is Ancient Mediterranean Religion?" In *Ancient Religions,* edited by Sarah Iles Johnston, 3–16. Cambridge, MA: Harvard University Press, 2007.

Graybill, Rhiannon. *Are We Not Men? Unstable Masculinity in the Hebrew Prophets.* New York: Oxford University Press, 2016.

Graybill, Rhiannon. "Fuzzy, Messy, Icky: The Edges of Consent in Hebrew Bible Rape Narratives and Rape Culture." *BCT* 15 (2019). https://www.bibleandcriticaltheory.com/issues/vol-15-no-2-2019-bible-and-critical-theory/fuzzy-messy-icky-the-edges-of-consent-in-hebrew-bible-rape-narratives-and-rape-culture/.

Graybill, Rhiannon. *Texts after Terror: Rape, Sexual Violence, and the Hebrew Bible.* New York: Oxford University Press, 2021.

Graybill, Rhiannon, Meredith Minister, and Beatrice Lawrence. "Sexual Violence in and around the Classroom." *Teaching Theology & Religion* 20 (2017): 70–88.

Grimké, Sarah. *Letters on the Equality of the Sexes and the Condition of Woman.* Boston: Isaac Knapp, 1838.

Gross, Jenny. "Archaeologists Uncover Decapitated Bodies from Roman Britain." *The New York Times.* June 2, 2021. https://www.nytimes.com/2021/06/02/world/europe/roman-burials-decapitated.html.

Gross, Rita. "Is the Goddess a Feminist?" In *Is the Goddess a Feminist? The Politics of South Asian Goddesses*, edited by Alf Hiltebeitel and Kathleen M. Erndl, 104–22. New York: NYU Press, 2000.

Groves, Isaac. "Rainbow Not Rainout: Crowd Enjoys Gay Pride Event." *Burlington Times-News*. October 11, 2015.

Grubb, Nancy. *Revelations: Art of the Apocalypse*. New York: Abbeville, 1997.

Gruen, Erich S. *Diaspora: Jews amidst Greeks and Romans*. Cambridge, MA: Harvard University Press, 2002.

Gstalter, Morgan. "North Carolina Gun Shop Puts up '4 Horsemen' Billboard to Slam Progressive Congresswomen." *The Hill*. July 30, 2019. https://thehill .com/homenews/house/455320-north-carolina-gun-shop-puts-up-4 -horsemen-billboard-to-slam-progressive.

Guest, Deryn. *When Deborah Met Jael: Lesbian Biblical Hermeneutics*. London: SCM, 2005.

Gundry, Robert H. "The New Jerusalem: People as Place, Not Place for People." *NovT* 29 (1987): 254–64.

Habel, Norman C., and Peter Trudinger. *Exploring Ecological Hermeneutics*. SymS 46. Atlanta: SBL, 2008.

Halberstam, Judith, and Del LaGrace Volcano. *The Drag King Book*. London: Serpent's Tail, 1999.

Hamburger, Jeffrey F. *St. John the Divine: The Deified Evangelist in Medieval Art and Theology*. Berkeley: University of California Press, 2002.

Hansen, Ryan Leif. *Silence and Praise: Rhetorical Cosmology and Political Theology in the Book of Revelation*. Minneapolis: Augsburg Fortress, 2014.

Harland, Philip A. "Honouring the Emperor or Assailing the Beast: Participation in Civic Life among Associations (Jewish, Christian and Other) in Asia Minor and the Apocalypse of John." *JSNT* 77 (2000): 99–121.

Hartocollis, Anemona. "Gender Pronouns Can Be Tricky on Campus: Harvard Is Making Them Stick." *The New York Times*. February 19, 2020. Sec. U.S. https://www.nytimes.com/2020/02/19/us/gender-pronouns-college .html.

Hays, Christopher B. "Gun Violence in America: A Theological Treatment for a Deadly Epidemic." In *God and Guns: The Bible against American Gun Culture*, edited by Christopher B. Hays and C. L. Crouch, 1–12. Louisville: Westminster John Knox, 2021.

Hearon, Holly E., and Philip Ruge-Jones, eds. *The Bible in Ancient and Modern Media: Story and Performance*. Eugene, OR: Cascade Books, 2009.

Heller, Meredith. *Queering Drag: Redefining the Discourse of Gender-Bending*. Bloomington: Indiana University Press, 2020.

Henning, Meghan R. *Hell Hath No Fury: Gender, Disability, and the Invention of Damned Bodies in Early Christian Literature*. New Haven: Yale University Press, 2021.

Hens-Piazza, Gina. *The New Historicism*. GBS, Old Testament Series. Minneapolis: Fortress, 2002.

Hernández, Juan, Jr. "A Scribal Solution to a Problematic Measurement in the Apocalypse." *NTS* 56 (2010): 273–78.

Hersch, Karen K. *The Roman Wedding: Ritual and Meaning in Antiquity*. Cambridge: Cambridge University Press, 2010.

Hersch, Karen K. "Violence in the Roman Wedding." In *The Discourse of Marriage in the Greco-Roman World*, edited by Jeffrey Beneker and Georgia Tsouvala, 68–93. Madison: University of Wisconsin Press, 2020.

Hess, Abigail Johnson. "U.S. Soccer Federation Announces Men's and Women's National Teams Will Be Offered the Same Contract." CNBC. September 15, 2021. https://www.cnbc.com/2021/09/15/us-soccer-federation-to-offer -men-and-women-players-same-contract.html.

Hesse, Josiah. "Apocalyptic Upbringing: How I Recovered from My Terrifying Evangelical Childhood." *The Guardian*. April 5, 2016. https://www .theguardian.com/world/2016/apr/05/religion-evangelical-christian -apocalypse-josiah-hesse.

Hezser, Catherine. *Jewish Slavery in Antiquity*. Oxford: Oxford University Press, 2006.

Hidalgo, Jacqueline M. *Revelation in Aztlán: Scriptures, Utopias, and the Chicano Movement*. New York: Palgrave Macmillan, 2016.

Hill, Alec. "The Most Troubling Parable: Why Does Jesus Say We Are Like Slaves?" *Christianity Today* 58 (2014): 76–79.

Hills, Megan C. "Snapchat's $1.3 Billion Drop in Value Is Linked to A Kardashian." *Forbes*. February 23, 2018. https://www.forbes.com/sites/meganhills1 /2018/02/23/snapchat-stock-value/.

Hitchcock, Alfred, et al. *The Birds*. Alfred J. Hitchcock Productions, 1963.

Hitchcock, Alfred, et al. *Rear Window*. Alfred J. Hitchcock Productions, 1954.

Hogan, Richard M., and John M. LeVoir. *Covenant of Love: Pope John Paul II on Sexuality, Marriage, and Family in the Modern World, with a Commentary on Familiaris Consortio*. San Francisco: Ignatius Press, 1992.

Hollyday, Joyce. *Clothed with the Sun: Biblical Women, Social Justice, and Us*. Louisville: Westminster John Knox, 1994.

hooks, bell. *Feminism Is for Everybody: Passionate Politics*. London: Pluto Press, 2000.

hooks, bell. *Feminist Theory: From Margin to Center*. 2nd ed. London: Pluto Press, 2000.

Hope, Valerie. *Death in Ancient Rome: A Sourcebook*. London: Routledge, 2007.

Hopkins, Denise Dombkowski. *Psalms, Books 2–3*. WCS 21. Collegeville, MN: Liturgical Press, 2016.

Hopkins, Dwight N. *Down, Up, and Over: Slave Religion and Black Theology*. Minneapolis: Fortress, 2000.

Hopkins, Dwight N. "Enslaved Black Women: A Theology of Justice and Reparations." In *Beyond Slavery: Overcoming Its Religious and Sexual Legacies*, edited by Bernadette J. Brooten with the editorial assistance of Jacqueline L. Hazelton, 289–303. New York: Palgrave Macmillan, 2010.

Hornsby, Teresa J., and Ken Stone, eds. *Bible Trouble: Queer Reading at the Boundaries of Biblical Scholarship.* Atlanta: SBL, 2011.

Horowitz, Juliana Menasce, and Abby Budiman. "Key Findings about Multiracial Identity in the U.S. as Harris Becomes Vice Presidential Nominee." *Pew Research Center* (blog). August 18, 2020. https://www.pewresearch.org/fact-tank/2020/08/18/key-findings-about-multiracial-identity-in-the-u-s-as-harris-becomes-vice-presidential-nominee/.

Horrox, Rosemary, trans. and ed. *The Black Death.* Manchester: Manchester University Press, 1994.

Howard-Brook, Wes, and Anthony Gwyther. *Unveiling Empire: Reading Revelation Then and Now.* Maryknoll, NY: Orbis Books, 1999.

Hsu, V. Jo. "(Trans)forming #MeToo: Toward a Networked Response to Gender Violence." *Women's Studies in Communication* 42 (July 3, 2019): 269–86.

Huber, Lynn R. "Gazing at the Whore: Reading Revelation Queerly." In *Bible Trouble: Queer Reading at the Boundaries of Biblical Scholarship*, edited by Teresa J. Hornsby and Ken Stone, 301–20. Atlanta: SBL, 2011.

Huber, Lynn R. *Like a Bride Adorned: Reading Metaphor in John's Apocalypse.* New York: T&T Clark, 2007.

Huber, Lynn R. "Making Men in Rev 2–3: Reading the Seven Messages in the Bath-Gymnasiums of Asia Minor." In *Stones, Bones, and the Sacred: Essays on Material Culture and Ancient Religion in Honor of Dennis E. Smith*, edited by Alan H. Cadwallader, 101–28. Atlanta: SBL Press, 2016.

Huber, Lynn R. "Revealing Christ in Revelation." In *Narrative Mode and Theological Claim in Johannine Literature: Essays in Honor of Gail R. O'Day*, edited by Lynn R. Huber, Susan E. Hylen, and William M. Wright IV, 95–108. BSNA 30. Atlanta: SBL Press, 2021.

Huber, Lynn R. "Sexually Explicit? Re-Reading Revelation's 144,000 Virgins as a Response to Roman Discourses." *Journal of Men, Masculinities and Spirituality* 2 (2008): 3–28.

Huber, Lynn R. *Thinking and Seeing with Women in Revelation.* LNTS 475. London: Bloomsbury, 2013.

Humez, Jean McMahon, ed. *Gifts of Power: The Writings of Rebecca Jackson, Black Visionary, Shaker Eldress.* Amherst: University of Massachusetts Press, 1987.

Humez, Jean McMahon, ed. *Mother's First-Born Daughters: Early Shaker Writings on Women and Religion.* Bloomington: Indiana University Press, 1993.

Hutzler, Alexandra. "Marjorie Taylor Greene Rebukes Vaccine Passports as 'Biden's Mark of the Beast.'" *Newsweek.* March 30, 2021. https://www.newsweek.com/marjorie-taylor-greene-rebukes-vaccine-passports-bidens-mark-beast-1579880.

Hylen, Susan E. "Feminist Interpretation of Revelation." In *The Oxford Handbook of the Book of Revelation*, edited by Craig R. Koester, 461–82. New York: Oxford University Press, 2020.

Hylen, Susan E. "Metaphor Matters: Violence and Ethics in Revelation." *CBQ* 73 (2011): 777–96.

Hylen, Susan E. "The Power and Problem of Revelation 18: The Rhetorical Function of Gender." In *Pregnant Passion: Gender, Sex, and Violence in the Bible*, edited by Cheryl A. Kirk-Duggan, 205–19. Atlanta: SBL, 2003.

Ilan, Tal, Lorena Miralles-Maciá, and Ronit Nikolsky, eds. *Rabbinic Literature.* The Bible and Women: An Encyclopaedia of Exegesis and Cultural History. Atlanta: SBL Press, 2022.

Immendörfer, Michael. *Ephesians and Artemis: The Cult of the Great Goddess of Ephesus as the Epistle's Context*. WUNT 2.436. Tübingen: Mohr Siebeck, 2017.

Ipsen, Avaren. *Sex Working and the Bible*. London: Routledge, 2014.

Isasi-Díaz, Ada María. *Mujerista Theology: A Theology for the Twenty-First Century.* Maryknoll, NY: Orbis Books, 1996.

Jackson, Rebecca. *Gifts of Power: The Writings of Rebecca Jackson, Black Visionary, Shaker Eldress*. Edited by Jean McMahon Humez. Amherst: University of Massachusetts Press, 1987.

Jacob, Sharon, and Jennifer T. Kaalund. "Flowing from Breast to Breast: An Examination of Dis/Placed Motherhood in African American and Indian Wet Nurses." In *Womanist Interpretations of the Bible: Expanding the Discourse*, edited by Gay L. Byron and Vanessa Lovelace, 209–38. Atlanta: SBL Press, 2016.

James, S. E., et al. "Executive Summary of the Report of the 2015 U.S. Transgender Survey." Washington, DC: National Center for Transgender Equality, 2016. https://transequality.org/sites/default/files/docs/usts/USTS-Executive-Summary-Dec17.pdf.

Jensen, Erik. *Barbarians in the Greek and Roman World*. Indianapolis: Hackett, 2018.

Jobling, David. *The Sense of Biblical Narrative: Three Structural Analyses in the Old Testament*. JSOTSup 7. Sheffield: University of Sheffield Press, 1978.

Jobling, David, and Tina Pippin, eds. *Semeia 59: Ideological Criticism of Biblical Texts*. Atlanta: Scholars Press, 1992.

Johns Hopkins Coronavirus Resource Center. "Johns Hopkins Coronavirus Resource Center." March 26, 2020. https://coronavirus.jhu.edu/.

Johns, Loren L. "Conceiving Violence: The Apocalypse of John and the Left Behind Series." *Direction* 34 (2005): 194–214.

Johns, Loren L. *The Lamb Christology of the Apocalypse of John: An Investigation into Its Origins and Rhetorical Force*. Eugene, OR: Wipf and Stock, 2014.

Johnson, Charles, Darrell Luster, and Ricky Luster. "I Know I've Been Sealed." *There Is a Guarantee in Jesus*. Gloryland Records, 1986.

Johnson, Elizabeth A. "God." In *Dictionary of Feminist Theologies*, edited by Letty M. Russell and J. Shannon Clarkson, 128–30. Louisville: Westminster John Knox, 1996.

Johnson, Elizabeth A. *She Who Is: The Mystery of God in Feminist Theological Discourse.* New York: Crossroad, 1992.

Johnston, Sarah Iles. "Mysteries." In *Ancient Religions,* edited by Sarah Iles Johnston, 98–111. Cambridge: Harvard University Press, 2007.

Johnston, Sarah Iles. *Restless Dead: Encounters Between the Living and the Dead in Ancient Greece.* Berkeley: University of California Press, 1999.

Jones, C. P. "Heracles at Smyrna." *American Journal of Numismatics Second Series* 2 (1990): 65–76.

Jones, C. P. "Stigma: Tattooing and Branding in Graeco-Roman Antiquity." *JRS* 77 (1987): 139–55.

Jordan, Miriam. "Migrants Separated from Their Children Will Be Allowed into U.S." *The New York Times.* May 3, 2021. Sec. U.S. https://www.nytimes.com /2021/05/03/us/migrant-family-separation.html.

Jozuka, Emiko, and Vivien Jones. "Japan's Hafu Stars Are Celebrated: But Some Mixed-Race People Say They Feel Like Foreigners in Their Own Country." CNN. September 23, 2020. https://www.cnn.com/2020/09/22/asia/japan -mixed-roots-hafu-dst-hnk-intl/index.html.

Junior, Nyasha. *An Introduction to Womanist Biblical Interpretation.* Louisville: Westminster John Knox, 2015.

Kamen, Deborah, and Sarah Levin-Richardson. "Lusty Ladies in the Roman Imaginary." In *Ancient Sex,* edited by Ruby Blondell and Kirk Ormand, 231–52. Columbus: Ohio State University Press, 2015.

Kananovich, Volha. " 'Execute Not Pardon': The *Pussy Riot* Case, Political Speech, and Blasphemy in Russian Law." *Communication Law and Policy* 20 (October 2, 2015): 343–422.

Kane, Paul, and Ed O'Keefe. "Republicans Vote to Rebuke Elizabeth Warren, Saying She Impugned Sessions's Character." *The Washington Post.* February 8, 2017. https://www.washingtonpost.com/news/powerpost/wp/2017/02/07/ republicans-vote-to-rebuke-elizabeth-warren-for-impugning-sessionss -character/.

Kaplan, Roberta, and Deborah Lipstadt. "Three Years Later, Charlottesville's Legacy of Neo-Nazi Hate Still Festers." CNN. August 12, 2020. https:// www.cnn.com/2020/08/11/opinions/charlottesville-three-years-later-hate -festers-lipstadt-kaplan/index.html.

Kaylor, Brian. "Campolo Urges Christians to Not Weep as Babylon Falls." *Word & Way.* May 19, 2020. https://wordandway.org/2020/05/19/campolo-as -babylon-falls/.

Keener, Craig S. *Revelation.* Grand Rapids: Zondervan, 2000.

Keller, Catherine. *Apocalypse Now and Then: A Feminist Guide to the End of the World.* Boston: Beacon, 1996.

Keller, Catherine. "The Breast, the Apocalypse, and the Colonial Journey." *JFSR* 10 (1994): 53–72.

Keller, Catherine. *Facing Apocalypse: Climate, Democracy, and Other Last Chances.* Maryknoll, NY: Orbis Books, 2021.

Keller, Catherine. *God and Power: Counter-Apocalyptic Journeys.* Minneapolis: Fortress, 2005.

Kelly, Benjamin. "Court Politics and Imperial Imagery in the Roman Principate." In *The Social Dynamics of Roman Imperial Imagery,* edited by Amy Russell and Monica Hellström, 128–58. Cambridge: Cambridge University Press, 2020.

Khan-Cullors, Patrisse, and Asha Bandele. *When They Call You a Terrorist: A Black Lives Matter Memoir.* New York: St. Martin's Press, 2018.

Kiel, Micah D. *Apocalyptic Ecology: The Book of Revelation, the Earth, and the Future.* Collegeville, MN: Liturgical Press, 2017.

Kiernan, Philip. *Roman Cult Images: The Lives and Worship of Idols from the Iron Age to Late Antiquity.* Cambridge: Cambridge University Press, 2020.

Kim, Jean K. "'Uncovering Her Wickedness': An Inter(Con)Textual Reading of Revelation 17 from a Postcolonial Feminist Perspective." *JSNT* 73 (1999): 61–81.

Kim, Jee-woon. *A Tale of Two Sisters.* B.O.M. Film Productions, 2003.

Kingkade, Tyler. "Chick-Fil-A Voted Out by Elon University Students, Booted from Other Campuses in North Carolina." *Huffington Post.* October 16, 2012. https://www.huffpost.com/entry/chick-fil-a-elon-university_n_1971376.

Kirk-Duggan, Cheryl. "Divine Puppeteer: Yahweh of Exodus." In *A Feminist Companion to Exodus to Deuteronomy,* edited by Athalya Brenner, 75–102. FCB 6. Sheffield: Sheffield Academic, 2000.

Kitzberger, Ingrid Rosa, ed. *Autobiographical Biblical Criticism: Between Text and Self.* Leiden: Deo, 2002.

Klawans, Jonathan. "Idolatry, Incest, and Impurity: Moral Defilement in Ancient Judaism." *JSJ* 29 (1998): 401–2.

Klein, Linda Kay. *Pure: Inside the Evangelical Movement That Shamed a Generation of Young Women and How I Broke Free.* New York: Simon and Schuster, 2019.

Knust, Jennifer Wright. *Abandoned to Lust: Sexual Slander and Ancient Christianity.* Gender, Theory, and Religion. New York: Columbia University Press, 2005.

Koch, Dietrich-Alex. "The God-Fearers between Facts and Fiction: Two Theosebeis-Inscriptions from Aphrodisias and Their Bearing for the New Testament." *ST* 60 (2006): 62–90.

Koester, Craig R. *Revelation: A New Translation with Introduction and Commentary.* AYB 38A. New Haven: Yale University Press, 2014.

Koester, Craig R. "Roman Slave Trade and the Critique of Babylon in Revelation 18." *CBQ* 70 (2008): 766–86.

Kotrosits, Maia. "Seeing Is Feeling: Revelation's Enthroned Lamb and Ancient Visual Affects." *BibInt* 22 (2014): 473–502.

Kovacs, Judith L., and Christopher Rowland. *Revelation: The Apocalypse of Jesus Christ.* Malden, MA: Blackwell, 2004.

Kraemer, Ross Shepard, and Mary Rose D'Angelo, eds. *Women and Christian Origins*. New York: Oxford University Press, 1999.

Krahmer, Shawn M. "The Virile Bride of Bernard of Clairvaux." *CH* 69 (2000): 304–27.

Kraybill, J. Nelson. *Imperial Cult and Commerce in John's Apocalypse*. Sheffield: Sheffield Academic, 1996.

Kyle, Donald G. *Spectacles of Death in Ancient Rome*. London: Routledge, 2012.

LaCugna, Catherine Mowry. *God for Us: The Trinity and Christian Life*. San Francisco: HarperCollins, 1991.

LaHaye, Tim. *Revelation Unveiled*. Grand Rapids: Zondervan, 2010.

LaHaye, Tim, and Jerry B. Jenkins. *Apollyon: The Destroyer Is Unleashed*. Wheaton, IL: Tyndale, 2000.

LaHaye, Tim, and Jerry B. Jenkins. *Kingdom Come: The Final Victory*. Carol Stream, IL: Tyndale, 2007.

LaHaye, Tim, and Jerry B. Jenkins. *Left Behind: A Novel of the Earth's Last Days*. Wheaton, IL: Tyndale, 1995.

Lam, Joseph. *Patterns of Sin in the Hebrew Bible: Metaphor, Culture, and the Making of a Religious Concept*. New York: Oxford University Press, 2015.

Lamp, Kathleen. "The *Ara Pacis Augustae*: Visual Rhetoric in Augustus' Principate." *Rhetoric Society Quarterly* 39 (2009): 1–24.

Latham, Jacob. " 'Fabulous Clap-Trap': Roman Masculinity, the Cult of Magna Mater, and Literary Constructions of the *galli* at Rome from the Late Republic to Late Antiquity." *JR* 92 (2012): 84–122.

Lebron, Christopher J. *The Making of Black Lives Matter: A Brief History of an Idea*. New York: Oxford University Press, 2017.

Lehoux, Daryn. "Drugs and the Delphic Oracle." *CW* 101 (2007): 41–56.

Lenthang, Marlene. "Atlanta Shooting and the Legacy of Misogyny and Racism against Asian Women." ABC News. March 21, 2021. https://abcnews.go.com/US/atlanta-shooting-legacy-misogyny-racism-asian-women/story?id=76533776.

Lerner, Gerda. *Creation of Feminist Consciousness: From the Middle Ages to Eighteen-Seventy*. New York: Oxford University Press, 1993.

Letteney, Mark, and Matthew D. C. Larsen. "A Roman Military Prison at Lambaesis." *SLA* 5 (2021): 65–102.

Levenson, Jon D. *Resurrection and the Restoration of Israel: The Ultimate Victory of the God of Life*. New Haven: Yale University Press, 2006.

Levick, Barbara. "The Roman Economy: Trade in Asia Minor and the Niche Market." *GR* 51 (2004): 180–98.

Levick, Barbara. "Women and Law." In *A Companion to Women in the Ancient World*, edited by Sharon L. James and Sheila Dillon, 96–106. West Sussex: John Wiley & Sons, 2012.

Levine, Amy-Jill. "Introduction." In *A Feminist Companion to the Apocalypse of John*, edited by Amy-Jill Levine with Maria Mayo Robbins, 1–16. FCNTECW 13. London: T&T Clark, 2009.

Levine, Amy-Jill. *The Misunderstood Jew: The Church and the Scandal of the Jewish Jesus*. San Francisco: HarperOne, 2006.

Levine, Amy-Jill, and Marc Zvi Brettler. *The Bible With and Without Jesus: How Jews and Christians Read the Same Stories Differently*. New York: HarperOne, 2020.

Levin-Richardson, Sarah. *The Brothel of Pompeii: Sex, Class, and Gender at the Margins of Roman Society*. Cambridge: Cambridge University Press, 2019.

Lillie, Celene. *The Rape of Eve: The Transformation of Roman Ideology in Three Early Christian Retellings of Genesis*. Minneapolis: Fortress, 2017.

Lilly, Ingrid Esther. "The Planet's Apocalypse: The Rhetoric of Climate Change." In *Apocalypses in Context: Apocalyptic Currents through History*, edited by Kelly J. Murphy and Justin Jeffcoat Schedtler, 359–80. Minneapolis: Fortress, 2016.

Lindsey, Hal. *The Late Great Planet Earth*. Grand Rapids: Zondervan, 1970.

Lisak, David, and Paul M. Miller. "Repeat Rape and Multiple Offending among Undetected Rapists." *Violence and Victims* 17 (2002): 73–84.

Lister, Kate. *A Curious History of Sex*. London: Unbound, 2020.

Lochrie, Karma. "Mystical Acts, Queer Tendencies." In *Constructing Medieval Sexuality*, edited by Karma Lochrie, Peggy McCracken, and James A. Schultz, 180–200. Minneapolis: University of Minnesota Press, 1997.

Long, D. Stephen. "Should We Call Donald Trump 'Antichrist'?" Opinion. ABC Religion & Ethics. June 8, 2020. https://www.abc.net.au/religion/stephen-long-should-we-call-trump-antichrist/12335450.

Long, Phillip J. *Jesus the Bridegroom: The Origin of the Eschatological Feast as a Wedding Banquet in the Synoptic Gospels*. Eugene, OR: Wipf and Stock, 2013.

Long, Thomas L. *AIDS and American Apocalypticism: The Cultural Semiotics of an Epidemic*. Albany: SUNY Press, 2012.

Longfellow, Brenda. *Roman Imperialism and Civic Patronage: Form, Meaning, and Ideology in Monumental Fountain Complexes*. Cambridge: Cambridge University Press, 2011.

Lopez, Davina C. "Victory and Visibility: Revelation's Imperial Textures and Monumental Logics." In *An Introduction to Empire in the New Testament*, edited by Adam Winn, 273–95. Atlanta: SBL Press, 2016.

Lorde, Audre. "The Master's Tools Will Never Dismantle the Master's House." In *Sister Outsider: Essays and Speeches*, 110–14. Berkeley: Crossing Press, 2004.

Lutz, Cora E. *Musonius Rufus: The Roman Socrates*. Vol. 10. YCS. New Haven: Yale University Press, 1947.

MacLean, Rose. *Freed Slaves and Roman Imperial Culture: Social Integration and the Transformation of Values*. Cambridge: Cambridge University Press, 2018.

Macumber, Heather. *Recovering the Monstrous in Revelation*. Lanham, MD: Lexington Books/Fortress, 2021.

Macumber, Heather. "The Threat of Empire: Monstrous Hybridity in Revelation 13." *BibInt* 27 (2019): 107–29.

Magie, David. *Roman Rule in Asia Minor: To the End of the Third Century after Christ*. Princeton: Princeton University Press, 1950.

Maier, Christl M. *Daughter Zion, Mother Zion: Gender, Space and the Sacred in Ancient Israel*. Minneapolis: Fortress, 2008.

Maier, Christl M., and Carolyn J. Sharp. *Prophecy and Power: Jeremiah in Feminist and Postcolonial Perspective*. London: Bloomsbury, 2013.

Maier, Christl M., and Nuria Calduch-Benages, eds. *The Writings and Later Wisdom Books*. The Bible and Women: An Encyclopaedia of Exegesis and Cultural History. Atlanta: SBL Press, 2014.

Maier, Harry O. *Picturing Paul in Empire: Imperial Image, Text and Persuasion in Colossians, Ephesians and the Pastoral Epistles*. London: T&T Clark, 2013.

Maier, Harry O. "Staging the Gaze: Early Christian Apocalypses and Narrative Self-Representation." *HTR* 90 (1997): 131–54.

Marchal, Joseph A. *Appalling Bodies: Queer Figures before and after Paul's Letters*. New York: Oxford University Press, 2019.

Marchal, Joseph A. "The Disgusting Apostle and a Queer Affect between Epistles and Audiences." In *Reading with Feeling: Affect Theory and the Bible*, edited by Fiona C. Black and Jennifer L. Koosed, 113–40. Atlanta: SBL Press, 2019.

Marchal, Joseph A. "Queer Studies and Critical Masculinity Studies in Feminist Biblical Studies." In *Feminist Biblical Studies in the Twentieth Century: Scholarship and Movement*, edited by Elisabeth Schüssler Fiorenza, 261–80. The Bible and Women: An Encyclopaedia of Exegesis and Cultural History. Atlanta: SBL Press, 2014.

Marek, Christian. *In the Land of a Thousand Gods: A History of Asia Minor in the Ancient World*. Translated by Steven Rendall. Princeton: Princeton University Press, 2016.

Marsh, Wendy, and Jen Leamon. "Babies Removed at Birth: What Professionals Can Learn from 'Women Like Me.'" *Child Abuse Review* 28 (January 1, 2019): 82–86.

Marshall, John W. *Parables of War: Reading John's Jewish Apocalypse*. Waterloo, ON: Wilfrid Laurier University Press, 2001.

Marshall, John W. "Who's on the Throne? Revelation in the Long Year." In *Heavenly Realms and Earthly Realities in Late Antique Religions*, edited by Ra'anan S. Boustan and Annette Yoshiko Reed, 123–41. Cambridge: Cambridge University Press, 2004.

Martin, Clarice J. "Polishing the Unclouded Mirror: A Womanist Reading of Revelation 18:13." In *From Every People and Nation: The Book of Revelation in Intercultural Perspective*, edited by David Rhoads, 82–109. Minneapolis: Fortress, 2005.

Martin, Clarice J. "Womanist Interpretations of the New Testament: The Quest for Holistic and Inclusive Translation and Interpretation." *JFSR* 6 (1990): 41–61.

Mason, Carol. *Killing for Life: The Apocalyptic Narrative of Pro-Life Politics*. Ithaca: Cornell University Press, 2002.

Mata, Roberto. "Border Crossing into the Promised Land: The Eschatological Migration of God's People in Revelation 2:1–3:22." In *Latinxs, the Bible, and Migration*, edited by Efraín Agosto and Jacqueline M. Hidalgo, 209–31. Cham, Switzerland: Palgrave Macmillan, 2018.

Matthews, Shelly. *First Converts: Rich Pagan Women and the Rhetoric of Mission in Early Judaism and Christianity*. Contraversions: Jews and Other Differences. Stanford: Stanford University Press, 2001.

Max, D. T. "The Public-Shaming Pandemic." *The New Yorker*. September 21, 2020. https://www.newyorker.com/magazine/2020/09/28/the-public-shaming -pandemic.

Mayer, Wendy. "Heirs of Roman Persecution: Common Threads in Discursive Strategies across Late Antiquity." In *Heirs of Roman Persecution: Studies on a Christian and Para-Christian Discourse in Late Antiquity*, edited by Éric Fournier and Wendy Mayer, 317–40. Abingdon: Routledge, 2019.

McCane, Byron R. "Simply Irresistible: Augustus, Herod, and the Empire." *JBL* 127 (2008): 725–35.

McFadden, Robert D. "Tim LaHaye Dies at 90: Fundamentalist Leader's Grisly Novels Sold Millions." *The New York Times*. July 25, 2016. https://www.ny times.com/2016/07/26/books/tim-lahaye-a-christian-fundamentalist -leader-dies-at-90.html.

McFague, Sallie. *Metaphorical Theology: Models of God in Religious Language*. Minneapolis: Fortress, 1982.

McFague, Sallie. *Models of God: Theology for an Ecological, Nuclear Age*. Philadelphia: Fortress, 1987.

McGinn, Thomas A. J. *The Economy of Prostitution in the Roman World: A Study of Social History and the Brothel*. Ann Arbor: University of Michigan Press, 2004.

McGinn, Thomas A. J. "Zoning Shame in the Roman City." In *Prostitutes and Courtesans in the Ancient World*, edited by Christopher A. Faraone and Laura K. McClure, 161–76. Madison: University of Wisconsin Press, 2006.

McGowan, Charis. "Chilean Anti-Rape Anthem Becomes International Feminist Phenomenon." *The Guardian*. December 6, 2019. https://www.theguardian .com/world/2019/dec/06/chilean-anti-rape-anthem-becomes-international -feminist-phenomenon.

McKinlay, Judith E. *Reframing Her: Biblical Women in Postcolonial Focus*. Sheffield: Sheffield Phoenix, 2004.

McKnight, Edgar V., and Elizabeth Struthers Malbon, eds. *The New Literary Criticism and the New Testament*. Valley Forge, PA: Trinity Press International, 1994.

McNemar, Richard, and Richard Treat. "The Lamb's Revelation." In *Millennial Praises: A Shaker Hymnal*, edited by Christian Goodwillie and Jane F. Crosthwaite. Amherst: University of Massachusetts Press, 2009.

Mekhennet, Souad. "As Anti-Semitic Incidents Rise in U.S., Group Launches New Online Tracking Tool." *The Washington Post*. February 1, 2020. Sec. National Security. https://www.washingtonpost.com/national-security/as -anti-semitic-incidents-rise-in-us-group-launches-new-online-tracking-tool /2020/02/01/71bc33bc-4452-11ea-b503-2b077c436617_story.html.

Mellor, Ronald. *ΘΕΑ ΡΩΜΗ: The Worship of the Goddess Roma in the Greek World.* Göttingen: Vandenhoeck & Ruprecht, 1975.

Mellott, Matthew. "To the Victor: Understanding the Calls to Be Victorious in Rev 2–3 in Light of Athletic and Gladiatorial Victory." PhD diss., Lutheran School of Theology at Chicago, 2019.

Mena, Peter Anthony. *Place and Identity in the Lives of Antony, Paul, and Mary of Egypt: Desert as Borderland.* Religion and Spatial Studies. Cham, Switzerland: Palgrave Macmillan, 2019.

Menéndez-Antuña, Luis. *Thinking Sex with the Great Whore: Deviant Sexualities and Empire in the Book of Revelation.* Abingdon: Routledge, 2018.

Meyers, Carol. *Rediscovering Eve: Ancient Israelite Women in Context.* New York: Oxford University Press, 2013.

Meyers, Carol, Toni Craven, and Ross S. Kraemer, eds. *Women in Scripture: A Dictionary of Named and Unnamed Women in the Hebrew Bible, the Apocryphal/Deuterocanonical Books, and the New Testament.* Boston: Houghton Mifflin, 2000/Grand Rapids: Eerdmans, 2001.

Migliozzi, Blacki, et al. "Record Wildfires on the West Coast Are Capping a Disastrous Decade." *The New York Times.* September 24, 2020. https://www.nytimes.com/interactive/2020/09/24/climate/fires-worst-year-california-oregon-washington.html.

Miller, John F. *Apollo, Augustus, and the Poets.* Cambridge: Cambridge University Press, 2009.

Miner, Terra Rae. "The State That Timber Built." *Oregon Humanities.* April 8, 2012. https://oregonhumanities.org/rll/magazine/here-spring-2012/the-state-that-timber-built/.

Moore, Stephen D. "The Beatific Vision as a Posing Exhibition: Revelation's Hypermasculine Deity." *JSNT* 60 (1995): 27–55.

Moore, Stephen D. *The Bible in Theory: Critical and Postcritical Essays.* Atlanta: SBL, 2010.

Moore, Stephen D. *Empire and Apocalypse: Postcolonialism and the New Testament.* Sheffield: Sheffield Phoenix, 2006.

Moore, Stephen D. *God's Beauty Parlor: And Other Queer Spaces in and around the Bible.* Stanford: Stanford University Press, 2001.

Moore, Stephen D. "Mimicry and Monstrosity." In *Untold Tales from the Book of Revelation: Sex and Gender, Empire and Ecology,* edited by Stephen D. Moore, 13–37. Atlanta: SBL, 2014.

Moore, Stephen D. *Poststructuralism and the New Testament: Derrida and Foucault at the Foot of the Cross.* Minneapolis: Fortress, 1994.

Moore, Stephen D. "Retching on Rome: Vomitous Loathing and Visceral Disgust in Affect Theory and the Apocalypse of John." *BibInt* 22 (2014): 503–28.

Moore, Stephen D., ed. *Untold Tales from the Book of Revelation: Sex and Gender, Empire and Ecology.* Atlanta: SBL, 2014.

Moore, Stephen D., and Janice Capel Anderson. "Taking It Like a Man: Masculinity in 4 Maccabees." *JBL* 117 (1998): 249–73.

Moss, Candida R. "The Man with the Flow of Power: Porous Bodies in Mark 5:25-34." *JBL* 129 (2010): 507–19.

Moss, Candida. *The Myth of Persecution: How Early Christians Invented a Story of Martyrdom*. New York: HarperOne, 2013.

Moss, Candida R., and Joel S. Baden. *Reconceiving Infertility: Biblical Perspectives on Procreation and Childlessness*. Princeton: Princeton University Press, 2015.

Moyise, Steve. "The Old Testament in the Book of Revelation." In *The Oxford Handbook of the Book of Revelation*, edited by Craig R. Koester, 83–100. New York: Oxford University Press, 2020.

Mulvey, Laura. "Visual Pleasure and Narrative Cinema." *Screen* 16 (1975): 6–18.

Muñoz, José Esteban. *Disidentifications: Queers of Color and the Performance of Politics*. Minneapolis: University of Minnesota Press, 1999.

Munro, Ealasaid. "Feminism: A Fourth Wave?" *Political Insight* (September 2013). https://journals.sagepub.com/doi/pdf/10.1111/2041-9066.12021.

Murray, James S. "The Urban Earthquake Imagery and Divine Judgment in John's Apocalypse." *NovT* 47 (2005): 142–61.

Mwombeki, Fidon R. "The Book of Revelation in Africa." *WW* 15 (1995): 145–50.

Myerowitz Levine, Molly. "The Gendered Grammar of Ancient Mediterranean Hair." In *Off with Her Head! The Denial of Women's Identity in Myth, Religion, and Culture*, edited by Howard Eilberg-Schwartz and Wendy Doniger, 76–130. Berkeley: University of California Press, 1995.

Mynott, Jeremy. *Birds in the Ancient World: Winged Words*. Oxford: Oxford University Press, 2018.

National Park Service. "Language of Slavery—Underground Railroad (U.S. National Park Service)." October 13, 2021. https://www.nps.gov/subjects/undergroundrailroad/language-of-slavery.htm.

Navarro Puerto, Mercedes, and Marinella Perroni, eds.; Amy-Jill Levine, English ed. *Gospels: Narrative and History*. The Bible and Women: An Encyclopaedia of Exegesis and Cultural History. Atlanta: SBL Press, 2015.

Nelavala, Surekha. "'Babylon the Great Mother of Whores' (Rev 17:5): A Postcolonial Feminist Perspective." *ExpTim* 121 (2009): 60–65.

Newby, Zahra. *Greek Athletics in the Roman World: Victory and Virtue*. Oxford: Oxford University Press, 2005.

Newman, Barbara. *Sister of Wisdom: St. Hildegard's Theology of the Feminine*. Berkeley: University of California Press, 1987.

Newsom, Carol A. *The Book of Job: A Contest of Moral Imaginations*. New York: Oxford University Press, 2003.

Niditch, Susan. "Ezekiel 40–48 in a Visionary Context." *CBQ* 48 (1986): 208–24.

Niditch, Susan. *"My Brother Esau Is a Hairy Man": Hair and Identity in Ancient Israel*. Oxford: Oxford University Press, 2008.

Nowell, Irene. *Women in the Old Testament*. Collegeville, MN: Liturgical Press, 1997.

Nutter, David. "The Rains of the Castamere." *Game of Thrones*. HBO. June 2, 2013.

Oakley, John Howard, and Rebecca H. Sinos. *The Wedding in Ancient Athens*. Madison: University of Wisconsin Press, 1993.

O'Brien, Julia M. "Joel." In *Theological Bible Commentary*, edited by Gail R. O'Day and David L. Petersen, 265–66. Louisville: Westminster John Knox, 2009.

O'Day, Gail R. "Jesus as Friend in the Gospel of John." *Int* 58 (2004): 144–57.

O'Day, Gail R. "Narrative Mode and Theological Claim: A Study in the Fourth Gospel." *JBL* 105 (1986): 657–68.

O'Day, Gail R. "Revelation." In *Theological Bible Commentary*, edited by Gail R. O'Day and David L. Petersen, 471–79. Louisville: Westminster John Knox, 2009.

O'Day, Gail R. "Teaching and Preaching the Book of Revelation." *WW* 25 (2005): 246–54.

O'Day, Gail R., and Susan Hylen. *John*. Louisville: Westminster John Knox, 2006.

O'Donnell, Paul. "For Some, the US Embassy's Move to Jerusalem Fulfills Divine Prophecy." *Religion News Service*. May 14, 2018. https://religionnews.com /2018/05/14/some-christians-and-jews-hail-embassy-move-to-jerusalem -as-key-to-a-biblical-plan/.

O'Hear, Natasha. "Images of Babylon: A Visual History of the Whore in Late Medieval and Early Modern Art; From the Margins." In *From the Margins 2: Women of the New Testament and Their Afterlives*, edited by Christine E. Joynes and Christopher C. Rowland, 311–33. Sheffield: Sheffield Phoenix, 2009.

O'Hear, Natasha, and Anthony O'Hear. *Picturing the Apocalypse: The Book of Revelation in the Arts over Two Millennia*. Oxford: Oxford University Press, 2015.

Økland, Jorunn. "Carnelian and Caryatids: Stone and Statuary in the Heavenly Sanctuary." In *Constructions of Space III: Biblical Spatiality and the Sacred*, edited by Jorunn Økland, J. Cornelius de Vos, and Karen J. Wenell, 184–214. London: Bloomsbury, 2016.

Økland, Jorunn. "Why Can't the Heavenly Miss Jerusalem Just Shut Up?" In *A Feminist Companion to the Apocalypse of John*, edited by Amy-Jill Levine with Maria Mayo Robbins, 88–105. FCNTECW 13. London: T&T Clark, 2009.

Olson, Alix. "Built Like That." *Built Like That*. Decatur, GA: Subtle Sister Productions, 2001.

Olson, Kelly. *Dress and the Roman Woman: Self-Presentation and Society*. London: Routledge, 2008.

Olson, Kelly. *Masculinity and Dress in Roman Antiquity*. Abingdon: Routledge, 2017.

Olson, Kelly. "Masculinity, Appearance, and Sexuality: Dandies in Roman Antiquity." *JHS* 23 (2014): 182–205.

Oring, Elliott. "Jokes on the Internet: Listing toward Lists." In *Folk Culture in the Digital Age: The Emergent Dynamics of Human Interaction*, edited by Trevor J. Blank, 98–118. Boulder: University Press of Colorado, 2012.

Pagels, Elaine. *The Origin of Satan*. New York: Vintage Books, 1995.

Pagels, Elaine. *Revelations: Visions, Prophecy, and Politics in the Book of Revelation.* New York: Penguin, 2012.

Pagels, Elaine. "The Social History of Satan, Part Three: John of Patmos and Ignatius of Antioch; Contrasting Visions of 'God's People'" *HTR* 99 (2006): 487–505.

Palmer, Erin. "Imagining Spaces: The Function of Imagined Space in Ezekiel and Revelation." Undergraduate Honors Thesis, Elon University, 2013.

Park, Rohun. "Revelation for Sale: An Intercultural Reading of Revelation 18 from an East Asian Perspective." *Bible and Critical Theory* 4 (2008): 25.1–12.

Parker, Angela N. *If God Still Breathes, Why Can't I? Black Lives Matter and Biblical Authority.* Grand Rapids: Eerdmans, 2021.

Patterson, Orlando. *Slavery and Social Death.* Cambridge, MA: Harvard University Press, 1982.

Peaslee, Emma. "Lawsuits Filed after Police Use Pepper Spray at North Carolina March to the Polls." *NPR.* November 3, 2020. https://www.npr.org/2020/11/03/930912025/lawsuits-filed-after-police-use-pepper-spray-at-north-carolina-march-to-the-poll.

Peckruhn, Heike. "Embodied Knowing: Body, Epistemology, Context, and Hermeneutics." In *What Is Constructive Theology? Histories, Methodologies, and Perspectives*, edited by Marion Grau and Jason Wyman, 77–101. London: T&T Clark, 2020.

Penchansky, David. "Deconstruction." In *The Oxford Encyclopedia of Biblical Interpretation*, edited by Steven McKenzie, 196–205. New York: Oxford University Press, 2013.

Pennington, Brian K. *Was Hinduism Invented? Britons, Indians, and the Colonial Construction of Religion.* Oxford: Oxford University Press, 2005.

Perry, Peter S. "The People of God in the Book of Revelation." In *The Oxford Handbook of the Book of Revelation*, edited by Craig R. Koester, 325–40. New York: Oxford University Press, 2020.

Perry, Peter S. *The Rhetoric of Digressions: Revelation 7:1-17 and 10:1–11:13 and Ancient Communication.* WUNT 2.268. Tübingen: Mohr Siebeck, 2009.

Peters, Rebecca Todd. *Solidarity Ethics: Transformation in a Globalized World.* Minneapolis: Fortress, 2014.

Peters, Rebecca Todd. *Trust Women: A Progressive Christian Argument for Reproductive Justice.* Boston: Beacon, 2018.

Petersen, David L. *The Prophetic Literature: An Introduction.* Louisville: Westminster John Knox, 2002.

Petro, Anthony M. *After the Wrath of God: AIDS, Sexuality, and American Religion.* Oxford: Oxford University Press, 2015.

Pippin, Tina. *Apocalyptic Bodies: The Biblical End of the World in Text and Image.* London: Routledge, 1999.

Pippin, Tina. *Death and Desire: The Rhetoric of Gender in the Apocalypse of John.* Louisville: Westminster John Knox, 1992.

Pippin, Tina. "Eros and the End: Reading for Gender in the Apocalypse of John." *Semeia* 59 (1992): 193–210.

Pippin, Tina. "The Heroine and the Whore: Fantasy and the Female in the Apocalypse of John." *Semeia* 60 (1992): 67–82.

Pippin, Tina. "Jezebel Re-Vamped." *Semeia* 69–70 (1995): 221–33.

Pippin, Tina. "Translation Happens: A Feminist Perspective on Translation Theories." In *Escaping Eden: New Feminist Perspectives on the Bible*, edited by Harold C. Washington, Susan Lochrie Graham, and Pamela Thimmes, 163–76. New York: NYU Press, 1999.

Pippin, Tina, and J. Michael Clark. "Revelation/Apocalypse." In *The Queer Bible Commentary*, edited by Deryn Guest, Robert E. Goss, Mona West, and Thomas Bohache, 753–68. London: SCM Press, 2006.

Plaskow, Judith. "Anti-Judaism in Feminist Christian Interpretation." In *Searching the Scriptures: A Feminist Introduction*, vol. 1, edited by Elisabeth Schüssler Fiorenza with the assistance of Shelly Matthews, 117–29. New York: Crossroad, 1993.

Pollini, Drusus. "A Bronze Statuette of Isis-Fortuna Panthea: A Syncretistic Goddess of Prosperity and Good Fortune." *Latomus* 4 (2003): 875–82.

Porter, Stanley E. "Paul Confronts Caesar with the Good News." In *Empire in the New Testament*, edited by Stanley E. Porter and Cynthia Long Westfall. Eugene, OR: Wipf and Stock, 2011.

Posner, Sarah. "'Obama the Antichrist' and End-Times Doctrine." *The Guardian*. November 18, 2011. https://www.guardian.co.uk/commentisfree/belief/2011/nov/18/obama-antichrist-end-times-doctrine.

Price, S. R. F. *Rituals and Power: The Roman Imperial Cult in Asia Minor*. Cambridge: Cambridge University Press, 1984.

Prothero, Donald R., and Robert M. Schoch. *Horns, Tusks, and Flippers: The Evolution of Hoofed Mammals*. Baltimore: Johns Hopkins University Press, 2002.

Pugh, Jeffrey C. "Fear on Display in Charlottesville." *Roanoke Times*. August 16, 2017. https://roanoke.com/opinion/commentary/pugh-fear-on-display-in-charlottesville/article_4e8adc62-2a5d-54a2-a65d-cf1bc9dec6c0.html.

Pui-lan, Kwok. *Postcolonial Imagination and Feminist Theology*. Louisville: Westminster John Knox, 2005.

Quiroga, Pedro López Barja de. "Freedmen Social Mobility in Roman Italy." *Historia: Zeitschrift Für Alte Geschichte* 44 (1995): 326–48.

Rainbow, Jesse. "Male μαστοί in Revelation 1:13." *JSNT* 30 (December 2007): 249–53.

Rampton, Martha. "Four Waves of Feminism." October 25, 2015. https://www.pacificu.edu/magazine/four-waves-feminism.

Rawson, Beryl. "Roman Concubinage and Other de Facto Marriages." *TAPA* 104 (1974): 279–305.

Reader, William W. "The Twelve Jewels of Revelation 21:19-20: Tradition History and Modern Interpretations." *JBL* 100 (1981): 433–57.

Redding, Jonathan D. *One Nation under Graham: Apocalyptic Rhetoric and American Exceptionalism*. Waco, TX: Baylor University Press, 2021.

Reddish, Mitchell G. *Revelation*. Smyth and Helwys Bible Commentary. Macon, GA: Smyth & Helwys, 2001.

Reinhartz, Adele. "The Hermeneutics of Chutzpah: A Disquisition on the Value/s of 'Critical Investigation of the Bible.'" *JBL* 140 (2021): 8–30.

Ress, Mary Judith. *Ecofeminism in Latin America*. Women from the Margins. Maryknoll, NY: Orbis Books, 2006.

Revised Common Lectionary Daily Readings: Proposed by the Consultation on Common Texts. Minneapolis: Augsburg Fortress, 2005.

Richard, Pablo. "Reading the *Apocalypse*: Resistance, Hope, and Liberation in Central America." In *From Every People and Nation: The Book of Revelation in Intercultural Perspective*, ed. David Rhoads, 146–64. Minneapolis: Fortress, 2005.

Richlin, Amy. *The Garden of Priapus: Sexuality and Aggression in Roman Humor*. Rev. ed. New York: Oxford University Press, 1992.

Richlin, Amy. "Not before Homosexuality: The Materiality of the *Cinaedus* and the Roman Law against Love between Men." *Journal of the History of Sexuality* 3 (April 1, 1993): 523–73.

Richlin, Amy. "Pliny's Brassiere." In *Roman Sexualities*, edited by Judith P. Hallett and Marilyn B. Skinner, 197–220. Princeton: Princeton University Press, 1997.

Richlin, Amy. *Slave Theater in the Roman Republic: Plautus and Popular Comedy*. Cambridge: Cambridge University Press, 2017.

Ringe, Sharon H. "When Women Interpret the Bible." In *Women's Bible Commentary*, edited by Carol A. Newsom, Sharon H. Ringe, and Jacqueline E. Lapsley. 3rd ed. Louisville: Westminster John Knox, 2012.

Rissi, Mathias. "The Rider on the White Horse: A Study of Revelation 6:1-8." *Int* 18 (October 1964): 407–18.

Robinson, Betsey A. "Fountains as Reservoirs of Myth and Memory." In *Myths on the Map: The Storied Landscapes of Ancient Greece*, edited by Greta Hawes, 178–203. Oxford: Oxford University Press, 2017.

Rodriguez, Jeanette. *Our Lady of Guadalupe: Faith and Empowerment among Mexican-American Women*. Austin: University of Texas Press, 2010.

Roose, Hanna. "The Fall of the 'Great Harlot' and the Fate of the Aging Prostitute: An Iconographic Approach to Revelation 18." In *Picturing the New Testament: Studies in Ancient Visual Images*, edited by Annette Weissenrieder, Friederike Wendt, and Petra von Gemünden, 228–52. Tübingen: Mohr Siebeck, 2005.

Rossetti, Christina. *The Face of the Deep: A Devotional Commentary on the Apocalypse*. London: SPCK, 1892.

Rossing, Barbara R. *The Choice between Two Cities: Whore, Bride, and Empire in the Apocalypse*. Harrisburg, PA: Trinity Press International, 1999.

Rossing, Barbara R. "For the Healing of the World: Reading *Revelation* Ecologically." In *From Every People and Nation: The Book of Revelation in Intercultural Perspective*, edited by David Rhoads, 165–82. Minneapolis: Fortress, 2005.

Rossing, Barbara R. *The Rapture Exposed: The Message of Hope in the Book of Revelation*. 2nd ed. New York: Basic Books, 2004.

Rountree, Kathryn. "Goddess Pilgrims as Tourists: Inscribing the Body through Sacred Travel." *Sociology of Religion* 63 (2002): 475–96.

Royalty, Robert M, Jr. "Etched or Sketched? Inscriptions and Erasures in the Messages to Sardis and Philadelphia (Rev. 3.1-13)." *JSNT* 27 (2005): 447–63.

Royalty, Robert M, Jr. *The Streets of Heaven: The Ideology of Wealth in the Apocalypse of John*. Macon, GA: Mercer University Press, 1998.

Ruether, Rosemary Radford. *Sexism and God-Talk: Toward a Feminist Theology*. Boston: Beacon, 1993.

Runions, Erin. *The Babylon Complex: Theopolitical Fantasies of War, Sex, and Sovereignty*. New York: Fordham University Press, 2014.

Runions, Erin. "Detranscendentalizing Decisionism: Political Theology after Gayatri Spivak." *JFSR* 25 (2009): 67–85.

Russell, Ben. *The Economics of the Roman Stone Trade*. Oxford: Oxford University Press, 2013.

Rutledge, David. *Reading Marginally: Feminism, Deconstruction and the Bible*. BibInt 21. Leiden: Brill, 1996.

Said, Edward W. *Orientalism*. New York: Knopf Doubleday, (1978) 2014.

Sakenfeld, Katharine Doob. *Just Wives? Stories of Power and Survival in the Old Testament and Today*. Louisville: Westminster John Knox, 2003.

Saller, Richard P. "Symbols of Gender and Status Hierarchies in the Roman Household." In *Women and Slaves in Greco-Roman Culture*, edited by Sandra R. Joshel and Sheila Murnaghan, 85–91. London: Routledge, 1998.

Sánchez, David A. *From Patmos to the Barrio: Subverting Imperial Myths*. Minneapolis: Fortress, 2008.

Sandnes, Karl Olav. "Seal and Baptism in Early Christianity." In *Ablution, Initiation, and Baptism: Late Antiquity, Early Judaism, and Early Christianity*, edited by David Hellholm, Tor Vegge, Øyvind Norderval, and Christer Hellholm, 1441–81. Berlin: De Gruyter, 2011.

Satlow, Michael L. *Jewish Marriage in Antiquity*. Princeton: Princeton University Press, 2001.

Sautman, Barry. "Big Thunder, Little Rain: The Yellow Peril Framing of the Pandemic Campaign against China." *Chinese Journal of International Law*. October 2, 2021. https://doi.org/10.1093/chinesejil/jmab023.

Schaefer, Kayleen. *Text Me When You Get Home: The Evolution and Triumph of Modern Female Friendship*. New York: Penguin, 2018.

Scheidel, Walter. "The Roman Slave Supply." In *The Cambridge World History of Slavery*, vol. 1: *The Ancient Mediterranean World*, edited by Keith Bradley and Paul Cartledge, 287–310. Cambridge: Cambridge University Press, 2011.

Scheidel, Walter. "Slavery." In *The Cambridge Companion to the Roman Economy*, edited by Walter Scheidel, 89–113. Cambridge: Cambridge University Press, 2012.

Scheidel, Walter, and Elijah Meeks. "ORBIS: The Stanford Geospatial Network Model of the Roman World." https://orbis.stanford.edu/#working.

Scheil, Andrew. *Babylon under Western Eyes: A Study of Allusion and Myth*. Toronto: University of Toronto Press, 2016.

Schellenberg, Ryan S. "Seeing the World Whole: Intertextuality and the New Jerusalem (Revelation 21–22)." *PRSt* 33 (Winter 2006): 467–76.

Schneider, Laurel. *Beyond Monotheism: A Theology of Multiplicity*. London: Routledge, 2007.

Schneiders, Sandra M. *The Revelatory Text: Interpreting the New Testament as Sacred Scripture*. Rev. ed. Collegeville, MN: Liturgical Press, 1999.

Scholz, Susanne, ed. *Feminist Interpretation of the Hebrew Bible in Retrospect*. Recent Research in Biblical Studies 7, 8, 9. Sheffield: Sheffield Phoenix, 2013, 2014, 2016.

Scholz, Susanne. "From the 'Woman's Bible' to the 'Women's Bible,' The History of Feminist Approaches to the Hebrew Bible." In *Introducing the Women's Hebrew Bible*, 12–32. IFT 13. New York: T&T Clark, 2007.

Schottroff, Luise. "Lydia: A New Quality of Power." In *Let the Oppressed Go Free: Feminist Perspectives on the New Testament*, translated by Annemarie S. Kidder, 131–37. Louisville: Westminster John Knox, 1993.

Schottroff, Luise. *Lydia's Impatient Sisters: A Feminist Social History of Early Christianity*. Translated by Barbara and Martin Rumscheidt. Louisville: Westminster John Knox, 1995.

Schreiner, Thomas R. "What Is the Mark of the Beast? (Revelation 13)." *Crossway*. October 8, 2018. https://www.crossway.org/articles/what-is-the-mark -of-the-beast-revelation-13/.

Schuler, Christof. "Local Elites in the Greek East." In *The Oxford Handbook of Roman Epigraphy*, edited by Christer Bruun and Jonathan Edmondson, 250–73. Oxford: Oxford University Press, 2015.

Schuller, Eileen, and Marie-Theres Wacker, eds. *Early Jewish Writings*. The Bible and Women: An Encyclopaedia of Exegesis and Cultural History. Atlanta: SBL Press, 2017.

Schüssler Fiorenza, Elisabeth. *The Book of Revelation: Justice and Judgment*. Minneapolis: Fortress, 1998.

Schüssler Fiorenza, Elisabeth. *Bread Not Stone: The Challenge of Feminist Biblical Interpretation*. 2nd ed. Boston: Beacon, 1995.

Schüssler Fiorenza, Elisabeth. *But She Said: Feminist Practices of Biblical Interpretation*. Boston: Beacon, 1992.

Schüssler Fiorenza, Elisabeth. *Empowering Memory and Movement: Thinking and Working across Borders*. Minneapolis: Augsburg Fortress, 2014.

Schüssler Fiorenza, Elisabeth, ed. *Feminist Biblical Studies in the Twentieth Century: Scholarship and Movement*. The Bible and Women: An Encyclopaedia of Exegesis and Cultural History. Atlanta: SBL Press, 2014.

Schüssler Fiorenza, Elisabeth. *In Memory of Her: A Feminist Theological Reconstruction of Christian Origins*. New York: Crossroad, 1983/1994.

Schüssler Fiorenza, Elisabeth. *Jesus: Miriam's Child, Sophia's Prophet; Critical Issues in Feminist Christology*. New York: Continuum, 1994.

Schüssler Fiorenza, Elisabeth. "New Testament Canon Formation and the Marginalization of Wo/Men." In *Gospels: Narrative and History*, edited by Mercedes Navarro Puerto, Marinella Perroni; Amy-Jill Levine, English ed., 19–30. The Bible and Women: An Encyclopaedia of Exegesis and Cultural History Atlanta: SBL Press, 2015.

Schüssler Fiorenza, Elisabeth. *The Power of the Word: Scripture and the Rhetoric of Empire*. Minneapolis: Fortress, 2007.

Schüssler Fiorenza, Elisabeth. *Revelation: Vision of a Just World*. Minneapolis: Fortress, 1991.

Schüssler Fiorenza, Elisabeth. *Wisdom Ways: Introducing Feminist Biblical Interpretation*. Maryknoll, NY: Orbis Books, 2001.

Schutte, P. J. W. "When *They*, *We*, and the *Passive* Become *I*—Introducing Autobiographical Biblical Criticism." *HTS Teologiese Studies / Theological Studies* 61 (2005): 401–16.

Sechrest, Love L. "Antitypes, Stereotypes, and Antetypes: Jezebel, the Sun Woman, and Contemporary Black Women." In *Womanist Interpretations of the Bible: Expanding the Discourse*, edited by Gay L. Byron and Vanessa Lovelace, 113–37. Atlanta: SBL Press, 2016.

Selvidge, Marla J. "Powerful and Powerless Women in the Apocalypse." *Neot* 26 (1992): 157–67.

Sestertius with Head of Domitian, 85. Coin, 85, 34.1415, Boston MFA: Ancient Greece and Rome. https://collections.mfa.org/objects/162166/sestertius-with-head-of-domitian.

Sex Workers Outreach Project. "How to Be an Ally to Sex Workers." 2019. https://swopusa.org/wp-content/uploads/2019/02/How_to_be_an_ally_draft_2.pdf.

Shaner, Katherine A. *Enslaved Leadership in Early Christianity*. New York: Oxford University Press, 2018.

Shelley, Mary. *Frankenstein: The 1818 Text*. New York: Penguin, 2018.

Sherwood, Yvonne. *A Biblical Text and Its Afterlives: The Survival of Jonah in Western Culture*. Cambridge: Cambridge University Press, 2000.

Sherwood, Yvonne. "Introduction." In *The Bible and Feminism: Remapping the Field*, edited by Yvonne Sherwood with the assistance of Anna Fisk. New York: Oxford University Press, 2017.

Sherwood, Yvonne. "Prophetic Scatology: Prophecy and the Art of Sensation." *Semeia* 82 (1998): 183–224.

Shields, Mary E. "Multiple Exposures: Body Rhetoric and Gender Characterization in Ezekiel 16." *JFSR* 14 (1998): 5–18.

Shoop, Marcia W. Mount. *Touchdowns for Jesus and Other Signs of Apocalypse: Lifting the Veil on Big-Time Sports*. Eugene, OR: Cascade Books, 2014.

Smallwood, E. Mary. *The Jews under Roman Rule: From Pompey to Diocletian; A Study in Political Relations*. 2nd ed. Leiden: Brill, 2001.

Smith, Kevin. *Dogma*. Lions Gate Films, 1999.

Smith, Mitzi J. "Race, Gender, and the Politics of 'Sass': Reading Mark 7:24-30 through a Womanist Lens of Intersectionality and Inter(Con)Textuality." In *Womanist Interpretations of the Bible: Expanding the Discourse*, edited by Gay L. Byron and Vanessa Lovelace, 95–112. Atlanta: Society of Biblical Literature, 2016.

Smith, Mitzi J. *Womanist Sass and Talk Back: Social (In)Justice, Intersectionality, and Biblical Interpretation*. Eugene, OR: Cascade Books, 2018.

Smith, R. R. R. "The Imperial Reliefs from the Sebasteion at Aphrodisias." *JRS* 77 (1987): 88–138.

Smith, R. R. R. "*Simulacra Gentium*: The *Ethne* from the Sebasteion at Aphrodisias." *JRS* 78 (1988): 50–77.

Smith, Shanell T. *Touched: For Survivors of Sexual Assault Like Me Who Have Been Hurt by Church Folk and for Those Who Will Care*. Minneapolis: Fortress, 2020.

Smith, Shanell T. *The Woman Babylon and the Marks of Empire: Reading Revelation with a Postcolonial Womanist Hermeneutics of Ambiveilence*. Minneapolis: Augsburg Fortress, 2014.

Sohn-Kronthaler, Michaela, and Ruth Albrecht, eds. *Faith and Feminism in Nineteenth-Century Religious Communities*. The Bible and Women: An Encyclopaedia of Exegesis and Cultural History. Atlanta: SBL Press, 2019.

Sojourner Truth. "Ain't I a Woman?" Modern History Sourcebook. https://sourcebooks.fordham.edu/mod/sojtruth-woman.asp.

Sostaita, Barbara. "Waste Land: For Migrants, Water Bottles Are a Matter of Life and Death." Bitch Media. January 14, 2022. https://www.bitchmedia.org/article/waste-land-for-migrants-water-bottles-are-a-matter-of-life-and-death.

Southern Poverty Law Center. "Y'all Means All." June 3, 2020. https://www.splcenter.org/news/2020/06/03/yall-means-all.

Spaeth, Barbette Stanley. "The Goddess Ceres in the *Ara Pacis Augustae* and the Carthage Relief." *AJA* 98 (1994): 65–100.

Staples, Ariadne. *From Good Goddess to Vestal Virgins: Sex and Category in Roman Religion*. London: Routledge, 1998.

Ștefan, Andreea. "The Case of Multiple Citizenship Holders in the Graeco-Roman East." In *Citizens in the Graeco-Roman World*, edited by Lucia Cecchet and Anna Busetto, 110–31. Mnemosyne Supplements, History and Archaeology of Classical Antiquity 407. Leiden: Brill, 2017.

Stenström, Hanna. "Feminists in Search for a Usable Future: Feminist Reception of the Book of Revelation." In *The Way the World Ends? The Apocalypse of John in Culture and Ideology*, edited by William John Lyons and Jorunn Økland, 240–66. Sheffield: Sheffield Phoenix, 2009.

Stenström, Hanna. "Is Salvation Only for True Men? On Gendered Imagery in the Book of Revelation." In *Imagery in the Book of Revelation*, edited by Michael Labahn and Outi Lehtipuu, 183–98. Leuven: Peeters, 2011.

Stevenson, Gregory. *Power and Place: Temple and Identity in the Book of Revelation.* Berlin: De Gruyter, 2001.

Stevenson, Gregory M. "Conceptual Background to Golden Crown Imagery in the Apocalypse of John (4:4, 10; 14:14)." *JBL* 114 (1995): 257–72.

Stow, Kenneth R. *The Jews in Rome: 1536–1551.* Leiden: Brill, 1995.

Stratton, Kimberly B. "Interrogating the Magic-Gender Connection." In *Daughters of Hecate: Women and Magic in the Ancient World*, edited by Kimberly B. Stratton and Dayna S. Kalleres, 1–37. New York: Oxford University Press, 2014.

Stryker, Susan. *Transgender History: The Roots of Today's Revolution.* 2nd ed. Berkeley: Seal Press, 2017.

Sutton, Matthew Avery. *American Apocalypse: A History of Modern Evangelicalism.* Cambridge, MA: Harvard University Press, 2014.

Swancutt, Diana M. "*Still* before Sexuality: 'Greek' Androgyny, the Roman Imperial Politics of Masculinity and the Roman Invention of the *Tribas*." In *Mapping Gender in Ancient Religious Discourses*, edited by Todd Penner and Caroline Vander Stichele, 11–61. BibInt 84. Boston: Brill, 2007.

Swartz, Michael D. "Chains of Tradition from *Avot* to the *'Avodah Piyutim*." In *Jews, Christians, and the Roman Empire: The Poetics of Power in Late Antiquity*, edited by Natalie B. Dohrmann and Annette Yoshiko Reed, 189–208. Philadelphia: University of Pennsylvania Press, 2013.

Taitz, Emily, Sondra Henry, and Cheryl Tallan. *The JPS Guide to Jewish Women 600 B.C.E.–1900 C.E.* Philadelphia: JPS, 2003.

Takács, Sarolta A. *Isis and Sarapis in the Roman World.* Leiden: Brill, 2015.

Taylor, Dorceta E. *Toxic Communities: Environmental Racism, Industrial Pollution, and Residential Mobility.* New York: NYU Press, 2014.

Taylor, Keeanga-Yamahtta. *From #Blacklivesmatter to Black Liberation.* Chicago: Haymarket Books, 2016.

Taylor, Marion Ann, and Agnes Choi, eds. *Handbook of Women Biblical Interpreters: A Historical and Biographical Guide.* Grand Rapids: Baker Academic, 2012.

Terpstra, Taco T. *Trading Communities in the Roman World: A Micro-Economic and Institutional Perspective.* Leiden: Brill, 2013.

Terrell, JoAnne Marie. "Our Mothers' Gardens: Discrete Sources of Reflection on the Cross in Womanist Christology." In *I Found God in Me: A Womanist Biblical Hermeneutics Reader*, edited by Mitzi J. Smith, 87–108. Eugene, OR: Cascade Books, 2015.

Tessera, Miriam Rita. "Philip Count of Flanders and Hildegard of Bingen: Crusading against the Saracens or Crusading against Deadly Sin?" In *Gendering the Crusades*, edited by Susan B. Edgington and Sarah Lambert, 77–93. New York: Columbia University Press, 2002.

Thimmes, Pamela. "Women Reading Women in the Apocalypse: Reading Scenario 1, the Letter to Thyatira (Rev. 2.18-29)." *CurBR* 2 (2003): 128–44.

Thistle Farms. "Our Mission." https://thistlefarms.org/pages/our-mission.

Thomas, Eric A. "The Futures Outside: Apocalyptic Epilogue Unveiled as Africana Queer Prologue." In *Sexual Disorientations: Queer Temporalities, Affects,*

Theologies, edited by Kent L. Brintnall, Joseph A. Marchal, and Stephen D. Moore, 90–112. New York: Fordham University Press, 2018.

Thompson, Leonard L. *The Book of Revelation: Apocalypse and Empire*. New York: Oxford University Press, 1990.

Thompson, Leonard L. "Spirit Possession: Revelation in Religious Studies." In *Reading the Book of Revelation: A Resource for Students*, edited by David L. Barr, 137–50. Atlanta: SBL, 2003.

Thunberg, Greta. "Transcript: Greta Thunberg's Speech at the U.N. Climate Action Summit." NPR.org. September 23, 2019. https://www.npr.org/2019/09/23/763452863/transcript-greta-thunbergs-speech-at-the-u-n-climate-action-summit.

Thurston, Bonnie. *Women in the New Testament: Questions and Commentary*. Companions to the New Testament. New York: Crossroad, 1998.

Tolbert, Mary Ann. "Social, Sociological, and Anthropological Methods." In *Searching the Scriptures: A Feminist Introduction*, vol. 1, edited by Elisabeth Schüssler Fiorenza with the assistance of Shelly Matthews, 255–71. New York: Crossroad, 1993.

Tompkins, Lucy. "Millions More People Got Access to Water: Can They Drink It?" *The New York Times*. December 2, 2021. Sec. World. https://www.nytimes.com/2021/12/02/world/clean-water-to-drink.html.

Trebilco, Paul. *The Early Christians in Ephesus from Paul to Ignatius*. Grand Rapids: Eerdmans, 2007.

Trebilco, Paul. *Jewish Communities in Asia Minor*. Cambridge: Cambridge University Press, 1991.

Trebilco, Paul. "Why Did the Early Christians Call Themselves ἡ Εκκλησία?" *NTS* 57 (2011): 440–60.

Trevett, Christine. *Montanism: Gender, Authority and the New Prophecy*. Cambridge: Cambridge University Press, 2002.

"The Trevor Project National Survey on LGBTQ Youth Mental Health 2020." https://www.thetrevorproject.org/survey-2020/.

Trible, Phyllis. *God and the Rhetoric of Sexuality*. OBT. Philadelphia: Fortress, 1978.

Trimble, Jennifer. "The Zoninus Collar and the Archaeology of Roman Slavery." *AJA* 120 (July 2016): 447–72.

Trotter, Jonathan. *The Jerusalem Temple in Diaspora: Jewish Practice and Thought during the Second Temple Period*. Leiden: Brill, 2019.

Ulmer, Rivka. "The Jerusalem Temple in *Pesiqta Rabbati*: From Creation to Apocalypse." *Hebr. Stud.* 51 (2010): 223–59.

UNESCO World Heritage Convention. "Villa Romana del Casale." https://whc.unesco.org/en/list/832/.

United Nations Refugee Agency. "Refugee Camps Explained." April 6, 2021. https://www.unrefugees.org/news/refugee-camps-explained/.

United States Department of Justice. "Justice Department Files Lawsuit against the Alamance County, North Carolina, Sheriff's Office." June 23, 2011.

https://www.justice.gov/opa/pr/justice-department-files-lawsuit-against
-alamance-county-north-carolina-sheriff-s-office.

Ustinova, Yulia. "To Live in Joy and Die with Hope: Experiential Aspects of Ancient Greek Mystery Rites." *BICS* 56 (2013): 105–23.

Vaid-Menon, Alok. "They Will Say." In *Femme in Public*. Self-published, 2017.

Vanden Eykel, Eric M. "No, the COVID-19 Vaccine Is Not Linked to the Mark of the Beast—But a First-Century Roman Tyrant Probably Is." *The Conversation*. April 7, 2021. https://theconversation.com/no-the-covid-19
-vaccine-is-not-linked-to-the-mark-of-the-beast-but-a-first-century-roman
-tyrant-probably-is-158288.

Vander Stichele, Caroline. "Re-Membering the Whore: The Fate of Babylon According to Revelation 17.16." In *Feminist Companion to the Apocalypse of John*, edited by Amy-Jill Levine with Maria Mayo Robbins, 106–20. FCNTECW 13. London: T&T Clark, 2009.

Vander Stichele, Caroline, and Todd Penner, eds. *Her Master's Tools? Feminist and Postcolonial Engagements of Historical-Critical Discourse*. Atlanta: SBL, 2005.

van Nijf, Onno. "Athletics and Paideia: Festivals and Physical Education in the World of Second Sophistic." In *Paideia: The World of the Second Sophistic*, edited by Barbara E. Borg, 203–28. Millennium Studies 2. Berlin: De Gruyter, 2004.

Vasser, Murray. "Bodies and Souls: The Case for Reading Revelation 18.13 as a Critique of the Slave Trade." *NTS* 64 (2018): 397–409.

Venkat, Rahul. "Biggest Stadium in the World: Venues in North Korea, India and the US in Top Three—Full List" Olympics.com. April 12, 2022. https://olympics.com/en/featured-news/largest-stadium-world-venue
-capacity-spectator-seats.

Vine, David. "Women's Labor, Sex Work and U.S. Military Bases Abroad." Salon. October 8, 2017. https://www.salon.com/2017/10/08/womens-labor-sex-work
-and-u-s-military-bases-abroad/.

Volkova, Elena. "Mater Nostra: The Anti-Blasphemy Message of the Feminist Punk Prayer." *Religion and Gender* 4 (2014): 202–8.

Wah, Carolyn R. "An Introduction to Research and Analysis of Jehovah's Witnesses: A View from the Watchtower." *RRelRes* 43 (2001): 161–74.

Walker, Alice. *In Search of Our Mothers' Gardens: Womanist Prose*. New York: Harcourt Brace Jovanovich, 1967, 1983.

Wallace-Hadrill, Andrew. "The Roman Imperial Court: Seen and Unseen in the Performance of Power." In *Royal Courts in Dynastic States and Empires*, edited by Jeroen Duindam, Tülay Artan, and Metin Kunt, 91–102. A Global Perspective. Leiden: Brill, 2011.

Walters, Jonathan. "Invading the Roman Body: Manliness and Impenetrability in Roman Thought." In *Roman Sexualities*, edited by Judith P. Hallett and Marilyn B. Skinner, 29–43. Princeton: Princeton University Press, 1997.

Walters, Jonathan. "'No More Than a Boy': The Shifting Construction of Masculinity from Ancient Greece to the Middle Ages." *Gender & History* 5 (1993): 20–33.

Weems, Renita J. *Just a Sister Away: A Womanist Vision of Women's Relationships in the Bible*. San Diego: Lura Media, 1988.

Weems, Renita J. "Reading *Her Way* through the Struggle: African American Women and the Bible." In *Stony the Road We Trod: African American Biblical Interpretation*, edited by Cain Hope Felder, 57–77. Minneapolis: Fortress, 1991.

Weiss-Wolf, Jennifer. *Periods Gone Public: Taking a Stand for Menstrual Equity*. New York: Arcade, 2017.

Westboro Baptist Church. "Westboro Baptist Church." 2020. https://www.godhatesfags.com/index.html.

Whisenant, Edgar C. *88 Reasons Why the Rapture Is in 1988*. Nashville: World Bible Society, 1988.

Whitaker, Robyn J. "Victim to Victor: The Appeal of Apocalyptic Hope." *Religions* 11 (September 2020): 1–11.

Whitaker, Robyn J. *Ekphrasis, Vision, and Persuasion in the Book of Revelation*. WUNT 2.410. Tübingen: Mohr Siebeck, 2015.

White, Jeremy, Amy Harmon, Danielle Ivory, Lauren Leatherby, Albert Sun, and Sarah Almukhtar. "How America Reached One Million Covid Deaths." *The New York Times*. May 13, 2022. https://www.nytimes.com/interactive/2022/05/13/us/covid-deaths-us-one-million.html.

Whitlock, Reta Ugena. "Introduction: Loving, Telling, and Reconstructing the South." In *Queer South Rising: Voices of a Contested Place*, edited by Reta Ugena Whitlock, xxi–xl. Charlotte: Information Age, 2013.

Wildfang, Robin Lorsch. *Rome's Vestal Virgins*. London: Routledge, 2006.

Williams, Craig A. *Roman Homosexuality*. 2nd ed. Oxford: Oxford University Press, 2010. 1st ed., 1999.

Williams, Wesley. "A Body Unlike Bodies: Transcendent Anthropomorphism in Ancient Semitic Tradition and Early Islam." *JAOS* 129 (2009): 19–44.

Wilson, Mark. *The Victor Sayings in the Book of Revelation*. Eugene, OR: Wipf and Stock, 2007.

Wiseman, Rob, Benjamin Neil, and Francesca Mazzilli. "Extreme Justice: Decapitations and Prone Burials in Three Late Roman Cemeteries at Knobb's Farm, Cambridgeshire." *Britannia* 52 (November 2021): 119–73.

Witherington, Ben, III. *Revelation*. NCBC. Cambridge: Cambridge University Press, 2003.

World Health Organization. "Gender, Climate Change and Health." https://www.who.int/globalchange/GenderClimateChangeHealthfinal.pdf.

Wurster, Herbert W., and Richard Loibl. *Apokalypse: Zwischen Himmel Und Hölle*. Regensburg: Friedrich Pustet, 2000.

Yarbro Collins, Adela. *Crisis and Catharsis: The Power of the Apocalypse*. Philadelphia: Westminster Press, 1984.

Yarbro Collins, Adela. "Feminine Symbolism in the Book of Revelation." *BibInt* 1 (1993): 20–33.

Yarbro Collins, Adela. "Revelation 18: Taunt-Song or Dirge?" In *L'Apocalypse johannique et l'Apocalyptique dans le Nouveau Testament*, edited by Jan Lambrecht 185–204. Leuven: Leuven University Press, 1980.

Yarbro Collins, Adela. "Vilification and Self-Definition in the Book of Revelation." *HTR* 79 (1986): 308–20.

Yee, Gale A., ed. *Judges and Method: New Approaches in Biblical Studies*. Minneapolis: Fortress, 1995.

Yegül, Fikret, and Diane Favro. *Roman Architecture and Urbanism: From the Origins to Late Antiquity*. Cambridge: Cambridge University Press, 2019.

Yeo, K.-K. "Hope for the Persecuted, Cooperation with the State, and Meaning for the Dissatisfied: Three Readings of *Revelation* from a Chinese Context." In *From Every People and Nation: The Book of Revelation in Intercultural Perspective*, edited by David Rhoads, 200–221. Minneapolis: Fortress, 2005.

Yeoman, Barry. "What Do Birds Do for Us?" *Audubon*. April 8, 2013. https://www.audubon.org/news/what-do-birds-do-us.

Zanker, Paul, and Bjorn C. Ewald. *Living with Myths: The Imagery of Roman Sarcophagi*. Translated by Julia Slater. Oxford: Oxford University Press, 2012.

Zaveri, Mihir. "Black Man Killed by Officer in Alabama Mall Shooting Was Not the Gunman, Police Now Say." *The New York Times*. November 24, 2018. https://www.nytimes.com/2018/11/24/us/alabama-mall-shooting.html.

Zeller, Benjamin E. *Heaven's Gate: America's UFO Religion*. New York: NYU Press, 2014.

Ziolkowski, John. "The Invention of the Tuba (Trumpet)." *CW* 92 (1999): 367–73.

Index of Scripture References and Other Ancient Writings

Other Ancient Writings

Dead Sea Scrolls

Joseph and Aseneth

Acts of Paul and Thecla

Apocalypse of Peter

Martyrdom of Polycarp

Passion of Perpetua

Shepherd of Hermas

Index of Subjects

666, 203–204

1000 years. *See* millennium

144,000, 97, 106–109, 111, 118, 130, 205–211, 213, 217, 222, 223, 224

Abaddon, 127, 129, 306

abominations, 78, 245, 248–249, 289, 334, 337. *See also* filth; unclean

Abu Ghraib, 271–272

abyss, lviii, 101, 125, 127, 130, 155, 157, 254, 284, 292, 306

adoption, 171

Ahmed, Sara, xlvii

AIDS/HIV, 232–234

altar, lxiii, 41, 49, 66, 74, 89–91, 101, 119, 120, 127, 129, 147, 148, 171, 182, 194, 198, 223, 227, 230, 233, 235, 286, 326

alter-empire, 67–68, 77, 79

amaze, amazement, lxi, 188, 244, 245, 252, 292

androcentric, androcentrism, xxxii, xxxviii, xl, 217–218

angel(s): lxxxiv, 3, 5, 7, 18, 26–28, 30, 33, 62n10, 70, 74, 77, 97, 99, 100, 101, 102, 106, 110, 119–123, 126, 127, 129–130, 135–144, 147–148,

153n17, 155, 159, 174–175, 176, 206, 207, 218–220, 223, 226, 227, 229–230, 231–235, 237, 241, 244–245, 252–254, 257, 264–265, 267, 274, 278, 293–295, 300–302, 306–307, 316, 320, 326, 328, 334–335, 340–341, 346–347

anger. *See* wrath

animal(s), lxxxvi, 72–74, 83, 86, 126–128, 152, 191–192, 206, 223, 233, 249, 276, 281, 308, 320, 342, 345. *See also* beasts; living creatures

anointed. *See* Messiah, messiahs

Antichrist, antichrists, 7, 84, 193–194, 194n23, 313

Antipas, lxxxi, 26, 41, 151, 194

antisemitism, 41–45, 110, 112, 304

Aphrodisias, xi, 12, 85, 88, 137

Aphrodite, 163n1, 165

apocalypse, 1–3, 8, 82, 117–118, 139, 175, 325–326

apocalyptic, liii, 1–2, 5, 18, 59, 92, 94, 122, 123, 124, 130, 132, 140, 153, 207, 227, 242, 252, 307, 312n15, 320, 325, 326

Apollo, 18, 129, 170–171, 175

Ark of the Covenant, 159–160

humor, xlv, xlvi, xlvi n9, lxxviii,
     186–187, 186n3, 192, 197. *See also*
     sarcasm
hybrid, hybridity, 68–69, 187, 189–190
Hylen, Susan E., xlviii n16, 302n48
hymn(s), 65–67, 77, 87, 114, 159–160,
     173, 175, 176, 228–229, 234–235,
     282, 285, 293, 296, 316, 348

idols, idolatry, 26–27, 47, 50–52, 54,
     107, 127, 131, 133–134, 182, 187,
     251, 328, 330–331, 347
imperial cults, lxvii–lxviv, 11, 23, 30,
     57, 66–69, 193, 196, 251, 253, 269,
     291
imperial family, lxxxii, 12, 193, 202,
     250
impurity, impurities, 209, 245, 249,
     265, 268, 284–285, 334. *See also*
     unclean
incense, 49, 73, 119–120, 148
iniquity. *See* sin(s)
intersectionality, xxv, liii, lxxiv, 144
Irenaeus, lxii, lxvi, lxxx, 84, 108, 171,
     203
Isis, lxxix, 165–167, 169, 170, 179
Ispen, Avaren, 259
Israel, Israelites, xx, lxxvii, lxxviii, 9,
     11, 12, 26, 30, 43, 47, 48, 49–50, 65,
     67, 74, 97, 100, 103–104, 106–112,
     114, 123, 130, 131, 133, 139, 141,
     149, 151, 157, 160, 169, 174, 177–
     180, 207, 208, 209, 219, 227–229,
     237, 247, 257, 268, 314, 319, 327,
     334, 335, 342

Jackson, Rebecca Cox, xlviii, 315,
     316–317
Jacob, Sharon, 172, 178
Jerome, 48
Jerusalem: lxxviii, 43, 48, 51, 59, 147,
     149, 157, 160, 169, 219, 237, 247,
     251, 258–259, 312, 314

heavenly, xlvii, xlix, liv, lxxxiii,
     lxxxviii, 28, 40–41, 69, 78, 108–
     110, 114, 149, 223, 229, 239, 247,
     267–268, 274, 278, 283, 289, 294,
     312, 317, 319, 323, 326–348
Jesus, xxi, xxv, xxxii–xxxiii, xlv, lvi,
     lxii–lxv, 2–6, 3n4, 9, 9n18, 12–14,
     19–20, 43, 65, 72, 84, 101, 103, 108,
     121, 123, 140, 146, 151, 154, 157–
     159, 166, 168–169, 171, 174, 176–
     177, 178–179, 209, 219, 220–221,
     238, 244–245, 251, 258, 283, 290,
     294, 297, 302, 304, 307, 314–315,
     329, 332, 347–348
Jewish, xx, xxv, xxvii, xxix–xxx, xxxiii,
     xxxix, liii, lix, lxiv, lxvi, lxvii n14,
     lxxiii, lxxvi–lxxix, lxxxii n66, 9, 14,
     15, 30, 42–45, 50, 85, 89, 104–105,
     107–112, 133, 139–140, 148, 150,
     175, 213n17, 221, 227, 236, 247, 264,
     282, 304, 308–309, 320, 325
Jezebel, xlviii, l, 27, 49–50, 49n55,
     52–53, 252, 284
Joachim of Fiore, 5, 7
John, xi, xlv, xlvii–xlviii, xlix, l–lii,
     lv, lxi–lxviii, lxxviii, lxxix, lxxx–
     lxxxvii, 1–2, 5–6, 8, 14–19, 23–24,
     43–44, 50, 53, 57–62, 68–69, 70, 98,
     104–106, 112, 123, 129, 135–144,
     148–149, 155, 160–161, 167, 176–
     177, 244, 340, 344, 346–349
Josephus, lxxvii, 61, 89, 149, 309, 325,
     334
Judaism, xxxii, lxviii, lxxvii, 44–45,
     110–112, 304
judgment, 7–8, 21, 52, 60, 95, 123, 132,
     144, 159, 177, 206, 218–220, 222,
     227, 231–236, 238, 241, 244–245,
     256–257, 263, 265, 272–274,
     278–279, 285–286, 302, 307, 317,
     320–321, 336, 342

Kaalund, Jennifer T., 172, 178

Authors

Lynn R. Huber is the Maude Sharpe Powell Professor of Religious Studies at Elon University in Elon, North Carolina. Originally from Portland, Oregon, Huber completed a BA in philosophy at Northwest Nazarene College in Nampa, Idaho, and an MDiv and PhD at Emory University in Atlanta, Georgia. Her first two books, *"Like a Bride Adorned": Reading Metaphor in John's Apocalypse* (2007) and *Thinking and Seeing with Women in Revelation* (2013), explore Revelation's use of gendered imagery and the ways the book invites interpreters to see along with these images.

Gail R. O'Day (1954–2018) was professor of New Testament and preaching and dean of Wake Forest School of Divinity from 2010 to 2018. In 1987–2010 she taught at Candler School of Theology, Emory University, where she was also an associate dean for seven years. O'Day's research focused on the Gospel of John and the book of Revelation. The author of several books, O'Day was also editor of *Journal of Biblical Literature* in 1999–2006 and general editor of the Society of Biblical Literature book series, Early Christianity and Its Literature, in 2009–2014. She was an ordained minister in the United Church of Christ.

Volume Editor

Amy-Jill Levine is Rabbi Stanley M. Kessler Distinguished Professor of New Testament and Jewish Studies, Hartford International University for Religion and Peace; University Professor of New Testament and Jewish Studies Emerita, Mary Jane Werthan Professor of Jewish Studies Emerita, Professor of New Testament Studies Emerita, Vanderbilt University. Her recent publications include *The Gospel of Luke* (with Ben Witherington III, the first biblical commentary by a Jew and an Evangelical), *The Jewish Annotated New Testament Second Edition* (co-edited with Marc Brettler), *The Bible With and Without Jesus: How Jews and Christians Read the Same Stories Differently* (with Marc Brettler), *The Pharisees* (co-edited with Joseph Sievers); and in the Beginner's Guide series, *Sermon on the Mount, Light of the World, Entering the Passion of Jesus, The Difficult Words of Jesus, Witness at the Cross*, and *Signs and Wonders*.

Series Editor

Barbara E. Reid, general editor of the Wisdom Commentary series, is a Dominican Sister of Grand Rapids, Michigan. She is the president of Catholic Theological Union and the first woman to hold the position. She has been a member of the CTU faculty since 1988 and also served as vice president and academic dean from 2009 to 2018. She holds a PhD in biblical studies from The Catholic University of America and was president of the Catholic Biblical Association in 2014–2015. Her most recent publications are *Luke 1–9* and *Luke 10–24*, co-authored with Shelly Matthews (WCS 43A, 43B; Liturgical Press, 2021); and *At the Table of Holy Wisdom: Global Hungers and Feminist Biblical Interpretation* (Paulist, 2023).